Canadian Perspectives
on the Sociology of Education

Canadian Perspectives
on the **Sociology** of **Education**

Edited by
Cynthia
Levine-Rasky

OXFORD
UNIVERSITY PRESS

OXFORD
UNIVERSITY PRESS

70 Wynford Drive, Don Mills, Ontario M3C 1J9

www.oupcanada.com

Oxford University Press is a department of the University of Oxford.
It furthers the University's objective of excellence in research, scholarship,
and education by publishing worldwide in

Oxford   New York
Auckland   Cape Town   Dar es Salaam   Hong Kong   Karachi
Kuala Lumpur   Madrid   Melbourne   Mexico City   Nairobi
New Delhi   Shanghai   Taipei   Toronto

With offices in
Argentina   Austria   Brazil   Chile   Czech Republic   France   Greece
Guatemala   Hungary   Italy   Japan   Poland   Portugal   Singapore
South Korea   Switzerland   Thailand   Turkey   Ukraine   Vietnam

Oxford is a trade mark of Oxford University Press
in the UK and in certain other countries

Published in Canada by Oxford University Press

Library and Archives Canada Cataloguing in Publication

Canadian perspectives on the sociology of education / edited by
Cynthia Levine-Rasky.

ISBN 978-0-19-542530-7

1. Educational sociology—Canada.   I. Levine-Rasky, Cynthia, 1958-
LC191.8.C2C35 2009   306.430971   C2008-905043-6

Cover image: Veer/LWA-Sharie Kennedy

This book is printed on permanent (acid-free) paper ∞.
Printed and bound in Canada

1 2 3 4 — 12 11 10 09

Contents

Part Three: Reforms and Consequences

Introduction

Every book starts life as a simple idea—sometimes nothing more than a desire to make something good that is one's own. Its development is a story in itself, often reflecting important chapters in the writer's or editor's professional (and personal) biography. This book is no exception. I can trace the idea to 1990, a couple of years after I had taken Lorna Erwin's undergraduate course in the sociology of education at York University and the year I commenced the PhD program in York's department of sociology. Soon after, Lorna was collecting material for a collection she was editing with David MacLennan; entitled *The Sociology of Education*, it was published by Copp Clark Longman in 1994. My hope was to be able to make a similar contribution some day.

My own commitment to the sociology of education had crystallized many years earlier, however. As a high-school student in the 1970s, I had attended a 'free school' in downtown Toronto called SEED. The name behind the acronym—'Share an Experience, Exploration and Discovery'—reflected the inspiration of the Hall–Dennis Report of 1968. This experience gave me a vantage point from which to criticize 'straight' schools and to imagine something better than forcing young people to attend formal institutions that seemed designed to strip away any capacity for original thinking. In graduate school I discovered an advantage in the outsider's position I had occupied in high school. In 2006 I contacted Harriet Wolff—one of the teachers at SEED who had had a strong influence on me—and told her about the enduring effect my high-school experience had had. (When she remarked that she found this 'extra-ordinary', I was amazed at how accurate my memory of her voice had been, even after 24 years.) Like Lorna, Harriet unknowingly contributed to both the idea behind this book and my desire to make something good that is my own.

An editor of an essay collection must balance her vision with respect for the individual contributors' voices. Certainly there is a wide variety of work here, from theoretical to empirical, addressing topics that range from school rules to the governance of education systems. However diverse they may be in the aspects of education they focus on, their interpretations, and their discursive approaches, one thing the contributors share is a basic concern for public education as a citizenship right, a common good to which we are all entitled. They also share what we might call a critical perspective: a commitment to exploring public education as an arena of conflict between the social agents invested in it—students, teachers, administrators, parents, activists, academics, policy-makers—and a set of social relations characterized by complex, often contradictory, processes.

This book reflects the breadth and depth of Canadian research in the sociology of education today. Canadian issues, data, problems, policies, and institutions are examined in almost every chapter, and much of the research breaks exciting new ground. The theory section, for example, reflects contemporary work on psychoanalysis, on intersectional theorizing, and on institutional theory. Other chapters present new research on subjects such as streaming in secondary schools, community placement in teacher education, 'diaspora literacy', and rural education. The impacts of educational inequalities on black, Aboriginal, lesbian/gay/bisexual/transgender, and working-class students are considered anew, in some cases for the first time in Canada. Finally, a variety of recent educational reforms are considered in terms of their implications for teachers, administrators, parents, and students, from the elementary to the university level. Each of the essays in this book engages with theory, policy, and social problems in a particular way, and all of them have the potential to influence the directions that the sociology of education in Canada will take in the future. The contributors are as diverse as their subjects. Drawn from across Canada, some are in the early stages of their careers and others are among the best established in the country. They are also diverse in the research methods they use. In these chapters, readers will discover possibilities for the development of their own academic voices. I hope the breadth of inquiry they represent will encourage readers to be active learners as they explore their own interests in research.

The book is divided into three parts under titles that deliberately integrate the abstract and the concrete. Part one presents six essays that sensitively blend theory with practice. In their introduction to New Institutional Theory, Scott Davies and David Zarifa trace how this theory developed from the thought of Max Weber, and discuss its value for studies in the sociology of education today. Jane Gaskell takes us through old and new feminist approaches to the sociology of education, providing a valuable overview and raising new questions for research and theorizing. Then Jo-Anne Dillabough explores what Pierre Bourdieu's theory of cultural reproduction can contribute to feminist sociology of education. Next, George Dei examines the theory and practice of anti-racism, raising pointed questions about its implications, skillfully synthesizing structural and cultural analyses. Joyce Barakett and Ayaz Naseem ask whether the goals of anti-racism education might be best served first by strengthening its critique of whiteness and second by strengthening its recognition of black and 'women of colour' feminist pedagogy. Lisa Farley and Judith Robertson also raise provocative questions in their chapter on the potential of psychoanalysis in education, in which they explore the intimate relationship between emotion and identity in teaching and learning.

Part two focuses on the subtle and not-so-subtle ways in which educational processes affect different groups of students. We open with a review of high-school streaming by Alison Taylor and Harvey Krahn, who confirm the pattern of inequality associated with differences in socio-economic status while identifying a number of interprovincial differences. Then Rebecca Raby reports on her research into the way school rules work on adolescent bodies, as well as students' responses to such rules. Jennifer Kelly and Lorin Yochim discuss the implications of the official curriculum for students who are members of racialized groups, specifically African Canadians; they propose that a more inclusive approach to literacy, emphasizing diasporic identities, could be beneficial for students of many different cultural backgrounds. The concept of culture is central to the next chapter as well; here, however, Verna St Denis explains how the emphasis on 'cultural authenticity' in Aboriginal education serves to distract attention from the more difficult issues of racism and socio-economic oppression. In his chapter, Gerald Walton describes the discrimination that students marginalized by sexual difference face. Urging school boards to adopt stronger policies against homophobic bullying, he also points out the risks that such bullying poses for all students, whatever their orientation. Wolfgang Lehmann looks at the ways working-class students experience university and negotiate the challenges of socio-economic marginalization. Then Jessica Ringrose takes up the question of gendered inequality, specifically the popularization of the 'post-feminist' notion that girls' success in school today has put boys at an educational disadvantage. She traces the emergence of such claims in the mass media and places them in their political context. Finally, Michael Corbett explores the consequences of educational reform for rural schools in Atlantic Canada, where small communities are already struggling to survive.

The third and last part concentrates on the politics of educational reform and their implications for teachers and students, especially with regard to equity issues. First, Claude Lessard and André Brassard provide a valuable overview of educational governance in Canada; readers will recognize many of the characteristics they identify in the chapters that follow. Next, Charles Ungerleider and Ernest Krieger look at the debates over education reform between the government of British Columbia and the BC Teachers' Federation. Among the issues at stake in such debates is the very purpose of public education. This controversy is reflected in Ann Vibert's chapter, in which she analyzes 'accountability' discourses and provides a forum for educators to reflect on the impact that such discourses have had on their critical practice. Goli Rezai-Rashti presents excerpts from interviews with a number of teachers and administrators on the specific consequences of the reforms introduced in Ontario after the 'common sense' revolution of 1995—consequences that have included not only intensification and reorganization of their work, but ultimately a loss of professional autonomy. The same reform program provides the backdrop for Kari Dehli's Foucauldian analysis of the political uses made of certain discursive categories (notably 'race' and 'parents') by the Ontario government and by one of its adversaries: a parents' organization advocating the reinvigoration of public schooling as a social good. The formidable challenges of teacher education are the subject of our penultimate chapter, in which Don Dippo and his colleagues examine one university faculty's efforts to build a relationship of true reciprocity between teacher candidates and the urban community in which many of them will practise. Finally, Claire Polster shifts the focus to post-secondary education. Her overview of the ongoing privatization of Canadian universities underlines the dangers that this trend poses for social equality; importantly, however, she also highlights the opportunities for resistance that it presents.

Reading these essays, I am reminded of the early inspiration that sparked my own intellectual curiosity about the sociology of education; I hope that readers will find similar inspiration in them. Together, the chapters that follow recall a wide-ranging conversation among colleagues. This book is an invitation to join us.

Contributors

Joyce Barakett is Professor, Department of Education, Concordia University.

Michael Corbett is Associate Professor, School of Education, Acadia University.

Scott Davies is Professor of Sociology and Ontario Research Chair in Educational Achievement at the Offord Centre for Child Studies, McMaster University.

Kari Dehli is Associate Professor and Chair of the Department of Sociology and Equity Studies in Education at the Ontario Institute for Studies in Education (OISE)/University of Toronto.

George Sefa Dei is Professor of Sociology and Equity Studies at the Ontario Institute for Studies in Education (OISE)/University of Toronto.

Jo-Anne Dillabough is University Reader in Sociology of Education and Cultural Studies, Faculty of Education, University of Cambridge.

Don Dippo is Associate Dean, Faculty of Education, York University.

Marcela Duran is Community Practicum Coordinator, Faculty of Education, York University.

Lisa Farley is Assistant Professor, Faculty of Education, York University.

Jane Gaskell is Professor and Dean, Ontario Institute for Studies in Education.

Jen Gilbert is Associate Professor, Faculty of Education, York University.

Jennifer R. Kelly is Associate Professor, Department of Educational Policy Studies, University of Alberta.

Harvey Krahn is Professor and Chair, Sociology Department, University of Alberta.

Ernest (Kit) Krieger is a recently retired history teacher who has served as President of the British Columbia Teachers' Federation and as a member of the Council of the BC College of Teachers.

Wolfgang Lehmann is Assistant Professor in the Department of Sociology at the University of Western Ontario.

Claude Lessard is Professor and Canada Research Chair on Occupations in Education, Université de Montréal.

M. Ayaz Naseem is Assistant Professor, Department of Education, Concordia University.

Alice Pitt is Dean of the Faculty of Education, York University.

Claire Polster is Associate Professor, Department of Sociology and Social Studies, University of Regina.

Rebecca Raby is Associate Professor, Department of Child and Youth Studies, Brock University.

Goli Rezai-Rashti is Associate Professor, Faculty of Education, University of Western Ontario.

Jessica Ringrose is Lecturer in Sociology of Education and Gender, Department of Educational Foundations and Policy Studies, Institute of Education, University of London.

Judith Robertson is Professor, Society Culture and Literacies, Faculty of Education, University of Ottawa.

Verna St. Denis is Associate Professor, Department of Educational Foundations, College of Education, University of Saskatchewn.

Alison Taylor is Professor, Educational Policy Studies, University of Alberta.

Charles Ungerleider is Professor of the Sociology of Education at the University of British Columbia and a former Deputy Minister of Education for the province.

Ann Vibert is Acting Director of the School of Education at Acadia University.

Gerald Walton is Assistant Professor in the Faculty of Education at Lakehead University.

Lorin G. Yochim is a doctoral student in the Department of Educational Policy Studies, University of Alberta, Edmonton.

David Zarifa is a doctoral candidate in the Department of Sociology, McMaster University.

Part One

Theory and Practice

CHAPTER 1

New Institutional Theory and the Weberian Tradition

Scott Davies and David Zarifa

New Institutional Theory (NIT) is an important framework in the sociology of educa-tion. This chapter situates NIT in the broad context of sociological theory, tracing its roots to the classic writings of Max Weber and highlighting three of Weber's core concepts. It illustrates NIT's insights by evaluating current notions of the 'knowledge-based economy' and discusses NIT's relation to other critical approaches.

Three Concepts from Weber

Max Weber (1864–1920) was a prolific German scholar who is widely considered one of the founders of classical sociological theory.[1] Weber made important contributions to a broad range of fields. Three of his signature concepts have been particularly useful for contemporary work in the sociology of education, and especially influential in the development of NIT.

Weber developed his concept of **bureaucracy** in response to the emergence of the large-scale, modern organization in the late 1800s. As organizations in every field—government, military, church administration, corporate business—grew in size, Weber observed, their structures became increasingly formal. More and more, organizations that might once have been governed by aristocrats were being run by hired officials, professional managers, and specialized experts. In Weber's ideal-typical bureaucracy, work was regulated by formal rules, positions were filled on the basis of open, standardized criteria (as opposed to personal favours or kinship networks), decisions were based on reason rather than personal whim, and officials' duties were separate from their outside lives. Although today the term 'bureaucracy' is often used disparag-ingly to evoke needless 'red tape' and inflexible rules, Weber saw bureaucratic organ-izations as more efficient and effective than their pre-modern forebears. By using impersonal criteria, officials could efficiently allocate people to positions for reasons of merit rather than nepotism. Forming explicit hierarchies of command made it possible to perform tasks more systematically and predictably.

A second important Weberian concept is **rationalization**. Writing at the turn of the twentieth century, Weber was struck by the declining influence of non-scientific (i.e., religious, supernatural) thinking in European affairs. In earlier times, when the great majority of humans had little if any control over their lives, the world was generally believed to be governed either by mysterious deities or by some kind of fate. By the early twentieth century, however, advances in science were forcing supernatural explanations to give way to the idea that the world operated on the basis of rational principles, along lines that could be predicted using science-based thinking. New rationalized orders, according to Weber, specified their purposes, defined the relationships between means and ends, standardized their systems of control, and regulated activity according to rule-like principles. Weber traced this trend to the growing pervasiveness of scientific, technical, and rationalist discourse. The spread of this culture, he argued, eroded traditional lifestyles and bolstered organizational forms that minimized individual discretion and emphasized systematization.

The third of Weber's core concepts is legitimacy. In his studies of political power, Weber found that the character of authority relations was dependent on social approval. He argued that rulers enjoyed a degree of power and authority, as long as the basis for their authority was socially accepted or generally agreed upon by their followers. Weber developed a famous typology that tied political authority to three ideal-typical sources of legitimacy. Leaders were said to have 'charismatic authority' when their followers were inspired by the exceptional personal qualities of their leaders. In contrast, 'traditional authority' was a form of leadership rooted in the sanctity of an immemorial and sacred tradition. The third type of authority—legal-rational—was power embedded in a set of procedures, principles, or laws. This last form of legitimacy, Weber believed, was increasingly prevalent in the modern world. Legal-rational forms of thinking were becoming integral to the governance of state institutions.

These three concepts can be fruitfully applied to understand the evolution of schooling in Canada. In the mid-nineteenth century, most schools were single-room operations run by a lone teacher, often without formal credentials; attendance was sporadic and students varied widely in age. By contrast, today's schools are bureaucratically organized according to an explicit chain of authority running from provincial ministries and departments to school boards, to individual principals, to classroom teachers. This bureaucratization serves to rationalize the everyday life of schools. Today's teachers are certified. Curriculum is approved by committees of appointed officials. Students are assessed with age-graded and increasingly standardized tests, and in order to graduate students must attend classes for a prescribed number of hours.

This rationalization also serves as a source of legitimacy. Think of what public schools implicitly demand from citizens. Every year Canadian schools require tens of billions in tax dollars in order to operate. Attendance is legally compulsory from the ages of 5 or 6 until at least the age of 16 (18 in some provinces). Schools expect society to recognize their diplomas as sanctified emblems certifying that graduates have been officially 'educated'. All this requires a large amount of legitimacy. Historians have shown how school officials toiled for decades to persuade taxpayers that the newly built public school systems of the mid-nineteenth century were worthy of public support (Prentice, 1977). To gain massive public funding and widespread political authorization, schools had to evolve in ways that would win them public recognition. As we will argue in the next section, they secured their legitimacy by becoming more bureaucratic and rationalized, to the extent that education today has become a motherhood item par excellence. Schooling of course provokes its share of intense political battles, but the issues at stake are now limited to specific areas—curriculum, hiring practices, methods of evaluation, funding formulae. Almost no one questions the abstract value of schooling or argues for abolition of the system. To understand how this state of affairs evolved over the past century, in the next section we will examine how New Institutional Theory has adapted Weber's key ideas.

The Core Concepts of NIT in Education

The application of NIT in the study of education is usually identified with the work of John Meyer and his colleagues.[2] Other branches of contemporary sociology of education have also drawn on Weber's ideas in their studies of credentialism, cultural capital, and classroom authority, but these innovative scholars were the first to use his concepts of bureaucracy, rationalization, and legitimacy to analyze the organization of contemporary schooling.[3]

From Bureaucracy to 'Loose Coupling'

NIT is fundamentally skeptical regarding 'functionalist' conceptions of educational bureaucracy. It questions any line of analysis, implicit or explicit, conservative or radical, that sees schools as directly fulfilling essential 'needs' for their surrounding communities. Most influential in the 1950s and 1960s, structural functionalism saw modern schools as formal mechanisms designed to instill in young people the cognitive abilities and core values vital to modern democracy. This reasoning continues to thrive in the 'human capital' theories that view schools as 'skill-producing machines' that efficiently train young people in the skills essential to the performance of most jobs. By contrast, the Marxist perspective sees schools as responding to the needs of capitalist employers by training future workers to be docile and by imposing an ideological hegemony on their students (for a classic statement, see Bowles and Gintis, 1976). While Marxism certainly diverges from structural functionalist and human capital theories, Meyer and his colleagues maintain that it shares with those theories a tendency to exaggerate the functional connections between schools and local economies, and to overstate schools' ability to socialize youth into adopting common values.[4]

Instead of imagining that schools perform essential roles for society, NIT emphasizes the *absence* of strong functional connections between schools and their surrounding communities. First, it notes that schools closely monitor and bureaucratize only some of their key attributes. They ensure that teachers are properly credentialled, that curricula are certified, and that courses are appropriately labelled and age-graded; virtually all Canadian public schools hire teachers with university degrees, teach standardized courses like math, science, and English, and are structured in a K–12 format. But their core activity—instruction—is far less closely regulated. Classroom activities are rarely subject to direct monitoring. Teachers for the most part do their jobs behind closed doors, away from the direct gaze of administrators, and enjoy substantial autonomy in their classrooms. Instead of closely monitoring instruction, schools rely on a 'logic of confidence' whereby administrators assume that classrooms are operating properly as long as they are staffed by certified teachers. Instructional quality is rarely measured directly, and when evaluations are done, they are highly ritualistic. Thus NIT portrays schools as examples of **loose coupling**: imposing rigid control on the formalities but scarcely regulating classroom activity at all.

A second instance of loose coupling identified by NIT is the relationship between schools and employers. Beyond the basics of literacy and numeracy, NIT argues, little of what is learned in school is directly applicable in the workplace. As Collins (1979) has pointed out, school content has historically evolved without the direct input of employers; instead it reflects the self-interest of educators, status groups, and the pressures of credential inflation. That is, after the primary grades in which literacy and numeracy are mastered, most course content has surprisingly little to do with the needs of employers. Consider university curricula: except for those pursuing professional specialties like engineering, business, or medicine, most students are enrolled in academic subjects in the arts and sciences—disciplines that were never intended as vehicles for vocational training. Their contents and conventions have been shaped by the interests of scholars, not the requests of workplace managers, and as a result they make far more sense to academics than to business owners. Only in some professional programs do non-academic authorities have organizational mechanisms that allow them to influence what is taught. Thus politicians and business groups may urge universities to teach more practical and job-oriented content, but norms of academic freedom grant professors considerable autonomy from those calls. Under these circumstances, employers generally influence universities in an indirect fashion, either by donating funds or by sponsoring research.

Schools thus resemble Weber's bureaucracy, but with a twist: instead of rationalizing their classroom procedures, they focus on building legitimacy. Thus they tend to put more effort into maintaining a positive image (through their hiring policies or course offerings, for instance) than into keeping an eye on what is actually conveyed to students in the classroom. Why? Part of the answer lies in schools' multiple and often ambiguous missions. In Canada schools are mandated not only to develop cognitive skills, but also to foster good citizenship, build character, and equalize opportunity. This complexity makes it difficult for schools to identify measurable 'outputs' or develop core processes (i.e., teaching techniques) that can be easily standardized and replicated.[5] Indeed, teaching defies any simple rationalizing process. Most educators believe that instruction is spoiled by overly rigid attempts to control it, and they often resist any intrusive monitoring of their professional practice in the classroom (Ingersoll, 2003). Theories of pedagogy have long recognized that teachers bring a variety of individual styles to the classroom, and few believe that a 'McDonaldized' system (Ritzer, 2004) of centrally controlling and standardizing teaching would improve student learning. As a result, schools elect to control formalities such as course descriptions and personnel certification, but leave the daily rhythms of the classroom to the trusted hands of teachers.

From Rationalization to Isomorphism

If the 'loose coupling' metaphor is correct, then schools are only partly bureaucratic: they control their formalities but do not rationalize their core process—instruction. How do such institutions maintain an image of legitimacy in a bureaucratic world that prizes efficiency and standardization? According to Meyer and his colleagues, they do so not by proving their instructional effectiveness, but by conforming to approved organizational templates. This practice recalls Weber's description of the 'rationalization' of the world, but again with a contemporary twist: schools rationalize their formalisms not to be efficient, but to conform to normative images of the proper school.

According to NIT, a century of mass schooling has fostered a common expectation that a 'school' will have clearly demarcated courses, age-based levels, certified instructors, student evaluations, and standardized curricula. An educational organization that fails to conform to this image can risk not being recognized as a 'school' at all. The 'free schools' of the 1960s and 1970s, for instance, were radically experimental organizations that de-structured education and abandoned recognizable courses, levels, accreditations, discipline codes, and tests in the hope of promoting more uninhibited and authentic learning. These schools were initially popular, but when authorities looked in vain for science classes, classes identified by grade level, teachers with bachelor's degrees, tests, or exams of any kind, they soon began to question such schools' legitimacy. By the mid-1970s most of the free schools had closed. It is important to note that the movement's failure was not a reflection of the schools' effectiveness: there was little systematic evidence that they were ineffective. Rather, free schools were faulted for being chaotic and difficult for authorities to control. The failure of this experiment taught mainstream schools a key lesson: to survive, they would have to conform to established conventions. The way for a new school to secure funding and accreditation was not to demonstrate its pedagogical efficacy—admittedly a difficult thing to do— but rather to imitate established schools. 'Loose coupling' is one consequence of this pattern. Schools conform to standard templates but rarely attempt to rationalize their instructional practices. As an example, virtually all Canadian high schools have a level called 'grade 10' and a course called 'history'. What actually happens in a grade 10 history class, however, can vary greatly from school to school. Though curricula are becoming more standardized, most teachers remain free to devise their own instructional techniques, examples, and tests. And schools rarely face closure on account of poor teaching. As long as the school offers a grade 10 history course, all is well. But imagine a high school without a course called 'history' or a level called 'grade 10'. Even if its instructors and students were exceptional, that school would attract the ire of officials and risk closure, regardless of its effectiveness.

Another consequence is a tendency towards **isomorphism**. Rewarded for conforming to current notions of certification and accountability, schools have come to resemble one another more and more over time. Historians of education have documented how widely schools differed in the nineteenth century, before the advent of mass public systems. Many types existed—grammar schools, family-run operations, local academies, private schools—and the people running them often had no formal certification. The creation of centralized school bureaucracies, however, greatly reduced such variety. Indeed, NIT researchers have found that schools gradually converged around a single organizational template. In the United States, most schools began to adopt a K–12 form, a certain set of course categories ('language', 'science', 'math', 'history'), certification systems for teachers, and standard credit requirements around the turn of the twentieth century. By the end of the century this isomorphism had become global, with schools around the world following much the same rule-bound pattern (see Meyer and Ramirez, 2000). By conforming to standardized bureaucratic templates, public schools can greatly enhance their chances of survival, even if their classroom practices are radically different from those of other schools.

From Legitimacy to Institutionalization

A century of isomorphism has elevated the basic form of 'school' to taken-for-granted status. Few people now question the legitimacy of age-grading, teacher certification, or basic course labels. In short, these elements of schooling have become **institutionalized**. A particular set of organizational arrangements and cultural rules is said to be institutionalized when it becomes ubiquitous and 'infused with value', that is, cherished beyond its immediate utility either for society in general or for powerful interests (see Scott, 2001). School organizations have become an arena in which a variety of groups pursue their interests—from state officials to professionals to business groups to unions to racial, sexual, and religious groups, majority and minority alike. Since Ivan Illich's famous manifesto for 'deschooling'(1970), published nearly 40 years ago, almost no one has called for the abolition of schools. Critics regularly fault schools for their alleged failure to live up to some ideal, offering blueprints to make them more equitable, more efficient, or higher quality. But virtually no one wants them to be dismantled altogether.

One dimension of schools' institutionalized character is what Meyer calls their 'charter': the power to have school credentials recognized as legitimate markers of social status. Schools have the authority to distinguish the 'educated' from the 'non-educated' by conferring credentials on students who satisfy their program requirements, regardless of whether they have actually mastered any basic skills. This consecration gives graduates a new social standing wherever credentials are institutionalized in labour markets. Whereas a century ago many fields lacked formal certifications of any kind, today credential requirements are nearly ubiquitous, with most jobs demanding some sort of educational requirement. In most job fields, a self-taught applicant can demonstrate the requisite skills but be nonetheless ineligible if they lack required credentials.

A further consequence of this institutionalization is that 'education' has come to be valued beyond its economic utility. Being governed by state institutions for a century and a half, schooling has been hailed as a 'public good', identified with all sorts of collective goals, including equality, social mobility, civil rights, societal progress, and individual human development. Whether schools have actually realized these ideals is less important than their association with them. The ability of schooling to tap into the public imagination has made education all things to all people. When contemporary critics bemoan schools' failure to live up to expectations, they almost always call for their reform, not their elimination. Calls for reform can actually bolster schools' legitimacy by making them appear relevant and up-to-date. For these reasons, today's schools are championed for reasons quite apart from their instrumental value.

Example: Universities in the Knowledge-Based Economy

In this section we will extend these three NIT concepts—loose coupling, isomorphism, and institutionalization—to the idea, frequently expressed by policy-makers today, that universities should increase their enrolments in service of the emerging 'knowledge-based economy' (KBE). We argue that this idea reflects the institutionalization of higher education in Canadian society rather than a realistic assessment of the connections between universities and the economy.

Policy-makers in most developed nations are heralding the emergence of a new type of economy (see Powell and Snellman, 2004) in which the production of goods and services will require more abstract and theory-based know-how. With professional, managerial, and technical work replacing jobs in agriculture and manufacturing, more and more workers are said to need sophisticated training. The burgeoning information technology sector requires particular scientific skills, while new service sectors demand upgraded reasoning and communication competencies. The prime generator of these new skills, according to this theory, is higher education. Advocates of KBE argue that more and more Canadians need college- and university-level training if they are to thrive in these changing times.

Calls for boosting university enrolment are not new, but today's policy-makers are advancing a more 'expansive' vision of higher education (see Schofer and Meyer, 2005). In previous eras higher education was seen as playing a limited role in society. Policy-makers believed that relatively few positions required advanced cognitive skills, and that a university education would be 'wasted' on individuals who were less capable or had menial jobs. Today, however, policy-makers believe that universities offer a novel path to societal prosperity. This new argument is premised on a more open-ended image of individual productivity. A university education, they believe, can stimulate creativity, innovation, and entrepreneurial ingenuity. Higher education is seen to nurture not only specific vocational skills, but also generic abilities that can manifest themselves in new types of productivity. Let universities encourage undirected individual development and good things will happen, policy-makers say. As a result, provinces are diverting monies to universities, particularly at the master's and doctoral levels, urging Canadians to raise their 'production' of graduates in order to match or surpass our international competitors.

There is some truth to these claims. Employment studies clearly show a shift over time from manufacturing and natural resources towards the professional, managerial, and technical sectors (e.g., Krahn and Lowe, 2002). Furthermore, post-secondary enrolments have grown substantially in many parts of the world over the last half-century

(Schofer and Meyer, 2005), and Canada is no exception. Between 1987 and 2000, full-time enrolment in community colleges and universities increased by 28 per cent and 16 per cent, respectively (Statistics Canada, 2003). Indeed, Canada is perhaps the most 'credentialled' nation in the world. In 2000, 41 per cent of Canadian adults possessed a college diploma or a university degree—a record unmatched by any other OECD nation (Statistics Canada, 2003: 144).

NIT, however, suggests several reasons to doubt that a further expansion of higher education is urgently needed. First, there is little evidence that university enrolments are tightly coupled with job market trends. If the KBE claims were accurate, enrolments in scientific and technological fields would be skyrocketing. Yet most Canadian university students are not entering the 'technical' disciplines. Almost 40 per cent of students choose the social sciences, compared to only 8 per cent for engineering and the applied sciences, and these proportions have been relatively stable over time (Statistics Canada, 2005a).

The lack of connection between economic needs and what is taught at universities is another reason for skepticism. As we mentioned earlier in this chapter, economic officials have almost no feedback processes to make their desires known to university officials (see Fuller and Rubinson, 1992). There are few policy instruments by which governments can coordinate university enrolments with human resource demands. As a result, most Canadian graduates from the humanities, social sciences, and even the natural sciences experience difficulty making the transition from school to work. Moreover, universities have yet to develop the kind of standardized testing or 'exit exam' regimes used by elementary and secondary systems to guarantee minimal skill levels among their graduates. Higher-education officials have not given priority to developing procedures to ascertain what their students have actually absorbed.[6]

Second, it is hard to tell how many university graduates directly utilize their learned skills on the job. Degrees clearly pay off in the labour market, as non-credentialled youth enter lower paying jobs and experience longer bouts of unemployment (Krahn, 1996). Why might this be the case? If human capital theory were correct, the abilities developed in school should be directly reflected in measures of occupational performance or income. But a body of empirical evidence suggests that credentials, rather than cognitive skills or grades per se, are better predictors (Berg, 1970; Collins, 1979; Brown, 2001). The 'credentialism' literature has argued that employers often hire university graduates simply because a degree serves as a convenient basis for selection in a crowded and competitive marketplace. When more university graduates take less prestigious positions, displacing job candidates who lack formal credentials, another dynamic process is set in motion: more youth are motivated to earn credentials. With rising numbers of graduates, degrees become less exclusive, and their relative worth declines. Education thus becomes a 'positional good' that is subject to inflation. Studies indeed find that many credentialled workers are underemployed and overqualified in their jobs (for Britain, see Wolf, 2002; for Canada, see Lehmann, 2005; Livingstone, 1998). While job–education matches are tighter in professional fields such as medicine, engineering, teaching, law, and computer science (Finnie, 2002: 14), these fields account for only a fraction of total enrolment.

Third, large-scale studies cast doubt on the assumption that higher education enrolments will directly promote national economic growth. International studies find it difficult to detect clear connections between rising post-secondary enrolments and national economic productivity (Meyer and Ramirez, 2000). In other words, while higher education pays off at the individual level, its 'aggregate' effects appear to be weaker. Policy-makers may be mistaken to think that the advantages enjoyed by degree-holders mean that they are fuelling the economy with vital skills. The relationship between a university education and job success may simply reflect the ongoing institutionalization of credentials in labour markets. Many employers regard credentials only as broad indicators of competence and trustworthiness, and are increasingly likely to view non-credentialled candidates as second-rate or untrustworthy (Wolf, 2002)—an unfortunate by-product of the preponderance of people with university credentials. Policy-makers are under pressure to demonstrate that universities are capable of nurturing high-quality skills on a mass level. But they are making no effort to tighten the connections between universities and local economies, whether by developing feedback instruments or by creating more vocational programs—a near-impossible exercise and one that might not be beneficial in any case. Instead, they are taking the easier path of regulating universities in ways that encourage isomorphism. That is, to meet the challenges of the KBE, policy-makers are requiring universities to demonstrate their 'quality assurance' and 'accountability' by self-reporting the qualifications of their professors, the standard nature of their degree programs, and their coursework requirements. If universities can conform to their stated expectations, they receive a badge of accreditation. By ceremonially conforming to new images of efficiency and quality, universities can signal their readiness for the KBE without changing their core instructional practices. This exercise in conformity grants legitimacy to post-secondary institutions just as it did for K–12 schools a century ago.

In summary, core NIT concepts such as loose coupling, isomorphism, and institutionalization are valuable extensions of Weber's classic ideas about bureaucracy, rationalization, and legitimacy. We applied them to argue that KBE policies overstate the links between universities and the economy. While the economy is undoubtedly changing and will continue to do so, universities are responding in ways that are only loosely coupled with economic forces, involve some forms of isomorphism, and reflect the continuing institutionalization of credentials in job markets.

Conclusions: NIT's Contributions and Challenges

Most of the scholars represented in this volume approach their subjects from a 'critical' perspective. The more widely the term 'critical' is used, however, the more variable its meaning becomes. Critical approaches today appear to fall into two camps: those focusing on manifestations of social inequality, particularly in the areas of race, gender, and sexual orientation, and those analyzing modern society from a comparative and historical vantage point. The former camp is usually linked to contemporary feminist and anti-racist scholars (e.g., Gaskell, 1992; James, 2005). The latter has its roots in the Frankfurt School, which blended Marxist and Weberian thought. Just as Weber drew on Marx (his work has often been likened to a debate with Marx's ghost), the Frankfurt School drew on Weber's notions of rationalization to analyze the culture of post–Second World War capitalism (Bottomore, 1984). Later social theorists such as Michel Foucault and Jürgen Habermas also extended Weber's ideas in their own critiques of modern society.

Both these camps of critical theory—one that exposes various bases of social inequality, and one that holistically critiques the character of modern social life—challenge dominant understandings of society. NIT clearly belongs in the second camp, finding an ancestor in Max Weber and offering an alternative view of the relationship between schools and society. As we have shown, NIT questions dominant assumptions about the economic utility of schools, and suggests that education is valued for other reasons, some quite noble (human rights, progress, equity, human potential), and some less noble (status competition). NIT offers a counter-image of schools as legitimacy-seekers rather than as skill-producing machines, and casts doubt on the faith that many have placed in KBE rhetoric. NIT offers a timely alternative for thinking about how schools relate to society.

But NIT still faces an important challenge: to develop an account of educational inequality. NIT effectively reveals links between schools and stratification systems, and the decoupling of normative ideals from actual school practice, but it has not yet examined how inequalities—of race, class, or gender—have been institutionalized in schools. Perhaps future generations of NIT scholars will borrow from the other camp of critical theory to develop a more complete theory of modern education.

Notes

1. For excellent summaries of Weber's writings, see Bendix (1960), Collins and Markowsky (1992), and Grabb (2006). For an effective application of the concept of bureaucracy, see Freidson (2001).

2. For a classic statement, see Meyer and Rowan (1978). For recent extensions, see Meyer et al. (1997) and Meyer and Ramirez (2000). For new applications by other scholars, see Baker and Wiseman (2006), Davies and Guppy (2006), and Meyer and Rowan (2006).

3. For studies of credentialism, see Collins (1979), Livingstone (1998), and Brown (2001). For studies of cultural capital, see Bourdieu and Passeron (1977) and Erickson (1991). For studies of classroom authority, see Pace and Hemmings (2006) and Roberts and Clifton (1995).

4. NIT thus has more affinity with studies that emphasize student resistance (e.g., Solomon, 1992) than those that assume the smooth socialization of youth (e.g., Bowles and Gintis, 1976).

5. We use the term 'output' to refer to entities that represent measured school effectiveness or outcomes of instruction. Policy-makers increasingly consider standardized test scores to be the best measure of learning and hence the principal output of schools. Professional educators often dispute the usefulness of such tests, claiming that they promote narrow forms of learning, encourage 'teaching to the test', and divert attention from educational goals that are less easily measured.

6. Wolf (2002: 237–42) and Cote and Allahar (2007) speculate that expanding enrolments may actually serve to dilute the quality of university education. In Canada, expansion has reduced average per-student funding and has substantially increased tuition fees, student–faculty ratios, and use of casual teaching staff (Statistics Canada, 2003). Students who have to work part-time to pay their fees may devote less time to their studies and have less contact with their professors as a consequence.

Glossary

bureaucracy: An ideal-type of organization that is predominant in modern societies, characterized by hierarchies of authority that compel action through prescribed norms, rules, or laws, rather than kinship ties or personal loyalties.

institutionalization: A process whereby an adopted action becomes taken for granted as the one way to organize, as opposed to procedures that are continually scrutinized and modified for their technical efficiency.

isomorphism: The gradual convergence of organizational forms that stems from an ongoing adoption of common components and processes. Over time, this conformity makes organizations increasingly similar to one another.

loose coupling: A type of organization in which formalisms are tightly controlled (e.g., teachers are certified, curriculum is approved), while core technical processes (e.g., classroom instruction) are only minimally monitored or regulated.

rationalization: A process in which social activity is transformed by systematic attempts to make it calculable, standardized, and efficient.

Study Questions

1. In what ways are schools bureaucratic? Identify aspects of school organization that embody what Weber meant by the term.
2. Think of an example of 'loose coupling' in your university. Do you know of any educational organizations that are 'tightly coupled'?
3. What features of your university are institutionalized? In what ways is it isomorphic with other Canadian universities?
4. According to New Institutional theorists, both Marxists and structural functionalists think about education in functional terms. Explain.

Recommended Readings

Baker, David P., and Alex Wiseman, eds. 2006. *The Impact of Comparative Education Research on Institutional Theory*. Oxford: Elsevier Science.

Davies, Scott, and Neil Guppy. 2006. *The Schooled Society: An Introduction to the Sociology of Education*. Toronto: Oxford University Press.

Grabb, Edward. 2006. *Theories of Social Inequality: Classical and Contemporary Perspectives*, 5th edn. Toronto: Nelson Thomson.

Meyer, H.D., and B. Rowan, eds. 2006. *The New Institutionalism and Education*. Albany: SUNY Press.

Schofer, Evan, and John W. Meyer, 2005. 'The Worldwide Expansion of Higher Education in the Twentieth Century', *American Sociological Review* 70: 898–920.

Recommended Websites

Website for Stanford University's Comparative Sociology Workshop and home to John Meyer and many of his Institutional Theory colleagues: http://www.stanford.edu/group/csw/

Verstehen: A reference site developed to assist undergraduates with Weber's core ideas: http://www.faculty.rsu.edu/~felwell/Theorists/Weber/Whome.htm

Educational Statistics Program at Statistics Canada: A site containing links for a wide array of statistical trends in Canadian education: http://www.statcan.ca/english/edu/edstat.htm

References

Axelrod, Paul, Paul Anisef, and Zeng Lin. 2001. 'Against All Odds? The Enduring Value of Liberal Education in Universities, Professions, and the Labour Market', *Canadian Journal of Higher Education* 31, 2: 47–77.

Baker, David P., and Alex Wiseman, eds. 2006. *The Impact of Comparative Education Research on Institutional Theory*. Oxford: Elsevier Science.

Becker, Gary S. 1993. *Human Capital: A Theoretical and Empirical Analysis with Special Reference to Education*, 3rd edn. Chicago: University of Chicago Press.

Bendix, Reinhard. 1960. *Max Weber: An Intellectual Portrait*. Garden City, NY: Anchor Books.

Berg, Ivar. 1970. *Education and Jobs: The Great Training Robbery*. New York: Praeger Publishers.

Bottomore, Tom. 1984. *The Frankfurt School*. London: Tavistock Publications.

Bourdieu, Pierre, and Jean-Claude Passeron. 1977. *Reproduction*. Beverly Hills, CA: Sage.

Bowles, Samuel, and Herbert Gintis. 1976. *Schooling in Capitalist America*. New York: Basic Books.

Brown, David K. 2001. 'The Social Sources of Educational Credentialism: Status Cultures, Labor Markets, and Organizations', *Sociology of Education* Extra Issue: 19–34.

Canadian Association of University Teachers (CAUT). 2005. *CAUT Almanac of Post-secondary Education 2005*. Ottawa: CAUT.

Collins, Randall. 1979. *The Credential Society: An Historical Sociology of Education and Stratification*. New York: Academic Press.

———, and Michael Markowsky. 1992. *The Discovery of Society*, 5th edn. New York: Random House.

Cote, James E., and Anton L. Allahar. 2007. *Ivory Tower Blues: A University System in Crisis*. Toronto: University of Toronto Press.

Davies, Scott, and Neil Guppy. 2006. *The Schooled Society: An Introduction to the Sociology of Education*. Toronto: Oxford University Press.

Erickson, Bonnie H. 1991. 'What is Good Taste Good For?', *Canadian Review of Sociology and Anthropology* 28: 255–78.

Finnie, Ross. 2002. *Early Labour Market Outcomes of Recent Canadian University Graduates by Discipline: A Longitudinal Cross-Cohort Analysis*. Ottawa: Statistics Canada.

Freidson, Eliot. 2001. *Professionalism: The Third Logic*. Chicago: University of Chicago Press.

Fuller, Bruce, and Richard Rubinson. 1992. *The Political Construction of Education: The State, School Expansion, and Economic Change*. New York: Praeger.

Gaskell, Jane. 1992. *Gender Matters from School to Work*. Toronto: OISE Press.

Grabb, Edward. 2006. *Theories of Social Inequality: Classical and Contemporary Perspectives*, 5th edn. Toronto: Nelson Thomson.

Illich, Ivan. 1970. *Deschooling Society*. New York: Harper and Row.

Ingersoll, Richard M. 2003. *Who Controls Teachers' Work? Power and Accountability in America's Schools*. Cambridge, MA: Harvard University Press.

James, Carl. 2005. *Race in Play: Understanding the Socio-Cultural World of Student Affairs*. Toronto: Canadian Scholars' Press.

Kerckhoff, Alan C. 2001. 'Education and Stratification Processes in Comparative Perspective', *Sociology of Education* 74: 3–18.

Krahn, Harvey. 1996. *School–Work Transitions: Changing Patterns and Research Needs*. Ottawa: Human Resources Development Canada.

————, and Graham Lowe. 2002. *Work, Industry and Canadian Society*, 4th edn. Toronto: Nelson Canada.

Labaree, David F. 1997. *How to Succeed in School without Really Learning: The Credentials Race in American Education*. New Haven: Yale University Press.

Lehmann, Wolfgang. 2005. 'I'm Still Scrubbing the Floor: Experiencing High School Based Youth Apprenticeships', *Work, Employment, and Society* 19, 1: 107–29.

Livingstone, David W. 1998. *The Education–Jobs Gap: Underemployment or Economic Democracy*. Boulder, CO: Westview Press.

Marquardt, Richard. 1998. *Enter at Your Own Risk: Canadian Youth and the Labour Market*. Toronto: Between the Lines.

Meyer, H.D., and B. Rowan, eds. 2006. *The New Institutionalism and Education*. Albany: SUNY Press.

Meyer, J., and B. Rowan. 1978. 'The Structure of Educational Organizations', in Marshall Meyer, ed., *Environments and Organizations*. San Francisco: Jossy Bass, 15–82.

————, John Boli, George M. Thomas, and Francisco O. Ramirez. 1997. 'World Society and the Nation-State', *American Journal of Sociology* 103, 1: 144–81.

————, and Francisco O. Ramirez. 2000. 'The World Institutionalization of Education', in Juergen Schriewer, ed., *Discourse Formation in Comparative Education*. Frankfurt: Peter Lang, 111–32.

Organisation for Economic Co-operation and Development (OECD). 2005. 'Productivity Levels and GDP per Capita—Data: Breakdown of GDP in Its Components and Differential in GDP per Capita and Their Decomposition'. Available at: http: //www.oecd.org/dataoecd/31/7/29880166.pdf. Accessed 15 April 2005.

Pace, Judith, and Annette Hemmings. 2006. *Classroom Authority: Theory, Research and Practice*. London: Lawrence Erlbaum and Associates.

Powell, Walter W., and Kaisa Snellman. 2004. 'The Knowledge Economy', *Annual Review of Sociology* 30: 199–220.

Prentice, Alison. 1977. *Education and Social Class in Mid-Nineteenth Century Upper Canada*. Toronto: McClelland and Stewart.

Ritzer, George. 2004. *The McDonaldization of Society*, Revised New Century Edition. Thousand Oaks, CA: Pine Forge Press.

Roberts, Lance W., and Rodney A. Clifton. 1995. 'Authority in Classrooms', in Roberts and Clifton, eds, *Crosscurrents: Contemporary Canadian Educational Issues*. Toronto: Nelson Canada, 459–69.

Schofer, Evan, and John W. Meyer. 2005. 'The Worldwide Expansion of Higher Education in the Twentieth Century', *American Sociological Review* 70: 898–920.

Scott, W. Richard. 2001. *Institutions and Organizations*, 2nd edn. Thousand Oaks, CA: Sage.

Solomon, Patrick. 1992. *Black Resistance in High School: Forging a Separatist Culture*. Albany: State University of New York Press

Statistics Canada. 2003. *Education Indicators in Canada: Report of the Pan-Canadian Education Indicators Program 2003*. Toronto: Canadian Education Statistics Council.

————. 2005a. 'University Qualifications Granted by Field of Study, by Sex'. Available at: <http: //www.statcan.ca/english/Pgdb/educ21.htm>. Accessed 13 March 2005.

————. 2005b. 'Productivity and Related Measures, by Business Sector (quarterly)'. Available at: <http://www.statcan.ca/english/Pgdb/econ78a.htm. Accessed 13 March 2005.

————. 2005c. 'Experienced Labour Force 15 Years and Over by Occupation (1991–2001 Censuses)'. Available at <http://www.statcan.ca/english/Pgdb/labor44.htm>. Accessed 15 April 2005.

Sweet, Robert, and Paul Anisef, eds. 2005. *Preparing for Postsecondary Education: New Roles for Governments and Families*. Kingston: McGill-Queen's University Press.

Taylor, Alison. 2001. 'Fellow Travellers' and 'True Believers': A Case Study of Religion and Politics in Alberta Schools', *Journal of Education Policy* 16, 1: 15–37.

Wolf, Alison. 2002. *Does Education Matter? Myths about Education and Economic Growth*. New York: Penguin.

CHAPTER 2

Feminist Approaches to the Sociology of Education in Canada

Jane Gaskell

The resurgence of the women's movement since the 1970s has affected all areas of sociology. It changed some of the questions that were being asked and destabilized some assumptions that had been taken for granted. The effect of **feminism** on educational scholarship has been particularly strong because most people, including government policy-makers, see education as a prerequisite for equal opportunity. When feminism demanded equal opportunity for women, education was one of the first areas targeted for reform and rethinking. Feminist scholars in the sociology of education have explored ways in which the organization of education disadvantages women, perpetuating the wage gap and women's lack of power in many spheres. It has also challenged the perception that education offers a route to equality, arguing that education reflects larger social forces and therefore cannot promote equality without profound changes in the economy, the family, and the culture.

The impact of feminism on the sociology of education in Canada was in part a product of the new questions it asked about educational institutions. Feminists wanted to understand the connections between education and other gendered patterns of inequality. They asked questions about the curriculum, the relative achievement of men and women, the economic consequences of educational attainment, and the careers of male and female educators. They wanted to know how sexuality was treated in schools, how male and female students related to one another in the playground, how the historical purposes of schooling had changed and how they had served men and women. The questions varied over time and from one feminist researcher to another, for feminism is not a single and unified way of looking at the world. Feminism is unified, however, in adding gender to the field of sociology of education.

The impact of feminism also reflected the challenge it put to the assumptions embedded in older sociological theories. Most obviously, feminism challenged the idea that the subordination of women was natural and inevitable, that it was biologically determined and could not be changed. From this starting point feminist theory branched into a variety of directions, as women tried to analyze their own experience, refine the conceptual tools necessary to articulate their points of view, and test out some of their suggestions for change in practice (Jagger and Rothenberg, 1984). A conversation grew in journals, books, classrooms, and conferences.

The women's movement that emerged around the world in the late 1960s was seen both by participants and by those looking in from the outside as a coherent effort to change the lives of women. But in fact—like any social movement—it was made up of people with different priorities and approaches. In many countries the principal issues were the wage gaps between men and women, segregation of the labour market by gender, and the taken-for-granted allocation of domestic labour to women. Some feminists focused on public representations of women as sexual objects and domestic help, and the power differences that shaped interactions between men and women. At the same time, women of colour pointed out how racial categories interacted with gendered categories to particularly disadvantage them, and women in developing nations examined how colonialism had changed the organization of gender difference.

There was agreement on many issues, but also disagreement about what to focus on and how to make sense of the workings of gender. 'Social movements are not entities that move with the unity of goals attributed to them by ideologues. Movements are systems of action, complex networks among the different levels and meanings of social action. Collective identity is not a datum or an essence, it is the outcome of exchanges, negotiations, decisions, and conflicts among actors.' (Melucci, 1996). The women's 'movement' represented a lot of different things to a lot of different people, even while it was described as one 'thing'.

In this essay I will explore some of the ways in which feminist thought has affected the sociology of education in Canada since the early 1970s. Rather than argue that any one perspective is the best or most powerful, I will examine three that have made a difference, showing how they developed and what questions they illuminate. The continuing dialogue among feminist perspectives makes the area a lively and important one for understanding the organization of education.

The points of view I will sketch out (and of course oversimplify) all start from the observation that women have less power than men. All three are concerned with understanding how educational institutions contribute to, or might reduce, this inequality. Where they disagree is in their understanding of gender 'difference', the assumptions they make, the questions they ask, and the kinds of research they have inspired. They can be summarized as follows:

1. Equal rights feminism sees gender differences as socially based—the product of nurture rather than nature—and seeks to minimize them in the belief that women should stand on an equal footing with men. It asks how schools, colleges, or universities overtly, subtly, or systemically discriminate against women and prevent them from reaching equality with men. Research in this tradition documents the inequalities in the treatment that girls and women receive, compared to boys and men, both in schools and in society.

2. Radical feminism recognizes many differences between women and men. What it questions is why and how men's experience is privileged over women's. It asks how knowledge, curriculum, and school structures have come to reflect male perspectives, and why the ways women learn and experience the world are undervalued. Research in this tradition documents the differences between men and women, and critiques the institutional structures that continue to exclude and devalue female characteristics and the people having them.

3. Poststructural or postmodern feminism points out that differences exist not just between men and women, but among and within groups of women and men. It is reflexive, making the reader aware that any observation about gender difference is constructed through **discourses** that make sense in context. Research in this tradition includes exploration of how factors like social class, race, ethnicity, language, and sexual preference shape and subdivide gender categories. It rethinks the nature of power in classrooms and educational institutions, showing its instability over time and place, and explores how students and educators develop a sense of identity in the context of changing curriculum and school structures.

Equal Rights Feminism

In 1970 the Royal Commission on the Status of Women produced a 300-page report that broke new ground in beginning to name the issues of concern to women in Canada (Royal Commission, 1970). It devoted a long chapter to education, based on extensive research into Canadian schools and universities. The Commission's approach is a good example of equal rights feminist analysis of the sociology of education.

The Commission's research showed women were receiving less education than men. More girls took commercial courses in high schools, more boys took mathematics and science, more young men went on to university, and then to medicine, law, and graduate degrees. The commission asked why, and looked for sociological answers. 'What are the variables that affect the educational enrolment and consequent occupational patterns of women? Why do so many girls complete junior matriculations and then drop out? Why do fewer girls than boys attend university?' (1970: 173)

Some of their findings involved straightforward discrimination: 'for boys and girls coming out of grade 13 into the first premedical year, there are three universities that demand a 10 percent higher academic qualification from the girls' (1970: 171). Other findings pointed to economic differences: even though female students earned less than their male counterparts in the summers, for instance, many were reluctant to take out a student loan for fear that it would become a 'negative dowry'. Among its conclusions the Report noted that equal rights for women depended on changes in child-rearing practices and family values, guidance counselling, and adult education.

The Commission also identified instances of systemic bias built into the system. It found that textbooks were rife with sexual stereotypes. Women were underrepresented in school books, and when they were represented, they were stereotyped in less active and powerful roles. Little girls in elementary school texts played with dolls while their brothers played baseball; mothers wore aprons and baked cookies, while fathers drove off to work; adult women were princesses and witches, while men were doctors and farmers. The Report concluded that 'a woman's creative and intellectual potential is either underplayed or ignored in the education of children from their earliest years. The sex roles described in these textbooks provide few challenging models for young girls, and they fail to create a sense of community between men and women as fellow human beings.' Other examples of sex role socialization included separate playground line-ups for girls and boys, the assignment of different chores to boys and girls, and having girls and boys form teams to compete against each other. Studies cited by the Commission showed that boys received more attention from teachers than girls and that teachers often had stereotyped expectations regarding the capacities and interests of male and female students.

Authors in the areas of child development and sociology of education at the time described 'sex role socialization' as an important function of schooling, and learning 'sex-appropriate' behaviours and traits in childhood as a prerequisite for mental health and smooth social functioning in adulthood (Parsons, 1942; Kagan, 1964).They believed that reinforcing gender differences was beneficial to both the individual and the society. The Commission, on the other hand, believed that sex differences were not biologically but socially based, and that sex-role stereotypes should be eliminated because they prevented women from achieving as much as men.

The Commission had an enormous impact on public consciousness, and a variety of policy changes were made in response to its recommendations. Since education was, then as now, a provincial rather than a federal responsibility, many different groups used the language of the Royal Commission in presenting their arguments at the provincial level. Ministries of education across the country appointed advisory groups on sexism and published guidelines for eliminating stereotyping in materials and in classroom practices. In 1974 British Columbia's ministry of education, which had appointed an advisory committee and a special advisor on sex discrimination, issued a directive called 'On the Equal Treatment of the Sexes: Guidelines for Educational Materials'. In 1976 the Quebec government published 'L'École sexiste c'est quoi?' And in the same year the Ontario ministry of education published 'Sex-Role Stereotyping and Women's Studies', a resource guide intended 'to assist educators in the ongoing task of developing a learning environment that is free from sex-role stereotyping of males and females and curriculum that accurately depicts the roles of women'. Among its recommendations were the following: 'Illustrations of groups should include both females and males'; 'Both males and females should be shown indoors and outdoors, in the home and at their places of work, with a wider range of occupational roles'; and 'When indoors, not all women need to wear an apron'(4). Alternative materials were developed and published.

These changes had an effect. By the early 1980s girls no longer had to take home economics while boys took industrial education, and formerly divided playgrounds were becoming integrated. Teachers were exposed to discussions of sex discrimination, and separate staffrooms for male and female teachers became less common. The critique of stereotyping had caught on. The idea that biology did not mean destiny, that equality meant open access and equal treatment, was increasingly accepted. The numbers of women in science and math, in universities, and in leadership positions in the teaching profession increased.

The gender gaps in school enrolment and achievement in Canada are significantly smaller today, but differences remain. Enrolments in professional faculties like law and medicine are much more equal than they were, and women now constitute well over half (about 60 per cent) of university students. Nursing remains overwhelmingly female, however, as does teaching. And women are still underrepresented not only in engineering and science but in leadership positions in education. The reasons for these differences are still being debated (Skelton, Francis, and Smulyan, 2006).

For example, when Larry Summers, the president of Harvard, claimed in 2005 that innate differences might account for women's underrepresentation in the sciences and mathematics, critics pointed to numerous studies of the ways those fields make it difficult for women to succeed. As Barton and Brickhouse put it, 'If one wants to understand why . . . access to many areas of science continues to be a struggle, one must look beyond achievement and examine more broadly how gendered identities are constructed and how they interact with an educational system that serves an important gatekeeping function' (2006: 227).

Meanwhile, concern about boys' performance in school has grown. Commissions in Ontario, Australia, and elsewhere are exploring the issues involved, trying to understand how gender continues to play out in the schools, and what might be done about it (Martino, 2006).

Radical Feminism

The belief that men and women, boys and girls, should be equally represented in all areas of education, and at all levels of study, is not universally shared by feminists. In the early 1970s many feminists were less interested in statistical and economic equality than in the politics of personal relationships and the struggle to see women's experiences, perspectives, and beliefs validated in the wider culture. These women asked questions about sexuality, housework, dress, language, and child-rearing. They were concerned with establishing non-hierarchical structures, governing by consensus, and recognizing difference as legitimate rather than problematic. The challenge for women was not just to become an equal part of the existing world; it was to invent new ways of living and new forms of knowledge that better reflected the ways in which women lived and worked (Taylor and Whittier, 1995).

Because the idea that women were different had been used to exclude them, many women had denied the differences attributed to them. But some feminists pointed out that denying difference had created a climate in which everyone was expected to conform to masculine models. Coeducation meant male education for everyone. There had been no shift in the power of women or the value attributed to them: just a general acceptance that they should be treated like men.

Feminist critics argued that values associated with women—nurturance, sociability, interdependence—were also important in schools, though they had too often been devalued by men. As Jeri Wine pointed out:

The large literature on psychological sex differences is highly problematic from a feminist perspective because of its apparent demonstration of the inferiority of the female. In this work, the guiding assumptions are that any characteristic that males have more of than do females is an essential characteristic, a mark of superiority, while any characteristic that females have more of is a sign of weakness, of inferiority. Women's investment in the interpersonal realm has been consistently devalued in psychology, our connectedness with others seen as pathological dependency needs, nurturance and interpersonal sensitivity defined as weakness (1982: 70).

These observations suggested that, instead of assuming women ought to become more like men, sociologists should pay more attention to women's differences from men—and the ways in which educational institutions devalue these characteristics. As Finn and Miles put it:

female characteristics, concerns, and abilities marginalized in industrial society, are necessarily central to the building of new more fully human society. The holistic, collective, intuitive, co-operative, emotional, nurturing, democratic, integrated, internal, and natural are affirmed against the over-valuation of the competitive, analytical, rational, hierarchical, fragmented, external and artificial. (1982: 13)

In a frequently quoted address to a group of female college graduates in 1977, the poet Adrienne Rich encapsulated this argument:

What you can learn here (and I mean not only here but at any college or in any university) is how men have perceived and organized their experience, their history, their ideas about social relationships, good and evil, sickness and health, etc. When you read or hear about 'great issues', 'major texts', 'the mainstream of western thought', you are hearing about what men, above all white men, in their male subjectivity, have decided is important. (1979: 232)

Mary O'Brien (1981) felicitously dubbed this curriculum the 'malestream'.

Sociologist Dorothy Smith (1990) argued that feminist sociologists should start from 'the standpoint of women' rather than sociology, exploring the questions that women would ask and making the assumptions that they would make. 'We do not begin with the categories and theories of the established discourse. . . . [R]ather a sociology for women must be able to explicate for women how their own social situation, their everyday world, is organized and determined' (220). If the usual sociological discourse reflects the point of view of the dominant class and group, a women's sociology needs to listen more carefully to the disadvantaged and outcast.

Smith's recent work with Allison Griffith on mothers and their interactions with the school system illustrates how the system can be rethought from a woman's point of view. Griffith and Smith (2005) point out that the system of formal schooling depends on the work of mothers. The principals they talked to viewed mothers as appendages of the educational system, some of whom were meeting the needs of that system by preparing their children well for school and some of whom were not. This dynamic has so shaped the way women see themselves as mothers that many have had difficulty recognizing any other grounds for valuing their work, especially if their children are struggling in the school environment. The job of the sociologist is to explain how this view of motherhood arose historically as schooling became universal and the assumption that women were primarily responsible for domestic work took root. Understanding the current organization of schooling in its context of family, economy, neighbourhood, and state makes it possible to imagine that it might be otherwise. Mothering might be valued for the self-confidence it generates in children, or the relationships it fosters with the church, or any number of other criteria. That schooling success becomes the criterion for judging family relations is an interesting, and gendered, social fact.

Some feminist theorists have argued that women and men learn in different ways, and that formal educational institutions do not provide enough space for women's 'ways of knowing'. In the 1970s, small, leaderless groups of women sharing their life experience constituted an enormously powerful and politically influential model of learning in the women's movement. The 'consciousness-raising' undertaken by these groups resembled the process that Paulo Freire called 'conscientization', combining political action and the active reconstruction of knowledge by learners. Belenky, Blythe, Goldberger, and Tarule (1986) wrote a very influential book outlining what they claimed was a distinctively female pattern of learning. On the basis of interviews with diverse women about how they learned, they argued that women came to under-standing through a series of stages, from silence to subjective knowledge to procedural knowledge and finally to 'constructed' knowledge. The authors concluded that in order to facilitate this growth, schools should emphasize 'connected knowing', rather than the dissemination of information in a traditional lecture format.

Discussions of 'feminist pedagogy' and feminist classrooms have not drawn such a clear line between the feminist and the traditional classroom. Feminist pedagogy tends to emphasize (a) questioning of the traditional authority relations between teacher and student, and (b) distrust of bureaucracy (Maher and Tetreault, 2001). It objects to the separation of the public classroom from private experience, and of emotion from reason, critiquing traditional classrooms for a one-dimensional view of knowledge that excludes women (as well as less privileged men).

In every curriculum area, the possibility of rethinking what counts as knowledge opens up new historical and sociological questions. Why is the language of domination and imposition so powerful in the science curriculum? Might it be replaced by 'conversations' with nature or 'a feeling for the organism' (Keller, 1985)? Why do individualized arguments about justice underpin our legal system and our tests of moral reasoning, when young women tend to use a more contextualized and collective reasoning that Gilligan (1982) termed 'the ethic of care'? Why are the public and the private spheres so clearly demarcated and gendered (Elshtain, 1981; Pateman, 1988)? Why do economic indicators ignore women's contributions to the domestic economy and take market value as a measure of worth (Cohen, 1982)?

Sex education is of particular interest to the feminist sociologist. All students learn a good deal about sexuality in school, even though sexuality itself is usually strictly regulated in schools (Epstein and Johnson, 1998). Public discourses about sexuality permeate and shape school environments, as Deirdre Kelly (2000) shows in her study of British Columbia secondary schools seeking to include teen mothers. The school can also challenge and reform those assumptions, creating safer spaces to explore critical feminist positions.

Finally, the emphasis on revaluing women's experience and work leads to a revised view of the connections between education and work. The usual assumption is that more education leads to a better job and more income. But women have frequently had more education than men, and it has not brought them better jobs or more income than men. In the early twentieth century, although women were less likely than men to attend university, they were more likely to graduate from high school and from elementary school. Yet their education did not gain them higher pay or better labour market chances than men. Gender inequalities and differences are built into both the structure of schooling and its links with the labour market (Gaskell, 1992).

Young women stayed in school in order to qualify for the jobs that were available to them—as office secretaries, as schoolteachers, as librarians. These jobs paid less than the equivalent trades and industrial jobs available to young men, even though they required higher levels of literacy. Moreover, young women received no pay while attending the various educational institutions that offered the necessary technical training; young men, by contrast, typically were paid as apprentices while learning their trades on the job.

Instead of arguing that equality will be achieved when there are as many girls as boys in mathematics and physics classes, radical feminism critiques the wages and prestige associated with the jobs that women have traditionally done. Equal-pay legislation has forced employers to recognize that the work women have done is underpaid in relation to the skills, education, and responsibility it entails. Daycare workers have been paid less than dog catchers; secretaries are paid less than male technicians with equal levels of education.

This second version of feminist thought makes the excellent point that central educational concepts like science, ethics, knowledge, curriculum, pedagogy, and labour markets are not neutral and necessary in the form they take. The educational structures we take for granted were established in a world where men had more power than women, and they reflect that fact in various often complicated ways. Sociologists can play an important role in analyzing the ways educational structures have been shaped by gender inequality, and suggesting what policies might lead to change.

Postmodern approaches

A third version of feminist thought, the one most prevalent in the academy today, does not assume a simple dichotomy between 'male' and 'female': instead, it holds the meaning of gender difference up to continual scrutiny. It recognizes that any talk about gender arises in a particular context, among a particular group of people, with a particular history. These discourses are often contradictory, they change over time, and they illuminate and privilege the experience of some people at the expense of others. A feminist analysis will focus on and disrupt the taken-for-grantedness of gender talk wherever it arises, and will look for ways to call it into question along with the power relations it reflects. It asks what gender means and how it is associated with power, without presuming to know what the answer will be.

This form of feminist analysis takes its force from a critique of **essentialism**, and hence of any simple 'revaluing of the female'. For 'the female' is not a single biologically defined thing. Valuing the female can mean glorifying characteristics that women have developed in response to male domination, denigrating useful 'male' characteristics, reinforcing restrictive biological dichotomies, and ignoring the diversity of the experiences and cultures that women and men can have.

Many of the early feminist texts from the 1970s, as bell hooks (1984) points out, focused on the plight of 'a select group of college-educated, middle and upper class, married white women—housewives bored with leisure, with the home, with children, with buying products, who wanted more out of life'. To define the experience of those particular women as 'women's' experience is to overgeneralize, falsely extending the experience of those with power to those without. In the context of the labour market, to analyze the economic disadvantage faced by 'women'—as if women constituted a homogeneous category—in relation to men is to ignore an increasing differentiation in economic advantage among women. When all women are cast as equally disadvantaged, particular pockets of poverty, for example among single mothers or Aboriginal women, become invisible, and professional women who are already relatively privileged may be the ones to benefit most. Furthermore, the implications of gender vary across cultural and linguistic groups, both in Canada and around the world (Trinh, 1989).

The point is not to define 'female experience' as any one thing, but to understand how gender relations have functioned as relations of power. In the end it is power relations that need to be examined, in all their forms. Gender should not be privileged over race, class, ability, ethnicity, nationality, or any factor that plays a part in shaping our lives. Since these things do not necessarily work the same way for men and women, we must look for gender relations as they coexist and interact with other relations of domination and exclusion.

A recent book by Marnina Gonick (2003), illustrates this approach. In *Between Femininities* Gonick examines how girls in the late elementary grades make sense of gender. She works with them as they make videos, talks to them informally, and takes notes on their comments, actions, and narratives. Her theoretical stance is set out at the beginning:

> Girlhood, far from signifying a universal, biological grounded condition of female experience, emerges instead within particular socio-historical material and discursive contexts. It is shaped and reshaped in complex ways through ongoing fantasized acts of relationality—with others, with idealized images and with both conceptual categories and practices. (2003: 6)

To understand what it means to be a girl in downtown Toronto at the beginning of the twenty-first century, she looks closely at the girls' language and the different contexts in which they use certain words and images, as well as their school and the popular culture they interact with. These young people are not committed to a single way of being; their identities are not fixed but multiple, unstable, and ambivalent.

Sociologists focus on how any particular school represents difference in its curriculum, its administrative structure, and its relations with the community. Is there a dominant version of femaleness or maleness? If so, how does it affect the way students and teachers see themselves? Does it normalize their identities or marginalize them? Move them closer to the centre of power or farther away?

Autobiographical texts are well suited to being clear about particular contexts and meanings. Those concerned about literacy are particularly attuned to the way language plays out through talk about gender, schooling, and knowledge. Ursula Kelly reflects on the cultural politics of literacy and sexuality, using her own experience in Atlantic Canada as a lens. She critiques the language around her, refusing 'the often taken for granted (mis)understanding of language as objective expression of thought and reality' (1997: 13). With these tools she examines identity, culture, desire, and pedagogy in schooling.

Another collection of mostly Canadian articles that consistently query the nature of difference and identity in schooling is *Dangerous Territories: Struggles for Difference and Equality in Education* (Roman and Eyre, 1997). Linda Eyre points out how even a curriculum designed to overcome homophobia can reinforce the assumptions that it is trying to critique. Analyzing the complications of classroom life, specific teaching strategies, and even fleeting bits of talk can tell us a great deal about the organization of schooling.

In such a complex context, curriculum must become multifaceted, to allow for multiple discourses. Empirical research can explore the extent to which this is occurring. Does the history curriculum include women's work in First Nations families in Labrador and pioneer women on the Prairies? Does the English curriculum examine Audre Lorde's poetry along with Virginia Woolf's novels and essays? Does the art and music that is studied include different cultures and places, exploring and validating the varieties of expression that are possible?

This third approach to feminist sociology of education emphasizes the shifting and local construction of identity, meaning, and power. For 'woman' is no fixed, unchanging category with a given meaning and power. The meaning of gender, its organization and relation to material and symbolic power shifts and changes. Schooling must therefore ensure that the curriculum and pedagogy enables all people to give voice to their experience, to analyze and understand it, and to connect it to the experience of others. Scholarship in this tradition explores the changing discourse about men and women, the different ways in which people have understood experience in schools, and the ways in which teachers can negotiate different discourses, as well as differences in privilege, to engage students in reflection.

Conclusion

Feminist sociologists seeking greater equality for female students and educators have called for a fundamental rethinking both of school as an institution and of our thinking about it. Feminist sociology has engaged with some of the most difficult and persistent concerns in our ongoing dialogue about education: who does the system serve, why, and how?

Feminism offers no simple answers. This chapter has stressed the differences between three feminist perspectives, but a good analysis could well incorporate elements from each of them: for instance, a historical account of how a particular school developed to serve a particular social group, a statistical analysis of who is most successful in that school, and a discursive account of individual students' views of themselves in that school could all coexist and illuminate the way gender works. Each perspective can offer important insights into both gender and education. Each is committed to changing the way schools work so that more people can benefit from them.

On the other hand, the different perspectives tend to be useful for different purposes. Questions informed by a concern for equality, for instance, are good at revealing basic patterns. What proportion of community college teachers are women? In what areas do they teach? What are the average incomes for men and women when they graduate from university? Such questions reveal little or nothing about the social dynamics behind those patterns, however, or the remedies that will make a difference.

In order to analyze the social dynamics that produce inequality for women, sociologists look for discrimination, institutionalized bias, and/or discursive patterns that associate power with particular understandings. Does the school experience respect and value the ways the women in them learn, think, and act? Is it a place where men feel more comfortable than women? Which girls find which classes interesting and lively, and why? How is the authority of the dominant texts maintained and challenged? Whose words are considered authoritative? Questions like these can provide key insights into the gendered nature of schooling.

Glossary

discourse: The language used within a particular context to refer to a specific subject area. A discourse of femininity is a set of statements and concepts that are concerned with femininity and have some coherence in a particular time and place.

essentialism: The belief that people have unchanging properties that are essential to what they are. In feminism, it is the belief that qualities of being female are intrinsic and natural rather than contingent, the product of cultural conditioning.

feminism: Belief in the social, political, and economic equality of men and women; a social movement, moral philosophy, and political theory that promotes the equality of women.

Study Questions

1. Take a look around the class in which you are reading this book. How many of your classmates are men and how many are women? Does one group speak more often than the other? How would you explain this pattern?
2. Find out how many of the full professors at your university are men and how many are women. How do you explain the numbers? Is this information easily available? If it is not, what might this tell you about the institution?

3. What single change in the field of education do you think would do the most to advance gender equality in Canada?
4. What change in education would be most helpful for Aboriginal women? For black women? For rural women? If your answer changes from one group to the next, explain why.
5. How do female undergraduates today feel about feminism? Would you call yourself a feminist? Why?
6. What do you think is the most important research question for feminism today? From which school of feminist thought does this question emerge?

Recommended Readings

Gonick, M. 2003. *Between Femininities: Ambivalence, Identity and the Education of Girls*. Albany: SUNY Press.
Kelly, D. 2000. *Pregnant with Meaning: Teen Mothers and the Politics of Inclusive Schooling*. New York: Peter Lang.
Reynolds, Cecilia, and Beth Young. 1995. *Women and Leadership*. Calgary: Detselig.
Skelton, C., B. Francis, and L. Smulyan, eds. 2006. *The Sage Handbook of Gender and Education*. London: Sage Publications.

Recommended Websites

The scholarly journal *Gender and Education*: http://www.tandf.co.uk/journals/titles/09540253. asp
Status of Women Canada: http://www.swc-cfc.gc.ca/index_e.html
Feminist educational research sites: http://carbon.cudenver.edu/~mryder/itc/fem_res.html
Centre for Women's Studies in Education at Ontario Institute for Studies in Education, University of Toronto: http://www.oise.utoronto.ca/cwse/resources.html

References

Barton, A., and N. Brickhouse. 2006. 'Engaging Girls in Science', in Skelton, Francis, and Smulyan (2006: 221–35).
Belenky, M., C. Blythe, N. Goldberger, and J. Tarule. 1986. *Women's Ways of Knowing: The Development of Self, Voice and Mind*. New York: Basic Books.
Cohen, M. 1982. 'Women's Paid Work: The North American and Western European Experience', *Labour/Le Travail* 8–9: 309–16.
Elshtain, J. 1981. *Public Man, Private Woman*. Princeton, N.J. Princeton University Press.
Epstein, D., and R. Johnson. 1998. *Schooling Sexualities*. Buckingham: Open University Press.
Finn, G., and A. Miles, eds. 1982. *Feminism in Canada*. Montreal: Black Rose.
Gaskell, J. 1992. *Gender Matters from School to Work*. Milton Keynes and Philadelphia: Open University Press.
Gilligan, C. 1982. *In a Different Voice*. Cambridge, MA: Harvard University Press.
Gonick, M. 2003. *Between Femininities: Ambivalence, Identity and the Education of Girls*. Albany: SUNY Press.
Griffith, A.I., and D.E. Smith. 2005. *Mothering for Schooling*. New York: RoutledgeFalmer.
hooks, bell. 1984. *Ain't I a Woman? Black Women and Feminism*. Boston: South End Press.
Jagger, A., and P. Rothenberg, eds. 1984. *Feminist Frameworks: Alternative Theoretical Accounts of the Relations between Women and Men*, 2nd edn. New York: McGraw Hill.

Kagan, J. 1964. 'Acquisition and Significance of Sex Typing and Sex Role Identity', in M.L. Hoffman and L.W. Hoffman, eds, *Child Development Research*. New York: Russell Sage.

Keller, E.F. 1985. *Reflections on Gender and Science*. New Haven: Yale University Press.

Kelly, D. 2000. *Pregnant with Meaning: Teen Mothers and the Politics of Inclusive Schooling*. New York: Peter Lang.

Kelly, U. 1997. *Schooling Desire: Literacy, Cultural Politics and Pedagogy*. New York: Routledge.

Maher, F., and M.K. Tetreault. 2001. *The Feminist Classroom: Dynamics of Gender, Race and Privilege*, Expanded edn. Lanham, MD: Rowman and Littlefield.

Martino, W. 2006. 'The "Right" Way to Educate Boys: Interrogating the Politics of Boys Education in Australia', in Skelton, Francis, and Smulyan (2006: 350–64).

Melucci, A. 1996. *Challenging Codes: Social Movements and Individual Needs in Contemporary Society*. Cambridge: Cambridge University Press.

O'Brien, M. 1981. *The Politics of Reproduction*. London: Routledge.

Parsons, T. 1942. 'Age and Sex in the Social Structure of the US', *American Sociological Review* 7: 604–12.

Pateman, C. 1988. *The Sexual Contract*. Palo Alto, CA: Stanford University Press.

Rich, A. 1979. *On Lies, Secrets and Silence: Selected Prose 1966–1978*. New York: Norton.

Roman, L., and L. Eyre, eds. 1997. *Dangerous Territories: Struggles for Difference and Equality in Education*. New York: Routledge.

Royal Commission on the Status of Women. 1970. *Report of the Royal Commission on the Status of Women*. Ottawa.

Skelton, C., B. Francis, and L. Smulyan, eds. 2006. *The Sage Handbook of Gender and Education*. London: Sage Publications.

Smith, D. 1990. 'Women's Work as Mothers: A New Look at the Relation of Class, Family and School Achievement', in F. Forman, M. O'Brien, J. Haddad, D. Hallman and P. Masters, eds, *Feminism and Education: A Canadian Perspective*. Toronto: Centre for Women's Studies, Ontario Institute for Studies in Education.

Taylor, V., and N. Whittier. 1995. 'Analytical Approaches to Social Movement Culture: The Culture of the Women's Movement', in H. Johnston and B. Klandermans, eds, *Social Movements and Culture*. Minneapolis: University of Minnesota Press, 163–87.

Trinh, T. 1989. *Woman, Native, Other: Writing Postcoloniality and Feminism*. Bloomington: Indiana University Press.

Wine, J. 1982. 'Gynocentric Values and Feminist Psychology', in G. Finn and A. Miles (1982).

CHAPTER 3

Culture, Self, and Society: Bourdieu and Feminist Sociology in Education

Jo-Anne Dillabough

Introduction

> Being included [in the state] as a man or woman, . . . we have embodied the historical struc-
> tures of the masculine order in the form of unconscious schemes of perception and appre-
> ciation. (Bourdieu, 1998a: 5)

This chapter seeks to open a window of illumination on the theoretical work of Pierre
Bourdieu (1930–2003), emphasizing the relationship between his broad conceptual
understandings of the state and the feminist sociology of education. In the current era
of postmodern and poststructuralist feminisms, Bourdieu is often read as a determinist
with little to offer contemporary feminist debates. In response to such critiques, I
would suggest that we have both underestimated and misrecognized Bourdieu's
conceptual potential for expanding the meanings attributed to the category of
'gender', particularly its enduring symbolic features, in the feminist sociology of education. I would also suggest that to consider Bourdieu an economic determinist, particularly in the last years of his academic career, may be to misrepresent his more recent
theoretical work on culture and the embodiment of gender which have extended his
theory of cultural reproduction quite substantially. In short, I will argue that a more
creative and empirical engagement with Bourdieu's work on 'masculine domination',
alongside an interdisciplinary reading of more recent cultural and social theories of
power, marks an important, albeit sometimes underestimated, advance for gender
studies and the feminist sociology of education.

The chapter is organized in five parts. The first section, intended for readers new
to Bourdieu's work, provides a brief overview of his concept of domination and his
links to the feminist sociology of education. Section two explores in greater detail his

contributions to the feminist sociology of education and identifies areas of related research in the field. Section three summarizes his theory of cultural production and the concept he referred to as 'classification struggle'. Section four outlines his account of masculine domination and its links to education. Finally, section five explores his view of the relationship between the political 'subject'/actor and the state. The chapter concludes by identifying some of the strengths and limitations of Bourdieu's theoretical work in relation to gender.

Bourdieu and the Feminist Sociology of Education

Summarizing Bourdieu's relevance for the feminist sociology of education poses fundamental intellectual challenges, not only because his work is far-reaching and highly interdisciplinary, but also because it has attracted numerous feminist critiques (see Adkins and Skeggs, 2004). Such critiques have been premised upon everything from second-wave feminist identity politics in the early 1980s to feminist poststructural responses to Marxist theories of the state at the end of the twentieth century (see McCall, 1992; McNay, 2004). A further difficulty is that in recent years, at least within sociology and gender studies, relatively few feminist sociologists have sought to investigate Bourdieu's work and its application to gender and education. Many have instead been attracted to less sociologically oriented theorists such as Foucault, Butler, Habberstalm, or Deleuze.

In any event, in seeking to consider Bourdieu's continued promise for the feminist sociology of education, we might start with the key conceptual questions that he posed throughout his career and refined in the latter part of his academic life. One such question concerns the relationship between domination and social class. Bourdieu's concern with domination took many forms, but one constant was the idea that Marxist accounts of the *direct* domination of the 'subordinate classes' by elites were too limited. In Bourdieu's later work, domination emerges as a form of indirect symbolic power operating in diverse cultural contexts (e.g., language, media, family relationships, academic disciplines) to reproduce not only class divisions but also social and cultural arrangements of all kinds (e.g., gender relations, educational policies of nation-states). This concept of domination was one of the most important theoretical components in Bourdieu's effort to develop a mature understanding of social inequality. As Curtis and Chodos write:

> Bourdieu attempted to mobilize the . . . conceptual repertoire he had developed over several decades to make sociology into an effective instrument of political critique. . . . Such a sociology would embrace its enemy—domination—mastering its characteristic idioms, its strategies and tactics, its feints and gestures, and turn the strength of domination against itself. (2002: 1)

In the 1990s Bourdieu channelled his lifelong concern with symbolic domination into what, in accordance with much second-wave feminist terminology, he called **'masculine domination'** (see Bourdieu, 1998a; see also classes and classifications in Bourdieu, 1984). Following a sustained interest in what it might mean for an individual to experience 'ideological subjection'—subjection through socialization within a given cultural **field**—Bourdieu (1990) argued that masculine domination finds its most substantial expression in the social 'institutions of modernity' (e.g., comprehensive schooling), where the maintenance of the social order remains a key national project. From this vantage point Bourdieu was able to pay particularly close attention to education, which he saw as a site of ideological socialization that was more likely to reproduce existing patterns of gender inequality than to challenge them (Bourdieu, 2001). In this understanding, masculine domination is made possible through historically inherited social and symbolic practices, which are reproduced across time (see also Bourdieu, 1977; Bourdieu and Passeron, 1977), and which always exceed, through deeply ingrained and resilient cultural practices, their own original intentions.

Within this system, however—as in Marx's account of the relations of production—contradictions persist over time, and these contradictions allow for the possibility of change such as the reconfiguration of gender relationships and the ways in which masculine domination is enacted. Thus the category 'gender' in Bourdieu's work, although it is enduring at the symbolic level (e.g., at the level of signs such as the white wedding dress), is also immensely flexible. In recent years, those gender theorists with a particular interest in social class have been particularly attracted to Bourdieu's theory of **cultural reproduction** as an aid to understanding the reproduction of unequal gender relations both in education and in the wider social world. This interest has been ignited by Bourdieu's later work which sought to develop a yet more subtle model of cultural reproduction (to be discussed later in the chapter) that seeks to recognize the powerful elements of history as it relates to some of the enduring features of culture expressed through class conflict, and their relationships to the changing category of gender, as opposed to any strict causal link between, for example, gender and class.

Bourdieu's Contributions

There are many ways in which Bourdieu's theoretical work has shaped, albeit indirectly, gender studies in education. In the first place, Bourdieu was an indirect and often unacknowledged intellectual mentor to some feminist sociologists of education in a period when they were facing a crisis of confidence in theorizing about the reproduction of gender inequality in schools. This crisis was fed by, among other things, the dynamics of global change; post-feminist claims that gender equity had already been substantially achieved; and the fact that some scholars—for example, some postmodernists and poststructuralists—now seemed more interested in questions of identity and the 'constitution of subjectivity' than of equity or class. For many, Bourdieu's notion of masculine domination—the idea that the history of masculine privilege provides a platform for the powerful use of state-generated symbols and codes (such as state endorsements of anti-abortion legislation, textbook images to 'man and wife', advertising, or policies supporting the heterosexual family) that serve to regulate the gendered consciousness of subjects—could be fruitfully combined with more pragmatic feminist concerns about gender inequalities in schools and society (e.g., Reay, 1998). This conjunction of ideas has proved very valuable in directing attention to what Bourdieu called the 'constancy of structure' in gender relations: the ways in which social relations and 'categories of understanding' about 'sex' and 'gender' (see Bourdieu, 1998a) reproduce a gendered division of labour. Here elements of constancy and change come together, are *embodied* in the consciousness of individuals, and enacted through class relations in education. Essentially, what this means is that while gender codes (male, female) shift over time through the impact of social change (e.g., the feminist movement), there remain enduring and resilient features of, and outcomes associated with, more traditional gender configurations that live on in public consciousness (such as the continued exploitation of young women in pornography and on the Internet, or the reality that most men still earn substantially more than women in the labour force). An educational concern with cultural **production**— the transmission and expression of class dispositions that assert, legitimize, and lead to the persistent production of often narrowly defined gender categories (the idea of the working-class girl as 'easy') and which maintain social stratification—has therefore always represented something quite different from a rigid meta-theoretical project that over-determines the classed subject, citizen, or gendered person in the liberal state. Rather, it has represented a sustained attempt to engage in what Fraser and Gordon (1995) have called a 'critical political semantic' (that is, a meaningful critique of the modern state and the roles that such symbolic markers of gender play in its operations). In this understanding, an individual's micro-negotiation of wider forms of culture in local contexts and macro-structural processes need to be seen as dialectically related. In other words, wider macro structures and local experiences come together to shape the meanings that circulate about gender in any given time and place. Within this understanding, the production of gender formations always emerges at the interface of macro and micro levels of social life. Change and stability operate at both levels in that there are always relatively stable forces at work, such as economic policies and ongoing stratification associated with global reforms, as well as transformations in the make-up of a very group or community at the local level. Yet any understanding of masculine domination must still be considered to fall within the remit of territory and space, even if that territory is tied, at least in part, to a global economic system. As Bourdieu writes: 'Integration into the state and the territory it controls is in fact the precondition for domination (as it can be readily seen in all situations of colonization)' (2001: 83).

Bourdieu's work has ignited debate in several key areas of feminist sociology of education. Among the topics of interest are the influence of social structure, sexuality, race, and social class on gender categories as they are expressed through educational and social inequality; the value of Bourdieu's sophisticated conceptual apparatus for our understanding of how the educational and social experiences of women differ from those of men; and, more recently, the role played by masculine domination in shaping those experiences. Although interest in Bourdieu has revived somewhat in recent years, sociological interest in theories of cultural reproduction subsided in the late 1980s, both in gender studies and in education. This decline of interest may have reflected the difficulty of deriving coherent, sustainable sociological positions from Bourdieu's theorizing. Nevertheless, his work has never ceased to suggest new theoretical directions for the feminist sociology of education. Recently, for example, scholars such as Kennelly (2008),

Reay (1998), and Reay and Lucey (2003) have referred to Bourdieu's notion of **habitus**—'a set of acquired patterns of thought, behaviour, and taste' (Marshall, 1994: s.v. 'habitus')—in their discussions of topics such as the tensions between schools and family life, the containment of minoritized youth in urban housing projects, and the formation and regulation of twenty-first-century youth movements through such forces as social class and neo-liberal ideals. Such scholars have also striven to understand how forms of educational knowledge (e.g., curricular content, academic disciplines) and the structure of work in education have been shaped by the historical legacies of masculine domination in relation to vast scales of global change (see Acker and Dillabough, 2007). Bourdieu's theoretical work has also proved useful to scholars wishing to challenge liberal or essentializing theories of gender identity, by helping them to identify the complex social processes that perpetuate inequality beyond an overly determined classed understanding of male control or the domination of women through masculine privilege (see Adkins, 2002; McNay, 1999). Theorists who have attempted to probe more deeply into the complex links between gender and class have helped to broaden and extend Bourdieu's theoretical reach by including other axes of social identification such as race, sexuality, and disability, which also shape gender inequality.

In recent years Bourdieu's work has served as an important stimulus for thinking about large-scale class shifts and novel forms of social inequality associated with globalization (see Bourdieu, 1998b; see also 2001). A recurring argument is that forms of neo-liberal and/or neo-conservative educational governance are increasingly cross-national and grounded in unequal gender relations. This claim calls for recognition of the need to further explore the relationship between educational structures (e.g., material access to education for girls), the emergence of either quite new or sedimented gender relationships in post-welfare economic regimes, and for the clear elucidation of the limits of social mobility for men and women. At the core of this relationship, Bourdieu argues, stand certain understandings of masculinity that have developed over time as advantages that privilege white middle-class boys and girls above all others. What is central, then, to Bourdieu's conception of masculine domination is that gender inequities are the product of the interaction between the social and historical practices of cultural reproduction, the general understandings about gender circulating in any given space and time, and the specific conditions of wider structural change.

In sum, Bourdieu's sociological account has benefited feminist sociologists of education by responding precisely to the limitations of other views of gender power, whether liberal, strong Marxist, or poststructuralist. Bourdieu's interdisciplinary perspective holds out the possibility of moving beyond such limitations. In a framework that takes into account the processes of cultural production, gender inequality can no longer be attributed to a singular explanatory factor, such as economic structures, language, or male culture in and of itself. Rather, Bourdieu offers a more subtle explanation that embraces the complex intertwining of culture and structure as social processes shaping gender inequality. Moreover, Bourdieu's account of symbolic power has materially assisted in the task of exploring how gender relations, which form part of the communicative structure of social life (i.e., discourses used in everyday life), can also be seen as cultural relations of symbolic power, embedded in a masculinized social history (Bourdieu, 1999; Mottier, 2002).

Bourdieu's Theory of Cultural Reproduction and Classification Struggles

Perhaps the most important aspect of Bourdieu's work for the feminist sociology of education is his theoretical use of material culture as a conceptual apparatus for understanding how social inequality persists and manifests itself in school and social life through the mechanism of production. The term **cultural production** refers to the socio-cultural processes in a given social 'field' that shape and ultimately produce, albeit in reconfigured forms, hierarchical social mechanisms that lead to gender inequality. These processes are grounded in communicative forms of culture (e.g., conversations) but are premised upon a historical understanding of the state as manifestly material[1] and strongly stratified. Particularly in Bourdieu's early work, such processes were seen primarily as material in form and concerned solely with labour power and interpreted within the realm of phenomenological experience— that is, as something transmitted and ultimately reproduced through interpretative repertoires of classed meanings which people carry with them as burdened historical subjects.

Individuals in this stratified context experience what Bourdieu called 'classification struggles': internalized conflicts provoked on a daily basis by their positioning in a stratified social order. In many liberal states these struggles centre on questions of identity (who am I, how should I behave, who is my friend, who is my enemy) that individuals must confront in relation to cultural status and social conflict in the wider context of class relations. As Bourdieu writes in relation to classification:

> The schemes of the habitus, the primary forms of classification, owe their specific efficacy to the fact that they function below the level of consciousness and language, beyond the reach of introspective scrutiny or control by the will. . . . They embed what some would mistakenly call values in the most automatic gestures or the apparently most insignificant techniques of the body—ways of walking or blowing one's nose, ways of eating or talking— and engage the most fundamental principles of construction and evaluation of the social world, those which most directly express the division of labour [which Marxist accounts always express in terms of a struggle over the means of production]. . . or the division of the work of domination, in divisions between bodies and between relations to the body which borrow more features than one, as if to give them the appearances of naturalness. (1984: 103)

Classification struggles arise in response both to everyday events and to pre-existing socio-cultural relations that are hierarchically framed but ultimately dynamic and at times deeply contradictory. The significance of the term 'classification struggle' is that it implicates individuals in the struggle over the production of culture as a form of both accommodation and resistance to dominant cultural and class norms, as well as in the conflictual and contradictory relations of power. Individuals, as both suffering and acting agents, are therefore involved in the making and remaking of their cultural worlds, but their interpretations are always constrained by social conditions. Now well-established, this Bourdieusian assumption casts doubt on any notion of the self as unconstrained or as an unfettered liberal agent. Indeed, as Bourdieu argued, all human beings must carry the lasting 'effects' of their history:

> The social world is . . . something which agents make at every moment; but they have no chance of unmaking and remaking it except on the basis of realistic knowledge of what it is and of what they can do to it by virtue of the position they occupy in it. (2001: 74)

The processes underlying cultural reproduction therefore never simply replicate existing forms of inequality. Cultural practices and forms of classification in any given field both subvert and reconstitute what Bourdieu called the 'constancy of structure in education': the persistence of state structures (e.g., neo-liberal educational policies) that continue to create novel forms of 'positional suffering'[2] as something inherited from the past and which are reshaped over time (Bourdieu, 1990).

In charting the ways in which the category of gender is reproduced over time, Bourdieu built on Husserl's idea of 'habituality' (*Habitualitat*). If the social order is reproduced through the cultural practices of individuals who carry with them the burden of their historical embeddedness and social experience, habits associated with masculine privilege are shaped, in part, by the normative architecture of culture and are reconstituted across time. In other words, habits are not simply patterns of behaviour or thought that are acquired and then manifested in the present: they are transmitted diachronically through cultural practices. What is important here is the idea of cultural practice as a form of interpretive understanding; habitus can be seen as a set of everyday normative practices for those who are, broadly speaking, operating in the same field and who view such practices as making practical sense (see Reay, 2004). It is not just a set of behaviours in the usual sense; it also includes embodied habits such as the way one gestures, dresses, or walks. Habitus 'is indicated in the bearing of the body (hexis) and in deeply ingrained habits of behavior, feeling and thought' (see Lovell, 2000: 12). Such deeply sedimented behaviours, dispositions, and practices—which Bourdieu later referred to as forms of embodiment—are the primary elements of cultural reproduction as they operate in the social world, through, for example, family life and the performance of sexuality.

Masculine Domination and Gender Studies in Education

In the late 1970s, prior to the cultural turn towards analyses of language in social thought and gender theory, one of the most influential approaches for the study of gender in education was the 'reproduction' or 'code' model (see also Arnot, 2002), in which structures shape state governance and social institutions and exert masculine power through capitalist relations. Many feminists interested in these ideas therefore equated capitalist relations with 'patriarchy' and identified such social relations in the structures of schooling. While Bourdieu saw capitalism as a vehicle for masculine domination, he seems to have been more interested in identifying how *symbolic culture* (the effects of signs and symbols) operates to reproduce social and educational inequality. He was also concerned with the ways in which cultural relations in any given site shape our notions of who we think we might be or become. The concept of domination was already central for Bourdieu, but it was when he focused on the social and historical conditions of masculine privilege that he exposed the links between culture and structure in the processes of cultural reproduction. What perhaps led some to see Bourdieu as overly deterministic with respect to gender and class categories were his frequent references to the sexual division of labour as the primary evidence of masculine domination (see Bourdieu, 1990, 1988, 1998a, 1998b, 2001). Later, however, he became increasingly interested in physical expressions, such as ways of walking or talking:

> it has to be posited that social agents are endowed with habitus, inscribed in their bodies by past experience . . . the agent is never completely the subject of his practices: through the dispositions and the belief which are the basis of engagement in the game, all the presuppositions constituting the practical axiomatics of the field (the epistemic doxa, for example) find their way into the seemingly most lucid intentions. (2001: 138)

Moreover, as Lovell (2000) suggests, Bourdieu's notion of gender performativity is not simply about transgressing authority. Rather, his view of the performance of masculinity has an anti-essentialist character in that male domination can be traced to historical ideas that are embodied by social actors in the present while still remaining differentiated in their articulations as they are expressed. Bourdieu writes:

> The schemes of the sexually characterized habitus are not 'fundamental structuring alternatives', as Goffman would have it, but historical and highly differentiated structures, arising from a social space that is itself highly differentiated, which reproduce themselves through learning processes linked to the experiences that agents have of the structures of these spaces. The insertion into different fields organized according to oppositions (strong/weak, big/small, fat/thin . . .) with the fundamental distinction between male and female and the secondary alternatives in which is it expressed is accompanied by the inscription in the body of a series of sexually characterized oppositions which are homologous among themselves. (1998a: 104)

Masculine domination cannot, therefore, represent a straightforward or objective derivative of contemporary social and cultural power formations or direct male power over women. It may be expressed and read in many different ways through social structures, discourses, social relations, and bodily representations (see Lovell, 2000). The fact is that these phenomena are differentiated and often hidden expressions of masculine domination and are present in diverse forms across time. When we are unaware of this differentiation, where it remains concealed, where we accept it as normal and natural, we are experiencing what Bourdieu (2001) refers to as 'symbolic violence':

> the objective structures and cognitive structures of a particularly well preserved androcentric society . . . provide instruments [for exposing symbolic violence] enabling one to understand some of the best concealed aspects of what those relations are in the economically most advanced societies. (2001: 7)

As vehicles for the assertion of masculine power over time, language and discourse were central to Bourdieu. What is distinctive about Bourdieu's notions of masculinized language and discourse is that he characterizes them as contingent on a cultural history of gender relations. Whereas some postmodern accounts of discourse create a disjuncture or impasse between discourse and the material elements of experience, Bourdieu was among the sociologists (others include McNay, Skeggs, and Adkins) who have focused on the relation between individual social experience grounded in social class relations and the formation and use of language (see Bettie, 2004). However, while Bourdieu saw these relationships as contingent upon material relations they could not always be seen as strictly temporal in their expression. As Adriana Caverero writes, 'the time of a life story is not reducible to the "time" of that life' (2000: 3). Like Caverero, Bourdieu is highly sensitive to history and the reproductive power of language over time.

Similarly, the time of masculine domination is not reducible to the time in which it is enacted or expressed. Masculine discourses (e.g., public male citizen, private female caregiver) are not straightforwardly measurable, objective forms of inequality that we can observe and recognize as they are asserted over time. Rather, they are naturalized in social and cultural space—as social and cultural history and as habitus: 'the habitus appears in one sense as each individual's characteristic set of dispositions for action. . . . But the habitus . . . is [also] the meeting point between institutions or bodies. . . . the way in which persons connect with the socio-cultural in such a way that the various [gender] games of life keep their meaning, keep being played' (Calhoun, 1995: 17).

According to Bourdieu (2001), then, masculine domination is manifested in the history of language, contemporary school texts, official knowledge, social and educational policies, contemporary media, and everyday human practices. It constitutes the essence of academic life and indeed some sociological theories (see Connell, 2007). In short, masculine domination helps to shape our understanding of the self and the citizen within the state. However, Bourdieu does not attempt to argue for a fixed notion of male or female selfhood but rather for a highly constrained individual who does not occupy the elusive liberal position of being able to choose whether they will oppress or not. Forms of domination are naturalized to the extent that they are unconscious and sometimes unrecognizable, and they are resisted to the extent that resistance is possible within a socio-cultural frame of constraints. As Mottier argues, masculine domination is concerned largely with the naturalization of symbolic forms of masculine power, the 'misrecognition of domination, and the mechanisms of social reproduction of this domination' (2002: 352).

Bourdieu's account of masculine domination has served several useful purposes for feminist sociologists. First, in contrast to strong Marxist accounts of inequality, which in the early 1980s were concerned largely with class and over-emphasized base–superstructure models[3] (see Robbins, 2002; see also Williams, 1977), Bourdieu's account of 'patriarchy' or 'masculine domination' does not focus solely on economic oppression exerted only by males. His more comprehensive account of gender inequality has allowed feminist sociologists in particular to move beyond purely economic accounts towards a more socio-cultural understanding of gender inequality and educational institutions, and their reproductive modes and functions (see Arnot, 2002; McLeod, 2003).

Second, in emphasizing the relationship between local cultures, macro-structures, and the economy, Bourdieu remained committed to a symbolic labour theory of the state wherein the sexual division of labour—as part of an accumulated history—might be seen as playing a fundamental role in the reproduction of gender inequality in the temporal present. Culture cannot therefore be eclipsed at the expense of a history of labour, colonialism, or material conditions:

> this noting of the trans-historical continuity of the relation of masculine domination . . . forces us to pose the always ignored question of the endlessly recommended historical *labour* which is necessary . . . to wrench masculine domination from history. . . . Above all, it forces one to see the futility of the strident calls of 'postmodern' philosophers for the 'supersession of dualisms'. These dualisms, deeply rooted in things (*structures*) and in bodies, do not spring from the simple effect of verbal naming and cannot be abolished by an act of performative magic, since the genders, far from being simple roles to be played at will, are inscribed in bodies and in a universe from which they derive their strength. (2001: 103)

Third, Bourdieu's ongoing emphasis on the role of social structures in the cultural reproduction of masculine domination exposes the historical role of the sexual division of labour in the maintenance and augmentation of symbolic capital and its gendered expression through the habitus. As a consequence, the idea of men or women as singular agents of oppression emerges as problematic and we see, through Bourdieu's eyes, the substantially constrained social actor located in a cultural milieu, an actor who has been shaped to perform particular kinds of domination and, perhaps where possible, to subvert them.

Fourth, Bourdieu's conceptual focus on symbolic modes of gender reproduction and the interpretive mediums that play some part in transmitting gender relations through a habitus and field of relationships has helped to explain how it is that elements of the gender order persist over time. Meaning-making, power formations, and the history of ideas are central to Bourdieu's theorizing about gender. Indeed, not unlike Raymond Williams in an earlier period, Bourdieu showed us how the socialized body expresses a 'logic of feeling' (Williams's 1977 term was a 'structure of feeling') that emanates from a moment long past but retains its symbolic effects. As Bourdieu writes:

> If it is quite illusory to believe that symbolic violence can be overcome with the weapons of consciousness and will alone, this is because the effect and conditions of its efficacy are durably and deeply embedded in the body in the form of dispositions. This is seen . . . in the case of . . . all relations built on that model, in which these durable inclinations of the socialized body are . . . experienced in the logic of feeling (filial love, fraternal love) or duty, which are often merged in the experience of respect and devotion and may live on long after the disappearance of their social conditions of production. (1998a: 39)

Here we begin to see the extent to which forms of domination are built into everyday life and might be understood as an 'invisible culture' (see also Moore, 2003) carrying with it the 'hypnotic power of domination' (Woolf, cited in Bourdieu, 1998a). In this way, masculine domination can be seen as permeating the cultural fields or spaces of local social institutions without diminishing the importance of the wider cultural, historical, and structural contexts that shape individuals' actions.

Fifth, unlike much contemporary continental social thought, Bourdieu's account fully engages structure even as it concentrates on determining the role of culture in the generation of meanings about 'gender' (see also McNay, 2000). As Lovell (2002) suggests, the range of such meanings is not inexhaustible. The idea of meaning as constantly proliferating beyond a material social reality, for example, is one point on which Bourdieu takes issue with the poststructural perspective. In his view, some post-modernist and poststructuralist accounts of masculine domination are poorly equipped to acknowledge the material aspects of experience, culturally derived meaning, and interpretation; therefore they fail to see that an interpretive reading of masculine domination is impossible without recognition of actual social practice, symbolic histories, or power relations. To separate masculine domination from its historical legacy and context is to objectify it and make it impossible to understand as an embedded representational knowledge form.

Finally, even more significant is Bourdieu's explicit recognition of the material relationship between discourse and social differentiation. This view of language emanates from an already existing set of material conditions that play some part in reproducing social stratification. It is crucial here to recognize that Bourdieu did not reject the idea of discourse as something that shapes the forms of masculine domina-tion in operation. Rather, he suggested that poststructural notions of discourse could be misleading if they failed to acknowledge the part played by language in the material processes of social differentiation (e.g., classifying and dividing practices)—the observ-able forms of differentiation that actually assert symbolic domination in social life (see McNay, 2000, 2004). It was therefore legitimate to be concerned with discourse in the Foucauldian sense (as a language–power relation), but this should not diminish the practical and ethical importance of understanding what the material and social conse-quences of that discourse might be. Discourse, in other words, is grounded in material relations; it is not simply text without historical memory or social meaning and it cannot be removed from the realm of social experience.

Enlarged Selves, Masculine Domination, and Bourdieu's 'Philosophy of the Subject'

> The individual [is] the locus of indissoluble identity—at least potentially self-sufficient, self-contained and self-moving. (Calhoun, 1995: 254)

Bourdieu's contributions point towards the power of structure as an enduring social reality. While he cannot be portrayed or indeed overdetermined as a hardened Marxist, his emphasis on structure means that he cannot be portrayed as a poststructuralist either, even though he paid respectful attention to many aspects of Foucault's work in his later writings. Indeed, his later ideas about the state and its late-twentieth-century power configurations clearly reflect that attention.

The similarities between many of the concepts formulated by Bourdieu and Foucault imply closer links and more shared intellectual influences than are typically suggested in the sociological literature. Thus it is not surprising that some feminist sociologists who have drawn on Bourdieu have also investigated the role of discourse in constituting the self and human subjectivity (a largely Foucauldian project) particularly within poststructural and more culturally oriented theories of power (see McLeod, 2003). Indeed, approaches to the study of gender through the destabilizing category of culture have been a persistent concern for third-wave feminist theorists in education. These more interdisciplinary accounts of gender (see McRobbie, 2004) allowed some later feminist reproduction theorists and cultural theorists to see gender identity as ontologically more complex than liberal theorists or strong modernist and particularly early Marxist accounts had suggested it was (see Arnot, 2002; McLeod and Kenway, 2004). Linking class to culture has therefore been an important step in extending our understanding of the legitimate 'citizen' as a 'who' rather than a 'what' in the descriptive sense (see Arendt, 1951). As Arendt wrote, 'the actor, the doer of deeds, is possible only if he is at the same time the speaker of words. In contrast to sign language, Arendtian speech remains close to the body as a symptom, to the semiotic', to that which is heterogenous to meaning and signification (cited in Zerilli, 1995: 180). Similarly, for Bourdieu gender identity emerges both as a meaningful representation and signification of culture, as 'human temporality concretely lived' (see Ricoeur, 2005), and as symbolic symptom of the social order. I would argue that Bourdieu here begins to offer insight into the philosophy of the subject (a theory of subjectivity) on sociological grounds and at the same time sheds light on a theoretical notion of identity that does not foreclose action or agency, but accepts that these are never unconstrained.

While respectful of some poststructural accounts, Bourdieu argues that poststructural representations of selfhood (the subject as regulated by language, the history of ideas, techniques of governance) pay little direct attention to issues of experience and the real subjects through whom language and power are generated (see also Lovell, 2000). Thus some poststructuralists may have missed the opportunity to advance a theory of identity that might explain why some individuals appear to enjoy greater 'freedom' and 'agency' than others, and are therefore in a social position precisely to articulate and assert their 'freedoms'. Bourdieu's point, I believe, is that no one is ultimately free. Individuals are certainly bound by their political, economic, and cultural circumstances. Nevertheless, members of privileged groups in the state will appear 'freer' than members of other, historically marginalized groups. In this way we can begin to view selfhood as something bound by social conditions rather than determined by them. Bourdieu therefore brings a larger and more relevant sociological account of gender identity to debates about the philosophy of the subject. He does not, for example, deny the importance of viewing the self as both actor and subject in the shaping of those social practices that lead to both inequality and subversion. Gender identity, in other words, is always contingent and permeable, as is the subversion of dominant or hegemonic understandings of gender in the ideological sense. In this way, Bourdieu endows subjects with the capacity to act in the social world through subversive practices without claiming a totalizing agency or an illusory, essentialist notion of freedom. This account of the self is particularly relevant for feminist theorists.

Against those who might contend that Bourdieu failed to develop a theory of the subject I would argue that his contribution was designed precisely to avoid 'an account of the self': rather, he set out to explain the social, historical, and cultural conditions within which the self is formed and reconstituted. It was towards the conditions and forms of meaning generated about the self that Bourdieu turned, rather than the self per se (McLeod, 2003). His interest was in developing a theory of power that would both operationalize and objectify power within a deeply masculinized state. A sociology of symbolic domination operating through bodies would challenge any liberal account of the free and unfettered subject, and, by extension, the concept of gender equality emerging from liberal feminism. Consequently, what we learn from Bourdieu about the 'self' is that context, conditions, and culture come together to shape all individuals through their understandings of themselves and others, as well as through the hierarchies of privilege within which they are embedded. Masculine domination is not located always in one site, and neither is it the sole property of men, just as the simple assertion of selfhood is not necessarily an 'act of domination' (see Butler, 1997) or a linguistic performance of naming, as some feminist poststructural accounts have suggested. Bourdieu writes: 'the work of symbolic construction is far more than a strictly performative operation of naming which orients . . . representations, starting with representations of the body. It is brought about and culminates in a profound and durable transformation of bodies (and minds)' (2001: 23). From Bourdieu's perspective, masculine privileging is a social relation, though not of an ungrounded, free-floating or indeterminate kind:

> Like Michel Foucault, who sought to rehistoricize sexuality against psychoanalytic naturalization, by describing [hidden aspects of the history of sexuality], in a *History of Sexuality*, conceived of . . . as a geneology of Western Man . . . , I have tried to link the unconscious which governs sexual relations, and the relations between the sexes . . . to the long and partly immobile history of the androcentric unconscious. But to carry through the project of understanding what it is that specifically characterizes the modern experience of sexuality, it is not sufficient, as Foucault supposed, to emphasize what differentiates it in particular from Greek or Roman antiquity. . . . Sexuality . . . is indeed a historical invention, but one which has developed progressively as the various fields and their specific logics became differentiated. (2001: 103–4)

Conclusion

As I have argued throughout this chapter, Bourdieu's account of masculine domination was part of his theory of cultural reproduction; it was never intended to stand alone as a theory of gender or gender relations. Setting out to develop a theory of social inequality that did not target or blame individuals, he focused primarily on the historical roles played by the state and its symbolic operations in the reproduction of inequality. This focus was central to all his work. However, some might argue that his emphasis more latterly on *masculinity* as the pivotal form of domination, particularly in *Masculine Domination*, tended to direct attention away from other potential explanations for widening our understanding of both the category of gender and gender inequality (see Curtis and Chodos, 2002). Consequently, gender and class remained privileged concepts, sometimes standing above other socio-cultural formations and identity markers, such as race and sexuality. Thus it could be argued that his understanding of late modern social movements, including feminism, was in some degree dated and restricted, as was his broad acceptance of race and post-colonial critiques of sociological theory. Not surprisingly, then, although some gender scholars revered Bourdieu's work, others reviled it. Those who had accused him of reductionism in his sociological theorizing charged that he was 'gender blind' and incapable of addressing the larger problem of female agency. Bourdieu was not alone in this respect; many male scholars schooled in postwar 'gender blind' neo-Marxist traditions have faced similar charges.

It would be unwarranted, however, to suggest that Bourdieu's quest for a nuanced understanding of domination was wholly unsuccessful. To his credit, Bourdieu did not seek to privilege one marginalized group over any other in assigning them types or magnitudes of domination. This was so because he believed that all groups are, to greater or lesser degrees, responding to a gendered habitus premised on different forms of domination. In other words, he did not argue that women, gay/queer and trans-gendered, and/or racialized groups are any more or less inclined to dominate than are white heterosexual men. Rather, he uncovered the *structures* of domination to which less privileged groups are exposed, and attempted to show how all of us come to embody those structures in everyday social practice, albeit in diverse and contradictory ways. In this way he moved beyond liberal identity politics to critique the liberal practice of privileging one identity over another, in order to expose the structural and psychic dimensions of domination that are normalized through a habitus. His central argument was that scholars have a political obligation to understand and make public the socio-cultural structures that have created a hierarchy of privilege. In short, Bourdieu moved beyond liberal accounts of the political subject, or simple gender and racial binaries, to expose the socio-cultural processes that reproduce hierarchy, differentiation, and inequality.

Contrary to many feminist critics, one could also argue that Bourdieu encouraged feminist sociologists to develop a theory of human agency that would allow women more dignity as social actors. He himself argued that late-twentieth-century social theorizing had largely failed to address the role played by pre-existing structures in shaping individuals' ability to 'act'. Agency is not something that someone either possesses or lacks. In Bourdieu's mind, women have been, and will always be, capable of taking action in some form or other. For a male scholar who spent a lifetime dispelling the liberal myths of agency and freedom, but not of action, this is a profoundly important point. But Bourdieu does not wish us to imagine that women are 'free unfettered authors of their own destiny' (see Weir, 1997; McNay, 2000). Instead, he wished us to understand and subvert the objective structures (e.g., gender discrimination in the workplace) that undermine women's ability to act, and that play a part in the formation of gendered subjectivities. Here he confronts both the socio-cultural organization of the state and its role in the shaping of the gendered self. Yet we must be wary, as Lovell (2000) suggests, not to use Bourdieu's account of masculine domination merely to construct women as 'capital bearing objects' who can be easily located in the private sphere, or as non-citizens who simply possess sexualized capital in relation to the formations of masculinity and femininity. For Lovell (2000), Bourdieu's account is in danger of constructing women as objects both of the market and of a highly sexualized state.

A related concern about work inspired by Bourdieu is that it tends to emphasize meta-theory at the expense of accounting for difference. Indeed, many have felt that a focus on class relations could not convincingly address issues of difference beyond gender and class (see Dillabough, 2001). Thus Bourdieu is sometimes read as a totalizing theorist of masculine domination and as an exponent of a meta-account of female subordination. An overarching criticism, therefore, is that Bourdieu, charmed by the lure of a theoretical determinism, failed both to account for the micro-negotiations of identity and change in schools and society, and to look beyond gender and class for more complex explanations of social inequality. Cornell writes: 'different women are differently situated with respect to power: while white women may experience oppression on account of their sex, they also share privilege on account of their race' (cited in Eichner, 2001: 11). Bourdieu's own work would have benefited considerably from a stronger analysis of race and colonialism in the symbolic production of masculine domination (see Connell, 2007).

Even so, Bourdieu remains one of the very few sociologists to recognize the theoretical tensions between structure and culture in the shaping of both society and the self. He was interested in the reproduction and reconfiguration of cultural meaning across time rather than the 'slippage of meaning' (see Eichner, 2001). For him, history, materiality, nature, and culture are inseparable in the study of self, society, and other. At this crossroads, Bourdieu's work contrasts starkly with that of thinkers such as Foucault, Agamben, Deleuze, Butler, and Derrida.

Bourdieu's socio-cultural account of masculine domination was designed to expose its operations, including the parts played by individuals who may enact domination even if they themselves are not fully aware that they are doing so. Essentially, this kind of theory explains how domination becomes practically possible at the same moment that it appears ethically unthinkable as conscious practice. It also exposes how changing *modes of cultural production* may establish, but do not predict, the limits within which gender identities may develop and take shape in society, as well as the actions of educational and social institutions towards them (see McNay, 2000).[4]

Today we need to re-engage with the theoretical value of Bourdieu's work as it might relate to the broader range of theories currently circulating and against which it might stimulate further novel contributions to the study of gender in education. Here I am particularly thinking of the work of Beverly Skeggs, Lisa Adkins, Terry Lovell, Sara Ahmed, and Lois McNay. We must also continue, as Bourdieu suggested throughout his academic life, to engage in acts of historization so that we can begin to trace the naturalization of symbolic culture over time and understand the reproduction of domination at both the symbolic and ontological levels. This kind of theoretical practice has not been the trend in recent years, largely because of the ways culture has been commodified as a tool of higher order analysis. Yet I maintain, following E.P. Thompson and Stuart Hall as well as Bourdieu, that culture, like class, is simultaneously discursive, relational, and stratified. Class cannot be eclipsed by culture, but neither should rigid assumptions about class as a strictly economic category be allowed to obscure the role that culture plays in the reproduction of gender inequality. Class is 'a relation' in that it can be identified only in relation to other classes, but it nevertheless must be seen as a contingent relation that possesses substantial symbolic and cultural power. As Thompson (1966) famously reminds us:

> Class is a social and cultural formation which cannot be defined abstractly, or in isolation, but only in terms of relationship with other classes; and ultimately, the definition can only be made in the medium of time—that is, action, reaction, change and conflict. . . . But class itself is not a thing, it is a happening.

To conclude, Bourdieu's theory of masculine domination offers an analytical scope beyond anything that a normative liberal account could provide, encompassing philosophy, cultural theory, phenomenology, existentialism, sociology, anthropology, and political economy, as well as the ontology of the subject. It stands as a highly focused, realistic, and generative attempt (McNay, 2000) to chart the problems of subordination, differentiation, and hierchy, and to expose the possibilities, as well as the limits, of gendered selfhood.

Notes

This chapter is a substantially revised version of an article published under the title 'Class, Culture and the "Predicaments of Masculine Domination": Pierre Bourdieu's Encounter with Contemporary Feminist Sociology', *British Journal of Sociology of Education* 25, 4: 489–506.

1. According to the materialist view, no cultural phenomenon or social relationship exists in isolation: therefore everything must be seen in its class relationship to other things—a relationship that is constantly shifting. Conflict and 'struggle' between two or more opposing relations among actors in a field can always be observed. A contradiction—that is, a struggle between oppositional sides or sets of ideas or concepts—is the source of persistent change. It is important to note that Bourdieu rejected any concept of progress through ongoing class conflict.
2. 'Positional suffering': suffering related to the status and position of the individual or group in a hierarchical society.
3. According to base–superstructure theory, society operates on two fundamental levels. The 'base' consists of the everyday cultural sites in which modes of production operate. The 'superstructure' is everything else in the social order (technology, culture, etc.).
4. While some argue that Bourdieu's impact on fields such as feminist sociology and feminist studies in the affluent West has been inconsistent (see, for example, Lovell, 2000), his theory of cultural production has been particularly influential in the field of gender and education and has had a substantial impact on feminists who have remained concerned with the state and class conflict as analytical categories (e.g., Reay, 2004; Lovell, 2000).

Glossary

cultural reproduction: The process by which cultural norms are transmitted and reproduced across generations. Reflecting the moral economy of a particular place or 'field' (see below), these norms are presented to actors in that field as normal and legitimate. They are bound up in class stratification and are usually endorsed by various privileged groups that wish to preserve their advantage. Among the institutions in which cultural reproduction takes place are the school, the church, and the family (e.g., through informal communication).

field: The concept of field is a term derived from Bourdieu's early work and refers to the idea that all state actors operate in a social realm made up of people who share, at least to some degree, a certain set of cultural norms. The field has many elements, but what is most important is that actors operate in the field in relation to the forces exerted by other actors. Hence the field provides the space for understanding how it is that certain 'logics of action' can take place only with particular spaces and places and in relation to social conflict.

habitus: A set of culturally acquired ways of thinking and patterns of behaviour, as well as the medium and mechanism for the development of 'tastes'. In an earlier period, habitus was understood to consist of those elements of culture that are grounded in individual habits and what Marcel Mauss, a predecessor of Bourdieu, referred to as 'body techniques'. For Bourdieu habitus represented the vehicle for the transmission and reproduction of values across time through even the simplest actions (e.g., ways of walking). As Okely (1978) wrote: 'within our school there could be no natural movement which might contradict what the authorities wanted'.

masculine domination: The expression of masculine privilege through everything from sexualized ways of walking or speaking to social institutions such as marriage. These relations are both contradictory to the degree that they may sometimes transgress norms if or when possible and sedimented (deeply ingrained codes of behaviour that are resilient to change), but an objective expression of these relations is central to the reproduction of gender inequality over time.

Study Questions

1. Why is it important for students interested in studying gender inequality to understand Bourdieu's theory of cultural production?
2. Is masculine domination something that individuals exert over others? Or is it a social process inherited from the past? Explain.
3. Define masculine domination as Bourdieu understood it.
4. Why is Bourdieu's theory of masculine domination useful to feminist theorists in education? What are some of its limitations?

Recommended Readings

Adkins, L., and B. Skeggs. 2002. *Feminism after Bourdieu*. Cambridge: Polity Press.

Bourdieu, P. 1977. *Outline of a Theory of Practice*. Cambridge University Press.

———. 1999. *The Weight of the World: Social Suffering in Contemporary Society*. Stanford, CA: Stanford University Press.

Fowler, B. 2000. 'Reading Pierre Bourdieu's Masculine Domination: Notes towards an Intersectional Analysis of Gender, Culture and Class', *Cultural Studies* 17, 3–4: 468–94.

Jenkins, R. 2000. *Pierre Bourdieu*, 2nd edn. London: Routledge.

Recommended Websites

'A Disconcerting Brevity: Pierre Bourdieu's Masculine Domination': http://www3.iath. virginia.edu/pmc/issue.503/13.3wallace.html

HyperBourdieu@WorldCatalogue—a multilingual bibliography: http://hyperbourdieu.jku.at/

'On Male Domination' by Pierre Bourdieu: http://mondediplo.com/1998/10/10bourdieu

References

Acker, S., and J. Dillabough. 2007. 'Women Learning to Labour in the "Male Emporium"', *Gender and Education* 19, 3: 297–316.

Adkins, L. 2002. *Revisions: Gender and Sexuality in Late Modernity*. Buckingham, UK: Open University Press.

———, and B. Skeggs. 2004. *Feminism after Bourdieu*. London: Blackwell.

Archer, M. 2000. *Agency and the Impoverishment of Humanity*. Cambridge: Cambridge University Press.

Arendt, H. 1957, 1971. *The Life of the Mind*, 2nd edn. New York: Penguin.

Arnot, M. 2002. *Reproducing Gender*. London: RoutledgeFalmer.

Bernstein, B. 1977. 'Aspects of the Relations between Education and Production', in *Class, Codes and Control*. Vol. 3. 2nd rev. edn. London: Routledge and Kegan Paul.

Bettie, J. 2003. *Women Without Class: Girls, Race and Identity*. Los Angeles: University of California Press.

Bourdieu, P. 1977. *Outline of a Theory of Practice*. Cambridge: Cambridge University Press.

———. 1984. *Distinction: A Social Critique of Judgement of Taste*. Stanford, CA: Stanford University Press.

———. 1990. 'La Domination masculine', *Actes de le Recherche en Sciences Sociales* 84: 2–31.

———. 1997. *Pascalian Meditations*. Stanford, CA: Stanford University Press.

———. 1998a. *Masculine Domination*. Stanford, CA: Stanford University Press.

———. 1998b. *Acts of Resistance: Against the Tyranny of the Market*, trans. Richard Nice. Cambridge: New Press and Polity Press.

———. 1999. *The Weight of the World: Social Suffering in Contemporary Society*. Cambridge: Polity Press and Blackwell.

———. 2001. 'Cultural Power', in L. Spillman, ed., *Cultural Sociology*. Oxford: Blackwell.

Butler, J. 1997. *Excitable Speech: A Politics of the Performative*. New York and London: Routledge.

Calhoun, C. 1995. *Contemporary Sociological Theory* [Readings]. Available at: <http:// www.nyu.edu/classess/Calhoun/Theory/paper-on-Bourdieu.htm>.

Cavarero, A. 2000. *Relating Narratives: Storytelling and Selfhood*. New York: Routledge.

Connell, R. 2007. *Southern Theory*. Cambridge: Polity Press.

Curtis, B., and H. Chodos. 2002. 'Pierre Bourdieu's Masculine Domination: A Critique', *Canadian Review of Sociology and Anthropology* 39, 2: 397–412.

Dillabough, J. 2001. 'Gender Theory in Education', in B. Francis and C. Skeleton, eds, *Investigating Gender*. Milton Keynes, UK: Open University Press.

———, and S. Acker. 2002. 'Globalization, Women's Work and Teacher Education: A Cross-national Analysis', *International Studies in the Sociology of Education* 12, 3: 227–60.

Eichner, M . 2001. 'On Postmodern Feminist Legal Theory', *Harvard Civil Rights–Civil Liberties Review* 36: 2–31.

Fraser, N., and L. Gordon. 1994. 'A Genealogy of Dependency: Tracing the Keyword of the U.S. Welfare State', *Signs* 19, 2: 33–60.

Foucault, M. 1986. *On the Uses of Pleasure*. Vol 2. *The History of Sexuality*. Harmondsworth: Viking Penguin.

Fowler, B. 2003. 'Reading Pierre Bourdieu's *Masculine Domination*: Notes towards an Intersectional Analysis of Gender, Culture and Class', *Cultural Studies* 17, 3–4: 468–94.

Kennelly, J. 2008. 'Youth Subcultural Theory and 21st Century Activism: Bourdieu's Contributions'. Unpublished dissertation. University of British Columbia.

Lovell, T. 2000. 'Thinking Feminism with and against Bourdieu', *Feminist Theory* 1, 1: 11–32.

McCall, L. 1992. 'Does Gender Fit? Bourdieu, Feminism and Conceptions of the Social Order', *Theory and Society* 21, 6: 837–62.

McLeod, J. 2003. 'Revisiting Gender, Habitus, and Social Field, or Why Bourdieu Now?' Paper presented to the Gender and Education Conference, UK.

———, and K.J. Kenway. 2004. 'Bourdieu's Reflexive Sociology and Aspects of "Points of View": Whose Reflexivity, Which Perspective?', *British Journal of Sociology of Education* 25, 4: 525–94.

McNay, L. 1999. 'Gender, Habitus, and the Field: Pierre Bourdieu and the Limits of Reflexivity Theory', *Theory, Culture and Society* 16: 95–117.

———. 2000. *Gender and Agency: Reconfiguring the Subject in Feminist and Social Theory*. Cambridge: Polity Press.

———. 2004. 'Agency and Experience: Gender as a Lived Relation', in Adkins and Skeggs (2004).

McRobbie, A. 2004. 'Notes on Bourdieu and Post Feminist Symbolic Violence', in Adkins and Skeggs (2004).

Marshall, G., ed. 1994. *The Concise Oxford Dictionary of Sociology*. Oxford: Oxford University Press.

Moi, T. 1991. 'Appropriating Bourdieu: Feminist Theory and Pierre Bourdieu's Sociology of Culture', *New Literary History* 22: 1017–49.

Moore, A. 2003. '"Cultural Capital", "Symbolic Violence" and the Arbitrary: Bourdieu's Exposure of Institutional Culturalism'. Paper presented at 'Bourdieu: The Legacy', Institute of Education, London.

Mottier, V. 2002. 'Masculine Domination: Gender and Power in Bourdieu's Writings', *Feminist Theory* 3, 3: 345–59.

Reay, D. 1998. *Class Work*. London: University College London Press.

———. 2004. 'It's All Becoming a Habitus', *British Journal of Sociology of Education* 25, 4: 431–47.

Ricoeur, P. 2005. *History, Memory and Forgetting*. Chicago: University of Chicago Press.

Robbins, D. 2002. 'On Bourdieu.' Paper presented to the symposium 'The Work of Pierre Bourdieu', Institute of Education, London.

Skeggs, B. 1997. *Formations of Class and Gender*. London: Sage.

———. 2004. *Class, Self, and Culture*. London: Routledge.

Spillman, L. 2001. 'Culture and Cultural Sociology', in Spillman, ed., *Cultural Sociology*. Oxford: Blackwell.

Thompson, E.P. 1966. *The Making of the English Working Class*. London: Random House.

Weir, A. 1997. *Sacrificial Logics*. New York: Routledge.

Williams, R. 1977. *Marxism and Literature*. London and New York: Oxford University Press.

Zerilli, L. 1995. 'The Arendtian Body', in B. Honig, ed., *Feminist Interpretations of Hannah Arendt*. University Park: Pennsylvania State Press.

CHAPTER 4

Theorizing Anti-racism

George J. Sefa Dei

Introduction

This chapter will present a theoretical and analytical perspective on anti-racism. I embark on this task fully aware of the tension, today, between the desire to move beyond **race** altogether and the recognition that until now only the racially privileged have been in a position to deny its existence. I assert from the outset that there is no single model of anti-racism, since to prescribe a single approach would be to limit the possibility of anti-racist practice. Having said this, I also acknowledge that any anti-racist practice must begin with an understanding of how central race is, how it intersects with other forms of difference, how it contributes to relations of domination and subordination, and how those asymmetrical power relations serve to position different bodies and their experiences in the larger web of systemic and institutionalized networks. Social oppression and marginalization are everyday experiences for racially minoritized bodies in our society. The collective quest for unity, harmony, and peace depends in large part on our ability to address the myriad ways in which asymmetrical power relations promote and sustain marginality and oppression. Institutionalized marginality and oppression produce lasting effects when certain members of society are denied access to valued goods and services by those who evoke difference in ways that demean their humanity and silence their needs and aspirations.

As educators we continually struggle to produce, interrogate, validate, and disseminate knowledge. We may work directly with race or we may deny its existence, but we can never honestly claim to be disinterested or neutral. Even silence does not signal a lack of position. Academic debate on issues of race and oppression can be healthy, provided we do not accuse those who disagree with us of disregard for 'excellence' or lack of academic rigour. In order to critically interrogate the possibilities and limits of any particular anti-racist theory, we need to know how it recognizes the centrality of race. What does it understand anti-racism to mean? Finally, how do we separate the discourse of anti-racism (i.e., anti-racist principles or ideas) from the questions/issues of scholarly gaze or individual focus? Critiques of anti-racist practice run the risk of reinforcing the dominant society's perspectives.

The sociology of anti-racism seeks to understand the culture of oppression and how the institutionalized marginality of racialized bodies sustains an enduring system of social injustice and inequity. Our focus on racial oppression should not be confused with 'race reductionism'. Race is our entry point into the culture of oppression, but we remain mindful of its intersections with other forms of difference. Hierarchies of race, class, gender, sexuality, (dis)ability, language, and religion all help to perpetuate systemic violence to bodies, particularly when these bodies are rendered 'structurally irrelevant' and their rights and privileges, along with the complexities of their cultural and historical identities, are either denied or negated. It is only by working within an integrative anti-racism framework that we can begin to explore the pernicious effects of racism and the way they are compounded by ethnicity, class, gender, sexuality, family, religion, culture, language, and history.

Behind my pursuit of an unapologetic anti-racist practice is an intellectual project to create space for the racially dominated to understand the terms of our oppression and to develop effective means of opposing and resisting it. In this context anti-racist practice could help minoritized bodies to transcend our marginality and work towards self-actualization and collective empowerment. This is why agency and resistance are key to sustaining anti-racist practice for the racially minoritized. But I am also interested in promoting a critical anti-racist practice that allows the dominant to question their own power and privilege, their complicity in the maintenance of structural inequity, and how positions of power and influence can be used to address social inequities. This approach to anti-racism is intended to build an effective power base from which racialized and dominant groups alike can work together for social change and transformation.

As a minority scholar and anti-racist practitioner, I believe in working for social justice. We should never allow ourselves—our abilities, our life, our spiritual purpose—to be sacrificed to conventional/dominant ideas about what constitutes 'valid', 'acceptable' knowledge. Some academics maintain that scholarship and activism should remain separate, but I believe they go hand in hand. Our institutions are such that we need 'academic warriors', 'academics with a conscience', people who are not afraid to risk the displeasure of their institutions. I will not argue that activist scholarship is something that everyone should practise. To take that stance would be to impose my own values and ideas on others. By the same token I do not expect those who disagree with me to presume that their standards of knowledge production and validation are the only legitimate ones. For me 'theory' is a living concept. We theorize in multiple ways. Anti-racist theory must be alive and it must compel action. Theory 'resides' in our everyday realities, and a good theory must be capable of responding to daily challenges.

Theorizing about anti-racism and its implications for the sociology of education is a worthwhile intellectual project. It is a legitimate way to interrogate power relations. It is disheartening, therefore, to hear such theorizing dismissed by critics who charge that it lacks conceptual and analytical clarity. We need to move beyond the quest for an objective, 'scientific', value-neutral exposition of the issues of race and anti-racist knowledge production. We need to ask new questions: Is there racism without race? And can we have racism without racists? Race has always been central to colonial and colonizing relations. Goldberg (1993) attests to how the European colonial powers used race to legitimize their domination of other groups. Racial-supremacist ideas developed to enforce the relations of dominance have continually been reproduced to serve the powerful while silencing the colonized. In writing about race and anti-racist knowledge I am always grateful to the listener, since being 'listened to' is something that oppressed bodies are not always guaranteed. Often we do not listen to each other, either because of arrogance or because we fear that hearing a 'different voice' will challenge our complacency and comfort. I recall a former student who pointed out to me that wisdom, patience, and piety inspire others to know. I believe these are also the ingredients of 'excellent' scholarship, and that those who think they know all the answers have no effect on knowledge production except to stunt the spirit (Wahab, 2006).

Transforming our institutions means using critical knowledge to challenge the dominance of Western knowledge, values, and ideas in the academy (see also Asante, 2006). It means challenging the dominance of Western thinking, which subsumes all other forms of thought and deems invalid any conception of social reality that is not framed within a Western Eurocentric paradigm. Of course, I understand that Western modes of thought are not monolithic. What I object to is their dominance. The way to challenge that dominance is by nurturing oppositional stances informed by our own subject positions and subjective experiences. The racially minoritized must define their identity through intellectual agency within the anti-racist discursive framework. This will affirm the epistemological relevance of the oppressed while subjecting their understanding of oppression to critical interrogation. An anti-racist discursive framework points to the site of oppression not simply as a point of reference but, more importantly, as a resource/knowledge base and source of agency. Anti-racism calls for intellectual rejuvenation, a resurgence of critical knowledge to subvert dominant thinking. To disrupt the dominance of Eurocentric knowledge and/or Westernity we need to create intellectual and political projects that will validate different knowledges.

Anti-racism as a Discursive Framework

A **discursive framework** is a reflection of both the powerful organizing effects of discourse and the way that social realities are continually changing, so that our understandings of social facts shift when new questions are posed. Certain questions are central to theorizing about an anti-racist framework. For example, how do we define race and racism? What understandings do learners bring to discussions of race and racism, and where do these ideas come from? Do learners make the important distinctions between racism and other forms of discrimination? And do they see and challenge the interconnections between racism and other forms of discrimination? How are questions of power and privilege engaged in discussion? Do learners recognize self-implication and complicity? Do they claim innocence? If so, why?

An anti-racist discursive framework highlights the processes of **racialization**—the processes responsible for the differential positioning of groups in the social order. As I argue in a recent book (2008), 'racialization' in this context refers to the ideological, material, and symbolic signification of different groups in the imagination of the dominant group. Racialization operates on the understanding that racial groups exist within hierarchies of power. Such hierarchies are meaningful only in competitive cultures, in which social institutions depend on racialized bodies in order to sustain themselves. In highly competitive, market-driven, individualistic societies, it is not enough to racialize individuals: the desired effects will be achieved only if the process is extended to groups. Social institutions such as schools, media, and the courts are never neutral or apolitical. They are implicated in broader social relations and networks establishing dominance and hegemony through the differential allocation of social wealth. Notwithstanding the constant denial of race, the concept of race is an important tool for rationalizing this unequal distribution of social wealth. In other words, race is not an innocent concept: it has historically been a medium for allocating rewards and punishment.

Race serves as a way of organizing social knowledge about ourselves, how we see each other as members of communities, and how we structure everyday life. In racialized communities it is through the use of racial images, symbols, and signifiers—including other forms of difference, such as class, gender, sexuality, and (dis)ability—that we order social meanings. Race cannot be understood only in its socially constitutive sense. It must also be understood as a fundamental way of material existence. It is in the economic conditions of everyday existence that race gains its currency. Rules are constantly being established to govern the way we organize our social relations (respect, rights, responsibilities) to ensure the existence of communities. Some of these rules help to transform our understandings of race through time. They also point to the fluidity and transformative possibilities of racial identities. The relations of race and racialized discourses to questions of material existence and how our bodies are implicated in every social relation serve to validate the dominant group's ways of knowing while devaluing or negating those of the oppressed. It is through a racialized prism that we make sense of the realities of everyday lived experiences, connections, and disconnections between oppressors and the oppressed. The mechanisms of racial power are 'invested, colonized, utilized, involuted, transformed, displaced, extended' through the oppressive activities of dominant groups (see Foucault, 1980: 99).

In the context of education, anti-racist theory addresses the connections between race, racialization, and social difference, particularly with respect to the imposition, enforcement, and resistance of hegemony. The starting position of such theorizing is that racism and racializing practices exist: they are realities that do not need to be proven in order to validate race knowledge (e.g., what constitutes racism, racial identities, racist practice, etc.). Rather, we focus on the politics of race denial as they play out in everyday institutional practices through the dominating particularities of whiteness and white privilege that serve to alienate students whose bodies are marked by racialized difference (see also Doyle-Wood, 2006a). This politics of denial constitutes a racial imposition and a covert racist practice. Denial is also a form of insidious racism that 'lies at the center, not the periphery; in the permanent, not in the fleeting; in the real lives of black and white people (and the nation-state itself), not in the sentimental caverns of the mind' (Bell, 1992: 198). The possibility of social and institutional transformation can emerge only through counter-oppositional paradigm shifts.

Proponents of transformative education insist that schooling should be understood and practised as a political activity, radical in nature. All learners engage with school differently, and the learner's identity is critical. As Doyle-Wood (2006b) notes, in the context of the racialized power relations that prevail in schools, the (re)claiming of the self through the collective is important. Hence the notion of difference is critical to theorizing anti-racist change in education and schooling. A truly decolonizing approach must speak to critical consciousness arising from multiple sites of difference—class, gender, sexuality, (dis)ability, etc. In fact, Doyle-Wood (2006b) sees 'the collective' as encompassing not just those who have been minoritized but the entire nation-state, since the society as a whole has been wounded by the processes of racialization over time. Critical/radical education can be a powerful force to resist and transcend the amputation of racial identities that takes place in institutional settings, including schools. By emphasizing alternative/counter-hegemonic paradigms, anti-racist education allows us to challenge the dehumanizing racist omissions and negations practised throughout the society. It also subverts the racist power relations that continue to afflict many of our institutions. Anti-racism asks why it is taken for granted that 'Canadian' means 'white' and explores how this assumption serves to neutralize whiteness to the point that whites themselves are not aware of their hegemony. A critical educational practice challenges the invisibility of the racially minoritized by asking whiteness to recognize itself as well as other racial identities.

In positing an 'anti-racist discursive framework' I find myself confronting a question posed by Tikly (2004) in a different context: 'how to go beyond the existing order of knowledge [while feeling] obliged simultaneously to work within its frameworks?' (192). The problem is that 'scientific' knowledge has discredited other ways of knowing. Thus when science is unable to explain a social phenomenon, it will deny the existence of that phenomenon—it does not question what constitutes 'valid' knowledge in the first place. In upholding race knowledge I am highlighting a form of knowledge regarding racial oppression that has been marginalized, suppressed, and de-legitimized by 'Western science' (see also Santos, 1999: 33, in another context). Anti-racist discourse is more than the use of language, signs, and symbols. It encompasses a range of social practices, at the heart of which is education, and how educational practices constitute individuals and groups as subjects. From an anti-racist perspective, education is a site of discursive struggle over competing versions of social reality. It is important to understand how power settles disagreements between competing claims to 'truth'.

To articulate an anti-racist discursive framework it is crucial to analyze power, knowledge, and the role of the subject in transformative education. The pursuit of social justice must be informed by a consciousness of one's existence as well as intellectual engagement and politics. Anti-racist discourse asserts that 'races' were historically constructed to facilitate the colonization project of the dominant Europeans.

Since then, numerous other sites of difference, including class, gender, (dis)ability, and sexuality, have served similar purposes. Anti-racist discourse affirms the power of racial and cultural perspectives (or reference points) in the analysis of social reality. Anti-racism acknowledges the saliency of race as a fundamental aspect of the lived experiences of the subjugated. It also works with a cultural perspective that foregrounds the agency and interests of racially minoritized subjects in narrating and resisting oppression. Usually, the perspectives of the racially dominant are passed on as objective and apolitical (see also critiques by Asante, 1999: 5, and 2003a: 37; and Akbar, 2003: 134–5, in related contexts). In positing that we are defined and confined by Eurocentric thought, Howard (2008) observes that such forms of knowledge production (by influencing the way we think and act) often serve as 'tools of domination'. What the West recognizes as knowledge is grounded in Eurocentric assumptions, epistemologies, axiologies, and aesthetics (see also Kershaw, 1992: 162; Mazama, 2001: 387).

Anti-racism theorists put forward a critique of colonial and imperial practices at both theoretical and political levels. They argue that race is relevant in explaining difference as a site both of power and of social inequality. Race cannot be subsumed or replaced with emerging understandings or categories of culture and politics. Even if few people today subscribe to biologistic/eugenic interpretations of society, we are nonetheless confronted with a 'resurgence of bio-political racism that uses cultural differences to explain social problems' (Tikly, 2004: 185). This is no accident. In fact it is a conscious attempt to deny the dominant group's power to name the 'Other' as different. An anti-racist discursive framework attempts to politicize social and cultural relations by engaging the broader socio-historical contexts within which everyday interactions between individuals and groups are structured. Anti-racism points to the asymmetrical power relations that structure these interactions and render subjects' identities (race, class, gender, sexuality, (dis)ability, etc.) relevant or irrelevant, depending on the politics at play. Far from denying or dismissing the significance of race, anti-racism theory argues that in order to respond to the pressing economic, political, and material challenges of our time, it is necessary to understand the role that race plays in them. The nature of social knowledge is such that to understand society we need to extend our discursive analysis beyond the economic and political to engage issues of culture and identity.

I noted in an earlier work (1996) that the primary concern of anti-racist discursive analysis is **equity**: the qualitative value of justice defined not only in terms of race but also in terms of other forms of difference such as class, gender, sexuality, (dis)ability, language, and culture. Anti-racism recognizes that institutions produce and reproduce inequalities through their regulatory mechanisms, disciplinary measures, and normalizing gaze. Indeed, schools, media, and legal systems are viewed in the anti-racist discursive framework as part of the institutional structure, sanctioned by society, that serves the material, political, and ideological interests of the state and capitalist relations of production. Schools, for example, are powerful institutional sites where the relationships between the state and its citizens are negotiated and/or contested. School policies are not innocent in this regard. In fact, the state relies on schools to regulate, rationalize, standardize, and clarify social life so as to manage social relations among citizens (see also Coe, 2005). Initiatives designed to transform schooling must therefore begin by addressing historic systemic inequities. An integrative anti-racist discursive approach critically examines the institutional structures that deliver education; that is, the structures for teaching, learning, and administration. It acknowledges the pedagogic requirement to confront the challenge of social diversity, and the urgent need for an educational system that is more inclusive and capable of responding to various minority concerns.

In addition, anti-racist discourse raises the issue of representation: the need for a multiplicity of voices, physical bodies, and perspectives to create and affirm social knowledge. An anti-racist discursive framework problematizes the marginalization of certain voices and ideas within societal institutions, as well as the delegitimation of the knowledge and experience of subordinate groups in everyday pedagogic and communicative practices. An anti-racist approach requires a critical understanding of how race, ethnicity, class, gender, sexuality, culture, language, and religion mediate the power of communal social practice and action. The framework stresses that power and resistant action are not the exclusive possessions of the dominant group, but also reside in/among minoritized, marginalized communities (see also Fanon, 1963; Foucault, 1980; Memmi, 1969, in other contexts). Discursive agency emerges from an understanding of the importance of locally produced communal knowledge embedded in local cultural history, daily human experiences, and social interactions. Subordinate groups develop a theoretical and practical conception of what 'difference' means as a legitimate entry point to engage in political practice for social change.

Within the anti-racist discursive framework there is an understanding that in any social context the effects of social policies and practices will be felt differently by different groups. It is therefore important to recognize the situational and contextual variations in the intensity of the experience of oppression and the impact of power for/on different groups, and the severity with which different issues will affect certain bodies, depending on the relative saliencies of their various identities. Thus, as I have argued elsewhere (2009, forthcoming), anti-racist practice calls for a re-thinking of the notions of 'multiplicity of oppressions' and 'intersectional analysis'.

Adopting an anti-racist gaze in institutional settings, specifically in schools, means scrutinizing the processes and structures through which education is delivered (curriculum, instruction, pedagogy, social organization of knowledge, policy, history of education, etc.). It means understanding the contestations that arise over knowledge, culture, values, and understandings of social relationships, and exploring the interplay of school culture, social climate, and environment that shape the 'learner'. The issues of responsibility and accountability place learners and educators in asymmetrical power relations in the school system. Corrigan (1990) long ago noted that schooling wounds all students through its normalizing routines, beginning with its negation of the space of family and the resistances and affirmative knowledges of local communities. The processes of knowledge production, interrogation, and validation can also serve to discipline minoritized and racialized bodies. The regulatory mechanism of schooling when enforced can come very close to a 'prison complex mentality' and the construction of the 'school-prison feeder road' especially when educators uncritically bring the panopticon gaze to certain bodies (see Foucault, 1977). In such cases the racialized, classed, gendered, and sexualized ideologies and tropes of schooling affect bodies differently. In fact, through their validation of knowledge that sustains a racialized ideology with differential outcomes, school policies can authorize and perpetuate racial hierarchies (see Henay, 2005).

Anti-racism and Questions of Materiality

An anti-racist framework also stipulates that we cannot dissociate discursive practices and their effects from material reality. In other words, everyday discourses have powerful material consequences, and questions of materiality can be understood only when ideas are engaged at both discursive and political levels. In order to understand the production and reproduction of racism today, we must ground our analyses firmly in the political economy of race knowledge production. For an anti-racist analysis, the interface of race, class, and political economy is crucial. Race cuts differently depending on one's social position and location. Historically, institutionalized oppression has been more beneficial to white men than white women, and to the white middle class than the white working class or poor, given the intersections of gender and class. Roediger (1991: 13) has also argued that 'status and privileges conferred by race could be used to make up for alienating exploitative class relationships' among whites. The economic as well as the political structures that sustain social domination must be transformed. Therefore it is not enough to focus on questions of culture, identity, and politics: attention must also be paid to the political economy of race, racism, and racial difference. Economic, political, spiritual, and cultural structures are intertwined. The political economy of race emphasizes the unequal relations of power in the production of knowledge and the economic and cultural structures of domination that sustain social inequities.

Where is class in the anti-racist analysis? If we acknowledge the influence of Marxist and neo-Marxist thought in contemporary progressive politics, class is everywhere. We can hardly grasp the larger political economic questions of globalization and transnationalism if we divorce race from class (or vice versa). I believe Neo-Marxist scholarship can contribute to the development of a contemporary anti-racist praxis. The important lesson of the racialization (and feminization) of poverty, and the differentiation in access to resources along the lines of race, class, and gender, is that materialism and consumerism always breed injustice. The exercise of social power requires social and material inequality. There is a dialectic of the material and non-material that must be acknowledged to make the pursuit of social justice a comprehensive undertaking. The consciousness of being is not simply an exercise in material accomplishment. Class-consciousness is a reflection of relative subject positions and incorporates cultural, spiritual, and emotional as well as political dimensions. If we believe that racial identity is part of the subjective being, then the link is a dialectic of race, class, and other forms of difference. The ideological stance that race, class, gender, sexuality, (dis)ability, and other forms of social difference shape subjective consciousness cannot be discounted. It is this shared, intertwined, and multiply grounded consciousness that may help propel anti-racist work for meaningful social change. It is within this consciousness that an anti-racist ideology committed to political action rests.

Anti-Racism and Embodiment of Knowledge

The anti-racist discursive framework also links race, identity, and representation in educational practice. In the context of an anti-racist discursive practice, 'bodies matter'. Bodies matter because of the link between identity and knowledge production. But bodies also matter because of the embeddedness and/or 'rootedness of racist ideologies in bodies' (Howard, 2006). As Howard (2006) contends, the white body is potentially prone to racism and this complicates any engagement in critical anti-racist work. The skin privilege of the white body gives rise to certain liabilities in any work that would be deemed anti-racist. This does not mean that white bodies cannot do anti-racist work, however. Engaging the self in anti-racist schooling and education work is a critical component of progressive work. Because white bodies are invested in systems of privilege, it is essential that dominant groups question their self-appointed and racialized neutrality. White society has long relied on the idea of a fractured, irresponsible black community to absolve it from any need to address broader systemic and structural questions of accountability and transparency.

In the context of bodies and the politics of educational transformation, Doyle-Wood (2006a) notes that what matters is not the colour of the person but the colour of the person's politics. Socially conservative views are no less dangerous when the body that holds them is minoritized. At the same time, if we are speaking about bodies whose politics must be anti-racist, liberatory, and transformative, then it is crucial that such bodies be bodies of colour. It is psychologically liberating for students to see experienced teachers who are members of a racial minority. At the same time, location is a critical factor when we are speaking about issues of race and power. A minoritized gaze is an informed gaze, with an alternative way of seeing and knowing. Today it matters a lot who teaches what (race, anti-racism, black Canadian literature, or Aboriginal history, for example).

Anti-Racism, Spiritual Knowing, and Non-Material Connections

An anti-racist discursive framework therefore gestures to more than the material world and/or the material reality. It seeks to reconnect the material and spiritual worlds that have been separated. It places spirituality at the heart of the pursuit of social justice. In working with spiritual ontologies and spiritual knowings anti-racists strategically and politically evoke a collective sense of being that propels individual and collective human action for common good. Equity work flows (and gains credibility) from the understanding of one's spiritual sense of being and place within a 'community' (however defined). Oppression damages not only the individual psyche but our collective will and power. It is through spiritual awareness and awakening that the oppressed can imagine, design, and carve out a hopeful future. We are encouraged to act because of a belief in hope, a triumph over despair, and a victorious future. As Asante cautions us,

> no example of oppression consciousness is stimulating in the progressive sense. Our history and future are only connected in victory. Struggle itself turns into oppressive consciousness when one cannot conceive of victory. (2003b: 65)

Developing a 'victorious consciousness' requires a strong sense of spiritual empower-ment, and recognition of spirituality as action-oriented. Thus an anti-racist discursive framework connects the material and non-material aspects of our lives, drawing on the synergies between mind, body, and soul. Conventional ways of knowledge production have sought to disembody the learner by separating the mind from the soul. Yet social oppression tends to cause deep material as well emotional, spiritual, and psychological damage to the oppressed. Anti-racism then becomes a practice to heal the soul and the mind, as well as the physical, mental, and spiritual damage brought on to the self and collective by the myriad forms of oppression.

Spirituality in anti-racism is not about believing in a higher moral authority. It is about respecting the sanctity of life and appreciating the humanity that we all share as the basis for working for social change. In bringing spirituality to discussions about anti-racism we are also challenging the dominance of Western epistemology and the propensity to dismiss some forms of knowing. Spirituality is part of our daily lives. It is an 'individual thing' and more, meaning that we must acknowledge our different spiritualities and what they mean for the collective. But spirituality in terms of the sense of self and personhood, the connection of the inner self to the outer self and group, means we should be able to address power relations. We cannot evade power questions when we speak about spirituality as a way of knowing the self and the connection of the self to the group. We begin anti-racist work knowing ourselves and what brings us to the pursuit of racial/social justice. The understanding of the collec-tive/community as 'communities of differences' stresses the unity of being, and a continuing search for mutual interdependence, linkages, and co-existence with the interface of society, culture, and nature. These connections make for a more humane existence, one that eschews control, oppression, and domination. Obviously, such a stance also requires a commitment to addressing key questions of social responsibility and ethics. Thus while anti-racist practice speaks about the power of healing and repairing the damage done by all forms of oppression, anti-racism moves to connect the self with the broader social, political, cultural, and spiritual realms of everyday existence. By acknowledging the power of spirituality, we are able to work with the agency and resistance of the oppressed.

In effect, a re-conceptualized anti-racist practice would have the spiritual as its foundation and make questions of economics, culture, and history the superstructure. This approach to anti-racist work cannot be viewed simply as a project of decoloniza-tion. It should also be seen as a critical discursive approach to unravelling power rela-tions of knowledge production, interrogation, validation, and dissemination. Among the new questions being asked are: What do marginalized people know about their own oppression? How do such voices speak about their resistances to oppression? How does conventional anti-racist politics allow local subjects to set/determine and articu-late their own priorities? By raising these questions, anti-racism becomes both a politics of knowledge production and a socialization of knowledge for social action. Admittedly, there is a need for intellectual rejuvenation, resurgence of critical thinking to subvert dominant and colonizing thinking. It is important that our understanding of the objective of anti-racism be untied from the privileging of Western Eurocentric knowledge and the pathologizing of the cultures, experiences, and human condition of the racially oppressed. Anti-racism cannot be an end in itself. Anti-racism should not be about the inevitability or desirability of a certain state of affairs. Rather, it must be a holistic political and intellectual agenda, complex and multifaceted. Anti-racism must reflect the lived realities and the cultural and political goals and aspirations both of racialized peoples and of the privileged. It should be a form of practice rooted in the moral and spiritual values that oppressed and dominant groups share.

Anti-racism and Social Transformation

The anti-racist discourse goes beyond critique to engage with the possibilities of social change. It is about both social critique and transformative political action. So what can we do as educators? First, we need to create safe and decolonized spaces for discussion both in the academy and in the public sphere. Among the forms of oppression that need to be brought into contemporary public discourse is the denial of race, including the role that institutionalized ideologies have played in creating a 'culture of silence' around the subject. Many people today are convinced that they cannot speak up about racial injustice for fear of jeopardizing whatever minor influence they might have in the spaces where decisions are actually made. If the academy is to help break this silence, we need to work on developing a truly democratic culture in which people can openly address the issues that matter to them without fear of repercussions.

Fostering a decolonized space in the academy will require nurturing 'multiple perspectives which [will] engage each dialectically in a process of mutual criticism and mutual correction' (Tucker, 1999: 16). In theorizing about communities, it is essential to put the identities, experiences, and histories of racialized subjects at the centre. And anti-racist discourse itself should encourage the oppressed to speak out about what they know. Too often, dominant groups have (mis)represented 'Others', with the result that the latter can find it difficult even to recognize themselves (ourselves) in the discourses that claim to portray their experiences and concerns.

The goal of anti-racist educational practice is to develop students' consciousness both of race and of the intersections between racial and other forms of oppression. To decolonize already colonized spaces, it is necessary to challenge the assumptions and thought processes underlying the dominant culture's efforts to control the production, validation, and dissemination of 'knowledge'—efforts that serve to ensure the reproduction of existing inequities among groups. Only by contextualizing and situating those efforts in the history of Eurocentric thought, so that we understand how our perceptions have been colonized and our inhumanity cultivated, can we begin to claim our humanity and the consciousness that comes with working politically to extricate ourselves from social oppression (see also Fanon, 1967: 10). Today we are beginning to understand how the 'everyday world' is conditioned by the complexities of race, class, gender, sexuality, language, and (dis)ability. For anti-racist and anti-colonial practitioners, questions of identity, representation, spirituality, indigenity, agency, and resistance are central to political practice.

Gramsci's (1971) work on the development of hegemony is informative for anti-racist struggles (see also Howard, 2008). Through their power and influence in societal institutions (e.g., schools, police force, justice system, media, etc.) dominant groups have created and certified as 'valid' a body of knowledge that has become hegemonic. This knowledge has come to be taken for granted as everyday 'common sense' among the dominant and the dominated (Howard, 2008; see also Hall, 1996), and it constitutes an increasing proportion of both groups' consciousness. The 'seizure of intellectual space' (Asante, 1998: 108) and the devaluing of Afrocentric perspectives by the West has been so complete that it is virtually impossible to challenge from within: oppositional discourses are easily dismissed once they have been filtered through the dominant prisms and paradigms. An anti-racist discursive framework makes it possible to recognize the experiences of the marginalized as legitimate sources of knowledge. There is power in understanding that the experiences of oppression position the racially oppressed to know differently.

The discourses that were the hallmarks of the Enlightenment—discourses of progress, reason, rationality, and civilization—were used to construct the 'Other' as inadequate, deficient, and incapable, deny his/her humanity, and legitimize everything from colonialism to enslavement and genocide. In the nineteenth century, advances in biology were co-opted to provide 'scientific' validation for the idea that certain groups (e.g., African/black people) were subhuman. As Tucker argues, the twentieth century challenged this biological racism—but it nonetheless ushered in 'a pernicious form of cultural racism which based its judgments of superiority and inferiority on essentially ethnocentric norms, thereby labeling other cultures as inferior' (1999: 5). Current anti-racist discourse and practice challenge the dominant culture's claims to a monopoly over truth, reason, and enlightenment, along with its control over the production, interrogation, validation, and dissemination of knowledge.

Education can be transformative to the extent that it challenges the dominant culture's efforts to pathologize racialized subjects. First, however, the academy must examine itself for hegemonic practices. Foucault's (1980) theorizing on discipline and punishment drew attention to the way schools use their power to regulate learners' lives. But power is not a fixed or stationary category. As Foucault (1980) argues, power does not belong to a particular class or institution, but is dispersed throughout society. Thus power can also be used both to resist marginalization and victimization and to recover histories of resistance that can help to subvert the dominant paradigms.

Anti-racism Implementation and Practice

In racialized communities, relations of domination are structured along lines of race, class, gender, sexuality, (dis)ability, age, language, culture, and religion. These relations are dictated not only by the history, cultural politics, and material relations of a society, but also by local actions and everyday discursive practices (see also Deliovsky, 2005: 12; Hall, 1997). The structure of dominance, privilege, and punishment affects bodies differently in our communities. An integrative anti-racist discursive framework allows educators to approach the challenges of difference and schooling from a critical point of view, understanding the different ways in which the socially constructed intersections of race, ethnicity, class, gender, sexuality, culture, language, and religion mediate the educational experiences of diverse bodies. An integrative anti-racist framework acknowledges the intersecting implications of a diverse group of learners within the macro-social politics of educational policy. This framework allows us to work with an understanding that knowledge production is fundamentally about questions of identity, culture, representation, and the politics of schooling.

While the sociology of education tends to investigate individual structures for educational delivery (i.e., structures for teaching, for learning, and for the administration of education), an anti-racist theoretical focus on the possibilities of subverting knowledge is associated with the 'macro-social politics of education'. This includes the cultural politics of schooling and broader macro-political processes and structures through which education is delivered (e.g., curriculum, social organization of knowledge, policy, history of education, etc.). By focusing on the contestations over knowledge, culture, values, and understandings, anti-racism brings to the fore the ways power plays out in educational and other institutional sites. The dynamics of everyday relations and the interplay of school culture, social climate, and environment shape the construction of learners' identities. An anti-racist gaze examines the ways in which learners' experience of schooling is racially, socially, politically, and culturally mediated. It also looks at how issues of responsibility and accountability connect with educational transformation: if students are socially responsible, they will fight injustice and inequality. Apart from the social and power relations of knowledge production, an anti-racist approach within the sociology of education also calls for the examination of ways in which structured differences within particular educational sites affect learning outcomes: for example, how differential access to resources contributes to disengagement, disaffection, and alienation from school among certain groups. An anti-racist approach puts students at the centre of educational research, policy-making, and teacher education. In addition to respecting students and listening to them, we must pay attention to the lessons they offer teachers about 'how to teach'.

Schools are, as Michelle Fine puts it, 'contested public spheres' (Fine, 1993; see also Apple, 1986, 1990, 1999; Apple and Weiss, 1983; Bourdieu and Passeron, 1977; Giroux, 1981). White privilege continues to manifest itself in countless ways, despite formal integration; and as Fine (2006) notes of the US in particular, racially minoritized students and parents are often held hostage to white parents and students who threaten to leave. Schools like these are not neutral territories, but arenas of powerful political desires. Hence **anti-racist education** highlights the social relations of power and social inequity in schooling.

For teachers I would argue that the challenge of minority education is not to do away with the notion of 'race' but rather to change the meanings we bring to that notion. The problem is not the concept of race in itself but the unequal relations of power that have been created around it in order to legitimize abuse and exploitation (see Tucker, 1999, for a related discussion of the concept of 'development'). Anti-racist discourse and practice should be about understanding the contemporary challenges of representation and identity and the role of power in mediating knowledge production. Anti-racism works with counter and alternative conceptions of 'difference' and 'Otherness'. Anti-racist discourse makes a crucial distinction between recognizing 'difference' and recognizing 'Otherness'. Difference is a positive identity that can be a source of strength, knowledge, power, and agency. We need to acknowledge difference in order to understand how we are affected by the asymmetrical power relations constructed around race, class, gender, sexuality, and other forms of difference. Of course it is crucial to recognize our similarities, the human qualities that we all share—but to focus only on our commonalities would be to ignore realities that have profound consequences for people's lives. 'Otherness', by contrast, is negative: not an identity that one claims for oneself or seeks to recognize in someone else. Rather, it is something constructed and imposed on those who look 'different' in order to prevent connection, to deny them resources or power, and to justify their subordination. At the same time, in establishing 'self/Other', 'us/them' distinctions, those who engage in this process of 'Othering' stake their own claim to membership in the dominant group. It is the failure to distinguish between 'difference' and 'Otherness' that leads some critics to charge that anti-racists, in drawing attention to the former, actually create problems of race and racism (see also Dei, 2006: 26).

Societies and schools in particular provide very few opportunities to explore critically how we think and feel about race and difference. The beginning of white racism, when Europeans first encountered people who looked 'different', is a critical juncture at which to explore the link between whiteness and racism. Whites grow into and embody their whiteness. They articulate their whiteness and white identity in relation to the racialized 'Other'. Hardening of racial divisions and stereotypes is a reflection of the unequal distribution of economic power and resources. Race is a historically and socially variable concept, and the complex social production of racial identities cannot be understood without a nuanced understanding of identity, representation, history, culture, and politics. An anti-racist discursive approach is about comprehending how racialized identities differ in form and function, depending on time and place (e.g., the performance/performativity of whiteness and racialized identities in complex social formations). Integrative anti-racist education pays particular attention to the myriad ways in which race, class, gender, sexuality, and (dis)ability intersect with one another at different historical moments. The anti-racism approach can help educators both to understand current racial, class, gender, and sexual oppressions and to challenge the Eurocentric/white racism that continues to privilege whiteness in our society.

Glossary

anti-racist education: Action-oriented education designed to combat racism and other forms of social oppression by focusing attention on the asymmetrical power relations that structure everyday interactions between individuals and groups in any society.

discursive framework: A comprehensive structure of ways of thinking (talking, writing, teaching, etc.) about a particular subject, organized—more or less consciously, by individuals or entire societies—so as to produce a particular effect.

equity: Justice or fairness, particularly with respect to race, class, gender, sexuality, (dis)ability, language, and culture.

race: A socio-political concept constructed for social control of subdominant groups.

racialization: The process by which the dominant imagination assigns particular ideological, material, and symbolic racial signification to different groups, then uses those meanings to position the groups in the social hierarchy.

Study Questions

1. How can educators with an anti-racist perspective disrupt the Western monologue and turn it into a conversation? How can we ensure that our academic work is actually relevant to oppressed peoples and not simply a matter of knowledge production for its own sake or a quest for personal recognition?
2. How does white defensiveness benefit institutionalized racism?
3. Discussions that in the past would have referred explicitly to race now tend to focus on 'equity' or 'diversity' instead. In what ways might this discursive shift be counterproductive?
4. How do we as individuals negotiate the relative saliencies of our different identities?
5. Different types of oppression have many things in common, but they are not equal in their consequences. Discuss.

Recommended Readings

Asante, M. 1998. *The Afrocentric Idea*. Philadelphia: Temple University Press.

Dei, G.J.S. 1996. *Anti-Racism Education: Theory and Practice*. Halifax, NS: Fernwood Publishing.

———. 2008. *Racists Beware: Uncovering Racial Politics in Contemporary Society*. Rotterdam: Sense Publishers.

Fanon, F. 1963. *The Wretched of the Earth*. New York: Grove Weidenfeld.

———. 1967. *Black Skin, White Masks*. New York: Grove Weidenfeld.

hooks, b. 1992. *Black Looks: Race and Representation*. Cambridge, MA: South End Press.

Recommended Websites

Canadian Race Relations Foundation: http://www.crr.ca

Centre for Integrative Anti-Racism Studies at the Ontario Institute for Studies in Education, University of Toronto: http://www.oise.utoronto.ca/ciars/index.html

National Anti-Racism Council of Canada: http://www.narcc.ca/index.html

National Youth Anti-Racism Network: http://www.antiracism.ca/

The Journal of Negro Education: http://www.journalnegroed.org/

References

Akbar, N. 2003. 'Africentric Social Sciences for Human Liberation', in A. Mazama, ed., *The Africentric Paradigm*. Trenton, NJ: African World Press, 131–43.

Apple, M. 1986. *Teachers and Texts: A Political Economy of Class and Gender Relations in Education*. New York: Routledge & Kegan Paul.

———. 1990. *Ideology and Curriculum*, 2nd edn. New York: Routledge.

———. 1999. *Power, Meaning and Identity: Essays in Critical Education Studies*. New York: Peter Lang.

———, and L. Weiss. 1983. 'Ideology and Practice in Schooling: A Political and Conceptual Introduction', in Apple and Weiss, *Ideology and Practice in Schooling*. Philadelphia: Temple University Press, 3–33.

Asante, M. 1998. *The Afrocentric Idea*. Revised and expanded edition. Philadelphia: Temple University Press.

———. 1999. *The Painful Demise of Eurocentrism: An Afrocentric Response to Critics*. Trenton, NJ: Africa World Press.

———. 2003a. 'The Afrocentric Idea', in A. Mazama, ed., *The Africentric Paradigm*. Trenton, NJ: African World Press, 37–53.

———. 2003b. *Afrocentricity: The Theory of Social Change*. Chicago: African American Images.

———. 2006. 'Cheikh Anta Diop: Resisting Westernity and Projecting Humanity'. Paper delivered at the 18th Annual Cheikh Anta Diop International conference, Philadelphia, 13–14 October.

Bell, D.A. 1992. *Faces at the Bottom of the Well: The Permanence of Racism*. New York: Basic Books.

Benjamin, L.A. 2003. 'The Black/Jamaican Criminal: The Making of Ideology'. PhD dissertation, Department of Sociology and Equity Studies, Ontario Institute for Studies in Education, University of Toronto.

Bourdieu, P., and J. Passeron. 1977. *Reproduction in Education, Society and Culture*. Beverly Hills, CA: Sage.

Coe, C. 2005. *Dilemmas of Culture in African Schools: Youth Nationalism and the Transformation of Knowledge*. Chicago: University of Chicago Press.

Corrigan, P. 1990. *Social Forms/Human Capacities: Essays in Authority and Difference*. London: Routledge.

Dei, G.J.S. 1996. *Anti-Racism Education: Theory and Practice*. Halifax, NS: Fernwood Publishing.

———. 1999. 'The Denial of Difference: Reframing Anti-Racist Praxis', *Race, Ethnicity and Education* 2, 1: 17–37.

———. 2006. 'We Cannot Be Colour-Blind: Race, Anti-racism and the Subversion of Dominant Thinking', in W. Ross and V. Ooka Pang, eds, *Race, Ethnicity, and Education*. New York: Greenwood Publishing, 25–42.

———. 2008. *Racists Beware: Uncovering Racial Politics in Contemporary Society*. Rotterdam: Sense Publishers.

———. 2009. 'Race, Racism and Anti-Racism: The Implications of Ideology for the Anti-Racist Project'. Forthcoming.

Deliovsky, K. 2005. 'Elsewhere from Here: Remapping the Territories of White Femininity'. PhD dissertation, Department of Sociology, McMaster University.

Doyle-Wood, S. 2006a. 'Comments on a Scholarship Grant Application'. Department of Sociology and Equity Studies, Ontario Institute for Studies in Education, University of Toronto, 7 October.

———. 2006b. *Chisani*. Toronto: Equitystorybooks.

Fanon, F. 1963. *The Wretched of the Earth*. New York: Grove Weidenfeld.

———. 1967. *Black Skin, White Mask*. New York: Grove Weidenfeld.

Fine, M. 1991. *Framing Dropouts: Notes on the Politics of an Urban Public High School*. New York: State University of New York Press.

———. 1993. '(Ap)parent Involvement: Reflections on Parents, Power and Urban Schools', *Teachers' College Record* 944: 682–710.

———. 2006. 'Dear Zora: A Letter to Zora Neale Hurston 50 Years after Brown'. Paper presented at the annual meeting of the American Educational Research Association, San Francisco, 6–12 April.

Foucault, M. 1977. *Discipline and Punish*. New York: Vintage Books.

———. 1980. *Power/Knowledge: Selected Interviews and Other Writings, 1972–1977*. New York: Pantheon Books.

Giroux, H. 1981. *Ideology, Culture and the Process of Schooling*. Philadelphia: Temple University Press.

Goldberg, T. 1993. *Racist Culture: Philosophy and the Politics of Meaning*. Cambridge, MA: Blackwell.

Gramsci, A. 1971. *Prison Notebooks*. London: Lawrence and Wishart.

Hall, S. 1996. 'Gramsci's Relevance for the Study of Race and Ethnicity', in D. Morley and K. Chen, eds, *Stuart Hall: Critical Dialogues in Cultural Studies*. London: Routledge, 411–40.

———. 1997. *Representations: Cultural Representations and Signifying Practices*. London: Sage Publications.

Henay, C. 2005. 'Who's Safe in Safe Schools? Race and the Ideology of Safety in the Ontario Safe Schools Act'. Master Research Paper, Department of Sociology and Equity Studies, Ontario Institute for Studies in Education, University of Toronto.

hooks, b. 1992. *Black Looks: Race and Representation*. Cambridge, MA: South End Press.

Howard, P. 2006. 'Comments on Thesis Proposal'. Department of Sociology and Equity Studies, Ontario Institute for Studies in Education, University of Toronto, 7 October.

———. 2008. 'Colliding Positions on What Counts as Racially Progressive: A Critical Race Africology of the Film, *Crash*', in P. Howard and G.J.S. Dei, *Crash Politics and Antiracism: Interrogations of Liberal Race Discourse*. New York: Peter Lang, 25–48.

Kershaw, T. 1992. 'Afrocentrism and the Afrocentric Method', *The Western Journal of Black Studies* 16, 3: 160–8.

Mazama, A. 2001. 'The Afrocentric Paradigm: Contours and Definitions', *Journal of Black Studies* 31, 4: 387–405.

Memmi, A. 1969. *The Colonizer and the Colonized*. Boston: Beacon Press.

Njamnjoh, F. 2004. 'From Publish or Perish to Publish and Perish: What Africa's 100 Best Books Tell Us about Publishing in Africa', *Journal of Asian and African Studies* 39, 5: 331–55.

Ogbu, John U. 2003. *Black American Students in an Affluent Suburb: A Study of Academic Disengagement*. Mahwah, NJ: Lawrence Erlbaum Associates.

Roediger, D. 1991. *The Wages of Whiteness*. London: Verso.

Santos, B. de Sousa. 1999. 'On Oppositional Postmodernism', in R. Munck and D. O'Hearn, eds, *Critical Development Theory: Contributions to the New Paradigm*. London: Zed Books, 29–43.

Tikly, L. 2004. 'Education and the New Imperialism', *Comparative Education* 40, 2: 171–98.

Tucker, V. 1999. 'The Myth of Development: A Critique of Eurocentric Discourse', in R. Munck and D. O'Hearn, eds, *Critical Development Theory: Contributions to the New Paradigm*. London: Zed Books, 1–26.

Wahab, A. 2006. Personal communication. Department of Sociology and Equity Studies, Ontario Institute for Studies in Education, University of Toronto, 7 October.

CHAPTER 5

Multicultural, Anti-racist Education and Black Feminist Pedagogy

Joyce Barakett and M. Ayaz Naseem

Given the continuing hostility towards anti-racism work, new knowledge must be produced to refocus attention and efforts on addressing social justice and equity issues. New knowledge should critically examine the socially constructed ways of making meaning in a racialized, gendered and classed world. (Dei, 2000: 25)

We begin this chapter with a brief look at the theory behind the concepts of multicultural and anti-racist education. We then critically engage with various interpretations of the relevance of the notion of whiteness for multicultural and anti-racist education. Finally, we consider the distinctive perspectives of black and women-of-colour feminism and discuss their relevance for critical multicultural and anti-racist pedagogy.

Theoretical Background

The relationship between anti-racist and multicultural education is open to debate. Some scholars (Duarte and Smith, 2000) see multicultural education as a forerunner of **anti-racist education**, now largely replaced by the latter. Others (e.g., Dei and Calliste, 2000, and Ghosh, 2002) maintain that the two concepts are often used interchangeably. By contrast, Grinter (2000) argues that they are not only separate but contradictory, standing in opposition to one another.

Dei (2002) notes the importance of putting the concepts of multiculturalism and anti-racism into social, historical, ideological, and political context. First, however, he argues that we need to understand 'race', which he considers to be socially constructed in a particular historical context. Racial identification is based not only on skin colour but also on social factors such as language, culture, and religion. The chief purpose of this socially created concept is to justify and maintain the unequal distribution of power in society. Racism is not simply an ideology but an ongoing, self-perpetuating process. Anti-racism, for its part,

> deals foremost with *equity*; that is, the qualitative value of justice. It deals with *representation*; that is, the need to have multiple voices and perspectives involved in the production of mainstream social knowledge. Anti-racism also examines institutional practices to see how institutions respond to the challenge of *diversity and difference*; understood as the intersections of race, gender, class, sexuality, language, culture and religion. (Dei, 2000: 34)

Many critical race theorists (Frankenberg, 1993; Dyer, 1997; Roediger, 1994; McLaren, 2000) have underlined the importance of challenging the unquestioned acceptance of whiteness and white privilege as the norm. What we need is a school system that will disrupt the dominance of whiteness.

Frankenberg provides a three-dimensional definition of whiteness: 'First, it is a location of structural advantage, of race privilege. Second, it is a "standpoint", a place from which white people look at themselves, at others, and at society. Third, "whiteness" refers to a set of cultural practices that are usually unmarked and unnamed' (1993: 1). That is, 'whiteness refers to set of locations that are historically, socially, politically, and culturally produced and, moreover, are intrinsically linked to unfolding relations of domination' (Frankenberg, 1993: 6). Similarly, McLaren (2000) argues that one of the most significant characteristics of whiteness is its invisibility. When whiteness is the norm against which all other cultures are measured, even supposedly 'multicultural' education is aimed more at educating the 'other' than at re-educating the white majority.

The author bell hooks has also discussed whiteness in terms of invisibility: 'In white supremacist society, white people can "safely" imagine that they are invisible to black people since the power they have historically asserted, and even now collectively assert over black people, accorded them the right to control the black gaze' (1992: 168). Although black people have been socialized to play along with this fantasy, in reality whiteness often inspires intense fear:

> As in the old days of racial segregation where black folks learned to 'wear the mask', many of us pretend to be comfortable in the face of whiteness only to turn our backs and give expression to intense levels of discomfort. Especially talked about is the representation of whiteness as terrorizing. (1992: 169)

How do we address the perpetuation of this debilitating, insidious feeling through the school curriculum and pedagogical practices?

Many Canadian scholars have contributed to the development of multicultural and anti-racist educational theory. White domination and power, Aboriginal struggles for social justice, and issues related to gendered teaching and learning in multicultural societies have been addressed in various studies (e.g., Ng, Staton, and Scane, 1995; Regnier, 1995; Barakett and Cleghorn, 2007; Dei, 1996; Dei and Calliste, 2000; Ng, 1995; Hoodfar, 1992; Ghosh, 1981, 2002). Rezai-Rashti (1995) examined the influential report of the Ontario Ministry of Education's Advisory Committee on Race

Relations (1987). Bedard has made an especially interesting contribution, suggesting that although the aim of multicultural pedagogies is to create an inclusive classroom environment, in reality they perpetuate existing institutional forms of racism; in his view, multiculturalism is unable 'to eradicate racism and create a Canadian White subject that does not base its identity on the bodies of non-White peoples' (2000: 51).

The academic discourse on multicultural and anti-racist education emphasizes the need for an approach to education that is critical, inclusive, and affirmative. So far, however, the pedagogical strategies inspired by that discourse have been largely ineffective. In our opinion, one reason those efforts have not been more successful is that they have been too narrowly focused. While multicultural education clearly aspires to take into account other forms of oppression (gender, social class, race, ethnicity, etc.), it foregrounds culture as the main unit and level of analysis. And while scholars of anti-racist education go to great lengths to argue that anti-racist education encompasses multiple modes and forms of oppression, it still foregrounds race as the main form of oppression. One of the prime objectives of this chapter is to clarify the conceptual and theoretical foundations on which we can build pedagogical strategies capable of addressing the multiple forms of oppression that exist in our society. We believe that the research conducted by black and **women-of-colour** feminists offers many insights that can help to bring theoretical and conceptual clarity to both multicultural and anti-racist education and pedagogical practice. In the following section we provide a brief overview of the insights from black and women-of-colour feminists that could help to demystify both multicultural and anti-racist education.

Black Feminism

Black feminists were the first to uncover the ethnocentrism and exclusionary universalism of the mainstream feminist movement. They problematized the singular notion of 'women' and pointed out that there is a deep and embedded relationship between sexism and racism. Central to their thinking was the idea that there is more than one kind of oppression, situation, condition, experience, and voice. They felt that the mainstream feminist movement was so embedded in the racist structures of the liberal discourse that it could not speak for black women. As the Combahee River Collective put it:

> We believe that sexual politics under patriarchy is as pervasive in Black women's lives as are the politics of class and race. We also often find it difficult to separate race from class from sex oppression because in our lives they are most often experienced simultaneously. (1982: 16)

In her book *Ain't I a Woman*, bell hooks wrote that 'black women have felt forced to choose between a black movement that primarily serves the interests of black male patriarchs, and a white women's movement which primarily serves the interests of racist white women' (1981: 9). Three years later, she suggested that 'feminist theory would have much to offer if it showed women ways in which racism and sexism are immutably connected rather than pitting one struggle against the other, or blatantly dismissing racism' (1984: 52).

Black feminists felt that the mainstream movement did not recognize their distinctive situation, condition, experience, and voice. They argued that, for black women, gender-, race-, and class-based oppression is not merely a sum of cumulative disadvantages—a matter of 'gender + race + class'. Rather, it should be understood as a product of multiple oppressions: 'gender ? race ? class' (Bryson, 1999). Multiplication makes for a very different experience than simple addition (Ghosh, 1981). Black feminists also contested the radical feminist conceptualization of patriarchy, arguing that it distorts the relationship between black men and black women. This relationship is not the same as the relationship between white males and females, nor is it standard in all situations; bell hooks (1984), for instance, argued that in concentrating on the white male as oppressor, feminists lose sight of the fact that black men have also been oppressors in their own right. Carby (1987) approached the question from a different angle:

> We can point to no single source of our oppression when white feminists emphasize patriarchy alone, we want to redefine the term and make it a more complex concept. Racism ensures that black men do not have the same relations to patriarchy/capitalist hierarchies as white men. (65)

Arguments such as these problematize the feminist 'standpoint theory', suggesting that the most useful feminist standpoint is that of black women. This is the case for three reasons. First, black women's situation at the bottom of the social, economic, and racial hierarchies means that they have a comprehensive view of the multiple locations in which oppression operates. Second, it enables black women to see the interconnections between different forms of oppression. Finally, it calls for a multifaceted approach to oppression, one that seeks to address not only gender inequalities but racial and social inequalities as well.

In addition, central to black feminism is the notion of multiple identities (as opposed to the unitary identity of 'woman'), each of which is embedded in a distinct culture and the insider/outsider position of women. Any denial of these identities will be self-defeating for feminism. It will essentially mean replacing one hegemonic narrative with another. As Lorde (1984) wrote in 'An Open Letter to Mary Daly' (author of *Gyn/Ecology: The Metaethics of Radical Feminism*, 1978):

> What you excluded from *Gyn/Ecology* dismissed my heritage and heritage of all other non European women, and denied the real connections that exist between all of us. . . . the oppression of women knows no ethnic or racial boundaries, true, but that does not mean it is identical within those differences. Nor do the reservoirs of our ancient power know these boundaries. To deal with one without even alluding to the other is to distort our commonality as well as our difference (1984: 68–70).

It was black feminists who pioneered the concept of identity politics in feminism. Black feminists also advocated that feminism should allow both equality and difference when organizing around/against specific oppressors. What black feminists like

Lorde and hooks argued was not that black women's perspectives should be added to the feminist narrative, but rather that not to do so would render feminist narratives incomplete and flawed.

In addition, black feminists argue that the state, especially in the West, has created a new form of racism that operates at the level of bureaucracies and institutions. This institutional racism takes the form of 'colour bars' in employment opportunities, health care, housing, education, and other social services. Racism in this sense has moved from being merely an individual prejudice to being a structural feature of the social system (Brah and Minhas, 1985). Institutional racism, when it combines with sexism and discrimination based on gender, produces oppression and exploitation that are both qualitatively and quantitatively different from the kinds that white women face.

Black feminists successfully challenged the totalizing discourse of Western (that is, white) feminism by identifying multiple locations, forms, and sources of oppression as well as multiple identities within a common gender. In so doing, however, they fell into some of the same totalizing and essentialist assumptions they had criticized in white feminists. Mirza (1997b), a British postmodern feminist, has argued that in deifying the black feminist standpoint, black women created a 'universal' that excluded other **women of colour** such as Asians, Chicanas, Aboriginal women, and those of mixed race. Black feminism has been preoccupied with the situation of African-American women and their 'journeys', to the exclusion even of other black women. The experiences of African-American women, for instance, are not the same as those of South African or Sudanese black women. Women of colour, while concurring with the basic premise of black feminism, have expressed their own concerns about the totalizing tendencies in black feminist discourse.

Women-of-Colour Feminism

Some women of colour in the United States feel that they have been defined through two kinds of 'narratives of racialization': those constructed by white scholars around Afro-Americans and those through which Afro-American women define themselves. As Alexander and Mohanty point out, the experiences of women of colour are 'recognized and acknowledged only to the extent that they resemble those of African-American women' (1997: xiv). While women of colour do recognize that racial solidarity is necessary, it is equally important to understand the multiple (local and global) locations and manifestations of power.

While women of colour are critical of **foundationalism** in black feminism, especially its universalizing and essentializing tendencies, they do not stand in opposition to black feminism. In fact they invoke the black feminist principle of multiple identities, voices, and narratives to insist that their experiences should also be recognized and heard. They also stand with the black feminists in their critique of the foundational white feminist thought and the academy. According to Alexander and Mohanty, 'serious intellectual, analytical, and political engagement with the theorization of women of colour has not occurred' (1997: xvi). Texts by women of colour are included in the white academy without any effort to reconceptualize the white, middle-class, gendered knowledge base that absorbs and silences the voices of women of colour. This effectively means that these narratives and theories 'are plausible and carry explanatory weight only in relation to our (their) *specific* experiences, but they have no use value in relation to the rest of the world' (Alexander and Mohanty, 1997: xvii). Other women of colour, especially those from parts of the world other than the Western hemisphere, maintain that their location outside the Western context contributes to their oppression at both individual and collective levels (Mohanty, 1990, 1993).

Black Feminist Pedagogy

The above account of the concerns of black and women-of-colour feminists provides a basis for modifying the conceptual frameworks developed in critical, multicultural, anti-racist pedagogy. Following bell hooks (1984, 1992), black feminist pedagogues have articulated a social theory of liberation: working through pedagogical agents of social change has the potential to overcome the multiple oppressions of racism, classism, and sexism. Central to **black feminist pedagogy** is the use of autobiography as a medium through which students and teachers can examine their own internalized racism (see Barakett and Cleghorn, 2007). As bell hooks has explained, insights from black feminist and critical pedagogy can be combined to develop a pedagogy that would encourage both students and teachers to think critically and participate in the learning process and knowledge creation. For hooks, it is of utmost importance that black women and women of colour be able to express and consciously foreground their fears and experiences of oppression. She refers to the structural workings and mechanisms of power and domination as **white supremacy** (hooks, 1992). According to hooks, 'whiteness' refers to the institutional privilege and advantage that excludes people of colour and marginalized groups from economic and political structures. It is essential that we teach black feminism to white students to help them recognize what it means to be *white* in a culture of 'white supremacist capitalist patriarchy'.

Lemons, a black male professor who teaches courses on black feminism to white students, applied the critical feminist pedagogical ideas in his class and found out that critical examination of white privilege in the classroom can contribute to personal, political, and pedagogical change: 'black feminist thought, as a social theory of liberation and pedagogical agent of social change can be a powerful tool toward the development of critical race consciousness in white students' (2004: 214).

Joseph (1995) argues that the best way to create equal and liberating educational structures is by bringing the history of oppressed groups such as blacks, Latinos, and Aboriginal people—their struggles, their values, their exploitation and oppression—into the educational process:

> I view the educational system as a system in its own right constituted by intrinsic imperatives, and capable of creating building blocks for radical changes in the structure of American capitalist society. It is in this spirit that I introduce the black feminist pedagogy that I feel complements and goes beyond the Marxist sociology of education. (1995: 464)

In Joseph's view, Afro-American women have their own ways of producing knowledge, relevant to them, based on their own experience—knowledge and interpretations of experience that differ tremendously from those of the dominant white male groups. Clearly, Joseph follows Paulo Freire in arguing for the development of political consciousness. '[P]olitical, social, and economic concepts, from a curriculum planned and taught by teachers possessing a black feminist perspective/consciousness would introduce a radical education methodological imperative' (1995: 465). In addition she makes a case for comparing the two existing conceptual systems: one of the oppressed and the other of the oppressor, with diametrically opposed values and beliefs. In this sense feminist pedagogy, especially black feminist pedagogy, implores us to examine the history and philosophy of each of these systems with the goal of developing an ideology that will help students to challenge the status quo and establish the conditions necessary for radical social and educational change to take place.

Let us now briefly summarize the main insights from black and women-of-colour feminists. First, there are multiple structures and locations of oppression, and different marginalized cultural, racial, class, ethnic, religious, and linguistic groups have different relationships both to these structures and to the dominant group. Second, the marginalized groups are not homogeneous: there are different forms and currents of oppression within each group that have to be taken into account. For example, members of marginalized groups are often forced to choose between the oppression that comes from inside their community and the oppression that comes from outside. Third, we cannot conflate the experiences of oppression of one group with those of another. For example, the experiences of Chicana and Asian women are different from those of African-American women. Similarly, the experiences of American Muslims after the attacks of September 2001 are *sui generis* and must be understood and analyzed as such. Fourth, different forms of oppression hit different groups with varying degrees of marginalizing/empowering force, depending on the historical, socio-political, and economic importance of that community in the society. Finally, marginalized groups will never be absolutely empowered. The degree of empowerment that can be achieved will depend on the power of the dominant group. Furthermore, empowerment itself will create tensions (even contradictions) within the individual and the group to which she belongs. This is famously characterized by Elizabeth Ellsworth's (1992) question 'Why doesn't this feel empowering?'

Luke echoes the concerns of black and women-of-colour feminists:

> Women's complex and multiple identities experienced *in* and *through* the discourses that define feminine gender identity, sexuality, ethnicity, class, or culture suggest that an understanding of women and the concept of femininity cannot be articulated in universal principles, but must come from women's individual voices articulated from various specific social and cultural locations. Hence, in feminisms generally and in feminist pedagogy particularly, the importance of 'positionality' of voice and experience is paramount. (1996: 290)

In addition, Luke's views of feminist pedagogy in general echo those of feminist pedagogues:

the feminist classroom tends to be more of a 'bottoms-up' than 'top-down' knowledge exchange. . . .The feminist pedagogue . . . does not see herself as authoritative arbiter of student interpretation and understanding. Instead, she emphasizes her own situatedness, her own partial 'take' on the world, and thus acknowledges her own experience and knowledge as no more and no less valid, 'better', or 'authentic' than those of the diversity of students in her class. . . . It makes knowledge production a collaborative class effort in which the feminist pedagogue has a specific body of knowledge to offer alongside women's equally situated knowledges and experiences. (1996: 293)

While we may concur with the focus on individual self, voice, and the importance of positionality, following Tastsoglou we reiterate that this in no way means that we want to 'divert attention from the larger social structures . . . and, therefore, from the need for collective struggles in society and in education' (2000: 98). Citing women-of-colour feminists such as Mohanty (1990), Tastsoglou sees classrooms as political and cultural sites where differently empowered social groups accommodate and contest different knowledge constructions. She further notes that classrooms mirror as well as reconstruct the divisions and inequalities and struggles of the larger society.

Insights from black and women-of-colour feminists encourage us to look for a collective, integrative analysis of oppressions and move towards a multi-centred educational experience aimed at meaningful, inclusive social change (Calliste and Dei, 2000; Dei, 1996). Pedagogically, they ask us to become what hooks (1994) calls 'engaged' teachers: active, critical, and self-reflexive, who hold 'difference' to be a basic condition for understanding both the self and the other.

Such a pedagogy can be meaningfully undertaken only in classrooms where both teachers and students feel it is safe to talk about various experiences of oppression. It is in safe spaces (classrooms) that teachers can explore ways in which the spaces between different kinds of oppression—cultural, economic, ethnic, racial, gender—can be bridged without suggesting that all experiences of oppression are the same. In other words, teachers must understand the multiple and even contradictory nature of students' subject positions while trying to give voice to them. Sinacore and Enns (2005) note that feminists of colour urge educators to deconstruct traditional pedagogies, and examine learning environments and power dimensions in teacher–student relationships. In other words, as Luke pointed out, the focus should be on the 'processes of education that demand that attention be drawn to the politics of those processes and to the broader political contexts within which they are situated' (1996: 293). The classroom should be a community of learners in which educators are consultants or resource people rather than controllers of the teaching–learning process. For them, course content must be 'inclusive and pluralistic' (Sinacore and Enns, 2005: 53).

Thus anti-racist black and women-of-colour feminists call for a pedagogy that includes multiple voices and encourages all marginalized groups to play central roles in the learning environment. In addition, all individuals in the classroom must struggle together to learn new ideas and models of scholarship.

Conclusion

The insights of black and women-of-colour feminists have a great deal to contribute to the development of an inclusive pedagogy—one capable of addressing the inadequate recognition of marginalized groups such as blacks, women of colour, Latinos, and Aboriginal people, and disrupting the association of whiteness with 'terror in the black imagination' (hooks, 1992). Our intention is not to propose a new concept of anti-racist discourse or pedagogy. Rather, we are seeking to integrate the interlocking aspects of critical multicultural, white, black, and women-of-colour feminist pedagogy in order to broaden the scope of anti-racist, critical scholarship in its efforts to transform traditional educational practice.

We must move beyond white–black discourse and address the connections between different kinds of oppression. What is essential is a pedagogy that can 'undo' the master narratives that do not acknowledge the identity of those who produced them. As Joseph puts it, 'A most radical approach to dealing with the problems of radical educational change would be to focus on blacks, Latinos, Native Americans— the domestic Third World people—as the vanguard' (1995: 463). This means that pedagogical practices must recognize marginalized groups' life experiences and perceptions as legitimate knowledge—indeed, acknowledge their ideas and practices as the basis of legitimate knowledge.

Glossary

anti-racist education: An active process in educational practice to eliminate individual, institutional, and systemic racism through an inclusive curriculum.

black feminist pedagogy: A social theory of liberation in which pedagogical agents of social change have the potential to overcome the multiple oppressions of racism, classism, and sexism, among other forms of oppression. Its central feature is autobiographical writing that enables students to examine their own internalized racism.

critical multicultural education: An approach to multicultural education that encourages students to reflect on an understanding of cultural differences and diversity. Classroom practices emphasize the sources of social injustices of racism and economic inequity.

foundational view: A characterization of a particular social group as essentially static, unchanging across time, space, culture, race, and/or class.

white supremacy: A set of cultural and social practices in which white people are systematically privileged or given advantage in society because of their skin colour.

women of colour: Women other than 'black' African Americans (or Canadians) who also experience oppression related to their skin colour. In the West, 'women of colour' include women of Caribbean, Asian, Indian, Middle Eastern, and Aboriginal descent, as well as those of mixed race.

Study Questions

1. How does bell hooks explain whiteness in the black imagination?
2. How can curriculum reform address the main requirements for a critical multicultural education and social justice?

3. Discuss some of the problems associated with the concepts of multicultural and anti-racist education.
4. How does black feminist pedagogy differ from critical pedagogy?
5. How can we use insights from black and women-of-colour feminists to develop a critical feminist pedagogy?

Recommended Readings

Davies, B. 1992. 'Women's Subjectivity and Feminist Stories', in C. Ellis and M. Flaherty, eds, *Investigating Subjectivity: Research on Lived Experience.* London: Sage, 53–76.

Grinter, R. 2000. 'Multicultural or Anti-Racist Education', in E.M. Duarte and S. Smith, eds, *Foundational Perspectives in Multicultural Education.* Don Mills, ON: Longman, 135–54.

Guy-Sheftall, B., ed. *Words of Fire: An Anthology of African-American Feminist Thought.* New York: New Press.

James, C. 2003. *Seeing Ourselves: Exploring Race, Ethnicity and Culture.* Toronto: Thomson Educational Publishing.

Ramanzanoglu, C. 1989. *Feminism and the Contradictions of Oppression.* London: Routledge.

Rodriguez, N. 1998. 'Emptying the Content of Whiteness: Toward an Understanding of the Relation between Whiteness and Pedagogy', in J. Kincheloe and S. Steinberg, eds, *White Reign: Deploying Whiteness in America.* New York: St. Martin's Press, 31–62.

Recommended Websites

Black American Feminisms: A Multidisciplinary Bibliography: http://www.library.ucsb.edu/subjects/blackfeminism/

Voices from the Gaps: Women Artists and Writers of Colour: http://voices.cla.umn.edu/

Resources on African-American Feminism: http://www.cddc.vt.edu/feminism/AfAm.html

Centre for the Study of Race, Politics and Culture: http://csrpc.uchicago.edu/

On bell hooks: http://education.miami.edu/ep/contemporaryed/Bell_Hooks/bell_hooks.html

References

Alexander, J., and C. Mohanty, eds. 1997. *Feminist Genealogies, Colonial Legacies, Democratic Futures.* New York: Routledge.

Barakett, J., and A. Cleghorn. 2007. *Sociology of Education: An Introductory View from Canada.* Scarborough, ON: Pearson Education.

Bedard, G. 2000. 'Deconstructing Whiteness: Pedagogical Implications for Anti-racism Education', in Dei and Calliste (2000: 41–56).

Brah, A., and R. Minhas. 1985. 'Structural Racism or Cultural Difference: Schooling for Asian Girls', in G. Weiner, ed., *Just a Bunch of Girls: Feminist Approaches to Schooling.* Milton Keynes: Open University Press, 14–26.

Bryson, V. 1999. *Feminist Debates: Issues of Theory and Political Practice.* New York: New York University Press.

Calliste, A., and G. Dei, eds. 2000. *Anti-Racist Feminism: Critical Race and Gender Studies.* Halifax: Fernwood Publishing.

Carby, H. 1987. 'Black Feminism and the Boundaries of Sisterhood', in M. Arnot and G. Weiner, eds, *Gender and the Practice of Schooling.* Basingstoke: Open University Press, 64–75.

Collins, P. 1990. *Black Feminist Thought: Knowledge, Consciousness, and the Politics of Empowerment*. New York: Routledge.

———. 1998. *Fighting Words: Black Women and the Search for Justice*. Minneapolis: University of Minnesota Press.

———. 2000. 'What's Going On? Black Feminist Thought and the Politics of Post-Modernism', in E. St. Pierre and W. Pillow, eds, *Working the Ruins: Feminist Poststructural Theory and Methods in Education*. New York and London: Routledge, 41–73.

Combahee River Collective. 1982. 'A Black Feminist Statement', in G.T. Hull et al., eds, *All the Women Are White, All the Blacks Are Men, but Some of Us Are Brave: Black Women's Studies*. New York: The Feminist Press, 13–22.

Daly, M. 1978. *Gyn/ecology: The Metaethics of Radical Feminism*. Boston: Beacon Press.

Davis, A. 1982. *Women, Race and Class*. London: Women's Press.

———. 1990. *Women, Culture and Politics*. London: Women's Press.

Dei, G. 1996. 'The Denial of Difference: Reframing Anti-racist Praxis', *Race Ethnicity and Education* 2, 1: 17–37.

———, and A. Calliste, eds. 2000. *Power, Knowledge and Anti-Racism Education*. Halifax: Fernwood Publishing.

Duarte, E., and S. Smith. 2000. *Foundational Perspectives in Multicultural Education*. New York: Longman Inc.

Dyer, R. 1997. *White*. New York: Routledge.

Ellsworth, E. 1992. 'Why Doesn't This Feel Empowering? Working Through the Myths of Critical Pedagogy', in C. Luke and J. Gore, eds, *Feminisms and Critical Pedagogies*. New York: Routledge, 90–119.

Frankenberg, R. 1993. *The Social Construction of Whiteness: White Women, Race Matters*. Minneapolis: University of Minnesota Press.

Ghosh, R. 1981. 'Minority within a Minority: On Being South Asian and Female in Canada', in G. Kurian and R. Ghosh, eds, *Women in the Family and Economy: An International Comparative Survey*. Westport, CT: Greenwood Press, 415–25.

——— . 2002. *Redefining Multicultural Education*. Toronto: Nelson.

Hoodfar, H. 1992. 'Feminist Anthropology and Critical Pedagogy: The Anthropology of Classrooms' Excluded Voices', *Canadian Journal of Education* 17, 3: 303–20.

hooks, b. 1981. *Ain't I a Woman: Black Women and Feminism*. Boston: South End Press.

———. 1984. *Feminist Theory: From Margin to Center*. Boston: South End Press.

———. 1988. *Talking Back: Thinking Feminist, Thinking Black*. Boston: South End Press.

———. 1992. 'Representation of Whiteness in the Black Imagination', in *Black Looks: Race and Representation*. Boston: South End Press, 165–78.

———. 1994. *Teaching to Transgress: Education as a Practice of Freedom*. New York: Routledge.

Joseph, G. 1995. 'Black Feminist Pedagogy and Schooling in Capitalist White America', in B. Guy-Sheftall, ed., *Words of Fire: An Anthology of African-American Feminist Thought*. New York: New Press.

Kincheloe, J., and S. Steinberg. 1998. 'Addressing the Crisis of Whiteness: Reconfiguring White Identity in a Pedagogy of Whiteness', in Kincheloe and Steinberg, eds, *White Reign: Deploying Whiteness in America*. New York: St Martin's Press, 3–29.

Lemons, G. 2004. 'When White Students Write about Being White: Challenging Whiteness in a Black Feminist Classroom', in V. Lea and J. Helfand, eds, *Identifying Race and Transforming Whiteness in the Classroom*. New York: Peter Lang, 213–33.

Lorde, A. 1984. *Sister Outsider: Essays and Speeches*. New York: Crossing Press.

Luke, C. 1996. 'Feminist Pedagogy Theory: Reflections on Power and Authority', *Educational Theory* 46, 3: 283–302.

McLaren, P. 2000. 'White Terror and Oppositional Agency: Towards a Critical Multiculturalism', in Duarte and Smith (2000: 213–42).

Mirza, H. 1997a. 'Introduction: Mapping a Genealogy of Black British Feminism', in Mirza (1997b: 1–28).

———, ed. 1997b. *Black British Feminism: A Reader*. London: Routledge.

Mohanty, C. 1990. 'On Race and Voice: Challenges for Liberal Education in the 1990s', *Cultural Critique* 14: 179–208.

Mohanty, S. 1993. 'The Epistemic Status of Cultural Identity: On *Beloved* and the Post-Colonial Tradition', *Cultural Critique* 24: 41–80.

Ng, R. 1995. 'Teaching against the Grain: Contradictions and Possibilities', in Ng et al. (1995: 129–52).

———, P. Staton, and J. Scane, eds. 1995. *Anti-Racism, Feminism, and Critical Approaches to Education*. Toronto: OISE Press.

Regnier, R. 1995. 'Warrior as Pedagogue, Pedagogue as Warrior: Reflections on Aboriginal Anti-Racist Pedagogy', in Ng et al. (1995: 67–86).

Rezai-Rashti, G. 1995. 'Multicultural Education, Anti-Racist Education, and Critical Pedagogy: Reflections on Everyday Practice', in Ng et al. (1995: 3–20).

Roediger, D. 1994. *Towards the Abolition of Whiteness: Essays on Race, Politics and Working Class History*. London: Verso.

Sinacore, A., and C. Enns. 2005. 'Diversity Feminisms: Postmodern, Women of Colour, Antiracist, Lesbian, Third-Wave, and Global Perspectives', in C. Enns and A. Sinacore, eds, *Teaching and Social Justice*. Washington, DC: American Sociological Association, 41–69.

Tastsoglou, E. 2000. 'Mapping the Unknowable: The Challenges and Rewards of Cultural, Political and Pedagogical Border Crossing', in Dei and Calliste (2000: 98–121).

CHAPTER 6

The Stranger Side of Education: A Dialogue with Psychoanalysis

Lisa Farley and Judith P. Robertson

Any history of the strange lessons that psychoanalysis offers to education needs to begin with Sigmund Freud. But why, readers may ask, should his ideas matter to *Canadian Perspectives on the Sociology of Education*? A letter written by Freud's wife Martha in the wake of his death in 1939 offers a glimpse of the human qualities he brought to his relationships, his life, and his work—qualities that we think he brings to education as well:

> How good . . . that you knew him when he was still in the prime of his life, for in the end he suffered terribly, so that even those who would most like to keep him forever had to wish for his release! And yet how terribly difficult it is to have to do without him. To continue to live without so much kindness and wisdom beside one! (Freud Museum, 2007)

If sociology offers education insight into the construction of individual identity through the internalization of social norms, what Freud brings to the discussion is a focus on internal conflict: a clamour of forces within the mind that both constrain human happiness and make it possible. We begin with a proposition central to Freud's conflict theory: that human beings move in ways that are beyond and can oppose our conscious intentions, that we are subjects of 'motivated irrationality' (Lear, 2005: 4).

But no sooner do we find this beginning than we must take a detour. On matters of education, Freud begins with a paradox. In an essay outlining the psychoanalytic technique to doctors, Freud (1937) goes so far as to define analysis as one of three '"impossible" professions in which, even before you begin, you can be sure that you will fall short of complete success'. The other two, he says, 'are education and government' (Freud, 1937: 203). That last remark is significant, for it suggests something elusive about education in terms of common perception, a quality outside the vocabulary of planning, management, and self-mastery. Following Freud, we begin by suggesting that if the teacher, like the analyst, can be sure to 'fall short of complete success', it is largely because of the unpredictable—and uneducable—quality of **the unconscious**.[1] Given this difficult beginning, it is little wonder that Freud's ideas have occupied a relatively minor chapter in the sociology of education. After all, what can we learn from someone who begins with the idea that education is impossible? How can we practise education with that idea in mind? For proponents of psychoanalysis, the idea of impossibility is strangely *good* news: according to Felman, it *opens up* 'unprecedented teaching possibilities, renewing both the questions and the practice of education' (1987: 70). What becomes possible is a study of the uncertainties and ambiguities of human responses that complicate any simple formulation of learning as a 'linear, one-way street' (Ellsworth, 1997: 50). Psychoanalytically, knowledge must take a detour through the internal conflicts of the teacher and learner. And as much as these interior detours can derail set paths of learning outlined in curriculum, they also make the journey richer, more complicated, and more alive.

Freud's youngest child, Anna Freud, played a significant role in bringing together the fields of psychoanalysis and education. Best known for her insistence on the effect of unconscious emotions on intellectual processes, she proposed three ways in which psychoanalysis can transform education: (1) by critiquing its methods; (2) by uncovering the conflicted inner realm of the human and the conflicted relations between the child and educator; and (3) by offering the possibility of repairing the injuries incurred through education (1935: 106). We particularly wish to highlight Anna Freud's bold effort to bring into the realm of educational discourse *something other* than conscious intention and reason. This 'something other' is none other than the unconscious—a way of re-imagining the miracle of 'mind' and mental life—and it is this that continues to inspire us now, more than 70 years later, to think of what interrupts understanding as the very ground of education itself. Psychoanalysis offers lessons in how to reconstruct the agony and ecstasy of childhood and the dynamic consequences of the early course of love. It suggests that we consider how children's and teachers' efforts to learn spring from sediments of early life: sediments such as desire, aggression, fear, neglect, or love—that structure our attachments to knowledge before the conscious effort to understand begins (Phillips, 1998).

We use Ms Freud's three lessons as a guide for a dialogue with education that will highlight key educational theorists who have found in psychoanalysis a unique language to express the emotional conflicts, uncertainties, missed meanings, silences, and unfamiliar openings that inevitably arise within individuals and social groups. We hope that our psychoanalytic dialogue will help to deepen understandings of schooling and society by exploring some of the 'unprecedented' possibilities opened by Freud's bold suggestion: *education is an impossible profession.*

Lesson 1: Reading Education (Critically) after Freud: Toward a 'Stranger' Education

Freud was a keen observer of individuals and groups in society, including the family and school and the unfamiliar part that desire plays in each. Observing the embodied symptoms of his patients (for example, 'feeling empty') and everyday linguistic mistakes, Freud suspected that something within the mind was interrupting people's conscious intentions. A well-known example is the 'Freudian slip' of the tongue, in which the intended meaning (e.g., 'mom') is betrayed by a slip ('mine'). The slip reveals a desire that is hidden from conscious view: in this case, the desire to have one's mother all to oneself. Beginning with observations of the everyday (and also the neurotic), Freud sketched out the idea of the unconscious—a container of forbidden desires and fears related to our earliest relationships—that becomes implicated (and hidden) in our conscious projects. Freud gave the name '**repression**' to the psychic mechanism that hides forbidden parts of the self from itself. In 'The Unconscious', he describes how repression can make life more livable: 'All the acts and manifestations which I notice in myself and do not know how to link up with the rest of my mental life must be judged as if they belonged to someone else' (1915a: 171). Freud uses the phrase '*as if*' because in fact these loose bits, or mental 'misfits', actually belong to the self. As one of the ego's first lines of defence, repression keeps away from consciousness a set of human terrors that, over and over, we try to disown.

Beginning with Freud, psychoanalysts have identified a list of overwhelming human terrors: wanting what is forbidden and fearing punishment (Freud); yearning for closure and fearing the destruction of self or others (Balint, Klein); fearing being dropped or violently jarred apart by mental breakdown (Winnicott); and the terrible sense—especially discernible in poetic writing—that our attempts at communication are always vulnerable to slippage, ambiguity, and disarray (Lacan, Kristeva). Whatever the terror, repression estranges us from the source of the fear and makes us 'strangers to ourselves', as Julia Kristeva (1991) puts it. Psychoanalysis, as theory and practice, invites us to become re-acquainted with and more hospitable to this 'stranger' within us all.

And yet it is not simply that lifting repression clears the way to an unencumbered existence, or that consciousness cures us of unconscious conflict. Indeed, from the viewpoint of psychoanalysis, enlightenment ideals of knowledge, understanding, and progress defend us against the inevitable and more interesting uncertainties that Freud dared to hold open. Adam Phillips suggests that in asking us to reflect on the meaning of human vulnerability, failure, and anomaly, psychoanalysis 'cures us of the notion of cure' (2002: xvi). On these terms, learning is more than a 'cure' for failure or ignorance; it is a passionate attachment to knowledge that originates in the contradictory desires to know and not to know. While teachers can encourage students to move in particular directions, and even use 'rubrics' to make these directions into objects that are explicitly spelled out in exchange for grades, it is impossible to predict what categories will incite the learner to learn. 'The Freudian child', Phillips suggests, 'can only be taught what he wants to know' (1998: 54). The common objects of knowledge in a curriculum/rubric may be exchanged for something decidedly different and private—incommunicable agents of the child's inner world (Cox, 2002). To the extent that the unconscious structures what we want to know, and that what we want to know feeds an unconscious need, education defined in terms of strategies and measurable outcomes may be an impossible profession indeed.

By now some readers may be getting nervous. What could it mean to say that education is not in control of its outcomes? A return to Felman may be helpful here, for she reminds us that impossibility is not synonymous with despair or apathy. Quite the contrary: impossibility, as Felman sees it, opens education to other possible lines of inquiry, to different ways of conceiving what happens in classrooms. A number of educators have begun to work these lines of inquiry, exploring the unruly operation of desire and its repression in educational practices. Here theorists observe education's woeful disregard of the interior events of learning, including desire, sexuality, dream, and fantasy-life. Of course, the critique of schooling and its repressive effects is a large field that is not exclusively psychoanalytic. But where psychoanalysis has played a significant role is in explaining how repression works on knowledge and in pedagogical relationships. Proponents of psychoanalysis bring to light the unconscious aspects of knowledge and classroom life: the repression of 'other' histories and voices in the curriculum (Pinar, 1973, 1993; Morris, 2001), the ways in which the teacher's memories of learning affect the pedagogical present (Britzman, 2003, 2006; Gallop, 1999), the unruly feelings of love and hate in teaching (Boldt, 2002; Britzman, 1998a; Gallop, 1999; Pajak, 1998; Tobin, 1997), the uses of fear and compliance in education (Block, 1999; Fenichel, 1954; de Forest, 1965); the emotional significance of student resistance (Britzman, 2006; Gilbert, 1998; Pitt, 2003; Todd, 2001); and the play of fantasy and desire in our uses of knowledge and language (Britzman, 2006; Robertson, 2000, 2002; Silin, 2006; Todd, 1997).

Accordingly, Elizabeth Ellsworth argues that those who think standard tests, curricular expectations, or linear models of development will make teaching straightforward or 'possible' forget the unconscious aspects of education that psychoanalysis brings to light. The problem is not development per se, but how developmental models tend to delimit 'who' the learner is, 'what' knowledge matters, and 'how' successful learning should proceed. Ellsworth argues that education is driven by this logic:

> The field of education is driven by research aimed at determining ever more exactly who the student is so that s/he can be more efficiently and effectively addressed. And such assumptions, desire, and research shape education's structures of address to its imagined audiences. They are structures of address designed, precisely, to make teaching possible. (1997: 58)

What drives theories of development, Ellsworth implies, is the promise of a perfect fit between curricular aims and what the learner 'gets' that erases the vulnerabilities that come with trying to know. Forgotten are the oddball ideas—what Freud (1908: 228) called 'grotesquely incorrect theories'—that are needed for creativity and agency beyond the school walls. Education loses its image of the child as someone alive, unpredictable, and personally interesting. Psychoanalysis, the stranger side of education, seeks to restore a more playful perspective. It calls attention to our many and surprising ways of giving significance to what we are given, ways of doing something more with our childhoods.

And so as much as psychoanalysis points to the rigidity with which education structures learning and learners, its emphasis on the unconscious also posits a theory of subjectivity that is, fortunately, capable of disrupting and moving beyond these structures. Among the strange reminders offered by psychoanalysis is the idea that unconscious conflict produces creativity in learning. Strangely, it is through ego defences—of which repression is one example—that we risk a relation to the world. On this view, we may read the stray impulses and baffling behaviours that crop up in childhood and adolescence as potentially resourceful: as responses to the ego's need to defend itself against the anxiety that learning sets into motion. Low and Palulis describe the educator's capacity to be curious about such detours in learning, and the learner, as 'learning to dwell in the unhomely' (2006: 49).

Here is where we think the concept of repression gets complicated and more interesting than a story of quashed desire. What is repressed never fully disappears, but rather takes a detour and returns to animate everyday conscious efforts: when we sit down to create a message, record a dream, sketch a memory, tune into a movie, hum the same song repeatedly, or speak our hopes and disappointments. As Ellsworth puts it: 'Repression . . . doesn't mean that some illicit desire or knowledge has been stuffed away, somewhere deeper inside ourselves, where it exists unchanged but forgotten. Repression means that some indestructible, illicit knowledge of our desire has been changed into something symbolically unrecognizable to our conscious selves' (1997: 60–1). Via repression, we can satisfy *and* relinquish a desire, simultaneously. In our third psychoanalytic lesson, for instance, we will see how language works at the level of the unconscious to fulfill this dual function: words both tap into our deepest desires and transform them into something more tolerable—'unrecognizable to our conscious selves'.

But repressed desire operates in the context of student/teacher relations as well. And with this point we have arrived at Anna Freud's second psychoanalytic lesson. It is to this lesson—which she refers to as 'the conflicted relations between child and educator'—that we now turn (1935: 129).

Lesson 2: On Transference and Counter-transference

At the age of 48, on a visit to his hometown in Moravia, Freud bumped into his former grammar-school teacher. Awe-struck, Freud remembered feeling something similar but even more intense as a student, and came to see that his feelings for his teacher were rooted in his earliest relations with his parents, combining intimate and ambivalent feelings of love and hate. Freud called this uncanny transportation of emotion from the past to the present '**transference**'. We find it defined in the 'Dora' case study:

> What are transferences? They are new editions or facsimiles of the impulses and fantasies that are to be awakened and rendered conscious as the analysis progresses, whose characteristic trait is the substitution of the person of the doctor for a person previously known to the patient. To put it another way: a whole series of earlier psychical experiences is brought to life not as something in the past, but as a current relationship with the doctor. (Freud, 1905: 534)

In transferring past psychical experiences onto the present analytic situation, the patient puts the analyst into the role of a beloved (and also feared and hated parent) and then relates to the analyst as s/he remembers the parent to have responded, or as s/he believes the parent should have responded. In this emotional trajectory, feelings travel from the patient to the doctor. But this is not the only direction in which transference works. At the same time a second transference may occur in which the patient *takes in* the 'good object' of the analyst and adds it to the crowded scene of internal object-relations, with the hope of strengthening an injured ego. What happens between a student and a teacher may involve three persons or no distinct persons at all. It may involve the past in the present. Or it may be the opposite of what it appears. Therefore the teacher needs to be attentive to what is *not* said in the interaction, to what we might call the 'pre-verbal' processes at work in developing classroom relationships.

Again Freud's experience offers an example of such processes. Recalling that meeting on the street several years later, Freud (1914) remembers how he and others sometimes imagined their teachers:

> We wooed them or turned away from them, we imagined sympathies or antipathies in them that probably did not exist, studied their characters and formed or distorted our own on the basis of theirs. They provoked our greatest rebelliousness and forced us into complete submission; we sought out their foibles, and were proud of their preferences, their knowledge and their justice. Basically we loved them very much if they gave us any reason to; I do not know whether all our teachers noticed that. But it cannot be denied that we faced them in a very special way, a way that might in some respects have been uncomfortable for them. (1914: 355)

Freud was puzzled about how students could have such strong feelings for their teachers even before developing a 'real' history with them. He came to understand that teachers stand in for children's first emotional objects (usually one or both parents) and so inherit ambivalent feelings, even before giving the child *reason* to feel any particular way (through special recognition or unjust punishment, for instance). The classroom, in Freud's view, oozes this messy emotional ambivalence from the beginning.

Educational theorists have since elaborated Freud's concept of transference to explore how students repeat early relationships, and the emotional conflicts they entail, with their teachers (Britzman, 1998a, 1998b, 2003, 2006; Cohler and Galatzer-Levy, 2006; Pitt, 2000, 2003, 2006; Todd, 2003). Britzman describes the transference as a crossroads of desire and power, which migrates from home to the classroom:

> Transference is perhaps the most central dynamic of time and space that organizes and stalls practices of learning. The compromised and condensed time of the transference catches the 'then and there' of the past and the 'here and now' of the present. As a mode of address, the message is derivative of something else, reminiscent of another scene but uncanny in its present urgency. (1998a: 33)

For Britzman, a student's relationship with the teacher is always once removed. The 'something else' of a student's attachment stems from the first parental relationship, now condensed and expressed in the 'here and now' of engagement with the teacher and her knowledge. Under the condition of the transference, the classroom is a very crowded place, full of bodies, pleasures, memories, and affects larger than the aims of curriculum. Indeed, transference scribbles over the lines of school routines.

Freud warned analysts to tread carefully in the deep pool of transference, insisting on emotional restraint. The analyst's task is to allow the patient to have an emotional experience without reciprocating feelings:

> You take care not to distract [the patient] from the love-transference, to frighten it away, or ruin it for the patient; but just as steadfastly you refrain from reciprocating. You hold onto the love-transference, but you treat it as something unreal, as a situation that has to be worked through in the therapy, taken back to its unconscious origins and made to help bring the most deeply buried aspects of [the patient's] erotic life up into the patient's consciousness. (1915b: 347)

In seeing the transference as 'something unreal', Freud reminds us that feelings—of both love and hate—belong to a time and place different from those of the analysis. The analyst must read the transference as a re-staging of conflicts from the patient's past (both real and imagined), provoked and enabled by the analyst. The latter is to remain neutral, responding to the patient's feelings with a *good analysis*, as opposed to emotional bias, reciprocity, or retaliation. Nonetheless, Freud knew that the difficult dynamics of transference would inevitably animate unconscious feelings on the part of the analyst, feelings such as narcissism, altruism, love, and hate. The problem for Freud was not the feelings themselves: it was the risk that that their unconscious expression—the '**counter-transference**'—would interrupt the 'playground of transference' that he wanted to reserve for *the patient*.

Since Freud's time psychoanalysts have paid increasing attention to the counter-transference as a significant feature of the therapeutic process (see Winnicott, 1960). This was especially important in the context of child analysis, since children demanded more than a 'blank screen' response from their analysts (Laplanche and Pontalis, 1973). (We note here how difficult it can be to 'remain neutral' to a child's request for a helping hand to, say, get a stalled toy moving again.) In this post-Freudian view, the concept of counter-transference still refers to the unconscious feelings aroused in the analyst. The difference is that non-neutral responses are recognized as essential to therapy (Winnicott, 1960) and the 'here and now' of the analytic relationship matters just as much as the projected past (Rank, 1996: 221).

The concept of counter-transference, in both the classical and post-Freudian senses, can also be seen operating in educational contexts. Jane Gallop has coined the term 'infantile pedagogy' to highlight the tangles of desire and hostility first experienced in childhood as they return in the pedagogical present (1999: 130). Similarly, Britzman (2003) argues that the teacher's experience of teaching is always inflected with her/his own history of learning. Following Gallop and Britzman, we might connect a teacher's effort to design a perfect lesson, or mark up a student's paper, with the teacher's memories of the child s/he once was, or wished to be. Robertson (2004) adds a layer of complication when she notes how the transferential relations at work in classrooms can take on a life of their own and result in a mind-boggling crisscrossing of identifications between students and their teacher. All three theorists put forward the idea that the classroom setting itself encourages transference and counter-transference, and that teachers may benefit from learning how to think analytically about pedagogy.

But building up this picture is not simple. Edward Pajak suggests a list of questions that teachers can use to probe their own counter-transference:

> Do we ever project onto students our own feelings of lack or inadequacy? . . . When we reprimand a student, are we really suppressing our own impulses? Do we admonish the child we once were, who now stands before us? Do we actively repress an empathic urge that we may feel at the moment in the name of duty? Is criticism of a colleague's behavior ever a reflection of our own internal state? . . . Can unexpressed anger ever be released and channeled toward improving the lives of our students? (1998: 12)

The compulsion to reprimand, punish, or avoid a student, to stifle an emotion in the name of institutional duty, to criticize, to try to improve the lives of others: all these may be seen as manifestations of the counter-transference.

Stephen Appel (1999) adds to Pajak's counter-transference list the experience of 'getting a headache'. Sometimes a headache really is just a headache, of course, but Appel reads his recurring migraines as symptomatic of his emotional life, which, as many teachers can attest, is also densely populated by (imagined) students. Appel noticed that he got headaches when he felt he had to be 'upbeat' for students, when they refused to pay attention, and when they discarded the course material (the course just happened to be on psychoanalysis and education!). Through self-reflection, Appel came to understand his migraines as products of two unconscious dynamics: (1) his repressed anger at students who did not respond to his 'furor to teach' Freud with a comparable furor to learn (Gardner, 1997: 3) and (2) his fantasy of rescuing Freud from their resistance. In a frank discussion with his students, Appel learned something about the emotional basis of their responses as well. He came to understand their 'resistance' as a defence against their fear of not knowing enough—a fear (ironically) provoked by the intensity of his desire for them to learn. Appel's insights didn't resolve students' anxious feelings, nor wholly curb his 'furor to teach', but his recognition of these group dynamics created an environment in which students could begin to risk real engagement with the material. And Appel's head ached a little less often.

To the extent that emotions operate outside the realm of conscious control, the counter-transference cannot be 'monitored' at all times, nor can it be effectively reduced with the right pedagogy. Teachers—like most human beings—typically possess highly accomplished ways of coping with the conflicts in their own emotional lives. But Paula M. Salvio (1999), in her book about the pedagogy of Anne Sexton, draws attention to the disquieting failure that can ensue when teachers lack educational support for learning about how their own counter-transferential processes can be used in meaningful ways. Too often, the glaring lack of institutional support in teacher education gives rise in the teaching profession to what Cathryn McConaghy calls 'exile and the art of escape in education' (2006: 82): depression, absenteeism, loss of voice, and in graver instances, substance addiction, breakdown, or even suicide.

The theory of counter-transference therefore highlights the risks inherent in education itself. Ellsworth lingers over this point: 'We can't just address that unconscious directly and ask it to speak or to get out of learning's [or teaching's] way' (1997: 59). One transference risk is that the teacher will channel her energies into bettering the lives of students at the expense of her own subjectivity. Salvio highlights the gendered quality of this 'lost-I feeling', and suggests that a feminine ideal poses risks for women in the caring professions (2006: 83). Anna Freud's (1936) study of 'altruistic surrender' uncovers the psychic pattern in which the 'altruistic' caregiver disassociates herself from her own unfulfilled desires and attributes them to others (children or students). Split off, the caregiver lives vicariously through others, sometimes quite apart from herself.

This 'altruistic mother' that for decades constituted the sanctioned, idealized image of the teacher is—from a psychoanalytic point of view—unable to contain the secret and unforeseen pleasures of words, knowledge, and teaching itself. Some theorists have read *eros in education* as emblematic of the woman teacher's resistance to the patriarchal dynamics of power that help to sustain the image of altruistic mother, emphasizing how the young rebellious teacher is passed on from home to school, and how—in a passionate psychic bid to recover her history—she turns the tables by falling in love with her students (Barreca and Denenholz Morse, 1997; Kelly, 1997; Gallop, 1999). In reading the dangers of intimacy in teaching and learning through the contested life of Sylvia Ashton-Warner, Robertson and McConaghy witness 'the difficult and ambiguous nature of postheterosexual attachments in women's biographies, [and] the violence of regulating excesses in women's lives' (2006: 13). Psychoanalysis, we think, offers a language to describe these emotional excesses and so complicates the more familiar (and stereotypical) 'cultural myths' of the teacher (Britzman, 1991: 6): 'altruistic mother', 'all-knowing', 'self-made', and without a mind of her own. It is a vocabulary that gives voice to the emotional life of the teacher and the conflicts that live there.

A second transference risk is the teacher's narcissism, which—though necessary in order to teach—is also a stubborn defence against students (Boldt, 2002; Britzman, 2006; Cohler and Galatzer-Levy, 2006; Pajak, 1998). Britzman (2006) identifies the problems that can arise when the teacher's love is projected not solely onto students, but onto the knowledge s/he hopes to convey. Thinking about her student teaching experience, Britzman finds something monstrous in her conscious effort to teach politics:

> I was involved in two furors: the furor to teach and the furor to teach my politics. I was convinced that teaching is a political activity and that my work was to convince my students of their political obligations. At the time, teaching was called a subversive activity. . . . I felt I had the answers without the thought of a terrific paradox: I railed against education as a banking method precisely as I banked on the message of consciousness raising. (2006: 118)

Britzman now sees that her counter-transference space was full of anxiety, self-doubt, and even anger at students 'sent to ruin my curriculum' (2006: 117). With the benefit of hindsight, she comes to a beautiful moment of recognition. Students *were* indeed engaged in the course—just not in the way that beginning teacher Britzman had imagined. Years later, she finds evidence of learning that her 'furor' had prevented her from recognizing: 'no matter how difficult the prose, how archaic the English, they read on, enjoying the suspense, identifying with what was monstrous in themselves and others, but not because they needed to change the world. Just the opposite, they wanted the world to take them in' (2006: 117). This psychoanalytic narrative reveals how heavy the curriculum can be with the teacher's fragile narcissism. Under the spell of enlightening others, the 'furor to teach' makes it difficult to notice students with minds of their own. But without such furor—and here is the conflict—teaching would be little more than 'going through the motions'.

Britzman challenges teachers not to choose one or the other side of this furor conflict (either to have furor or to leave it at the door). Instead, she dares us to recognize furor as a necessary fiction, as both a blind spot and a potential source of insight in thinking about teaching. The counter-transference can be pedagogical, Britzman argues, when it lends insight into the unconscious conflicts that both structure and distort our relations to the self and others in educational sites. Assigning an unconscious to the shadow texts of teaching is a good place to start. In Appel's example, the counter-transference, initially experienced as a migraine, became the grounds for insight into the unspoken fantasies and fears alive in his classroom. It may be that there is no way out of the unconscious dynamics we bring to each other; yet the language of the transference and the counter-transference may open a way *in* to this 'shadow side' of pedagogy that is, oftentimes, also 'stranger' than fiction.

Lesson 3: Narrating Ambivalence: Toward a Pedagogy of Reparation

So far we have emphasized the unconscious aspects of the student–teacher relationship, including both aggressive and tender feelings. In our third lesson we will look at one possible outcome of ambivalent feelings: what Melanie Klein (1937) called a 'drive to reparation'. Analysts and educators alike have posited **reparation** as a painful labour through which the subject attempts to make amends—to restore or to compensate for the losses that inevitably come with living, loving, and learning. Three big questions organize psychoanalytic and educational literature on this concept. First, where do reparative impulses come from? Second, what do reparative impulses have to do with teaching and learning? Third—and this returns us to Anna Freud—how can education repair the interference, or 'cognitive dissonance', that learning invokes? In *Beyond the Pleasure Principle*, Freud (1920) wondered about the human capacity to find pleasure in the face of both everyday difficulties and profound losses in our lives. Freud illustrated this idea by describing a game invented by his toddler grandson, little Ernst. During times when Ernst's mother needed to be absent (as invariably all mothers do), Freud noticed that Ernst would play this game over and over with intense pleasure. The game involved throwing a wooden reel over the edge of a curtained cot so that it was out of sight. Ernst accompanied this first move by calling out 'o-o-o-o', which Freud later interpreted to mean *'fort'* ('gone'). Freud imagines the anger (and pleasure) that Ernst experiences when he tosses away the reel: 'Alright, go away! I don't need you; I'm sending you away myself'. Ernst would then pull the reel back into sight and towards himself, this time hollering a joyful *'Da!'* ('There!'). By repeating the dynamics of disappearance and re-appearance, Ernst actively symbolized his relationship to his mother, and in particular the idea that even when she was physically gone, she could be made virtually present in play, through representation. Through this little game of hide-and-seek, Freud proposed a human capacity to make from unpleasurable experiences meanings that are more acceptable to the ego. He referred to this 'capacity' as an 'urge to psychically process powerful experiences'. Here Freud approaches Klein's later formulation of 'the urge to reparation', which involves mitigating difficult feelings with other symbols and signifiers (such as a toy or a book), allowing such feelings 'to be remembered and to be processed in the psyche' (1920: 53–5).

It was not Freud but Klein (1937) who elaborated the concept of reparation.[2] Following Freud, she suggests that guilt (i.e., the 'drive for reparation') originates in the effort to work through the anxiety of losing a loved (and hated) object (as little Ernst tried to do through his game with the wooden reel). But Klein emphasized the impulse to destroy (Freud's controversial 'death drive') as a key feature of the infant's psyche and her/his capacity for reparation. It is important to point out that the destruction here is not literal: it is not a matter of aggressive action but of aggressive *fantasies* that are unconscious and expressed (symptomatically) in ordinary baby behaviours such as sucking, biting, pulling, screaming, and crying. Klein argued that in moments of aggressive fantasy, the infant believes that s/he 'has really destroyed' the caregiver; and un-thinkable anxiety ensues (1937: 61, emphasis in original). It is through this early fantasy of aggression towards a loved object that guilt, or the 'drive for reparation', is born. With this formulation, Klein offers an answer to our first question: from where do reparative impulses come? Reparation, Klein says, is the second layer of imagination needed to cope with, and to make good from, the human capacity (also a tendency) to do harm, both real and imagined.

Educational theorists have turned to these twin dynamics—destruction and reparation—to explore the emotional underbelly of seemingly ordinary educational activities (lecturing, reading, writing), objects (toys, books, the curriculum) and student responses (resistance, negation, guilt, and identification with the aggressor) (Britzman, 2006; Gilbert, 1998; Grumet, 1998, 2006; Phillips, 1998; Pitt, 2000, 2003, 2006; Robertson, 1997; Salvio, 2006; Silin, 2006; Todd, 2001). They highlight the student's emotional uses of knowledge, which, as Phillips argues, often begin with a wish to destroy the knowledge on offer:

> The student attacks the subject with questions and criticisms, and finds out what's left after the assault; whatever survives this critique—this hatred—is felt to be of real substance (resilient, incorruptible, worth banking on). In this way, the student makes (or fails to make) [knowledge] true for her. (1998: 56)

What remains after the symbolic destruction of knowledge is a sense of its existence, or place, in social or cultural reality where it can be put to work in the service of creative and satisfying ends. If all goes well, the fantasy of having destroyed knowledge (and the ensuing anxiety) will be mitigated by the opposing impulse: knowledge can be engaged as something *real*, as opposed to something conveniently *ideal* (see Winnicott, 1969). Remember that Anna Freud's psychoanalytic lessons for education began with a 'critique' of its methods. Before we can become curious about the ambivalences and uncertainties that arise in the process of education, we may first need to challenge its practices.

Madeleine R. Grumet's essay 'Romantic Research: Why We Love to Read with Others' focuses on the reparative significance of words and how they can help us work through the ambivalence of early relationships—relationships fraught with both anxiety and pleasure. Like Freud, Grumet refers to childhood games or 'melodies' of 'wheeeee!', 'up we go', and 'peek-a-boo' to illustrate how symbols such as words allow us to make and maintain connections to beloved others whom we also fear losing (2006: 212). As Grumet writes:

> The romance of reading invites us to recuperate our losses. As we enter into the fictive world and emerge from it, we experience the opportunity to reconsider the boundaries and exclusions that sustain our social identities. . . .The text serves (as do other forms of art) to mediate the distance between self and other. . . . (2006: 221)

For Grumet and other proponents of psychoanalysis, the beauty of language is not that it moves us away from early non-linguistic experiences to increasingly sophisticated forms, but rather that it is a way back to those experiences. Reading, in this context, is more than a technical exercise; it is a psychic bridge that connects us to the deepest structures of our minds, our bodies, and our relationships to others: all replete with the ambivalence and anxiety that mark psychical life.

Judith Robertson and Jonathan Silin have written about language—and the arts of reading and writing—on precisely these terms. Robertson (1997, 2000, 2002) has connected the vitality of books to two psychic structures mobilized in reading: the fantasies of the earliest years of life, and the structures of address of the text in which the unconscious reads via verbal associations and sounds. For instance, in one essay Robertson analyzes the 'structural conditions' of the children's book *Goodnight Moon* and shows how its linguistic form and sequence help the child cope with otherwise unbearable psychical experiences: in this case, the terrors awakened at bedtime (2000: 211). Like any good transitional object, such as a well-worn blanket, Robertson suggests how the bedtime story mediates the terrifying transition from waking to dreaming, a transition rife with hallucinations that animate bedroom shadows. Reading is an invitation to 'the would-be-sleeper' to work through the risks posed by closing one's eyes: losing control, feeling abandoned, being swallowed by darkness (Robertson, 2000: 203). To return to Klein, the storybook may be read as a reparative work that both awakens children's terrors and if all goes well, puts them to bed, at least for the night.

In a different context, Silin (2006) tries to understand his struggles with reading, and later writing, as linked to the emotional ambivalence implied in narrating the self.

In a story about periods, commas, and paragraphs, Silin describes a primary ambivalence central to his literacy experience: a tension between the desires 'to authorize [his] own life' and still to be recognized by his father:

> Nightly responsibility for editing my homework alternates between my mother and my father, the former far more patient and the latter always insistent that I understand the principles underlying his corrections. I am impatient, easily frustrated, and unwilling to internalize the lessons they struggle to teach me. In the end, I am never quite sure who is the real author of these anguished collaborations. They reflect my deep ambivalence about being held accountable for my own words, my own life.
>
> This reluctance to claim my ideas on paper, I now believe, was connected in some complicated and still incomprehensible way to my recalcitrant and unacceptable sexuality. The written word was both the medium that tied me to my parents in endless battles over periods, commas, and paragraphs and the medium that eventually allowed me to see myself as an independent agent with a unique story to tell. (2006: 234)

Rhetorically speaking, the present tense in which Silin narrates his experience is a beautiful example of the 'condensed time of the transference' explored earlier. The narrative also captures something of the crushing conventions of language and Silin's defiance of those conventions as central to his entry into sexuality and sociality. Of particular interest with regard to the concept of reparation is the way Silin uses the medium of language to 'process in the psyche' childhood experiences of ambivalence, anxiety, and conflict (Freud, 1920: 55). Words do not change the past, nor can they rescue us from the necessary disruptions of growing up. But they may help us endure psychical losses in so far as they enable us to 'articulate authority within a potentially frustrating space' (Robertson, 2000: 210).

Of course, the pedagogical demand that children like Silin use grammatical conventions such as periods, commas, and paragraphs is justified. Psychoanalysis simply highlights how such requirements can be felt as demands to let go of a sense of the self—perhaps what Winnicott calls the 'true' self—which the child is not ready to sacrifice in the name of growing up.[3] Winnicott develops this point, noting the emotional value of silence, or *not* communicating: 'Although healthy persons communicate and enjoy communicating, the other fact is equally true, that *each individual is an isolate, permanently non-communicating, permanently unknown, in fact unfound*' (1965: 187, emphasis in original). Winnicott highlights a key tension here: the drive to symbolize experience through the shared human discourse of language is *countered by* a need to preserve the 'isolate' and 'non-communicating' aspects of the self; this is what he calls 'the right not to communicate' (1965: 179). Jacques Lacan further complicates our understanding of language through his emphasis on 'the abject'—the terrors of inner experience that disrupt and exceed symbolic substitution (Felman, 1987). This marks another difficult psychoanalytic lesson for education: as much as language represents freedom of expression, it can also be experienced as intrusive, inadequate to its task, and downright disappointing.

We have now come full circle, arriving back at Anna Freud's question of what it would mean to repair the harm—or what she would call 'interference'—that learning entails. A key part of this reparative work involves creating potential spaces for symbolization, in which raw experiences (desires, pleasures, anxieties) can be engaged through representational forms that are more acceptable and less devastating to the ego. As Winnicott and Lacan remind us, educators may also need to recognize the value of unarticulated states of being that resist communication in language. Psychoanalysis dares educators to 'clear a space that recognizes the value of linguistic *incompetence* as well as *fluency*, verbal *insufficiency* as well as communicative *competence*' (Silin, 2006: 233, emphasis added). This theory of learning, instead of travelling the familiar 'linear, one-way street' of stage-theories of development, moves back and forth between dynamic positions (Ellsworth, 1997: 50). Psychoanalytically, language is the means by which we re-connect with repressed material in ourselves, even as words inevitably fail to represent that material. Language is not only how we can make what is gone, here: it is how we can make what is not yet, now, and open what is now to meanings not yet made.

Impossible Pedagogy

It is tempting to think that psychoanalysis can fully account for the unconscious and thus help educators to manage, or master, all that goes on in the classroom. But in fact it does just the opposite: it reminds teachers of the very impossibility of educating and shakes up the assumption that students and teachers will be on the same path to understanding. Something unconscious exceeds and interrupts the conscious project to know. At issue in the psychoanalytic classroom is not which strategies can guarantee active or critical learning—where learning is already a pre-established outcome—but rather how the unconscious opens education to what cannot be known in advance, and to conflicts that both animate and interrupt conscious efforts to teach and to learn. Psychoanalysis invites us to explore why affect as well as cognition matters to pedagogical relationships. It introduces an emotional complexity that requires teachers to consider the meaning of uncertainty, silence, and resistance in the classroom and to tolerate what we cannot know in trying to teach others. Desiring and resisting, loving and hating, destroying and repairing: these are the fundamentals of psychoanalytic education. Seventy years after Freud suggested that education is an impossible profession, that idea can still serve to open education to its stranger side, to the interplay of desire and its discontents, and—if all goes well—to a horizon of infinite possibility and surprise.

Notes

1. Socrates begins his teaching of the slave boy and *Meno* with a similar assertion of education's impossibility: '. . . Meno, you are a rascal. Here you are asking me to give you my "teaching", I who claim that there is no such thing as teaching, only recollection' (14). The idea here is that Socratic education is a matter of drawing out of the student that which already lies within. In a much more recent history, Shoshana Felman returns to this dialogue and the

impossibility of education: '[E]very true pedagogue is in effect an anti-pedagogue. . . . [E]very pedagogy stems from its confrontation of the impossibility of teaching' (1987: 72). In saying so, Felman is reminding us that failure is not only inevitable to teaching; she is also reminding us that the goal of teaching is not simply to transfer knowledge from curriculum to student. Confronting the impossibility of teaching means recognizing the multiplicity of meanings students make in relation to knowledge, and so requires educators to notice the otherness of the process of learning and the person who is the learner. Our chapter returns to this interminable concept, impossible education, once again.

2. For an introduction to Klein's contribution to object–relations psychoanalysis, see Juliet Mitchell's (1986) 'Introduction' in *The Selected Melanie Klein*.

3. Freud's early definition of education follows precisely this trajectory: 'an incitement to the conquest of the pleasure principle, and to its replacement by the reality principle' (1911: 41). Psychoanalytically speaking, education must cause the ego 'discontents' in its demand for the renunciation of immediate forms of pleasure.

Glossary

counter-transference: The stirring of unconscious material in one person as it arises in response to another person's transference material.

reparation: A psychic process, described by Melanie Klein, driven by the urge to make amends for destructive fantasies.

repression: A psychic defence that keeps forbidden ideas, wishes, impulses, and fantasies out of conscious awareness.

the unconscious: Psychic material that is not present to conscious awareness.

transference: The projection of unconscious conflicts, wishes, fantasies, and fears from one person onto another.

Study Questions

1. Based on your own history of learning (and teaching), discuss Freud's claim that education is an impossible profession. If he was right, what can it mean to teach and to learn?

2. Freud's theory of repression refers to the psychic process by which difficult ideas are buried deep in the unconscious, hidden from view. How might this process inform your thinking about the sociology of education? In what ways might the concept of repression operate at the level of schooling and society?

3. 'Transference' was Freud's term for the movement of (past) conflicts into (present) situations. Have you noticed the 'transference' of conflict in your own history of learning? Why might this be significant for studies in education?

4. Examine the assumptions and emotional investments you bring to the act of reading. How does reading for the purpose of learning differ from reading for pleasure? Have you ever fallen in love with a book? How do words on a page have the capacity to draw us in, touch us, and/or tear us apart?

5. Psychoanalysis links everyday activities—such as reading or writing—to our earliest relations and unconscious conflicts. How does this idea help you think about times when students do not learn, or when learning is difficult?

Recommended Readings

Freud, A. 1935/1979. *Psychoanalysis for Teachers and Parents*, trans. B. Low. New York: Norton.

Freud, S. 1914/2006. 'On the Psychology of the Grammar-School Boy', in S. Whiteside, trans., and A. Phillips, ed., *The Penguin Freud Reader*. London: Penguin Books, 354–7.

Phillips, A. 1998. *The Beast in the Nursery*. London: Faber and Faber.

Recommended Websites

Freud Museum, London: http://www.freud.org.uk/

Freud Abstracts, New York Freudian Society and Training Institute: http://nyfreudian.org/society_00.html

Sigmund Freud: online resources: http://www.freudfile.org/resources.html

References

Appel, S. 1999. 'The Teacher's Headache', in S. Appel, ed., *Psychoanalysis and Pedagogy*. Westport, CT: Bergin and Garvey, 133–46.

Balint, E. 1993. *Before I Was I: Psychoanalysis and the Imagination*, eds. J. Mitchell and M. Parsons. eds. London: Free Association Books.

Barreca, R., and D. Denenholz Morse, eds. 1997. *The Erotics of Instruction*. Lebanon, NH: University Press of New England.

Benzaquén, A.S. 1998. 'Freud, Little Hans, and the Desire for Knowledge', *Journal of Curriculum Theorizing* 14, 2: 43–52.

Block, A.A. 1999. *It's Okay Ma, I'm Only Bleeding: Education as a Practice of Social Violence against Children*. New York: Peter Lang.

Boldt, G. 2002. 'Oedipal and Other Conflicts', *Contemporary Issues in Early Childhood* 3, 3: 365–82.

———. 2006. 'Parenting and the Narcissistic Demands of Whiteness', in Boldt and Salvio (2006: 143–60).

———, and Salvio, P.M., eds. 2006. *Love's Return: Psychoanalytic Essays on Childhood, Teaching and Learning*. New York: Routledge.

Britzman, D. 1991. *Practice Makes Practice: A Critical Study of Learning to Teach*. Albany, NY: State University of New York Press.

———. 1998a. *Lost Subjects, Contested Objects: Toward a Psychoanalytic Inquiry of Learning*. Albany, NY: State University of New York Press.

———. 1998b. 'Some Observations on the Work of Learning', *Journal of Curriculum Theorizing* 14: 53–9.

———. 2003. *After-Education: Anna Freud, Melanie Klein, and Psychoanalytic Histories of Learning*. New York: State University of New York Press.

———. 2006. *Novel Education: Psychoanalytic Studies of Learning and Not Learning*. New York: Peter Lang.

Cohler, B.J., and R.M. Galatzer-Levy. 2006. 'Love in the Classroom: Desire and Transference in Learning and Teaching', in Boldt and Salvio (2006: 243–65).

Cox, O.C. 2002. 'A Lacanian Look at English Elegance: Some Reflections on Ian McEwan's *Enduring Love*', *International Journal of Psychoanalysis* 83, 1153–67.

de Forest, I. 1965. *The Leaven of Love: The Development of the Psychoanalytic Theory and Technique of Sándor Ferenczi*. Hamden, CT: Archon Books.

Ellsworth, E. 1997. *Teaching Positions: Difference, Pedagogy, and the Power of Address*. New York: Teacher's College Press.

Felman, S. 1987. 'Psychoanalysis and Education: Teaching Terminable and Interminable', in *Jacques Lacan and the Adventure of Insight: Psychoanalysis in Contemporary Culture*. Cambridge, MA: Harvard University Press, 53–97.

Fenichel, O. 1954. 'The Means of Education', in H. Fenichel and D. Rapaport, eds, *The Collected Papers of Otto Fenichel*. Second Series. New York: Norton, 324–34.

Freud, A. 1935/1979. *Psycho-analysis for Teachers and Parents*, trans. B. Low. New York: Norton.

———. 1936/1998. 'A Form of Altruism', in R. Ekins and R. Freeman, eds, *Collected Writings: Anna Freud*. London: Penguin, 24–34.

Freud, S. 1905/2006. 'Fragment of an Analysis of Hysteria (Dora)', in S. Whiteside, trans., and A. Phillips, ed., *The Penguin Freud Reader*. London: Penguin Books, 435–540.

———. 1908/2006. 'On the Sexual Theories of Children', in S. Whiteside, trans., and A. Phillips, ed., *The Psychology of Love*. London: Penguin Books, 221–37.

———. 1911/1991. 'Formulations on the Two Principles of Mental Functioning', in J. Strachey, trans., and A. Richards, ed., *On Metapsychology: Penguin Freud Library* Vol. 11. London: Penguin, 31–44.

———. 1914/2006. 'On the Psychology of the Grammar-School Boy', in S. Whiteside, trans., and A. Phillips, ed., *The Penguin Freud Reader*. London: Penguin Books, 354–57.

———. 1915a/1991. 'The Unconscious', in J. Strachey, trans., and A. Richards, ed., *On Metapsychology: Penguin Freud Library*. Vol. 11. London: Penguin Books, 159–222.

———. 1915b/2006. 'Observations on Love in Transference', in S. Whiteside, trans., and A. Phillips, ed., *The Penguin Freud Reader*. London: Penguin Books, 341–53.

———. 1920/2003. 'Beyond the Pleasure Principle', in J. Reddick, trans., and A. Phillips, ed., *Beyond the Pleasure Principle and Other Writings*. London: Penguin Books, 43–102.

———. 1937/2002. 'Analysis Terminable and Interminable', in A. Bance, trans., and A. Phillips, ed., *Wild Analysis*. London: Penguin Books, 173–208.

Freud Museum London. 2007. Available at: <http://www.freud.org.uk>. Accessed 23 February.

Gallop, J. 1999. 'Knot a Love Story', in Stephen Appel, ed., *Psychoanalysis and Pedagogy*. Westport, CT: Bergin & Garvey, 125–132.

Gardner, M.R. 1997. *On Trying to Teach: The Mind in Correspondence*. Hillsdale, NJ: Analytic Press.

Gilbert, J. 1998. 'Reading Colorblindness: Negation as an Engagement with Social Difference', *Journal of Curriculum Theorizing* 14, 2: 29–34.

Grumet, M.R. 1998. 'Lost Places, Potential Spaces, and Possible Worlds: Why We Read Books with Other People', *Journal of Curriculum Theorizing* 14, 2: 24–8.

———. 2006. 'Romantic Research: Why We Love to Read', in Boldt and Salvio (2006: 207–25). (Essay originally published in 1999.)

Kelly, U. 1997. *Schooling Desire: Literacy, Cultural Politics and Pedagogy*. New York: Routledge.

Klein, M. 1937/1964. 'Love, Guilt and Reparation', in M. Klein and J. Riviere [Lectures], *Love, Hate and Reparation*. London: Norton, 57–119.

Kristeva, J. 1991. *Strangers to Ourselves*, trans. L.S. Roudiaz. New York: Columbia University Press.

Laplanche J., and J.B. Pontalis. 1973. *The Language of Psychoanalysis*, trans. D.N. Smith. Paris: Presses Universitaries de France.

Lear, J. 2005. *Freud*. New York: Routledge.

Low, M., and P. Palulis. 2006. 'Of Pedagogy and/as *Différance*: A Letter from Derrida', *Journal of Curriculum Theorizing* 22, 1: 45–60.

McConaghy, C. 2006. 'Teaching's Intimacies', in J.P. Robertson and C. McConaghy, eds, *Provocations: Sylvia Ashton-Warner and Excitability in Education*. New York: Peter Lang Inc., 63–94.

Mitchell, J. 1986. 'Introduction', in J. Mitchell, ed., *The Selected Melanie Klein*. New York: The Free Press, 9–32.

Morris, M. 2001. *Curriculum and the Holocaust: Competing Sites of Memory and Representation*. Mahwah, NJ: Lawrence Erlbaum.

Pajak, E. 1998. 'Exploring the "Shadow Side" of Teaching', *Journal of Curriculum Theorizing* 14, 2: 8–14.

Phillips, A. 1998. *The Beast in the Nursery*. London: Faber & Faber.

———. 2002. 'Introduction', in A. Bance, trans., and A. Phillips, ed., *Wild Analysis*. London: Penguin Books, vii–xxv.

Pinar, W.F. 1973/1995. 'Mr. Bennett and Mrs. Brown', in *Autobiography, Politics, and Sexuality: Essays in Curriculum Theory 1972–1992*. New York: Peter Lang, 13–18.

———. 1993. 'Notes on Understanding Curriculum as a Racial Text', in C. McCarthy and W. Critchlow, eds, *Race, Identity and Representation in Education*. New York: Routledge, 60–70.

Pitt, A.J. 2000. 'Hide and Seek: The Play of the Personal in Education', *Changing English* 7, 1: 65–74.

———. 2003. *The Play of the Personal: Psychoanalytic Narratives of Feminist Education*. New York: Peter Lang.

———. 2006. 'Mother Love's Education', in Boldt and Salvio (2006: 87–105).

Rank, O. 1996. *A Psychology of Difference: The American Lectures*, ed. R. Kramer. Princeton, NJ: Princeton University Press.

Robertson, J.P. 1997. 'Fantasy's Confines: Popular Culture and the Education of the Female Primary School Teacher', *Canadian Journal of Education* 22, 2: 123–43.

———. 2000. 'Sleeplessness in the Great Green Room: Getting Way under the Covers with *Goodnight Moon*', *Children's Literature Association Quarterly* 25, 4: 203–13.

———. 2002. 'What Happens to Our Wishes: Magical Thinking in Harry Potter', *Children's Literature Association Quarterly* 26, 4: 198–211.

———. 2004. 'Teaching in Your Dreams: Screenplay Pedagogy and Margarethe von Trotta's *The Second Awakening of Christa Klages*', *Canadian Journal of Film Studies* 13, 2: 74–92.

———, and C. McConaghy, eds. 2006. *Provocations: Sylvia Ashton-Warner and Excitability in Education*. New York: Peter Lang Inc.

Salvio, P.M. 1999. 'Teacher of "Weird Abundance": Portrait of the Pedagogical Tactics of Anne Sexton', *Cultural Studies* 13, 4: 639–60.

———. 2006. 'On the Vicissitudes of Love and Hate: Anne Sexton's Pedagogy of Loss and Reparation', in Boldt and Salvio (2006: 65–86).

Silin, J.G. 2006. 'Reading, Writing and the Wrath of My Father', in Boldt and Salvio (2006: 227–41).

Tobin, J. 1997. 'The Missing Discourse of Pleasure and Desire', in J. Tobin, ed., *Making a Place for Pleasure in Early Childhood Education*. New Haven, CT: Yale University Press, 1–37.

Todd, S., ed. 1997. *Learning Desire: Perspectives on Pedagogy, Culture, and the Unsaid*. New York: Routledge.

———. 2001. 'Guilt, Suffering and Responsibility', *Journal of the Philosophy of Education* 35, 4: 597–614.

———. 2003. *Learning from the Other: Levinas, Psychoanalysis and Ethical Possibilities in Education*. Albany: State University of New York Press.

Winnicott, D.W. 1960/1990. 'Counter-Transference', in *The Maturational Processes and the Facilitating Environment*. London: Karnac Books, 158–65.

———. 1965/1990. 'Communicating and Not-communicating Leading to a Study of Certain Opposites', in *The Maturational Processes and the Facilitating Environment*. London: Karnac Books, 179–92.

———. 1969/1971. 'The Use of an Object and Relating through Identifications', in *Playing and Reality*, 86–94

Part Two

Process and Equity

CHAPTER 7

Streaming in/for the New Economy

Alison Taylor and Harvey Krahn

Introduction

> [D]espite marked expansion of all educational systems under study, in most countries there has been little change in socioeconomic inequality of educational opportunity. . . . The stability in the association between social origins and educational transitions . . . indicates that educational selection persistently favors children of privileged social origins. (Shavit and Blossfield, 1993: 19, 21)

Practices that stratify students include ability testing, **streaming/tracking**, and the charging of tuition fees. In the past, streaming was a topic of intense debate within academic and policy communities, but recent discussions have been somewhat muted. Policy-makers suggest that schools are becoming less stratified as they focus on preparing young people for the knowledge economy. However, it is difficult to say if this is the case.

On one hand, the expansion of higher education encourages de-stratification. On the other hand, opportunities for **stratification** increase with the spread of standardized testing and expanding accountability regimes. While curriculum is becoming increasingly standardized as a result of interprovincial initiatives, the growth of the school choice movement has led to increasing differentiation among schools themselves (e.g., charter and other independent schools). Finally, even as school systems around the world are increasingly subjected to international comparisons, there is some evidence that control over educational decision-making is becoming increasingly decentralized. It is difficult to tell whether this combination of trends is likely to result in a more or less stratified system.

This chapter looks at how streaming currently works in several different provinces across Canada as part of our larger interest in the equity implications of shifts in education policy over time. To try to make sense of current policy and practice, we examine data from a national survey of 15-year-old high-school students conducted in 2000 by Statistics Canada and compare those findings with previous research on high-school streaming.

How Streaming Works

Traditionally, educational stratification in high schools has been known as 'streaming' in Canada and 'tracking' in the United States. Streaming is the practice of sorting students into different ability groups, typically an upper stream bound for post-secondary schooling and lower tiers offering vocational training (Davies and Guppy, 2006: 74).

The form that streaming takes depends on the level of schooling. At the elementary level, streaming usually involves placing students labelled 'behavioural, slow learning, and learning disabled' in special education classes; at the secondary level it involves distributing students across various types and levels of courses (Curtis, Livingstone, and Smaller, 1992). Students take different levels (e.g., 'general' or 'advanced') of core or required subjects (e.g., math, science, English), and choose different option courses (e.g., trades-related courses, second languages) that, in combination, lead toward different post-secondary and labour market outcomes. Choice of program (e.g., French immersion) and choice of school (e.g., private school) are two other forms of streaming.

Although the provincial governments play an important role in the development of elementary and secondary curriculum in Canada, decisions affecting the distribution of students (e.g., the scheduling of different courses) are usually made at the level of the school district and school. Students are generally encouraged rather than required to enrol in different levels of courses, and make their decisions on the basis of previous grades and input from subject teachers. In other words, the streaming process is largely informal. Writing about the US, Oakes (2005: 43) notes that practices may not be consistent 'even within a single school', and do not necessarily reflect 'school or district policies'. For example, in a school where there is extensive streaming in core subjects, unstreamed classes (e.g., options) may also become homogeneous. Or there may be too few students to justify offering a single-stream class. Thus streaming (and de-streaming) is not always intentional. Unlike many of their European counterparts, Canada's education systems have been relatively open. Single-stream schools are rare, and high schools in most provinces offer the same general credential to graduates regardless of course stream. Davies and Guppy (2006) suggest that, in Europe as well as Canada, the general trend has been toward de-stratification. However, Ireson and Hallam (2001) observe that England and Wales since the late 1990s have reintroduced **ability grouping** in response to concerns about the relatively poor performance of students on international tests. Meanwhile, some North American writers (e.g., Gidney, 1999; Lucas, 1999; Oakes, 2005) argue that overt and formal streaming systems have

simply been replaced by more covert and multi-dimensional systems of in-school stratification that continue to limit opportunity and mobility for some groups.

Trends in Streaming Policy: The Case of Ontario

The shifts that Ontario's education policy has undergone since the early 1960s reflect
overall trends across the country. The 1962 Robarts Plan was introduced in response to
criticisms that high-school programs were overly academic and were not producing the
technical skills that Canada needed if it was to compete internationally (Gidney, 1999).
Accordingly, the program of studies was reorganized so that students had three choices:
a two-year practical program, a four-year program for those intending to enter the
labour market or community college, and a five-year program leading to university.
The decision to pass or fail a student depended on his or her performance across all
courses, and there was little mobility across streams (Gidney, 1999).

Six years later, interest in progressive child-centred education and concerns about
rigid streaming were reflected in the 1968 Hall–Dennis Report. In response to its
recommendations the province introduced individual timetables and a credit system
that gave students more flexibility, made more options available, and abolished
program streams, though courses continued to be offered at different levels of difficulty. By the late 1970s however, the Ontario and other provincial governments were
once again raising the requirements for high-school graduation, reinstituting provincial exams, and increasing streaming of students (Gaskell, 1991).

A decade later, concern about high dropout rates and some graduates' limited
literacy, along with perceptions that 'general level' (non-university) courses had little
relevance and denied equal opportunity to poor children, were reflected in the influential 1987 Radwanski report (the *Ontario Study of the Relevance of Education and the
Issue of Dropouts*). Describing streaming as 'a social injustice, a theoretical error, and a
practical failure'(1987: 152), it called for a common un-streamed curriculum from
grades 1 through 12. Two years later, the province's Liberal government announced
plans to develop new provincial benchmarks for grades 3 and 6 and abolish streaming
in grade 9.

The NDP government of Bob Rae began destreaming grade 9 in 1993. Two years
later, a Royal Commission on Learning (RCL) recommended eliminating grade 13,
increasing the number of required high-school courses, and providing one stream of
courses designed for university preparation and another, of equal quality, emphasizing
applications and connections outside the classroom. But Ontario's policy shifted once
again with the 1995 election. The Mike Harris Conservatives introduced curriculum
changes that included the re-streaming of grade 9, a new four-year high-school
program, an increase in the number of compulsory credits, and the requirement that
students pass a grade 10 literacy test in order to graduate.

Gidney (1999: 240) describes the latter changes as representing a 'reassertion of
more traditional views'. However, government representatives would argue that they
were moving towards de-stratification by offering courses geared to different learning
styles, strengths, and aspirations. Students in grades 9 and 10 were offered Academic or

Applied courses, while grade 11 and 12 students could take Workplace, College, University/College (U/C), or University 'destination' courses. The aim was to increase graduation rates and promote success for all young people by better preparing them for future destinations and encouraging them to make realistic career choices. Even so, the new five-year graduation rate for the first cohort was only 70 per cent—down from 78 per cent before the program was reorganized (King, Warren, Boyer, and Chin, 2005).

The fluctuations in Ontario's policy reflect the ongoing debate between those who would minimize streaming and delay it as long as possible in order to maximize students' choices, and those who believe that the differing abilities of students call for more streams and earlier channelling (cf. Davies and Guppy, 2006). This debate recalls the one that took place in the early 1900s between John Dewey, the well-known proponent of progressive education, and 'the social efficiency' advocate David Snedden over whether vocational and liberal education should be separate (Dewey and Snedden, 1977). Similar issues underlie contemporary debates about streaming.

Arguments for and against Streaming

Debates about the content and organization of secondary-school programs continue to centre on economic concerns. For example, the trend toward further de-stratification of high schools and a shift of **educational selection** from the secondary to the postsecondary level in some ways fit with the vision of a *knowledge economy* that demands highly skilled labour. By contrast, arguments for more vocational streaming, particularly in periods when intermediate skills are in short supply, reflect concern that schools are not providing enough opportunities for students to explore trades and technical careers. Across Canada, the current approach to streaming encourages students to choose the courses that best fit their further education and labour market plans and attempts to make students more aware of the different career pathways they might follow. However, since streaming has been seen both as a *solution to* and a *cause of* human capital problems in the past, it is important to look carefully at the arguments for and against it. Arguments in favour of streaming frequently reflect the belief that school programs should be designed to meet the needs of diverse students. Ireson and Hallam (2001) suggest that calls for streaming in the first half of the twentieth century in England grew out of the intelligence testing movement, which justified ability grouping as a way of providing education consistent with differing innate abilities. For example, after sketching the development of an 'average' person, a 'bright' person, and a 'slow' person, Whipple (1936) argued that schools should be organized to prepare students for their positions in society. Ability grouping was also seen as a mechanism for dealing with the increasing range of individual differences that came with growing secondary-school enrolments.

In a less functionalist vein, proponents of streaming have also argued that students learn better and develop more positive attitudes when grouped with others like themselves, and that teachers are better able to accommodate students when those with similar needs are grouped in more homogeneous classes. In fact, teachers have often been strong advocates of streaming. In Ontario they resisted (at least initially) the de-streaming of grade 9 (Robertson, Cowell, and Olson, 1998; Ross, McKeiver, and Hogaboam-Grey, 1997). And a survey of Ontario secondary-school teachers in 1999 regarding school reforms introduced in the 1990s found that respondents were positive about only two reforms—the creation of school councils and a return to streaming (Ontario Secondary School Teachers' Federation, 2000).

By contrast, critics of streaming have asked troubling questions about who gets into what stream, how various streams differ in terms of content and process, and where the different streams lead. The core criticism is that streaming tends to increase inequity. In the US, according to Oakes, 'virtually every study' found 'poor and minority students . . . in disproportionately large percentages in the bottom groups' (2005: 64). Davies and Guppy (2006) report similar Canadian research showing that students from wealthier and more advantaged family backgrounds are disproportionately inclined to enter academic programs while students from poorer and less advantaged family origins enter vocational programs in disproportionate numbers. In the 1980s in Ontario, roughly 90 per cent of students from professional families were enrolled in Advanced-level (university-bound) programs, compared to approximately 50 per cent of students with parents in unskilled occupations (Curtis et al., 1992: 13). An Ontario Ministry of Education study from the late 1980s noted that, whereas more than 60 per cent of secondary-school graduates overall were enrolled in Advanced programs, the majority of high-school dropouts had been enrolled in General (49 per cent) and Basic (12 per cent) programs (Karp, 1988).

A Toronto District School Board study of the students enrolled in Basic, General, and Advanced secondary-school program streams in 1991–2 found disproportionately high proportions of male, black, and Aboriginal students in non-university tracks and of Asian students in the university stream (Yau, Cheng, and Ziegler, 1993: i). Furthermore, 65 per cent of students in the Advanced program listed their parents' highest education level as university or college, compared to only 38 per cent at the General level and 34 per cent in Basic programs. In the Canadian context, therefore, socio-economic status and race/ethnicity do appear to influence streaming decisions within schools.

Concern about which students are in particular streams would not be so great if levels of self-esteem and quality of materials, instruction, and resources were similar across streams. But there is evidence that this is not the case (Oakes, 2005; Curtis et al., 1992; Osborne, 1999). Drawing on **cultural reproduction** perspectives (e.g., Bourdieu and Passeron, 1990), critics suggest that students in university-bound streams have more opportunity to develop valuable cultural and social capital through the acquisition of high-status knowledge and the opportunity to learn with similar peers. Teachers working in those streams tend to emphasize 'critical thinking, independent work, active participation, self-direction, and creativity', while those working in lower-level streams emphasize 'students getting along with one another, working quietly, improving study habits, being punctual, and conforming to classroom rules and expectations' (Oakes, 2005: 85). Students located in different streams also tend to make friends within their own stream, which in turn may affect their attitudes toward school and their aspirations (Lucas and Gamoran, 2002). In sum, different streams can result in different 'cognitive and non-cognitive outcomes' (Oakes, 2005: 201).

Describing the outcomes associated with Ontario's various curriculum streams in the 1980s, Curtis et al. (1992) noted that students in vocational streams were expected to have high rates of early school leaving and low rates of employment in program-related areas after leaving school. They also noted that few of these students entered apprenticeship programs. Oakes agrees that the knowledge and behaviours taught to low-track students 'have little exchange value in a social or economic sense' (2005: 92). She adds that outcomes for students tracked into non-university courses also include lower self-esteem (because of the stigma attached to lower streams) and lower levels of aspirations, controlling for social class, ability, and pre-track enrolment attitudes (2005: 8). While acknowledging the difficulty of asserting a causal direction between track and attitudes, she notes that different kinds of attitudes toward schooling tend to cluster at various track levels, and that attitudes of students in 'lower' tracks worsen as they move from junior to senior high school (2005: 139).

Because much of the research on streaming discussed above was conducted in the 1970s and 1980s, it is important to ask whether the patterns observed then are still apparent today. For example, Curtis et al. noted that the proportion of students in Basic-level programs in Ontario in grade 9 declined from 19 per cent in 1980 to 10 per cent in 1987, while the proportion in Advanced-level programs increased from 52 to 64 per cent (1992: 94–5). In the US context, Lucas and Gamoran report that the proportion of sophomores in college preparation programs increased from 40 per cent in 1980 to 68 per cent in 1990. They suggest that there was a 'dismantling of overarching tracks' nationally during this period (2002: 174). This leads us to ask whether streaming is still an issue in Canada today.

Based on his research in the US, Lucas suggests that, although the current stratification system is more hidden, students' prospects still resemble those under the 'old regime with its overarching programs' (1999: 114). In the Canadian context, questions also continue to arise about the consequences of streaming with respect to post-secondary education (PSE). For example, a 2001 report by Alberta Learning notes that factors associated with early school leaving include enrolment in the Integrated Occupational Program (a non-PSE-bound stream). It further notes that, of those passing Math 14 and 24 (leading to very limited PSE options), only 35 per cent went on to complete high school on time, compared to 56 per cent of the entire cohort (Alberta Learning, 2001).

These more recent studies are admittedly limited in number. Nevertheless, they suggest that despite changes in streaming policies over time (cf. Loveless, 1999), inequality persists, and that questions about the role of schooling in structuring inequality are still valid. This chapter contributes to this research tradition by providing a detailed snapshot of the extent of streaming in four Canadian provinces in the year 2000. It also explores the relationship between socio-demographic and location variables and course/stream placement.

The *Youth in Transition Survey* (YITS)

Method

The *Youth in Transition Survey* (YITS) is a national longitudinal survey of 15- and 18-year-olds, conducted by Statistics Canada. Baseline data were collected in 2000, then follow-up surveys were conducted with each cohort in 2002 and 2004. Our study is based on the information collected from and about the sample members who were 15 years old in April/May 2000. These young people were randomly selected via a stratified probability sample that initially sampled 1,241 Canadian schools (schools in the northern territories and on Indian reservations were excluded) and then selected students within these schools who completed questionnaires in class. A parallel telephone survey collected family-related information from their parents, while a third component of the study collected data about the schools from senior administrators in each school. When appropriately weighted to correct for over-sampling in smaller provinces and for non-response, the 26,063 teenagers in this unique student–parent–school database represent all the 15-year-olds living in Canada in 2000—a population of more than 348,000.[1]

Among many other questions, these students were asked to identify the level of their 'current or most recently taken' math, science, and English courses (answers were chosen from lists specific to each province). We made numerous telephone calls to provincial departments of education and teacher associations to determine whether the response categories used would have been understandable to the respondents (given ongoing curriculum changes in several jurisdictions) and to confirm that certain levels of courses were prerequisites for university entrance, college entrance, or work destinations. These conversations were extremely useful, since they frequently revealed distinct differences between provincial educational policies and practices. Based on this contextual information, we eliminated six provinces from our analysis because we felt that the YITS response categories for these provinces might have been problematic for students.[2] Our final analysis focused on four provinces: British Columbia, Alberta, Saskatchewan, and Ontario. In addition, to ensure comparability, we restricted our analysis to 15-year-olds enrolled in grade 10 (82 per cent of all 15-year-old YITS respondents).

Predicting post-secondary destinations based on grade 10 course selection would be difficult if there were a great deal of mobility across streams in later grades. But conversations with provincial government and teacher association representatives, along with previous research (Curtis et al., 1992; Lucas, 1999), convinced us that mobility between streams is limited and that movement that limits PSE options is more common than movement that enhances those options. Hence for each course (math, science, English), we categorized students in two groups, according to whether their grade 10 course selection was likely to restrict or keep open their PSE options (particularly university). We decided not to differentiate further because the line between college and university course streams typically appeared to be better defined than that between college and workplace-oriented streams. Appendix A (page 119) describes in more detail how course levels were coded.[3] Unfortunately, YITS questionnaires did not collect information on the students' optional courses; therefore, we were unable to address questions related to the extent of 'vocational' streaming.

Findings
Subject streaming

Table 7.1 shows the proportion of grade 10 students in four provinces with all PSE options open, based on math, science, and English course levels. Although the proportions are calculated in two different ways (because some data were missing),[4] several basic patterns emerge. First, the proportion of students with open PSE options is typically highest in English, while the proportion with open PSE options based on math course level is always lowest. As a result, when we focus on those students who have open PSE options in all three of these courses (row 4 in Table 7.1), in each province it is math that has the most restrictive effect on PSE options.

Table 7.1   Percentage of grade 10 students with PSE options open, based on level of grade 10 course(s) by province

Subject	Ontario[2]		Saskatchewan[2]		Alberta[2]		British Columbia[2]	
Math	70	(76)	90	(96)	62	(66)	72	(79)
Science	73	(78)	93	(99)	83	(88)	80	(86)
English	76	(82)	93	(99)	79	(84)	88	(99)
All three subjects[1]	64	(70)	87	(96)	59	(63)	66	(77)
N	9,172	(8,287)	854	(780)	2,273	(2,103)	3,162	(2,716)

[1]Percentage of students taking university-preparation courses in all three subjects.
[2]For each province, the first column shows percentages of the total sample of grade 10 students (i.e., study participants who did not answer the question, or who answered 'another level', are included and counted as *not* being in a university-preparation course). The second column contains percentages based on the smaller sub-sample of 15-year-olds who did identify the specific type of course in which they were enrolled.

These findings are consistent with the observation that mathematics departments in secondary schools tend to favour streaming, while English departments usually prefer more heterogeneous groupings (Loveless, 1999). Wheelock (1992) confirms that in the US math is often the last outpost of rigid tracking. In Canada a provincial teachers' association representative commented that math is the main 'gatekeeping' course for university entrance (personal communication, December 2006).

Provincial differences
The proportion of students with all PSE options open ranged from a high of 87 per cent in Saskatchewan to a low of 59 per cent in Alberta; the figures for British Columbia and

Ontario were 66 and 64 per cent, respectively. As we have already noted, in every case the subject most likely to be associated with restriction of options was math.

These findings are in line with those of other research conducted in 1999 as part of the School Achievement Indicators Program (SAIP) by the Council of Ministers of Education Canada (CMEC). Teachers in different provinces were asked to what extent they agreed or disagreed with the statement 'high school students should be streamed into different programs based on their abilities' (CMEC, 1999: 53). In the four provinces that are the focus of this study, the proportions of teachers agreeing were as follows: Saskatchewan 56 per cent, British Columbia 57 per cent, Alberta 83 per cent, and Ontario 93 per cent. Teacher attitudes recorded around the time of the YITS survey therefore seem consistent with the data on the extent of streaming across provinces.

Provincial government policies also appear to play an important role in promoting certain educational values and practices. For example, a Saskatchewan Education report stated that the province's 'approach to education focuses on inclusion and de-emphasizes streaming' (2000: 76). As evidence, it added that 46 per cent of Saskatchewan schools had only one stream for 16-year-olds in 1999, whereas the Canadian average was 22 per cent. An earlier document (Saskatchewan Education, 1992) began with the assumption that 'there are alternatives to homogeneous grouping practices that do not isolate students and do not foster stereotypes or limit teacher expectations' (1992: 4) and promoted a policy approach that 'empowers the teacher to make adjustments in approved educational programs to accommodate variations in student needs' (1992: 1).

Nevertheless, internal and external pressures may lead to a narrowing of provincial differences in the future. For example, the Saskatchewan Teachers' Federation (STF, 2005) recently invited Saskatchewan Learning to join it in investigating the feasibility of introducing academic, technical, or practical programs for students in grades 11 and 12. Discussion with government representatives suggested that the province might be moving towards a system in which applied and pure math streams would lead to technical institutes and universities, respectively (personal communication, December 2006). At the time of the YITS survey in 2000, Saskatchewan curriculum was not aligned with the Western and Northern Canadian Protocol (WNCP), a plan to build a common curriculum framework for the four western provinces and three territories. It will be interesting to see how implementation of this plan will affect policies and practices related to streaming. For example, WNCP work on math curricula in grades 10 to 12 reportedly recommends three streams that are related to students' destinations or pathways, similar to the Ontario approach (ibid.).

Policies regarding evaluation of high-school students may also influence streaming practices. In Alberta, for example, students in grade 12 courses leading to a high-school diploma[5] write provincial exams that are worth half of their final grade. By contrast, final grades for more than three-quarters of Saskatchewan students are determined by classroom teachers. For the remaining quarter of students, grades are determined as in Alberta (50 per cent teacher, 50 per cent provincial exam). The difference may have something to do with the fact that in Saskatchewan provincial exams are not differentiated by course stream as they are in Alberta. Further research is needed to account for provincial differences in the use of streaming, but we may speculate that the pressure imposed on schools to 'continuously improve' their results may be a contributing factor.

Gender

Table 7.2 highlights gender differences in streaming. We see that the proportion of students with open PSE options (all three subjects) is slightly higher for females than for males in Ontario, Saskatchewan, and Alberta, while this pattern is reversed in British Columbia. But it is important to note that the gender differences are not very large. This finding is supported by other international and national data, suggesting that gender differences in educational attainment have decreased significantly in recent decades (Shavit and Blossfield, 1993; Davies and Guppy, 2006). However, we note that YITS data are limited to academic course streams. If we also considered practical arts options and apprenticeship programs, we would see more of a gender divide in enrolments (Taylor, 2007). Further, program enrolments in post-secondary institutions reveal distinct differences in the 'pathways' followed by males and females (Statistics Canada, 2003).

Table 7.2   Percentages of grade 10 students with PSE options open (all three subjects)[1] by gender by province

Gender	Ontario	Saskatchewan	Alberta	British Columbia
Female	67	90	61	65
Male	60	85	56	67
Total	64	87	59	66

[1]For each province, percentages are based on the total sample of grade 10 students (i.e., study participants who did not answer the question are included and counted as not being in a university-preparation course).

Parents' education and income

Previous research showing strong links between students' course levels and their parents' education are clearly confirmed in our analysis of YITS data. We distinguished between two groups of 15-year-olds: those from families in which neither parent had acquired a university degree and those from families in which one or both parents had completed university. Table 7.3 shows that, in each of the four provinces, young people from university-educated families were much more likely to have open PSE options. In Ontario, four out of five (81 per cent) of the 15-year-olds with at least one university-educated parent were in university-targeted math, science, and English courses, compared to only 57 per cent of those from families in which neither parent had a degree. Table 7.4 tells a similar story about the reproduction of educational inequality across generations. While the differences are not as pronounced as those shown in

Table 7.3, we can still see that in all four provinces young people from more affluent families are more likely to be enrolled in grade 10 courses that will keep their post-secondary options open.

As we noted earlier, previous research has found a strong connection between course stream and parental education (Yau et al., 1993; Curtis et al., 1992; Oakes, 2005). Although course streams have become more difficult to identify, and there is some evidence that educational selection is moving to a later stage,[6] it appears that this relationship continues to hold. This confirms the findings of other studies that even

Table 7.3   Percentages of grade 10 students with PSE options open (all three subjects)[1] by parents' education by province

Parents' Education[2]	Ontario	Saskatchewan	Alberta	British Columbia
No degrees	57	86	52	61
One or two degrees	81	93	79	77
Total	64	87	59	66

[1]For each province, percentages are based on the total sample of grade 10 students (i.e., study participants who did not answer the question are included and counted as not being in a university-preparation course).
[2]Neither parent has a university degree versus one or both parents have a degree.

Table 7.4   Percentages of grade 10 students with PSE options open (all three subjects)[1] by family income by province

Family Income	Ontario	Saskatchewan	Alberta	British Columbia
<$30,000	49	83	50	59
$30,000–$44,999	52	`83	52	60
$45,000–$59,999	59	88	53	60
$60,000–$74,999	65	93	56	70
$75,000–$89,999	70	89	62	69
$90,000+	73	89	68	73
Total	64	87	59	66

[1]For each province, percentages are based on the total sample of grade 10 students (i.e., study participants who did not answer the question are included and counted as not being in a university-preparation course).

though the average level of educational attainment has risen in North America, inequality of educational opportunity between different social strata persists (Shavit and Blossfield, 1993).

Visible minority, immigrant, and first language

Previous research has suggested that students from certain visible minority groups, along with those for whom English is a second language, are disproportionately placed in streams that restrict PSE options (Curtis et al., 1992; Oakes, 2005). In fact, however, our YITS findings (see Table 7.5) show that visible minority and immigrant students are more likely than non-visible-minority and Canadian-born students to have open PSE options. Equally surprising, but in line with the immigrant and visible minority status results, is the finding that the proportion of students taking courses leading to more open PSE options is lower among those whose first language is English (or French) than among those whose first language is not English. These differences are not nearly as pronounced as those observed for parents' education and income.

Table 7.5   Percentages of grade 10 students with PSE options open (all three subjects)[1] by visible minority status, immigrant status, and first language by province

	Ontario	Saskatchewan	Alberta	British Columbia
Visible Minority				
Yes	69	—[2]	69	71
No	62	88	57	64
Immigrant Parent				
Yes	68	85	62	70
No	62	88	58	64
First Language				
English/French	62	87	58	65
Other language	70	—[2]	68	70
Total	64	87	59	66

[1]For each province, percentages are based on the total sample of grade 10 students (i.e., study participants who did not answer the question are included and counted as not being in a university-preparation course).
[2]Small sub-samples make estimates unreliable.

These findings run counter to those of writers who have documented the disadvantages faced by particular groups within the school system (for research on English-language learners, see Derwing, DeCorby, Ichikawa, and Jamieson, 1999; Watt and

Roessingh, 2001). A limitation of the YITS survey is that it does not indicate when students whose first language is not English entered the Canadian school system, whether they were in English Language Learner (ELL) programs, and for how long. We are also unable to disaggregate results to explore ethnic/racialized group differences (e.g., between black and Asian students, between Aboriginal and white students). Other writers suggest that these differences are important; see Dei, Mazucca, McIsaac, and Zine (1997), on black youth, and Castellano, Davis, and Lahache (2000) on Aboriginal youth.

However, the YITS findings are supported by a US study (Lucas and Gamoran, 2002) that looked at course-based indicators of tracking in 1990 and found no net racial differences in the likelihood of students' being assigned to college-track courses. More specifically, they report that Hispanics and blacks were as likely as whites to be on the college track once other covariates (e.g., social class and prior achievement) were controlled for. However, Asians were more likely to enter the college preparation track than whites. Our findings regarding stream placement of visible minority immigrant youth are also consistent with those of a study, based on the same YITS data, in which 77 per cent of those students expressed university aspirations, as compared to just 60 per cent of Canadian-born non-visible minority youth (Krahn and Taylor, 2005).

School size and school type

Table 7.6 compares patterns of streaming in schools of different sizes and types. One might expect to find a correlation between the number of course streams available and the size of the school, with the smallest high schools (generally in rural areas) offering the fewest choices. For example, a 1980 Ontario study found that three-quarters of students in large urban centres were in academic programs, compared to just half of rural students (Anisef, Paasche, and Turrittin, 1980). Our analysis of the YITS data suggests a similar pattern, at least in some provinces. Only 45 per cent of 15-year-olds in the smallest Ontario schools had all their PSE options open, compared to 66 per cent in the province's largest schools. A similar pattern can be seen in BC, although the difference between the smallest schools and the others is not as large. This effect was not apparent in either Alberta or Saskatchewan, however.[7]

YITS questionnaires for school administrators asked if the school was non-sectarian (no religious affiliation) or sectarian/separate (including Catholic and private religious schools). When we link these school-level data with student data (see bottom panel of Table 7.6), we find that a somewhat higher proportion of students in sectarian/separate schools have all PSE options open. Although this variable has not been a focus of previous Canadian research, a recent US study found a similar pattern, with Catholic schools tending to take a more inclusive approach to ability grouping (Hallinan and Ellison, 2006). Further research on sectarian/non-sectarian differences in the Canadian context is needed, however, since Catholic schools in the US are private.

Net impact of all predictor variables

As some of our discussion above has suggested, the various factors influencing the extent of streaming among grade 10 students in these four provinces are inter-related. For example, university-educated parents also tend to have higher incomes than parents without degrees. For this reason we will conclude our discussion of YITS

Table 7.6   Percentages of grade 10 students with PSE options open (all three subjects)[1] by school size and school type by province

	Ontario	Saskatchewan	Alberta	British Columbia
No. of students in school				
≤ 400	45	89	62	58
401–800	55	85	59	64
801–1,200	65	88	53	68
1,201–1,600	68	86	61	65
1,601 +	66	88	58	69
School Type				
Non-sectarian	61	87	57	66
Sectarian/separate	68	89	67	69
Total	64	87	59	66

[1]For each province, percentages are based on the total sample of grade 10 students (i.e., study participants who did not answer the question are included and counted as not being in a university-preparation course).

findings with a multivariate analysis of the determinants of open PSE options. Table 7.7 displays a logistic regression equation, with 11 predictor variables, that essentially reinforces the tentative conclusions we have drawn above.

Taking the effects of the other predictor variables into account, we find that province of residence has the strongest impact on the chance that a 15-year-old will have all PSE options open in grade 10. Young people living in Saskatchewan are much more likely than their peers in Ontario, British Columbia, and Alberta to have wide-open PSE options. When we control for province of residence and other variables in this equation, the next strongest effect is associated with parental education. The chance of having all PSE options open is two and one-half times higher for 15-year-olds who have at least one university-educated parent than it is for those whose parents did not complete university. Family income also has a statistically significant net effect.

Young women are more likely than young men to have open PSE options, other things being equal. The same is true of visible minority immigrant youth,[8] young people attending sectarian schools, and those enrolled in larger schools (which essentially explains away the small community size finding). But compared to the effects of family background (parents' education and income) these effects are not as strong.

Table 7.7   Logistic regression of PSE options open (all three subjects)[1] on selected predictor variables

Predictor Variable	Odds Ratio	(P)
British Columbia[2]	0.215	.000
Alberta[2]	0.156	.000
Ontario[2]	0.176	.000
Gender (female = 1)	1.308	.000
Visible minority immigrant (yes = 1)	1.186	.008
Parents university educated (yes = 1)	2.516	.000
Family income ($60,000 + = 1)	1.567	.000
First language (English = 1)	0.834	.004
School type (sectarian = 1)	1.264	.000
School size (800 + = 1)	1.224	.000
Community size (100,000 + = 1)	1.061	.144
Nagelkirche R^2 = 0.109		

[1]Binary variable (all three PSE options open = 1); N = 9,882.
[2]Saskatchewan is the reference category.

Discussion

This study contributes several important insights to ongoing debates about course streaming in Canada. Not only is much of the previous Canadian research dated, but many of the studies have been small in scale and have not addressed provincial differences. For all its limitations, the YITS database has great value for examining course streaming in the four provinces highlighted in this chapter. An interesting picture of high-school streams emerges from our analysis.

First, our finding that students' academic placement is strongly related to parents' education and family income makes it clear that social inequality in education persists. Partly because of this persistent inequality, there is a continuing need to debate policies and practices related to streaming.

Second, there are sizeable provincial differences in the extent to which students are streamed into non-university pathways. A grade 10 student in Saskatchewan is much more likely to have all his or her university options open than a student in British Columbia, Ontario, or Alberta. Interestingly, Saskatchewan's high-school non-completion rate of 7 per cent by the age of 20 is reported to be the lowest in Canada (Statistics Canada, 2002). The rates for other provinces examined in this study were 10 per cent for Ontario, and 13 per cent for both British Columbia and Alberta. In conjunction with streaming data, these findings raise important questions about how educational policies and practices combine to affect students' educational attainment.

Third, moving beyond the statistical data, conversations with educational representatives across Canada suggest that there may be increasing pressures on provinces to engage in streaming. Increasing student diversity and shrinking resources in classrooms tend to increase teacher support for streaming. Increasing emphasis on performance on international and national standardized tests, along with interprovincial projects to harmonize curriculum, may also serve to promote streaming as administrators and educators seek ways to improve their results.

When compared to findings of previous studies of streaming, our study indicates that there have been changes in high-school streaming patterns and processes. Educational selection does appear to be moving from the secondary to the post-secondary level (Davies and Guppy, 2006). For example, Alberta is one of the only provinces that offers a high-school certification that will not lead to post-secondary education. Further, new curriculum streams are being promoted as 'different but equal'. At the same time, universities, and to some extent colleges, reportedly use certain courses (e.g., pure math) as 'gatekeeper' courses. Demand for university places continues to outstrip supply and therefore higher-education providers seek ways to differentiate among students. This process involves the designation of required courses (e.g., pure as opposed to applied math), comparison of student grades (preferably linked to standardized tests), and the privileging of elite high-school courses and programs like Advanced Placement and International Baccalaureate.

Even as secondary schooling becomes less stratified, then, stratification continues at the post-secondary level. The topic of post-secondary streaming warrants further research (cf. Tamburino, 2005). In Canada as elsewhere, it seems, educational systems tend to open up 'step-by-step from the bottom up' (Shavit and Blossfield, 1997: 14). In other words, a more open post-secondary system appears to require de-streaming at the secondary level. Longitudinal studies following students from high school to post-secondary destinations would be very valuable.

Other forms of streaming in secondary schools—notably 'vocational' streaming—also raise questions. Educational policy-makers are increasingly interested in giving high-school students the opportunity to explore and prepare for various careers through co-operative education and high-school apprenticeship programs. At the same time, secondary schools today offer fewer traditional 'vocational' courses than they did in the past, and more courses related to professions such as computer science or psychology. Again, post-secondary institutions as well as high-school staff play an important role in determining how these courses are valued and the extent of mobility across streams. Although Canada does not have the kind of rigid vocational streaming observed in countries like Germany, legitimate questions can be asked about whether increased policy interest in vocational education may enable the educational system 'to absorb disadvantaged groups at the secondary level without disturbing the basic social interests of advantaged groups at higher levels in the school system' (Shavit and Blossfield, 1997: 14). More research into non-academic course streaming and its relationship to academic course streaming is needed to answer this question.

While our analysis of the YITS data suggested strong links between socio-economic status and course stream, the influence of visible minority status, immigrant status, and first language appears to be less strong. Students from these groups were somewhat more, rather than less, likely to have all PSE options open, in contrast to earlier findings (Curtis et al., 1992). But we need to be careful in our interpretation since differences between student groups (e.g., black, Asian, Aboriginal) warrant further attention. The influence of language also requires further investigation. For example, the age at which a student is integrated into an English-language school would be of critical importance, as well as the levels of ELL resources and support available.

In sum, the YITS data related to academic course streaming provide valuable information. Our study of those data suggests that the most important influences on student placement are provincial high-school program/policy and parents' socio-economic status. Further, de-stratification within secondary schools appears to be a slow process that is highly dependent on expanding access to higher education.

Appendix A: Coding Course Levels

Grade 10 mathematics, science, and English courses offered in the four provinces in 2000 were categorized as:

1 = open post-secondary options (including university)

2 = more restricted post-secondary options

	Ontario	Saskatchewan	Alberta	British Columbia
1	Academic	Regular, Advanced	10/20/30, 10 Pure (Math)	Academic, International Baccalaureate/ Advanced Placement, Communications (English)
2	Applied	Modified, Alternative	10 Applied (Math), 13/23/33 (English), 14/24 (Math, Science), 16/26 (IOP)	Applied (Math, Science), Introductory (Math), A Stream (Math), General (Science)

Notes

The *Youth in Transition Survey* (YITS) data analyzed in this chapter were collected by Statistics Canada and accessed via the University of Alberta Research Data Centre (RDC). The opinions expressed are those of the authors, not of Statistics Canada. We gratefully acknowledge the research assistance provided by Julie Hudson, Diane Wishart, and Polly Madsen. We are also grateful to representatives from provincial education ministries, teachers' federations, and the Council of Ministers of Education for their cooperation in this research.

1. All the results reported in this chapter are based on weighted sample analyses. Approximately 30,000 teenagers completed the YITS/PISA questionnaires; about 26,000 parents took part in the telephone survey. Response rates were very high in all components of this study: 94 per cent for schools; 87 per cent for students; 91 per cent for parents.
2. Lucas and Gamoran (2002) observed some differences when they compared student-reported track indicators and data from schools about the courses in which the students were enrolled. They concluded that student self-reports may be more accurate as indicators of social-psychological aspects of tracking while course-based indicators may measure the structure more precisely. But even course-based indicators can be problematic. For example, if students are taking courses at different levels, it may be more difficult to develop an overall measure of their school placement.
3. In some cases it was not completely clear whether taking a particular level of course would restrict students' PSE options. For example, Charlton (1999) notes that 'applied' and 'academic' courses in Ontario are equally challenging and are intended to equip a student at the end of grade 10 for any of the 'destination' streams of grades 11 and 12. However, Pinto (2006) writes that 'though there is no explicit link articulated in the policy between streaming by learning styles in grades 9/10 and destination-based streaming in grades 11/12, in practice such a connection exists. Many courses in grades 11/12 require certain prerequisites, creating a continuum between the two streaming systems' (81). Similarly, in Alberta the 'applied math course' was intended to lead to university, but in practice universities have not accepted this course. Interestingly, the Council of Ministers of Education Canada (2004) transfer guide states: 'For maximum flexibility for admission to the university sector, students taking Applied Mathematics [10, 20, 30] should also include a second language (e.g., European, Asian, Aboriginal languages, or either English or French)'. For this reason, a provincial teachers' association representative suggested that taking an applied math course may restrict students' post-secondary options (Personal communication, May 2006).
4. For each province, the first column contains percentages of the *total* sample of grade 10 students. In other words, study participants who did not answer the question, or who answered 'another level' (between 4 and 7 per cent chose this response) are included and counted as *not* being in a university-preparation course. The second column contains percentages based on the smaller sub-sample of 15-year-olds who did identify the specific type of course in which they were enrolled.
5. Alberta students may enrol in a stream of courses leading to a certificate of achievement, which requires 80 credits instead of the 100 required for a high-school diploma.
6. The clearest evidence that educational selection is occurring later is the decline over time across provinces in the number of course streams that do not lead to college or university. The division seems to be stronger between college and university streams than between work-destined and post-secondary streams. We can assume that this is largely related to increasing demand for higher education. YITS data suggest that 61 per cent of 15-year-olds

and 64 per cent of their parents expect the student to acquire one or more university degrees (Krahn and Taylor, 2005).

7. We also checked to see if community size affected the likelihood of streaming. We found a slightly higher percentage of grade 10 students in the very largest communities (Toronto and Vancouver) had all their post-secondary options open, based on their math, science, and English courses. However, the effect was quite weak and, as Table 7.7 demonstrates, not statistically significant when school size and other predictor variables are controlled for.

8. In Table 7.5 we examined separately the effects of immigrant status and visible minority status. Since we observed a very similar pattern (not surprisingly, since many immigrant youth are from visible minority backgrounds), we combined the two measures for the multivariate analysis. Table 7.5 compares young people who are *both* immigrants and from visible minority backgrounds with all other young people.

Glossary

ability grouping: The placing of students in homogeneous groups based on perceived academic ability.

cultural reproduction: The idea that class culture can serve to perpetuate inequality. For example, school practices that reward familiarity with middle-class culture will help to reproduce students' class locations. The fact that different groups have access to different types of cultural capital reinforces their differential status. Bourdieu and Passeron's (1990) classic text *Reproduction in Education, Society and Culture* exemplifies this theoretical approach.

educational selection: See stratification.

stratification: The hierarchical ranking of students according to ability. Streaming/tracking is a traditional form of educational stratification in high schools.

streaming/tracking: The practice of organizing students in distinct groups for subjects studied according to particular measures of ability. Each stream receives the type of instruction deemed appropriate to the students' ability and the school's (spoken or unspoken) assessment of their future prospects.

Study Questions

1. Why is it important to examine streaming policies? What is your personal position on this practice?
2. Do you think streaming matters as much today as it did when your parents were young?
3. What are the key arguments for and against different forms of streaming?
4. What are the most interesting provincial differences in the YITS findings and what might explain them?
5. What could families and schools do to counter the negative effects of streaming?

Recommended Readings

Curtis, B., D. Livingstone, and H. Smaller. 1992. *Stacking the Deck: The Streaming of Working-Class Kids in Ontario Schools*. Toronto: Our Schools/Our Selves.

Loveless, T. 1999. *The Tracking Wars*. Washington, DC: Brookings Institution Press.

Oakes, J. 2005. *Keeping Track: How Schools Structure Inequality*. New Haven: Yale University Press.

Recommended Websites

Articles on ability grouping: http://ericae.net/edo/ED290542.htm

Bibliography of materials related to ability grouping: http://www.indiana.edu/~reading/ieo/bibs/ability.html

The US publication *Rethinking Schools*: http://www.rethinkingschools.org/archive/19_04/res2194.shtml

UK National Literacy Trust site: http://www.literacytrust.org.uk/Research/stream.html

Ministry of Education websites in Canada: http://www.cmec.ca/educmin.en.stm

References

Alberta Learning. 2001. *Removing Barriers to High School Completion: Final Report*. Prepared by System Improvement and Reporting, Edmonton. September.

Anisef, P., J. Paasche, A. Turrittin. 1980. *Is the Die Cast? Educational Achievements and Work Destinations of Ontario Youth*. Toronto: Ministry of Colleges and Universities.

Bourdieu, P., and J.C. Passeron. 1990. *Reproduction in Education, Society and Culture*, 2nd edn, trans. R. Nice. London: Sage.

Castellano, M., L. Davis, and L. Lahache. 2000. *Aboriginal Education: Fulfilling the Promise*. Vancouver: University of British Columbia Press.

Charlton, J. 1999. 'Leadership Challenges of Secondary School Reform', *Orbit* 30, 1: 30.

Council of Ministers of Education Canada (CMEC). 1999. *Science Learning: The Canadian Context*. Available at: www.cmec.ca. Accessed January 2007.

————. 2004. *Secondary Education in Canada: A Student Transfer Guide, 9th edition, 2004–05*. Available at: www.cmec.ca/tguide/2004/index.en.html. Accessed December 2006.

Curtis, B., D. Livingstone, and H. Smaller. 1992. *Stacking the Deck: The Streaming of Working-Class Kids in Ontario Schools*. Toronto: Our Schools/Our Selves.

Davies, S., and N. Guppy. 2006. *The Schooled Society*. Don Mills, ON: Oxford University Press.

Dei, G., J. Mazucca, E. McIsaac, and J. Zine. 1997. *Reconstructing 'Drop-Out': A Critical Ethnography of the Dynamics of Black Students' Disengagement from School*. Toronto: University of Toronto Press.

Derwing, T., E. DeCorby, J. Ichikawa, and K. Jamieson. 1999. 'Some Factors that Affect the Success of ESL High School Students', *Canadian Modern Language Review* 55, 4: 532–47.

Dewey, J., and D. Snedden. 1977. 'Two Communications: David Snedden and John Dewey', *Curriculum Inquiry* 7, 1: 33–60.

Gaskell, J. 1991. 'Education as Preparation for Work in Canada: Structure, Policy, and Student Response', in D. Ashton and G. Lowe, eds, *Making Their Way: Education, Training and the Labour Market in Canada and Britain*. Buckingham: Open University Press, 61–84.

Gidney, R. 1999. *From Hope to Harris: The Reshaping of Ontario's Schools*. Toronto: University of Toronto Press.

Hallinan, M., and B. Ellison. 2006. 'The Practice of Ability Grouping: Sector Differences in Implementation', in M. Hallinan, ed., *School Sector and Student Outcomes*. Notre Dame: University of Notre Dame Press, 125–52.

Ireson, J., and S. Hallam. 2001. *Ability Grouping in Education*. London: Sage.

Karp, E. 1988. *The Drop-Out Phenomenon in Ontario Schools*. Prepared for the Ministry of Education, Toronto, Ontario.

King, A., W. Warren, J. Boyer, and P. Chin. 2005. *Double Cohort Study: Phase 4 Report*. Prepared for the Ontario Ministry of Education by Social Program Evaluation Group, Queen's University, Kingston, Ontario.

Krahn, H., and A. Taylor. 2005. 'Resilient Teenagers: Explaining the High Educational Aspirations of Visible Minority Immigrant Youth in Canada', *Journal of International Migration and Integration* 6, 3/4: 405–34.

Loveless, T. 1999. *The Tracking Wars*. Washington, DC: Brookings Institution Press.

Lucas, S.R. 1999. *Tracking Inequality: Stratification and Mobility in American High Schools*. New York: Teachers College Press.

———, and A. Gamoran. 2002. 'Tracking and the achievement gap', in J. Chubb and T. Loveless, eds, *Bridging the Achievement Gap*. Washington, DC: Brookings Institution Press, 171–98.

Oakes, J. 2005. *Keeping Track: How Schools Structure Inequality*. New Haven: Yale University Press.

Ontario Secondary School Teachers' Federation. 2000. *Impact 2000: Report of the Impact of Government Reforms on Education*. Toronto: OSSTF.

Osborne, K. 1999. *Education: A Guide to the Canadian School Debate—Or Who Wants What and Why?* Toronto: Penguin.

Pinto, L. 2006. 'The Streaming of Working Class and Minority Students in Ontario', *Our Schools/Our Selves* 15, 2: 79–89.

Radwanski, G. 1987. *Ontario Study of the Relevance of Education and the Issue of Dropouts*. Prepared for Ministry of Education, Toronto, Ontario.

Robertson, C., B. Cowell, and J. Olson. 1998. 'A Case Study of Integration and Destreaming, Teachers and Students in an Ontario Secondary School Respond', *Journal of Curriculum Studies* 30, 6: 691–717.

Ross, J.A., S. McKeiver, and A. Hogaboam-Grey. 1997. 'Fluctuations in Teacher Efficacy during Implementation of Destreaming', *Canadian Journal of Education* 22, 3: 283.

Saskatchewan Education. 1992. 'The Adaptive Dimension in Core Curriculum'. Available at: www.sasked.gov.sk.ca. Accessed January 2007.

———. 2000. 'Saskatchewan Education Indicators: Kindergarten to Grade 12'. Available at: www.sasked.gov.sk.ca. Accessed January 2007.

Saskatchewan Teachers' Federation (STF). 2005. 'Report to Councilors on Disposition of Council Resolutions'. Available from STF, Saskatoon, SK.

Shavit, Y., and H. Blossfield. 1993. *Persistent Inequality: Changing Educational Attainment in 13 Countries*. Boulder, CO: Westview Press.

Statistics Canada. 2002. 'Youth in Transition Survey, 2000', *The Daily*. 23 January 2002. Available at: www.statcan.ca. Accessed January 2007.

———. 2003. 'University Enrolment by Field of Study', *The Daily*. 31 March 2003. Available at www.statcan.ca. Accessed January 2007.

Tamburino, A. 2005. 'Different but Equal? Post Secondary Streaming in Ontario: A Comparison of the Labour Market Outcomes of College and University Students'. Paper presented at The Future of Lifelong Learning and Work conference, OISE/UT, June.

Taylor, A. 2007. *Pathways for Youth to the Labour Market: An Overview of High School Initiatives*. Prepared for Canadian Policy Research Networks. Ottawa: Ontario.

Watt, D., and H. Roessingh. 2001. 'The Dynamics of ESL Dropout: Plus ça change . . .', *Canadian Modern Language Review* 58, 2: 203–22.

Wheelock, A. 1992. *Crossing the Tracks: How 'Untracking' Can Save America's Schools*. New York: The New Press.

Whipple, G.M., ed. 1936. *The 35th Yearbook of the National Society for the Study of Education. Part 1: The Grouping of Pupils*. Bloomington, IL: Public School Publishing Company.

Yau, M., M. Cheng, and S. Ziegler. 1993. 'The 1991 Every Secondary Student Survey, Part III: Program Level and Student Achievement'. Toronto: Toronto District School Board.

CHAPTER 8

School Rules, Bodily Discipline, Embodied Resistance

Rebecca Raby

Introduction

Of all the ways in which schools regulate students' bodies, one of the most direct is through school rules. Most North American secondary schools require attendance. Students must follow timetables; they are also told where they may eat and when, where and when they may talk or listen to music, and what they can and cannot wear. In Ontario they are required to stand for the national anthem, and in some metropolitan schools they must wear identity tags. Punishment for breaking the rules may take the form of detention or suspension. These are just some of the ways in which schools use rules to govern students' bodies.

In this chapter I will explore three specific areas of rule-based bodily discipline: dress, 'public displays of affection' (PDAs), and bodily needs. I will examine a selection of school rules and responses to them gathered through nine focus groups with secondary students in southern Ontario. Throughout this analysis, I will refer to the classic work of Michel Foucault and the more recent scholarship of Nancy Lesko to consider how schools attempt to discipline 'unruly' adolescent bodies and how students both reproduce and resist such efforts to contain them. The role of the body in such **resistance** will also be briefly considered in light of the notion of desire described by Gilles Deleuze and Felix Guattari. Finally, bodies are not all treated in the same way within such disciplinary environments as the school—the rules and the manner of their enforcement serve to normalize certain bodies and to marginalize others.

Theoretical Background

Michel Foucault's writings cover a broad range of topics related to the exercise of power. Foucault understood power not as a force held by some over others but rather as something that is enacted by all of us—in the language we use, for example, and in the ways we discipline ourselves and others. Through such processes, power produces knowledge, or the truths we believe about the world, and governs our behaviour. He was particularly interested in the way people internalize institutional processes such as observation, evaluation, management, and normalization and use them to regulate themselves (Foucault, 1977, 1978). In addition, Foucault observed that power is always intertwined with resistance to these processes. On these points, the high-school environment offers many examples.

When we are discussing the discipline of the body in the context of secondary school, we are talking about the bodies of young people, specifically adolescents. The American educational theorist Nancy Lesko draws on Foucault to argue that one of the most prominent **discourses** regarding adolescence centres on the idea that teenagers 'are controlled by their hormones and, therefore, dangerously out of control' (1996a: 150). Hence adolescence is assumed to be inevitably fraught with crisis. Like the historic discourse depicting women as unpredictable and potentially uncontrollable as a result of the vagaries of their reproductive systems, such discourses effectively pathologize bodily change and allow the more 'rational' (adult) subject to know, judge, and attempt to control those who are 'out of control' (adolescents). Some social theorists, such as Norbert Elias, argue that growing up requires that young people 'develop civilized bodies and become full and acceptable members of society' (Shilling, 1993) through exposure to adult forces of socialization such as school rules. Others (e.g., Simpson, 2000) caution that we must ask who determines what is acceptable and whose behaviour is judged problematic, and with what effects.

Lesko problematizes the idea that hormones explain adolescents' behaviour. Our understandings of the body are as much cultural and political as they are biological (Burr, 1995). It is only over the last century and a half that adolescence has come to be considered a naturally fraught stage in the life course (Lesko, 1996b), and social assumptions regarding adolescents can vary widely, depending on circumstances. For example, in periods of high demand for labour, such as during the Second World War, young people have been considered competent, capable, and independent; but in periods of low demand (e.g., when unemployment is high) they have been seen as dependent, irresponsible, and in need of extensive training before being entrusted with an adult job (Finn, 2001). What these examples underscore is that our perceptions of young people's bodies and behaviours depend on the prevailing social and economic conditions, which are often contradictory. According to the currently dominant discourses, adolescents are unstable and prone to social problems; yet they are also valued both as consumers and as future adults (Raby, 2002). It is up to the school both to control them and to teach them the self-discipline required if they are to become 'civilized' adults in the future. Present obedience and future self-discipline are the contradictory premises on which most school rules are based (Lewis, 1999; Raby, 2005).

School rules and their application also serve to establish what is considered 'normal'. For example, Pierre Bourdieu (1984) suggests that the school is not 'neutral' in its treatment of students but rather rewards those with what he calls '**cultural capital**': the values, skills, and dispositions deemed valuable by the dominant (middle) class. Students who are familiar and comfortable with the society's dominant values as reflected in school rules usually know how to negotiate them (Nelson, 1996). Those who, for one reason or another, do not follow the rules may be 'deemed deficient in cultural capital' and their bodies regulated in order 'to reform these perceived deficiencies' (Morris, 2005). Similarly, various researchers have found that rules are more likely to be enforced on racialized youth (Ferguson et al., 2005; MacDonell and Martin, 1986; Ruck and Wortley, 2002); others, that enforcement is gendered (Pomerantz, 2007; Robinson, 1992). According to Morris enforcement varies depending on the student's specific constellation of gender, race, and class (Morris, 2005).

How do young people respond to schools' efforts to discipline their bodies? While students frequently accept and even embrace school rules (Knesting and Waldron, 2006; Raby and Domitrek, 2007), they also challenge or resist them (Simpson, 2000; Vavrus and Cole, 2002). Obviously, the most direct way of challenging a school rule is by breaking it—a response that is often considered a sign of deviance. For some researchers, however, rule-breaking represents resistance to school-based inequalities (Willis, 1977).

Rule-breaking frequently involves strategic deployment of the body. In her ethnography of primary and secondary schools in Britain, Brenda Simpson found that children often invoked 'the fragility, sickness or "wild nature" of [their] bodies . . . , either formally or informally, to circumvent school rules' (2000: 71), producing sick notes in order to facilitate visits to the washroom or get around requirements regarding physical education. The body was also used in smaller acts of defiance: among boys, resistance was expressed primarily through behaviour such as spitting, making faces, drumming their fingers on the table, or breaking wind, while among girls resistance most often took the form of challenges to school dress codes. Simpson argues that because efforts to control and discipline are focused on students' bodies, it is through their bodies that students will resist those efforts.

We have already noted that Foucault considered power and resistance to be inseparable. As Leslie Thiele argues, the struggle between the two was central to Foucault's thought: 'it is the human condition to exist within a system of power; it is the human potential to incessantly resist its reach, relocate its boundaries, and challenge its authority' (Thiele, 1990: 918). This struggle is about ensuring the *opportunity* to struggle, to change social conditions, and to make self-creation possible. Butz and Ripmeester (1999) note that resistance is sometimes directly oppositional as some rule-breaking might suggest, and sometimes partial or 'off-kilter'. Off-kilter resistance is more subtle and indirect, often taking the form of alternative modes of thinking that complicate dominant discourses. Among students, examples of off-kilter resistance might include citing the authority of the parent to counter that of the teacher, challenging a teacher in the neutral setting of the hallway rather than the classroom, or temporarily going along with a teacher's demands in one matter in order to win greater freedom in another. According to Butz and Ripmeester (1999), off-kilter resistance is flexible, tentative, temporary (but also ongoing), and cunning; successful practitioners both work with and circumvent current power relations. Although some (e.g., Lash, 1991) have argued that Foucault's framework casts bodies as primarily passive, resistance—whether direct, indirect, or partial—offers another lens through which to interpret students' bodily engagement with their school rules.

Finally, we can also examine the role of the body in processes of resistance quite differently through the work of Deleuze and Guattari (1983). While Foucault understood our desires as being *produced* through power relations, Deleuze and Guattari consider desire as its own force, or 'will to power' (Lash, 1991). Such desire can be seen as fuelling **'lines of flight'**, or disruptions to the categories and binaries that attempt to contain social life, ultimately in the interests of the capitalist state (Deleuze and Guattari, 1983). Here desire is a force in its own right, expressed through the body (Fleming, 2002; Lash, 1991). In this case, school rules can be understood as institutional efforts to contain young people's expressions of bodily desire.

Data Collection

The textual data reported in this chapter were collected in 2003 in Ontario, where a controversial province-wide Code of Conduct (2001) included a series of automatic consequences for certain rule infractions.[1] In addition, school boards have codes of conduct that reflect the provincial Code and establish more local parameters. Within the region under study, the school board has its own code of conduct and requires that each school have its own code. Codes at all three levels are developed by administrators and teachers, with representation from parents and students. In all, codes of conduct cover a wide range of behaviours and often list the consequences of rule infractions. Although some codes include explanations for each rule, in general the rules are presented as a series of 'no's.

The region under study consists of several small cities interspersed with farmland, and its main industries are agriculture, manufacturing, tourism, and commercial services. Residents are predominantly Canadian-born; the largest non-Anglo ethnic groups are German, Italian, and French Canadian (Canada, 2006). All but one of the region's 22 public, non-Catholic, English-language secondary schools are represented in this textual study. Their codes of conduct—provided by the school board as per the Access to Information Act—differ in length, completeness, and style of presentation. However, three schools in the region do have the same dress and discipline codes, and overall the codes varied little from school to school.

The 21 codes of conduct were read through several times, both by me and by a research assistant, in search of recurring patterns in the way the rules were presented and, when relevant, how they were justified. Codes were then formally charted to highlight the prominence of certain rules and the relative rarity of others across schools. All codes were read through a final time in order to identify any inconsistent cases that had been overlooked in the original searches for themes.

In addition, nine focus groups were conducted with public secondary students in this region over the summers of 2004 and 2005: six of them were organized through non-school organizations and clubs and three through informal contacts. In all cases, the intent was to access a variety of young people outside the school environment. Students were generally between the ages of 14 and 18[2] and represented a wide range of social groups (see Appendix A on page 138). Because all the participants in each group were acquainted with one another, the chances were good that the groups would reflect the way meaning is made among peers. In some groups one or two participants tended to dominate the discussion; however, short questionnaires distributed at the end of each session, asking for additional feedback, gave other students a chance to express their views. Participants were offered refreshments and a $10 honorarium. They were also given the option of choosing their own pseudonyms.

Each session was tape-recorded and roughly transcribed on-site, then more thoroughly transcribed later. All transcripts were then coded twice, by me and by a research assistant. Working independently, we each identified a number of themes that were eventually organized into broader categories, three of which are discussed here.

Codes of Conduct

Dress codes

Dress codes are the most obvious example of rules focused on the body. Although one school in the study uses school uniforms, this discussion will concentrate on general (non-uniform) dress codes. Among the requirements of these codes were the following: no gang-related clothing; no ripped or torn clothing; no winter jackets, non-religious headgear, or hoods (some schools allow hats, but not in assemblies or during the national anthem); no beachwear or other distracting clothing; no clothing promoting hatred or advertising tobacco, alcohol, or drugs; and no jewelry such as spiked bracelets, dog collars, or heavy chains that could be used as weapons. When explanations for these rules are given, they tend to emphasize safety, respect for others, and respect for self (for a more detailed discussion of self-respect, see Raby, 2005). Although disputes over these matters can take up significant school time, administrators often consider dress code compliance to be an important symbol of order and discipline (Morris, 2005; Robinson, 1992), as well as good preparation for future success. In the focus groups, participants objected to various aspects of their schools' dress codes, but opposition was by no means consistent; discussions tended to centre on three general themes: rights to individual expression, girls' provocative dress, and practical considerations.

Adolescents are not the only people in our culture who see a strong link between presentation of self, particularly in dress and adornment, and self-identity. However, young people may be particularly likely to focus on dress because it is an accessible and easily changeable form of communication. Students who considered dress integral to self-expression often talked about dress codes as infringing on their rights:

Focus Group 8
Ben: Remember, there used to be a guy [who went to] a Catholic school and he dyed his hair like, I dunno, some crazy colour. And they wouldn't let him do exams. . . . he

was gonna take them to court for [that], like under his right as a Catholic person he like was . . .

Fernando: He has the right to go to Catholic school.

Ben: . . . the right to go to a Catholic school, no matter what. And it was a breach of his, you know . . .

Fernando: Expression.

Ben: expression . . .

Focus Group 4

Nicole: . . . if a girl wants to dress like a sleaze then she should be allowed to 'cause that is part of Canada and part of our Charter of Rights and Freedoms.

In these instances students criticized dress codes by appealing to the discourses of individual rights and freedom of expression.

In keeping with the quotation from Group 4, Lesko (1988: 123) observes that the body (and how it is dressed) is central to the construction of identity, particularly for young women; yet dress codes thwart this 'process of bodily identity construction' by emphasizing modesty and attempting to control sexuality. In her study of girls' culture at an American Roman Catholic school, she focused on cultural subgroups to point out how girls within and across these groups would accept some of the school's attempts to control their bodies and would challenge others, particularly through bodily expressions. Lesko (1988) argues that it is primarily through their 'bodily expressions' that young people engage with oppressive structures. Morris (2005) similarly found that students at a middle school in Texas considered their uniform dress code uncomfortable and stifling their creativity. They resisted by wearing their shirts untucked and their pants low—the normative style in the students' own communities, especially for Latino and black youth. Thus by enforcing a strict dress code the school was reinforcing not only the distinction between its own culture and the students' local class and ethnic cultures, but also the students' sense of 'the school as an alien, unfairly punitive institution' (2005: 43), and consequently their resistance.

Dress codes are also designed to contain sexuality (Lesko, 1988; Tait, 2000). In the region under study, the primary target of concern was girls' dress. Many codes explicitly referred to clothing that might be a 'distraction'. The term can be interpreted in a number of ways, but generally seems to refer to girls' sexually provocative dress. Dress codes imply that girls' sexuality manifests itself in 'problematic' bodily display, and that boys' sexuality is such that anything likely to arouse it must be hidden from their gaze. Australian theorist Gordon Tait suggests that the objective behind secondary schools' efforts to discipline young people's sexuality is to 'produce adults who can manage their own sex' (2000: 87)—a comment that is also relevant to the following section on personal displays of affection. Clearly such discipline is also specifically gendered, grounded in heterosexuality, and quite directly addressing the body.

While students were concerned with the details and policing of dress codes, frequently challenged the codes, and occasionally criticized their differential application among girls (noting specifically that bigger and more 'developed' girls were more likely than others to be singled out for regulation), most supported the enforcement of some kind of dress code for girls. In fact, female respondents were occasionally quite vocal about their discomfort at seeing too much of other girls' bodies:

> Nicole (Focus Group 4): This girl that was in my tech class in grade nine. We all sat on stools and she'd sit in front of me and she'd pull her thong out of her pants, so you could see it when she sat down. I'm just like—[*look of surprise*]. And then I'd, like, ask her 'Could you not do that?' and [she'd say] 'Look somewhere else!' It's like 'Where else do you look?' [*chuckles*] There!

> Marjory (Focus Group 5): I like the dress code [rules] a lot 'cause I don't appreciate the girls wearing like . . . [*group agreeing*] the midriff and the thong. I don't like seeing that.

Through such comments, these participants echo the school codes of conduct, sometimes even reproducing the language of self-respect, thus marginalizing girls who cross the fine line between attractive and 'slutty' and positioning themselves as 'acceptable'. These comments also illustrate that school rules can be enlisted in students' processes of regulating themselves and others.

Morris (2005) also notes that the dress regulations are aimed mainly at girls. In addition, however, he found that African-American girls were much more likely than others to be told to act more 'lady-like', even when the others were dressing and behaving in much the same way. Similarly, Morris found that it was black and Latino boys who were disciplined for 'gang wear', even though their gang involvement was no greater than that of other groups. The same pattern emerged in my own study and is examined below under 'other bodies'.

Finally, dress also arose in relation to the question of practicality in that certain rules were seen as problematic because they were considered impractical. For instance, students feel that they should be able to wear jackets when it is cold inside, and tank tops when it is hot. In such instances, it is through recourse to the body that the students challenge the rules, a point that I will develop shortly with regard to more general rules.

Public displays of affection

> Within this disempowering environment of educational imperative and external control, student sexual cultures become imbued with significance as adult-free and education-free zones where students collectively negotiate what is acceptable/desirable and what is 'too much'. (Kehily, 2004: 214)

Some schools also have specific rules against 'public displays of affection' (PDAs): one code, for instance, listed 'embracing, kissing and hugging' as 'not appropriate for school', and another stated that 'no public displays of affection are permitted.' Again the emphasis is on controlling young people's sexuality and ensuring appropriate comportment of bodies within the school. The rules themselves are frequently vague on what they mean by 'public displays of affection', but the focus group participants understood the term to refer to hand-holding and kissing. Many objected to what they considered heavy-handed application of the rule. Yet most also drew a line at excessive displays of affection, such as heavy 'making out' or 'having sex' in the hall.

> Focus Group 4
> Nicole: . . . I dunno, it's a shady one again 'cause, you know, it's fine if, like, you know, somebody wants to give their boyfriend or girlfriend a kiss goodbye. But if you're like deep throat tonguing in the hallway . . .

> Focus Group 2
> Amy: Like, even if you were with your boyfriend walking down the hallway . . .
> Lindsey: Holding hands.
> Amy: Yeah, holding his hand, you get yelled at for it.
> Lindsey: You get like detention.
> RR: And why is that stupid?
> Lindsey: It's retarded [*sic*], 'cause why couldn't I—I can understand [*inaudible*] . . .
> Male voice [*unidentifiable*]: Why can't I hold my girlfriend's hand?
> Amy: [*continues from Lindsey's comment*] . . . kissing and being all over each other in the hallway.
> Lindsey: Like I understand about kissing, making out and groping and stuff like that, but you should be able to hold his hand [*Everyone talking*] . . .
> James: Or give someone a hug if you haven't seen someone in a long time or something.

Once again students experience teachers and administrators as uncomfortable with any bodily display of affection, intent on using this rule to prevent all physical contact. Although the students share the teachers' concern about certain activities, they feel that the rule is too broad and that some PDAs should be acceptable.

Rules that forbid hugging and kissing may indeed reflect middle-class, middle-aged discomfort with the body and visions of teens running out of control, consumed by their sexuality (Tait, 2000). They also may be intended to foster a school environment that is rational, self-disciplined, and separate from the body. In fact, various school rules present the school as similar to a place of business, preparing students for the world of work. The rules thus attempt to construct the school space as a professional one that is separate both from the street (McLaren, 1986) and from young people's private lives. Yet the school is also the living space where students spend a significant portion of the day, and many of them do not have access to any private space at all. In this context PDAs may be quite important for some young people, and over-zealous interpretation of such rules may represent a significant intrusion. Evidently, students both challenge and reproduce this position.

Practical needs and the body

Finally, students frequently mentioned practical needs and the way school rules can interfere with activities like eating, visiting the bathroom, or getting to the next class on time. Although local codes of conduct do not include procedures for getting to the bathroom, many schools do have rules about who may be in the halls and when, and many teachers have developed protocols for bathroom visits that some students find infantilizing and impractical. In addition most schools regulate where and when students can eat. Students report frequently breaking this rule, either because they need to eat between classes or because they don't like eating in the lunchroom. The 'no backpacks' rule can make it hard to get to class on time because it means a stop at the lockers on the way.

Some students said that boredom leads them to seek alternative stimulation, frequently through breaking rules. Also, as we have seen, dress rules such as 'no heavy coats' or 'no spaghetti straps' are sometimes blamed for causing physical discomfort. Emotional needs were also discussed, including the need to cry (Focus Group 4) and to work off excess aggression (Focus Group 2).

Ethnographer Brenda Simpson observes that in both primary and secondary schools, the discipline of the body is often framed as a matter of safety and 'caring for the pupil' (2000). Simpson argues that teachers have resorted to these discourses of safety and care because corporal punishment is no longer an option. These explanations are particularly common in the context of rules such as the ones banning coats (they can hide weapons) and backpacks (people can trip on them). In fact, students were most willing to accept rules as fair when they were explained in terms of safety.

In many cases, however, even those 'safety' rules can seem impractical when they interfere with students' own bodily needs. Occasionally students will negotiate with individual teachers for special arrangements or enlist the support of their parents. Most often, though, in such instances participants reported that they simply break the rules. I will return to the subject of students' reactions in the discussion of resistance below, but first I will address the creation and regulation of 'other' bodies through the deployment of school rules.

'Other' bodies: Class, race, and ethnicity

Both the content and the application of school rules may result in exclusion as well as discipline, specifically around inequalities of class, race, and gender. For example, some dress codes are quite vague, couched in middle-class language that can leave some students uncertain of what is expected (Raby, 2005):

> Students should be clean and neatly dressed in a manner which maintains the good moral tone of the school.

> Dress which is suggestive, offensive or otherwise inappropriate is, of course, unacceptable.

> . . . good common sense, good taste, decency and socially acceptable attire.

The fact that the standards of 'good taste', 'common sense', or 'social acceptability' are left undefined means that it's up to teachers and administrators to decide who is and who is not compliant. Pierre Bourdieu (1984) reminds us that taste is not neutral but a reflection of cultural capital; 'good taste' is a subjective value, and within schools it is commonly defined in terms of middle-class ideals (Lareau, 2003). In short, language that presumes a shared understanding or previous knowledge effectively marginalizes those who are not 'in the know' or who value a different kind of taste.

School rules themselves thus have the potential to create 'other' bodies through their use of vague, middle-class language and references to specific types of clothing (e.g., gang-related), which in practice may be read onto some bodies but not others. Students' experiences of the application of school rules also suggest that in certain contexts, specific bodies are singled out as 'different': girls who are larger or more 'developed' than most, young people in non-conformist dress, and new immigrants.

The class background of focus group participants was not always easy to determine[3] and was only occasionally referenced directly in group discussions. However, participants frequently made it clear that they were aware of the ways in which rules can be seen to reward those with cultural, economic, and social capital.[4] First, six groups discussed class inequality in the context of rules against ripped or torn clothing, expressing concern about students who might not have the money to buy new clothes. Fernando, in Group 8, related how a friend of his was mocked by school staff and suspended for wearing torn pants when he couldn't afford to buy new ones. Focus Group 7 discussed how a student's clothing led their school to call Family and Children's Services (FACS):

> Bacon Boy: . . . the school likes to call FACS on people.
> The Flag: And that's bad just for, like, what they're wearing.
> Bacon Boy: Like my friend . . . got the FACS called on him 'cause his shoes weren't properly fitted. He got FACS called on him.
> The Flag: Yeah, they worry about the outside stuff.

Several focus groups debated whether uniforms promote equality or (because of their cost) inequality. By contrast, one female student in Group 5 associated 'respectable' clothing—defined as clothing that's not 'too trashy'—with wealthier people.

Second, a number of participants discussed favouritism towards members of students' council, athletes, cheerleaders, high academic achievers, and friends of teachers/administrators.

> Focus Group 1
> Patricia: I was on student council for a lot of years and so the teachers really like me a lot, like I'm one of the favourite students, but it's really unfair [*girls laugh*]. No, it's extremely unfair 'cause I'm no better than any other student. Like, I've broken rules, I've done all the stuff but, like, I should have been kicked off of student council and stuff because my grades were too low to be on it, but they didn't do anything because they liked me already . . . a lot of students are like that. Like people—if you get on student council you're pretty much good for high school [*laughs; girls laugh*] because they look at that as something better and we get benefits and stuff [. . .] it's pretty bad, like it's not fair at all.

Students who are well-integrated into accepted school activities and perform well at sports, academics, and social networking are thus seen to be advantaged. By contrast, participants noted the over-policing of marginalized students, including immigrant/racial minority youth, or those who seemingly belong to a particular alter-native subculture, such as stoners, punks, goths, skaters, or (left-wing) political teens.

Over-regulation and unequal discipline of immigrant/racial minority youth has been noted in other studies as well. For example, in Canada, both MacDonell and Martin (1986) and Ruck and Wortley (2002) found that non-white students perceived inequalities in the application of school discipline. Investigating early school-leaving among minority youth, Ontario researchers Ferguson et al. (2005) also found striking examples of racism in young people's experiences of school discipline.[5]

The new immigrant youth in Focus Group 8 discussed racism against non-white students, including administrators' assumption that any gathering of new immigrant students must be a gang:

> Latino Heat: I'm hanging out with people—like I'm hanging out with all Spanish kids. They
> don't like that. Or all the black people are hanging out with black people and they
> don't like that.
> RR: So what do they do?
> Latino Heat: They just tell you to go somewhere else. Like 'don't hang out around in one
> place'.
> Moe: Yeah. Yeah.
> [. . .]
> Latino Heat: At my school . . . we're always talking in Spanish. So [the vice-principal] goes
> 'Oh no, you always try to speak in English.' And one day I was speaking Spanish with
> my friend and he came to me and he told me not to speak in Spanish. He speak in
> Spanish . . .
> RR: He was speaking to you in Spanish.
> Latino Heat: Yeah. And he told me he was taking Spanish lessons because they thought we
> were, like, forming a gang and all that.

Students described teachers who surrendered to their prejudices as contradictory, since they were supposedly teaching tolerance and inclusiveness. It is interesting to note that codes of conduct in many Toronto schools include anti-harassment policies directly related to racism and the importance of respecting diversity, but this was not the case in the region under study.

Uncontainable bodies?

As we have seen, a number of rules have been designed and applied specifically to contain young people's bodily display, sexual bodies, and bodily needs inside the school. Such rules are not always applied consistently or fairly, partly because of inter-sections of gender, class, and race. We have also seen that a number of students concur with the containment and regulation of other students' bodies in terms of dress, PDAs, and physical safety. At the same time, there were many instances in which students challenged rules, and various ethnographic studies have identified similar challenges in the school (Lesko, 1988; McLaren, 1986; Morris, 2005; Simpson, 2000).

Participants felt completely disconnected from the rule-creation process and appeared to have little idea of how to formally appeal an unfair rule or application of a rule, though some did mention the possibility of drawing on the support of their parents (a 'back-up' resource reflecting the family's cultural capital). Nonetheless, several focus groups cited instances of more traditionally conceptualized resistance in the form of civil disobedience. For instance, some students staged a walkout as part of an unsuccessful effort to lobby for a football team. In another case students refused to stand for the anthem. And friends of a boy who had been suspended for wearing a skirt showed their solidarity by going to school in skirts the next day. The only success story, however, involved a campaign of communal non-compliance mounted after a new vice-principal introduced a system of hall passes, which was dropped when it was ignored by students and teachers alike.

For the most part, however, challenges to school rules were informal and reflected the Foucauldian model of resistance as continual struggle. Students frequently spoke up when they found a rule or its application to be unfair, although they found it much more productive to negotiate the loosening of a rule with a teacher than with a principal or vice-principal; the fact that they thought strategically in deciding which teachers were open to negotiation suggests a kind of 'off-kilter' resistance (Butz and Ripmeester, 1999). Students also struggled against the rules by breaking them. In some cases they saw this rule-breaking as inherently wrong, but they also frequently justified their infractions by reference to compelling bodily and personal needs—in effect, using a rival discourse to legitimate their challenge. This too can be considered a form of 'off-kilter' resistance:

> Focus Group 9
> Allison: . . . Like you might be at school and . . . something really shitty happens. Like, you're not gonna want to go to class in tears. . . . Like I had a friend who was going through a lot of family crises. She went to class and just walked out, because she could not deal with it. Every time you looked at her, she was in tears.

> Focus Group 2
> Mark: Well, you know how classes are like four minutes apart? . . . Well, I was always the last one to get to class . . . and this one time when I was just half a minute late . . . he suspended me . . . And it was just really, really stupid . . . because there was three flights of stairs [*inaudible*] and some of my classes were like on one end and [at] the other in the far end [of the school . . .] So it was hard for me to get there on time even running, 'cause you couldn't run in the friggin' school.

In cases like these, institutional efforts to contain students' bodies are challenged by students' construction of those needs as legitimate. Of course, rule-breaking also individualizes and therefore de-politicizes students' challenges to the rules (Willis, 1977), confirms discourses depicting young people as unthinkingly rebellious, and may lead to the imposition of additional rules or stricter enforcement. Clearly, such resistance cannot be expected to produce large-scale social change. Rather, it is best understood as a continuing process of struggle and negotiation. It can also be seen to reflect the participation of the body itself.

Recent theorists have tried to build a bridge between a social constructionist understanding of the body as contextual and constructed, and an understanding of the body itself as an actor (Tuana, 2001). Tuana argues that 'human ways of knowing, our concepts, meanings of terms, and modes of reasoning, are grounded in patterns of bodily being' (2001: 229). How we give meaning to and interact with the material world is cultural, yet at the same time, culture is not disconnected from the effects of the material world. In some of this rule-breaking, then, we can perhaps see the body itself as a participant: asserting needs which challenge the order and structure of the institution. In this sense resistance that is based on bodily practicality, including sexuality, can be rethought as manifestations of desire which are enacted through, or even by, the body.

Reflecting this perspective, and quite distinct from Foucault, Deleuze and Guattari see desire as escaping discourse and overflowing the social/institutional boundaries that try to categorize and contain people (Deleuze and Guattari, 1983; Tarulli and Skott-Myhre, 2006). The lived immediacy of young people's desire can thus be understood as a 'line of flight' that unsettles and disrupts, even as we attempt to contain its disruptions (e.g., through school rules). It is young people living their desire, often through their bodies and often through necessity, that disrupts the rules intended to contain them. Seen from this perspective, the dynamics of resistance are reversed: it is not the students who are reacting to (resisting or rebelling against) the rules, but the rules that are reacting to the lived expression of young people's desire. The immediacy of young people's bodily needs and desires (including those related to their embeddedness in racialized, classed, and gendered categories) eludes the schools' attempts to contain them.

Conclusion

This chapter has examined institutional efforts to regulate adolescent bodies through school rules concerning dress, physical displays of affection, and activities such as eating or running in the halls. Within these rules, we see how the containment of bodies is a key element of many schools' codes of conduct but that it is also through the body that rules may be negotiated, challenged, undermined, and resisted—through understandings of embodied self-expression, by appeal to practical bodily needs, and through recognition and critique of the 'othering' of certain bodies, for instance.

Ultimately, this analysis raises questions about the efficacy of school rules. What are they trying to accomplish? How are they interpreted by the young people who must live a significant portion of their lives in schools? What do these rules teach young people about their bodies and how they need to be managed within our society's institutional spaces? Students' acceptance of most rules suggests that for the most part the schools are succeeding in their efforts to produce 'civilized' citizens. But the process leaves little room for sexualized bodies, creative bodies, or practical bodily needs. It is not surprising therefore that students also chafe against, try to elude, and sometimes directly challenge the rules—rule-breaking that in turn reinforces popular views of adolescents as inherently unstable and rebellious. Finally, codes of conduct and their application may be used not only to curtail bodily expression but to identify certain bodies as more acceptable than others.

Appendix A: Focus Groups

#1 Youth centre	In a mall in a small city.
	All participants white.
	15–17 years.
	Five females, two males.
	Economic backgrounds unavailable.
#2 Street youth	At a drop-in and shelter for street youth in a small city.
	Participants were primarily white.[6]
	16–21 years.
	Four females, ten males.
	Economically marginalized youth.
#3 Political youth	Friends in a political group.
	All participants white.
	16–18 years.
	Three males.
	Middle- to upper-class, professional parents.
#4 Performing arts	Members of an organized performing arts group in a small city.
	All participants white.
	One 13-year-old, the remaining members 16–17.
	Three females, one male.
	Middle- to upper-class, professional parents.
#5 French group	Participants located informally, all attending a French public school.
	All participants white.
	15–18 years.
	Four females.
	Working-class parents (trades and service industry).
#6 Catholic group	Participants located informally, all attending public Catholic school.
	All participants white.
	17–18 years.
	Two females, two males.
	Middle-class, professional parents.
#7 Boys and girls club	Drop-in centre for young people located in a small city.
	All participants white.
	13–16 years.
	Four females, two males.
	Economically marginalized.

#8 New immigrant group	Weekly program for new immigrant youth in a small city.
	One participant Latin American, two from North Africa, one from East Africa, remaining three also non-white.
	15–18 years.
	Two female, five male.
	Working- and middle-class parents.
#9 LGBTTQ group	Weekly group for lesbian, gay, bisexual, transgender, two-spirited, queer, and questioning teens.
	Seven white, one black, one Asian youth.
	15–19 years.
	Five males, four females.
	A range of class backgrounds.

Notes

Research for this chapter was conducted with support from the Social Sciences and Humanities Research Council of Canada.

1. At the time of writing (spring 2008) this code had been revised.
2. There were two exceptions. Focus Group 2 included several young people over 18 and no longer in secondary school while Focus Group 7 included three participants in middle school.
3. Participants in groups 3–9 were directly asked (on paper) about their parents' occupations, although some respondents did not respond. Participants in group 2 may have come from more middle-class homes, but were in economically marginal circumstances at the time of the study.
4. Cultural capital can be translated into economic capital as it can bring economic rewards. Social capital refers to having valuable social bonds between people.
5. Ken Bhattacharjee (2003) finds that students with learning disabilities also experience such inequalities.
6. Participants were not asked their racial identity.

Glossary

cultural capital: The values, skills, dispositions, and tastes deemed valuable by the dominant social class and consequently rewarded through social institutions such as schools.

discourse: Defined by Burr (1995: 48) as 'a set of meanings, metaphors, representations, images, stories, statements and so on that in some way together produce a particular version of events [places and people]'. Discourses are specific to historical and cultural contexts, mutually supporting (though also at times contradicting), and powerfully influential, in that they construct how we think about the world around us.

lines of flight: A term coined by Gilles Deleuze and Felix Guattari, referring to flight from, or disruption of, the categories through which the institutions of the capitalist state attempt to contain us.

resistance: Some—most Marxists, for example—see resistance as a direct challenge to oppressive social structures. Others, such as Foucault, understand resistance as including more limited struggle (e.g., in the context of interpersonal power relations). Resistance of this second type often takes indirect forms (e.g., negotiation rather than direct challenge, or highlighting alternative discourses) and can be described as 'off-kilter'.

Study Questions

1. What assumptions does Canadian society hold about teenagers? Are they the same for males and females? For teens from different racial backgrounds? How might some of these assumptions influence the way teenagers' behaviour (such as rule-breaking) is interpreted?
2. What are some reasons behind school rules such as the ones discussed in this chapter? Are these reasons always legitimate?
3. Why do young people break school rules? What do differing explanations of rule-breaking assume about adolescents? When (if ever) is it legitimate for young people to break rules?
4. What do school rules assume about adolescents and adolescent bodies? What do they teach young people about how bodies should be managed within institutional spaces and what kinds of bodies are considered acceptable? Are there times when such education is valuable?
5. What is gained and what is lost through the containment of bodies, specifically teenaged bodies? What channels are available for students to challenge such containment?

Recommended Readings

Lareau, Annette. 2003. *Unequal Childhoods: Class, Race and Family Life*. Berkeley: University of California Press.

Lesko, Nancy. 1996. 'Denaturalizing Adolescence: The Politics of Contemporary Representations', *Youth and Society* 28: 139–161.

Morris, Edward W. 2005. '"Tuck in That Shirt!" Race, Class, Gender and Discipline in an Urban School', *Sociological Perspectives* 48: 25–48.

Simpson, Brenda. 2000. 'Regulation and Resistance: Children's Embodiment during the Primary–Secondary School Transition', in A. Prout, ed., *The Body, Childhood and Society*. Hampshire, UK: MacMillan Press, 60–78.

Tait, Gordon. 2000. *Youth, Sex and Government*. New York: Peter Lang Publishing.

Recommended Websites

Ontario Code of Conduct: http://www.edu.gov.on.ca/eng/document/brochure/conduct/conduct.html

An introduction to Foucault: http://www.theory.org.uk/ctr-fouc.htm

Report on early school leavers' disengagement from secondary school: http://www.edu.gov.ca/eng/parents/schoolleavers.pdf

Essay: 'Finding space for resistant subcultures': http://www.rochester.edu/in_visible_culture/issue2/butz.htm

References

Bhattacharjee, K. 2003. *The Ontario Safe Schools Act: School Discipline and Discrimination*. Toronto: Ontario Human Rights Commission.

Bourdieu, P. 1984. *Distinction: A Social Critique of the Judgment of Taste,* trans. R. Nice. Cambridge, MA: Harvard University Press.

Burr, V. 1995. *An Introduction to Social Constructionism.* London: Routledge.

Butz, D., and M. Ripmeester. 1999. 'Finding Space for Resistant Subcultures', *Invisible Culture: An Electronic Journal for Visual Studies* 2 (23 pages).

Deleuze, G., and F. Guattari. 1983. *Anti-Oedipus: Capitalism and Schizophrenia.* Minneapolis: University of Minnesota Press.

Ferguson, B., K. Tilleczek, K. Boydell, and A. Rummens. 2005. *Early School Leavers: Understanding the Lived Reality of Student Disengagement from Secondary School.* Toronto: Community Health Systems Resource Group.

Finn, J. 2001. 'Text and Turbulence: Representing Adolescence as Pathology in the Human Services', *Childhood: A Global Journal of Child Research* 8, 2: 167–90.

Fleming, P. 2002. '"Lines of Flight": A History of Resistance and the Thematic of Ethics, Death and Animality', *Ephemera* 2, 3: 193–208.

Foucault, M. 1977. *Discipline and Punish: The Birth of the Prison.* London: Penguin Books.

———. 1978. 'Governmentality', in G. Burchell, C. Gordon, and P. Miller, eds, *The Foucault Effect: Studies in Governmentality.* Chicago: University of Chicago Press, 87–104.

Government of Canada. 2006. *Innovation in Canada.*

Government of Ontario. 2001. 'Code of Conduct'. Toronto: Queen's Printer, 1–11.

Kehily, M.J. 2004. 'Gender and Sexuality: Continuities and Change for Girls in School', in A. Harris, ed., *All About the Girl: Culture, Power and Identity.* New York: Routledge, 205–18.

Knesting, K., and N. Waldron. 2006. 'Willing to Play the Game: How At-risk Students Persist in School', *Psychology in the Schools* 43, 5: 599–611.

Lareau, A. 2003. *Unequal Childhoods: Class, Race and Family Life.* Berkeley: University of California Press.

Lash, S. 1991. 'Genealogy and the Body: Foucault/Deleuze/Nietzsche', in M. Featherstone, M. Hepworth, and B.S. Turner, eds, *The Body: Social Process and Cultural Theory.* London: Sage, 256–80.

Lesko, N. 1988. 'The Curriculum of the Body: Lessons from a Catholic High School', in L.G. Roman, L.K. Christian Smith, and E. Ellsworth, eds, *Becoming Feminine: The Politics of Popular Culture.* London: Falmer Press, 123–42.

———. 1996a. 'Denaturalizing Adolescence: The Politics of Contemporary Representations', *Youth and Society* 28, 2: 139–61.

———. 1996b. 'Past, Present and Future Conceptions of Adolescence', *Educational Theory* 46, 4: 453–72.

Lewis, R. 1999. 'Preparing Students for Democratic Citizenship: Codes of Conduct in Victoria's "Schools of the Future"', *Educational Research and Evaluation* 5, 1: 41–61.

MacDonell, A.J., and W.B.W Martin. 1986. 'Student Orientations to School Rules', *The Alberta Journal of Educational Research* 32, 1: 51–65.

McLaren, P. 1986. *Schooling as a Ritual Performance: Towards a Political Economy of Educational Symbols and Gestures.* London: Routledge.

Morris, E.W. 2005. '"Tuck in That Shirt!" Race, Class, Gender and Discipline in an Urban School', *Sociological Perspectives* 48, 1: 25–48.

Nelson, R.W. 1996. 'Deviance and Discipline in the Classroom', in B. Schissel and L. Mahood, eds, *Social Control in Canada: Issues in the Social Construction of Deviance.* Toronto: Oxford University Press, 373–402.

Pomerantz, S. 2007. 'Cleavage in a Tank Top: Bodily Prohibition and the Discourses of School Dress Codes', *Alberta Journal of Educational Research* 53, 4: 373–86.

Raby, R. 2002. 'A Tangle of Discourses: Girls Negotiating Adolescence', *Journal of Youth Studies* 5, 4: 425–50.

———. 2005. 'Polite, Well-dressed and on Time: Secondary School Conduct Codes and the Production of Docile Citizens', *Canadian Review of Sociology and Anthropology* 42, 1: 71–92.

———, and J. Domitrek. 2007. 'Slippery as Fish. But Already Caught? Secondary Students' Engagement with School Rules', *Canadian Journal of Education* 30, 3: 931–58.

Robinson, K.H. 1992. 'Class-room Discipline: Power, Resistance and Gender. A Look at Teacher Perspectives', *Gender and Education* 4, 3: 273–88.

Ruck, M.D., and S. Wortley. 2002. 'Racial and Ethnic Minority High School Students' Perceptions of School Disciplinary Practices: A Look at Some Canadian Findings', *Journal of Youth and Adolescence* 31, 3: 185–95.

Shilling, C. 1993. *The Body and Social Theory*. London: Sage.

Simpson, B. 2000. 'Regulation and Resistance: Children's Embodiment during the Primary–Secondary School Transition', in A. Prout, ed., *The Body, Childhood and Society*. Hampshire, UK: MacMillan Press, 60–78.

Tait, G. 2000. *Youth, Sex and Government*. New York: Peter Lang Publishing.

Tarulli, D., and H. Skott-Myhre. 2006. 'The Immanent Rights of the Multitude: An Ontological Framework for Conceptualizing the Issue of Child and Youth Rights', *International Journal of Children's Rights* 14, 2: 187–201.

Thiele, L.P. 1990. 'The Agony of Politics: The Nietzschean Roots of Foucault's Thought', *American Political Science Review* 84, 3: 907–25.

Tuana, N. 2001. 'Material Locations: An Interactionist Alternative to Realism/Social Constructivism', in N. Tuana and S. Morgan, eds. *Engendering rationalities*. New York: State University of New York Press, 221–43.

Vavrus, F., and K. Cole. 2002. '"I Didn't Do Nothin": The Discursive Construction of School Suspension', *The Urban Review* 34, 2: 87–111.

Willis, P. 1977. *Learning to Labour*. Farnborough, UK: Saxon House.

CHAPTER 9

African-Canadian Students, Identity, and Diaspora Literacy

Jennifer R. Kelly and Lorin G. Yochim

Introduction

Any discussion of curriculum, according to Herbert Kliebard, must address four questions: Why should we teach this rather than that? Who should have access to what knowledge? What rules should govern the teaching of that knowledge? And how should the various parts of the curriculum be interrelated? (1992: 174). These philosophical questions are central to the discussion that follows. Although Kliebard's questions were posed in the context of the United States, they are just as relevant in Canada. The issues of power associated with the selection and transmission of knowledge are especially important when the learners are a racialized group, in this case African Canadians. 'At the heart of the educational process', writes sociologist Rob Moore, lie

> the curriculum and the crucial question, 'What should we teach?' Whatever we intend to do with education, or believe is happening because of it, occurs by virtue of the transmission of knowledge intended to transform the learner. This points to something broader than teaching method: a curriculum is an organization of knowledge involving the selection of content and also the structuring of the relationships within content. (2004: 147)

Because curriculum is socially constructed, it involves not just the reproduction of knowledge in the neo-Marxist sense (Bowles and Gintis, 1976), but also the production of knowledge through the cultural dynamics that operate at school sites and beyond. Curriculum is formed in part through the power relations experienced by groups racialized as 'black' within 'white' society.

This chapter has developed out of our experiences both as teachers (K–12 and Higher Education) and as researchers conducting various empirical studies of African-Canadian students and their experiences of curriculum and schooling (Kelly, 1998, 2004; Brown and Kelly, 2001). Across those projects as well as others conducted in various provinces (Dei et al., 2000; Solomon, 1992; James, 1990; BLAC, 1994), African-Canadian students have consistently expressed concern over inadequate recognition of their racialized and historically constituted identities (collective as well as individual); issues of **representation** within the nation-state; questions of official and unofficial knowledge; and the need for more content explicitly relevant to people of African descent, as well as problems such as stereotyping and low expectations. Furthermore, during this research it became evident that the term 'African Canadian', though useful for purposes of categorization, is not adequate to represent a highly heterogeneous group of people whose identities and identifications are fragmented by class, gender, ability, and sexuality. The question at the heart of this chapter—what does it mean to produce curriculum that responds to the racialized identifications of African-Canadian students?—encapsulates all these issues and concerns.

Our aim is to present an overview of the issues—racialized identities, segregation, and anti-racism; nation-state and belonging; representation, receptivity, and content—and then to propose a way of working through these issues via a newer approach to curriculum and pedagogy that we call **diaspora literacy**.

Racialized Identities and Identification: Who Is an African Canadian?

'African Canadians' are people of African descent whose heritage can more rightly be identified as *diasporan* in that they or their ancestors have been displaced from the African continent at least once. For many there have been several re-scatterings as ancestors and parents have moved to and from North America, the Caribbean, and Europe. Thus the students encompassed by this descriptor are heterogeneous in terms of heritage as well as experience. An 'African-Canadian student' is any student of African descent with familial links to continental Africa, the Caribbean, South America, the United States, or Canada (Clarke, 1996: 118). While the students discussed in this chapter are identified as African Canadian, this label is only the latest in a long line of socially constituted identifiers, including 'Ethiopian', 'Negro', 'coloured', and 'black'. Some of the name changes can be traced to historical colonialism and imperialism as well as more recent exercises of geopolitical power. In recent times this has been accomplished largely through a process of **mediazation** that has established the cultural presence of the United States around the globe. Issues around naming have become particularly important in recent years as movement among and between the world's populations continues to increase.

Over the past 20 years or so we have come to understand that identities are not singular and fixed; rather, they are complex and fluid (Hall, 1990). It is now clear that identity is made in different ways in different social spaces, depending on who is involved, and that racialized identities—no less than identities related to class, gender, sexuality, and ability—are socially constituted. It is equally clear that, even today, the identities constructed around students of African descent may reflect the influence of historical classifications 'associated with practices such as slavery, servitude and colonialism' (Bonilla-Silva, 1997: 471). Thus a teacher may attribute low achievement on the part of an African-Canadian student to some characteristic supposedly inherent in 'those people'—perhaps laziness, or a motivational deficit. Such traces of history can be regarded as 'the underlying rules or "grammar" that structure consciousness . . . and, as such, regulate the ways in which we categorize, organize, select and configure the material and cultural resources we employ in our social behaviour' (Moore, 2004: 81). For many African-Canadian students, the dominance of this habitus (Bourdieu, 1977) means they are not only classed in the traditional sense of the term, but also racialized.

Far from recognizing this racialized habitus, however, Canadian school systems strive to represent themselves as race-neutral zones, bastions of pluralism and equality that reinforce depoliticized interpretations and perceptions of race and racialization. Whether or not one accepts this claim to depoliticization, the myth of benign pluralism has significant impact on the design and implementation of school policy and curricula. In this sanitized scenario, race is portrayed as an objective, yet irrelevant, identity marker that is unproblematic and inconsequential in the day-to-day activities of the school. Often the result of this approach is 'colour-blindness', or what Virginia Chalmers (1997) calls 'sameness as different colour', whereby individual students' success is said to be determined solely by academic 'merit'. In other words, the assumption is that students' potential for success is not affected in any way by their ethnic background or the colour of their skin. It is their failure to recognize the racialized element of identities that enables school administrators in general to disregard the socially constituted relationship between a student's racialized identity and his or her perception and reception of mainstream curriculum.

Drawing on data generated through various research projects, we argue that individual and group identity markers involving race and colour significantly affect a student's perception of school, self, and other. Blackness becomes a salient feature in the school context when discourses on blackness are shared and disputed intersubjectively in the school and the society. For black students, one's skin colour is a distinguishing feature, a marker that connotes historically derived meanings, beliefs, stereotypes, and curiosities. As Brown and Kelly argue, it is 'as identity is filtered and interpreted through the mask of difference' that 'colour . . . becomes a relevant feature' (2001: 507). What is often not recognized in discussions of curricula is that one must insist not only on cultural diversity of 'school knowledge' but also on its inherent relational aspect. School knowledge is socially produced, deeply imbued with human interests, and deeply implicated in the unequal social relations outside the school doors. In linking curricula with the descriptor 'African-Canadian students' we make the assumption that despite their heterogeneity there are also common socially constituted concerns that can be taken up within a common curriculum.

The heterogeneous nature of experiences is also reflected in provincial differences. Because curriculum is constitutionally a provincial rather than a federal responsibility, the African-Canadian students' curricular responses vary from province to province. So, for example, in the mid-1990s, clear deficiencies in Nova Scotia's school policies and curriculum were identified by Castor Williams, Chairman of the 1994 Black Learner Advisory Committee (BLAC) report. For him, 'African Canadian culture is often relegated to an inferior status by schools thus hiding our group's true historic struggle for survival, liberation and enhancement' (1994: 18). By contrast, during the same time period the Ontario Ministry of Education (although still open to criticism) was sufficiently aware of racialized issues to state in its *Guidelines for Antiracism and Ethnocultural Equity in School Boards* that 'much of the traditional curriculum focuses on the values, experiences, achievements and perspectives of white-European members of Canadian society and excludes or distorts those of other groups in Canada' (1993: 13).

Some liberal educators think it polite to avoid recognition of racialized identifications; but research suggests that such avoidance makes no difference to students who are unable to produce themselves as non-racialized (for examples see Dei et al., 1995; James, 1990; Kelly, 1998). For example, the following student explains how racialization—i.e., attribution of raced meanings to everyday experiences—occurs:

Student 1: . . . I was kind of like in with the blacks. I was friends with a [lot] of people outside the blacks. But it was kind of like a safeguard to stay with the blacks all the time. And I am still kind of same way . . . For me it's kind of safe. I feel safer if I am like that.
JK: When you say safer, what do you mean?
Student 1: If I was to hang around with like a bunch of white kids I wouldn't feel so [safe]guarded. Um; I would feel kind of—I don't know how to explain it. Like kind of by myself. I guess you could say. Like subjected to anything at all.

Further, students apply these discursively constituted, racialized categorizations not only to themselves but also, at times, to others, positioning them as racialized subjects. While the school would like to perceive all students as sharing a single identity as 'just students', narrative evidence makes it clear that African-Canadian students perceive their schoolmates as well as themselves in racialized terms:

Student 2: They call them brown. I don't [know] why.
JK: So you have brown and you have black. What else do you have?
Student 2: Whites, and like Orientals.
JK: Oh Orientals. And Oriental is?
Student 2: That's everything from like Asia.

From Segregation to Anti-racism: Historical Responses of the State

Most sociologists of education accept the premise that curriculum is socially produced and historically located. If we concur, then we must acknowledge the historical relationship (however limited it may have been) between mainstream curriculum and African-Canadian students. From the early days of common schools in the mid-nineteenth century, African-Canadian students were set apart from the mainstream in terms of funding, aims, and objectives of education. Historically, one of the essential reference points in the relationship between African-Canadian students and the curriculum is the 1850 Common School Act (Canada West), which mandated the establishment of separate schools for 'coloured people':

> [It] should be the duty of the Municipal Council of any Town ship and of the Board of School Trustees of any City, Town or Incorporated Village on the application in writing, of 12 or more resident's heads of families, to authorize the establishment of one, or more, Separate Schools for Protestants, Roman Catholics or coloured people. (cited in Walker, 1980: 110)

As a result of the Act, African-Canadian students with access to a separate school could be legally excluded from the common system and where no separate school existed, permission to attend the common school had to be obtained from the white community. With funding allocated on the basis of population, separate black schools often could not afford the breadth of curriculum available in other areas. On the other hand, it should be noted that the degree of segregation varied between provinces and sometimes within them. In Ontario, for example, integration was the norm in Toronto and the eastern part of the province, although the Act stayed on the books in Ontario until 1964.

Over the years, various special curricula have been advocated for African-Canadian students. The most consistent recommendations have focused on multiculturalism, anti-racism, and—in contrast to the Euro-centrism of mainstream curricula—a philosophical stance known as Afro-centrism or, more recently, Afri-centrism. While each of these approaches has had some success in terms of outcomes for students, each has also been heavily critiqued. For example, poststructuralist and critical cultural studies theorists (Gilroy, 2000) have questioned as 'essentialist' the Afri-centric idea of a single collective 'African Consciousness'. Afri-centric theorist Molefi Asante, however, argues that, 'in the context of White racial hierarchy and domination', to acknowledge fragmentation within **black identity** would amount to 'accept[ing] a White definition of Blackness' (2001: 847). Afri-centrism also underlies recent campaigns for 'black-focused' schools in Ontario and other provinces. However, as Andrew Allen cautions, 'the last thing we want to do is replace a Eurocentric curriculum with an exclusively Africentric approach. We want to respect children of all backgrounds in our curriculum' (cited in Brown, 2006: 4).

In Canada, multicultural education developed out of the multicultural policy passed in 1971. Various sociologists have discussed the ambiguity that surrounds the concept of multiculturalism in Canada (Moodley, 1992). Some educators have understood this approach as a way of improving the self-concept of minority children by including aspects of their heritage (dress, dance, diet) and presence in the curriculum. Others view multicultural education as a 'palliative which does little to recognize the real needs of language education, inequality of access, and of the racism which differentiates between physically assimilable minorities and visible ones' (Moodley, 1992: 89). The racialized experiences of African-Canadian students are taken to be a matter of culture rather than race, and the idea that race might be a social construct of any significance is denied. Those who experience racial bias are considered responsible for their own marginalized predicament and, by extension, their future prospects. Discussions concerning Canadian multicultural education and curriculum are further exacerbated by the fact that Canada has no national multicultural education policy, leaving the development of any such framework to the individual provinces. Curriculum pertaining to students of African descent falls outside the traditional conception of multicultural curriculum that has only recently started to move away from its two main models: (1) an ethno-cultural support service model as in Ontario and Nova Scotia; and (2) the heritage/international/second-language model used in Saskatchewan, Alberta, and Manitoba (Henry and Tator, 1991). Underlying this ambivalence of purpose in multicultural education and curriculum is the fact that, in general, Canadian society pays only lip service to pluralism. Thus while multiculturalism is advocated at the educational and ideological levels, it rarely ascends into the higher echelons of political power.

Nation-State and Belonging

Like most liberal-democratic societies, Canada fosters an expectation—indeed, an ideology—of 'a nation-state in which individuals from all ethnic, cultural and racial groups are able to participate fully' (Banks, 1986: 3). In order to deny their claims for inclusion in the curriculum, African Canadians must be constructed as 'Other', a 'special interest group' with demands that are contrary to the 'greater good' of the nation-state. By implication, groups that coalesce around an ethnic or racial identity are seen as competing with the nation-state and therefore threatening to its patriarchal role (Enloe, 1973). Evident too are tensions between the universalistic Enlightenment concept of the nation as a voluntary association or contractual entity and a more particularistic German Romantic notion of a 'predetermined community bound by blood and heredity' (Malik, 1996: 131).

In Canada, as in many white settler societies (Razack, 2002), education has traditionally been concerned with transmitting ideas and symbols integral to nation–building. The principal vehicle for this purpose is the curriculum, described by Schick and St. Denis as 'one of the significant discourses through which white privilege and "difference" are normalized' (2005: 298). As Durkheim argued in the nineteenth century, education is primarily about socialization and development of a collective consciousness. Although he saw it as the primary task of education to promote socialization, his vision of social order is not generally understood to have centred on any specific norms of race, class, gender, or sexuality.

Benedict Anderson (1983) proposed that a nation is 'imagined' into existence. School curricula play an essential role in that process. African Canadians, however, are not regarded as part of the historical continuum that is imagined to have brought contemporary Canada into being. Nor are curricula the only social sites where the presence of African Canadians is denied. Thus African Canadians turn to 'African-American texts and historical cultural icons to define their own experiences (a fact which can seduce the unwary into believing that no uniquely African-Canadian perspective exists)' (Clarke, 1996: 57).

The notion that there are no uniquely African-Canadian experiences is reflected in the ways in which African-Canadian students talk about their own identity. For some, the curriculum's failure to recognize the black presence in Canadian history reinforces the sense of blackness as a marker of 'the Other', as set apart from the Canadian norm. Even students whose ancestry is historically rooted in Canada often find it hard to identify any symbolic representation in Canadian society with which they can align themselves. Therefore many youth perceive Canadian identity as problematic and/or not readily available. In addition, we can surmise that official citizenship does not automatically lead to recognition of self or acceptance by others as 'Canadian'.

JK: You wouldn't call yourself a Canadian?
Student 3: Not here I don't suppose. Well I always go . . . 'Cuz I am born here so I don't want to lead anyone [on]. Usually I say I am born here. But obviously my mum's from [the Caribbean]. 'Cuz usually . . . that's what people are asking. I figured that out. 'Cuz they don't expect [*pause*] to hear that you are Canadian. They just know what they want to hear. Like whether you are born here or not. I've learnt that. 'Cuz some people always ask you. If I say, 'Oh, I am Canadian?', they will say, 'Oh well where are your parents from?' Or something like that. They ask you a further question. So I usually always put in a [quali-fying] sentence. Depending on who it is.
JK: Who it is?
Student 3: It depends I guess like [*pause*] I don't know. If a white person asks me normally I'd say [*pause*] 'Cuz I guess normally I do say I am [Caribbean]. 'Cuz Canadian to them [*pause*] most of them don't understand what that means. But to a black person, especially if they are not from here. I usually tell them I am born here, but where my mum's from 'cuz that's what they want to know.

Provisional alliances and affinities are dependent on context, so that while at times students' need to identify themselves as black is paramount, at other times a national identity related to geographic region emerges as a qualifier of or an explanation for their blackness. These national identities emerge at times when a relation of domina-tion is most evident, as in the example above where Student 3 is not accepted as authentically Canadian. Recent research by Reitz and Banerji (2007), based on data from the 2001 census, highlights the way assumptions about a sense of 'belonging' are affected by the dynamics of racialization, so that some members of racialized minori-ties are slower to identify with Canada than are those of (white) European origin.

Representation, Receptivity, and Content

Today, in the first decade of the twenty-first century, it is probably safe to say that the most powerful cultural influence on young African Canadians' construction of their identity is hip-hop culture—a US-dominated hegemonic representation of black life and lived experiences. Though clearly not part of the formal curriculum, hip-hop culture works alongside it to produce forms of knowledge and stereotypes that are no less, if not more, effective than those delivered by teachers. Cultural forms such as hip-hop offer not only entertainment and pleasure, but also knowledge and under-standings that young people can use to give meaning to their school lives. Consider the implications of the phrase 'keeping it real'. Some students, especially males, clearly place knowledge learned in school in a separate category from the 'real' everyday knowledge garnered through direct experiences. Students often feel that their 'real' knowledge is treated as illegitimate in relation to school-legitimated knowledge. In the following extract, three male students express how they see learning through experi-ence in comparison with school knowledge. For them, you don't have to go to Harvard to produce poetry:

> Student 4: I saw this guy [on TV] . . . [He] was supposed to be the biggest drug dealer in Washington [and he] was in jail . . . this was someone who hasn't been to high school. And the way this guy talked, he blew me away, he was brilliant.
> Student 5: People who are harassed most by the cops on a daily basis, they begin to know how things work for themselves and how to get around certain questions.
> Student 6: It's like Tupac. Most people who went to Harvard will be like 'blah blah, I can write this', [but] Tupac knows [how to write poetry].

Here meaning is no longer something to be sought exclusively within the text itself—where structuralism would locate it. Now the analysis of meaning has to expand to include the reader's position as a subject within a specific social context—a subjec-tivity that will reflect, among other things, his or her class, gender, and ethnicity.

Receptivity to texts has been a problem for many students of African descent. There is no guarantee that two students will understand a given text in the same way, let alone a student and a teacher. So it can be argued that the ways in which students construct meaning in the classroom are conditioned by their social experiences outside the classroom. The traditional understanding of classroom learning saw students as passive, as empty containers waiting to be filled with information. Now we know that students come to school with values, histories, and perceptions that will help to shape the meaning created within the classroom. In one research project Jennifer found that many of the books presented by language arts teachers as exemplars of a humanist, anti-racism perspective—books such as *The Cay* or *To Kill a Mockingbird*—were inter-preted in quite a different way by black students, who took the fact that the principal characters were 'white' to mean that the black characters were necessarily subsumed and subjugated. From their point of view, therefore, these texts did not interrupt racist representations, but rather perpetuated them.

Diaspora Literacy and Curriculum

Having outlined some of the issues that make school curricula problematic for African-Canadian students, we would now like to propose a new approach to content and pedagogy that addresses some of those issues. Although the issues range widely, there are some points of convergence around matters of identity and identification. First, we need to challenge the notion that black identity is unitary and argue instead for recognition of heterogeneity. What is different about the 'diaspora literacy' approach is that it makes identity formation an explicit topic of discussion.

Other theorists have also identified the tension between identification and curriculum as problematic. As George Sefa Dei argues, 'students attribute the difficulties they have in negotiating their individual self and group identity to a very narrow school curriculum. They complain about schools not linking questions of identity with schooling' (1996: 51). Drawing from sociology, cultural studies, and critical theory, diaspora literacy highlights African diasporan identities as a way of encouraging social understanding and literacy.

Use of the term *diaspora* in the African context is relatively recent, but the concept goes back a long way, as Asante makes clear:

> African intellectuals have used the term Diaspora more prominently since the 1950s when large numbers of African scholars and activists began adopting [it] as a statement of solidarity with the struggles of the African continent. Although there had been from the earliest times a sense of belonging to Africa in the writings of Edward Blyden, Martin Delany, Abdias do Nascimento, Marcus Garvey, and others, it was the liberation of the African continent that brought into existence a new era of pride and dignity. (2004: 3)

What we are proposing is an approach to curriculum that allows for recognition of lived experiences and at the same time refuses to accept without analysis the term 'African Canadian'. In particular we want to encourage the development of a pedagogy that would allow students to read a text in terms of what it excludes as well as what it includes. In this kind of 'dialogic' reading, meaning is arrived at through the bringing together of many voices, some of which support the dominant narrative and some of which resist it. Ultimately, the goal is to develop 'a politicized citizenry capable of fighting for various forms of public life . . . to develop the cooperative/social intelligence necessary for democracy and freedom' (McLaren and Sleeter, 1995: 362).

In this context the emphasis should be on heterogeneity rather than homogeneity—especially when we take into account the fragmentation that occurs when racial identity combines with class, gender, sexuality, and nationality. In challenging the notion of black identity as fixed or predictable, this approach reflects the rise of poststructuralist theory in the sociology of education (Apple, 1996) as the focus of analysis shifted from social reproduction towards discourse and identity formation. Linking cultural studies with analysis of black youth identity formation opens us 'to the theoretical possibilities for understanding education as a political, pedagogical practice that unfolds in a wide range of shifting and overlapping sites of learning' (Giroux, 1996: 15). Exploring black diaspora literacy is a starting point towards understanding a collectivity that spans geographic boundaries and makes it possible to place black identity in relation to other national and ethnic identities. Diasporic identity is transnational; according to Gilroy, it 'offers a way to imagine a more complex ecologically sophisticated and organic concept of identity than offered by the contending options of genealogy' (1997: 339). Drawing again on Gilroy's understanding of 'diaspora' (a scattering of peoples) in conjunction with an understanding of literacy as the need to read and understand the world (Freire, 1993), we are able to re-theorize curricula in a way that offers possibilities for working with knowledge of and about African Canadians as well as other racialized and diasporic communities. Starting conceptually with 'culture', Gilroy's work suggests that we should think of culture formation as occurring via 'routes' rather than 'roots'. The concept of diaspora offers the opportunity to reinterpret the relationship not just between identity and location, but also between nationality and geographic origin. It allows us to conceive of sharing a space that is not just geographic but discursive.

Further, such an open reading allows us to analyze the political and the social aspects of identity and to see how representation of sameness and difference become part of meaning making and everyday culture. Conceptually, this use of diaspora helps us understand the intersections of ethnicity, class, religion, and gender in identity formation. So it can be argued that diaspora offers the opportunity to re-theorize and articulate ideas of nation, nationalism, and pluralism within the field of education, particularly in terms of pedagogy and curricula. Thus we are encouraged to ask: In a pluralistic and historically multicultural society such as Canada, how can we develop within our classrooms a complex and heterogeneous understanding of students' cultural and racialized identity formation and their sense of belonging?

A diaspora-focused curriculum offers a way to work with students whose identities are hybrid rather than unified, complex rather than singular; whose cultural heritage is elsewhere but who are now firmly part of what is commonly seen as the Canadian *mosaic*, but that might be better conceptualized as a kind of *amoebic* social entity. Why this conceptual shift? Whereas *mosaic* suggests an amalgam of fragments that form a coherent and beautiful, if somewhat jagged, artistic whole, *amoeba* evokes an image of society as a somewhat less attractive, unicellular organism that is fluid and open to change, able to absorb disparate entities into itself. We would argue that diaspora literacy foregrounds issues around 'identity' and 'mobility' in a more overt and coherent way than either the official or the hidden curriculum permitted in the past. It allows for an understanding of how history, politics, and culture inform the availability and/or construction of identities and, furthermore, how movement across geographic areas (re)translates and blurs these same selves.

Within our conceptualization of diaspora literacy there is recognition that schools are spaces of learning, sites where knowledge is produced, exchanged, and transferred, places where students meet and learn from each other. This kind of informal learning is especially significant for African-Canadian youth today, given the dominance of US media culture and the cross-border proliferation of discourses on black youth culture through mediazation and popular representations (Thompson, 1990; Kelly, 2004).

Figure 9.1 identifies five ways in which a curriculum focused on diaspora literacy might respond to the critiques of mainstream curricula voiced by students of African descent. These five components can be used in an initial exploration of the dimensions of diaspora literacy. Three of them represent approaches to knowledge (cultural politics, power, historicity) while the other two relate to pedagogy (dialogue, dialectic). Each of the five is linked with the others so that together they form a pedagogical whole. To explore this unity we will start by examining the various nodes in more detail.

Figure 9.1   Diaspora literacy

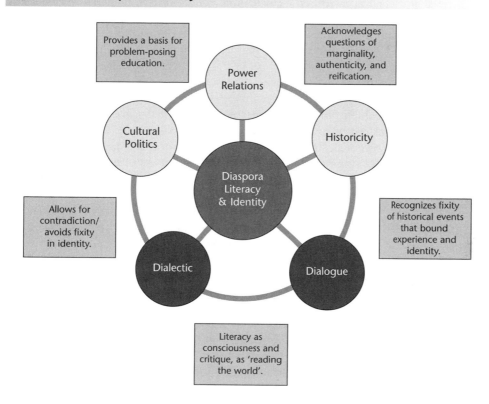

Note: The three light grey balloons represent knowledge elements; the two dark grey balloons, pedagogical/skill elements. As the five articulate with one another, the wheel links each one to all the others. Each of the outer boxes is positioned between two balloons to indicate how the two balloons relate to one another. In the case of the box between 'dialectic' and 'dialogue', both are relevant to the notion of 'literacy as consciousness and critique'. The box between 'cultural politics' and 'dialectic' explains how the pedagogical technique and the knowledge element work together. The pattern is the same for the rest of the boxes.

Dialogue, Dialectic, and Power Relations

An overly simplistic or conventional approach to teaching that sees knowledge as nothing more than a body of information or isolated 'facts' to be transmitted makes for a dry, boring classroom. One student described her preferred pedagogical style this way:

> The classes I love are the ones [where you] get to debate, say your opinion. . . . Not these classes where you have to sit there and listen to the teachers and if you talk you are in trouble. . . . Classes should be more [about] participation from the students. . . . [Sometimes] it's like listening to a dictator up there, and you can't say nothing.

We also want to highlight how, as a pedagogical strategy, project work gives students in general greater choice within the curriculum. For minority students, however, it also provides an opportunity to learn about peoples and cultures other than those designated as important in the official curriculum. As another student indicated in her interview, projects leave it up to students to highlight their own 'ethnic' perspective:

Zora: You have to do it on your own.

The project approach encourages a broader view of knowledge and offers students the opportunity to introduce some of their own special knowledge into a Eurocentric curriculum. Though not all students availed themselves of this opportunity, those who were sensitive to the dominant European focus found it a useful strategy.

Another way to open up the complexities of issues surrounding a diaspora curriculum is through the use of dialogue and dialectic. A consistent critique among the students interviewed was the lack of dialogue within the classroom, especially on the topic of identities. As Paulo Freire (1993) pointed out, dialogue is central to the project of education, since it is only through the exchange of ideas that we can work towards transformative change. Yet we cannot take it for granted that students will enter the classroom with the skills needed to take part in such a dialogue. Thus diaspora literacy highlights identity as both a topic of discussion and a starting-point for the development of a deeper, more critically reflective mode of analysis. Adoption of such a curriculum would foreground issues involving cultural identity and geographic mobility in a more coherent way than has previously been possible. In this new framework, culture is regarded as evolving rather than absolute. Such an understanding recognizes the contextualization and re-contextualization of movements of peoples across geographic borders. A curriculum that combines cultural studies with critical pedagogy can recognize the value of hybridity and heterogeneity over biological sameness—the old value that reinforced cultural and racial stereotypes.

The next component in this holistic formation is dialectic. Dialectic can be understood as the unity of analysis and synthesis that emerges at every stage of diaspora literacy. More specifically, it involves breaking down and identifying the model's various parts and coming to a new understanding based on the interactions among them.

A dialectical approach allows for the recognition of contradictions within identity that more traditional, unproblematic notions of identity did not acknowledge. Dialectical theorizing recognizes that social problems are not isolated phenomena, attributable to individual or group deficits, or some lack in the social structure itself. Rather, it sees problems as part of the shifting interaction between individual and society. So it can be argued that the individual, a social actor, both creates and is created by the social universe of which he/she is a part. Neither individual nor society is given priority in analysis. Dialectical thinking attempts to tease out the histories and relations of accepted appearances and meanings, tracing interactions from the whole to the parts, from the system inward to the event (Darder, Baltadano, and Torres, 2003). In this way, critical theory helps us focus simultaneously on both sides of a social contradiction and thus to develop a curriculum that is meaningful and affirming for African-Canadian students and other traditionally marginalized groups.

A recurring theme in a curriculum focused on diaspora literacy is power, both in the sense of agency and in the sense of constraint. This theoretical position recognizes the importance of resistance in the lives of peoples of African descent.

Historicity

'Historicity' represents an approach to knowledge that emphasizes the role of history in identity formation. This approach makes it possible to recognize the aspects of African identity that virtually everyone of African descent shares to some degree: namely, the experiences of racialization, colonialism, and imperialism. Underlying and reinforcing issues of racialization are the ways in which knowledge is constructed via the official and unofficial curricula. What is missing from the official curriculum is a vast body of knowledge that encompasses not only Africa and its diaspora but also the specific experiences of African Canadians in Canada. Historical representations of people of African descent in North America tend to focus on slavery and the Underground Railway, erasing the diversity of African-Canadian experiences. In the context of diaspora literacy, however, the historical formation of different African communities in Canada can be explored, along with the factors, including racialization, that have contributed to the formation of present-day African-Canadian identities. Understanding how different groups within a society come to be formed would be valuable in itself, of course; but it would also allow for fresh thinking about the idea of 'community', including recognition of the diversity of experiences within the group described as African Canadian. For example, the fact that racism was an obvious aspect of African-Canadian life in early twentieth-century Alberta did not prevent interaction between black and other communities. It is worth noting Linebaugh and Rediker's insight that 'fixed, static notions of race, ethnicity, and nationality among historians have obscured a vital world of cooperation and accomplishment within a multi-racial, multiethnic, international working class' (1990: 225). They continue:

> [H]istorians who consciously posit static and immutable differences between workers black and white, Irish and English, slave and free in the early modern era have frequently failed to study the actual points of contact, overlap and cooperation between their idealized types. (226)

Thus Canadian students are rarely, if ever, introduced to African Canadians such as Mifflin Gibbs, Mary Shadd, or Stanley Grizzle, pioneers of human rights in Canada who were active members of the mainstream society. Nor are they told anything about the hybrid heritage of Sir James Douglas (the 'Father' of British Columbia).[1]

As Ellen Swartz points out in her discussion of the 'master script' in school curriculum, even when 'historically excluded "others" are . . . included in standard classroom texts', it is 'in very limited and constricted ways', without reference to broader issues (1992: 343). Typically, the interaction that takes place between communities is simply ignored. Even if we were focusing on African-Canadian history, it would be essential to recognize that the African-Canadian community did not develop in isolation but rather in relation to and with other social groups. Thus an account of 'white Canadian history' that fails to recognize the contributions of non-European groups is not merely incomplete but false. At the same time there is a tendency to treat the history taught in schools as if it were 'fact' rather than social interpretation. At a minimum, students need to learn how to question interpretations of the experience of marginalized and racialized groups that are presented as if they were straightforwardly factual.

Willinsky (1999), in his work on the connections between culture, race, and nation, argues for a 'postnationalism' in which these categories would no longer be regarded as natural divisions of humankind. Instead, the curriculum would emphasize the idea of Canada as the product of the civil and political choices made by the people who actually live here, rather than—as is the case at present—the product of a compact between two founding cultures. As Willinsky views it, a postnationalist imagination would see the categories of 'culture', 'race', and 'nation' not as realities but as 'elaborate means for claiming place and position, for establishing an advantage, for policing a boundary'—in effect, for 'justif[ying] inequalities' (1999: 97). Willinsky's approach allows for an 'opening up', a de-naturalization and de-sanitization, of the descriptor 'Canadian'.

Cultural Politics

The last component of the diaspora literacy model is what theorists call 'cultural politics': the ways in which culture works to empower some groups and constrain others, to situate some groups at the centre and move others to the margins, to ascribe 'authenticity' to some and to limit or remove it from others. For example, the emergence of a discourse around authenticity in high schools demands that students position themselves and others in relation to that discourse. In doing so, they already experience the tensions inherent in the process of representation. This experience opens the door to the understanding that discourses of similarity and difference are never as straightforward as they appear to be.

This point was illustrated in the course of one research project when the school organized a 'multicultural' event at which students were invited to 'represent' their various cultures. Focusing on food, dress, and dance, such celebrations are typical of the neutral multiculturalism that has been encouraged by government, and they are intended to be a form of affirmation. But the black students had difficulty finding a common cultural heritage to represent, and this led us to question the wisdom of such exercises. Indeed, the idea of representing a shared black identity seems absurd, given students' limited knowledge of both Africa and the diaspora—let alone the complex relations between the two. Under pressure to identify what gave them a sense of common identity, they fell back on music and the standard images of contemporary black youth constructed by the dominant cultural industries. The exercise might have had greater depth had the students been exposed to a more historically informed, complex, and heterogeneous understanding of blackness. In trying to perform a 'universal' black identity, however, they illustrated a tension that McCarthy (1997) refers to as 'nonsynchrony': a condition in which identities are never fully aligned in time and space.

We use the term 'representation' to refer to both the process of creating meaning from a given sign or signs and the product of that activity (O'Sullivan et al., 1994). Understanding the politics of representation requires an analysis of the construction of media images, power, and economics that allows us to draw out contradictions. By taking such realms of culture into account, diaspora literacy has the potential to heighten awareness of how ideology operates in any society and to bring to the forefront the ways in which domination is concealed and harnessed to serve sectional interests and dominant groups (Giddens, 1979).

Conclusion

The new approach to curriculum that we are advocating is not simply a matter of replacing negative images of people of African descent with positive ones. For one thing, as Nieto points out, 'Idealizing our ancestors, romanticizing their struggles, or presenting them as only heroes and saints is both dishonest and insulting to students' (1995: 209). Another reason for honesty is suggested by Stuart Hall (1997), who, drawing on Derrida, reminds us that meaning is unstable: therefore we can never be sure how students will interpret an image—even one that has been coded as positive.

A curriculum centred on diaspora literacy, by contrast, would help students appreciate the complexity of identity. A curriculum encompassing the concept of African diaspora would foreground issues around cultural identity and geographic mobility in a more coherent way than either official or unofficial curricula allowed for in the past. In this new framework, 'Canadian culture' would appear not as an absolute but as something in the process of evolution—more like an *amoeba* than a *mosaic*. Such an understanding recognizes the contextualization and re-contextualization of movements of peoples across geographic boundaries. A curriculum informed by cultural studies (see Gilroy, 1997, 2000; Hall, 1990, 1997) and critical pedagogy (see Freire, 1993) could emphasize hybridity and heterogeneity rather than homogeneity and stereotypes.

Although this chapter has focused on African-Canadian students, diaspora literacy is an inclusive approach that can be adapted for use with other diasporic communities. It has the potential to enable all students to develop a more nuanced understanding of black (or Chinese or East Indian) identities and to recognize that identities in general are complex and heterogeneous rather than simple and homogeneous. In the classroom, diaspora literacy offers a way to work with students whose cultural heritage may well be elsewhere but who are now firmly part of Canada. All students can learn more about identity and citizenship through exploration of diasporic identities. Such an approach can make a place for the experiences of people of African descent within the official curriculum and allow teachers to intervene in the process of identity formation that students are already engaged in as they educate themselves and others about the issues that have shaped their lives.

Note

This chapter draws on earlier research discussed in Brown and Kelly (2001) and Kelly (1998, 2004).

1. Mifflin Gibbs (1823–1915) was 'among the first of a long line of successful, if not wealthy, businessmen who helped shape the destiny of British Columbia' (<http://bhcsbc.org/historical_gibbs.html>). Mary Ann Shadd (1823–93) was the 'first black woman in North America to edit a weekly paper' and 'complemented her active anti-slavery efforts and editorials with articles on women and their contributions' (<http://collectioncanada.ca/women/002026-204-e.html>). Stanley Grizzle (b. 1918), who worked for many years as a railway porter, became a labour activist, a citizen court judge, and a member of the Order of Canada; in 2007 a Toronto park was named in his honour. For more on Sir James Douglas, visit the Black Historical and Cultural Society of British Columbia's excellent website at <http://www.bhcsbc.org/historical_douglas.html>.

Glossary

black identity: A fluid concept, in keeping with Stuart Hall's notion of identity as 'more the product of the marking of difference and exclusion than . . . the sign of an identical, naturally constituted unity' (2000: 17). This understanding makes problematic not only the concept of black identity in itself but also the notion of black 'community' and the idea that black students will somehow be automatically drawn to one another (Kelly, 2001: 4). It also recognizes how identity is affected by historical inheritance: i.e., the commonality of historical experiences that informs the present-day lives of racialized individuals and groups. Related to this, the notion of mediazation has significant impact on black identity formation in Canada (Hall, 2000: 10).

diaspora: The term generally used to refer to dispersed peoples, languages, or cultures formerly concentrated in a relatively bounded geographical space. Originally used to refer to the Jewish people, in the age of 'globalized' mobility 'diaspora' is commonly applied to groups ranging from Ukrainians to Chinese to those of African descent. For cultural theorists such as Paul Gilroy, 'the concept . . . involves "creolized, syncretized, hybridized and chronically impure cultural forms"' (cited in Barker, 2002: 75).

literacy: Originally, the ability to decode text, but understood in the Freirian sense as far more—not just 'reading the word' but reading the world, a process that encompasses both consciousness and critique.

mediazation: Defined by Thompson as 'the process by which the transmission of symbolic forms becomes increasingly mediated by the technical and institutional apparatuses of the media industries' (1990: 3).

representation: Defined by du Gay et al. as 'the practice of constructing meaning through the use of signs and language' (1997: 24). To analyze representation is to look at how the meanings associated with particular things, physical or otherwise, are expanded by association with other 'discourses or semantic networks', and how those things are marked as similar to or different from others (24–5).

Study Questions

1. Should the identities of African-Canadian students be explicitly recognized in the classroom? How? And by whom? Would this be the responsibility of the teacher or of the local African-Canadian community?
2. Should teachers directly address historical experiences that might be painful or disturbing for students or their communities? If so, how might this be most effectively accomplished?
3. How might you react if students asked you to help them gain recognition for a school group that would restrict participation to African Canadians? How would you explain your action to (a) various student groups and (b) your principal?
4. If a parent complained that the textbook used in your class was Eurocentric, how might you respond? What if a parent complained that your methods were 'too sensitive' or 'too multicultural'? What practical strategies might you use to address such issues (a) with parents and (b) in the classroom?
5. What advantages or disadvantages might there be for (a) sociologists of education and (b) classroom teachers in a curriculum that moved beyond the traditional focus on social reproduction to examination of identity?

Recommended Readings

Dei, S.G. 1996. *Antiracism Education: Theory and Practice*. Halifax: Fernwood Publishing.

Gilroy, P. 2000. *Against Race: Imagining Political Culture beyond the Color Line*. Cambridge, MA: Harvard University Press.

Mathieu, S.-J. 2001. 'North of the Colour Line: Sleeping Car Porters and the Battle against Jim Crow on Canadian Rails, 1880–1920', *Labour/Le Travail* 47: 9–41. Available at: <http://www.historycooperative.org/journals/llt/47/02mathie.html>. Accessed 18 May 2007.

McCarthy, C. 1997. 'Nonsynchrony and Social Difference: An Alternative to the Current Radical Accounts of Race and Schooling', in A.H. Halsey, H. Lauder, P. Brown, and A.S. Wells, eds, *Education, Culture, Economy, Society*. Oxford: Oxford University Press, 541–56.

Winks, R. 1997. *Blacks in Canada: A History*, 2nd edn. Montreal: McGill-Queen's University Press.

Recommended Websites

The Black Historical and Cultural Society of British Columbia (BHCS): http://bhcsbc.org/index.html

The CBC Archives 'Africville: Expropriating Nova Scotia's Blacks': http://archives.cbc.ca/IDD-1-69-96/life_society/africville/

Remembering Nova Scotia's Black Loyalists: http://museum.gov.ns.ca/blackloyalists/struggle.htm

The Ontario Black History Society (OBHS): http://www.blackhistorysociety.ca/

The Canadian Race Relations Foundation (CRR): http://www.crr.ca/

The Northern Alberta Alliance on Race Relations (NAARR): http://www.naarr.org/

References

Anderson, B. 1983. *Imagined Communities: Reflections on the Origin and Spread of Nationalism.* London: Verso.

Apple, M. 1996. 'Power, Meaning and Identity: Critical Sociology of Education in the United States', *British Journal Sociology of Education* 17, 2: 125–44.

Asante, M.K. 2001. 'Against Race: Imagining Political Culture beyond the Colour Line' [Review of the book *Between Camps*], *Journal of Black Studies* 31, 6: 847–51.

———. 2004. 'Africa and Its Diaspora: Forging Ideas of an African Renaissance', in First Conference of Intellectuals of Africa and Its Diaspora. Dakar, Senegal. 6–9 October. Available at: <http://www.kametrenaissance.com/Molefi-English-Doc2.html>.

Banks, J. 1986. 'Multicultural Education: Developments, Paradigms and Goals', in J. Banks and J. Lynch, eds, *Multicultural Education in Western Societies*. Westport, CT: Praeger, 2–28.

Barker, C. 2002. *Making Sense of Cultural Studies: Central Problems and Critical Debates*. London: Sage Publications.

Black Learners Advisory Committee. 1994. *BLAC Report on Education: Redressing Inequality— Empowering Black Learners*. Halifax: BLAC.

Bonilla-Silva, E. 1997. 'Rethinking Racism: Towards a Structural Interpretation', *American Sociological Review* 62, 3: 465–80.

Bourdieu, P. 1977. 'Cultural Reproduction and Social Reproduction', in J. Karabel and A.H. Halsey, eds, *Power and Ideology in Education*. New York: Oxford University Press, 487–511.

Bowles, S., and H. Gintis. 1976. *Schooling in Capitalist America*. New York: Basic Books.

Brathwaite, K., and C. James, eds. 1996. *Educating African Canadians*. Toronto: James Lorimer.

Brown, D., and J. Kelly. 2001. 'Curriculum and the Classroom: Private and Public Spaces', *British Journal of Sociology of Education* 22, 4: 501–18.

Brown, L. 2006. 'Making Blacks Feel at Home at School: Program Designed to Boost Marks Includes Math Unit on Racial Profiling', *Toronto Star*, 19 July: A01.

Calliste, A. 1987. 'Sleeping Car Porters in Canada: An Ethnically Submerged Split Labour Market', *Canadian Ethnic Studies* 19, 1: 1–20.

———. 1996. 'African Canadians' Organizing for Educational Change', in Brathwaite and James (1996: 87–106).

Chalmers, V. 1997. 'White Out: Multicultural Performances in a Progressive School', in M. Fine, L. Weis, L. Powell, and L. M. Wong, eds, *Off White: Readings on Race, Power, and Society*. New York: Routledge, 66–78.

Clarke, G.E. 1996. 'Must All Blackness Be American?: Locating Canada in Borden's "Tightrope Time", or Nationalizing Gilroy's Black Atlantic', *Canadian Ethnic Studies* 28, 3 Special Issue: 56–71.

Curtis, B. 1988. *Building the Educational State*. Toronto: University of Toronto Press.

Darder, A., M. Baltodana, and R.D. Torres. 2003. 'Critical Pedagogy: An Introduction', in *The Critical Pedagogy Reader*. New York: Routledge, 1–21.

Darroch, G. 1979. 'Another Look at Ethnicity, Stratification and Social Mobility in Canada', *Canadian Journal of Sociology* 4, 1: 1–25.

Dei, S.G. 1996. *Antiracism Education: Theory and Practice*. Halifax: Fernwood Publishing.

———. 1996. 'Listening to Voices: Developing a Pedagogy of Change from the Narratives of African Canadian Students and Parents', in Brathwaite and James (1996: 32–57).

———, I.M. James, L.L. Karumanchery, S. James-Wilson, and J. Zine. 2000. *Removing the Margins: The Challenges and Possibilities of Inclusive Schooling*. Toronto: Canadian Scholars' Press Inc.

du Gay, P., S. Hall, L. Janes, H. Mackay, and K. Negus. 1997. *Doing Cultural Studies: The Story of the Sony Walkman*. London: Sage Publications.

Enloe, C. 1973. *Ethnic Conflict and Political Development*. Boston: Little Brown.

Freire, P. 1993. *Pedagogy of the Oppressed*. New York: Continuum.

Giddens, A. 1979. *Central Problems in Social Theory: Action Structure and Contradiction in Social Analysis*. London: MacMillan.

Gillespie, M. 1995. *Television, Ethnicity and Cultural Change*. London: Routledge.

Gilroy, P. 1997. 'Diaspora and the Detours of Identity', in K.Woodward, ed, *Identity and Difference*. London: Sage Publications, 299–346.

———. 2000. *Between Camps: Nations, Cultures and the Allure of Race*. London: Penguin.

Giroux, H. 1996. *Fugitive Cultures: Race, Violence and Youth*. New York: Routledge.

Hall, S. 1990. 'Cultural Identity and Diaspora', in J. Rutherford, ed., *Identity, Community, Culture and Difference*. London: Lawrence and Wishart, 222–37.

———, ed. 1997. *Representation: Cultural Representation and Signifying Practices*. London: Sage.

———. 2000. 'Who Needs "Identity"?', in Paul du Gay, Jessica Evane, and Peter Redman, eds, *Identity: A Reader*. London: Sage Publications, 15–30.

Henry, F., and C. Tator. 1991. *Multicultural Education: Translating Policy into Practice*. Ottawa: Department of Multiculturalism and Citizenship.

hooks, b. 1990. 'Postmodern Blackness', *Postmodern Culture* 1, 1: 1–14.

James, C. 1990. *Making It: Black Youth, Racism and Career Aspirations in a Big City*. Oakville, ON: Mosaic.

———, and K. Brathwaite. 1996. 'The Education of African Canadians: Issues, Contexts, Expectations', in *Educating African Canadians* (1996: 13–31).

Kelly, J. 1998. *Under the Gaze: Learning to Be Black in White Society*. Halifax: Fernwood Press.

———. 2001. 'Borrowed Blackness: A Case Study of Black Identity and Cultural Formation among a Group of African Canadian High School Students'. PhD dissertation, University of Alberta, Edmonton, Canada.

———. 2004. *Borrowed Identities*. New York: Peter Lang.

King, J.E. 1992. 'Africentrism and Multiculturalism: Conflict or Consonance', *The Journal of Negro Education* 61, 3: 317–40.

Kliebard, H. 1992. 'Curriculum Theory: Give Me a "for instance"', in *Forging the American Curriculum*. New York: Routledge, 168–82.

Linebaugh, P., and M. Rediker. 1990. 'The Many Headed Hydra: Sailors, Slaves and the Atlantic Working Class in the Eighteenth Century', *Journal of Historical Sociology* 13, 3: L 225–52.

McCarthy, C. 1997. 'Nonsynchrony and Social Difference: An Alternative to the Current Radical Accounts of Race and Schooling', in A.H. Halsey, H. Lauder, P. Brown, and A., S. Wells, eds, *Education, Culture, Economy, Society*. Oxford: Oxford University Press, 541–56.

———, and W. Critchlow. 1993. 'Theories of Identity, Theories of Representation, Theories of Race', in *Race, Identity, and Representation in Education*. New York: Routledge, xiii–xxix.

McLaren, P.L., and C.E. Sleeter. 1995. *Multicultural Education, Critical Pedagogy and the Politics of Difference*. New York: State University of New York Press.

Malik, K. 1996. *The Meaning of Race*. Hampshire, UK: MacMillan Press.

Mathieu, S.-J. 2001. 'North of the Colour Line: Sleeping Car Porters and the Battle against Jim Crow on Canadian Rails, 1880–1920', *Labour/Le Travail* 47: 9–41. Available at: <http://www.historycooperative.org/journals/llt/47/02mathie.html>. Accessed 18 May 2007.

Miles, R. 1982. *Racism and Migrant Labour*. London: Routledge and Kegan Paul.

Moore, R. 2004. *Education and Society: Issues and Explanations in the Sociology of Education*. Cambridge: Polity Press.

Moodley, K. 1992. *Beyond Multicultural Education: International Perspectives*. Calgary: Detselig Enterprises.

Nieto, S. 1995. 'From Brown Heroes to Assimilationist Agendas Reconsidering the Critiques of Multicultural Education', in C. Sleeter and P. McLaren, eds, *Multicultural Education, Critical Pedagogy, and the Politics of Difference*. New York: SUNY Press, 191–221.

Ontario Ministry of Education and Training. 1993. 'Antiracism and Ethnocultural Equity in School Boards: Guidelines for Policy Development and Implementation'. Ministry of Education and Training. Toronto: OMET. Available at: <http://www.edu.gov.on.ca/eng/document/curricul/antiraci/antire.pdf>. Accessed 18 May 2007.

O'Sullivan, T., J. Hartley, D. Saunders, M. Montgomery, and J. Fiske, eds. 1994. *Key Concepts in Communication and Cultural Studies*. London: Routledge.

Porter, J. 1967. *The Vertical Mosaic*. Toronto: University of Toronto Press.

Razack, S. 2002. *Race, Space and the Law: Unmapping a White Settler Society*. Toronto: Between the Lines.

Reitz, J.G., and R. Banerjee. 2007. 'Racial Inequality, Social Cohesion and Policy Issues in Canada', in K. Banting, T.J. Courchene, and F.L. Seidle, eds, *Belonging? Diversity, recognition & shared citizenship in Canada*. Montreal: Institute for Research on Public Policy, 1–57.

Schick, C., and V. St. Denis. 2005. 'Troubling Nationalist Discourses', *Canadian Journal of Education* 28, 3: 295–317.

Solomon, P. 1992. *Black Resistance in High School: Forging a Separatist Culture*. New York: State University of New York Press.

Stevenson, N. 1997. *Understanding Media Cultures*. London: Sage Publications.

Swartz, E. 1992. 'Emancipatory Narratives: Rewriting the Master Script in the School Curriculum', *Journal of Negro Education* 61, 3: 341–56.

Thomas, D. 2002. 'Modern Blackness: What We Are and What We Hope to Be', *Small Acts* 6, 2: 1–15. Available at: <http://muse.jhu.edu/journals/small_axe/v006/2.2thomas.html>. Accessed 24 July 2006.

Thompson, J.B. 1990. *Ideology and Modern Culture: Critical Social Theory in the Era of Mass Communication*. Cambridge: Polity Press.

Walker, J. 1980. *A History of Blacks in Canada*. Ottawa: Supply and Services.

Waters, M. 1994. *Modern Sociological Theory*. London: Sage.

Willinsky, J. 1999. 'Curriculum after Culture, Race, and Nation', *Discourse Studies in the Cultural Politics of Education* 20, 1: 89–112.

CHAPTER 10

Rethinking Culture Theory in Aboriginal Education

Verna St. Denis

> Will teaching Native culture remedy the many wounds of oppression?
>
> (Hermes, 2005: 23)

Introduction

In their book *The Colour of Democracy: Racism in Canadian Society*, Henry, Tator, Mattis, and Rees state that 'the legacy of centuries of dispossession, oppression, and exploitation directed at the Aboriginal peoples of Canada is the direct result of pervasive and intractable racism' (1996: 64). They refer to the documentation provided in various historical and contemporary reports in areas such as law and justice, child welfare, Aboriginal women, the economy, land claim processes, and residential schools. But when racialized conflict between Aboriginal and white Canadians erupts in a way that makes it clear that collective action is required, more often than not what is recommended is not anti-racism education but cross-cultural awareness or race-relations training for the primarily 'white' service providers, including police officers, social workers, and teachers. Usually the recommended cross-cultural awareness or race-relations training does not include a critical race theory analysis that might explore 'how a regime of white supremacy and its subordination of people of color have been created and maintained' (Ladson-Billings, 1999: 14). Rather than acknowledging the need for a critical examination of how and why race matters in our society, it is often suggested that it is Aboriginal people and their culture that must be explained to and understood by those in position of racial dominance. A recent example is the Stonechild Inquiry that recommends race-relations training that will include 'information about Aboriginal culture, history, societal and family structures' (Wright, 2004: 213).

This chapter explores how the culture concept and the discipline of anthropology came to occupy such an important role in the conceptualizing and theorizing in the lives of Aboriginal people and especially in Aboriginal education. This knowledge is important because of the effects that the culture concept and discipline has had on the capacity for defining and suggesting solutions to Aboriginal educational problems. For example, in both explaining and seeking solutions to low achievement and high dropout rates for Aboriginal students, the call is usually made for **'culturally relevant' education** rather than the need for a critical race and class analysis. This chapter will suggest that a cultural framework of analysis is partial and inadequate on its own for explaining Aboriginal educational failures and that culturally based solutions can inadvertently contribute to further problems.

Current concepts of Aboriginal education and the sub-discipline of educational anthropology evolved during the same time period and are as related as are anthropologists and Indians in North America. As has been observed, the discipline of anthropology was 'invented across the "red/white" color line' (Michaelson, 1999: xvi). Both Aboriginal and American-Indian educators have acknowledged the predominance of the culture concept and anthropology in Aboriginal and American-Indian education. In a review of literature on American-Indian education, Deyhle and Swisher (1997: 117) observed that, 'over the past 30 years, we found that the largest body of research was grounded in educational anthropology and sociology'. Furthermore they state that this research 'used the concept of culture as a framework for the analysis of schooling and the behaviour of Indian students, parents and their communities' (ibid.).

In the 1960s much of the educational anthropology literature suggested that racialized minority children failed in school because their cultural beliefs and practices predisposed them to failure, and they were, therefore, described as being 'culturally deprived' or even 'deviant' (McDermott, 1997). In the 1970s some adjustments were made to the cultural framework for analyzing educational failure, suggesting that it was not so much that some children were culturally deprived or culturally disadvantaged but that their way of life was merely 'culturally different'—not better or worse than that valued by schools, but definitely different (McDermott, 1997). The subsequent educational interventions suggested that cultural differences needed to be celebrated rather than eradicated. This shift in emphasis was meant to advantage Aboriginal and American-Indian children whose culture would now be celebrated and observed through research that would focus on learning styles and acculturation processes.

This shift towards prescribing the celebration of cultural difference as a means to bring about educational equality provided a foundation for the growing focus on the importance and necessity of cultural and language revitalization for Aboriginal students. American-Indian educators and researchers Tippeconnic and Swisher note that, 'beginning in the 1960s and into the 70s a revival of "Indianness" in the classroom was now encouraged' (1992: 75). In a Canadian review of policy on Aboriginal education, Abele, Dittburner, and Graham also explain that between 1967 and 1982 Aboriginal education was increasingly regarded as a 'means for the revitalization of Indian cultures and economies' (2000: 8).

As part of this cultural revitalization, the provision of culturally relevant education assumed great importance for improving the educational success of Aboriginal students, and the health and well-being of Aboriginal communities in general. This shift to regarding education as the means to revitalize Aboriginal culture and language is often attributed to processes of decolonization and, in Canada, to the policy outlined in 'Indian Control of Indian Education' (National Indian Brotherhood, 1972). The idea that culture and language could be revitalized, and that Aboriginal people needed a 'positive' cultural identity as a prerequisite to success in education and in life more generally, can also be understood to be derivative of anthropological concepts and theorizing.

In writing this chapter, I have been informed by my own experiences and professional knowledge as an Aboriginal teacher and educator. By the time I arrived on campus as a university student in the late 1970s, the move towards decolonizing education by Aboriginal people in Canada was already moving forward with the adoption of the policy position outlined in 'Indian Control of Indian Education' (National Indian Brotherhood, 1972). With the recognition of this policy came the establishment of Indian cultural centres, Indian Teacher Education programs, cultural survival schools, and Indian and Native Studies departments across the country (Posluns, 2007). It was a very exciting time for us Aboriginal students since we could now pursue specialized studies in Aboriginal education and Native Studies.

In 1978 I enrolled in the Indian Teacher Education Program at the University of Saskatchewan. I was going to become an 'Indian' teacher. I was younger than most students in the program at that time, and, although both my parents had spoken Cree, I myself was not fluent in Cree. Indian Teacher Education programs were at the forefront in calling for the cultural and language revitalization of Indian cultures, and Indian teachers were to play a significant role in this revitalization. In this educational context I sensed I was in trouble—I was well aware that my lack of fluency in my indigenous language placed me at a disadvantage. The analysis offered here in this chapter is one attempt to make sense of this 'trouble'.

I didn't realize back then the role that anthropological concepts and theory had in the formulations of Aboriginal education through notions like '**cultural discontinuity**', 'cultural relevance', 'cultural difference', and 'acculturation/**enculturation**'. As a student and teacher of Aboriginal education and Native Studies, I never imagined that studying anthropology and its concepts would be useful in unravelling some of the ways in which we interpret the problems and solutions we have named and pursued in Aboriginal education.

Although I have now been involved in Aboriginal education for almost three decades, it is only in the past decade that I realized I needed to know more about anthropology. I had avoided learning about anthropology partly because anthropology and history were two mainstream disciplines that Native Studies and Aboriginal education had rallied against in the 1970s and 1980s. I regarded the discipline of anthropology, as some in late 1960s referred to it, as the 'child of colonialism' (Gough, in Caulfield, 1969: 182) and therefore not worthy of attention. It was Rosaldo's *Culture and Truth: The Remaking of Social Analysis* (1989) that introduced me to a critique of classic notions in anthropology. Reading this book marked the beginning of my efforts to develop an understanding of how anthropologically informed social analysis has impacted the development of Aboriginal education. This chapter offers an analysis of how those of us in Aboriginal education have been historically and discursively constituted within and by anthropological theory and research.

I began to understand that the social and cultural analysis prevalent when I first enrolled in the Indian Teacher Education Program was informed not only by 'Indian philosophy and worldview' but also by the social and cultural analysis practised by American anthropologists who combined psychology and anthropology through their focus on culture and personality and acculturation studies. The culture and personality movement and acculturation studies inspired psychologists and anthropologists who were interested in cross-cultural education, and who contributed to the development of educational anthropology. In turn, the social and cultural analysis offered by scholars of educational anthropology influenced the conceptualizing of Aboriginal/Indian education. As someone who has been involved in Aboriginal/Indian education for almost 30 years, I find there is still much to learn about this legacy of anthropological ideas, concepts, problems, and solutions that helped to shape Indian education.

European Philosophical and Intellectual Legacies

Culture is . . . itself the illness to which it proposes a cure.

(Eagleton, 2000: 31)

Although reading Rosaldo's *Culture and Truth* may have marked the beginning of my journey to understand the influence of anthropology on Aboriginal education, my introduction to a study of the culture concept occurred within a graduate philosophy course taught by German professor Wolfgang Welsch. Among the various European philosophers we studied, the work of the German Romantic philosopher Johann Gottfried Herder (1774/1967) stood out. Later, as I developed a broader understanding of the history of anthropology, and the anthropology of Franz Boas in particular, Herder's importance in conceptualizing modern notions of culture and nation became apparent (Eagleton, 2000; Malik, 1996; Williams 1976; Young, 1995). As is often the case in intellectual history, the legacy of Herder's ideas is complex, as one can make a link between his ideas of culture and nation as a justification for xenophobia through articulations of 'cultural racism' and his ideas of the value of diverse cultures as support for acknowledging the right for cultures/nations to exist.

Efforts to develop a history of the culture concept invariably require attempts to make sense of the relationships between the varied usages of the concepts of 'culture' and 'civilization', and 'Romanticism' and 'Primitivism' within European thought and social practice. In regard to the concept of Primitivism, anthropologist Diamond (1964: 127) explains, 'the search for the primitive is as old as civilization. It is the search for the utopia of the past, projected into the future; it is paradise lost and paradise regained, with civilization being the middle term'. On the other hand, De Zengotita describes Romanticism as 'the effort of the alienated modern mind to refuse itself, as alienated, and so re-fuse itself, as embodied in the world' and 'marked by its oppositionality' (1989: 75). Herder and his ideas are often described as constitutive of Romanticism.

Both Romanticism and Primitivism have influenced our understanding of 'culture' and 'civilization' through articulations of self and Other. Scholarly writing about the history of the development of modern notions of culture is often situated within histories of Romanticism if not Primitivism. Although Romanticism and Primitivism are two different social and intellectual developments, there is some overlap and similarities between these two schools of thought. And although neither Romanticism nor Primitivism has been consistently or constantly invoked in European imagination and fantasies of the Other, one of their recurring and enduring emphases is a valorization of the Other, as a way to critique and register dissatisfaction with European society (Stocking, 1986).

Herder is described by anthropologist Del Hymes as a 'seminal Enlightenment figure in the German tradition, a man who developed a sympathetic understanding of the validity of diverse cultures' (1969: 19). Robert Young (1995) also situates Herder within a 'romantic reaction against the grand claims of civilizations, in which the word "culture" was used as an alternative word to express other kinds of human development, other criteria for human well-being' (37). Herder conceptualized 'culture' as the 'uniquely distinct' way of life, values, and beliefs of a people; culture was what distinguished one people from another (1774, 44f.). Herder is regarded as the first to speak 'of "cultures" in the plural: the specific and variable cultures of different nations and periods' (Williams, 1976: 89) and of 'national and traditional cultures' (Williams, 1976: 89) as opposed to 'civilization'.

Herder's conceptualization of 'culture' has lent itself to a belief in '**cultural essentialism**' and 'cultural determinism' that is elaborated upon in Boasian anthropology. Herder suggested that

> The nature of a people found expression through its *volksgeist*—the unchanging spirit of a people refined through history. What gave unity to the life and culture of a people was the continuity of this original spirit. The *volksgeist* was expressed through myths, songs and sagas that carried the eternal heritage of a people, far removed from the ephemera of science and modernity. Myths and legends represented a cultural heritage that reached back to the origins of a people and, if conserved, could rejuvenate its spirit. (Malik, 1996: 78; italics in original)

This notion of an unchanging spirit that could be rejuvenated through the songs, myths, and legends of a people is a concept of culture that would be reinforced and built upon in functional anthropology, and, in turn, is a concept of culture that suggests the possibility of cultural revitalization. It suggests an essential culture that is able to exist in the realm of the spiritual.

Herder also signalled language as important to the delineation of a nation, because within language dwells a people's 'entire world of tradition, history, religion, principles of existence; its whole heart and soul' (Herder, in Malik, 1996: 78–9). This idea that the culture of a people is invoked through its language and stories is further developed in the efforts made in Aboriginal education to participate in cultural and language revitalization, as it was also an idea brewing within anthropological studies of culture and personality and acculturation.

Another of Herder's beliefs was in the 'incommensurability of the values of different cultures and societies' (Malik, 1996: 78). Herder rationalized prejudice because it encouraged people of a similar culture/nation to stay together, providing a glue of sorts:

> Prejudice is good, at its right time: for it makes for happiness. It forces peoples together to their centre, makes them firmer at their stem, more flourishing in their kind, more fervent and happier too in their inclinations and aims. (Herder, 1774, 44f)

This idea of the incommensurability of different cultures would eventually propel and motivate anthropology's interest in what makes people different. The idea would lend itself not only to an exaggeration of human difference but also a negative evaluation of these differences, making possible notions like folks who suffer not from colonial oppression but from 'cultural incongruence', and 'cultural discontinuity', both of which were seen as tangible threats to cultural self-preservation despite whatever cultural exchanges and accommodations have been made by cultural Others (Biolsi, 1997).

The idea of the 'incommensurability' of cultures led anthropologists in search of 'an Indian culture incommensurably alien from [their own]' (Biolsi, 1997: 140)—in other words, the search for the 'real' Indian (Biolsi, 1997; Waldram, 2004). The belief in twentieth-century social analysis about the incommensurability of different cultures encourages a trivializing of the impact of colonial oppression by attributing the effects and the conditions of oppression to this very factor of incommensurability. In the example of Aboriginal people, effects of oppression are cast as 'value conflicts' between white and Indian cultures, suggesting that inequality is inevitable, and merely an effect of different orientations to work, education, and family. When the effects of oppression are attributed to a 'conflict of values' it is easy to see how the remedy then becomes cross-cultural awareness training or a 'race'-relations program that does not disrupt the status quo of structural inequality while seemingly responding.

Understanding American Anthropological Legacies

> We owe our modern notion of culture in large part to nationalism and colonialism, along with the growth of an anthropology in the service of imperial power.
>
> (Eagleton, 2000: 26)

This section of the chapter provides a broad overview of some key ideas and concepts central to a social analysis informed by classic anthropology. Beginning students of anthropology are soon apprised of the enormous influence of Franz Boas on anthropology and more specifically on American anthropology (Darnell, 2000; Stocking, 1968/82; Vincent, 1990). Part of his legacy includes challenging scientific racism and its assumptions of a 'single hierarchical evolutionary sequence' (Stocking, 1974: 18) in which those of European ancestry were above and ahead of everyone else. Boas, who drew his inspiration from Herder, suggested that human difference could be better understood through a notion of culture as 'relativistic, pluralistic, holistic, integrated, and historically conditioned' (Stocking, 1974: 19). This relativistic and pluralistic stance towards human diversity was intended to discourage the moral and social evaluations of those designated as Other (Stocking, 1968), including Indigenous and Aboriginal people whose 'difference' could be assessed as 'equally valid' (Malik, 1996:

152). Drawing on a Herderian notion of 'specific and variable cultures' (Williams, 1976: 89) Boas shifted anthropological and social analysis from culture to culture*s*.

Along with the idea of many equally valid cultures, Boas also believed that 'culture conditioned people to behave in culturally specific ways' (Willis, 1969: 137). A Boasian concept of culture was

> synonymous not so much with conscious activity as with unconscious tradition. He drew on the Romantic Herderian vision of culture as heritage and habit, the role of which was to allow the past to shape the present. Tradition and history moulded an individual's behaviour. (Malik, 1996: 154)

Through concepts like 'enculturation', this idea of a culture as a conditioning process became a central concept in educational anthropology, and suggested research into the 'enculturation processes' of culturally different students, families, and communities. In addition, this idea that culture is a conditioning process implied that it is not people who create culture through the conditions of their everyday lives, but rather 'culture' that creates people. It is as if culture is an object with its own agency divorced from people. This objectification of culture also suggests that culture is something to be 'lost' and 'found'. It is as if people are no longer agents; culture happens to them. A notion like 'cultural determinism' then becomes possible. Cultural determinism has been used to justify racism; hence the notion of 'cultural racism' (Hall, 1982; Gilroy, 1990) that becomes another way to justify discrimination.

Culture as a conditioning process and as an entity outside human life is also a foundational belief of functional anthropology, a form of anthropology popularized by Boas' students, including Ruth Benedict and Alfred Kroeber. For example, Benedict promoted the idea that 'the vast proportion of all individuals who are born into any society always [assume] the behaviour dictated by that society' (Benedict, in Malik, 1996: 163). Kroeber also promoted the idea that culture 'was not the conscious creation of humanity but the unconscious product of human activity which stood above and beyond society' (Malik, 1996: 162).

This idea of culture as an entity outside of people provides a foundation for the belief in the potential for 'cultural revitalization' and the very idea that culture can be retrieved. While the idea that culture resides deep inside one's 'core' may be reassuring in the early stages of an engagement with cultural revitalization, when that 'traditional' culture fails to appear or reveal itself, it can be very troubling. This failure of culture to appear becomes a very different kind of problem. It is a problem long familiar to those anthropologists who have been keenly interested in 'authentic' and 'real' Indians or the 'primitive', and for whom evidence of 'cultural change' would suggest otherwise, namely that culture is mutable.

Many have critiqued anthropologists' interest and fetishization of the most exotic and primitive Other (e.g., Biolsi, 1997; Caulfield, 1969; Deloria, 1969; Rosaldo, 1989). The implications for regarding cultural change as a threat and as a negative process continue to have repercussions for 'Others' such as Aboriginal people. Anthropologists, such as Boas and his students, responded in several ways to evidence of cultural change. At times, they ignored this evidence (Keesing, 1990), asserting, 'essential culture-ness lives on despite the outward changes in their lives' (Keesing, 1990: 48); at other times, they interpreted change as a sign of psychological duress in the primitive Other (DuBois, 1955; Waldram, 2004). Not only was cultural change regarded as dangerous for the 'primitive' Other, but 'rapid' cultural change was regarded as even more detrimental. Culture was something primitive people 'had', and it was understood that 'primitive' people needed culture more than 'civilized' people did. As Stocking explains, Boas 'felt that civilized men were in important respects less bound by tradition than primitives' (Stocking, 1968: 226).

Boas also claimed that 'we cannot remodel, without serious emotional resistance, any of the fundamental lines of thought and actions which are determined by our early education, and which form the subconscious basis of all our activities' (Boas, in Stocking, 1968: 226). Boas further believed that people 'learned less by instruction than imitation because they constitute the whole series of well-established habits according to which the necessary actions of everyday life are performed' (Boas, in Stocking, 1968: 227). As Stocking explains,

> It was in this context that the idea of culture, which once connoted all that freed man from the blind weight of tradition, was now identified with that very burden, and that burden was seen as functional to the continuing daily existence of individuals in any culture and at every level of civilization. (1968: 227)

Educational anthropology would embrace the above ideas and to a large degree so would Aboriginal education. This conceptualization has resulted in that claim that it is 'cultural discontinuity' between the school and the Aboriginal family and community, and the inability of Aboriginal students to make adequate cultural adjustments, that causes high levels of school failure for Aboriginal students despite evidence that racism and classism are equally if not more compelling reasons for these levels of school failure (Ledlow, 1992). Culturally relevant education rather than anti-oppressive education have become common-sense solutions. As well, the idea that 'primitives' learn less by instruction than by imitation led to research focusing on understanding different 'learning styles' and with the effect of creating a new set of stereotypes about the nature of Aboriginal learning styles.

The interest in cultural change, particularly in rapid cultural change that could allegedly result in psychological trauma for the cultural Other, became a focus of study for anthropologists interested in acculturation. Anthropology and psychology were brought together in both culture and personality studies as well as studies of acculturation. Benedict 'ignited' culture and personality studies within anthropology (Caffrey, 1989). For example, in her book *The Chrysanthemum and the Sword* (1946), Benedict compared and contrasted basic traits of American culture with Japanese culture. Benedict also described cultures as exhibiting different types of personalities, contrasting, for example, 'introverted' and 'extroverted' cultures. Another student of Boas, Margaret Mead, was also an early contributor to studies of culture and personality. Mead took the 'two psychological traits of cooperation and competition, and compared their strength, variations, and relationships among thirteen different cultures' (Caffrey, 1989: 242). Benedict's anthropological social analysis applied 'psychological' terms, which formerly had been only applied to describe individuals, to describe configurations of all peoples within the culture. Her notion of cultures as personality types 'surfaced in the psychological literature of the 1970s and 1980s with sweeping generalizations of *the* Aboriginal personality (Waldram, 2004: 9, original italics).

This method of anthropological social analysis, exemplified by Benedict and Mead, compared and contrasted cultures as a whole and paved the way for cross-cultural comparisons that continue to remain popular in educational research. In particular, this method has been used as a way of explaining the low academic achievement of Aboriginal students. This particular comparative emphasis in anthropological studies has a profound effect on understanding Aboriginal culture and education:

> Forcing Aboriginal peoples into a single, uniform, and implicitly homogenous variable category to be contrasted with another, similarly homogeneous category, the non-Aboriginal or 'white', is a strong convention in comparative research. (Waldram, 2004: 8)

In the late 1950s and 1960s, these studies comparing cultures lent themselves to the type of anthropology pursued in the developing sub-discipline of educational anthropology in which caricatures of white middle-class cultural values would be compared with Indian cultural values (e.g., DuBois, 1955; Hawthorne, 1967).

Acculturation studies, on the other hand, promoted ideas that the retention of 'indigenous belief systems' was essential for Indians to adequately adjust to rapid social change (Waldram, 2004). Anthropologists were often not interested in documenting the creative and successful ways in which Indians were making cultural adaptations to their continually changing environments (Deloria, 1969). This was especially the case if anthropologists were particularly interested in finding the most 'incommensurable' and exotic Indian (Biolsi, 1997). Further advancing the belief that culture was a 'cure', studies of acculturation, such as those conducted among the Hopi, claimed that 'Personality disorders and social breakdown characterize Hopi communities that have lost their values and their ceremonies' (Thompson, 1946: 210, in Waldram, 2004: 37). This idea that Indian culture is 'lost' and that Indians have lost their culture is a deceptively benign but very common way to refer to the effects of colonial and racial oppression on Aboriginal people. In acculturation studies, suggesting that 'maintaining essential, internal cultural integrity' (Thompson, 1950, in Waldram, 2004: 35) is necessary for exploited and colonized people has become a popular and common way to blame the victim of oppression.

The problem of inequality is now attributed to the Indian who does not have 'cultural integrity' rather than the social, economic, and political context that does not recognize the human rights of Aboriginal people. Acculturation, and culture and personality studies, contributed to reducing the effects of colonial and racial oppression to a problem of an identity crisis. Restoring the Indian has become the imperative rather than ensuring social and political justice. The anthropological interest in a timeless and unchanging cultural Indian demeans Aboriginal and American-Indian peoples who have had to constantly adjust to and live with the context of ongoing and normalized racism. For example, Mead explains that Benedict was not as interested in adaptations to cultural change as she was in 'listening for the older culture beneath the *broken phrases of the new*' (Mead, 1974: 30, italics added). The idea that cultural adaptation is regarded as 'broken' relegates Indians as interesting to the degree that they can serve as windows to the past, ignoring the effects of colonization by aiming to celebrate and recoup as much 'traditional' culture as possible.

As many have stated, Boas and his many students 'never showed any real interest in studying the *situation* of conquest and exploitation (Caulfield, 1969: 184, italics in original). This failure by the anthropology of that time to explore the consequences and situation of exploitation continued to have repercussions for at least the early years in the development of Aboriginal education by and for Aboriginal people. Rather than examining the situation of conquest and exploitation, anthropologists like Benedict were more interested in bringing attention to 'the desperate urgency of doing anthropological field work before the last precious and irretrievable memories of traditional American Indian cultures were carried to the grave' (Mead, 1974: 3). Mead explains that Benedict's anthropology 'made the breakdown and disappearance of the traditional culture vivid and irreparable. But she was not sentimental about the possibility of preserving Indian societies or romantic about Indians who had been disinherited' (Mead, 1974: 5). Kroeber also asked: 'Why should we preserve Mohave values when they themselves cannot preserve them, and their descendants will likely be indifferent? It is the future of our own world culture that can be enriched by the preservation of these values, and our ultimate understandings grow wider as well as deeper' (Kroeber, in Mead, 1974: 48). Here we have an anthropology that cared more about 'Indian culture' than the people of that culture, yet another example of the belief in a culture as something outside and existing independently of its people.

This background knowledge of anthropology provides a basis to better understand the published conference proceedings of the first conference of educational anthropology. That conference helped initiate the field of Educational Anthropology, which has had its own set of implications for Aboriginal education.

The Legacy of Educational Anthropology

> We observe the desperate struggles of a Negro who is driven to discover the meaning of black identity. White civilization and European culture have forced an existential deviation on the Negro. I shall demonstrate elsewhere that what is often called the black soul is a white man's artifact.
>
> (Fanon, 1986: 16)

In 1954, the anthropologist George Spindler hosted a conference that brought together several educators and anthropologists; among them were anthropologists Margaret Mead, Alfred Kroeber, and Cora DuBois. Several papers were presented, along with remarks by formal discussants; conference proceedings were published in the book *Education and Anthropology* (Spindler, 1955a) and later republished in the edited collection, *Education and Culture: Anthropological Approaches* (Spindler, 1963).

In the opening comments, Spindler remarks, 'no "educational anthropology" exists at present' (1955a: 5). He explains that part of the task of the conference was to further the development of an exploratory framework for the development of education and anthropology through 'their concepts, data, methods, and problems' (Spindler, 1955b: v). Some of the many concepts utilized in the papers and the discussions that followed included ones familiar to those who work in the area of Aboriginal education, including: cultural transmission; enculturation; acculturation; cultural awareness; bicultural, monocultural, and intercultural learners; cultural gap; and cultural discontinuity.

Conference participants acknowledged that the discipline of psychology made it possible to combine educational and anthropological interests (Frank, 1955). Participants agreed that exploring cultural processes of socialization was one way in which anthropology could contribute to education. Socialization processes were understood to vary from culture to culture, and it was those 'differences' that could form the basis of investigation in developing educational anthropology. Building on acculturation and personality studies in anthropology, educational anthropology would also explore processes of cultural change, cultural adaptation, and cultural continuity. Knowledge of socialization practices and processes could in turn help educators and schools assist culturally different students adjust to change.

Quillen, who at the time was dean of the Stanford School of Education, suggested that anthropological knowledge of the processes of cultural continuity could further understanding of education as a cultural process. Through the combination of psychology and anthropology, schools and education are described as places 'concerned with the transmission, conservation, and extension of culture' (Quillen, 1955: 2). Rather than family and community as places where culture is learned, education and schools are looked upon as 'the instrument through which cultures perpetuated themselves. It is the process through which the members of a society assure themselves that the behaviour necessary to continue their culture is learned' (Quillen, 1955: 1). The idea that education and schools are important places for 'cultural transmission' is articulated here in a way that would come to have enormous significance for Aboriginal people a decade later, as they sought involvement in how and what their children would be taught in school.

There are two implications from this proposed relationship between culture and education that have taken hold within current conceptualizations of Aboriginal education. First, that cultural continuity is seen as necessary for the survival and success of Aboriginal students and people in general; and second, that schools are regarded as the site where this will happen. This idea that schools and education are the site for cultural continuity and cultural transmission has become accepted wisdom in Aboriginal education (see, e.g., Royal Commission on Aboriginal Peoples, 1996). Through the conceptual framework of educational anthropology, schools are increasingly instructed to become a place where 'culturally relevant' education should occur so as to ensure cultural continuity and cultural transmission for the Aboriginal child. But in light of massive cultural change in regards to how Aboriginal people live, the task of providing culturally relevant education can prove to be perplexing and challenging for the well-intentioned Aboriginal teacher who asks, 'what is it exactly that you want to be taught in the classroom, the parents say let's teach culture in a classroom, but they don't come out and say what they mean by culture' (Friesen and Orr, 1995: 22). In the context of ongoing cultural change, this line of questioning remains relevant, but it is also the legacy of an anthropology that was once intent on 'reconstructing traditional culture' (Asad, in Stocking, 1991: 318).

By combining psychology and anthropology, the field of educational anthropology would pursue investigations that would seek to explain the impact of differences between the cultural values and beliefs of the culturally different child and the teacher. Allusions to Benedict's 'patterns of culture' and personality formation are evident in Spindler's suggestion that anthropology could help educators understand how culture shaped 'behavioural compulsion and perception and the variable forms these patterns take' (1955: 11). It was proposed that this cultural knowledge could help teachers understand how 'imitation, participation, communication, and informal methods' socialize members into one's culture, as well as how 'cultural motivation, incentives, values and school learning' are related (Quillen, 1955: 3).

Four decades later, this theorizing about difference has, more often than not, resulted in the production of stereotypes and classist and racist constructions of the culturally different child (Laroque, 1991; Razack, 1998). This anthropological orientation to understanding 'difference' is now used to endorse the current demand that human service providers be 'culturally competent' in their delivery of services. Without examining the impact of racism and classism, this requirement for cultural competency has the potential to repeat stereotypes of Aboriginal people rather than focusing on how racial dominance and poverty continue to detrimentally impact Aboriginal people (Razack, 1998; Schick and St. Denis, 2005).

To elucidate further the nature of the theorizing at this 1954 conference, I will discuss in detail the paper presented by the anthropologist Cora DuBois, entitled 'Some Notions on Learning Intercultural Understanding' (1955). There is no single straightforward trajectory to understanding how, when, and why the concept of culture, as opposed to the need for social and political justice, has come to occupy such a large role in articulating Aboriginal education, but the theorizing and conceptualizing in the DuBois paper provides one avenue to that understanding.

DuBois's paper, which is representative of thinking at the conference, explores the challenges that face intercultural learners. She begins by distinguishing between 'international education' and 'intercultural' education. To distinguish between these two forms of education, DuBois suggests that the culture concept, embedded in the concept 'intercultural', is associated with the 'primitive', while the 'nation' concept, embedded in the concept 'international', is associated with 'complex' societies. This distinction underlies the examples she presents in which she compares and contrasts the experiences of a white American child of missionaries born in India and raised by Indian nurses, as opposed to the experiences of an African village boy who is sent away to boarding school in Africa. DuBois describes the experiences of both in terms of intercultural learning, but it is implied in her thinking that the white child of missionaries is also, and more importantly, an international learner. The politics of this articulation of culture as a concept associated with the Other, and the nation as a concept associated with the civilized person, has a long history not only in anthropology but in

Western and European thinking in general. It is not common for those in a position of racial dominance to risk relativizing their own way of life by describing it as a 'culture': as Eagleton puts it, 'One's own way of life is simply human; it is other people who are ethnic, idiosyncratic, culturally peculiar' (2000: 27).

In order to discuss the potential and unique challenges faced by each category of learner, DuBois makes distinctions first between two types of intercultural learners—the bicultural learner and the monocultural learner—and second, between two types of bicultural learners. According to DuBois, the white American child of missionaries and the African village child sent to the boarding school, described above, offer 'dramatically different' examples of bicultural learning (1955: 94). Given that anthropological theory had already established that change is not good for the cultural Other, that the potential for psychological disequilibrium is great in light of cultural change, and that anthropologists were not interested in creative adaptations the cultural Other were making in response to change, then it makes sense that DuBois 'knew', and we now know, which of these two children would fare better in this process of bicultural learning.

In DuBois's hypothetical case, the American child is presumed to be able to resolve any potential cultural conflict resulting from being raised by Indian nurses in India. With a bit of reintegration into the American cultural milieu, the white child will be able to resolve any cultural discrepancies he or she may have suffered. This line of reasoning parallels DuBois's distinction between those who have 'nations' and those who have 'culture'. When one is 'civilized' and therefore 'superior', one is not encumbered by culture, one can rise above culture. But it is a different story for the African child who is forever relegated, according to DuBois, to an 'identity crisis'. DuBois claims that it is unlikely that the African child with a boarding school education will successfully manage the negotiations required to live by the standards and practices of two cultures. DuBois hypothesizes that the social discontinuities between the boarding school environment and the home village will aversely affect the African child's life and 'that this child will not be able to resolve the two systems of rewards and penalties'(1955: 94). This idea of the cultural Other who is unable to resolve two system of rewards and penalties erases any acknowledgment of the racist and classist applications of rewards and penalties.

In terms of penalties, a review of literature found that racism against Aboriginal students unfolded though the unfair and rigid application of school rules and procedures that, as a result, enabled and encouraged 'dropping out' among Aboriginal students (St. Denis and Hampton, 2002). Not only are rules often rigidly and unfairly applied to Aboriginal students, but Aboriginal students are often subjected to harsher penalties than racially dominant students. An American study found glaring inequalities and discrimination in the public schools towards racial minority students, including Native American students. Minority students were suspended or expelled in disproportionate numbers and had less access to advanced classes or programs for gifted students (Gordon, Piana, and Keleher, 2000). Brady (1996) also found that one's socioeconomic status shapes and limits the quality of education. Low-income students report that 'school administrators are uneven in their enforcement of school rules, often giving harsher penalties for rule infractions to lower income students than are the norm for their higher income peers' (Brady, 1996: 5).

One way in which rewards are also distributed unequally based on class and race is through expectations for success or failure. Again, a review of literature reveals that teachers often have low expectations of Aboriginal and American-Indian students (Ambler, 1997; Delpit, 1995; Hall, 1993; Strong, 1998; Tirado, 2001; Wilson, 1991). Low expectations justifies lack of instruction and attention to Aboriginal students. Tirado (2001) found that teachers have a tendency to size up American-Indian students as underachievers; they don't expect the kids to do anything, so they don't teach them. Wilson found that 'even before teachers knew the [Aboriginal] students, they prejudged them. They could not have imagined that these students would ever be successful. Students were classified as unable to cope with a heavy academic load' (1991: 379). As a result, Aboriginal students are often placed disproportionately in vocational or special needs classes (Wilson, 1991). Rather than encouraging an examination of the ways in which class and racial bias impact educational processes, the legacy of the 1954 conference of anthropologists and educators has resulted in a large body of educational research primarily interested in 'culture' as the explanatory concept for understanding how the culturally Other would or would not adjust to school.

The ability to adapt to cultural change is a major theme in DuBois's theorizing as she shifts her analysis to the monocultural learner who is described as a member of a society or culture that is undergoing rapid social change. DuBois (1955) explains that monocultural learners are faced with trying to resolve discrepancies in values, beliefs, attitudes, and knowledge between their home and the school, which can result in their experiencing psychological problems. In the event of rapid social change, social tension can result, which brings on 'social dysphoria' (DuBois, 1955: 96) or in current language an identity crisis. The idea that the cultural Other is not able to make cultural adjustments without a great deal of trauma is an idea that continues to have a negative effect on discussions of how to improve educational achievement for Aboriginal students. To a large extent these discussions tend to promote a stereotyped idea of the Aboriginal student as vulnerable and non-resilient and enables the avoidance of addressing the far more difficult questions of racism and classism in education.

This idea of the Aboriginal cultural Other as unwilling and unable to adapt to changing social, economic, and political contexts is a long entrenched assumption that justifies oppression and inequality. For example, Sarah Carter (1986, 1996), a prairie Canadian historian, challenges the taken-for-granted assumption that Aboriginal people were unwilling and unable to adapt to a farming-based economy. Carter uncovers the extent to which white settlers and the Canadian government colluded to ensure that Aboriginal farmers failed at farming. The introduction of the pass and permit system prevented Aboriginal farmers from succeeding by limiting their ability to purchase farm machinery, limiting what produce they could grow, and limiting when and where they could sell their produce.

The All Hallows School in British Columbia, a boarding school attended by both Aboriginal and white girls between 1884 and 1920, described in the work of Barman (1986), provides another historical and educational example of unwarranted assumptions about Aboriginal people unwilling and unable to adapt to change. The establishment of the All Hallows School was a case in which Aboriginal parents welcomed change and the opportunity to adjust to a changing world by requesting that a school be established for their girls.

Because of inadequate financial resources, the All Hallows School could only function if white girls were allowed to attend alongside Indian girls. In the first years of the school, the Indian and white girls seemed content with their integrated schooling situation. Then a white parent protested about this integrated situation, so the effort was made to separate the white and Indian girls. But in his annual report, the bishop in charge of the school commented that the Indian girls were as intellectually capable as the white girls, claiming that at times the Indian girls had 'the answers all respects being equal, and sometimes superior, to anything that could be expected from white children of the same age' (Barman, 1986: 117). Not only did the Indian girls achieve academically, but they also could from time to time serve as junior teachers, and their ability to learn the practices of another culture was demonstrated in two Indian girls, who alongside eight white girls passed the Royal Academy of Music exam.

These Indian girls did not seem to suffer any crisis due to the culture difference between the school and their home and community. When the Indian girls returned home for holidays and summer vacation, they often freely maintained contact with the teachers through letters. At least for one Indian girl, the only source of cultural conflict involved the dilemma of attending a potlatch even though it was 'forbidden by law' (Barman, 1986: 118). In a letter to the sisters at the school, this student tried to persuade them that the potlatch is not something they should be afraid of because it is just 'our way of praying' (Barman, 1986: 119).

Eventually the Indian and white girls were physically separated, although still offered equally challenging academic programs. But then the curriculum for the Indian girls shifted from a full academic program to one that included teaching them how to weave baskets. Finally, a shift in government policy lead to closing the school, a policy change justified by a larger concern that it was unwise to offer Indians an education that would allow them 'to compete industrially with our people' (Minister of Indian Affairs, 1897, in Barman, 1986: 120). Throughout the proceeding decades, Aboriginal people continued to be denied the high-quality education for which First Nations treaty negotiators assumed they had signed on. The inability of an anthropology and in turn an educational anthropology to acknowledge the effects of 'conquest and exploitation' of the cultural Other continues to reverberate.

As Biolsi (1997) explains, anthropologists such as those present at the time of that 1954 conference were typically not interested in Indians who accepted that change was inevitable. As a result, these examples of Indian farmers and the All Hallows School would not have drawn their attention. Not only were anthropologists not interested in Indians wanting to figure out how to adapt to the changing world around them, but anthropologists also typically maligned these Indians for not being 'real' Indians (Biolsi, 1997; Waldram, 2004).

Conclusion

> More powerful than their knowledge of cultural difference is their knowledge of the big
> picture—the context of socio-economic and cultural oppression of Native Americans.
>
> (Hermes, 2005: 21)

We started out a few decades ago in Aboriginal education believing that we could address the effects of racialization and colonization by affirming and validating the cultural traditions and heritage of Aboriginal peoples. There is increasing evidence that those efforts have limitations. As I have argued elsewhere, cultural revitalization encourages misdiagnoses of the problem (St. Denis, 2004). It places far too much responsibility on the marginalized and oppressed to change yet again, and once again lets those in positions of dominance off the hook for being accountable for ongoing discrimination. It is to the advantage of the status quo to have Aboriginal people preoccupied with matters of authenticity. If cultural authenticity is the problem then we don't have to look at what is the immensely more difficult task of challenging the conscious and unconscious ways in which the ideology of white identity as superior is normalized and naturalized in our schools and nation, both in the past and in the present (Francis, 1997; Willinsky, 1998).

Instead of doing anti-racism education that explores why and how race matters, we can end up doing cross-cultural awareness training that often has the effect of encouraging the belief that the cultural difference of the Aboriginal 'Other' is the problem. Offering cultural awareness workshops can also provide another opportunity for non-Aboriginals to resent and resist Aboriginal people. Offering cultural awareness education has become the mainstream thinking about proper solutions to educational and social inequality. In her research exploring the qualities of effective teachers of American Indians, Hermes, an American-Indian educator, found that 'more powerful than [teachers'] knowledge of cultural difference is their knowledge of the big picture—the context of socioeconomic and cultural oppression of Native Americans' (2005: 21). We often hear that addressing racism or doing anti-racism education is too negative and that we need to focus on a more positive approach. However, that often means tinkering with the status quo. As Kaomea suggests, when schools offer benign lessons in Hawaiian arts, crafts, and values, this approach tends to erase Hawaiian suffering, hardship, and oppression. 'It is time to tell more uncomfortable stories' (Kaomea, 2003: 23).

Glossary

cultural discontinuity: The incongruence and disjunctures resulting from differences between schooling practices, teacher values, and the socialization practices and values of the culturally different student.

cultural essentialism: The assumption that in spite of social change, particular cultural characteristics and behaviours remain enduringly and consistently constitutive of culturally and ethnically diverse groups.

culturally relevant education: A subdiscipline of anthropology that·studies relationships between the socialization processes of culturally diverse groups and schooling practices.

enculturation: The process by which a cultural group inducts and socializes its members to its values, beliefs, and practices.

Study Questions

1. Why does the author argue that the call to provide culturally relevant education for Aboriginal students is problematic?

2. What does the author believe is the most appropriate goal in Aboriginal education?

3. How did the discipline of anthropology come to exert such influence on approaches to Aboriginal education? What was that influence?

4. This chapter argues against the idea that culturally relevant education for Aboriginal students will prevent their cultural discontinuity and preserve an authentic Aboriginal culture. Do you agree or disagree? What barriers do you believe exist in reforming that approach?

5. How does the author criticize common uses of the term 'culture'? What is her preferred use?

Recommended Readings

Kaomea, J. 2003. 'Reading Erasures and Making the Familiar Strange: Defamiliarizing Methods or Research in Formerly Colonized and Historically Oppressed Communities', *Educational Researcher* 32, 2: 14–25.

Ladson-Billings, G. 1999. 'Just What Is Critical Race Theory, and What's It Doing in a Nice Field like Education?', in L. Parker, D. Deyhle, and S. Villenas, eds, *Race Is . . . Race Isn't: Critical Race Theory and Qualitative Studies in Education*. Boulder, CO: Westview Press, 7–30.

Posluns, M. 2007. *Speaking with Authority: The Emergence of the Vocabulary of First Nations' Self-government*. New York: Routledge.

Razack, S. 1998. *Looking White People in the Eye: Race, Class and Gender in the Courtrooms and the Classrooms*. Toronto: University of Toronto Press.

St. Denis, V. 2004. 'Real Indians: Cultural Revitalization and Fundamentalism in Aboriginal Education', in C. Schick, J. Jaffe, and A. Watkinson, eds, *Contesting Fundamentalisms*. Halifax, NS: Fernwood, 35–47.

Recommended Websites

First Nations University of Canada: http://www.firstnationsuniversity.ca/

First Nations Education Council: http://www.cepn-fnec.com/index_e.aspx

Canadian Council on Learning (Topic: Aboriginal Learning): http://www.ccl-cca.ca/CCL/Topic/AboriginalLearning/?Language=EN

Coalition for the Advancement of Aboriginal Studies: http://www.edu.yorku.ca:8080/%7Ecaas/index.htm

First Nations, Métis, and Inuit Educational Resources: http://www.goodminds.com/

References

Abele, F., C. Dittburner, and K.A. Graham. 2000. *Towards a Shared Understanding in the Policy Discussion about Aboriginal Education*, in M.B. Castellano, L. Davis, and L. Lahache, eds, *Aboriginal Education: Fulfilling the Promise*. Vancouver and Toronto: University of British Columbia Press, 3–24.

Ambler, M. 1997. 'Without Racism: Indian Students Could Be Both Indian and Students', *Tribal College Journal* 8, 4: 8–11. Available at: <http://www.tribalcollegejournal.org/themag/backissues/spring97/spring97ee.html>. Accessed 8 October 2002.

Barman, J. 1986. 'Separate and Unequal: Indian and White Girls at All Hallows School, 1884–1920', in J. Barman, Y. Hebert, and D. McCaskill, eds, *Indian Education in Canada, Volume 1: The Legacy*. Vancouver: University of British Columbia Press.

Biolsi, T. 1997. 'The Anthropological Construction of "Indians": Haviland Scudder Mekeel and the Search for the Primitive in Lakota Country', in Thomas Biolsi and L.J. Zimmerman, eds, *Indians and Anthropologists: Vine Deloria Jr. and the Critique of Anthropology*. Tucson: University of Arizona Press, 133–59.

Brady, P. 1996. 'Native Dropouts and Non-Native Dropouts in Canada: Two Solitudes or a Solitude Shared?', *Journal of American Indian Education* 35, 2: 10–20. Available at: <http://jaie.asu.edu/v35/V35S2nat.htm>. Accessed 2 October 2002.

Caffrey, M.M. 1989. *Ruth Benedict: Stranger in This Land*. Austin, TX: University of Texas Press.

Carter, S. 1986. '"We Must Farm to Enable Us to Live": The Plains Cree and Agriculture to 1900', in R.B. Morrison and C.R. Wilson, eds, *Native Peoples: The Canadian Experience*. Toronto: McClelland and Stewart, 444–70.

———. 1996. 'First Nations Women in Prairie Canada in the Early Reserve Years, the 1870s to the 1920s: A Preliminary Inquiry', in C. Miller and P. Chuchryk, eds, *Women of the First Nations: Power, Wisdom, and Strength*. Winnipeg: University of Manitoba Press, 51–75.

Caulfield, M.D. 1969. 'Culture and Imperialism: Proposing a New Dialectic', in D. Hymes, ed., *Reinventing Anthropology*. New York: Pantheon Books, 182–212.

Darnell, R. 2000. *And Along Came Boas: Continuity and Revolution in Americanist Anthropology*. Amsterdam: J. Benjamins.

Deloria, V., Jr. 1969/1988. *Custer Died for Your Sins: An Indian Manifesto*. Norman, OK: University of Oklahoma Press.

Delpit, L. 1995. *Educating Other People's Children: Cultural Conflict in the Classroom*. New York: New Press.

Deyhle, D. 1992. 'Constructing Failure and Maintaining Cultural Identity: Navajo and Ute School Leavers', *Journal of American Indian Education* 31: 24–47.

———, and K. Swisher. 1997. 'Research in American Indian and Alaska Native Education: From Assimilation to Self-determination', *Educational Review* 22: 113–94.

De Zengotita, T. 1989. 'Speakers of Being: Romantic Refusion and Cultural Anthropology', in Stocking (1989: 74–123).

Diamond, S. 1964. 'Introduction: The Uses of the Primitive', in Stanley Diamond, ed., *Primitive Views of the World*. New York: Columbia University Press, v–xxiv.

DuBois, C. 1955. 'Some Notions on Learning Intercultural Understanding', in Spindler (1955a: 89–126).

Eagleton, T. 2000. *The Idea of Culture*. Oxford: Blackwell Manifestos.

Fanon, F. 1986. *Black Skin, White Masks*. London: Pluto Press.

Francis, D. 1997. *National Dreams: Myth, Memory and Canadian History*. Vancouver: Arsenal Pulp Press.

Frank, L.K. 1955. 'Preface', in Spindler (1955a: vii–xi).

Friesen, D.W., and J. Orr. 1995. 'Northern Aboriginal Teachers' Voices'. Unpublished manu-script, University of Regina, Saskatchewan.

Gordon, R., L.D. Piana, and T. Keleher. 2000. *Facing the Consequences: An Examination of Racial Discrimination in U.S. Public Schools*. Oakland, CA: ERASE Initiative, Applied Research Center.

Hall, J.L. 1993. 'What Can We Expect from Minority Students?', *Contemporary Education* 64, 3: 180–2.

Henry, F., C. Tator, W. Mattis, and T. Rees. 1996. *The Colour of Democracy: Racism in Canadian Society*. Toronto: Harcourt Brace.

Herder, J.G. 1774/1967. *Another Philosophy of History Concerning the Development of Mankind*. Translation of *Auch eine Philosophie der Geschichte zur Bildung der Menschheit*. Frankfurt am Main: Suhrkamp.

Hermes, M. 2005. 'Complicating Discontinuity: What about Poverty?', *Curriculum Inquiry* 35, 1: 9–26.

Hymes, D. 1969. 'The Use of Anthropology: Critical, Political, Personal', in D. Hymes, ed., *Reinventing Anthropology*. New York: Pantheon Books, 3–79.

Kaomea, J. 2003. 'Reading Erasures and Making the Familiar Strange: Defamiliarizing Methods for Research in Formerly Colonized and Historically Oppressed Communities', *Educational Researcher* 32, 2: 14–25.

Keesing, R. 1990. 'Theories of Culture Revisited', *Canberra Anthropology* 13, 2: 46–60.

Ladson-Billings, G. 1999. 'Just What Is Critical Race Theory, and What's It Doing in a Nice Field like Education?', in L. Parker, D. Deyhle, and S. Villenas, eds, *Race Is . . . Race Isn't: Critical Race Theory and Qualitative Studies in Education*. Boulder, CO: Westview Press, 7–30.

Larocque, E. 1991. 'Racism Runs through Canadian Society', in O. McKague, ed., *Racism in Canada*. Saskatoon: Fifth House, 73–6.

Ledlow, S. 1992. 'Is Cultural Discontinuity an Adequate Explanation for Dropping Out?', *Journal of American Indian Education* 31: 21–36.

McDermott, R.P. 1997. 'Achieving School Failure, 1972–1997', in G. Spindler, ed., *Education and Cultural Process: Anthropological Approaches*, 3rd edn. Prospect Heights, IL: Waveland Press, 110–35.

Malik, K. 1996. *The Meaning of Race: Race, History and Culture in Western Society*. New York: New York University Press.

Mead, M. 1974. *Ruth Benedict: A Humanist in Anthropology*. New York: Columbia University Press.

Michaelson, S. 1999. *The Limits of Multiculturalism: Interrogating the Origins of American Anthropology*. Minneapolis: University of Minnesota Press.

National Indian Brotherhood. 1972. 'Indian Control of Indian Education'. Ottawa: National Indian Brotherhood.

Posluns, M. 2007. *Speaking with Authority: The Emergence of the Vocabulary of First Nations' Self-Government*. New York: Routledge.

Quillen, J.I. 1955. 'An Introduction to Anthropology and Education', in Spindler (1955a: 1–4).

Razack, S. 1998. *Looking White People in the Eye: Race, Class and Gender in the Courtrooms and the Classrooms*. Toronto: University of Toronto Press.

Rosaldo, R. 1989. *Culture and Truth: The Remaking of Social Analysis*. Boston: Beacon Press.

Royal Commission on Aboriginal Peoples. 1996. *Report on the Royal Commission on Aboriginal Peoples*. 5 vols. Ottawa: Canada Communications Group.

Schick, C., and V. St. Denis. 2005. 'Troubling National Discourses in Anti-racist Curricular Planning', *Canadian Journal of Education* 28, 3: 295–317.

Spindler, G. 1955a. *Education and Anthropology*. Stanford: Stanford University Press.

———. 1955b. 'Anthropology and Education: An Overview', in Spindler (1955a: 5–22).

———. 1963. *Education and Culture: Anthropological Approaches*. New York: Holt, Rinehart and Winston.

St. Denis, V. 2004. 'Real Indians: Cultural Revitalization and Fundamentalism in Aboriginal Education', in C. Schick, J. Jaffe, and A. Watkinson, eds. *Contesting Fundamentalisms*. Halifax, NS: Fernwood, 35–47.

———, and E. Hampton. 2002. 'Literature Review on Racism and the Effects on Aboriginal Education'. Prepared for Minister's National Working Group on Education, Indian and Northern Affairs Canada. Ottawa.

Stocking, G.W., Jr. 1968/1982. *Race, Culture and Evolution: Essays in the History of Anthropology*. Chicago: University of Chicago Press.

———. 1986. 'Essays on Culture and Personality', in Stocking, ed., *History of Anthropology*. Vol. 4. *Malinowski, Rivers, Benedict and Others: Essays on Culture and Personality*. Madison: University of Wisconsin Press, 3–12.

———. 1989. *History of Anthropology*. Vol. 6. *Romantic Motives: Essays on Anthropological Sensibility*. Madison: University of Wisconsin Press.

———. 1989a. 'Romantic Motives and the History of Anthropology', in Stocking (1989: 3–9).

———. 1989b. 'The Ethnographic Sensibility of the 1920s and the Dualism of the Anthropological Tradition', in Stocking (1989: 208–76).

Strong, W.C. 1998. 'Low Expectations by Teachers within an Academic Context'. Paper presented at the Annual Meeting of the American Educational Research Association, San Diego, CA. (ERIC Document Research Service No. ED 420 62)

Tippeconnic, J.W., III, and K. Swisher. 1992. 'American Indian Education', in M.C. Alkin, ed., *Encyclopedia of Education Research*. New York: MacMillan, 75–8.

Tirado, M. 2001. 'Left Behind: Are Public Schools Failing Indian Kids?', *American Indian Report* 17: 12–15. Available at Wilson Web. Accessed 9 October 2002.

Trouillet, M.R. 1991. 'Anthropology and the Savage Slot: The Poetics and Politics of Otherness', in R.G. Fox, ed., *Recapturing anthropology: Working in the Present*. Santa Fe, NM: School of American Press, 17–44.

Waldram, J. 2004. *Revenge of the Windigo: The Construction of the Mind and Mental Health of North American Aboriginal Peoples*. Toronto: University of Toronto Press.

Williams, R. 1976. *Marxism and Literature*. New York: Oxford University Press.

———. 1983. *Keywords: A Vocabulary of Culture and Society*, Rev. edn. New York: Oxford University Press.

Willinsky, John. 1998. *Learning to Divide the World: Education at Empire's End*. Minneapolis: University of Minnesota Press.

Willis, W.S., Jr. 1969. 'Skeletons in the Anthropological Closet', in D. Hymes, ed., *Reinventing Anthropology*. New York: Pantheon Books, 121–52.

Wilson, P. 1991. 'Trauma of Sioux Indian High School Students', *Anthropology and Education Quarterly* 22: 367–83.

Wright, D.H. 2004. *Report of the Commission of Inquiry into Matters relating to the Death of Neil Stonechild*. Available at <http://www.stonechildinquiry.ca/>.

Young, R.C. 1995. *Colonial Desire: Hybridity in Theory, Culture and Race*. New York: Routledge.

Zenter, H. 1973. *The Indian Identity Crisis: Inquires into the Problems and Prospects of Societal Development among Native Peoples*. Calgary: Strayer Publications.

CHAPTER 11

Homophobia, Heterosexism, and Heteronormativity in Schools

Gerald Walton

Defining Homophobia

Most people in North America today would probably recognize the word **homophobia**, if only because it has been used in popular TV shows such as *Will and Grace* and *Law and Order: Special Victims Unit*. It is also likely that most of them would define it as fear or hatred of homosexuality. If asked to explain those feelings, some might suggest that the majority of homophobes are men who do not want to be the objects of other men's sexual desire. Such an explanation would not be incorrect, but it is far from complete.

The term 'homophobia' was coined by George Weinberg in the 1960s (Elia, 2005). At that time, homosexuality was widely considered to be a form of sexual deviance and was listed as such in the *Diagnostic and Statistical Manual of Mental Disorders* (DSM), a catalogue of psychological and psychiatric disorders published by the American Psychological Association. It was not removed from the list of mental disorders until 1973—four years after Canada had decriminalized homosexual relations between consenting adults. The decision to remove the 'mental disorder' label followed heated debate among intellectuals and medical practitioners, as well as persistent lobbying from gay and lesbian groups across North America. Cressida Heyes (2005) suggests that it was during this period that the term 'homophobia' gained widespread currency as part of a strategy to draw attention to the negative attitudes and social stigmatization that homosexuals face. From a medical point of view, the claim that homosexuals (to use a medicalized term) are sexually deviant or mentally ill was invalidated and characterized as prejudicial.[1] In 1984 social psychologist Gregory Herek (1984) suggested that individual attitudes towards homosexuals were shaped by the nature of the individual's interaction with homosexuals (or lack of such interaction). Herek also identified what has become known as *internalized* homophobia: a kind of defensive homophobia in which individuals project their anxieties about their own same-sex attractions, desires, or fantasies onto others who are perceived to be homosexual. In such cases homophobic violence could be understood as an expression of inner conflict.

People who express prejudice or bigotry towards gays and lesbians (to use more contemporary terms) are often called *homophobes*. Overt violence (typically, but not necessarily, physical) is commonly referred to as *gay bashing*. Bashers are young men who get together in small groups and go to areas known for their large gay populations to taunt or beat up 'faggots' or 'queers'. In Vancouver in 2001, for instance, Aaron Webster was kicked and beat to death by a group of four such men in Vancouver's Stanley Park. In 1998 in Wyoming, 22-year-old student Matthew Shepard was tortured and beaten to death by two young men. And in 2007, two gay men were murdered within days of each other in Halifax (Moore, 2007). Although the motives behind the Halifax murders have yet to be determined, there is no question about the Webster and Shepard cases: both men were targeted and murdered specifically because they were gay. The men who target gay men (or those they perceive to be gay) for such violence are typically young. This suggests that their own sexual identities may be immature and easily threatened. Such vulnerability is precisely what displays of masculine bravado are intended to mask. The fact that most gay bashing is carried out by small groups of young men is a good indicator that a follow-the-leader mentality likely comes into play. Rarely do men behave in such socially irresponsible and violent ways when they are not with their friends.

Such men should be held responsible for their actions. But there is more to homophobia than either individual or group psychology. There is also pervasive social prejudice based on rigid gender expectations. As Michael Kimmel astutely points out, 'men prove their manhood in the eyes of other men' (2000: 214), in part by continually demonstrating their heterosexual orientation. In other words, the normative identity of 'man' necessitates homophobia among men.

In addition to motivating violence, homophobia strongly influences how people act, communicate, and function in the world. Males are taught from boyhood to suppress their feelings, to 'tough it out'. Appearing masculine is equated with being straight. Most boys learn to present themselves as tough and masculine specifically so that they will not be perceived as gay. People tend to perceive 'feminine' characteristics in boys as flaws that should be corrected. Parents might express shame when their sons do not conform to expectations of masculinity. For boys and men, homophobia is a powerful agent of social control and an effective way to undermine others' sense of masculinity. Thus boys and young men often use words like *faggot* and *queer* to bully other boys and young men. The culture of masculinity and the homophobic bullying that maintains it have been implicated in both routine forms of school violence and sensational and extreme forms, such as school shootings (Newman et al., 2004).

The two perpetrators of the 1999 'Columbine massacre' are known to have been frequent victims of bullies at a high school rife with violence that faculty and administration largely ignored (Brown and Merritt, 2002; Larkin, 2007; Newman et al., 2004). Homophobic slurs were a routine feature of the bullying that the shooters endured. The fact that all school shooters have been boys or young men has been largely ignored, but it is significant, suggesting that there is something about the socialization of boys and men that encourages the use of violence as a response to conflict (Katz, 2006). From this perspective, school shootings are merely an extreme expression of the masculine bravado and violence that have become normalized in a culture that glorifies men's use of guns to assert power.

But homophobia is not just a male phenomenon. It also plays a normative role in shaping the gender identities of females. Most females are taught that a 'proper' girl is 'feminine' and submissive. The aggressive behaviour that is considered desirable in boys and men is generally unacceptable in girls and women (except perhaps in sports). Aggressive females are often assumed to be lesbians regardless of their actual **sexual orientation**. In short, homophobia is a powerful agent of social control for girls and women as well as boys and men.

Gender Identity and Gender Performance

For most people in society, **gender identity**—boy or girl, man or woman—is unproblematic. From birth, most children are labelled and treated as either boys or girls, depending on their external physiology, and most accept their designated gender. People usually assume that sex (male or female) corresponds to gender (boy or girl, man or woman), and that humans naturally identify themselves as one or the other. Such assumptions are usually correct—but only because individuals are conditioned to identify themselves and 'perform' the script considered appropriate to their assigned gender.

The concept of gender performance is usually associated with the work of Judith Butler (1990). From clothing choices to manners of walking and speaking, most people clearly demonstrate their self-identification as boys or girls, men or women. Butler refers to this as *performativity*. Most people probably do not even recognize that they are performing a role because they have been trained to do so since birth. Even today, male babies are wrapped in blue blankets and females in pink ones. These choices are dictated not by 'nature' but by culture. Similarly, boy babies are often described as 'strong' and girl babies are described as 'sweet'. These **attributions** are the foundations of gender normativity, drawing attention to what it means to be a 'boy' or a 'girl' in the current cultural and historical contexts and shaping our notions of what is 'normal' and 'natural' (Devor, 2007). According to Meyer (2006), what gives rise to homophobic harassment and violence is not the violation of any sexual 'law', but rather the contravention of normative gender expectations. Yet if the performance of masculinity and femininity was 'natural' to boys and girls respectively, there would be no need for social controls to ensure gender-normative behaviour. Nor would the gender scripts for boys, girls, men, and women vary throughout history or across cultures, as they clearly do. In short, gender performance does not come 'naturally' but is socially constructed and enforced. Homophobia is one mechanism by which gender performance, like sexuality and **sexual orientation identity**, is regulated and shaped.

People whose gender identity (boy/man; girl/woman) does not match their biological sex (male/female) are known as transgender. The term does not refer to a particular type of sexuality: transgender people can be gay, lesbian, bisexual, or asexual.

Transgender youth are at particular risk of attack and exclusion. Every province in Canada guarantees human rights on the basis of sexual orientation, but so far none offers protection against rights violations based on gender identity. Even in gay and lesbian communities, prejudice and violence against transgender people are not uncommon.

Homophobia in Schools

School is the primary site where boys and girls learn to 'perform' the gender scripts assigned to them in a society where heterosexuality is the norm. The phrase *compulsory heterosexuality* was coined by the poet Adrienne Rich (1986) in the context of the patriarchal control of women's sexuality. Today, however, it is used in a broader sense to refer to the hegemony of heterosexuality in society. The compulsory nature of heterosexuality is particularly evident in schools, where atypical gender performance is usually interpreted as evidence of homosexuality. For girls and boys alike, failure to conform often means marginalization in school communities.

Some efforts to enforce heterosexuality are probably motivated by moral or religious conviction. In 1997 the school board in Surrey, BC, banned from classroom use three children's books because, in its view, their depiction of families with same-sex parents was inappropriate. When the ban was appealed, the board commissioned a survey of parents, which reported that a majority opposed the use of the books in schools. However, the validity of the survey was doubtful (see British Columbia Library Association Intellectual Freedom Committee, n.d.), and in 1998 the BC Supreme Court overturned the ban, ruling that because it likely reflected the personal religious views of some board members and parents, it violated the separation of church and state required by the School Act. The Surrey board appealed, maintaining that the ban had nothing to do with religious views and pointing to details such as grammatical inconsistencies as reasons for finding the books 'inappropriate'.

Despite legal initiatives in Canada intended to foster equality, gays and lesbians continue to face social prejudice. At school, students who are lesbian, gay, bisexual, and transgender (LGBT) are routinely subjected to homophobic comments not just from other students but sometimes even from staff, with the result that the school becomes a hostile environment. As Kumashiro (2001) points out, the intersection of racism and homophobia places students of colour at even greater risk of discrimination and harassment. Youth who are LGBT and disabled (Thompson, 2004) and/or Aboriginal (Raymond, 2005; Heavy Runner, 2001) also face double or even triple levels of social oppression. Nor is the hostility limited to those who identify themselves as LGBT. Merely to be perceived as LGBT is enough to put a student at risk of abuse, regardless of his or her actual orientation. Thus homophobia in schools is a threat to all students (Elia, 2005; Epstein and Johnson, 1994; Macgillivray, 2004; O'Conor, 1995).

The case of Azmi Jubran, which generated a wealth of media attention and a precedent-setting Supreme Court ruling, is a key example of how homophobia can be used against straight students as a bullying tactic. A former student of the North Vancouver School District (NVSD), he was routinely targeted for verbal and physical assault, much of it homophobic, even though he identified himself as straight. In 1996, Azmi filed a human rights complaint against the school district for failing to provide protection from violence, which included pushing, shoving, and having holes burned in his shirt. Although the BC Supreme Court accepted the NVSD's argument that since Azmi was not gay, he was not entitled to human rights protections on the basis of sexual orientation, in 2005, the Supreme Court of Canada finally affirmed that school districts are obligated to provide safe learning environments free of harassment. As Justice Risa Levine of the BC Court of Appeal explained, 'discrimination focuses not on the actual characteristics of the person but on the attitudes, prejudices and stereotypes of others that impose limitations on that person's human dignity, respect, and right to equality' (quoted in Teeter, 2005). In 2006 the NVSD drafted and implemented a policy aimed at 'raising awareness and improving the understanding of the lives of people who are identified as gay, lesbian, bisexual, transgender, or who are questioning their sexual orientation or gender identity' (North Vancouver School District, 2006).

Human rights codes and the Charter of Rights and Freedoms, as well as recent changes to the Marriage Act, have helped to curb discrimination. But schools remain sites where casual expressions of social prejudice are still largely accepted. Catchphrases such as 'That's so gay!' and 'Don't be a homo!' have become standard schoolyard insults. Yet few administrators have had the courage to spearhead policies and programs targeting homophobic violence specifically. In 2003, for instance, only four of 60 school districts in BC mentioned the word *homophobia* in their safe schools policies and only two (Greater Victoria and Vancouver) included suggestions for education about gender and sexual diversity. As of 2008, six districts have policies specifically designed to curb homophobia. The rest continue to rely on generic anti-bullying policies. Since homophobic bullying threatens all students, however, continued reliance on generic policies constitutes a failure to adequately address violence in schools. As Macgillivray (2004) argues, creating a school culture of inclusion and safety for all children means ensuring that diversity of gender and sexual orientation is addressed alongside other forms of social difference both in administrative policies and in educational programs.

Heterosexism and Heteronormativity

Less familiar than *homophobia* are the terms **heterosexism** and (especially) **heteronormativity**. In a course I taught in the Faculty of Education at Simon Fraser University in 2006 and 2007, a handful of students said they had heard of heterosexism, but no one claimed to be familiar with the idea of heteronormativity.

Central to 'isms' such as sexism and racism is the notion that members of one group are innately superior to non-members and therefore are entitled to discriminate against those 'others'. Thus men have tended to enjoy certain privileges at the expense of women, and in many countries of the world, white people have (at a minimum) felt entitled to advantages they would deny to people of colour. In the same way, heterosexism privileges heterosexuals at the expense of gay and lesbian people. Before 2005, for example, marriage in Canada was an overtly heterosexist institution, reserved for straight couples. Today, Canada is one of only five countries in the world that have extended the privilege of marriage—hence legal recognition—to gay and lesbian couples. (The first was the Netherlands, in 2001; Belgium followed in 2003, and Canada, Spain, and South Africa in 2005. A small number of US states recognize same-sex marriage, among them California and Massachusetts.) Countries such as Honduras and Uganda, however, have explicitly prohibited legal recognition of same-sex unions, as have several US states. The fact that most US states and the federal government have steadfastly upheld marriage as a heterosexual privilege calls into question the country's hegemonic rhetoric about equality and freedom for all.

In Canada, conservative religious and political groups opposed the extension of marriage to same-sex couples, but challenges based on the Charter of Rights and Freedoms eventually prevailed. The first same-sex couple to be legally married in Canada was Kevin Bourassa and Joe Varnell, whose wedding in January 2001 was legally recognized two years later (Equal Marriage for same sex couples, 2004). Although conservative groups maintain that gays and lesbians undermine marriage and the family, Bourassa and Varnell (2007) point out that the extension of marriage to gay and lesbian couples has served to raise marriage rates, which until then had been in decline.

In most regions of the world marriage remains a heterosexist institution, and heterosexism remains well-entrenched in attitudes and values even in countries that now recognize same-sex marriage. The underlying assumption, as both Gerald Unks (1995) and Gregory Herek (1992) point out, is that heterosexuality is the default position: everyone is assumed to be heterosexual until proven (or self-declared) other-wise. The consequences of this assumption, however, are not limited to mere disre-gard or social invisibility for gays and lesbians. At the extreme, heterosexism explicitly portrays non-heterosexuals as deviant, immoral, and/or mentally ill. Religious funda-mentalists can be particularly vitriolic, as I discovered when I joined a conservative evangelical church in the late 1980s (Walton, 2006; for more on religious bigotry against gays and lesbians see Bawer, 1997; Hedges, 2006; Herman, 1997). Far more commonly, however, heterosexism operates through the usual channels of social regulation, specifically the norms and values expected of individuals as members of societies and communities. For instance, heterosexual couples have the privilege of expressing their sexual orientation identities in public without having to fear hostile reactions. In most circumstances, straight couples can hold hands in public without worrying that someone will accuse them of 'flaunting' their sexuality. The idea that it is a privilege to go about one's daily business without thinking about one's social identities (race, gender, sexual orientation) can be hard to appreciate in a country such as Canada, where the rhetoric of equality disguises the fact that certain groups of people are routinely stigmatized. Privilege itself tends to make the marginalization and oppression of others invisible to the privileged. In fact, *heterosexist* is arguably more accurate than *homophobic* as a description of the oppression that gays and lesbians experience in a society where heterosexuality is the unquestioned norm and anything else is automatically defined as 'abnormal'. Changes in social attitudes and legal provisions are clear evidence that what is considered 'normal' is a social construct that shifts over time. But norms of sexuality and gender are deeply entrenched in society.

In schools, heteronormativity compels gay and lesbian students to make choices that most straight students do not have to make. Gay and lesbian students must decide whether to conform and 'pass' as straight at school functions, not to attend at all, or to attend and risk being ostracized by peers and sanctioned by school authorities. Students in same-sex relationships often avoid public displays of affection (such as holding hands) at school, and will sometimes use opposite-sex pronouns when referring to their intimate relationships. The choices that individual students make depend on their circumstances and must be accepted as valid even if they do not advance the social equality of LGBT students.

Some students, however, actively challenge mainstream expectations. In 2002, for example, an Ontario student named Marc Hall sued his Catholic high school for prohibiting him from attending its prom with his then boyfriend (Smith, 2002). An Ontario Superior Court eventually ruled in his favour. The Hall case drew attention to one common heterosexist practice that otherwise would have gone unchallenged. But there are many more. The simple omission of gay and lesbian material from curricula and library resources, for instance, serves to reproduce and perpetuate heteronormative beliefs and values, teaching students that only straight relationships are acceptable in the public realm, and only heterosexuality is 'normal' in the private realm.

Homophobia, heterosexism, and heteronormativity are evident in campaigns against equality of gays and lesbians with heterosexuals. In 1997, for example, conservative Christian organizations dismissed as 'politically correct' a campaign by the British Columbia Teachers' Federation (BCTF) and others to address homophobia and heterosexism in BC schools, and suggested that concerns about homophobia were nothing more than a smokescreen for efforts to destroy the 'normal' and 'traditional'. In addition, conservative groups charged that the Ministry of Education and the BCTF were trying to take away the rights of parents to educate their children on issues such as sexuality. Meanwhile, the lack of resources for LGBT students and families meant that some students and families were not represented in the school curricula and culture.

Why do schools need policies specific to homophobia? The answer is simple: if violence were generic rather than specific to particular groups of students who are marginalized because of particular social differences, then a generic policy might be enough to curb violence in schools. But violence is rarely generic. Rather, it is usually directed against particular students who are perceived as different and therefore inferior. Verbal bullying often takes the form of homophobic labels such as 'faggot', 'dyke', and 'queer'. These names are often attached not only to self-identified LGBT students but also to other students who are different in some way, regardless of their actual sexual orientation or gender identity. Strategies to address LGBT issues in schools need not be limited to anti-homophobia initiatives such as codes of conduct on verbal violence, although these are important. Equally beneficial to all students are pro-LGBT initiatives that foster inclusion and representation of LGBT students on a par with straight counterparts. Gay Straight Alliances (GSAs), for example, are student-organized and student-led associations that work 'to advance the understanding of homosexualities, to reduce heterosexism, and to support the welfare of sexual minorities in schools and communities' (Lipkin, 2005: 354). The first GSAs were organized in the US in the late 1980s, and as of 2007, more than 3,000 GSAs had registered with the American-based Gay, Lesbian, and

Straight Education Network (GLSEN, 2007). Several Canadian high schools currently have a GSA. Many student groups do similar advocacy work but might not be called GSAs, opting instead for titles such as Diversity Club. Collectively, these student-focused initiatives indicate a strong movement towards transforming schools into learning environments that are inclusive of difference, specifically where gender identity and sexual orientation are concerned.

Contested Language and the Controversies of 'Queer'

Historically, words such as 'faggot', 'dyke', and 'queer' have been used as blunt verbal tools to demean, ridicule, or ostracize individuals or, more generally, to regulate 'gender performance'. Yet, some LGBT people also use these words for themselves. This practice is a subject of controversy in LGBT communities. Critics see it as an expression of internalized homophobia that perpetuates negative stereotypes. Defenders, however, maintain that embracing words such as 'queer' and 'dyke' transforms them from weapons of denigration to tools of empowerment. This is especially true in the case of 'queer', which has a long list of connotations such as 'odd', 'unusual', and 'irregular'. In short, many people adopt 'queer' as a self-identity to challenge social norms and, as Lipkin (2000: 103) puts it, to emphasize the fact that they are 'not straight'.

Those who claim 'queer' as an identity do not deny that the word is often used as a weapon. Nor do they underestimate the pain inflicted on children in particular by those who use it to demean them. Instead, queers co-opt words such as 'fag', 'dyke', and 'queer' in order to subvert their power to do harm. The contradiction, as Lipkin (2000) points out, is that as more people embrace 'queer' as an identity, its value as an instrument of resistance is likely to erode.

Conclusion

This chapter has offered an overview of the discrimination that LGBT students typically experience in schools. Despite the prevalence of homophobia in school environments, some LGBT students choose to be out. But many remain 'in the closet', hiding their sexuality and identities from their families, teachers, and peers for fear of being kicked out of their homes and ostracized at school. Even students who identify themselves as straight often choose to keep their relationships with LGBT friends or family members in the closet for fear of ostracism by association.

Staying in the closet may be a matter of survival for some students, even if it comes with significant costs. Closeted youth lose out on the chance simply to be themselves, especially when it comes to public expressions of young love and lust. They are also 'at risk' for a range of educational, sexual, and emotional difficulties. Rates of both suicidal ideation and suicide itself are higher for LGBT youth than for their non-LGBT counterparts (Russell, 2003; McCreary Centre Society, 1999). But, as we have seen, homophobic bullying can be no less devastating for straight-identified youth. Hamed Nastoh, for instance, identified himself as straight, but in 2000 he jumped off Vancouver's Pattullo Bridge to escape the torments he faced at school. Since then, his mother has become an advocate of anti-bullying and anti-homophobia initiatives in schools. LGBT youth of ethnic, cultural, and racialized minority backgrounds are doubly vulnerable (Kumashiro, 2001).

Despite the routinization of homophobia and its intersections with other forms of social oppression, such as racism, not all LGBT youth experience oppression to the same degree. Some LGBT youth are fortunate enough to have supportive families and affirming schools. But those who do not should not necessarily be considered passive victims. Agency and resiliency are equally important considerations. Ream and Savin-Williams emphasize the overall resiliency of LGBT youth and 'their development of a positive sense of self in spite of experiences of heterosexism, homophobia, and intolerance of variations in gender expression' (2005: 724). While acknowledging the consequences of the oppression that many LGBT youth experience, Grace and Wells (2008) suggest that, in addition to understanding the ways in which LGBT youth might be 'at-risk', embracing the affirming notion that they are also 'at-promise' is also crucial.

A number of programs have been designed specifically to help LGBT learners fulfill their promise. An example is the Triangle program established by the Toronto District School Board in the mid-1990s to provide a safe learning environment for students who have been severely marginalized in mainstream schools. According to its website, the program provides a space 'where [LGBT] youth can learn and earn credits in a safe, harassment-free, equity-based environment', and where 'LGBT literature, history, persons and issues' are recognized and celebrated. The fact that this program exists is a clear indication of the risks that LGBT students face in regular schools—risks that teachers have been either unwilling or unable to address—and the need for resources, affirmation, and homophobia-free learning environments.

As beneficial as the Triangle program may be for its students, segregation does not challenge homophobia and heterosexism in regular schools. Nor does it help students who are still in the closet, or who are targeted for abuse because they have LGBT friends or family members. Thus it is crucial to emphasize once again that homophobia is a threat to all students. Strategies to combat homophobia and heterosexism cannot be limited to generic codes of student conduct and special initiatives such as the Triangle program.

Only a handful of school districts in Canada today have the necessary programs in place. This is not surprising, given that school trustees' positions depend on the support of municipal voters, and that to address homophobia seriously would be to risk losing some of that support. In light of the recent legal victories of Azmi Jubran and Marc Hall, however, districts that have not taken action are leaving themselves vulnerable to similar lawsuits. It has now been established that LGBT students and those who come from families with LGBT members have both the legal and the moral right to learn in environments that are safe and welcoming, and to attend school events with their same-sex partners. Policies that uphold these rights are thus highly political and contested, as is education itself.

Note

1. Although a minority of psychiatrists and psychologists continue to spread the mental-illness theory of homosexuality, the American Psychological Association (APA) denounces them on the grounds that they pander to social prejudice and conservative values.

Glossary

attribution: The assignment of particular characteristics or identities to other people on the basis of assumptions. For instance, gender is attributed to individuals on the basis of outward appearance, comportment, voice, mannerisms, and clothes.

gender identity: The gender by which individuals self-identify: boy or girl, man or woman. Although gender identity is presumed to correspond to biological sex (male or female), the existence of transgender, transsexual, and intersexed individuals demonstrates that such a correspondence is socially constructed and can be inaccurate.

heteronormativity: A term used to refer to processes, practices, and values that normalize heterosexuality in society and its institutions, obscuring the fact that it is socially constructed and continually reinforced.

heterosexism: Discrimination or prejudice based on the notion that everyone is or should be heterosexual, and that social and legal privileges should be accorded only to heterosexuals. Heterosexism is also known as heterosexual privilege.

homophobia: In general, fear and/or hatred of homosexuality; a prejudicial attitude and cultural bias expressed either through discriminatory behaviour or through verbal and/or physical violence.

sexual orientation: Categories of sexual attraction, fantasy, desire, and behaviour, usually classified as homosexual (same sex), heterosexual (opposite sex), or bisexual (both sexes). Sexual orientation is related to sexual orientation identity but not necessarily synonymous with it.

sexual orientation identity: How individuals identify their sexual orientation (usually gay, lesbian, straight, or bi), regardless of actual sexual behaviour. Many straight-identified people have same-sex attractions, fantasies, and sexual activity. Many gay or lesbian people have opposite-sex attractions, fantasies, and sexual activity. Thus sexual orientation identity is not necessarily the same as actual sexual orientation.

Study Questions

1. Why are anti-homophobia policies and programs important for all students?
2. What does it mean to be identified as a member of a stigmatized group in society? How and why are some individuals and groups stigmatized and not others?
3. How does homophobia influence individual behaviour? Explain with examples for boys and men, and girls and women.
4. Historical evidence indicates that transgender people have existed in numerous cultures. What does this mean for Western notions of sexuality and gender?
5. Regardless of your actual sexual orientation, hold hands with someone of your own gender in public for five minutes. Then write a paragraph describing where you chose to perform the exercise, how you chose a partner, how the latter responded to your request, and how you felt during the activity. Describe the reactions that you noticed from others. If you choose not to take part in this activity, explain why (even if only to yourself). What does

your choice reveal about the various dimensions of homophobia in society? Discuss the risks and benefits of assigning this exercise to students in school.

Recommended Readings

Gay and Lesbian Educators of BC. *Challenging Homophobia: A Teachers' Resource Book*, 2nd edn. (Copies may be ordered through the GALE BC website listed below.)

School district policies in British Columbia on LGBT issues (also accessible through the GALE BC site).

Schrader, Alvin M., and KristopherWells. 2007. *Challenging Silence, Challenging Censorship*. Ottawa: Canadian Teachers' Federation.

Sears, James T., ed. 2005. *Gay, Lesbian, and Transgender Issues in Education: Programs, Policies, and Practices*. Binghamton, NY: Harrington Park Press.

Recommended Websites

Equality for Gays and Lesbians Everywhere (EGALE): http://www.egale.ca/

Gay and Lesbian Educators of BC (see their publications): http://www.galebc.org/main.htm

International Day against Homophobia (Canada): http://www.homophobiaday.org/

It's Elementary: Talking about Gay Issues in School (website of the 1996 US documentary): http://www.womedia.org/itselementary.htm

Jackson Katz: http://www.jacksonkatz.com/

PFLAG (formerly Parents, Families and Friends of Lesbians and Gays): http://www.pflagcanada.ca

Triangle Program of the Toronto District School Board: http://schools.tdsb.on.ca/triangle/

References

Bawer, Bruce. 1997. *Stealing Jesus: How Fundamentalism Betrays Christianity*. New York: Crown.

Bourassa, Kevin, and Joe Varnell. 2007. 'Gay Marriage Bolsters Institute in Canada: Statistics Canada Shows Marriage Foes Are Wrong'. Available at: <http://www.samesexmarriage.ca/advocacy/sta170107.htm>. Accessed 6 June 2008.

British Columbia Library Association Intellectual Freedom Committee. n.d. Available at: <http://www.bclibrary.ca/bcla/ifc/censorshipbc/1990.html#onedad>. Accessed 6 June 2008.

Brown, Brooks, and Rob Merritt. 2002. *No Easy Answers: The Truth Behind Death at Columbine*. New York: Lantern.

Butler, Judith. 1990. *Gender Trouble: Feminism and the Subversion of Identity*. New York: Routledge.

Devor, Aaron. 2007. 'How Many Sexes? How Many Genders? When Two Are Not Enough'. Available at: <http://web.uvic.ca/~ahdevor/HowMany/HowMany.html>. Accessed 9 June 2008.

Elia, John P. 2005. 'Homophobia', in James T. Sears, ed., *Youth, Education, and Sexualities: An International Encyclopedia*. Westport, CT: Greenwood, 413–17.

Epstein, Debbie, and Richard Johnson. 1994. 'On the Straight and the Narrow: The Heterosexual Presumption, Homophobias and Schools', in Debbie Epstein, ed., *Challenging Lesbian and Gay Inequalities in Education*. Buckingham, UK: Open University Press, 197–230.

Equal Marriage for same sex couples. 2004. 'The First Legal Gay Marriage Is Now Certified'. Available at: <http://www.samesexmarriage.ca/legal/ontario_case/cer300604.htm>. Accessed 6 June 2008.

Gay, Lesbian, and Straight Education Network (GLSEN). 2007. Available at: <http://www.glsen.org/cgi-bin/iowa/all/news/record/1876.html. Accessed 6 June 2008.

Grace, André, and Kristopher Wells. 2008. 'Using Sexual-Minority Youth Resilience Research to Inform Queer Critical Theory Building and Educational Policymaking'. Paper presented at the conference of the Canadian Society for the Study of Education, Vancouver, BC.

Heavy Runner, Raven. 2001. 'First Nations, Queer, and Education', in Kevin K. Kumashiro, ed., *Troubling Intersections of Race and Sexuality: Queer Students of Color and Anti-Oppressive Education*. Lanham, MD: Rowman & Littlefield, 131–3.

Hedges, Chris. 2006. *American Fascists: The Christian Right and the War on America*. New York: Free Press.

Herek, Gregory M. 1984. 'Beyond "Homophobia": A Social Psychological Perspective on Attitudes toward Lesbians and Gay Men', *Journal of Homosexuality* 10, 1–2: 1–21.

———. 1992. 'The Social Context of Hate Crimes: Notes on Cultural Heterosexism', in Herek and Kevin T. Berrill, eds, *Hate Crimes: Confronting Violence against Lesbians and Gay Men*. Newbury Park, CA: Sage, 89–104.

Herman, Didi. 1997. *The Antigay Agenda: Orthodox Vision and the Christian Right*. Chicago: University of Chicago.

Heyes, Cressida. 2005. 'Same Sex Marriage and Homophobia'. University of Alberta: Express News. Available at <http://www.expressnews.ualberta.ca/article.cfm?id=6383>. Accessed 5 May 2008.

Katz, Jackson. 2006. 'Coverage of "School Shootings" Avoids the Central Issue', *Dallas Morning News*. 16 October. Available at: http://www.jacksonkatz.com/pub_coverage.html>. Accessed 9 June 2008.

Kimmel, Michael. 2000. 'Masculinity as Homophobia: Fear, Shame, and Silence in the Construction of Gender Identity', in Maurianne Adams et al., eds, *Readings for Diversity and Social Justice: An Anthology on Racism, Anti-Semitism, Sexism, Heterosexism, Ableism, and Classism*. New York: Routledge, 213–19.

Kumashiro, Kevin K., ed. 2001. *Troubling Intersections of Race and Sexuality: Queer Students of Color and Anti-oppressive Education*. Lanham, MD: Rowman & Littlefield.

Larkin, Ralph W. 2007. *Comprehending Columbine*. Philadelphia: Temple.

Lipkin, Arthur. 2000. 'Why Use That Word? Adolescents and Queer Identity', in Michael Sadowski, ed., *Adolescents at School: Perspectives on Youth, Identity, and Education*. Cambridge, MA: Harvard Education Press, 102–5.

———. 2005. 'Gay–Straight Alliances', in James T. Sears, ed., *Youth, Education, and Sexualities: An International Encyclopedia*. Westport, CT: Greenwood, 354–8.

McCreary Centre Society. 1999. *Being Out: Lesbian, Gay, Bisexual, and Transgender Youth in BC. An Adolescent Health Survey*. Burnaby, BC: McCreary Centre Society.

Macgillivray, Ian K. 2004. *Sexual Orientation and School Policy: A Practical Guide for Teachers, Administrators, and Community Activists*. Lanham, MD: Rowman & Littlefield.

Meyer, E. 2006. 'Gendered Harassment in North America: School-based Interventions for Reducing Homophobia and Heterosexism', in C. Mitchell and F. Leach, eds, *Combating Gender Violence in and around Schools*. Stoke-on-Trent, UK: Trentham Books, 43–50.

Moore, Oliver. 2007. 'Gay Cruising Areas on Alert after Killings: Halifax Homosexual Community in Shock after Two Men Found Dead in Similar Circumstances', *Globe and Mail*, 15 May, 3.

Newman, C.S., C. Fox, D.J. Harding, J. Mehta, and W. Roth. 2004. *Rampage: The Social Roots of School Shootings*. New York, NY: Basic Books.

North Vancouver School District. 2006. *Policy 412—Homophobia.* Available at: <http://www.nvsd44.bc.ca/Administration/PoliciesAndProcedures/Series400/Policy%20412. aspx>. Accessed 9 June 2008.

O'Conor, Andi. 1995. 'Who Gets Called Queer in School? Lesbian, Gay, and Bisexual Teenagers, Homophobia, and High School', in Gerald Unks, ed., *The Gay Teen: Educational Practice and Theory for Lesbian, Gay, and Bisexual Adolescents.* New York: Routledge, 95–101.

Raymond, Victor J. 2005. 'Native and Indigenous LGBT Youth', in James T. Sears, ed., *Youth, Education, and Sexualities: An International Encyclopedia.* Westport, CT: Greenwood, 585–9.

Ream, Geoffrey L., and Ritch C. Savin-Williams. 2005. 'Resiliency', in James T. Sears, ed., *Youth, Education, and Sexualities: An International Encyclopedia.* Westport, CT: Greenwood, 724–7.

Rich, Adrienne. 1986. *Blood, Bread, and Poetry: Selected Prose 1979–1985.* New York: Norton.

Russell, Stephen T. 2003. 'Sexual Minority Youth and Suicide Risk', *American Behavioural Scientist* 46: 1241–57.

Smith, Graeme. 2002. 'Gay Teen Wins Prom Fight'. *Globe and Mail*, 11 May, A1, A10.

Teeter, Brad. 2005. 'Victory after All: North Van School Board Liable for "Hellish" High School Experience'. *Xtra West* 14 April: 7–8.

Thompson, Scott Anthony. 2004. 'Operation "Special": Interrogating the Queer Production of Everyday Myths in Special Education', in James McNinch and Mary Cronin, eds, *I Could Not Speak My Heart: Education and Social Justice for Gay and Lesbian Youth.* Regina, SK: University of Regina, 273–88.

Unks, Gerald. 1995. 'Thinking about the Gay Teen', in Unks, ed., *The Gay Teen: Educational Practice and Theory for Lesbian, Gay, and Bisexual Adolescents.* New York: Routledge, 3–12.

Walton, Gerald. 2006. '"Fag Church": Men Who Integrate Gay and Christian Identities', *Journal of Homosexuality* 51, 2: 1–17.

CHAPTER 12

Class Encounters: Working-Class Students at University

Wolfgang Lehmann

Introduction

It has been argued that globalization makes higher education essential for both national economic competitiveness and individual success. Countries like Canada, which cannot compete in global markets on the basis of low-cost production, must focus on the development of innovative, value-added products and services, and for this they require a highly educated workforce. In response, most provincial governments in Canada have pledged (if not always delivered) increased funding for post-secondary education.

Meanwhile, theorists like Giddens (1990) and Beck (1992) have argued that we have entered a period of late modernity, in which structural factors such as gender, race, and social class no longer determine the individual life course to the extent that they once did. Rather, people today must largely determine their own life course through continuous reflexive engagement with the social environment. As a result, the transitions from high school to work or further education have changed: traditional participation patterns no longer apply, and gender, class, and race are no longer reliable predictors of educational pathways.

In Canada, participation in all levels of post-secondary education is increasing. In fact, Canada now has the most highly educated workforce of all countries in the Organization for Economic Co-operation and Development (OECD, 2000). This trend toward post-secondary education has been particularly pronounced at the university level. Reviewing data on educational aspirations, Davies (2005: 151) found that 57 per cent of Canadian parents expected their offspring to attend university and only 12 per cent did not foresee any post-secondary education in their children's future. Although actual enrolment figures are not as high as parental expectations, they do follow suit. In 1998, 65 per cent of all Canadians aged 18 to 21 who were no longer in high school had enrolled in post-secondary education at some point during the previous five years. Of them, 43 per cent were at university (Knighton and Mirza, 2002: 27).

Although the increase in post-secondary enrolment and the push for university are evident across gender, race, ethnicity, and social-class categories, access to university is still significantly constrained by social-class background (Andres et al., 1999; Anisef et al., 2000; Krahn, 2004b; Wanner, 2005). Rising tuition fees have put university out of reach for many young people from low-income families. Furthermore, low-income families in particular have been found to overestimate the costs and underestimate the benefits of a university education (Junor and Usher, 2002; Usher, 2005). Empirical studies, however, have shown that the most important predictor of university access is not family income per se, but parental educational attainment. Having at least one parent with a university degree significantly increases the likelihood that a young person will attend university. The 'massification' of higher education in recent decades has done little to change this relationship. Not surprisingly, therefore, most research on social class and higher education has focused on access. Yet it is equally important to investigate whether social class continues to be an important factor once a working-class student has actually entered university. This chapter analyzes the expectations, hopes, and fears of newly enrolled working-class first-generation university students (i.e., students who are the first in their families to attend university) for evidence of unique class-based concerns and coping strategies.

Social Class and University

The persistent relationship between social-class background and educational attainment has been variously explained as the product of cost–benefit calculations (Goldthorpe, 1996); educational structures, streaming processes, and teaching strategies that disadvantage working-class students (Bowles and Gintis, 1976; Oakes, 2005; Rist, 1977); working-class students' own disengagement from and resistance to education (Willis, 1977); and a fundamental cultural clash between the working-class world of those students and the middle-class culture of the schools (Bourdieu and Passeron, 1977).

The latter perspective, informed by the work of the late French theorist Pierre Bourdieu, has been increasingly reflected in research investigating educational experiences of working-class students. Bourdieu's work is central to our understanding of the **cultural reproduction of social inequality**, which rests on the idea that structural conditions (e.g., social institutions) interact with individual actions and choices to create outcomes that reproduce and perpetuate social inequalities. It was Bourdieu (1977, 1990) who developed the concept of **habitus**: a set of acquired patterns of thought, behaviour, and taste, informed by class background, that constitutes the individual's sense of self within the social structure. In addition habitus creates dispositions to understand the world, and hence to behave, in certain ways. For instance, someone from a family that has always worked in construction or some other manual employment will be more likely to continue that pattern than to consider a career as a doctor or lawyer (and vice versa). To put it simply, our upbringing and social environment lead us to see the world and our place in it in particular ways, which in turn create dispositions to act, interpret experiences, and think in particular ways. The concept of habitus provides a framework that can account for the active formation of dispositions towards certain educational and occupational choices, and explain how these dispositions are rooted in social structure (Hodkinson and Sparkes, 1997). For instance, habitus has been shown to influence families' engagement with the school system and their interaction with teachers and other school staff (Lareau, 2003); high school students' educational and career dispositions (Andres, 1993); their choices between academic and vocational-track programs (Lehmann, 2005); and the nature of the expectations they have regarding university (Lehmann, 2004).

Interestingly, the disadvantages that working-class students experience in secondary school are not so immediately evident at the post-secondary level. For instance, Canadian studies of university dropouts have found little indication of class differences in the decision to leave university without graduating (Grayson, 1997; Krahn, 2004a; Butlin, 2000). This suggests that working-class students at university may already have undergone selection processes that make them less like their non-university, working-class peers and more like their middle-class fellow students.

These findings notwithstanding, other studies in Canada and elsewhere indicate that we still need to consider issues of social class in order to understand the university experiences of first-generation, working-class students. For instance, Lehmann (2004) found that Canadian high-school students who were to be the first in their families to attend university expressed uncertainty and expected the experience to be difficult. Their social origins and biographies led them to fear both that they would not be able to fit in and that they might fail their courses. By contrast, their peers with university-educated parents looked forward to university with excited anticipation. Other studies in the US and the UK have found that the concerns expressed to Lehmann (2004) tend to be borne out at university.

In 2005, as part of a series entitled 'Class Matters', the *New York Times* published a feature article on 'The College Dropout Boom'. The article stated that almost one in three Americans in their mid-twenties was a college dropout and that most came from poor and working-class families (Leonhardt, 2005). Berger and Milem (1999) found that students from families with higher incomes were more likely to become socially and academically integrated early on in university and thus to develop a greater institutional commitment, which in turn made them less likely to drop out. Analyzing longitudinal data from the US national study of college students, a data set that provides information on students' activities, aspirations, and attainment from first-year college through early adulthood, Walpole (2003) found that students with low socio-economic status (SES) studied less than others, spent more time working at off-campus jobs, had lower levels of academic involvement, and had lower grade averages while at university. Similarly, the follow-up study, conducted nine years after university entry, found lower levels of educational attainment, lower aspirations for further education, and lower incomes in the low-SES group.

Qualitative ethnographic and interview-based research has also found that students from working-class backgrounds often become cultural outsiders. They have difficulty connecting with their more privileged peers and integrating into university life, and are prone to fears of academic inadequacy. In a study of working-class students at an elite law school, Granfield (1991) found that the most successful students overcame their outsider status by mimicking their middle-class peers' dress, manners of speech, and career ambitions, while downplaying their social-class backgrounds. Similarly, Aries and Seider (2005) noted that lower-income students at a prestigious private university in the US had trouble connecting with their wealthy peers and becoming properly integrated into university life. The authors concluded that the feelings of 'inadequacy, inferiority and intimidation' were greatest among the first-generation students, most of whom were 'lacking in cultural capital' (Aries and Seider, 2005: 440).

This review of the literature suggests several key research questions. What do working-class first-generation students expect of university? Do they anticipate trouble becoming socially and academically integrated? Do they feel that they have to overcome their class background in order to succeed at university? Or do they feel that their social background gives them unique strengths and motivation that will actually help them succeed?

The Study

The data presented in this chapter are taken from the first phase of a three-year longitudinal study conducted at a large, research-intensive university in Ontario. In this phase, 75 newly enrolled first-generation, working-class students were interviewed soon after arriving on campus, between early September and mid-October 2005. Participants were recruited through advertisements in the student newspaper, posters around campus, and announcements made in first-year classes across all the disciplines offered at the university. Candidates were screened to ensure that they were the first in their families to attend university, came from moderate- to low-income backgrounds, and had parents who were employed in working- or lower-middle-class occupations. Although the selection process was not random, the sample was carefully constructed to be as representative as possible.

More women than men responded to the call for participants. Although efforts were made to find more men, in the end only 22 of the participants (30 per cent) were male. In addition, roughly 30 per cent of the participants were visible minorities.

The 75 interviews were conducted in offices and classrooms on campus; each lasted between 45 minutes and two hours. All interviews were audio-taped, transcribed, and analyzed using qualitative data analysis software.

The extracts quoted in the following analysis follow the interview transcripts as closely as possible, with a few minor editorial changes to make them more readable. Pseudonyms are used throughout to protect the confidentiality and anonymity of the research participants.

Going to University

Research in the social-structural tradition finds consistent evidence that social class is still a barrier to university access. Once this barrier has been overcome, first-generation, working-class students' reasons for being at university at first sight appear quite similar to those expected from middle-class students. A substantial majority of the students interviewed in this study insisted that they had always—or at least for a very long time—known they wanted to go to university. Some said they had developed an interest in a specific professional career in elementary or secondary school as a result of a career project, for example. In other instances, the participants were less clear on why they always knew they wanted to go to university, but referred to a mix of parental wishes, academic interests, and labour-market realities:

> Becky: In high school, at least my high school, they really drill it into you to go to university. If you go to college, or if you go to work, or if you're an apprentice, then you're not going to have a good future.

> Hilary: It was always 100 per cent 'I want to go to university'. I never even considered college, never. I don't know why. It was frowned upon . . . you know, people are like 'Oh yeah, college . . . '.

Equally important, streaming and tracking processes in high school tend to cement educational trajectories, as the following quotation suggests:

> Joan: I think the way the school system is set up . . . you have two different streams and you either go academic or applied. And so with my teachers kind of assuming it, I think I kind of assumed it as well. Just 'okay, well I'm smart enough', so I'm in these classes and these are the ones that I'm taking and all through it's like academic and then it turns into university. And so it just—I don't know, it becomes an expectation.

Yet when the various narratives are further deconstructed, multiple meanings emerge that betray the participants' class origins and reveal their fears regarding academic and social integration. All these issues can be interpreted as arising from a specific class habitus in which going to university is not the norm.

Decision-Making and Habitus

For many first-generation students it is their perception of their parents' class status that motivates them to strive for social mobility through higher education. Here Ed describes how his parents' employment in casual labour has always motivated him to do better and improve his class status:

> Ed: I planned on [going to university] as far as I can remember . . . always wanted one of the prestigious jobs. [. . .] Ah, because I got to see them [parents] working and it, it's not something that they love to do. . . . I think my dad and my mom used to tell me to work hard . . . to make sure that I didn't end up in a job that didn't lead anywhere.

Similarly, Alissa's decision to study at university was motivated by her understanding of her parents' social and employment situation and by their insistence that she get a better job and, one would assume, a better life than theirs:

Alissa: [Both my parents] do factory work, so . . . I see how tough it is. They're always complaining about back problems or something. [Going to university] wasn't even like an issue when I was younger: it was just 'You're done high school, you're going to university . . . Get a degree, you'll get a good job.'

Parents' desire for upward mobility is probably most succinctly expressed by Justin:

Justin: [My parents] just said 'Do what you want, as long as you're not working in a foundry like me,' that's what my dad said. . . . [My] dad always says, 'Just giving you what I didn't have.'

Many of the participants referred to social networks they had established outside the family, with peers, guidance counsellors, and, perhaps most important, teachers. The following quotations indicate that social capital played a role in working-class youths' career plans and especially their decision to consider university:

Irene: With my tight group of friends, if I didn't go [to university], I'd feel kind of . . . I don't know, I'd feel odd.

Tiffany: At lunch period we'd just kind of bring our lunch [to our biology teacher] and eat while we'd talk and take notes or bring questions and stuff and a lot of times it actually led into, you know, the university aspect of biology, like what kind of jobs could I get from this or, 'Um, did you study this in university' and stuff like that or 'How much more in depth do you go in university on this subject. [. . .] She always told the group of students that would come to the tutorials like we all could make it if we just, you know, put our minds to it.

Monica: My English teacher I was pretty close with too and she definitely helped me out, 'cause I'm thinking of being an English teacher . . . she was definitely influential.

The last two quotations in particular reflect the way specific teachers can act as catalysts for career and educational goals and help students feel more comfortable about the university. The fact that teaching was one of the participants' most commonly mentioned career goals underlines the role that teachers can play in overcoming **cultural capital** deficiencies and providing 'credible' role models.

Habitus Dislocation

Many first-generation students expressed concern that their class background would create challenges that students with university-educated parents do not face. In some cases the concern centred on not knowing what to expect from university:

Brenda: I left high school really unsure. I didn't know anyone here . . . I'd never seen a university before [*laughs*]. I had no idea what I was coming for. I guess actually I felt unprepared.

In other cases students expressed regret that their parents' ability to help them through the transition to university life was limited because they themselves had never experienced it. At the same time some felt guilty for thinking that way about their parents, and this only increased their stress:

Amber: I know that [my parents] feel bad and I'm sure they wish they could help me, 'cause they know that I stress out . . . but they'd have no idea with the classes I'm taking now . . . I guess it's something you just deal with [*laughs*].

The perception that their parents did not understand the demands placed on university students was a particular concern for those students who could not rely on their parents for financial support and expected they would have to work through much if not all their time at university:

Jennie: Sometimes they don't really understand the demands . . . how much work I really have to do. Sometimes . . . I'll be up late finishing something off, and they'll say 'Oh, go to bed, it's late, you can work on it tomorrow.' And I'm like: 'You haven't gone to university, you don't understand how much I really need to get done tonight.' So in that way, I don't think they're really on the same level with me, [they don't know] how . . . heavy a workload I actually have. . . . They just see me, like la-de-dah, doing well, coasting along. . . . They probably view it as being a lot easier than it is, just 'cause they don't really have anything to base it on.

Martina: I think it's important for students not to work while they're in university. And I wish that my family was able to support me that way. I can't say that I'm not happy with the way I've grown up. And I have respect for that—you know, [the fact] that I have to work. [But] I really think that it affects my studies a lot [. . .] and that it's going to cut into my social time [and the] down time [I need] to be able to focus on the next day's lectures.

Among the challenges unique to working-class university students, therefore, is that of reconciling the conflict between the desire for social mobility and the fear of class 'betrayal'. This problem is sometimes discussed as one of **habitus dislocation** (Baxter and Britton, 2001; Lehmann, 2007).

Baxter and Britton have described the uncertainty and anxiety that first-generation university students experience when they enter the unfamiliar terrain of university as 'a painful dislocation between an old and newly developing habitus, which are ranked hierarchically and carry connotations of inferiority and superiority' (2001: 99). Some of the first-generation students were keenly aware of these challenges. Maggie, for instance, began to see her parents (and herself) in a new light when she compared their occupational attainments with the attainments of her residence peers' parents:

Maggie: I was the last one in our suite to go through that conversation: 'What do your parents do?' My parents definitely had the lowest-class jobs, but I'd never thought of that before. [. . .] [My roommates] were all so surprised that I was the first [to go to university].

Navjot's comments reflect her discomfort at the prospect of having to disclose her background:

> Navjot: [When the study was announced in class], a girl beside me [said], 'Both my parents went [to university] and my grandparents went.' She was saying it in a way—as if she couldn't believe that there were people out there [whose parents didn't go] I'm uncomfortable with [being a first-generation student] just because of what people might think, but I'm not . . . really quite sure what other people really think.

Many other study participants echoed these feelings of difference. Yet almost everybody claimed to feel well integrated and to be thoroughly enjoying the social relationships they had formed so far. Given that the interviews took place within the first few weeks of the academic year, it's likely that the overall positive feelings regarding social integration and newly formed friendships had something to do with the exhilaration of adopting a new lifestyle and the exuberance of orientation events. Not surprisingly, those who had moved into residence were most enthusiastic about their social experiences. But at this point the new relationships were still superficial enough that family backgrounds and histories had not yet become major issues. When pressed in the interview to say whether they thought their working-class backgrounds might affect their relationships, participants either rejected that idea altogether or suggested that any friends who would judge them by their class background were not worth having. Nonetheless, most did mention social-class differences in one way or another:

> Abby: [In residence] everyone seems pretty nice, but I know a lot of them aren't on OSAP [Ontario Student Assistance Program]. A lot of people don't even know what OSAP is. A lot of people have never even had a job. It's so different from what I have experienced . . . I've worked for [nearly] four years of my life, and they have no idea what being average is like, you know? They're just pulling out, like, $20s and $50s out of their butts . . . I could never ever do that.

Few participants, however, reflected on social-class differences as poignantly as Kate. Interviewed in mid-October, she suggested that attitudes had already begun to change, now that the exuberance of the first few weeks had passed:

> Kate: You're meeting this person for the first time . . . and you're thinking, 'OK, they just moved here too.' [. . .] It takes a while before people realize—'Oh well, her mom doesn't have a job.' Or 'Oh, her dad works 24-hour shifts so she can be here.' It definitely kinda conflicts friendships. [. . .] And eventually you realize . . . we're not [*laughing*] really friends, 'cause we're from two totally different backgrounds. . . . As soon as people find out the financial background, things become different. Money's huge when it comes to university. It plays a part in everything.

For other first-generation students the sense of habitus dislocation expressed itself mainly in the form of exaggerated fears about their academic abilities:

Karen: In grade twelve my lowest mark was a ninety-five. [. . .] I'm so worried . . . cause I know that it's so much harder and there's so many more expectations and . . . the stuff that you could [do] in high school just won't cut it anymore. [. . .] I'm definitely worried.

Mary: I'm afraid of the tests and the exams 'cause . . . high school didn't really prepare me . . . I don't know what to expect in the exams and stuff. [. . .] So it's kinda scary and I don't know how to study . . . I bought books to teach you how to study and stuff [. . .] but I still don't know what to expect. I'm just afraid of the tests and the exams.

Abby: I guess I fear . . . flunking out or just not being smart enough. [. . .] What if I'm really not university material?

It's worth noting that all the interviews were completed within the first six weeks of the term: therefore the fears discussed by Karen, Mary, and Abby likely had less to do with their actual performance on tests or assignments than with a habitus-based sense of uncertainty and disconnection from the academic environment.

Overcoming Disadvantage

Independence, work ethic, and value for money

Elsewhere I have argued that the experience of habitus dislocation may help to explain why many first-generation and particularly working-class students drop out of university within a few weeks or months and despite solid academic performance up to their departure (Lehmann, 2007). By contrast, most of the participants in this study insisted that their social background and lower-income status were not disadvantages. Although many conceded in the interviews that social-class background might affect some students, they also insisted that it had no influence on *their* university experience and achievement:

Jillian: I guess I never considered that people who were upper-class or had more money . . . were better. So it doesn't really concern me to say that, you know, my parents don't work in a profession, or I wasn't raised in a home where, you know, we had all the luxuries, because I don't put any real value in that. I don't think that really has any weight.

Jessie probably sums it up most poignantly in her response to the question whether she ever feels disadvantaged, like an outsider, or pressured to keep up with wealthier peers:

Jessie: Well screw it what other people think about me, I'm here for school. I'm not here for some kind of fashion show.

In fact, most participants appeared to think of their economic disadvantage in positive terms:

Joe: [My parents are] 110 per cent, they're that extra 10 per cent [more] supportive than I think a normal parent would be, one who has gone to university, 'cause they know you can do it. And my parents just want me to do the best I can . . . they'd do anything, I guess.

> Brian: I have a bit of pride in it [being working-class]. I'm proud of the fact that my family has really worked. . . . Not to say that being a financial analyst isn't work, but I think [I have] a different work ethic because of the way I was brought up. You know . . . I'm used to doing hard physical labour for 8 hours a day, which most people aren't.

A related factor that emerged quite strongly in the interviews was the notion of a strong work ethic and independence or maturity as a unique working-class value or virtue that will help these students succeed at university. Although family background was generally not seen as a liability at university, the discourses on advantages were firmly rooted in social-class comparisons with their more affluent—or, as some called them, 'spoiled'—peers. Interestingly, the first-generation students turned common assumptions on their heads: having fewer family resources to draw upon and needing a job to support one's studies were seen as advantages rather than disadvantages:

> Josh: I feel that I'm kind of mature beyond my years. [. . .] I was in a working environment that was very rigid, I was working with older people and I learned a lot from them [. . .] But here . . . well, in a way it's frustrating to see . . . the unappreciation [sic] for hard work [. . .] I guess unless their parents are willing to support them all their life, it's going to be a pretty big wake-up call when they decide to actually work for their money.

In most instances, these perceptions were informed by a strong 'value-for-money' ethos:

> Julia: I think it's a lot easier for me to go and get stuff done because I'm paying for it. I know a lot of students [whose] parents pay for it, so they're like 'ah whatever.' But for me it's 'I have to do well.' So I have to go to class. That gives me more incentive to do stuff.

> Walter: There's a lot of rich kids [here] and maybe that's why they don't care about their marks: 'cause mommy and daddy will just pay for university; but I had to pay seven thousand dollars to get in here, and I don't want to lose [that money]. [Financially I'm worse off], but academically I feel a bit better 'cause I guess that they're just partying and I'm actually working.

These comments reflect a strong rational choice perspective (Goldthorpe, 1996), which is not surprising, given the relatively high costs of a university education for a low-SES family. A similar cost–benefit perspective can be detected in the ways the first-generation students in this study talked about their long-term educational and career goals.

Instrumentalism and Ambitious Career Goals
It has been argued that university retention depends on full integration into the culture of the university and relatively high commitment to the institution (Pascarella and Terenzini, 1991; Tinto, 1987). It has also been argued that an overly **instrumental** orientation—one that sees university exclusively as preparation for employment—is detrimental to successful integration and retention (e.g., Longwell-Grice, 2003). In this

first phase of the study, however, it seemed that the instrumental perspective was a powerful class-based response to the uncertainties and risks first-generation students associated with university:

Anabel: If I had money and a guaranteed job, like my dad [I wouldn't go to university]. But that's not the case.

Alissa: I [want to] wake up in the morning [and look forward to going to work], like, 'I get to do that again!', Not like, 'Oh God, Tim Horton's again!' [*laughs*]. I hate my life [*laughs*] . . . I want to be satisfied with the job that I have. [That's why] I went to university.

The second and third rounds of interviews in this longitudinal study will try to determine whether these instrumental attitudes toward university persisted and, if so, whether they became a liability. Without a doubt, the instrumental view of university is encouraged by a pervasive public discourse that equates career and life success with increasingly high levels of formal education. Therefore it is not surprising that the majority of participants in this study discussed very ambitious plans, usually involving post-graduate degrees and careers in professions like medicine, law, or education. The fact that all these professions depend on formal educational credentials, however, betrays the students' class backgrounds. Conspicuously absent from the plans of most participants were careers requiring high levels of social capital (e.g., in management) or not directly linked to clearly defined occupations. Teaching was a popular career choice for many. We may speculate that students without academic role models in their immediate families will often look to teachers instead. In many cases, however, formal acknowledgement of the relationship between higher education and life success is tempered by a class-habitus that may already be pushing them in other directions:

Alicia: At the same time I'm not really sure yet if I really do want to complete a degree. Because that's . . . quite a bit of time in my life. . . . Is university really going to make a difference in the long run? Is it really going to open up doors? I don't really know the answer. You know, other things are important in life [too]. You're only young once and there's a lot of things to do out there. And I don't know if I really want to work in a lab or an office and get paid a lot. . . . I could be doing something else for lower pay but possibly a happier life. So I don't know.

Abby: I didn't take high school seriously at all, 'cause I didn't know how university was. . . . Now that I'm here, it's like 'Holy crap, that's a lot of work' and . . . I think college would have been an easier thing for me. . . . College is more hands on, [and] can direct you right into a job. But university is just books . . . learning, learning, learning, [then] you get your degree, and from there you choose something, and most likely you might have to go into a program in college anyway to get to somewhere where you'd want to go, right?

Bob: [When I took] the year off, it was kind of nice because I could just go to work and get my pay check and then afterwards I didn't have to worry about reading chapters 3 through 5 in this text book. I could just relax and do nothing.

Previous research has shown that first-generation students leave university for the same reasons suggested by these three students: the overwhelming commitment associated with four years of university, the perception of non-university alternatives as more attractive, and the lure of more immediate employment and income (see Lehmann, 2007).

Discussion

For almost all participants, the decision to study at university was in some way enforced by a pervasive public discourse that equates life course success with higher education. The social mobility so desired by these students and especially their parents is seen as attainable only with university credentials. But the chances of achieving social mobility through educational attainment are uncertain for first-generation students. Previous research on university dropouts found that first-generation students were more likely than traditional students to leave very early, in some cases within two months of enrolling. They were also more likely to leave university despite solid academic performance. 'Not fitting in', 'not feeling university', and 'not being able to relate to these people' were key reasons for withdrawing. Some first-generation students who dropped out also said that their university experience actually confirmed that they needed more hands-on, applied post-secondary education, which many found at community colleges or in apprenticeships (Lehmann, 2007). The findings presented in this study suggest that the seeds for these decisions may be sown within a few weeks of starting university. Many newly enrolled first-generation students expressed uncertainty and anxiety about their decision to come to university and about their ability to successfully complete their degree. And many had already begun to imagine alternatives such as college or employment.

Not surprisingly, almost all first-generation, working-class students in this study reflected in one way or another on their class position. Some perceived their background as a disadvantage, whether because they could not expect either academic or financial help from their parents, because they were obliged to work as well as to study, or because they could not afford to spend money carelessly. A substantial number, however, interpreted their class status as an advantage or blessing in disguise (some associated being the first university student in the family with relatively low academic pressures and high motivation).

These findings strongly support a cultural understanding of social class, as suggested by Bourdieu (1977, 1990). Although the concept of habitus has been criticized as overly deterministic, Bourdieu himself always interpreted it as an 'open system of dispositions that is constantly subjected to experiences, and therefore constantly affected by them in a way that either reinforces or modifies its structures' (Bourdieu and Wacquant, 1992: 133). He was quick to add, however, that the circumstances and experiences that most people will encounter in life are more likely to reinforce their habitus than to transform it. The experiences of most first-generation students in this study are consistent with the understanding of habitus as an 'open system of dispositions' that nevertheless ultimately reinforces itself. Attending university is increasingly recognized as a necessity, if not a norm, by many young people, regardless of their social-class background. Yet the culture of the university often remains somewhat mystifying for those who have been traditionally excluded from it. Thus young people whose decision to study at university represents a break with the social-structural confines created by their habitus nevertheless continue to interpret their experiences and circumstances at university through the lens of their specific class habitus.

For some of the participants in the study, the uncertainties, worries, and fears that had already formed so early in their time at university can be interpreted as a slowly developing form of habitus-based self-censorship. Although 'objectively' (e.g., based on their educational achievements at high school) their ambitious occupational aspirations were justified and university was the 'right' place for them to be, their experience there had already led them to question both their abilities and their goals, and some had already begun to talk about other educational options. According to Quinn, the dropout decisions of working-class university students in the UK may represent 'a form of loyalty to working-class culture' (2004: 70). By contrast, participants in the Ontario study appeared to think of their commitment to education as an expression of their working-class loyalty. These findings are echoed in a study of low-SES students at an elite private university in the US who affirmed their working-class identities with pride and drew on them as a source of strength (Aries and Seider, 2005).

As the importance of formal education is increasingly stressed and universities continue their efforts to recruit students from diverse backgrounds, attention should be paid to the ways in which university experiences are shaped by family background. Do first-generation, working-class students who persist at university reshape their conceptions of themselves, their dispositions, and ultimately their habitus? Do they 'become' middle-class, or do they affirm working-class identities with pride and use them as a source of strength, as some of the participants in this study have suggested? Do those who leave without graduating do so because of alienation from university and loyalty to the working class? Future phases of data collection in this longitudinal project will provide further insights into the factors that do and do not contribute to the success of first-generation, working-class university students.

Glossary

cultural capital: The assorted advantages (e.g., knowledge, language skills, general attitudes) that give the middle class access to the dominant culture.

cultural reproduction of social inequality: The idea that structural conditions (e.g., social institutions) interact with individual actions and choices to produce outcomes that perpetuate social inequalities. The education system is particularly important, as it functions to reproduce the culture of the dominant class.

instrumentalism: An attitude towards a job or other activity that sees it only as a means to an end (e.g., as a way of earning a living).

habitus: The set of patterns of thought, behaviour, and taste, informed by class background, that constitutes the individual's sense of self within the social structure and disposes him or her to understand the world, and to act, in certain ways.

habitus dislocation: The 'fish out of water' feeling that we get when we encounter a social situation or context for which our habitus has not prepared us.

Study Questions

1. Why did you decide to come to university? Do you think your decision is related to your habitus?
2. How important do you think financial concerns are for first-generation, working-class students? Would lowering tuition fees or providing more student funding make a significant difference in the numbers of low-SES students who attend university and complete their degrees?
3. Should first-generation students adapt to the culture of the university, or should the culture of the university change to become more open to non-traditional students?
4. Discuss the following comment: 'University simply is not for everybody. After all, we need people who pick up garbage, cut our hair, build our houses, and make our cars.'
5. This chapter focuses on issues of social class. Do you think gender, race, ethnicity, or sexual orientation has a more profound effect on students' experiences at university?

Recommended Readings

Archer, Louise, Merryn Hutchings, and Alistair Ross, eds. 2003. *Higher Education and Social Class: Issues of Exclusion and Inclusion*. London: RoutledgeFalmer.
Lehmann, Wolfgang. 2007. *Choosing to Labour? School–Work Transitions and Social Class*. Montreal and Kingston: McGill-Queen's University Press.
Pascarella, Ernest T., and Patrick T. Terenzini. 2005. *How College Affects Students: A Third Decade of Research*, 2nd edn. San Francisco: Jossey-Bass.
Sadovnik, Alan R., ed. 2007. *Sociology of Education: A Critical Reader*. New York and London: Routledge.
Sweet, Robert, and Paul Anisef, eds. 2005. *Preparing for Post-Secondary Education: New Roles for Governments and Families*. Montreal and Kingston: McGill-Queen's University Press.

Recommended Websites

Canadian Millennium Scholarship Foundation: http://www.milleniumscholarships.ca
School–Work Transitions Project: http://www.arts.ualberta.ca/transition/
Job Futures: http://www.jobfutures.ca/
Educational Policy Institute (EPI): http://www.educationalpolicy.org/

References

Andres, L. 1993. 'Life Trajectories, Action, and Negotiating the Transition from High School', in P. Anisef and P. Axelrod, eds., *Transitions: Schooling and Employment in Canada*. Toronto: Thompson Educational Publishing, 137–57.
———, P. Anisef, H. Krahn, D. Looker, and V. Thiessen. 1999. 'The Persistence of Social Structure: Cohort, Class and Gender Effects on the Occupational Aspirations and Expectations of Canadian Youth', *Journal of Youth Studies* 2, 3: 261–82.
Anisef, P., P. Axelrod, E. Baichman-Anisef, C. James, and A. Turrittin. 2000. *Opportunity and Uncertainty: Life Course Experiences of the Class of '73*. Toronto: University of Toronto Press.
Aries, E., and M. Seider. 2005. 'The Interactive Relationship between Class Identity and the College Experience: The Case of Lower Income Students', *Qualitative Sociology* 28, 4: 419–43.

Baxter, A., and C. Britton. 2001. 'Risk, Identity and Change: Becoming a Mature Student', *International Studies in Sociology of Education* 11, 1: 87–101.

Beck, U. 1992. *Risk Society: Towards a New Modernity*. London: Sage Publications.

Berger, J.B., and J.F. Milem. 1999. 'The Role of Student Involvement and Perceptions of Integration in a Causal Model of Student Persistence', *Research in Higher Education* 40, 6: 641–64.

Bourdieu, P. 1977. *Outline of a Theory of Practice*. New York: Cambridge University Press.

———. 1990. *The Logic of Practice*. Cambridge: Polity.

———, and J.C. Passeron. 1977. *Reproduction in Education, Society, and Culture*. London: Sage.

———, and L.J. Wacquant. 1992. *An Invitation to Reflexive Sociology*. Chicago: University of Chicago Press.

Bowles, S., and H. Gintis. 1976. *Schooling in Capitalist America*. New York: Basic Books.

Butlin, G. 2000. 'Determinants of University and Community College Leaving', *Education Quarterly Review* 6, 4: 8–23.

Davies, S. 2005. 'A Revolution of Expectations? Three Key Trends in the SAEP Data', in R. Sweet and P. Anisef, eds, *Preparing for Post-secondary Education: New Roles for Government and Families*. Montreal and Kingston: McGill-Queen's University Press, 149–65.

Giddens, A. 1990. *The Consequences of Modernity*. Stanford: Stanford University Press.

Goldthorpe, J. 1996. 'Class Analysis and the Reorientation of Class Theory: The Case of Persisting Differentials in Educational Attainment', *British Journal of Sociology of Education* 47, 3: 481–505.

Granfield, R. 1991. 'Making It by Faking It: Working-Class Students in an Elite Academic Environment', *Journal of Contemporary Ethnography* 20, 3: 331–51.

Grayson, J.P. 1997. 'Academic Achievement of First-Generation Students in a Canadian University', *Research in Higher Education* 38, 6: 659–76.

Hodkinson, P., and A.C. Sparkes. 1997. 'Careership: A Sociological Theory of Career Decision Making', *British Journal of Sociology of Education* 18, 1: 29–44.

Junor, S., and A. Usher. 2002. *The Price of Knowledge: Access and Student Finance in Canada*. Montreal: Canadian Millennium Scholarship Foundation.

Knighton, T., and S. Mirza. 2002. 'Post-Secondary Participation: The Effects of Parents' Education and Household Income', *Education Quarterly Review* 8, 3: 25–32.

Krahn, H. 2004a. *Access to Post-secondary Education in Alberta*. Annual Meeting of the Canadian Sociology and Anthropology Association. University of Manitoba, Winnipeg, 2–5 June.

———. 2004b. 'Choose Your Parents Carefully: Social Class, Post-Secondary Education, and Occupational Outcomes', in J. Curtis, E. Grabb, and N. Guppy, eds, *Social Inequality in Canada: Patterns, Problems, and Policies*. Toronto: Pearson Prentice Hall, 187–203.

Lareau, A. 2003. *Unequal Childhoods: Class, Race and Family Life*. Berkeley: University of California Press.

Lehmann, W. 2004. '"For Some Reason I Get a Little Scared": Structure, Agency, and Risk in School–Work Transitions', *Journal of Youth Studies* 7, 4: 379–96.

———. 2005. 'Choosing to Labour: Structure and Agency in School–Work Transitions', *Canadian Journal of Sociology* 30, 3: 325–50.

———. 2007. '"I Just Didn't Feel like I Fit In": The Role of Habitus in University Drop-out Decisions', *Canadian Journal of Higher Education* 37, 2: 89–110.

Leonhardt, D. 2005. 'The College Dropout Boom', in *Class Matters*. New York: Times Books.

Longwell-Grice, R. 2003. 'Get a Job: Working Class Students Discuss the Purpose of College', *College Student Affairs Journal* 23, 1: 40–53.

Oakes, J. 2005. *Keeping Track: How Schools Structure Inequality*, 2nd edn. New Haven and London: Yale University Press.

Organisation for Economic Co-operation and Development. 2000. *Education at a Glance: OECD Indicators*. Paris: OECD.

Pascarella, E.T., and P.T. Terenzin. 1991. *How College Affects Students: Findings and Insights from Twenty Years of Research*. San Francisco: Jossey-Bass.

Quinn, J. 2004. 'Understanding Working-Class "Drop-out" from Higher Education through a Sociocultural Lens: Cultural Narratives and Local Contexts', *International Studies in Sociology of Education* 14, 1: 57–73.

Rist, R.C. 1977. 'On Understanding the Processes of Schooling: The Contributions of Labeling Theory', in J. Karabel and A.H. Halsey, eds, *Power and Ideology in Education*. New York: Oxford University Press, 292–305.

Sennett, R., and J. Cobb. 1972. *The Hidden Injuries of Class*. New York: Knopf.

Tinto, V. 1987. *Leaving College: Rethinking the Causes and Cures of Student Attrition*. Chicago and London: University of Chicago Press.

Usher, A. 2005. *A Little Knowledge Is a Dangerous Thing: How Perceptions of Costs and Benefits Affect Access to Education*. Washington, Toronto, and Melbourne: Educational Policy Institute.

Walpole, M. 2003. 'Socioeconomic Status and College: How SES Affects College Experiences and Outcomes', *Review of Higher Education* 27, 1: 45–73.

Wanner, R.A. 2005. 'Twentieth-Century Trends in Occupational Attainment in Canada', *Canadian Journal of Sociology* 30, 4: 441–69.

Willis, P. 1977. *Learning to Labour: How Working Class Kids Get Working Class Jobs*. Farnborough: Saxon House.

CHAPTER 13

'The Future Is Female': The Post-feminist Panic over Failing Boys

Jessica Ringrose

Introduction

This chapter begins by examining the development of 'educational feminism' and the struggles to gain educational equality for girls in the UK and Canada during the first two waves of feminism. It then traces the controversy that erupted in the 1990s when exam results indicated that girls were catching up to and even outperforming boys in school—a 'moral panic' over 'failing boys' that continues today and has international reach (Ali et al., 2004; Davison et al., 2004; Epstein et al., 1998; Francis and Skelton, 2005). The chapter discusses how measures of exam performance by gender are now used internationally to 'prove' that boys are failing and to support claims that girls' unparalleled success is a sign that feminist interventions in schooling may have gone 'too far' (Francis, 2005: 9; Arnot et al., 1999).

My central argument is that the educational **discourse** around 'failing boys' has directly contributed to a reactive, celebratory post-feminist discourse around *over*-successful girls. The latter discourse is characterized as **post-feminist** because it assumes that feminism has won the battle for equality, and treats boys and men as victims of the cultural shifts that have established the new 'gender order' (Connell, 1987). As Angela McRobbie argues, post-feminist discourses

> actively draw on and invoke feminism as that which can be taken into account in order to suggest that equality is achieved, in order to install a whole repertoire of meanings which emphasize that it is no longer needed, a spent force. (2004: 4)

Focusing on media coverage in Canada and the UK, I will trace how educational debates are fuelling a seductive 'girl power' discourse that belies continuing gender inequalities. More specifically, I will examine how girls' educational success is being used as evidence for two questionable propositions: that individual success is attainable, and that current educational policies are working in the face of the growing economic insecurity associated with deindustrialization and globalization. I will suggest that the 'successful girls' discourse obscures the connections between educational achievement and factors such as class, race, ethnicity, religion, citizenship, and location, ignoring the huge disparities in girls' educational access and attainment in different parts of the world (Aikman and Unterhalter, 2005; Francis and Skeleton, 2005; Gillborn and Mirza, 2000).

The Rise of 'Educational Feminism'

Education has been a core issue for women's activism for centuries (Gamble, 2001). Early proto-feminist texts like Mary Wollstonecraft's *Vindication of the Rights of Women* (1792) dealt at length with questions of female education, partly in response to Rousseau's notion that what girls needed to learn was how to look after men. Well into the nineteenth century, however, activists focused almost exclusively on middle-class women and girls (Sanders, 2001: 17). Even in the developed world, women's access to secondary and, especially, higher education in many cases continued to be limited until the twentieth century (Weiner et al., 1997); at Cambridge, women were not granted full degrees until 1948. And access to education is still a problem in many developing countries (Aikman and Unterhalter, 2005).

Educational equality became a primary goal of the women's movement in the twentieth century (Arnot et al., 1999). In the UK, the Education Act of 1944, which established the principle of free secondary education for all, prepared the way (Weiner et al., 1997) for a series of 'equal opportunity' laws put in place from the 1970s onward, including the Equal Pay Act (1970), the Sex Discrimination Act (1975), and the Race Relations Act (1976) (Arnot et al., 1999). Arnot et al. (1999: 7) note that in the UK in particular, the development of 'educational feminism' was central to the post-war era of social democracy. Meanwhile in Canada feminists across the country challenged sexist policies and practices in education after the Royal Commission on the Status of Women published its report in 1970 (Eyre and Gaskell, 2004).

Feminists internationally at this time pointed out that girls and women were marginalized in many aspects of education (Weiner et al., 1997; Eyre and Gaskell, 2004). Some focused on the curriculum, the limited range of girls' subject choices, or female students' generally poor performance in mathematics and science (Kelly, 1981, 1985; Harding, 1983; Northam, 1982; Walkerdine, 1989; Riddell, 1989). Others (e.g., Whyte, 1983; Whyte et al., 1985; Weiner, 1985) looked at the school experience: matters such as sexual harassment, lack of space and attention in the classroom (Spender, 1982; Stanworth, 1981), and whether girls and boys should be educated together or separately (Arnot, 1984; Whyte et al., 1985).

Arnot, David, and Weiner (1999) suggest that the educational feminism of this period launched a global social movement demanding not only a 'gender blind approach to education' but equality of outcome and gender equity in society. Programs intended to redress the balance were established across the developed world, virtually always by individual teachers and groups such as GAMMA (Girls/Gender and Mathematics Association; Paechter, 1998). In the UK and Canada, the relative decentralization of education meant that feminist education initiatives tended to be localized, with little sustained funding (Weiner et al., 1997; Eyre and Gaskell, 2004). In Canada, efforts to encourage more equal participation of girls and boys across the range of subject areas met with some success. However, 'deeper structural changes and substantive modifications to curriculum to incorporate women's knowledge and experience proved . . . difficult to implement' (Eyre and Gaskell, 2004: 6).

Some countries saw modest improvements as liberal feminists, in particular, entered the policy field and gained a certain amount of leverage. This was especially noticeable in Australia, where a class of what became known as 'femocrats' working with the national government grew and assumed influential positions (Eisenstein, 1996).

With their focus on 'equal opportunities' as a key indicator of progress for girls and women, liberal feminists expressed concern that most girls were choosing subjects such as home economics and languages, and that the few who did take math and sciences tended to 'underperform' in those subjects; yet research at the time showed girls were actually not under-performing in any subject at the primary level, and that they were outperforming boys in subjects like English at the secondary level (Walkerdine, 1989). What happened next was quite extraordinary.

Failing Boys: The Post-feminist Panic

In England and Wales, equal opportunity in education was finally formalized in 1988 with the introduction of a 'National Curriculum'. For the first time, girls and boys had to take the same core subjects until they reached school-leaving age. 'League tables' (public statistical tables)—introduced to gauge performance across gender in the wake of this policy change—showed indisputably that girls were not only outperforming boys in language subjects but were also catching up in math and sciences more rapidly than boys were catching up in languages. In 1995 girls had gained a head start over boys in mathematics and science by the age of seven: in math 81 per cent of girls had reached the expected level compared with 77 per cent of boys; in science the percentages were 86 and 83 per cent, respectively (Arnot et al., 1999). By 1996 public debate increasingly reflected the new facts of gender equality:

- In English, girls outperformed boys at ages 7, 11, and 14; results in math and science were broadly similar.
- Girls were more successful than boys at every level.
- Girls were succeeding in traditional 'boys' subjects' such as technology, math, and chemistry (adapted from Jackson, 1998: 78).

According to Arnot and Phipps (2004), these results were touted as representing one of the most important changes in the history of social inequality in the UK. Claims about boys' *under*-performance and girls' *over*-performance were exaggerated and played upon by the UK press (Epstein et al., 1998). Headlines ranged from 'Girls doing well while boys feel neglected' to 'Is the future female?', with reports claiming that boys' 'under-achievement . . . has become one of the biggest challenges facing society today' (*Guardian*, 1995; *Panorama*, BBC1, 1995; *Times Educational Supplement*, 1997, cited in Cohen, 1998). The most recent British research indicates that the ensuing 'moral panic' over boys continues to 'dominate the current gender agenda, and channel debate into a narrow set of perspectives associated with the policy drive to raise "standards" in education' (Ali et al., 2004: 1). This was visible, for instance, in the four-year (2000–4) UK Department for Education and Skills project 'Raising Boys' Achievement Project', described by Younger and Warrington (2005) as 'a "holistic" school resource developed to help boys succeed'. The same concerns underpin the 2007 UK Department for Children, Schools and Families 'topic paper', 'Gender and Education: The Evidence on Pupils in England' (DCSF, 2007), which primarily explores the 'gender gap' (a concept used as shorthand for the truth claim that girls outperform boys) and 'boys' underachievement'. The report largely neglects other salient and ongoing gender issues such as gendered, sexist, sexualized, and homophobic classroom and schooling environments (Francis, 2005; McNeil and White, 2007; Renold, 2005; Ringrose, 2008b) and the continuing substantial pay gap facing girls after school (Weaver, 2006; Women and Work Commission, 2006).

A similar pattern emerged in Canada following the introduction in 1993 of the School Achievement Indicators Program (SAIP), which analyzes achievement levels in mathematics, sciences, reading, and writing. At that time, concern was expressed that boys were falling behind girls in literacy and reading (Davison et al., 2004). The evidence of gender disparity in grades was not as clear as in the UK case because of regional differences in the test data. Nevertheless, the Canadian government also pointed to the results of tests conducted by the Programme for International Student Assessment (PISA, 2003) reporting that 'girls performed significantly better than boys on the reading test . . . in all ten Canadian provinces'. Although it noted that 'few significant differences were found' in math and science, the government still pointed to the reading results as grounds for concern that 'boys [were] lagging behind girls' (Statistics Canada, 2004).

According to Bouchard, Boily, and Proulx (2003), articles reporting boys' school-related problems became increasingly common in Canada's English-language press following the release of a report by the hyper-conservative Fraser Institute entitled *Boys, Girls and Grades: Academic Gender Balance in British Columbia's Secondary Schools* (Cowley and Easton, 1999). Although the report drew attention to the fact that girls were still constrained in their choice of subject—'stereotypical course preferences (the very thing gender-equity initiatives were developed to combat) remain firmly entrenched'—the point picked up by the media and made into a news story was the suggestion that 'girls and boys do not, on average, fair [sic] equally well in our secondary schools'. Finding that 'on average girls out-perform boys by statistically significant margins on nearly all of the Report Card indicators', the authors of the Fraser Institute report raised what they called 'a provocative question: Are girls actually learning more or are school based assessments *systematically biased against boys*?' (Cowley and Easton, 1999: 8; emphasis added).

Concern about the possibility of a bias against boys reinforced fears that that too many teachers were women, and that testing methods and school environments generally were therefore too 'feminine', signalling the rise of what Bouchard, Boily, and Proulx (2003) call a 'masculinist' discourse around 'school success by gender'. Before long the 'failing boys' panic had spread across Canada, generating a spate of articles with headlines like 'La misère scolaire des garçons' (Gagnon, 1999) and 'It's time to give boys our attention' (quoted in Bouchard et al., 2003). Canadian educational researchers note that the media-driven 'perception among some parents/guardians and educators that boys in school are being shortchanged' has been taken up by provinces and school boards, which are making the development of new curricular and instructional plans for improving boys' literacy a priority (Davison et al., 2004: 50; Wallace, 2007).

In the UK, Michele Cohen (1998) has written instructively about the complex representational politics of the 'failing boys' debate. First she draws on historical data to argue that the longstanding idea of boys' academic superiority is a myth: 'boys have always underachieved and more importantly, this underachievement has never been seriously addressed' (1998: 20; Davison et al. [2004] have reported similar findings for Canada). The reason that boys' underachievement had never before been identified as a problem, according to Cohen, was that historically their successes were attributed to their innate intellect and ability, while their failures were attributed to external factors such as 'femininized' teaching methods. In the case of girls the scenarios were reversed: successes were attributed to the same external factors (such as feminized teaching methods) that were injurious to boys, while failures were attributed to innate intellect and ability.

Cohen's work is significant for several reasons. First, she reminds us that it is historically inaccurate to suggest that underachievement among boys is something new. As Valerie Walkerdine (1989) has found, the reason that girls were rarely identified as 'brilliant' in the past had nothing to do with the quality of their performance in comparison with boys'; rather, teachers and parents alike assumed that girls' successes reflected external factors rather than their innate abilities (Walkerdine, 1994, 1989, 1990). Second, Cohen points out that girls' recent achievements have tended not to be valued for their own sake, but rather for what they seem to tell us about boys (that they are falling behind). Third, Cohen draws attention to the tendency to blame boys' problems on a feminized system created by feminists.

Outrage over the 'feminization of education', or strategies aimed at addressing sexism and gender stereotyping as they affect girls, has taken centre stage in the media (Bouchard et al., 2003; Lingard, 2003), as Susan Ormiston reported in a story on 'The Gender Gap' (CBC News, 2003):

> . . . it was the girls we were most worried about 10 years ago. They were falling behind boys in science or math. Teachers and the women's movement came up with a cottage industry of strategies. Girls-only physics classes, math and science camps, and female role models aimed at closing that gap. . . . The efforts with girls worked. Today 30 per cent of engineering students at Canadian universities are young women. More women then men are applying to medical schools. The demographics are rapidly shifting. 'I can tell you that across the developed world, countries are looking very closely at this issue, trying to figure

out strategies and innovative policies and approaches that will work for boys.' You don't have to convince Doug Trimble . . . respected principal . . . at Cecil B. Stirling elementary school, he launched his own boys' strategy. 'It's great what we've done for girls, but boys, we're not doing what we need to for boys in school,' Trimble says. '[It's a] common fact. People can't argue. Can't debate that one.'

Bouchard et al. analyze the dynamics of this 'masculinist' discourse as follows:

> The cornerstone of the discourse is the women's movement has achieved gender equality and that, as a result of the battle waged by women, they have managed in the space of a few decades to catch up to men in virtually every field. Women have allegedly gone beyond equality and relegated men to second place, even in fields that were traditional male domains. (2003: 26)

As Taft (2004) explains it, the post-feminist argument goes roughly as follows: 'girls and women are doing fine [and] feminism is unnecessary'; not only have girls attained 'all the power they could ever want', but—as a result of feminist interventions such as math and science camps, the emergence of strong female role models, and the apparent feminization of school and work alike—they may actually 'have *too much* power in the world' today (Taft, 2004: 72, emphasis added; see also Adkins, 2002; Francis and Skelton, 2005).

Concern that the introduction of supposedly new, more feminine modes of testing (fewer 'sudden death' exams), and 'softer' subjects (like sociology or drama) has been bad for boys is also evident in the UK (Phillips, 2002). In 2002 a columnist with the *Daily Mail* suggested that 'wholesale feminisation' had made the education system 'unfair and discriminatory against boys' (Phillips, 2002). Four years later, *The Times* published yet another story on how 'Boys are being failed by our schools', citing an academic who once again blamed a 'feminised' system and teachers who, instead of encouraging the development of 'male traits such as competitiveness and leadership . . . celebrate qualities more closely associated with girls, such as methodical working and attentiveness in class' (Clarke, 2006). In addition to recommending recruitment of 'more male teachers, particularly to primary schools', Dr Tony Sewell called for 'replacement of some coursework with final exams and a greater emphasis on outdoor adventure in the curriculum'. The article quoted Sewell as follows: 'We have challenged the 1950s patriarchy and rightly said this is not a man's world. But we have thrown the boy out with the bath water. . . . It's a question of balance and I believe it has gone too far the other way' (*The Times*, 2006).

Once again the concern is expressed that feminism has 'gone too far'. Similarly, Australian research has identified a discursive shift away from the idea that girls need help in order to 'measure up to' boys and towards the 'masculinist' idea that girls are 'actively succeeding, and even beating boys in male educational terrain' (Foster, 2000: 207; Kenway, 1997; Lingard, 2003). Becky Francis (2006) notes that the US has been relatively slow to take up the issue because of its focus on ethnic inequality, but that generalized concern over 'boys' underachievement' has been increasing with the publication of books such as Hoff-Sommers' *The War against Boys: How Misguided Feminism*

Is Harming Our Young Men (2000) and a 2006 national survey finding that 'young boys [are] failing across the US' (Swicord, 2006). The central question, then, is why the 'failing boys' panic continues to hold centre stage in international educational debates.

Why Compare Boys' and Girls' Achievements?

Gendered comparisons have become commonplace in most Western countries over the past few decades, in the wake of a massive restructuring of education systems sparked by rapid changes in the global economy and labour markets (Giddens, 1998). Improving student achievement is seen as a crucial part of the effort to make the nation-state marketable; schools are under increasing pressure to produce a suitably skilled and adaptable work force (David, 2004).

Efforts to improve school 'effectiveness' by setting quantifiable goals and measuring performance are consonant with 'neo-liberal' governments' emphasis on individual attainment and flexibility as the keys to both educational and career success in a global context of social, economic, and political transformation and instability (Morley and Rassool, 1999; Francis, 2006; Walkerdine and Ringrose, 2006). According to Benjamin (2003), the international preoccupation with testing is producing a 'techno-rationalist' culture of 'curricular fundamentalism' in which schools and teachers are required to aim for specific, quantifiable versions of 'achievement'. Educational policy discourses that focus on performance and measures of excellence have flourished in current economic and governmental contexts (Francis and Skelton, 2005; Youdell, 2004; see also Department for Children, Schools and Families, 2003).

Assessment-driven policies promote testing and performance measures as the keys to improving standards and effectiveness in schooling, whether at the institutional, the group, or the individual level (Fairclough, 2000). Internationally, the results of standardized tests are used to lend weight not only to neo-liberal discourses of excellence and success (Apple, 2006) but to governments' claims of success at addressing issues of social exclusion and inequality. Comparative evidence showing that girls outperform boys on standard tests is used as 'proof' of gender equality (David, 2004).

Comparisons of girls' and boys' test performances construct a 'gender gap' that is statistically evidenced only at the higher levels of assessment and 'simply does not exist' in any generalizable form (Gorard et al., 1999: 11). In the UK the narrow parameters of the gender and achievement debate, focused on test results, make it possible to use the fact that girls' performance at certain levels exceeds boys' as evidence that gender equity has been attained or even surpassed (Francis, 2005: 9). In the Canadian context SAIP, PISA, and provincial exam results (primarily for reading) are likewise used to present a story of girls excelling at boys' expense. And even though concern over boys' 'underachievement' has dominated public debates on education for at least a decade, headlines continue to present such findings as groundbreaking and 'shocking'.

A recent *Observer* headline proclaimed that 'Exam results *reveal* gender gulf in schools' (Hill, 2005). Drawing on data from the Department for Education and Skills, the article stated that A-level results from 1,500 schools showed girls to be 'up to 115 percent more likely to achieve an A or B grade than boys':

The shocking extent of under-achievement by boys in some of Britain's leading schools has been revealed in a report which for the *first time* shows the huge differences in the performance of girls and boys across the country.' (Hill, 2005: 1; emphasis added)

In Canada as well, concern has been sustained by stories with titles like 'School System Failing Boys' and 'Gender Gap' (CBC News, 2006, 2003). In 2006 a Canadian Press story on the results of grade 3 tests appeared in Toronto under the headline 'Girls outperforming boys, tests show' (*Metro*, 2006). This statement was true with respect to reading and writing—but these were not the only skills tested. As the article itself reported,

for the first time since the test has been administered, boys in Grade 3 scored higher in math. This trend follows in high school, where more males performed at or above the provincial average in the Grade 9 math assessment.

Thus media headlines continue to sensationalize gender differences, creating a gender 'see-saw' around boys' failure that sets up the contrasting story of girls' success (Collins et al., 2000). I will unpack the conceptual problems underlying such comparisons in the next section.

The Problem with Comparing 'Boys' and 'Girls'

Framing the debate over gender and achievement through a narrow binary conception of gender sets up the unitary category of 'girl' against the unitary category 'boy'. Liberal feminism, which concentrates on the promotion of *equality* for girls and women with boys and men, actually promotes simplistic gender binaries by emphasizing comparisons between the sexes. This encourages the 'sex war' mentality (boys' failure vs girls' success, and vice versa) that plays out in the educational debates on gender (Jackson, 1998). At the same time, more than two decades of anti-racist, post-colonial, black, and critical race feminist theory have clearly shown the conceptual weakness of such analysis, which ignores the way gender is differentiated by other 'intersecting' or 'articulating' axes of experience and identity, or the many other social discourses that produce inequalities of social class, race, and ethnicity (Bhavnani, 1997; Brah, 2001; Carby, 1982; Collins, 1998; Mohanty, 1991; Wing, 2000). Gender treated as a stand-alone variable, without reference to economic and cultural factors, can be used to prove either inequality or equality. Social class, ethnicity, race, and culture are conveniently obscured, even though many critics suggest that these factors are much stronger than gender as predictors of performance in school (Gillborn and Mirza, 2000; Lucey, 2001; Jackson, 1998; Reay, 2001). Thus to use gender as an undifferentiated, monolithic, essentialized category of analysis is to gravely misrepresent the issues involved in school achievement. Several educational researchers note that it is difficult to develop a convincing analysis of the way class and race affect rates of achievement in Canada because data disaggregated by race, class, socio-economic status, and so on are not readily available (Wallace, 2007). But this is precisely the type of complex analysis that is required if we are to get at the truth behind the now hegemonic 'masculinist' discourse that all boys are failing in Canadian schools (Bouchard et al., 2003).

Scholars in the UK have used **intersectional analysis**, looking at class and race alongside gender, to deconstruct the 'successful girls' discourse. They have shown that the high achievements of some (primarily white) middle-class girls are increasingly employed to fuel a story of girls' overarching success (Gillborn and Mirza, 2000; Youdell, 2004). The 'failing boys/successful girls' discourse hides the reality that middle-class white boys continue to succeed at school alongside their female counterparts, while many working-class and black boys continue to experience difficulty with educational performance. According to David Gillborn (2004: 13), the overall gap in achievement between black and white students in the UK is greater now than it was a decade ago, while Bangladeshi and Pakistani students fell even further behind their white peers in the 1990s.

The specific ways in which the 'successful girls' discourse serves to conceal continuing class inequalities in the UK are articulated by Walkerdine, Lucey, and Melody (2001: 112) in their study *Growing Up Girl*, which analyzes how exam results from high-achieving girls at high-achieving schools have been used to obscure the degree to which achievement is always a 'class related phenomenon'. Presenting longitudinal data on UK girls from both working- and middle-class backgrounds in order to demonstrate how class cultures continue to shape educational outcomes for girls, they argue that attainment figures based on gender alone serve to hide the class component: 'The resounding success by girls that has been spoken of in recent years is primarily about middle class girls' (2001: 112).

Walkerdine et al. also describe how girls and feminism are blamed for larger social problems that are in fact consequences of deindustrialization:

> It was formerly relatively easy for boys to obtain employment that did not require high levels of literacy, a particular accent or stylish attractiveness. . . . However, fewer of those kinds of jobs exist in affluent countries and so boys are now being pushed to remake themselves as literate, adaptable and presentable: it is this that has produced a crisis for 'working-class masculinity' and it is this that sets girls' educational achievement as a particular problem in the present. . . . *It is as though the success of girls has somehow been responsible for the dramatic and distressing changes that have happened over the last twenty or so years.* (Walkerdine et al., 2001: 112, emphasis added)

In effect, sensational generalizations about girls' success prevent nuanced analysis of deindustrialization, globalization, and accompanying processes: apparently it is easier, in the new post-feminist cultural space, simply to blame feminism. Indeed, 'in this gendered terrain, girls, women, and the feminine can be held accountable for all manner of cultural effects, as the beneficiaries of a shifting "gender order"' (Connell, 1987), in ways that pre-empt any wider critique of neo-liberal educational policies and testing regimes in school. At the same time, amidst the crisis of masculinity, the success of the feminine can be used to legitimize the brutal new regimes of testing and achievement. As another Canadian commentator frames the issues:

After decades of focusing on finding ways to ensure girls weren't kept behind on the basis of their gender, statistics show it's the boys who are falling behind. . . . barriers that once kept girls out of universities are crumbling and girls are now gaining access based on good marks and merit. Increasingly, universities are trolling for students who not only have high grades but who are well-rounded people. . . . many girls have developed good multi-tasking skills through balancing school, sports, work and volunteering, giving them an advantage. . . . while we've done a very good job of challenging stereotypes that limit girls' potential to be whatever they have the skills and determination to become, as a society we've allowed tired old myths of what it means to be a male to remain standing and now boys are paying the price. (Connell, 2005)

The shift in focus from the failing boy to the successful girl also marks a shift away from a problem-oriented discourse—the idea that economic globalization poses a problem for males—towards a success-based discourse of femininity. In a neo-liberal context that associates both economic and familial success with a self-made, rational, adaptable subject, qualities typically ascribed to femininity—flexibility, malleability, capacity for self-reinvention—have a central place (Walkerdine and Ringrose, 2006). The gender shifts we are witnessing require that both men and women increasingly perform what Lisa Adkins (1995) has called an 'aesthetics of femininity' and adaptation. By contrast, Diane Reay (2001: 165) suggests that in education (a key site in the production of upward mobility), with its 'growing emphasis on measured outputs, competition and entrepreneurship, it is primarily the assertiveness and authority of masculinity rather than the aesthetics of femininity that is required and rewarded'. The task for girls, then, is somehow to juggle feminine and masculine attributes, succeeding academically while remaining distinctly feminine (Walkerdine et al., 2001; Renold and Allen, 2006). This is the new, specifically middle-class ideal of productive femininity that girls and women must perform as students and workers in an increasingly neo-liberalized society (Walkerdine and Ringrose, 2006). In this way femininity is marshalled to sustain an educational arena obsessed with academic achievement.

The Future Is Female

Today we are witnessing a 'proliferation' of discourse (Foucault, 1980) about successful girls that is not bounded within the 'field' or 'domain' of education (Bourdieu and Wacquant, 1992). The reach of the educational discourses about successful girls is increasingly wide and exceedingly powerful, spreading in complex ways through the realm of globalized popular culture. It confirms and co-constructs a neo-liberal discourse of personal performance, choice, and freedom, along with its complementary discourse or 'rationale' of individual responsibility for failure in the 'global education race' (Mahoney, 1998; McRobbie, 2004; Rose, 1999; Walkerdine and Ringrose, 2006).

As Aapola, Gonick, and Harris suggest, writing in the Norwegian, US, and Australian contexts respectively, governments in many countries are entrenching a 'failing boys and successful girls' dichotomy through 'shifts in policies which re-focus on the educational needs, body image, mental health and leadership for boys in light of the argument that young women are outperforming young men in school and beyond in almost every aspect of personal development' (2005: 8). Members of the British Labour party think-tank Demos have suggested repeatedly that that the 'future is female' (Walkerdine et al., 2001). The Canadian Council of Ministers of Education, which administers the SAIP, has likewise registered concern that women will 'eventually leap ahead of men in the education, jobs and earnings race' (cited in Froese-Germain, 2004).

Unsurprisingly, this line of reasoning in educational research and policy-making continues to resonate with conservative news media. A 2004 *Guardian* article reported UK School Standards Minister David Miliband's statement that across the UK, 'there has been a *revolution* in educational achievement over the last 30 years', of which girls had been the 'primary drivers and beneficiaries' (Smithers, 2004, emphasis added). Anxieties over the long-range implications of girls' educational success appear to have heightened recently in the UK media, with headlines like 'Girls Beat Boys at School, Now They Get Higher Pay':

> They have been outperforming boys at GCSE, A-level and in university for years. But now girls are doing better at work too, earning more than boys in the first eight years of their careers. Between 22 and 29, women earn 0.1% more on average than men, with the pay gap not opening up until they hit their thirties. . . . (Rozenberg and Bennett, 2006)

In 2003 a cover story in the US *Business Week* with the title 'The new gender gap' discussed 'alpha femmes' and described girls' achievement as 'a kind of scholastic Roman Empire alongside boys' languishing Greece' (cited in Froese-Germain, 2004). Another cover story, this one from the *New York Times*, in April 2007 focused on the problems of high-achieving 'Super Girls' who have to balance academic excellence with being slim and pretty; but the headline continued to buttress the claim of girls' overarching success (Rimer, 2007). The most recent headlines scream, once again, 'The future is female' (BBC, 2007) and claim that men will have to 'readjust' to the new qualities that will be centre stage in the new 'care economy' within which women are set to thrive.[1]

Furthermore, girls' success is presented as a *global* phenomenon. The idea that girls everywhere are getting ahead is evident in three separate 2003 BBC news reports of a survey conducted by the Organization for Economic Co-Operation and Development (OECD). The first story proclaimed a new '*Global* gender gap in education' based on findings that 'girls out-performed boys in reading at the age of 15 in all 43 countries [studied]', reporting that women have 'overtaken men at every level of education' (BBC News, 2003a, emphasis added). Success at school was directly connected to success at work in the article's representation of these issues: 'They [girls] are better at school, much more likely to go to university and are expecting to take the better-paid jobs.' A second story about the same survey lamented that 'In the space of a generation, boys have gone from expecting to be the best at school, to an assumption that they will be the worst. . . . around the world girls are winning the academic race' (BBC News, 2003b). Such claims of global equality fly in the face of the fact that the UN's Millennium Development Goal that all girls should receive at least primary education was missed by a huge margin in 2005 (Aikman and Unterhalter, 2005). Yet another story, 'Girls Top of the Class Worldwide', claimed that 'the 1990s [saw] a remarkable change in women's expectations and achievements', noting in the UK '63% of girls expect to have white collar, high skilled jobs by the time they are 30, compared to only 51% of boys' (BBC News, 2003c). This chapter, however, has argued that the revolutionary changes reported by the media do not represent a revolution at all: instead, they emphasize the representational dimensions of discourses of gender and achievement that position girls as unambiguous winners, objects of both fear and desire in a brave new post-feminist world. These stories also illustrate how the high achievements of some economically privileged girls in Western countries are being used to fuel a dangerously oversimplified story of widespread female success.

Conclusions

In the wake of the decade-long panic over failing boys, the 'successful girls' discourse has flourished because it supports neo-liberal arguments in favour of adaptation to market forces and globalized insecurities. According to the new story, the future is female: girls who have 'made it' are held up as proof that individual success is possible and the current test-based educational regime is working (McRobbie, 2004). The 'failing boys' discourse, based almost entirely on gender-differentiated test results, hammers home what Foster (2000) calls a 'presumptive equality': new common-sense understandings or assumptions that women have achieved equality with or even surpassed men in society. Girls' success in schooling is represented as the dawn of a brave new 'post-feminist' world in which gender inequality no longer exists and the 'kind of young woman celebrated for her "desire, determination and confidence"' has the opportunity to 'take charge of her life, seize chances, and achieve her goals' (Harris, 2004: 1). This celebratory discourse of girlhood is an international phenomenon, gripping both the affluent West and the developing world, where 'governments and NGOs also look to the minds and bodies of young women for whom education comes to promise enormous economic and demographic rewards' (McRobbie, 2004: 6).

More critical educational research, however, suggests that when girls are positioned as 'not a problem', the resources that should be devoted to addressing their needs at school are diverted to the 'boys' agenda, with devastating consequences (Cruddas and Haddock, 2005; Osler et al., 2002). Increasingly, post-feminist assumptions about girl power, gender equality, and feminine success encourage an overall denial of sexism, acceptance of double standards (e.g., around balancing beauty and brains), and pathologization of those 'other' girls who are not educationally successful, particularly the ones positioned as 'at risk' of pregnancy, welfare dependency, and criminality (Chesney-Lind and Irwin, 2004; Harris, 2004; Jackson, 2006; Ringrose, 2006; Worall, 2004). There is also neglect of myriad other issues such as heterosexualized competition, bullying, truancy, self-harm, eating disorders, depression, and even suicide (Francis, 2005; Meyer, 2006; Ringrose, 2008a). Girls and boys alike face massive contradictions in an educational context where 'masculine' assertiveness and performance are rewarded, but it is girls who are seen as most successful in these respects (Reay, 2001).

How are girls navigating the contradictory demands to live up to both the neo-liberal ideal of success and the traditional ideals of femininity? New research is exploring the contradictions that make negotiating these subject positions impossible: being the 'bright and the beautiful', the 'nurturer and aggressor', the 'hetero-feminine desirable and successful learner', 'the sexy, assertive and high achieving "supergirl"' (Archer, 2005; Renold and Allen, 2006; Ringrose and Walkerdine, 2007; Walkerdine, 2007; Youdell, 2006).

We need much more research, however, to map out all the implications of the post-feminist discourse of successful girls (in education and beyond) around the world. (Taft, 2004; Francis, 2005). To assume that girls' success is a global phenomenon, with girls everywhere getting ahead, is to deny both the vast gender inequalities in access to schooling in the developing world and the differential rates of success among girls in (over)developed countries like the UK and Canada. In such countries educational success and 'excellence' are still largely the preserve of middle-class students, regardless of their gender, who benefit from the 'cultural capital' of their parents (Lucey and Reay, 2002). We need to work out the complex effects of the neo-liberal discourse of successful girls in both the developed and developing worlds. What are the consequences of the myth of girls' success in places where fundamental human rights and access to education still have not been achieved? Mapping local contexts of educational access and gendered politics of equality is crucial for understanding the complex and uneven effects of globalization (see Aikman and Unterhalter, 2005).

In this difficult representational context, how can feminists continue to complicate and disrupt these claims to gender equality? Feminist analysis that focuses on simple gender binaries is complicit in the neo-liberal effort to legitimize an ethos of hierarchical achievement, competition, and marketization at the level of the individual, the school, and the community. A commitment to more intersectional analysis that takes into account the ways class, race, culture, location, and other factors intersect with gender to influence girls' and boys' experiences of schooling (Jackson, 1998) is necessary to disrupt the seductive discourse of 'successful girls' and 'failing boys'.

Note

1. The article goes on to suggest machines will displace men (which men?) 'from many of today's information economy jobs, just as they already have in agriculture and manufacturing'. The argument is there will still be employment in 'softer interpersonal skills' in 'child care, elderly care, nursing or other personal services', pointing to the global trends in increasing service-oriented work, which is feminized, casualized, and poorly paid. Indeed the article ends by noting 'there is nothing to guarantee female-dominated jobs will be better paid than they are now'. This should pique questions for us as educators about the global complexities of labour markets that demand qualities that mirror femininity, like adaptation, flexibility, and compliance. Moreover, the positioning of girls and women (and we need to ask which girls and women) as coming out better in this context of overall dropping wages and poorly paid jobs, might be viewed more clearly as an ideological trend of the 'gender wars' in education (http://www.campbell-kibler.com/Gender_Wars.htm) and broader culture, where the abstract 'girls against boys' logic obscures deeper economic and cultural shifts towards a growth in poorly paid service-oriented jobs in the 'care economy'.

Glossary

discourse: In Foucauldian thought, discourses are 'socially organized frameworks of meaning that define categories and specify domains of what can be said and done' (Burman cited in Paechter, 2001: 41). They are regimes of knowledge that create 'conditions of possibility' for knowing the self and others. Discourses enable varying levels of power; as one feminist commentator has suggested: 'Power is exercised within discourses in the ways in which they constitute and govern individual subjects' (Weedon, 1987: 113).

intersectional analysis: According to Collins, the framework of intersectionality may be used to 'think through social institutions, organizational structures, patterns of social interactions and other social practices on all levels of social organization' (1998: 117, 205). Intersectional analysis reveals how multiple discourses and axes of group and personal identity such as race, citizenship, class, sexuality, and gender afford differential access to power and affect the individual's chances of success.

post-feminist/post-feminism: Terms associated with postmodernist, post-foundationalist efforts to destabilize and deconstruct gender (Brooks, 1997; Gamble, 2001), but also with an anti-feminist 'backlash' (Whelehan, 1995) that has appropriated feminist ideas and language for use in discourses proclaiming that girls and women have now won or even surpassed total equality with boys and men. Post-feminism is a conceptual tool that helps us to grasp the complex implications of various feminist discourses circulating in popular culture and beyond.

Study Questions

1. What is 'post-feminism'? Does this concept help us to understand the rise of the discourses of 'failing boys' and 'successful girls'?
2. Discuss some of the reasons why governments compare the academic achievements of boys and girls. How are gendered rates of achievement used to construct arguments about school effectiveness and educational standards?
3. Explore why it is problematic to compare girls' and boys' educational achievements.
4. What is intersectional analysis and how can it help us to think about the multiple social factors that might impact students' achievement?
5. Explore the CBC news story on the 'Gender Gap' found at: http://www.cbc.ca/news/background/gendergap/. Which strategies are suggested for helping boys? How are girls' successes in school represented in the story?
6. Explore the BBC news story 'The Future Is Female' found at: http://news.bbc.co.uk/1/hi/business/6518241.stm. How do these types of stories contribute to gender anxieties?

Recommended Reading

Aikman, S., and E. Unterhalter. 2005. *Beyond Access: Transforming Policy and Practice for Gender Equality in Education*. London: Oxfam.

Arnot, M. 2002. *Reproducing Gender? Critical Essays on Educational Theory and Feminist Politics*, London: RoutledgeFalmer.

Bourne, P.B., and C. Reynolds. 2005. 'Theme Issue on Girls, Boys, and Schooling', *Orbit: OISE/UT's Magazine for Schools* 34, 1. Available at: http://www1.oise.utoronto.ca/cwse/worbit.html.

Epstein, D., et al. 1998. *Failing Boys: Issue in Gender and Achievement*. Buckingham, UK: Open University Press.

Francis, B., and C. Skeleton. 2001. *Investigating Gender: Contemporary Perspectives in Education*. Buckingham, UK: Open University Press.

———, and ———. 2005. *Reassessing Gender and Achievement: Questioning Contemporary Key Debates*. London: Routledge.

Recommended Websites

Statistics Canada report, 'The Gap in Achievement between Boys and Girls': http://www. statcan.ca/english/freepub/81-004-XIE/200410/mafe.htm

Department for Education and Skills (UK), 'The Standards Site': http://www.standards. dfes.gov.uk/genderandachievement/goodpractice/

Education Sector (US) report, 'The Truth about Boys and Girls': http://www. educationsector.org/analysis/analysis_show.htm?doc_id=378705

Oxfam Report, 'Gender Equality in Education: Beyond Access': http://www.oxfam. org.uk/what_we_do/issues/education/genderequality_education.htm

References

Aapola, S., M. Gonick, and M. Harris. 2005. *Young Femininity: Girlhood, Power and Social Change*. Basingstoke, UK: Palgrave.

Adkins, L. 1995. *Gendered Work: Sexuality, Family and the Labour Market*. Buckingham, UK: Open University Press.

———. 2002. *Revisions: Gender and Sexuality in Late Modernity*. Buckingham, UK, and Philadelphia: Open University Press.

Aikman, S., and E. Unterhalter. 2005. *Beyond Access: Transforming Policy and Practice for Gender Equality in Education*. London: OXFAM.

Ali, S., S. Benjamin, and M. Muthner. 2004. *The Politics of Gender and Education: Critical Perspectives*. Basingstoke, UK: Palgrave.

Apple, M. 2006. 'Understanding and Interrupting Neoliberalism and Neoconservativism in Education', *Pedagogies* 1, 1: 21–6.

Archer, L. 2005. 'The Impossibility of Girls' Educational "Success": Entanglements of Gender, "Race", Class and Sexuality in the Production and Problematisation of Educational Femininities'. Paper presented at ESRC seminar series 'Girls and Education: 3–16'. Cardiff University. November.

Arnot, M. 1984. 'How Shall We Educate Our Sons?', in R. Deem, ed., *Co-Education Reconsidered*. Milton Keynes & Philadelphia: Open University Press, 37–56.

———. 2002. *Reproducing Gender? Critical Essays on Educational Theory and Feminist Politics*. London: RoutledgeFalmer.

———, and A. Phipps. 2004. 'Gender and Education in the UK'. Available at: <http://portal.unesco.org/education/en/files/25755/10739011441Gender_and_Education_in _the_UK.doc/Gender%2Band%2BEducation%2Bin%2Bthe%2BUK.doc>.

———, and J. Dillabough, eds. 2000. *Challenging Democracy? International perspectives on gender, education and citizenship*. London: RoutledgeFalmer.

———, M. David, and G. Weiner. 1999. *Closing the Gender Gap: Post-war Education and Social Change*. Cambridge: Polity Press.

BBC News. 2003a. 'Global Gender Gap in Education'. Available at: <http://news.bbc.co.uk/1/hi/education/3037844.stm>. Accessed July 2005.

————. 2003b. 'School Works to Help Boys'. Available at: <http://news.bbc.co.uk/1/hi/education/3114208.stm>. Accessed July 2005.

————. 2003c. 'Girls Top of the Class Worldwide'. Available at: <http://news.bbc.co.uk/1/hi/education/3110594.stm>. Accessed July 2005.

————. 2007. 'The Future Is Female'. Available at: <http://news.bbc.co.uk/1/hi/business/6518241.stm>.

Benjamin, S. 2003. 'What Counts as "Success"? Hierarchical Discourses in a Girls' Comprehensive School', *Discourse* 24, 1: 105–18.

Bhavnani, K.K. 1997. 'Women's Studies and Its Interconnections with "Race", Ethnicity and Sexuality', in Diane Richardson and Victoria Robinson, eds, *Introducing Women's Studies: The Second Edition*. London: Macmillan Press.

Bouchard, P., I. Boily, and M. Proulx. 2003. 'School Success by Gender: A Catalyst for the Masculinist Discourse'. Available at: <http://www.swc-cfc.gc.ca/pubs/pubspr/0662882857/index_e.html>.

Bourdieu, P., and L.J.D. Wacquant. 1992. *An Invitation to Reflexive Sociology*. Chicago: Chicago University Press.

Brah, A. 2001. 'Difference, Diversity, Differentiation', in K.K. Bhavnani, ed., *Feminism and Race*. London: Oxford University Press.

Brooks, A. 1997. *Postfeminisms: Feminism, Cultural Theory and Cultural Forms*. New York: Routledge.

Carby, H. 1982. 'White Women Listen! Black Feminism and Boundaries of Sisterhood', in P. Gilroy, ed., *The Empire Strikes Back*. London: Hutchinson, 212–35.

CBC News. 2003. 'Gender Gap'. Available at: <http://www.cbc.ca/news/background/gendergap/>.

————. 2006. 'School System Failing Boys'. Available at: <http://www.cbc.ca/canada/saskatchewan/story/2006/06/07/sk-boys-schools060607.html>. Accessed 4 May 2007.

Chesney-Lind, M., and K. Irwin. 2004. 'From Badness to Mean-ness: Popular Constructions of Contemporary Girlhood', in A. Harris, ed., *All about the Girl: Culture, Power and Identity*. New York: Routledge, 45–56.

Clarke, L. 2006. 'Boys Are Being Failed by Our Schools'. *The Times*. 13 June. Available at: <http://www.dailymail.co.uk/news/article-390319/Boys-failed-schools.html>.

Cohen, M. 1998. 'A Habit of Healthy Idleness: Boys' Underachievement in Historical Perspective', in D. Epstein, J. Elwood, V. Hey, and J. Maw, eds, *Failing Boys? Issues in Gender and Achievement*. Buckingham, UK: Open University Press.

Collins, C., J. Kenway, and J. McLeod. 2000. 'Gender Debates We Still Have to Have', *Australian Educational Researcher* 27, 3: 37–48.

Collins, P.H. 1998. *Fighting Words: Black Women and the Search for Justice*. Minneapolis: University of Minnesota Press.

Connell, H. 2005. 'We're Leaving the Boys Behind'. *London Free Press*. Available at: <http://lfpress.ca/newsstand/Opinion/Columnists/Connell_Helen/2005/09/24/1233060.html>.

Connell, R.W. 1987. *Gender and Power*. Cambridge: Polity.

Cowley, P., and S.T. Easton. 1999. 'Boys, Girls, and Grades: Academic Gender Balance in British Columbia Secondary Schools'. The Fraser Institute. Available at: <http://www.fraserinstitute.org/Commerce.web/publication_details.aspx?pubID=2528>.

Cruddas, L., and L. Haddock. 2005. 'Engaging Girls' Voices: Learning as Social Practice', in G. Lloyd, *Problem Girls: Understanding and Supporting Troubled and Troublesome Girls and Young Women*. London: RoutledgeFalmer, 161–71.

David, M. 2004. 'A Feminist Critique of Public Policy Discourses about Educational Effectiveness', in Ali et al. (2004: 9–29).

Davison, K.G., T.A. Lovell, B.W. Frank, and A.B. Vibert. 2004. 'Boys and Underachievement in the Canadian Context: No Proof for Panic', in Ali et al. (2004: 50–64).

DCSF. 2003. 'Raising Boys' Achievement'. At <http://www-rba.educ.cam.ac.uk/index.html>.

———. 2007. 'Gender and Education: The Evidence on Pupils in England'. Available at: <http://www.dfes.gov.uk/research/data/uploadfiles/RTP01-07.pdf>.

Dei, G.S. 1996. *Anti-Racism Education: Theory and Practice*. Halifax: Fernwood Publishing.

Eisenstein, H. 1996. *Inside Agitators: Australian Femocrats and the State (Women in the Political Economy)*. Philadelphia: Temple University Press.

Epstein, D., J. Elwood, V. Hey, and J. Maw. 1998. *Failing Boys? Issues in Gender and Achievement*. Buckingham, UK: Open University Press.

Eyre, L., and J. Gaskell. 2004. 'Gender Equity and Education Policy in Canada, 1970–2000', *Orbit: OISE/UT's Magazine for Schools* 34, 1.

Fairclough, N. 2000. *New Labour, New Language?* London: Routledge.

Foster, V. 2000. 'Is Female Educational "Success" Destabilizing the Male Learner-Citizen?', in M. Arnot and J.A. Dillabough, eds, *Challenging Democracy, International Perspectives on Gender, Education and Citizenship*. London: RoutledgeFalmer, 203–15.

Foucault, M. 1980. *Power/Knowledge: Selected Interviews and Other Writings, 1972–77*, trans. C. Gordon, L. Marshall, J. Mepham, and K. Soper, ed. C. Gordon. New York: Pantheon Books.

———. 1982. 'The Subject of Power', in H. Dreyfus and P. Rabinow, eds, *Michel Foucault: Beyond Structuralism and Hermeneutics*. Brighton: Harvester.

Francis, B. 2005. 'Not Know/ing Their Place: Girls' Classroom Behaviour', in G. Lloyd, ed., *Problem Girls: Understanding and Supporting Troubled and Troublesome Girls and Young Women*. London: RoutledgeFalmer, 9–22.

———. 2006. 'Heroes or Zeroes? The Construction of the Boys' Achievement Debate within Neo-liberal Policy Discourse', *Journal of Education Policy* 21: 187–99.

———, and C. Skelton. 2005. *Reassessing Gender and Achievement: Questioning Contemporary Key Debates*. London: Routledge.

Froese-Germain, B. 2004. 'Are Schools Really Shortchanging Boys? Reality Check on the New Gender Gap', *Orbit: OISE/UT's Magazine for Schools* 34, 1: 3–5.

Gagnon, L. 1999. 'La Misère scolaire des garçons', *La Presse*, 16 and 25 October.

Gamble, S. 2001. *The Routledge Companion to Feminism and Postfeminism*. New York: Routledge.

Giddens, A. 1998. *The Third Way: The Renewal of Social Democracy*. Cambridge: Polity Press.

Gillborn, D. 2004. 'Racism, Policy and Contemporary Schooling: Current Inequities and Future Possibilities', *Sage Race Relations Abstracts* 29, 2: 5–33.

———, and H. Mirza. 2000. *Educational Inequality: Mapping Race, Class and Gender*. London: HMI.

Gorard, S., G. Rees, and J. Salisbury. 1999. 'Reappraising the Apparent Underachievement of Boys at School'. *Gender and Education* 11, 4: 141–54.

Harding, J. 1983. *Switched Off: The Science Education of Girls*. New York: Longman.

Harris, A. 2004. *Future Girl: Young Women in the Twenty-first Century*. New York: Routledge.

Hill, A. 2005. 'Exam Results Reveal Gender Gulf in Schools', *The Observer*, 15 May.

Hoff-Somers, C. 2000. *The War against Boys: How Misguided Feminism Is Harming Our Young Men*. New York: Simon and Schuster.

Jackson, C. 2006. *Lads and Ladettes in School: Gender and a Fear of Failure*. Maidenhead, UK: Open University Press.

Jackson, D. 1998. 'Breaking out of the Binary Trap: Boys' Underachievement, Schooling and Gender Relations', in Epstein et al. (1998: 77–95).

Kelly, A., ed. 1981. *The Missing Half: Girls and Science Education*. Manchester: Manchester University Press.

———. 1985. 'The Construction of Masculine Science', *British Journal of Sociology of Education* 6, 2: 133–54.

Kenway, J. 1997. *Will Boys Be Boys? Boys' Education in the Context of Gender Reform*. Australian Curriculum Studies Association, Deakin West, ACT.

Lingard, B. 2003. 'Where to in Gender Policy in Education after Recuperative Masculinity Politics?' *International Journal of Inclusive Education* 7, 1: 33–56.

Lucey, H. 2001. 'Social Class, Gender and Schooling', in B. Francis and C. Skelton, eds, *Investigating Gender: Contemporary Perspectives in Education*. Buckingham, UK: Open University Press, 177–88.

———, and D. Reay. 2002. 'Carrying the Beacon of Excellence: Social Class Differentiation and Anxiety at a Time of Transition', *Journal of Education Policy* 17, 3: 321–36.

Mac an Ghaill, M. 1994. *The Making of Men: Masculinities, Sexualities and Schooling*. Buckingham, UK: Open University Press.

McNeil, R., and H. White. 2007. 'Sexist Bullying and Teenage Attitudes towards Violence'. Paper presented at 'Gender Equality Duty: Are Schools Ready?' Conference, London, 20 March 2007.

McRobbie, A. 2001. 'Sweet Smell of Success? New Ways of Being Young Women'. Unpublished address to 'A New Girl Order? Young Women and the Future of Feminist Inquiry' Conference, London, 12–14 November.

———. 2004. 'Notes on Postfeminism and Popular Culture: Bridget Jones and the New Gender Regime', in A. Harris, ed., *All About the Girl: Culture, Power and Identity*. New York: Routledge, 3–14.

Mahoney, P. 1998. 'Girls Will Be Girls and Boys Will Be First', in Epstein et al. (1998).

Meyer, E. 2006. 'Gendered Harassment in North America: Recognising Homophobia and Heterosexism among Students', in F. Leach and C. Mitchell, eds, *Combatting Gender Violence in and around Schools*. Stoke on Kent, UK: Trentham Books.

Mohanty, C.T. 1991. 'Under Western Eyes: Feminist Scholarship and Colonial Discourses', in C.T. Mohanty, A. Russo, and L. Torres, eds, *Third World Women and the Politics of Feminism*. Bloomington: Indiana University Press, 51–80.

Morley, L., and N. Rassool. 1999. *School Effectiveness: Fracturing the Discourse*. Brighton and London: Falmer Press.

Northam, J. 1982, 'Girls and Boys in Primary Maths Books', *Education* 10, 1 (Spring): 11–14.

Osler, A., C. Street, M. Lall, and C. Vincent. 2002. *Not a Problem? Girls and Exclusion from School*. London: Joseph Rowntree Foundation.

Paechter, C. 1998. *Educating the Other: Gender, Power and Schooling*. London: Routledge.

———. 2001. 'Using Poststructuralist Ideas in Gender Theory and Research', in B. Francis and C. Skelton, eds, *Investigating Gender: Contemporary Perspectives in Rducation*. Buckingham, UK: Open University Press, 41–5.

Phillips, M. 2002. 'The Feminisation of Education'. *The Daily Mail*, 19 August. Available at: <http://pws.prserv.net/mpjr/mp/dm190802.htm>.

Pilcher, J., and I. Whelehan. 2004. *50 Key Concepts in Gender Studies*. Thousand Oaks, CA: Sage.

PISA (OECD Programme for International Student Assessment). 2003. Available at: <http://www.pisa.oecd.org/pages/0,2987,en_32252351_32235731_1_1_1_1_1,00.html>.

Reay, D. 2001. 'The Paradox of Contemporary Femininities in Education: Combining Fluidity with Fixity', in B. Francis and C. Skelton, eds, *Investigating Gender: Contemporary Perspectives in Education*. Buckingham, UK: Open University Press.

Renold, E. 2005. *Girls, Boys and Junior Sexualities: Exploring Children's Gender and Sexual Relations in the Primary School*. London: RoutledgeFalmer.

———, and A. Allan. 2006. 'Bright and Beautiful: High-achieving Girls, Ambivalent Femininities and the Feminisation of Success', *Discourse: Studies in the Cultural Politics of Education* 27, 4: 457–73.

Riddell, S. 1989/2005. 'Pupils, Resistance and Gender Codes: A Study of Classroom Encounters', in C. Skelton and B. Francis, eds, *A Feminist Critique of Education*. London: RoutledgeFalmer, 11–24.

Rimer, S. 2007. 'AMAZING +: Driven to Excel; For Girls, It's Be Yourself, and Be Perfect, Too'. *New York Times*. 1 April. Available at: <http://select.nytimes.com/gst/abstract.html?res=F10912FD35540C728CDDAD0894DF404482>.

Ringrose, J. 2006. 'A New Universal Mean Girl: Examining the Discursive Construction and Social Regulation of a New Feminine Pathology', *Feminism and Psychology* 16, 4: 405–24.

———. 2008a. '"Just Be Friends": Exploring the Limitations of Educational Bully Discourses and Practices for Understanding Teen Girls' Heterosexualized Friendships and Conflicts', *British Journal of Sociology of Education* (forthcoming).

———. 2008b. '"Every Time She Bends over She Pulls up Her Thong": Teen Girls Negotiating Discourses of Competitive, Heterosexualized Aggression', *Girlhood Studies: An Interdisciplinary Journal* (forthcoming).

———, and V. Walkerdine. 2007. 'Exploring Some Contemporary Dilemmas of Femininity and Girlhood in the West', in C.A. Mitchell and J. Reid-Walsh, eds, *Girl Culture: An Encyclopedia*. Westport, CT: Greenwood.

Rose, N. 1999. *Powers of Freedom: Reframing Political Thought*. Cambridge: Cambridge University Press.

Rozenberg, G., and R. Bennett. 2006. 'Girls Beat Boys at School, Now They Get Higher Pay', *The Times*, 27 October. Available at: <http://www.timesonline.co.uk/tol/news/uk/article615102.ece>.

Sanders, V. 2001. 'First Wave Feminism', in Gamble (2001).

Segal, L. 1999. *Why Feminism? Gender, Psychology, Politics*. London: Polity Press.

Smithers, R. 2004. 'Minister Backs Split-Sex Lessons in Some Subjects', *The Guardian*, 17 November.

Spender, D. 1982. *Invisible Women: The Schooling Scandal*. London: Writers and Readers Publishing Cooperative.

Squires, J. 1999. *Gender in Political Theory*. Cambridge: Polity.

Stanworth, M. 1981. *Gender and Schooling: A Study of Sexual Divisions in the Classroom*. London: Hutchinson.

Statistics Canada. 2004. 'The Gap in Achievement between Boys and Girls'. Available at: <http://www.statcan.ca/english/freepub/81-004-XIE/200410/mafe.htm>.

Swicord, J. 2006. 'Survey Finds Young Boys Failing in Schools across the US'. Available at: <http://www.voanews.com/english/archive/2006-04/2006-04-13-voa4.cfm?CFID=138742099&CFTOKEN=19806460>.

Taft, J. 2004. 'Girl Power Politics: Pop-Culture Barriers and Organizational Resistance', in Harris (2004: 69–78).

Walkerdine, V. 1989. *Counting Girls Out*. London: Virago.

———. 2007. *Children, Gender, Video Games: Towards a Relational Approach to Multimedia*. London: Palgrave.

————, H. Lucey, and J. Melody. 2001. *Growing up Girl: Psychosocial Explorations of Gender and Class*. London: Palgrave.

————, and J. Ringrose. 2006. 'Femininities: Reclassifying Upward Mobility and the Neo-liberal Subject', in B. Francis and C. Skelton, eds, *The Sage Handbook of Gender and Education*. Thousand Oaks, CA: Sage, 31–46.

Wallace, J. 2007. 'Inclusive Schooling and Gender'. Paper presented at the Canadian Teachers' Federation Conference, Ottawa, 4–6 May.

Weaver, M. 2006. 'UK Pay Gap among Worst in Europe'. *The Guardian*, 27 February. Available at: <http://www.guardian.co.uk/politics/2006/feb/27/1>.

Weedon, C. 1987. *Feminist Practice and Poststructuralist Theory*. New York: Blackwell.

Weiner, G. 1985. *Just a Bunch of Girls*. Milton Keynes and Philadelphia: Open University Press.

————, M. Arnot, and M. David. 1997. 'Is the Future Female? Female Success, Male Disadvantage and Changing Gender Patterns in Education', in A.H. Halsey, P. Brown, H. Lauder, and A. Stuart-Wells, eds, *Education: Culture, Economy and Society*. Oxford: Oxford University Press, 620–30.

Whelehan, I. 1995. *Feminist Thought: From the Second Wave to 'Postfeminism'*. New York: New York University Press.

Whyte, J. 1983. *Beyond the Wendy House: Sex Role Stereotyping in Primary Schools*. York: Longman.

————, R. Deem, and M. Cruickshank. 1985. *Girl Friendly Schooling*. New York: Routledge.

Wing, A.K. 2000. *Global Critical Race Feminism: An International Reader*. New York: New York University Press.

Wollstonecraft, M. 1792/1975. *A Vindication of the Rights of Women*, ed. Miriam Kramnick. London: Penguin.

Women and Work Commission. 2006. 'Shaping a Fairer Future'. Executive Summary. Available at: <http://www.equalities.gov.uk/women_work/women_work_commission.htm>.

Worrall, A. 2004. 'Twisted Sisters, Laddettes, and the New Penology: The Social Construction of "Violent Girls"', in C. Alder and A. Worrall, eds, *Girls' Violence: Myths and Realities*. New York: SUNY Press, 41–60.

Youdell, D. 2004. 'Engineering Education Markets, Constituting Schools, and Subjectivating Students: The Bureaucratic, Institutional, and Classroom Dimensions of Educational Triage', *Journal of Education Policy* 19, 4: 407–32.

————. 2006. *Impossible Bodies, Impossible Selves: Exclusions and Student Subjectivities*. London: Springer.

Younger, M., and M. Warrington. 2005. *Raising Boys' Achievement*. London: Department for Education and Skills. Research Report 636. Available at <http://www.dfes.gov.uk/research/data/uploadfiles/RR636.pdf>.

CHAPTER 14

The Road to School Leads Out of Town: Rurality and Schooling in Atlantic Canada

Michael Corbett

Introduction: Retrieving a Sociology of Rural Education

The sociology of education in Canada—indeed, the entire field of educational thought—is essentially an urban enterprise. Rurality is treated as historical and vestigial, as the space that modernity leaves behind. The case is much the same in the United States, as a small cadre of educational theorists have been arguing for some years (Theobald, 1997; DeYoung, 1995; Howley and Eckman, 1997; Haas and Nachtigal, 1998). If their work has had a core theoretical thread, it is to be found in **communitarianism** and the general view that modernity erodes the social base of contemporary America (Etzioni, 1991; Putnam, 2000). Typically, this literature represents an attempt to preserve the integrity of rural schools and rural communities and to argue that the malaise in modern education can somehow be set right by returning to the core values represented by good rural schools. Additionally, strong rural schools and rural communities will ensure that vast rural lands will be protected from undesirable and ecologically dangerous industrial and development practices (Theobald, 1997).

In Canada there is no real 'field' of rural education. Rather there is a handful of sociologists of education whose work encompasses rural areas. There are also a few Canadian anglophone sociologists who are seeking either to understand the contemporary transformation of rural communities (Epp, 2001; Reimer, 2007; Matthews, 1976; Ommer et al., 2007; Winson and Leach, 2002) or to push theorizing about Canadian rurality beyond its romantic roots in a naïve communitarianism (Bonner, 1997). What I want to suggest in this chapter is that Matthews' rural Newfoundland quip that 'the road to school leads out of town' captures a dynamic that can help us understand how to develop rural educational policy that is both distinct and cognizant of the extent to which rural and urban places are being simultaneously transformed by global forces of change.

In recent years rurality has largely disappeared from the academic map. Early work in rural sociology, heavily influenced by Georg Simmel, the Chicago School, and anthropology, tended to focus on the fundamental differences between urban and rural lifeways as revealed through the methodological medium of community studies. As early as the 1960s, sociologists were raising fundamental questions about the distinction between the rural and the urban in industrial societies (Pahl, 1966; Williams, 1973; Hoggart, 1990). In the 1970s, rural sociology was revived through linkages to Marxist theorizing (and particularly dependency theory) and development and peasant studies in which scholars analyzed the spatial dynamics of capitalist development and the production of metropolitan core regions and peripheral hinterland regions. However, this brand of theoretical and empirical work came to be read as yet another discourse of inevitable victimization, in this case the victimization of rural dwellers (Southcott, 1999). In his 1998 *Dictionary of Sociology*, Gordon Marshall comments that rural sociology generally has become a moribund field.

> Rural sociology has been powerfully influenced by anti-urbanism, producing a stereotypical view of rural society as stable and harmonious . . . much mainstream rural sociology remains obstinately wedded to the old (anti-urban) paradigm, or is little more than abstracted empiricism. (Marshall, 1998: 574)

Rural sociology then is considered to be under-theorized, over-empiricized, mobilized as an ideological tool by both right and left, and stuck in romantic notions of traditional community life that have been superseded by contemporary forces of social change. At the 2006 International Sociological Association World Congress of Sociology in Durban, there was no active rural sociology research committee or working group in evidence. Work that might formerly have fallen under the rubric of rural sociology has been located in research committees dedicated to topics such as Community Research, the Sociology of Migration, the Sociology of Agriculture and Food, and Regional and Urban Development.

Additionally, rurality has been associated with a special kind of place attachment; indeed this is a large part of the romantic foundation of rural sociology criticized by Marshall and others. Influential social theorists such as Anthony Giddens and Zygmunt Bauman have promoted the idea that place is becoming less important or even unimportant as global postmodernity unfolds. The specific positions of each of these two grand sociological theorists are distinct, but their views on the decreasing significance of place are quite similar. Bauman analyzes the increasing importance of mobility in contemporary societies. Wiborg (2004) puts it this way: 'The central place of mobility in modern society, according to Bauman (1992), prevents the development of strong affection for any particular place because the places we occupy are no more than temporary stations.'

As moderns, or postmoderns, Bauman argues that we necessarily become Simmel's quintessential 'strangers', people whose alterity becomes normal and who look at social situations from a vantage point outside traditional community and culture. The thing is that everyone else is also a stranger and everyone else is on the move—at least everyone who can afford to move and who is not 'glocalized' (Bauman, 1998).

Glocalized immobile victims are stuck in place and represent yet another form of waste (in this case 'human waste' [Bauman, 2004]) generated by 'fast capitalism' (Agger, 1989). In this sense, the noble rural dweller of traditional communitiarian thought and middle-class rural romanticism (Williams, 1973) and antimodernism (McKay, 1994) has been transformed into the ultimate victim of the incessant uprooting and mobilization. The romance of the rural is not gone, but it has been cosmopolitanized or infused with non-local content (Beck, 2007). 'Winners' are able to control their movement, while 'losers' are either trapped in a spatially bounded home place or pushed into other places by forces beyond their control. Thus, I have argued that formal education generally, and rural education particularly, are best understood in terms of the mobilization of populations (Corbett, 2005, 2006a, 2007c). In other words, rural schooling is fundamentally concerned with efficiently shifting labour from rural to urban areas.

For Giddens, place has become increasingly 'phantasmagorical' as modern humans have been 'disembedded' and herded aboard the seductive 'juggernaut' of late modernity. In a cocoon of abstract expert systems that range from the growing multitude of professions to the modern home, connected to pipelines of energy and information, late moderns are at once contained and freed. We enjoy a high level of comfort, but as individuals we are largely cut off from and ignorant of the knowledges and systems on which that comfort depends. As a result, the late modern self is constructed not out of traditional identities and socialization patterns rooted in a particular landscape, but rather out of more abstract, trust-focused, mediated relationships existing in 'expert systems.'

As Stockdale (2004) points out, for rural people entry into the local labour market has typically meant engaging local networks of face-to-face trust relationships often based on kinship. Today, however, economic and cultural conditions in most industrialized countries are such that rural youth require credentials from key gatekeepers in expert and abstract certification systems in order to access labour markets. In contrast to informal, face-to-face, trust-based systems, these systems (of which educational institutions are prime examples) may have very few and very tenuous local connections. Thus, the trust systems and cultural-capital evaluation mechanisms through which a worker used to 'get a job' (particularly a crucial first job) are challenged by emerging credential systems like the formal education system. In rural places this transition is relatively recent. Institutions of formal education are, I will argue here, generally understood to be what Giddens calls 'mechanisms of **disembedding**' (1990: 24–9). The traditional rural community is often cited as the quintessential opposite of the placeless, faceless city (Williams, 1973).

On the other hand, recent decades have seen the rise of what has been called the 'spatial turn' in social theory. As space and place have attracted increased attention, the grand temporal narratives that had dismissed place and rurality as vestiges of an earlier time have been called into question. In his analysis of recent developments in rural studies, Martin Phillips (2002) essentially argues that as a consequence scholarship in the field is caught between the theoretical poles of postmodernism/**poststructuralism** and political economy, both of which have tended to position rurality as a victim space within multinational capitalism. As Thomson (2006) comments, there is mounting evidence that place may not be as 'phantasmagorical' and unimportant as Giddens and Bauman contend.

Formal education has been considered one part of the final solution to what Cubberley called the 'rural problem'. At the same time, rurality has come to be understood as posing a distinct set of political, economic, and spatial problems for the development of contemporary states. Still, it is clear that rural communities and their inhabitants often hang on long after they have served their purpose for capital. Rural dwellers have become one face of a larger resistance movement founded on emerging forms of identity construction that challenge the logic and hegemony of established institutionally conferred identity positions (Castells, 2004; deCerteau, 1984). In Castells' terms, the 'power of identity' and the more open configurations of sociability represented by virtual networks, affinity groups, and new social movements mobilize resistance to economic globalization, and other forms of transportation and communication generate new opportunities and challenges for self-construction.

The quintessential symbol of this phenomenon is the small farming or fishing community holding out against the alleged economic rationality that would move its inhabitants along to some other place. As Epp (2001) points out, this is why grain elevators and rural schools have become flashpoints for the identity politics of rural resistance in Canada. At the same time, environmental degradation, resource extraction and harvesting, common property and access rights, and other social issues have been framed in terms of rural citizens' entitlements—entitlements typically founded on longstanding residence. Michael Woods calls this new political configuration 'the politics of the rural', a politics in which 'it is notable that many rural advocacy groups are concerned with both social issues and development issues and that debates over rural social issues and development issues are increasingly framed around questions of rural identity, the meaning of rural community and the rights of rural citizens' (2006: 580).

The Road to School Leads Out of Town

Of the handful of rural education studies that have been conducted in Canada, most have been atheoretical analyses carried out under the auspices of Statistics Canada (Dupuy, Mayer, and Morissette, 2000; Finnie, Lascelles, and Sweetman, 2005; Frenette, 2003; Tremblay, 2001); in addition there have been a few isolated and mostly independent analyses of particular rural education questions in particular regions. Indeed, the landscape of rural education scholarship with a sociological focus resembles much of rural Canada itself in its diversity and isolation. This is not the case elsewhere in the world, however. In Europe and Australia a number of studies in rural education have recently been published, mainly in the *Journal of Rural Studies* and *Sociologia Ruralis*. In the United States a few rural education scholars have also been analyzing education in rural areas in the *Journal of Research in Rural Education* and the *Rural Educator*.

One important area of research and theorizing in the sociology of rural education has been the connection between formal education and the spatial reordering of rural places. Some of this research is community-focused, informed by the revival of communitarian traditions in the 1980s under the general leadership of the eminent US sociologist Amitai Etzioni. Scholars in this tradition have argued that instead of eliminating rural schools in favour of amalgamated and consolidated large school options, we should be using small rural schools as a model for a kind of educational practice that is connected to the land and cultural traditions in particular geographic communities. For instance, Paul Theobald (1997) argues that the United States took a wrong turn from the start in choosing to follow the liberal individualist philosophy of John Locke rather than the more pro-social and community-conscious ideas of other social philosophers such as Montesquieu. The focus on liberal individualism led to the development of social institutions that inculcate competitive, self-interested values, which in turn end up supporting industrial capitalism, social fragmentation, and atomization. In the case of education, the result has been a commodification of learning, with heavy emphasis on testing and competition for individual advancement. Meanwhile, the communities in which individuals live have come to be increasingly meaningless and tangential to the central business of personal advancement. The ultimate result of this ethos, and the economic and social practices that follow from it, is that rural places come to be marginalized in a modern society just as rural labour is marginalized within an industrial economy.

In the 1980s when communitarianism (Etzioni, 1988) and critical pedagogy (McLaren and Giroux, 1990) emerged as legitimate philosophical standpoints in the United States, longstanding debates about education and place in the field of rural education came to be framed in terms of larger structural questions rather than the narrow interests of community-bound rural dwellers. Even so, rurality occupies an ambivalent position in the context of the larger forces of capitalist economic development and the general movement away from traditional forms of face-to-face interaction. While rural education has continued to present particular challenges (e.g., low rates of post-secondary participation, pressure for school consolidation, urban-centric curriculum, high rates of early school leaving, etc.), it has become increasingly difficult to separate the challenges faced in rural areas from those faced in other socially marginalized spaces (Theobald, 2005).

In fact, a good deal of the American research in rural education has been focused on the survival struggles of particular schools, most of which are small in size and believed to be essential to the sustainability of their local communities. These studies have found common ground around issues of school size (Corbett and Mulcahy, 2006; Howley and Eckman, 1997; Howley and Howley, 2004, 2006) and progressive place-based educational practice (Gruenewald, 2003; Shelton, 2005; Theobald, 1997). A key limitation of sociological work in rural education has been its particularity, which obviously is problematic for generic theory (Ching and Creed, 1997; Kincheloe and Pinar, 1991). Nevertheless, most rural students do share at least one common educational reality, and that is the necessity of out-migration from a community where they and their families have deep roots and strong place attachments, in order to pursue higher education. While educational success has always been connected to social mobility, with all its attendant losses and problems,[1] in rural areas geographic relocation is also part of the picture.

Since the mid-1980s a number of studies in the United States have investigated the conflict between becoming formally educated and remaining connected to one's rural community. These studies have shown conclusively that the road to school does indeed lead out of town; in fact, the further one pursues formal education the farther away one is likely to end up (Corbett, 2007c). Attitudes towards school success therefore tend to be ambivalent, particularly in working-class families that have limited historical success in institutions of formal education and deep historical connections to the local geography, lifeways, and resources (Brandau and Collins, 1994; Hektner, 1995; Porter, 1996).

As part of a complex of what Giddens (1990) variously calls 'abstract systems', 'expert systems', and 'institutions of disembedding', schooling is regarded by many rural families with a skepticism similar to that reserved for government agencies and state regulatory bureaucracies. Nonetheless, the educational process offers individuals opportunity and choice. The result is a deep ambivalence about the whole process of schooling that operates simultaneously at several levels. First of all, formal education has historically worked well as a vehicle for those wanting to take their talents elsewhere, but such a vehicle is little use to those who want to stay in the rural community. Notwithstanding persistent moral panic about school dropouts (Gaskell and Kelly, 1996), formal education is not necessarily an advantage in rural economic and cultural markets. In other words, the idea that there will be an occupational or social status 'pay-off' at the end of an extended trajectory of formal education is not accepted by many rural communities and families.

Second, formal secondary and (especially) post-secondary education often serves as a kind of certification that particular individuals have developed sufficient cultural capital to function in markets beyond the local community. To develop this capital through the channels of formal education rather than the practice of family traditions is likely to mean abandoning some of those localized practices. Notably, one typically needs to leave behind the place-based practical skills and linguistic patterns necessary for smooth integration into adult society in the community in favour of the 'impractical' academic abstractions and 'space-based' virtual connections to multiple networks (Corbett, 2007a). In this way formal education drives deep wedges between many school-successful and mobility-focused children and their families and friends. At best, there is a deep ambivalence about the process of becoming educated, while at the same time becoming less pragmatically able or—as Daniel Cottom (2003) puts it— becoming 'stupid' as a natural by-product of formal education.

Third, rural people may tend to regard those who pursue formal education as in a sense 'going over to the dark side'. As Kincheloe and Pinar (1991) and Ching and Creed (1997) found in their studies of identity in the American south, formal education is associated with the kind of urban-centric social policy and resource-management manipulation that led to the decline of traditional industries and rural lifeworlds. Rural folks' distinction between 'common sense' and 'bullshit' might be instructive here. Common sense is the practical knowledge that the everyday person possesses without specialized training. It is acquired through experience and immersion in situations. Bullshit is the impractical theoretical knowledge produced and used by those removed from 'real life' (the farm, the factory floor, the fishing boat) to control and restrict the common sense practitioners. Formal education is seen in this context as the preparation ground for the institutional bullshit discourses in which rural common sense will eventually be complicated, marginalized, and even destroyed by rules and regulations.

To become formally educated is to enter a world of theory and generality in which one's home place is subsumed within an enormous matrix of places, markets, networks—the virtual and real complex of mobile 'scapes and flows' described by John Urry (2000). In this matrix, traditional industries, lifeways, and communities are merely means to larger ends, and it is no big deal when a school closes or a small community (or farm, or fishery, or woodlot) dies. The dark side is the perspective from which such events are historical necessities and tiny data points on a large scatter plot. This process is often understood as the work of a conspiracy of 'educated' urban interests out to destabilize and deskill rural communities (Epp, 2001). As one of my informants said, 'it's these educated people who make the rules that give all the fish to these corporations; that's where their science and their conservation have brought us.'

Rural Education and the Progressive Tradition

From my perspective, the central problem in the sociology of rural education and perhaps in rural educational thought more generally is the role of place. The deep rural education traditions connecting school both to community and to practical work go back at least to Dewey (1899/1980) and the beginnings of progressive education. Dewey's legacy is the orientation of formal education towards pragmatic activity in particular communities. As Mayher (1990) points out, most of our truly powerful learning occurs when we are engaged in activities that consume us, in which we are fully absorbed. Csikszentmihalyi (1990) has essentially made the same argument with his concept of 'flow'—the timeless state of deep concentration and commitment that permits real learning. The idea that learning begins with the experience of the child, and that different social contexts will afford different opportunities for learning, has given rise to a multitude of theories, movements, and research traditions, from child-centred education and the child study movement to emancipatory and activist pedagogies, situated cognition, activity theory, and place-based education.[2] Kieran Egan (1997) characterizes all these as 'socialization' theories of education, because they essentially focus on integrating young people into some existing or emerging social configuration.

Dewey's progressive/pragmatic approach offered rural teachers a way to resolve some of the fundamental tension between the demands of a tradition based on classical or 'essential' content[3] and the needs of rural communities that depended on the acquisition and refinement of practical skills (Davey, 1978; Gaffield, 1987; Harris, 1998; Corbett, 2001). Dewey provided the foundation for the development of contemporary ideas of place-based education[4] focused on the rural locality as the crucible of experience and on the kinds of 'working intelligence' (Rose, 2004) or embodied cultural capital (Bourdieu, 1984) that count as pragmatic in particular rural contexts.

There is, however, another side to the progressive movement, and it offers a different resolution to the tension between place and educational standardization. In Cubberley's (1922) classic formulation of the 'rural school problem', the school was understood as a key transitional mechanism that would serve both to introduce modernity and science into agricultural production (and by extension other forms of primary resource production) and to develop the skills and inculcate the attitudes necessary to make rural youth useful to urban capital. Without that preparation, a rural youth would be just one more dysfunctional misfit among the hoards of 'others' imagined by the nineteenth- and early-twentieth-century social reformers—children of immigrants, ethnic minorities, and the industrial working classes; intellectually and morally 'deficient' and 'defective' children; and the increasingly differentiated masses of what Donzelot (1979) called 'dangerous children/children in danger'.

More recently Tom Popkewitz (1998), in his analysis of the *Teach for America* program, referred to what he called the 'urban/rural child'. The modern incarnation of the child who in the past would have been considered educationally problematic by association with deficient social, cultural, or geographic communities (whether urban ghetto or rural backwater), the urban/rural child is understood to stand outside the frame of normality represented by the well-adjusted, well-resourced child who can reasonably be expected to meet educational age norms. In this way rural schools have come to be classified among the spaces that diverge from middle-class norms.

Similar kinds of spatial problems have arisen around accountability regimes designed for the global knowledge economy: the fact that not all places are equally amenable to educational standardization creates regional gaps in tested performance. I see two large areas of concern in Canadian rural education today. First, international educational and economic organizations, notably the OECD, have developed assessment and system comparison tools such as the Programme for International Student Assessment (PISA) and the Trends in International Mathematics and Science Study (TIMSS), and national assessment systems have been developed to articulate with those models—in Canada's case under the auspices of the Council of Ministers of Education Canada (CMEC). More recently, most Canadian provinces have developed assessment and curriculum delivery systems designed to produce outcomes in line with national and international standards. The new emphasis on academic achievement as measured by standardized instruments poses a direct challenge for experience-based, contextually sensitive education, especially in rural areas.[5] The upshot is that the central purpose of schooling is academic achievement as measured by standardized instruments. In general, test scores increase from east to west across Canada, mirroring trends in provincial wealth and the percentages of provincial populations living in rural regions. The second area of concern is a Canadian variant of the United States' No Child Left Behind program. It is now generally recognized that academic achievement is strongly influenced by contextual variables. In the United States this has led to a sometimes contradictory focus on raising standardized test scores in schools where academic achievement tends to be weak. Not surprisingly, many of these schools operate in neighbourhoods with high proportions of economically disadvantaged families. The chief levers of school reform today are neo-liberal school-choice schemes and the publication of individual schools' test results, on the basis of which funds have sometimes been diverted from poorly performing schools towards more successful ones. It soon became clear, however, that this 'naming and shaming' strategy was disastrous for students who lacked the resources to switch schools and 'choose' their way to a better education. As a consequence, additional resources have been shifted toward poorly performing schools in a variety of ways. In Canada school choice has effectively penetrated many urban jurisdictions, and right-wing policy analysts argue that this development ought to be pushed further. In rural areas and in small towns, a variety of compensatory and inclusionary programs have been designed to accommodate children from formerly marginalized groups within comprehensive schools (typically the only option in regions where population density is low). In Nova Scotia this initiative has been named 'closing the gap' (Government of Nova Scotia, 2006).

Against various socialization theories (Egan, 1997) is counterposed what I would characterize as an urban-focused classical education that essentially ignores place. Kieran Egan calls this the Platonic idea of 'the truth about reality' (1997: 12–15). Instead of attempting to socialize students or develop curriculum content out of their experience, proponents of the Platonic vision focus on engagement with ideas and texts that have stood the test of time and that represent the best of the Western cultural tradition. 'Culture' in this context is to be understood in the nineteenth-century sense, as 'the body of achievements in the various creative arts assumed to have moral and aesthetic value (as distinct from mere "entertainment"), their proper appreciation, and the body of knowledge necessary for their proper appreciation' (Hobsbawm, 2006: 101). In this tradition, formal education was part of a larger process of modernization that transformed rural life and geography through mechanization of natural resource extraction processes and at the same time released tradition-bound 'rustics' from what Marx and Engels called the 'idiocy of rural life'. The ensuing process of urbanization, which is now global in scale, has continued to the point where Davis (2004) claims that the majority of the world's population now inhabits expanding slum-ridden conurbations.

The seductive imagined spaces of urban life and the persistent discourse of rural decline (Corbett, 2006a) have led many, if not most, contemporary rural youth to think of the places they inhabit in negative terms: as less exciting than urban places (Theobald, 1992; Baeck, 2004), less sustainable, and generally not the places where 'successful' people end up. As a 'cultural bridge' (DeYoung, 1995) to urban spaces, the rural school is a transitional space where youth are taught definitions of success that include protracted formal education, immersion in locally ungrounded curricular abstractions, and the desire for mobility, the need to avoid getting stuck in a boring and unsustainable home place. Educationally successful students in rural communities 'enjoy the highest social status and power' (Vanderbeck and Dunkley, 2003: 255) by understanding the complex hierarchies of place and developing the ability to straddle the boundaries of identity, culture, and school (Carter, 2006; Corbett, 2007a).

Acquiring this knowledge is not easy. The social distinctions of class, race, and gender mediate the extent to which individual young people are able to take advantage of the educational path away from their rural origins. At the same time, discourses of postmodern social instability and insecurity may lead some rural youth to conclude that no matter how difficult life at home may be, at least it offers a level of security that would be impossible to achieve in an urban place (Corbett, 2007a;

Kelly, 1993). Established structures of masculinity, notions of what constitutes appropriate work for men and women, gendered work opportunity, and traditional apprenticeship socialization patterns also serve to make the educational route out of the community appear more or less attractive and convenient, depending on individual circumstances. It is widely recognized that rural women are more likely than rural men to migrate to urban areas and acquire more educational credentials (Ni Laoire, 2001; Dahlstrom, 1996). For instance, in a recent study of gendered educational trajectories in one Canadian coastal community, women who remained in the local area were twice as likely as their male counterparts to have completed high school, but as a group they earned less than half as much income (Corbett, 2007b).

Conclusion

The relationship between formal education and rural-to-urban migration poses a difficult policy conundrum. On one hand it seems obvious that rural people who wish to improve their life chances in the contemporary economy need higher education, and that out-migration is required to obtain it. On the other hand it is arguable that the abstract skills acquired through higher education are crucial to keeping rural communities vibrant.

Both of these contentions are problematic. As Theobald (1997) argues, individualism has been a guiding ideology for educational thought and practice in the United States from the beginning, in the sense that it has promoted training young people to advance themselves as autonomous, competitive individuals, undercutting the values of community and stewardship. By focusing schooling on the acquisition of personal credentials and educational capital, communities encourage their young to leave for places where the markets for those credentials are more lucrative. Theobald and many other rural educational activists and scholars are resistant to the idea that education represents a capital market in which individuals do battle for scarce resources. Yet educational processes have become thoroughly commodified over the last several decades in most parts of the Western world. It is very difficult to argue that young people should not do what appears to be in their individual interest and acquire as much formal education as possible; immobility and limited employment options hardly amount to an appropriate set of principles around which to organize any system of schooling.

Second, the idea that the development of a rural community can be separated from the educational achievement of its youth is equally problematic. There are at least two lines of sociological thinking here. One of these holds that rural communities are diminished by the brain drain that formal education entails; thus the better the system is at educating all children and youth, the more likely they will be to leave. The second line of thinking is that as children progress through school, the area of study ought to become increasingly global in nature. The child begins studying his or her family, then moves outward in concentric circles, eventually encountering global studies and increasingly placeless abstractions. Developmentally, this educational trajectory is understood as moving from the concrete to the abstract, with the local representing the simple and the concrete. This 'expanding horizons' curriculum (Wade, 2002) tends to ensure that adolescents and high-school students never focus seriously on the problems that confront their immediate communities.

Finally, the multifarious non-standard transitions from childhood to adulthood (Buckingham, 2000; Lesko, 2001) and from school to work (Looker and Dwyer, 1999) noted by contemporary sociologists and youth studies scholars are as prevalent in rural communities as anywhere else. The fluidity of the boundaries between childhood and adulthood today makes it possible to move back and forth between places and between identity positions. For example, it is now common for young adults to move in and out of the family home, or back and forth between work and school. These fluid and more vaguely defined norms surrounding transitions to adulthood and the construction of personally meaningful and sustainable life projects (Giddens, 1990) emerge as young people interact with global consumer culture, mediated leisure, emerging flexible labour markets, and the multiple identity possibilities all of this entails. In rural communities where longstanding gendered identity expectations and family responsibilities often play a part in young people's career and educational decision-making processes, these decisions have become increasingly risky and difficult.

The persistent paradox in rural education is that, out-migration notwithstanding, improving the educational performance of rural youth is good both for individuals and for their communities. Rural communities need better-educated populations if they are to prosper in contemporary economic conditions. In other words, rural communities need the kinds of people who are most likely to leave.[6] This is what makes recent policy discussions on the subject of keeping rural youth in their communities deeply problematic. My own research has shown that there is at least one coastal community where a strong proportion of the youth population actually does remain close to home.[7] Most of these young people are male and most of them possess low levels of formal education.

Nobody seems to have a clear idea about how to invest in rural youth in such a way as to both educate them well and keep them from moving away. Some of the discourse around this question is simplistic and nostalgic and appears to amount to developing 'local' educational programming that would effectively limit the options for some rural students to those available at hand. Community-based vocational training may be appropriate for a small minority of youth at the secondary-school level, however, a more appropriate challenge might be to: (1) support and persuade these youth to seek higher education and a more cosmopolitan experience, and (2) to create the conditions that would make the return to rural communities both attractive and feasible. I will conclude with seven specific policy suggestions which I think are supported by current research in rural education. It must be noted, however, that these suggestions are predicated on the assumption that rural communities are valuable to the Canadian social fabric.

First, it is essential that a wide range of publicly funded services be maintained in rural communities in order to draw their young people back following post-secondary education. If the state effectively abandons rural places, young people who have become accustomed to a wide range of services and opportunities will be all the less likely to return home. In addition, since public-sector jobs often require post-secondary educational credentials, retaining government services means retaining good rural jobs. Keeping small rural schools functioning, changing, and vibrant is crucial to rural communities' survival.

Second, since Canada's particular rural geography can represent a fundamental barrier to post-secondary education in some regions (Frenette, 2003), a special form of student financial aid should be made available to offset the additional costs that rural post-secondary students often face. This aid could take the form of residential bursaries that would help defray relocation and away-from-home living costs. Third, satellite campuses in rural areas and on-line program delivery could reduce the need for relocation in some cases. Fourth, programs that tie student support to commitments to return to rural areas (one such program is currently being piloted in Manitoba) could provide financial incentives to rural youth to return. Fifth, keeping a lid on post-secondary tuition costs would substantially benefit rural youth who already face higher overall costs than most urban and suburban youth do. This is particularly important for young people whose families do not have a tradition of pursuing post-secondary education and who may be reluctant to pay costs that they perceive to be too high.

My final two recommendations are directed to K–12 programming. First, the curriculum in rural schools should emphasize place-based educational initiatives and entrepreneurship. Broadly conceived entrepreneurial programming[8] is essential to develop the skills youth will need to create new opportunities in changing times. As for place-based education, this is now well established as a framework for developing curriculum and pedagogy (Gruenewald, 2003; Theobald, 1997) that engage children in real-world problems that matter and have real consequences (Shelton, 2005) within the places where they live. Vermont has actually developed a way to combine place-based education with the more standard educational outcome expectations (Jennings, Swindler, and Koliba, 2005). Finally, a new emphasis on geography and environmental studies could help rural youth develop their sense of place and understanding of globalization, as well as an ethic of stewardship and caring for natural spaces.

In post-traditional rural communities and rural schools, the opportunities and challenges posed by present conditions complicate the difficulties and contradictions of the rural schooling that have existed from the establishment of the Canadian education state (Curtis, 1988) in the mid- to late nineteenth century. The 'rural school problem' of the early twentieth century began with the plan to use the schools to introduce science and technical rationality into agriculture. This 'problem' had morphed by mid-century into an ongoing effort to educate redundant rural labour forces out of the countryside altogether. More recently, rural schooling has expanded its scope to serve a wider clientele and in more culturally inclusive ways while at the same time serving a wider range of socialization functions. Ironically, this has led to what Bauman (1991) calls a deep-seated ambivalence as we come to realize that every problem construction and every blanket policy solution has consequences we can never foresee. As Canada has become what Davies and Guppy (2006) call a 'schooled society' we continue to struggle with the difficult tension between an education that will benefit the local community and at the same time will provide rural young people with the intellectual, social, and geographic mobility opportunities they need.

Notes

1. A number of studies have examined the part that formal education plays in the processes of identity transformation (particularly at the level of language performance and literacy learning; Delpit and Dowdy, 2002) and leaving home not only for rural youth but for working-class youth in general (Dews and Law, 1995). This process is additionally challenging when race is added to the mix (hooks, 1994; Deyhle and Margonis, 1995).

2. For analysis of the long romance with this broadly based pedagogical movement (also known as Progressivism) see Cremin (1961), Tyack (1974), Egan (2002), and Tyack and Cuban (1995). Many observers have shown that it has become a virtual orthodoxy in teacher education institutions (see Labaree, 2004; Ravitch, 2002; Neatby, 1953).

3. Hlebowitsh's (2005) distinction between forms of 'traditional' curriculum that are perennialist (focused on relatively timeless classical content) and those that are essentialist (focused on a changing core of essential knowledge) is instructive here.

4. Traditions of place-based education in Atlantic Canada can be traced to the early and middle decades of the twentieth century in the work of progressive rural educators like Loran DeWolfe (Norman, 1989), Elizabeth Murray (Harris, 1998), and Jimmie Tompkins and Moses Coady, the founders of the Antigonish Movement (Lotz, 2001).

5. It may be no coincidence that the Atlantic provinces, which as a group tend to produce the country's lowest scores, also have the lowest average and median incomes in Canada. While it is now generally understood that academic achievement and particularly standardized test scores reflect the influence of contextual factors, these scores are still treated as the gold standard (see Corbett, 2004, 2006b).

6. There is, though, some debate about whether or not rural individuals actually improve their life circumstances by acquiring more education and by relocating. Bollman (1999), Corbett (2007c), and Pittman et al. (1999) found that the linkage between formal education and higher incomes in North American rural communities is weaker than in urban places. Chapman et al. (1998) have also questioned whether those who leave rural communities actually improve their occupational status.

7. This discussion raises the question of what counts as staying and leaving, which in turn raises questions about the constitution and boundaries of 'community'. For a discussion of how this dilemma may be addressed by spatially problematizing the idea of community, see Corbett (2005).

8. I mean here entrepreneurship that goes beyond the traditional business sense of the term and encompasses the idea of 'social entrepreneurship', or the application of creativity and resources to persistent social problems.

Glossary

communitarianism: A social philosophy that developed in the latter decades of the twentieth century in reaction to the apparent hegemony of liberal individualism. With the fall of the socialist regime, the former Soviet Union, many social critics began to make claims about how liberal individualism had emerged as the only viable and resilient social philosophy. Amatai Etzioni and others launched their challenge to this hegemony by claiming that community and an engaged collective life (civil society) remain the foundation of a strong society.

disembedding: the concept, developed by British sociologist Anthony Giddens, that individuals in modern societies are no longer bound by the ties of tradition, obligation, and place that 'embedded' them in particular social and geographic locations. There are two central mechanisms of disembedding in modern societies: symbolic tokens (e.g., money) and expert systems (e.g., modern educational or health-care institutions). These have taken control of forms of expertise and knowledge formerly held by individuals themselves who are now forced to place their trust in experts and symbolic token systems rather than in face-to-face relations.

poststructuralism: A broadly based attempt to undo, question, and deconstruct the grand project of social science to establish understandings of core social processes such as language, social class, and human cognition. Most poststructuralists argue that meaning cannot be separated from the particular context and power relations that produced it. Because context is the key to meaning-making, it is problematic to generate context-free structural systems for understanding how meaning is produced.

Study Questions

1. In this chapter, the author alludes to the 'discourse of decline'. What impact do you think the discourse of decline might have on young people growing up and going to school in particular rural and urban communities?
2. Is it true that schools educate rural youth to leave their home communities? Is this a problem, or is it actually a solution?
3. What do you think are the impacts of standardized testing on/in rural communities?
4. What role, if any, should schools play in community development?
5. Do schools foster individualism and an acquisitive consumerist mentality in students?

Recommended Reading

Bonner, K. 1997. *A Great Place to Raise Kids: Interpretation, Science and the Urban–Rural Debate*. Montreal and Kingston: McGill-Queen's University Press.

Ching, B., and G.W. Creed, eds. 1997. *Knowing Your Place: Rural Identity and Cultural Hierarchy*. New York: Routledge.

Corbett, M. 2007. *Learning to Leave: The Irony of Schooling in a Coastal Community*. Halifax: Fernwood.

Giddens, A. 1990. *The Consequences of Modernity*. Stanford: Stanford University Press.

Theobald, P. 1997. *Teaching the Commons: Place, Pride and the Renewal of Community*. Boulder, CO: Westview Press.

Recommended Websites

The Rural School and Community Trust (USA): http://www.ruraledu.org/site/c.beJMIZOCIrH/b.497215/k.CBA7/Home.htm

The Rural Education Special Interest Group of the American Educational Research Association: http://mkb.myweb.uga.edu/ruralsig/conferences.html

References

Agger, B. 1989. *Fast Capitalism*. Champaign: University of Illinois Press.

Baeck, U. 2004. 'The Urban Ethos: Locality and Youth in North Norway', *Young: The Nordic Journal of Youth Research* 12, 2: 99–115.

Bauman, Z. 1991. *Modernity and Ambivalence*. Ithaca: Cornell University Press.

———. 1992. *Imitations of Postmodernity*. London and New York: Routledge.

———. 1998. *Globalization: The Human Consequences*. London: Polity.

———. 2004. *Wasted Lives: Modernity and Its Outcasts*. London: Polity.

Beck, U. 2007. *Cosmopolitan Vision*. London: Polity.

Bollman, R. 1999. 'Human Capital and Rural Development: What Are the Linkages?', in N. Walford, J.C. Everett, and D. Napton, eds, *Reshaping the Countryside: Perceptions and Processes of Rural Change*. New York: CABI Publishing.

Bonner, K. 1997. *A Great Place to Raise Kids: Interpretation, Science and the Urban–Rural Debate*. Montreal and Kingston: McGill-Queens University Press.

Brandau, D., and J. Collins. 1994. 'Texts, Social Relations and Work-Based Scepticism about Schooling: An Ethnographic Analysis', *Anthropology and Education Quarterly* 25, 2: 118–36.

Buckingham, D. 2000. *After the Death of Childhood: Growing up in the Age of Electronic Media*. London: Polity.

Carter, P. 2006. 'Straddling Boundaries: Identity, Culture and School', *Sociology of Education* 79 (October): 304–28.

Castells, M. 2004. *The Power of Identity: Economy, Society and Culture*. Volume 2 of *The Information Age: Economy, Society and Culture*, 2nd edn. Oxford: Blackwell.

Chapman, P., E. Phimister, M. Shucksmith, R. Upward, and V. Vera-Toscano. 1998. *Poverty and Exclusion in Rural Britain: The Dynamics of Low Income and Employment*. York, UK: Joseph Rowntree Foundation.

Ching, B., and G.W. Creed, eds. 1997. *Knowing Your Place: Rural Identity and Cultural Hierarchy*. New York: Routledge.

Corbett, M. 2004. 'Knowing a Duck from a Goose in an Age of Smoke and Mirrors: Education in the Real World', *Our Schools/Ourselves* 13, 2: 95–122.

———. 2005. 'Rural Education and Out-migration: The Case of a Coastal Community', *Canadian Journal of Education* 28, 1/2: 52–72.

———. 2006a. 'Educating the Country out of the Child and Educating the Child out of the Country: An Excursion in Spectrology', *Alberta Journal of Educational Research* 52, 4: 286–98.

———. 2006b. 'Riding the Tiger in Nova Scotia: Educational Accountability on the Edge of a Runaway World', *Our Schools/Ourselves* 15, 3: 57–74.

———. 2007a. 'Learning and Dreaming in Space and Place: Identity and Rural Schooling', *Canadian Journal of Education* 30, 3: 771–92.

———. 2007b. 'So Much Potential: Women and Out-migration in an Atlantic Canadian Coastal Community', *The Journal of Rural Studies* 23, 4: 430–42.

———. 2007c. *Learning to Leave: The Irony of Schooling in a Coastal Community*. Halifax: Fernwood Press.

———, and Mulcahy, D. 2006. 'Education on a Human Scale: Small Rural Schools in a Modern Context', Wolfville, NS: Acadia Centre for Rural Education. Available at: <http://www.holidaymedia.ca/transcontinental/documents/2/Education%20On%20Human%20Side.PDF>. Accessed 7 January 2007.

Cottom, D. 2003. *Why Education Is Useless*. Philadelphia: University of Pennsylvania Press.

Cremin, L. 1961. *The Transformation of the School: Progressivism in American Education, 1876–1957*. New York: Knopf.

Csikszentmihalyi, M. 1990. *Flow: The Psychology of Optimal Experience*. New York: Harper Perennial.

Cubberley, E. 1922. *Rural Life and Education: A Study of the Rural-school Problem as a Phase of the Rural-life Problem*. Boston: Houghton Mifflin.

Curtis, B. 1988. *Building the Educational State: Canada West 1836–71*. London, ON: Althouse.

Dahlstrom, M. 1996. 'Young Women in a Male Periphery—Experiences from the Scandinavian North', *Journal of Rural Studies* 12, 3: 259–71.

Davey, I. 1978. 'The Rhythm of Work and the Rhythm of School', in N. McDonald and A. Chaiton, eds, *Egerton Ryerson and His Times*. Toronto: Macmillan.

Davis, M. 2004. 'Planet of Slums: Urban Involution and the Informal Proletariat', *New Left Review* 26 (March/April): 5–34.

deCerteau 1984. *The Practice of Everyday Life*. Berkeley: University of California Press.

Delpit, L., and J.K. Dowdy, eds. 2002. *Skin That We Speak: Thoughts on Language and Culture in the Classroom*. New York: New Press.

Dewey, J. 1899/1980. *The School and Society*, ed. J. Boydston. Carbondale: Southern Illionis University Press.

Dews, B., and C. Law, eds. 1995. *This Fine Place So Far from Home: Voices of Academics from the Working Class*. Philadelphia: Temple University Press.

Deyhle, D., and F. Margonis. 1995. 'Navajo Mothers and Daughters: Schools, Jobs, and the Family', *Anthropology and Education Quarterly* 26, 2: 135–67.

DeYoung, A. 1995. 'Constructing and Staffing the Cultural Bridge: The School as Change Agent in Rural Appalachia', *Anthropology and Education Quarterly* 26, 2: 168–92.

Donzelot, J. 1979. *The Policing of Families*. New York: Pantheon.

Dupuy, R., F. Mayer, and R. Morissette. 2000. *Rural Youth: Stayers, Leavers and Return Migrants*. Catalogue 11F0019MPE no. 152. Ottawa: Statistics Canada.

Egan, K. 1997. *The Educated Mind: How Cognitive Tools Shape Our Understanding*. Chicago: University of Chicago Press.

———. 2002. *Getting It Wrong from the Beginning: Our Progressive Inheritance from Herbert Spencer, John Dewey and Jean Piaget*. New Haven: Yale University Press.

Epp, R. 2001. 'The Political Deskilling of Rural Communities', in Epp and D. Whitson, eds, *Writing off the Rural West: Globalization, Governments and the Transformation of Rural Communities*. Edmonton: University of Alberta Press, 301–24.

Etzioni, A. 1991. *A Responsive Society: Collected Essays on Guiding Deliberate Social Change*. San Francisco: Jossey-Bass.

Finnie, R., F. Lascelles, and A. Sweetman. 2005. *Who Goes? The Direct and Indirect Effects of Family Background on Access to Post-secondary Education*. January. 11F0019MIE, No. 237, Ottawa: Statistics Canada.

Frenette, M. 2003. *Access to College and University: Does Distance Matter?* Analytical Studies Research Paper Series. June. 11F0019, No. 201, Ottawa: Statistics Canada.

Gaffield, C. 1987. *Language, Schooling and Cultural Conflict: The Origins of the French Language Controversy in Ontario*. Kingston and Montreal: McGill-Queens University Press.

Gaskell, J., and D. Kelly, eds. 1996. *Debating Dropouts: Critical Policy and Research Perspectives on School Leaving*. New York: Teachers College Press.

Giddens, A. 1990. *The Consequences of Modernity*. Stanford: Stanford University Press.

Glendinning, A., M. Nuttall, L. Hendry, M. Kloep, and S. Wood. 2003. 'Rural Communities and Well-being: A Good Place to Grow Up?', *The Sociological Review* 51, 1: 129–56.

Government of Nova Scotia. 2006. *Learning for Life 2: Brighter Futures Together*. Halifax: Department of Education.

Gruenewald, D. 2003. 'Foundations of Place: A Multidisciplinary Framework for Place-Conscious Education', *American Educational Research Journal* 40, 3: 619–54.

Haas, T., and P. Nachtigal. 1998. *Place Value: An Educator's Guide to Good Literature on Rural Lifeways, Environments and Purposes of Education*. Charleston, WV: ERIC Clearinghouse on Rural Education and Small Schools.

Harris, C. 1998. *A Sense of Themselves: Elizabeth Murray's Leadership in School and Community*. Halifax: Fernwood Press.

Hawley, G., H. Harmon, and G. Leopold. 1996. 'Rural Scholars or Bright Rednecks? Aspirations for a Sense of Place among Rural Youth in Appalachia', *Journal of Research in Rural Education* 12, 3: 150–60.

Hektner, J. 1995. 'When Moving up Implies Moving out: Rural Adolescent Conflict in the Transition to Adulthood', *Journal for Research in Rural Education* 11, 1: 3–14.

Hlebowitsh, P. 2005. *Designing the School Curriculum*. Boston: Pearson.

Hobsbawm, E. 2006. 'Culture and Gender in European Bourgeois Society 1870–1914', in D. Olson and M. Cole, eds, *Technology, Literacy and the Evolution of Society: Implications of the Work of Jack Goody*. Mahwah, NJ: Lawrence Erlbaum.

Hoggart, K. 1990. 'Let's Do Away with Rural', *Journal of Rural Studies* 6, 3: 245–57.

hooks, b. 1994. *Teaching to Transgress*. New York: Routledge.

Howley, C., and J. Eckman. 1997. *Sustainable Small Schools: A Handbook for Rural Communities*. Charlestown, WV: ERIC Clearinghouse on Rural Education and Small Schools.

———, and A. Howley. 2004. 'School Size and the Influence of Socioeconomic Status on Student Achievement: Confronting the Threat of Size Bias in National Data Sets'. *Education Policy Analysis Archives*, 12, 52. Available at: <http://epaa.asu.edu/epaa/v12n52/v12n52.pdf>. Accessed 27 December 2006.

———, and ———. 2006. 'Small Schools and the Pressure to Consolidate', *Educational Policy Analysis Archives* 14, 10. Available at: <http://epaa.asu.edu/epaa/v14n10.>. Accessed 27 December 2006.

Jamieson, L. 2000. 'Migration, Place and Class: Youth in a Rural Area', *The Sociological Review* 48, 2: 203–23.

Jennings, N., S. Swidler, and C. Koliba. 2005. 'Place-Based Education in the Standards-Based Reform Era—Conflict or Complement?', *American Journal of Education*, 112, 1: 44–65.

Jones, G. 1995. *Leaving Home*. Milton Keynes: The Open University.

———. 1999. 'The Same People in the Same Places? Socio-spatial Identities and Migration in Youth', *Sociology* 33, 1: 1–22.

Kelly, U. 1993. *Marketing Place*. Black Point, NS: Fernwood.

Kincheloe, J., and W. Pinar, eds. 1991. *Curriculum as Social Psychoanalysis: The Significance of Place*. Albany: State University of New York.

Labaree, D. 2004. *The Trouble with Ed Schools*. New Haven: Yale University Press.

Lambert, M., K. Zeman, M. Allen, and P. Bussière. 2004. *Who Pursues Postsecondary Education, Who Leaves and Why: Results from the Youth in Transition Survey*. Catalogue no. 81-595-MIE2004026. Ottawa: Statistics Canada.

Lesko, N. 2001. *Act Your Age! A Cultural Construction of Adolescence*. New York: RoutledgeFalmer.

Looker, D., and P. Dwyer 1998. 'Education and Negotiated Reality: Complexities Facing Rural Youth in the 1990s', *Youth and Society* 1, 1: 5–22.

Lotz, J., and M. Welton. 1997. *Father Jimmie: The Life and Times of Father Jimmie Tompkins*. Wreck Cove, NS: Wreck Cove Books.

McLaren, P., and H. Giroux. 1990. 'Critical Pedagogy and Rural Education: A Challenge from Poland', *Peabody Journal of Education* 67, 4: 154–65.

Marshall, G. 1998. *The Oxford Dictionary of Sociology*. Oxford: Oxford University Press.

Matthews, R. 1976. *'There's No Better Place Than Here': Social Change in Three Newfoundland Communities*. Toronto: Peter Martin Associates.

———. 1993. *Controlling Common Property: Regulating Canada's East Coast Fishery*. Toronto: University of Toronto Press.

Mayher, J. 1990. *Uncommon Sense: Theoretical Practice in Language Education*. Portsmouth, NH: Heinemann.

Neatby, H. 1953. *So Little for the Mind*. Toronto: Clark Irwin and Company.

Ni Laoire, C. 2001. 'A Matter of Life and Death? Men, Masculinities and Staying "Behind" in Rural Ireland', *Sociologia Ruralis* 41, 2: 220–36.

Norman, J. 1989. *Loran Arthur DeWolfe and the Reform of Education in Nova Scotia 1891–1959*. Truro, NS: Atlantic Early Learning Productions.

Ommer, R., and the Coasts under Stress Research Team. 2007. *Coasts under Stress*. Montreal and Kingston: McGill–Queens University Press.

Pahl, R.E. 1966. 'The Rural–Urban Continuum', *Sociologica Ruralis* 6: 299–339.

Phillips, M. 2002. 'Distant Bodies? Rural Studies, Political Economy and Poststructuralism', *Sociologia Ruralis* 42, 2: 81–105.

Pinar, W., W.M. Reynolds, P. Slattery, and P.M. Taubman. 1995. *Understanding Curriculum*. New York: Peter Lang.

Pittman, R.B., D. McGinty, and C.I. Gersti-Pepin. 1999. 'Educational Attainment, Economic Progress and the Goals of Education in Rural Communities', *Journal of Research in Rural Education* 15, 1:19–30.

Popkewitz, T. 1998. *Struggling for the Soul: The Politics of Schooling and the Construction of the Teacher*. New York: Teachers College Press.

Porter, M. 1996. 'Moving Mountains: Reform, Resistance and Resiliency in an Appalachian Kentucky High School', *Journal of Research in Rural Education* 12, 2: 107–15.

Putnam, R. 2000. *Bowling Alone: The Collapse and Revival of American Community*. New York: Simon & Schuster.

Ravitch, D. 2002. 'Education after the Culture Wars', *Daedalus* 131, 3: 5–21.

Reimer, W., ed. 2007. *Our Diverse Cities: Rural Communities*. Ottawa: Metropolis Project.

Shelton, J. 2005. *Consequential Learning: A Public Approach to Better Schools*. Montgomery AL: New South Books.

Southcott, C. 1999. 'The Study of Regional Inequality in Quebec and English Canada: A Comparative Analysis of Perspectives', *Canadian Journal of Sociology* 24, 4: 457–84.

Stockdale, A. 2002. 'Out-migration for Rural Scotland: The Importance of Family and Social Networks', *Sociologia Ruralis* 42, 1: 41–64.

———. 2004. 'Rural Out-migration: Community Consequences and Individual Migrant Experiences', *Sociologia Ruralis* 44, 2: 167–94.

Theobald, P. 1997. *Teaching the Commons: Place, Pride and the Renewal of Community*. Boulder, CO: Westview Press.

———. 2005. 'Urban and Rural Schools: Overcoming Lingering Obstacles', *Phi Delta Kappan* 87, 2: 116–22.

Thomson, P. 2006. 'Miners, Diggers, Ferals and Show-men: School–Community Projects That Affirm and Unsettle Identities and Place?', *British Journal of Sociology of Education* 27, 1: 81–96.

Tremblay, J. 2001. *Rural youth migration between 1971 and 1996*. Working paper #44, Catalogue# 21-601-MIE01044. Ottawa: Statistics Canada.

Tyack, D. 1974. *The One Best System: A History of American Urban Education*. Cambridge, MA: Harvard University Press.

———, and Cuban, L. 1995. *Tinkering toward Utopia: A Century of Public School Reform*. Cambridge, MA: Harvard University Press.

Urry, J. 2000. *Sociology beyond Societies: Mobilities for the 21st Century*. London and New York: Routledge.

Vanderbeck, R., and C. Dunkley. 2003. 'Young People's Narratives of Rural–Urban Difference', *Children's Geographies* 1, 2: 241–59.

Wade, R. 2002. 'Beyond Expanding Horizons: New Curriculum Directions for Elementary Social Studies', *The Elementary School Journal* 103, 2: 115–30.

Wiborg A. 2004. 'Place, Nature and Migration: Students' Attachment to their Home Places', *Sociologia Ruralis* 44, 4: 416–32.

Williams, R. 1973. *The Country and the City*. Frogmore, St. Albans, UK: Paladin.

Winson, A., and B. Leach. 2002. *Contingent Work, Disrupted Lives: Labour and Community in the New Rural Economy*. Toronto: University of Toronto Press.

Wotherspoon, T. 1998. 'Education Place and the Sustainability of Rural Communities in Saskatchewan', *Journal of Research in Rural Education* 14, 3: 131–41.

Part Three

Reforms and Consequences

CHAPTER 15

Education Governance in Canada, 1990–2003: Trends and Significance

Claude Lessard with André Brassard

Introduction

This chapter examines the education policies of Canada's various provinces and territories from the perspective of **governance** and its evolution. The principal questions of
interest to us fall into two groups. First, how is power in education exercised across the
country? What legislative and regulatory frameworks are involved? How do we characterize it? Has education governance changed since 1990? Second, can we identify any
common trends in the various policies? Is there anything that could be called a
'Canadian trend'? Or have there been several distinct evolutions, specific to individual
provinces and territories or subgroups, reflecting different general, political, or education cultures? The present analysis is a start towards answering these questions. The
empirical data[1] that are its subject matter are thirteen 25- to 60-page narratives of
educational policy change, one for each of the ten provinces and three territories that
make up Canada. Covering the years from 1990 to 2003 for each jurisdiction (see
references below), they were constructed by research teams representing universities
from various regions, with each team taking responsibility for different provinces or
territories. The narratives themselves were based primarily on current and historical
documentary data available through archives and websites of ministries of education
and related government education units, provincial professional organizations, and
public interest groups (teacher federations, trustee associations), academic research in
universities, and the news media.

Governance was one of ten pan-Canadian policy themes identified in an initial
analysis of common focuses of policy debate and change over the period covered by
the narratives (Chan et al., 2003). After reviewing all the original narratives to get a
sense of the whole, we identified the major trends in governance across the country.

In the first section we discuss the concept of governance itself. In the second we present the principal elements of the structural framework we used to compare the governance systems in place across Canada. This framework, based on Weber's 'ideal type', may be somewhat Quebec-centric, since the Quebec system is the one we know best. Nevertheless, we think it illuminates the elements common to all of Canada's education systems: a three-part structure and democratic, community-based participation. These two characteristics, which we call the vertical and horizontal axes of governance, constitute Canada's institutional heritage, 'the traces of our origins', to borrow an expression from Merrien (1990), and are the starting point for our comparative study. In the third section we identify and describe the principal trends in education governance, and in the last section, we analyze the meaning of those trends.

Governance

The term 'governance' is very much in fashion these days. It is not neutral or unequivocal. Nor is the movement to substitute 'governance' for 'government', both in everyday language and in more specialized contexts. The notion of government is grounded in the action of governing—making decisions that engage a collectivity, determining the directions for policy change and taking the action required to bring change about—exercised by an identifiable person or group with legitimate authority in a given public arena. 'Governance', by contrast, has multiple meanings, both descriptive and prescriptive.

A central element in the concept of governance is the idea that governments no longer have a monopoly on legitimate power: other bodies may contribute to the maintenance of order within the state and may take part in its economic and social regulation. In this sense, 'governance' refers to the capacity to coordinate interdependent activities and/or to effect change without having the legal authority to order it. While 'government' in its strict sense involves elected officials or legitimate representatives, 'governance' enlarges the decision-making circle to include other actors, sectors, or organizations—and does so in such a way as to give the decisions made an air of legitimacy and create an impression of efficacy and efficiency in their implementation. 'Governance' is, in a sense, a way of referring to policy-making processes based on a network of organizations and actors at various political arenas, local, central, or intermediate. In this 'open' political vision, the state works in partnership with other actors in order to bring about an action for which the responsibility, authority, costs, and risks are all shared. In this sense the state is becoming more strategic.

If states are pressed to move from government to governance, it is because there is a 'problem'—or, if one prefers, because some people claim there is a problem. Recall that in 1975, a report commissioned by the Trilateral Commission and entitled 'The Crisis of Democracy: Report on the Governability of Democracies' maintained that the state was in crisis because of the widening gap between ever-increasing social demands and the finite resources controlled by the state. To resolve that crisis, the authors of that report argued that the state must be transformed. In this way we moved from a state whose principal task was to redistribute resources to one that favoured liberaliza-tion, deregulation of markets, and privatization of the public sector. We note that, from the beginning, the idea of a crisis in governance was framed within the neo-liberal discourse (Saldomando, 2000: 3).

Descriptively, as Van Haecht (2004) emphasizes, governance covers a set of phenomena revealing that the public sphere has lost its legitimacy and centrality, and that public action is no longer effective or efficient. Prescriptively, therefore, 'good' governance shows a way out of the crisis faced by the welfare state, now seen as 'ungovernable'. This good governance would see the state give some of its functions to other actors, to work as a mediator and as part of a network. As Merrien (1998: 63) puts it: 'the new "good" governance is characterized by the movement from guardianship to contracts, from centralization to decentralization, from the State as redistributor to the State as regulator, from the management of public service to management according to market principles, from public "guidance" to cooperation between the public and private actors, etc.'

Two sets of principles lend legitimacy to the concept of governance: those of liberal democracy and participatory democracy (Gilbert, 2003). First, liberal—especially neo-liberal—principles demand that contemporary states, in order to ensure the well-being of their citizens, become competitive on an international scale. To that end, national economies must work to attract foreign capital and encourage technological innovation, while the state must put in place arrangements that promote competition and accountability: quasi-marketplaces for service delivery, accountability of the actors involved, contractual relationships between those actors and others (performance contracts), decentralization, and a client-centred approach emphasizing extending choice for users of public services. In this liberal vision, it is the goal of the state to manage and optimize economic and social resources, to promote adjustment to the new global realities, and to enhance the efficacy of state institutions. In this scenario the market and the democratic state support one another, the first providing the second with the means to produce the necessary political results.

However, according to Gilbert (2003) and Saldomando (2003), we can imagine democratic governance that focuses on making democracy and the marketplace evolve more positively towards equity and social justice. Following this point of view, which is wrapped up with concerns about basic democracy and social solidarity, governance should actively work to correct social injustices and strengthen participatory democ-racy. Here 'good' governance redistributes power and integrates excluded groups; it also helps to empower various actors and increases their institutional and political power. This form of governance enhances the capacity to find compromises and build local consensus. In this vision, decentralization is seen as promoting local control and increasing democratic power at the level of the people concerned.

As we see, governance concerns the relationships between the market, the state, and the 'community' (or civil society). It is, in its actual development, strongly embedded in ideologies and prescriptions. We must be careful in our use of it. We will hold onto the notion that governance concerns the capacity of the state to coordinate interdependent activities and to make change without the legal authority to order the change, while seeking to increase the decision-making circle to include other actors, sectors, or organizations in order to increase the legitimacy of decisions and the efficacy and efficiency of their implementation. As we will see in the section that follows, Canada's institutional heritage in education governance includes a strong element of local participatory community-based democracy.

Education Governance in Canada: The Essential Elements

It is important to note from the beginning that education in Canada is a provincial and territorial responsibility. Although the federal government provides substantial funding for post-secondary education and intervenes through specific funding programs that it directs—the Millennium Scholarships for students, Canadian Research Chairs, organizations funding research, the Canadian Council on Learning— it has no authority over primary and secondary education. There is no such thing as 'Canadian education policy', even if some federal mandarins have dreamt for decades of putting one in place in order to develop a workforce better equipped to meet the demands of the global economy. Control of education remains with the provinces and territories. Is there, in these jurisdictions, a structural framework of powers and responsibilities?

A Three-Level Structure of Responsibilities and Powers

Historically, the governance of the education system has taken place on three levels: those of the central authority (i.e., the province/territory), the intermediate authority—which may be called either a school board or a school district, depending on whether it is local or regional—and the individual school. The central authority is the provincial or territorial government in the form of the Ministry of Education. In general the central authority defines the direction and priorities of the system, as well as the education services that people have the right to demand. It is this authority that creates, empowers, and regulates the intermediate and local levels, to which it provides the necessary material and financial resources. Although direct responsibility for the schools lies with the school board (or district), it is the central authority that determines their institutional status, and it determines their functioning in multiple ways— for example, by establishing the norms for the training and tenure of school personnel. Historically, its involvement in curriculum has varied, but at a minimum the central authority has usually outlined the overall goals and objectives for the curriculum, set the norms for student progress, and established the procedures for assessment and certification of that progress. In certain cases the provincial authorities have gone further, producing uniform programs for all school boards. In general, the central authority also establishes policies and norms for other education services offered to students, notably specialized services for those with special needs. In addition, the central authority often exerts *a posteriori* control by requiring that all students pass exams in certain areas in order to obtain certification. As we will see in the next section, the dominant trend is to reinforce the central authority in these matters, and not to let them flow to the intermediate or local authorities.

The school board (or district), the intermediate authority, has judicial status, but in many provinces it is a decentralized entity. Each school board is administered by a council whose members are elected by the population of the territory. The school board has the legal power to deliberate and make decisions. It also has the authority to levy taxes on property for school purposes, although in many provinces this authority has been reduced over the last 25 years. Today it is usually the province that pays for core services and capital facilities; the exceptions are Quebec, Manitoba, and Saskatchewan. In Quebec the province provides 85 per cent of the funding for public schools and the remaining 15 per cent comes from local property taxes. In Manitoba the corresponding percentages are 60 (province) and 40 (school board). In Saskatchewan the province provides 40 per cent from general revenue, and the remainder comes from local property taxes. One of the school board's primary responsibilities is to ensure that all students in its jurisdiction receive the services they are entitled to, in conformity with the general policy directions, specific prescriptions, and frameworks defined by the central authority.

Finally, it is the mission of the school, whether primary or secondary, to provide the required education services to everyone with a right to them. The school is a creation of the school board and must work within the framework it provides. The relationship between schools and school boards may be characterized as a dialectic of support and control.

This tri-level governance structure is found across Canada. The dynamic relationships between the levels and their relative weight may vary from province to province, but we are always in a three-way political game—sometimes zero-sum, sometimes with possibilities of expansion. In Canada, when centralization/decentralization is discussed, it is essential to be clear about the levels involved and the type of political game in question: for example, are we talking about decentralizing the powers of the central authority towards the school board, or those of the school board towards the schools? Does the game involve centralizing certain powers within the central authority, while decentralizing others from the school boards to the schools? Do we increase one level's responsibilities without changing those of the others? It is in the answers to these questions that the precise configuration of governance in each case can be seen.

Participatory democracy

As the outline above suggests, the structure of the education system in the various provinces and territories of Canada has tended to be strongly vertical. This tendency persists today. Historically, however, this structure has not been exclusively bureaucratic and centralized. Indeed, each level in the governance structure has always been seen as a locus of democratic participation, whether provincial, regional, or local. The members of the provincial legislature and the school trustees who administer the intermediate level are all elected and thus have democratic legitimacy (even if rates of participation in school board elections are low in some regions). Meetings of the school boards are open to the public. At the level of the school, participation may take the form of consultation, recommendation, or decision-making. In Canada the concept of schooling is grounded in a community ideology: not only should the school function as an education community, but it must be community-based in the sense that it is linked with the community it serves, primarily through the participation of parents, but also through exchanges with other community organizations.

Education governance in Canada thus reflects its long history: its rests on a tri-level structure, and the intermediate and local levels must conform to the rules set by the central level. Governance is exercised by the central authority and the school board through the establishment of norms (control being both *a priori* and *a posteriori*) and by a system of democratic and community participation that traditionally and ideologically is very important. In what directions is education governance evolving? We will examine this question in the next section.

Principal Trends in Education Governance

The relationship between the three traditional levels of education governance is changing. In its place a new hybrid mode of regulating education is emerging. There are several interrelated phenomena at work here, and to understand the dynamics involved, we must first look at them one by one:

1. Reductions in the numbers of school boards through amalgamation, with merged boards taking responsibility for larger territories; this trend calls into question both the need for an intermediate level in the school pyramid and the idea of 'local democratic government';
2. Deconfessionalization of school structures in Quebec and Newfoundland and Labrador, reaffirming the importance of a common education for all as an element of social cohesion;
3. A combination of decentralization and centralization designed to increase students' success by giving schools and teachers what has been described as 'structured autonomy', with a centralized curriculum and standardized assessment;
4. A greater role for parents in school governance through school councils;
5. Increasing school choice and offering parents alternative forms of education (charter schools, private schools, home schooling); and
6. Partnerships between government, municipal, private, and community organizations intended to maximize integration of the services needed to support at-risk populations.

We will analyze each of these elements in turn.

Amalgamation

Historically, as we noted in the preceding section, school boards served as a form of local democratic government and embodied the community values in education. In certain cases and for certain subjects, the school boards were also able to provide a modest counterweight to the provincial authority. The cuts in numbers and reorganization of school boards raise questions not only about what will be 'local' in the future, but about the democratic legitimacy of authorities further and further removed from the schools and parents they are supposed to serve.

Table 15.1 outlines the cuts to the intermediate level made by each province between 1992 and 2004. As the remaining boards are reorganized to cover ever-larger territories, relationships among the various actors will tend to become less personal, and the sense of a shared education culture is likely to weaken.

Table 15.1   School board/district by province, 1992–2004 (numbers include francophone boards)

Province	Date Implemented	Legislation and Background Documents	Reduction	Number in Year of Implementation
British Columbia	1996		75 to 59	60
Alberta	1994, 1995		141 to 71	66
Saskatchewan	1998, 2004		119 to 100	82
Manitoba	1993, 1998, 2001	Bill 14: Public School Modernization Act	57 to 36	36
Ontario	1997	Bill 104: Fewer School Boards Act	129 to 72	72
Quebec	1997	Bill 109	160 to 72	69
New Brunswick	1992, 1996		42 to 0; 0 to 14	14 district councils
Nova Scotia	1996, 2000	School Board Boundary Review (2000)	22 to 7	7 regional
Prince Edward Island	1994		5 to 3	3
Newfoundland and Labrador	1996	Bill 8 (Royal Commission 1992)	27 to 11; 11 to 5	5

Source: Chan et al., 2003.

It is interesting to note that Saskatchewan, with a population of less than one million, continued to have more school boards than any other province even after the mergers of 1998. All the evidence suggests that the reason has nothing to do with population, but rather with a strong belief in community participation and local management. Saskatchewan and Manitoba were the only provinces where the mergers were voluntary (at least in the beginning); elsewhere the mergers were imposed by the provincial government.

The move towards amalgamation is hardly recent. Throughout the demographic changes and population movements (urbanization, rural exodus) of the last century, most provincial authorities at some point have tried administrative restructuring in an effort to respond to the education needs of the population wherever it might be congregating. (Similar adjustments have been made in the size of schools, notably high schools.) Amalgamation of school boards appears to be a long-term trend. It did not develop overnight, although the most recent mergers involved new dimensions specific to the context of the 1990s.

But demographic changes were not the only reason for amalgamation, particularly during the 1990s. Looking to reduce their budget deficits, all the provinces made huge cuts in education. At a time when the public sector in general was frequently criticized for its alleged 'bureaucratic inefficiencies', most people involved in school board mergers were willing to try reducing the layers of 'bureaucracy' and middle management in order to save money for 'direct services' at the school level. Unfortunately, we don't know of any pan-Canadian studies that would allow us to determine whether school board mergers actually led to substantial savings.

Economic considerations aside, the merger phenomenon also has a political dimension that may have consequences for the medium term. Reducing the number of school boards has meant reducing the number of school board commissioners as well. As a consequence the merged school boards, the commissioners, and the intermediate political actors all lose some of their political clout. Some provinces have taken advantage of the merger process to reduce the number of commissioners elected to each district. In Toronto there is now only one trustee elected for each 300,000 students. And Nova Scotia is conducting a pilot project that would further diminish the democratic legitimacy of the intermediate level, creating a centralized administrative structure and two education sub-units that are integrated into the single administrative structure. Managed by administrators appointed by the minister of Education, rather than democratically elected trustees, this is a 'de-concentrated' rather than a decentralized administrative structure. Recall that New Brunswick, during the 1990s, under the McKenna administration, abolished the school boards and replaced them with an intermediate authority that reported directly to the Minister of Education; but the boards were recreated under the Lord administration, when the courts ruled them back into existence.

Deconfessionalization

In two provinces amalgamation has led to a restructuring of the intermediate level on the basis of something other than religion. In Newfoundland and Labrador two referendums were needed to amend article 17 of the 1949 Confederation agreement, and the process of deconfessionalization was strongly resisted by the Catholic and Protestant churches alike. In Quebec, however, the reorganization of the education system along linguistic rather than religious lines was accomplished without any major difficulties or systematic obstruction by either the Catholic or the Protestant churches. Apparently the argument for social cohesion at the heart of a civil society that is growing ever more pluralist and diverse was widely accepted in Quebec. In Newfoundland and Labrador, demographic constraints and the desire to maintain public education across the territory weighed heavily on the deconfessionalization process. In these provinces, the debate on this question revived the idea of public service associated with public education for all under the responsibility of the province and the school boards.

Centralization and decentralization

Centralization and decentralization are an inseparable couple. In most of the provinces, school funding, curricula, and testing have all become more centralized since 1990 (Quebec is an exception, but only because its funding system was centralized in the 1960s). For example, since 1995 school boards in Alberta may no longer levy taxes on the people they serve: instead, they must go before the government-controlled Alberta School Foundation Fund in order to obtain the funding necessary to carry out their mandate. This significant change was upheld by the Supreme Court of Canada in 2000. In the same vein, with Bill 160—the Education Quality Improvement Act, passed in 1997—Ontario's Harris government centralized education financing: all school taxes (personal or commercial) collected are now managed by the government, which also oversees their distribution. One might think that this would increase social equity and reduce financial inequalities between school boards, but in reality it does neither. In both provinces, centralization of school financing has allowed government to make significant cuts in education budgets and has reduced school boards' ability to manoeuvre in their negotiations with the teachers' unions.

To arrive at the same result—budget cuts—the Liberal government of British Columbia modified the funding formula by moving several important budget items into supplementary categories, the management of which is left to the discretion of the school boards. Justified in the name of flexible management, this arrangement places a number of programs (ESL, geographic equity, services for special needs students) at risk. It also opens the door to entrepreneurship at the school board level or partnerships with businesses in order to generate additional revenues. We cannot infer from these developments that British Columbia is 'centralizing' its education financing as Ontario and Alberta have. Nevertheless, like those provinces, British Columbia is seeking to increase its control of the financial costs of education and to reduce the amount of money flowing towards the school boards. In 2002–3, Manitoba too adopted a new form of financing (Funding of Schools Program, FSP), allegedly simpler and clearer but also better able to target certain equity priorities. There is no evidence that this arrangement entails greater centralization of financing, however.

By contrast, it appears that no province or territory has escaped centralization of the curriculum and standardized testing. This strong trend is characteristic of governance based on results (see the following section). The move towards centralized curricula across the country, including Saskatchewan, is more recent in English Canada than in Quebec, for the simple reason that Quebec began the centralization process at the time of the Quiet Revolution and has had a strongly centralized curriculum since the 1980s. On the other hand, the notion of governance based on results is as new for Quebec as it is for the rest of the country.

As for decentralization, it is not always easy to identify general trends. Are we talking about decentralization from the ministry to the school boards, or from the school boards to the schools, or both at the same time? In British Columbia, for example, provincial bargaining is still the norm, although powers in the area of human resource management were delegated to the school boards in the name of flexible management. Decentralization went much further in Alberta in the 1980s, when much of the Edmonton school board's power was transferred to the schools for which it was responsible: since then, 75 per cent of school budgets have been allocated and managed directly by the schools. In Quebec, school councils are not only consultative bodies; they also have decision-making power over issues such as school budgets and improvement plans, the time allocated for various subjects in the curriculum, self-financing, and local partnerships.

Parental participation

If the school boards are becoming political and administrative entities that are further and further removed from the 'local' milieu, it seems appropriate that provisions should be made for parents to play a larger role in the management of schools. And this is what the provinces and territories did during the 1990s; see Table 15.2.

Like school board amalgamation, parental and community participation is hardly new. Before the 1990s the schools had tried to establish channels of communication with parents, to take into account their values and expectations, and obtain their support and involvement, either in informal ways or through consultative committees or parent assemblies. The new dimension introduced in the 1990s was the idea that parents could help to improve the schools, and their children's academic results, if the schools and their actors—teachers and principals—were more formally accountable to parents. Not every school has pursued this idea to the same degree, but a managerial logic inspired by the 'new public management' is now widespread. If we had to represent this change visually, we might imagine a continuum with the school as a community of practice, rich in its endogenous education culture, at one end and the school as a managerial entity, keenly aware of efficacy and efficiency norms, at the other. Reality is hybrid, but the trend in education policies, to the extent that they are inspired by the 'new public management' philosophy, is to push schools towards the managerial end.

The development of school councils raises many questions. First, is this a strategy to limit the power and influence of internal education actors—teachers and principals—to the benefit of parent users and consumers of education services? Where decision-making powers have been transferred to school councils, reducing the powers of school boards, could this be seen as a step towards limiting the power of the teachers' unions? Does the long campaign waged in the 1980s and 1990s by the Quebec teachers' union, the Fédération des enseignants des commissions scolaires, against all forms of decentralization of school board powers—the intermediate level bargaining unit—support this interpretation?[2]

Second, doesn't the request, made just about everywhere, that school councils develop improvement plans that take into account quantitative parameters set by provincial governments, make these councils the tool of a central administration seeking to 'align' the various levels of the education system to conform to abstract norms of results and effectiveness? What room to manoeuvre—or real power—do school councils have in relation to school boards and ministerial authorities? In the end, is the role of school councils to adapt school board's prescriptions and provincial government policies to the context of particular schools? Everything suggests that, with few exceptions, school councils are not real counter-balances and do not have strong autonomous political powers—at least, not for the moment.

Table 15.2 School councils in Canada by province and territory

Province Name of Council	Date	Legislation and Background Documents	Composition
British Columbia School Planning Councils	2002	Bill 34 School Board Flexibility Bill	3 parents, 1 teacher, the principal
Alberta School Councils	1995	School Act; revised Policy 1.8.3 (2003)	1 principal, 1 or more teachers, 1 student, parents of students in the school, another parent or community member
Manitoba Advisory Councils for School Leadership	1995, 1996	Education Administration Act	7 members with 2/3 parents and 1/3 non-parents including community members. Teachers and staff may be elected but may not number more than the community members
Ontario School Councils	1995	Policy/Program Memorandum No. 122	The principal, 1 teacher, parent representatives, non-parent community members
Quebec School Councils	1998	Bill 180 (1997)	Students, parents, teachers, staff, and community representatives Principal ex-officio
New Brunswick	2001	Amendment of the Education Act	Parents District education councils
Nova Scotia School Advisory Councils	1996		Students, parents, teachers, staff and community representatives
Prince Edward Island School Councils	1995	Section 66 of the School Act	Parents, teachers, and the principal Students may also be represented
Newfoundland and Labrador School Councils	1996	Royal Commission (1992); Bill 48, Section 26 of the Education Act	Parents, teachers, and the principal have an advisory role
Yukon School Councils	1990	Education Act	Parent and community members First Nations representation guaranteed

Source: Chan et al., 2003.

Third, in the context of budget restrictions, do the school councils represent a way of making local actors responsible for finding additional funds? Or, as Weiner (2003) suggests, are they symptoms of a furtive privatization of public education financing? Fourth, have the relationships between school boards and schools been fundamentally transformed by the creation of school councils? Have schools, thanks to the councils, 'won' room to manoeuvre and a certain degree of freedom from school boards? It is difficult to answer these questions for all of Canada. The decision-making powers entrusted to Quebec's school councils, for example, have in some places shaken up the traditional hierarchical relationship between the school board's administrative centre and the schools. From now on, the school boards and the centralized services must operate on a client-centred basis and show the necessity and value of the services they intend to provide to the schools. Another example comes from Edmonton, where under a new 'site-based management' plan schools define their needs and priorities and the school boards provide the necessary support. These questions can be summarized as one: does decentralization—or 'structured autonomy'—increase local powers, or does it paradoxically strengthen the central power, especially in the context of a strong movement towards common curricula and standard assessment systems?

School choice

If school boards must increasingly adopt a client-centred approach in their relationships with the school, the same is true for schools in their exchanges with parents. Without doubt, one of the net gains in power for parents is the increase in school choice. Alberta led the way, eliminating all jurisdictional boundaries in 1996. Now Alberta parents may register their children wherever they wish, as long as space is available. In addition, since 1994 the government has permitted the establishment of charter schools (non-profit schools that operate within the public system but have their own individual mandates), giving parents real choice in education. In 2007 Alberta had 17 charter schools.

Independent or private schools vary widely: some have a particular religious, philosophical, or pedagogical focus; others specialize in 'cramming'; while others work with the elite. These schools receive 50 per cent of the per-student funding allotted to their public counterparts in British Columbia, Alberta, Saskatchewan, Manitoba, and Quebec. In Ontario all Roman Catholic schools have been fully funded since 1986, but other private schools receive no direct funding. A tax credit for the parents of children attending private schools, introduced in 2001, was cancelled before it had been fully implemented. In Quebec, private schools attract 20 per cent of students at the secondary level. Within the public system, school choice exists as long as there are places available. In fact, declining numbers of students have meant increasing competition among schools—a situation that was once quite rare. It is also possible to enrol a child in a school managed by a different school board in order to obtain specific services, as long as space is available. In Quebec, as no doubt elsewhere, well-informed parents can usually find a way into the schools of their choice. By moving their children, parents can effectively 'punish' a school they judge to be inferior. The success of the secondary school 'report cards' prepared and published by the Fraser Institute and the Economic Institute of Montreal shows that a large number of parents behave as consumers in terms of education and are ready to exert pressure to exercise, at a reasonable cost, their freedom to choose. Manitoba has also moved to increase school choice in recent years. Finally, we should also mention the home schooling movement, which may be marginal but still represents an additional choice available to parents, and the obligation, since 1990, to ensure that official-language minorities have control of their own schools. These agreements led to the creation of francophone school boards where the need existed.

All these moves in the direction of increasing school choice have strengthened parents' power to influence their children's schools. They have also served to increase the competition between schools, obliging them to establish their positions in the school 'marketplace' and to strategize accordingly. School choice is not a new reality. Middle-class parents have often taken the local schools into account when deciding where to live. And well-educated parents, familiar with the school system, have long intervened on behalf of their children to secure a particular school, teacher, or course. Until recently, though, concern for social equity and the integrity of the public system has generally led ministerial authorities not to encourage such behaviour. This is no longer the case. We know the refrain: competition is good, the client is king (or queen), the system will change if enough dissatisfied parents pull their children out of public schools, the most effective strategy is to rely on the pressure exerted by parent consumers, etc. But we should not overestimate the importance of this phenomenon. School choice is specific to large urban centres. In less populated or rural areas the priority is not to maximize parents' choice but rather to ensure that everyone can receive a basic education, as close to the family as possible and at a reasonable cost. In demographic situations where the talk is of service cuts and mergers rather than expansion, diversification, and competition, choice is a luxury that no one can afford. Nevertheless, the expansion of school choice in urban areas forces the public schools to submit to the law of the 'market'. And that constitutes an important change in the regulation of the system.

Partnership

The sixth and last of the trends identified above is the encouragement of partnership between the public education system and other parts of the society, both public and private. The term can be ambiguous, however. In some contexts 'partnership' means sharing knowledge and power with the broader public, especially the local community. In others it means turning over to the private sector certain tasks in order to make the system more efficient and effective. Moving closer to the private sector may involve the management of both schools and certain school programs, such as professional training. Some see the latter especially as a step towards privatization and the subordination of education to the labour market.

'Partnership' in the first sense is associated with increasing democratic participation; this is the sense in which the term is used in Saskatchewan, in the territories, and in several urban centres where there is a great deal of poverty. 'Partnership' in the second sense is associated with 'integration of services', or what the Americans call 'full service schools': a move away from the 'silo' model of public service delivery and towards integration with other sectors. The Manitoba School Improvement Program, which brings together various internal and external education partners and is directed by a non-governmental, independent non-profit organization, is an example of this trend.

Nova Scotia has also experimented with this model. But a project known as 'Triple P' (for 'public–private partnership')—in which private entrepreneurs would construct a number of high-tech schools and then rent them to the government—was abandoned in 2000, following a change of government. And the education department's contract with the 'Knowledge House'—a private company specializing in electronic learning—had barely been signed when the company collapsed amid allegations of scandal. So far, then, despite copious rhetoric for and against 'partnerships' with the private sector, such arrangements remain uncommon. We are still a long way away from seeing basic education turned over to private enterprise.

The CMEC: A Fourth Level of Governance?

The Council of Ministers of Education Canada (CMEC) was created by the provinces and territories in 1967 to speak for Canadian educators and facilitate interprovincial coordination, as well as exchanges between the federal government and pan-Canadian education organizations. Today its main objective is to improve students' performance as measured by numerical indicators and international standards.

There are three ways of looking at the CMEC. On the one hand, it can be seen as the expression of the provinces' desire to protect their traditional autonomy in matters of education by joining forces to ward off against any intrusion by the federal government. In this scenario the provinces' common interest is to keep the federal government out and to protect their exclusive jurisdiction in education. On the other hand, CMEC can be seen as a forum for an ongoing Canada-wide 'conversation' that is conducive to the development of a common language, similar perspectives on common problems, and collaboration in areas such as curriculum and learning assessment, all of which translates into a kind of **policy convergence**. A third vision would see the CMEC as opening the way for the provinces to play an international role in education matters, enabling them to take advantage of the globalization and the marketing of education.

In the Victoria declaration (1999), the education ministers agreed on the following priorities:

- emphasizing education outcomes;
- exchanging information regarding best practices;
- collaborating on curricula;
- promoting policy research
- strengthening post-secondary activities and improving access to them;
- supporting international activities;
- facilitating interprovincial mobility for post-secondary students; and
- strengthening the CMEC's role in facilitating collaboration with the federal government.

In addition the Victoria declaration set out five explicit goals: 'accountability, quality of education, accessibility, mobility and responding to the needs of learners' (CMEC, 1999). These priorities have been translated into five specific actions constituting what the CMEC calls its 'basic pan-Canadian strategy':

- supporting the School Achievement Indicators Program, which assesses the performance of 13- and 16-year-olds in mathematics, reading, writing, and science;
- maintaining the Statistical Data Collection on education system outputs;
- exchanging information regarding areas such as information technologies, open learning, and copyright, as well as research and development in education;
- producing reports and publications on various aspects of education in Canada; and
- increasing mobility of post-secondary students through provincial and territorial agreements on the knowledge acquired.

In the same vein, several provinces and territories have worked together on curriculum matters. The Atlantic Provinces Education Foundation brings together the education authorities of the four Atlantic provinces to develop, implement, and follow-up on an outcome-based curriculum. As well, the Council of Atlantic Ministers of Education and Training (CAMET) was recently created, while the Western Canadian Protocol Project is working towards the adoption of a common outcome-based primary and secondary school curriculum across all the western provinces and territories.

The CMEC also manages Canada's participation in PISA, the program for international student assessment. Certification of Canada's 'world-class' status facilitates the export of Canadian education to different areas of the world, particularly Asia and Latin America. There is a world market and Canadian education authorities want a share of it.

To these initiatives should be added the Canadian Council on Learning (CCL), created in 2004 by the federal government with a budget of $100 million over five years. Directed by Paul Cappon, former executive director of the CMEC, the CCL is intended to help build a 'knowledge railway' that, like the CPR, will connect the nation from sea to sea. As part of this effort the CCL has created a 'composite learning index' that allows cross-country comparisons, as well as five research centres, each located in a different region of the country and dedicated to a particular theme: Work and Learning, Early Childhood Learning, Adult Learning, Aboriginal Learning, Health and Learning. The fact that the CCL is funded by the federal government gives it an important role in structuring the political discourse regarding education in Canada, as well as the research being done in this area.

Together, all these developments attest to the importance now attributed to outcomes and performance assessment according to explicit standards and norms. A province's position relative to the Canadian average, or to the scores of other OECD countries, thus becomes an important element in public discussion about education. Increasingly caught up in the globalization of education, Canada's education systems are incorporating the performance and efficiency ethics associated with that movement.

The convergence in education policies suggested by these developments, particularly in the areas of curriculum and assessment, may well contribute to the pan-Canadian coordination and regulation that the federal government has dreamed of for decades. The trend towards governance based on outcomes, embodied in the CMEC and CCL, both manifests and reinforces similar orientations among the education systems of the different provinces and territories.

Significance of the Trends Observed

Education governance in Canada has traditionally had two axes: one vertical and one horizontal. The phenomena described in the preceding sections reinforce both these axes and at the same time encourage further regulation of education. Regulation, or vertical governance, frames in a systematic and systemic way the activities of the players within the system who have the power to initiate action along the horizontal axis (notably through school councils) that allows for adjustment among the diverse logics of school actors, parents, and the principles of the 'market' and school choice—but only within a corridor defined by the superior (vertical) power.

The reinforcing of the vertical axis of governance reflects both the actual control exercised by the central authority and the quality control it has gained through the centralization of curriculum and the demand for specific outcomes imposed by policies at all levels of the system and made operational by the top of the bureaucratic pyramid of the education system. Contributing to this reinforcement are the CEMC, the CCL, the performance indicators, the centralization of financing, and the trend towards amalgamation of school boards.

The intensification of the horizontal axis reflects the mobilization of various school actors (internal and external) in the context of site-based management, increased participation by parents and the community, and improvement plans designed and carried out by the schools and their local community partners. It is also linked to increasing local or regional competition for students, which is exacerbated by widely publicized school rankings. On this second axis, several significant developments have taken place: the reinforcement of parental participation, the introduction of local tools of accountability, greater parental school choice, and the development of an educational 'marketplace'.

Canada's provinces and territories seem to be evolving, although to differing degrees and on different timetables, as a result of the intensification and strengthening of the two axes of regulation. However, even if we can see common tendencies in terms of education policies, it is important to recognize that the various provinces and territories do not start from the same point, they do not travel at the same speed, and they all have their own political trajectories and historical pathways.

Here the concept of **path dependency** (Palier and Bonoli, 1999; Merrien, 2000) may be useful. Developed to explain institutional stability and resistance to change, the theory of path dependency draws attention to the way institutions, policies, and ways of thinking inherited from the past can restrain the range of political options available in the present. Saskatchewan, for example, has resisted the neo-liberal 'common sense revolution' launched by the Klein government of Alberta in 1992 and subsequently picked up in Ontario by the Harris Conservatives and BC by the Campbell Liberals. Even though it was exposed to the same neo-liberal winds as those provinces, Saskatchewan continued along its own path in education, a path marked by concern for social equity and participatory community-based democracy. Quebec, during the first half of the 1990s, seemed to want to 're-establish the principle of equal opportunity' (as put forward by the Estates General on Education of 1996); however, in the decade following and until today, education seems to be caught up in the neo-liberal current, starting with the adoption of a law on the 'modernization' of the state in 2000 and the arrival in power of the Charest government (2003).

The provinces situated at the two extremes of the continuum have adopted radically different strategies, one group focusing on confrontation, notably with the internal actors in the education system, and the other continuing to rely on collaboration and consensus-building. The former are working within the strict confines of representative democracy, while the latter continue to prefer the participatory, community-based democracy inherited from the past.

As we have noted in preceding sections, the last decade has been marked by various forms of centralization, especially with respect to curriculum and assessment, to such a degree that a third axis is required to represent the growing role of the central state. This is not easy to accomplish because there are several dimensions to this centralization: not just curriculum and assessment but also financing, labour agreements, norms for managing equipment, and so on. Notwithstanding these difficulties, and for hypothetical purposes only, Figure 15.1 shows the intersections of the centralization/

Figure 15.1 Types of governance and centralization/ decentralization of education in Canada

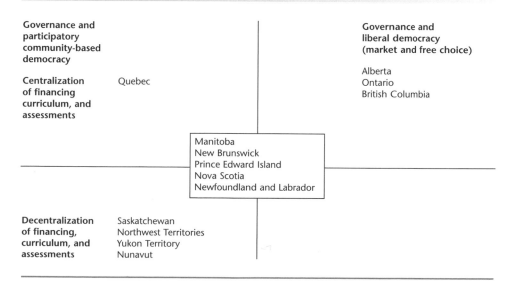

decentralization dimension (in financing, curriculum, and assessment) with the two kinds of governance identified. If a pan-Canadian trend could be teased out, it would be moving both upwards (towards centralization) and to the right (in the direction of a neo-liberal, confrontational type of governance)—which is where we find the richest Canadian provinces (Alberta, Ontario, British Columbia) and where Quebec may end up if its civil society, traditionally more social-democratic, does not act to modify the course set by the Charest government. The positions of the provinces in the 'centre' may be debatable. However, it is important to recognize that political rhetoric may not always be an accurate reflection of reality. As well, the history and reality of Canada are such that the neo-liberal rhetoric has come up against significant counterbalances: the Official Languages Act and multiculturalism, Native issues, the geographic dispersion of a small population over an immense territory, and demographic evolutions have all imposed various constraints on models of education governance, whatever the political rhetoric of the decision-makers.

Notes

1. The project was undertaken as Sub-Project 2 of a longitudinal study of policies and conditions affecting the lives of school personnel across Canada. The overall study, entitled 'Current Trends in the Evolution of School Personnel in Canadian Elementary and Secondary Schools', is funded by the Social Sciences and Humanities Research Council of Canada through its Major Collaborative Research Initiatives program.
2. One reason the teachers' unions have opposed decentralization is that they see it as representing a return to the arbitrary exercise of authority by the local boss, now disguised in the modern costume of 'flexibility'. Another is the risk that the 'national' education service will be dismantled or privatized.

Glossary

governance: The capacity to coordinate interdependent activities and/or to realize change without the legal authority to order it. It is a means of conceiving the construction of policies based on a network of organizations and actors who move into various political arenas, be they local, central, or intermediate.

path dependency: Auto-reinforcement as a choice, a way of doing something, or as a system of thinking long-term within a given framework; traces of origins that explain institutional stability and continuity.

policy convergence: Increase in the similarities between policies across political jurisdictions over time.

Study Questions

1. How would you define the concept of governance? What are the principal sources of its legitimacy?
2. What do you think of the hypothesis of a 'fourth level' of governance in Canadian education?
3. How is power in education exercised within the legislative and regulatory frameworks of the different provinces and territories? How do we characterize it?

4. What is the significance of the trends identified in this chapter?
5. Are there common trends in the various provincial policies? Does a 'Canadian trend' even exist?

Recommended Reading

Éducation et Sociétés, international francophone review of the sociology of education, published by the group 'proces de socialisation' of l'Association Internationale des Sociologues de langue française.

Levin, B. 2005. *Governing Education*. Toronto: University of Toronto Press.

Merrien, F.-X. 2000/2. 'La Restructuration des Etats providence: "sentier de dépendance", ou tournant néo-libéral? Une interprétation néo-institutionnaliste', *Recherches sociologiques* 31, 2: 29–44.

Recommended Websites

The Fraser Institute, conservative policy think-tank: http://www.fraserinstitute.ca
Canadian Centre for Policy Alternatives: http://www.policyalternatives.ca
Canadian Council on Learning: http://www.ccl-cca.ca
Organization for Economic Co-Operation and Development: http://www.oecd.org

References

Brassard, A., C. Lessard, and J. Lusignan. 2003. 'La Liberté de choix existe déjà au Québec', in M. Venne, ed. *L'annuaire du Québec*. Montréal: Fides, 439–52.

———, A. Chené, and C. Lessard. 1999. 'L'École publique a-t-elle un avenir?', *Carrefours de l'éducation* 8 (July–December): 26–54.

Chan, A.S., D. Fisher, and K. Rubenson. 2003. 'Preliminary Synthesis of Trends in Education Policy in Canada', manuscript. Centre for Policy Studies in Higher Education and Training (CHET, University of British Columbia). 29 Oct.

Gilbert, L. 2003. 'La Structuration de la gouvernance de l'éducation au Bénin. Analyse du point de vue des acteurs et des processus en cours'. PhD dissertation, Department of Education, Université de Montréal.

Lessard, C. 2000. 'Nouvelle Régulation de l'éducation et évolution du travail enseignant', *Revue Recherche et Formation* INRP, Paris 35: 91–111.

———. 2000/2. 'Nouvelles Régulations et professions de l'éducation, présentation', *Éducation et Sociétés, Revue internationale de sociologie de l'éducation* 6: 5–19.

———. 2003. 'L'École, communauté de sens ou produit de consommation', *Télescope, l'Observatoire de l'Administration Publique* ENAP 10, 2: 12–17.

Levin, B. 2005. *Governing Education*. Toronto: University of Toronto Press.

Merrien, F.-X. 1990. 'État et politiques sociales: contribution à une théorie "néo-institutionnaliste"', *Sociologie du travail* 3: 267–94.

———. 1998. 'De la gouvernance et des États Providence contemporains', *Revue internationale des Sciences Sociales* 155: 61–71.

———. 2000/2. 'La Restructuration des États providence: "sentier de dépendance" ou tournant néo-libéral? Une interprétation néo-institutionnaliste', *Recherches sociologiques* 31, 2: 29–44.

Palier, B., and G. Bonoli. 1999. 'Phénomènes de *Path Dependence* et réformes des systèmes de protection sociale', *Revue Française de science politique* 49, 3: 399–420.

Saldomando, A. 2000. *Coopération et gouvernance, une analyse empirique.* Actes de la journée d'études de l'Équipe CEDIM-FCAR Mondialisation, gouvernance et État de droit tenue à l'Université du Québec à Montréal.

Van Haecht, A. 2004. 'La Notion de gouvernance en perspective critique: réflexion sur les systèmes d'éducation actuels', *Politiques d'éducation et de formation, analyses et comparaisons internationales* 10: 11–19.

Weiner, H. 2003. 'Le Financement de l'éducation publique—une privatisation furtive?'. 14th Annual CAPSLE conference, Jasper, AB.

CHAPTER 16

British Columbia: Whose Education? What Reform?

Charles Ungerleider and Ernest Krieger

In recent years British Columbia has experienced dramatic reductions in its dropout rates,[1] and BC students have performed very well on international student assessments.[2] Yet too many of the province's students still leave school early and do not return, and too many graduates say they did not find their school experience challenging or relevant. Moreover, there are significant performance and graduation gaps between groups of students (Aman, 2006; Jago, 2006; Imagine BC, 2006). Whether these realities demand **reform** of the system depends on what one means by reform. Some call for restructuring, reorganization, and transformation of education; others favour changes, modifications, amendments, or alterations. Though they may differ in their opinions about the extent and nature of the reforms required—and about who is responsible for carrying them out—few deny the need for improvement. In British Columbia, however, education **policy** is contested ground.

To comprehend education policy in British Columbia requires examination of the relationship between the British Columbia Teachers' Federation (BCTF), the union representing the province's public school teachers, and various provincial governments. Relations have been strained under regimes of all stripes. For almost a quarter of a century, the BCTF and successive Social Credit governments fought what have been characterized as the 'school wars' (Kilian, 1985; Kuehn, 1988; Ungerleider, 1987, 1994).

A self-described social justice union, the BCTF—more than any other provincial **teachers' union**—is animated by the spirit of George S. Counts, the sociologist and critical friend of the Progressive movement who promoted social reconstruction through education. Counts believed that schools should be involved in every aspect of society, including politics, economics, and ethics. He advocated labour unions and believed that schools, by working with such groups, could change society. In a critique of **progressive** education, Counts charged that its accomplishments—its attention to children and the interests of the learner; its defence of activity as the root of education;

its conception of learning in relation to life situations and character growth; and its advocacy for the rights of children—reflected an excellent but inadequate conception of learning. Counts believed that anything calling itself 'progressive' must have a conception of the direction in which it wants to progress, and that 'there is no good education apart from the conception of the nature of the good society.' If progressive education was to be genuinely progressive, he argued, it would need to emancipate itself from the influence of the liberal-minded upper middle class, to

> face squarely and courageously every social issue, come to grips with life in all of its stark reality, establish an organic relation with the community, develop a realistic and comprehensive theory of welfare, fashion a compelling and challenging vision of human destiny, and become somewhat less frightened than it is today at the bogeys of *imposition* and *indoctrination*.

The great weakness of progressive education, according to Counts, 'lies in the fact that it has elaborated no theory of social welfare, unless it be that of anarchy or extreme individualism' (Counts, 1932).

Over the years the BCTF (2006a) has pursued its agenda of social justice in British Columbia by arguing in support of federal (1974) and provincial (1975) affirmative action for women, French-language instruction for both English- and French-speaking students (1975), the establishment of a dental health program for students (1975), the provision of family planning information and services (1975), negotiated Indian land claims settlements (1976), minority and Native language instruction (1976), provincially established pre-school education centres (1976), full public funding for the Planned Parenthood Association (1980) and Medicare (1981), the concept of a guaranteed annual income (1985), a tourist boycott of Brazil to protest the killing of street children (1994), and amendment of the Criminal Code to ban female genital mutilation (1996). The list of things it has opposed is almost as long, including organizations limiting membership on the basis of sex, race, or creed (1974), racial discrimination (1975), the location of a nuclear submarine base at Bangor, Washington (1975), restricted admission to private schools receiving public funding (1978), deregulation of the telephone system (1991), deficit reduction through cuts to social spending (1995), and cuts in federal transfer payments to post-secondary institutions (1996).

Apparently the BCTF is either reluctant or unable to negotiate the middle ground. Over the years it has strenuously opposed standardized testing, most moves towards increased parental involvement, and increased involvement of the private sector in public education. And in the 1990s, conflicts between the BCTF and government (New Democratic as well as Liberal) continued regarding provincial testing, school accreditation, and the role of the British Columbia College of Teachers (Ungerleider, 2003).

In 2001 the British Columbia Liberal Party swept into power under the slogan of a 'New Era' for the province that was intended to draw a clear distinction between the Liberals and the New Democrats who had governed the province for the preceding 10 years—a remarkably long period for a centre-left party to hold power in a province that for all but three of the preceding 50 years had been governed by coalitions of conservatives, neo-conservatives, and neo-liberals who, by avoiding electoral divisions among themselves, had managed to prevent the social democrats from forming government. In their policy document 'Promising a New Era for British Columbia', the British Columbia Liberal Party proclaimed 'a vision for hope and prosperity for the next decade and beyond'. With regard to education the Liberals had promised that, if elected, they would

- restore education as an essential service under the Labour Code, to ensure that no child's right to an education is denied during school strikes and lockouts;
- maintain and increase education funding levels by increasing revenues through economic growth;
- establish specific goals and outcomes to measure the success of educators in public schooling;
- devote more of each education dollar to improving the quality of education, and less to bureaucracy;
- support more flexibility and choice in public schooling;
- give local school boards more autonomy and control over the delivery of education services, subject to provincial curriculum and testing standards;
- give school boards multi-year funding envelopes, to improve long-term education planning and budgeting;
- work with educators and employers to expand job training and skills development opportunities;
- maintain current funding arrangements for independent schools;
- provide teachers with more technology training;
- eliminate the PST on basic school supplies purchased by Parent Advisory Councils, which volunteer their time and effort to raise money for public schools;
- guarantee that parents of students attending schools are entitled to volunteer their services, provided it does not result in the displacement of existing staff services;
- put more computers in schools and increase resources to improve computer literacy for students of all ages;
- ensure that music, arts, and physical education curriculums are fully funded in BC's public schools; and
- improve school accreditations (BC Liberal Party, n.d.).

Once in office, however, the Liberals embarked on a path that was anything but new. Their 'New Era' initiatives in education exemplified the neo-liberal values to which the Campbell government, like its Social Credit predecessors, subscribed:

- Choice, as a manifestation of freedom, is a virtue in its own right and the means by which individuals are able to express their approval or disapproval.
- The most important criterion by which public policy should be judged is its **productive efficiency**.
- Public regulation or provision of services should be eschewed in favour of private entrepreneurialism.
- Considerations of social equity should not fetter the economic interests of individuals.

In April 2002 the Campbell government introduced legislation to amend the School Act and implement changes consistent with the party's campaign promises. Bill 34, the School Amendment Act 2002, was described by the education minister as following through on the government's commitments to

> improve student achievement by enhancing parental involvement in children's schools, by providing parents and students with more choice about what school they would like to attend, by lifting spending restrictions that have tied the hands of school boards and by giving school boards more autonomy in the management of their local affairs while making them more publicly accountable for student success. (Debates of the Legislative Assembly, 2002a, 2002c)

Choice

In its 'New Era' document the Liberal party had promised to 'support more flexibility and choice in public schooling'. In May 2002 the Liberal government passed Bill 34. Among other measures, the legislation gave students the right to attend any school in the province, subject only to the availability of space. Describing the plan as a stimulus to the improvement of schools, the government said that it would permit parents to express their support for schools by voting with their feet. Yet many of the province's urban school districts already had long-established boundary policies that provided for student mobility where space allowed.

The Liberals had assured that choice would be high on the reform agenda by appointing as deputy minister of education Emery Dosdall in 2001. A former school superintendent in the Langley school district, Dosdall had been a champion of site-based management there in the 1980s. He later became a superintendent in Edmonton, where he gained a national reputation for promoting choice and specialty schools—including fine arts schools, sports academies, and even confessional institutions—within a system that blurred the traditional boundaries between public and private schools. Edmonton boasted the country's highest rates of public satisfaction with schools (Edmonton Public Schools, 2008). In British Columbia, by contrast, satisfaction was middling despite achievement and graduation rates that ranked among the best in Canada (British Columbia Ministry of Education, n.d.). The Campbell government's encouragement of a wider range of choices within and between school districts, combined with the School Act amendments providing for greater student mobility, signalled that Dosdall intended to bring the Edmonton model to British Columbia (Goldman, 1999).

More than five years on, however, school choice remains largely an urban phenomenon. One reason is the obvious difficulty that offering choice would pose for rural communities with only one high school (with declining enrolment at that). Another is the fact that the funding increases offered by the Liberal government have been modest, and in the first years were more than offset by legislated salary increases for teachers, rising energy and transportation costs, and a doubling of the premiums paid by the province for the benefits owed to school board employees. Furthermore, many of the 'choice' programs that did exist (such as fine arts schools and sports academies) were threatened when the BC Supreme Court ruled, in 2006, that the collection of fees for special courses and programs violated the School Act; this decision was soon amended, however (see p. 284 below).

Productive Efficiency

The School Amendment Act of 2002 also provided for the establishment of a school planning council (SPC) in every public school in the province. The mandate of these councils was to monitor the schools' performance and develop detailed annual plans for improvement, which would then become the basis of annual 'accountability contrasts' between the ministry and the school boards. School boards were required to consult with the SPCs about the educational services and programs offered and the allocation of resources, as well as matters covered by the boards' annual 'accountability contracts' with the ministry. The legislation was designed in anticipation of organized opposition from the Teachers' Federation (BCTF, 2002b, 2002c). Stipulating that each SPC should consist of the school principal and three parents but only one teacher, it required that the teacher representative be elected by secret ballot; it also provided that, should the teachers refuse to elect one of their number to represent them, the school board would appoint one. In addition, the legislation explicitly denied all school employees the right to serve as parent-representatives on any SPC.

Relations between the BCTF and the provincial organization of parents, the BC Confederation of Parent Advisory Councils, had long been strained. At the local level, however, relations between parents and teachers were generally positive. Hence teachers were divided over how best to respond to the SPCs.[3] The vast majority of BCTF locals initially sanctioned participation. But in the fall of 2006 delegates to the federation's Annual General Meeting voted to end participation in both SPCs and district accountability contracts (BCTF, 2006c). By early 2007 few if any schools had teachers sitting on their SPCs. Nevertheless the Campbell government forbade school districts to devise alternative models for school–parent cooperation. SPCs without teachers continued to be the only officially sanctioned planning committees.

At the centre of the dispute between the union and the government was the question of accountability (BCTF, 2006b). The ministry defined accountability in terms of measurable targets in areas such as literacy, numeracy, graduation rates, and social responsibility. Among the cornerstones of its accountability framework were the School Planning Councils (Debates of the Legislative Assembly, 2002d), final examinations in most academic subjects to be written by students not just in grade 12 but (as of 2003) grades 10 and 11 as well; annual provincial assessments of reading and writing achievement among children in grades 4 and 7; and satisfaction surveys completed by parents, students, and teachers (Debates of the Legislative Assembly, 2002b; BCTF, 2002d, 2002f, 2002a) .

The BCTF, however, opposed not just standardized testing but any model based on outcomes to the exclusion of inputs. It argued that student achievement reflects socioeconomic factors and criticized the ministry's accountability contracts, expanded testing regime, and Foundation Skills Assessment as a competitive model that ignores the factors influencing students' achievement. BCTF fears were fuelled by the conservative Fraser Institute's annual ranking of schools on the basis of provincial test results, exam participation figures, and graduation rates, designed to facilitate comparison by the public (BCTF, 2002e). Believing that the long-term Liberal agenda favoured private over public education, the Federation was concerned that the government had abandoned long-standing provincial commitments to equity of both resources and opportunity for students. The BCTF defines accountability as government's responsibility to provide adequate resources, especially for disadvantaged students.

As for the annual satisfaction surveys to be completed by parents, students, and teachers, the BCTF tried to persuade the government to include some questions related to funding, class size, and resources. When that effort failed, the BCTF directed its members to boycott the annual surveys (BCTF, 2006b).

Labour Relations

From the beginning of their mandate, the Liberals viewed both the 40,000-member British Columbia Teachers' Federation and its collective agreements as obstacles to their education reform agenda.

BCTF politics had also posed challenges for the New Democrats who had preceded the Liberals in office. Union activists could not forgive the NDP for replacing local bargaining with provincial bargaining in 1994 and reducing the number of school districts from 75 to 59 in 1995. The provincial teachers' contract, legislated over the objections of trustees in 1998, expired with the NDP government in 2001. Attempts were made to renew the contract before the provincial election, but to no avail. Neither of the first two rounds of provincial bargaining had produced a negotiated settlement between the BCTF and the BC Public Schools Employers' Association (BCPSEA) and there was no confidence that the third round would be any different.

In November 2001, BC teachers began a province-wide work-to-rule campaign to advance the BCTF's demands regarding class size and composition. Finally, in late January 2002, the Liberal government legislated an end to the province-wide work-to-rule campaign by imposing a new collective agreement (Bill 28, the Public Education Flexibility and Choice Act, 2002) that provided for a 7 per cent pay increase over three years.[4]

The BC Principals and Vice-Principals' Association, the BC Confederation of Parent Advisory Councils, and senior staff at the district level all supported the government, but that certainly was not the case with teachers. The Public Education Choice and Flexibility Act, 2002, removed the class size and composition provisions that since 1989 had been arguably the most cherished elements in teachers' contracts.

Emery Dosdall had advocated site-based management during his tenure as superintendent of Langley in the late 1980s. Under this model the authority to determine classroom composition fell to principals. But that authority was limited by contractual limits on class size and a provision requiring additional resources or further reductions in class size for classrooms with three or more special needs students. BC administrators had launched an assault on class size provisions in earlier rounds of collective bargaining, arguing that such provisions served the interests of teachers rather than students, and led districts to deny students access to their preferred neighbourhood schools and courses. From 1988 to 1994 contracts had been negotiated locally, and as a result class size and composition provisions varied from district to district. Ministry funding, on the other hand, was based on a provincial formula that gave no consideration to local contractual differences.[5] Class size and composition provisions were major expenses for school boards. There could be little increase in the authority of parents or principals at the site level unless these provisions were stripped from teachers' contracts.

The Liberal government therefore legislated removal of all provisions pertaining to class size and composition from contracts and denied teachers the right to negotiate such terms in the future. Interestingly, the 2002 legislation did include class size limits for the primary grades, albeit slightly higher than the limits stipulated in the 1998 contract; no such provisions were made for secondary schools, however. In 2001 Bill 18, the Skills Development and Labour Statutes Amendment Act, made teaching an essential service—although subsequent rulings by the Labour Relations Board have indicated that teachers can still withdraw many services and even close schools for short periods of time.

In the immediate wake of the legislated contract, teachers engaged in an illegal one-day protest. They withdrew their services and joined other public sector employees on picket lines in communities throughout the province. With nearly four years remaining in the Liberal mandate and no effective opposition in the provincial legislature, BC teachers had little choice but to return to their schools and contemplate long-term responses to their predicament.

Since Bill 28

Teacher activists were split over how to respond to this legislative assault. Although some leaders at both the provincial and local levels called for continued job action, others pointed out that it would take years of political action and public advocacy to regain the rights lost in January 2002. To advance this long-term strategy, the BCTF established a Public Education Advocacy Fund (the 2006 allocation to this fund was approximately $750,000), held public education conferences for parents and like-minded trustees on the benefits of small classes, and collected data on the numbers of teachers—particularly specialists such as librarians, counsellors, ESL, and special education resource teachers—lost as a result of the Liberal actions. It sponsored the formation of a 'Coalition for Public Education' whose ranks included a retired superintendent, a sympathetic parent, and a former church leader, as well as former BCTF President David Chudnovsky. Furthermore, the BCTF abandoned its long-time policy of avoiding overt involvement in provincial elections. In 2005 the BCTF and its locals registered as third-parties engaged in campaigning. Having joined the BC Federation of Labour on a trial basis in 2002, it made the relationship permanent in 2006.

By the fall of 2005 the educational and political landscapes in British Columbia had changed dramatically. The election of May 2005 had returned the BC legislature to its polarized norm, with the New Democrats rising phoenix-like and winning 36 of 79 seats, though still not enough to prevent the Liberals from forming a second majority government. The deficit that had provided the rationale for attacking public sector contracts had given way to an economic upturn fuelled by a booming energy sector and record-breaking commodity prices.

In 2005, teachers were again at the bargaining table and were determined to regain the ground lost in 2002. Facing poor prospects of achieving a negotiated provincial settlement, the BCTF held a special Representative Assembly in August and decided, subject to a membership vote, to commence an escalating job action in September.

That action initially affected only a small number of administrative activities, but the Liberals acted swiftly, once again using legislation to impose a contract. The collective agreement that had expired the previous June was extended for a year with no salary increase. Although nothing in the legislation gave teachers reason to hope that their concerns over class size and composition would be addressed, Premier Campbell did offer to establish a 'roundtable' at which major partner groups could engage in policy discussions (Debates of the Legislative Assembly, 21 November 2005).

The BCTF initially rejected the offer because it was concerned that the roundtable would include too many government allies and too few teachers. Later the roundtable was to play a major role in advancing the Federation's goal of reinstating class size limits and resources for students with special needs.

Teachers responded to the imposition of yet another contract by walking out of their schools. The Liberals insisted that they would not negotiate with a union engaged in an illegal strike. Perhaps they assumed that the union would back down under public pressure and threat of court sanctions, as had the Hospital Employees Union in an earlier conflict over the legislated elimination of clauses from collectively bargained contracts in the health care sector.

From the outset, however, public opinion was on the teachers' side. Government actions that had been accepted as necessary in 2001 because of economic circumstances at that time appeared arbitrary and mean-spirited in the fall of 2005. In President Jinny Sims, the BCTF had a spokesperson who kept the teachers' message simple and focused on student learning conditions. After two weeks, despite a court ruling that the strike was illegal, public support for the teachers was higher than it had been at the start of the action.

Premier Campbell relented and the BCTF ended the strike after he agreed to appoint arbitrator Vince Ready to address matters arising from the dispute. Ready's recommendations were revealed in stages over the following nine months. They included compensation for some of the pay lost during the strike in the form of a rebate for premiums paid into their long-term disability program. In addition, the Campbell government directed to the school districts the money it had saved during the strike, targeting the funds to address issues of learning resources and class composition. This move (another of Ready's recommendations) gave new impetus to the BCTF campaign for improved learning conditions.

The 2005 dispute framed the terms of reference for the education roundtable. Campbell attended the meetings and agreed that class size and composition could be discussed. By the spring of 2006 a new policy framework had been passed into law, establishing firm class size limits for Grades 4 through 7 and more flexible limits for secondary grades. The BCTF's influence, so diminished in the early years of the Liberal mandate, was restored at least to the point where the Campbell government was willing to take steps that would diminish management flexibility and parent control. In the winter of 2006–7 the BCTF launched a campaign drawing public attention to what it saw as the government's failure to provide the funds necessary to significantly improve learning conditions in the classroom.

Entrepreneurialism

An expression of the value placed on economic entrepreneurialism by the BC Liberals can be found in the School Act. In 2002 an amendment to the Act permitted school boards to establish businesses in order to raise the funds needed to provide services to students.

Critics charged that public school districts were ill-prepared for such activity. They also expressed concern that boards seeking to establish businesses would be using scarce public funds for that purpose but would not be accountable to the people. A number of districts established businesses to operate schools in Asia that would offer a certificate of high-school graduation to fee-paying students. But Asian markets proved challenging to penetrate and by 2005 every district involved in such ventures had reported losses.[6]

Entrepreneurial initiatives are not new to BC schools. West Vancouver introduced programs for fee-paying international students as early as the 1980s, and several other districts (mostly urban) followed suit. International student programs continue to represent the lion's share of non-government revenue for school boards. Urban and affluent districts have had obvious advantages in recruiting foreign students, the vast majority of whom came from Asia. In 2006 West Vancouver, one of Canada's most affluent communities, derived more than 20 per cent of its total revenue from the international students, who represented 8 per cent of enrolments. But few districts were able to increase their revenues by more than 2 or 3 per cent, and most rural districts gained virtually nothing (Kuehn, 2007). Nevertheless, the international student phenomenon has had a profound effect on the educational landscape, since affluent and urban districts, whose students already have more social capital than their rural and northern counterparts, now have a funding advantage that further skews opportunities in a system that was historically based on the principle of equity.

Social Equity

British Columbia's School Act prohibits school boards from charging fees for any educational program that contributes to a student's graduation. Yet in the past many boards charged fees for purposes not intended by the Act. For example, students in carpentry and sewing courses were routinely charged for the materials they used, senior math students were required to purchase graphic calculators for courses, and many students had to pay for workbooks. Fees for band and fine arts programs were numerous. At the government's urging, boards created 'choice' programs, such as fine arts and sports academies, expanding fee schedules.

John Young, a former high-school principal and long-time Victoria school trustee, took the Victoria School Board to court over its practice of charging course and program fees. In 1997 the courts ruled in *McDonald and Chamak v. S.D.#61 (Gr. Victoria)* that such fees violated the School Act and since then Victoria schools have done without them. But most boards ignored the ruling. Therefore Young pressed his challenge again, and in 2006 the province's Supreme Court (British Columbia Supreme Court, 2006) confirmed the fee ban. This time the ministry issued a formal statement of its expectation that boards would comply with the ruling. Young estimated that boards were collecting some $15 million in illegal fees every year, but the actual figure was certainly much higher. West Vancouver, with only 1 per cent of the province's students, collected more than $2 million in fees in 2005–6. The provincial education minister initially ruled out additional government funding to make up for the lost revenue, but since then boards have been reimbursed for one year's worth of summer-school fees. In addition, recognizing that the prohibition of fees might impede the development of 'choice' programs, the Ministry gave school boards the authority to collect fees for some special programs, including academics.

Education Finance and Reform

The Liberal government and the BCTF have sharply contrasting views regarding the adequacy of education funding. The government repeatedly states that funding is at record high levels and that the trend toward lower enrolment has further enriched the system as more dollars are distributed among fewer students. The BCTF counters that funding has not kept up with the increasing costs imposed by the government on school boards; as evidence it points to the fact that from 2001 through 2005 the reductions in the teaching force were steeper than the declines in student enrolment.

In 2002 the Campbell government ended the long-standing practice of 'targeting' funding for special needs students and removed ceilings on administrative spending, citing reasons of flexibility and local autonomy. The removal of class size and composition provisions from the provincial collective agreement in 2002 meant that school boards had still fewer limitations on where to spend their revenue.

Throughout the Liberal government's time in office, defenders of its education policy have rightly claimed that more dollars were flowing to school districts, while critics have rightly argued that fewer dollars were being directed into classrooms in the form of teaching staff. This situation raises the question whether education reform can be achieved without measures to ensure that resources are directed to areas where improvement is sought. The fact that no additional funding has been targeted towards the government's stated goal of advancing student achievement raises the further question of whether that goal was really a smokescreen for the actual goal of advancing the ideological position outlined earlier in this chapter.

Is Education Reform Possible in British Columbia?

The path of education reform in British Columbia is profoundly influenced by the ideologies of the central players in the province's education system and by the relationships between those players. Most governments in the province have found it difficult to work with the BCTF. The Liberals, however—because of their neo-conservative bent, their often contemptuous approach to organized labour, and their determination to advance their reform agenda regardless of its reception among those affected by it—have had more difficulty than most.

The ideologies of the Liberal government and the British Columbia Teachers' Federation are situated close to the opposite ends of the spectrum. The Liberals' ideal would be an education system dedicated above all to the development of individual capital. For them, the purpose of schooling is to equip individuals with the knowledge and skills required to maximize their potential to earn and compete in a global economy (British Columbia OIC 1280/89, 1989).

In advocating choice and flexibility, the Liberals espouse the values of the marketplace. The educational marketplace thrives when consumer choice is maximized and the service providers (schools and boards or districts) compete with one another for clients. District accountability contracts requiring specific and measurable goals, patterned after private sector models, are designed to give 'consumers' (parents and students) the information they need to make informed choices. Numerical evidence of students' achievement allows government to assure the public that their tax dollars are well spent.

The British Columbia Teachers' Federation's view of education is based on a different ideal. The union asserts that the purpose of public education is to reduce social differences and advance social cohesion. Rejecting measures of achievement that don't take into account differences arising from social inequality, the BCTF outlines its view of the mandate of public education as follows:

> The broad prime aim of the public school system should be to further the growth and development of every individual to the end that he/she will become a self-reliant, self-disciplined, participating member with a sense of social and environmental responsibility within a democratic, pluralistic society. (BCTF, 2007–8: 47)

Achieving consensus among the various education groups in BC is a challenge. Clearly the influence of the BCTF over government policy has waned under the Liberals. Government has advanced its choice and accountability agenda despite the Federation's opposition. A motion of non-confidence in Deputy Minister Dosdall, passed by the 2005 BCTF AGM, along with the political struggle surrounding the labour dispute of the same year, deepened the conflict and distrust between the parties.

Early in its mandate the Campbell government sought to enlist parents as allies in the quest for educational reform. Funding to the BC Confederation of Parent Advisory Councils (BCCPAC) was increased substantially and parents' influence was enhanced with the creation of School Planning Councils and district accountability contracts. The Liberals instituted a model of district reviews to replace a school accreditation system that had many critics. Parents were appointed to district review teams and the extent of parental involvement in the school district became one of the measures of district success. The BCCPAC proved a reliable ally for the government and supported many of its initiatives, including its attack on teacher collective agreements and its efforts to increase flexibility at the school level.[7] On the other hand, the BCTF found a receptive audience among parents when it criticized government actions that in its view reduced services to students, particularly those with special needs.

School boards, though created by the School Act, are rooted in local community politics. School trustees have been on the defensive under the Liberals, who have never clearly refuted rumours of further board mergers to come. Trustees are a varied group: some are staunchly pro-Liberal and others are staunchly opposed. Most school boards avoid political engagement because they lack the skills or the will, or they fear they would lose in the exchange. From 2001 to 2004, however, the Vancouver School Board was dominated by the Coalition of Progressive Electors (COPE), a civic party situated to the left of the provincial New Democrats. The COPE trustees were strong critics of the Liberals, particularly on issues of funding. But most school boards are uncomfortable with political strife, and the parent BC School Trustees Association rarely takes positions that would alienate some member boards or government.

In 2005 the education ministry floated the notion of 'repurposing' school boards and sponsored regional discussions on the topic. But the precise nature of that 'repurposing'—which could have meant either expanding or reducing the role of school boards—was never defined. Generally, trustees were suspicious that repurposing would entail additional responsibilities without additional funding. In 2007 the government redefined school boards as boards of education, expanding their mandates to permit them to offer pre-school programs (Education Statutes Amendment Act, 2007).

The 60 BC school superintendents are powerful influences in their districts, but they have not found a collective voice to inject into policy discussions at the provincial level. Their provincial organization, the BC School Superintendents' Association, limits its role to promoting leadership and professional development for its members. The 2006 court decision denying most of the school fees levied by boards in the province led to unprecedented cooperation among boards in metropolitan Vancouver. But, as a rule, superintendents are watchful of their individual autonomy and don't regard themselves as a collective influence at the provincial level. Although hired by local boards, their authority is derived from the School Act. Like trustees, superintendents may be wary of challenging the ministry for fear of reprisal. In 2007 the Liberal government altered provincial legislation to increase the accountability of school superintendents (School [Student Achievement Enabling] Amendment Act, 2007).

School-based administrators number approximately 2,200 and are organized in the BC Principals and Vice-Principals' Association. According to Emery Dosdell's educational philosophy they are the major leaders of educational reform and, for the most part, BCPVPA members ally themselves with the ministry. School-based administrators were vocal supporters of the move to eliminate class size and composition provisions in the name of flexibility, and enjoyed their greatest influence in early 2002, when the government legislated major changes to teacher contracts.

The decision by the Campbell government to re-introduce class size and composition regulations following the teachers' strike of 2005 was a rare reversal of policy. In 2002 the same government had granted school administrators what they had long requested: an end to the restrictive contract provisions that were deemed to impede sound management, including the effective and efficient allocation of resources. Three years later the Liberals were faced with growing challenges from the BCTF and allied parents, claiming that the loss of those provisions had diverted scarce resources from classrooms. Nonetheless, at the learning roundtable the BCTF representatives were the only participants demanding that the government address class size and composition; all the rest, including parents, defended the status quo. It is not clear whether the Liberal reversal represented a change in philosophy or a political accommodation to the BCTF. What is clear is that the politics of education in BC preclude change rooted in consensus. The Ministry and the teachers' union are separated by a deep ideological divide regarding the nature and purpose of public education, while other partner groups, lacking a tradition of political engagement, rarely attempt to assert any influence themselves. When the provincial government acts, therefore, it acts unilaterally, certain only that its initiatives will be opposed by the teachers whose support is essential if change is to take place.

And yet, as we noted at the beginning of this chapter, dropout rates in British Columbia have declined, graduation rates have increased, and student performance has improved in several areas in recent years. These improvements have been achieved despite the ideological differences between the union and the government, largely through the efforts of individual teachers. One can only speculate about the magnitude of the improvements that might be achieved were the government and the union able to reach consensus about some of the issues that divide them.

Notes

1. Between 1991–3 and 2002–5, the proportion of British Columbians aged 20–24 without a high school diploma and not in school declined from 13.3 per cent to 7.5 per cent (Bowlby, 2005).

2. Of the 41 countries participating in the PISA mathematics assessment only two performed better than Canada. Of the Canadian jurisdictions only Alberta outperformed British Columbia (Human Resources and Skills Development Canada, Council of Ministers of Education, Canada, and Statistics Canada, 2004).

3. The split was most evident in Vancouver, which has both a secondary and an elementary teachers' local. The elementary teachers boycotted the SPCs, but the secondary teachers participated.

4. The Campbell government's strong response to the teachers' strike was only one part of a comprehensive approach to the challenges posed by organized labour. Enjoying a strong mandate (the Liberals controlled 77 of the 79 seats in the BC legislature), no effective opposition (Gordon Campbell denied the New Democrats the status of official opposition and

hence the resources that would have accompanied such status) and tepid public support for public servants' wage demands, the Liberals were able to make major changes in the collective agreements of health care workers and government employees as well as teachers.

5. Lack of discipline by school boards and their willingness to agree to terms of employment that they could not afford were major reasons that the NDP legislated province-wide bargaining in 1994.

6. New Westminster school district, one of the most aggressive entrepreneurial districts in the province, reported losses of over $1 million, causing Minister Shirley Bond to call for a review of district practices.

7. However, it is debatable whether BCCPAC extends its influence to the district level, where district and school parent advisory committees tend to be more attuned to local rather than provincial issues.

Glossary

reform: A change for the better as a consequence of correcting faults.

policy: An authorized course of action toward a goal or goals.

productive efficiency: The highest possible output given a particular level of input.

progressive: A political philosophy of progress and reform.

teachers' union: A formal association of teachers formed under labour legislation for the purpose of maintaining or improving the conditions of their employment.

Study Questions

1. What educational reforms have been implemented in your province or territory? How would you account for the similarities and differences between those reforms and the ones pursued by the Liberal government in British Columbia?

2. Compare the issues pursued by the provincial or territorial government in your jurisdiction with those pursued by the Council of Ministers of Education (CMEC), 'the national voice of education in Canada' (www.cmec.ca/).

3. What factors determine the extent to which parents, superintendents, trustees, and school administrators influence education policy in your jurisdiction?

4. To what extent can legislation provide a framework for effective education reform and cooperation among key partners in public education?

5. The British Columbia Teachers' Federation has been described as a social justice union. How would you characterize the orientation of the teachers' organization(s) in your jurisdiction? Why?

6. Is it possible for a government to advance education reform policies in the face of opposition from a collective of teachers?

Recommended Readings

Counts, G.S. 1932. 'Dare Progressive Education Be Progressive?', *Progressive Education* 9, 4: 257–63.

Kelly, D.M., and G. Minnes-Brandes. 2001. 'Shifting Out of "Neutral": Beginning Teachers' Struggles with Teaching for Social Justice', *Canadian Journal of Education* 26, 4: 437–54.

Levin, B. 2005. *Governing Education*. Toronto: University of Toronto Press.

Poole, W. 2002. 'Barriers to "New Unionism" in Canadian Teacher Unions'. Society for the Advancement of Excellence in Education. Available at: <http://www.saee.ca/policy/D_019_DDB_LON.php>.

Recommended Websites

Legislative Assembly of the province of British Columbia: http://www.leg.bc.ca/index.htm
British Columbia Teachers' Federation: http://www.bctf.bc.ca/
The Canadian Education Association: http://www.cea-ace.ca/
The Council of Ministers of Education—Canada: http://www.cmec.ca/

References

Aman, C.L. 2006. 'Exploring the Influence of School and Community Relationships on the Performance of Aboriginal Students in British Columbia Public Schools'. Unpublished dissertation. Department of Educational Studies, University of British Columbia.

BC Liberal Party. n.d. 'A New Era for British Columbia: A Vision for Hope & Prosperity for the Next Decade and Beyond'. Liberal Party of British Columbia.

Bill 18: The Skills Development and Labour Statutes Amendment Act, 2001. Available at: <http://www.leg.bc.ca/37th2nd/amend/gov18-2.htm>. Accessed June 2008.

Bill 28: The Public Education Flexibility and Choice Act, 2002. Available at: <http://www.leg.bc.ca/HANSARD/37th2nd/h20127a.htm#bill28-C>. Accessed June 2008.

Bill 34: School Amendment Act, 2002. Legislative Assembly of British Columbia. Available at: <http://www.leg.bc.ca/37th3rd/3rd_read/gov34-3.htm>. Accessed 10 January 2007.

Bowlby, G. 2005. 'Provincial Drop-out Rates—Trends and Consequences', *Education Matters* 2, 4. Statistics Canada Catalogue no. 81-004 XIE. Available at: <http://www.statcan.ca/english/freepub/81-004-XIE/2005004/drop.htm#table2>. Accessed 14 January 2007.

British Columbia Ministry of Education. 2007. 'New Legislation Allows School Fees for Some Courses'. News release. 26 March. Available at: <http://www2.news.gov.bc.ca/news_releases_2005-2009/2007EDU0033-000312.htm>.

———. n.d. 'Satisfaction Survey'. Available at: <www.bced.gov.bc.ca/sat_survey/>.

British Columbia OIC 1280/89. 1989. *Mandate for the School System*. System of Education Policy Order. Available at: <http://www.bced.gov.bc.ca/legislation/schoollaw/d/oic_1280-89.pdf>. Accessed 30 July 2008.

British Columbia Supreme Court. 2006. *Young v. British Columbia (Minister of Education)*, 2006 BCSC 1415. Available at: <http://www.canlii.org/bc/cas/bcsc/2006/2006bcsc1415.html>. Accessed 13 January 2007.

British Columbia Teachers' Federation (BCTF). 2002a. 'Foundation Skills Assessment: Opting Out Is an Option. School Staff Alert'. 19 April. Available at: <http://bctf.ca/publications/SchoolStaffAlert.aspx?id=3796>. Accessed 13 January 2007.

———. 2002b. 'School Planning Councils Migrate West—And Why We Need to Pay Attention'. School Staff Alert. 6 June. Available at: <http://bctf.ca/publications/SchoolStaffAlert.aspx?id=3812>. Accessed 13 January 2007.

———. 2002c. 'School Planning Councils—There's No Hurry'. School Staff Alert. 19 June. Available at: <http://bctf.ca/publications/SchoolStaffAlert.aspx?id=3814>. Accessed 13 January 2007.

————. 2002d. 'Ministry Surveys Do Not Address the Concerns of Most Teachers'. 6 March. School Staff Alert. Available at: <http://bctf.ca/publications/SchoolStaffAlert.aspx?id=3766>. Accessed 13 January 2007.

————. 2002e. 'Slanted Reality: The Fraser Institute Rankings'. School Staff Alert. 7 March. Available at: <http://bctf.ca/publications/SchoolStaffAlert.aspx?id=3768>. Accessed 13 January 2007.

————. 2002f. 'BCTF Advice on Ministry Satisfaction Surveys'. School Staff Alert. 8 March. Available at: <http://bctf.ca/publications/SchoolStaffAlert.aspx?id=3770>. Accessed 13 January 2007.

————. 2006a. 'Every Kid Counts: Members' Guide to the BCTF 2006–7'. Vancouver: BCTF.

————. 2006b. 'Teachers Not Participating in School Planning Councils'. School Staff Alert. 10 November.   Available at: <http://bctf.ca/publications/SchoolStaffAlert.aspx?id=8510>. Accessed June 2008.

————. 2006c. 'Accountability.' Available at: <http://bctf.ca/IssuesInEducation.aspx?id=5528>. Accessed 13 January 2007.

————. 2006d. 'School Planning Councils'. Available at: <http://www.bctf.bc.ca/ IssuesInEducation.aspx?id=5700>. Accessed 13 January 2007.

————. 2007–8. 'Member's Guide 47'. Available at: <http://bctf.ca/uploadedFiles/ About_Us/Members_Guide/guide.pdf>. Accessed June 2008.

Counts, G.S. 1932. 'Dare Progressive Education Be Progressive?', *Progressive Education* 9, 4: 257–63.

Debates of the Legislative Assembly (Hansard). 2002a. 5 March (3, 20). Available at: <http://www.leg.bc.ca/hansard/37th3rd/h20305p.htm#1526>. Accessed 27 January 2007.

————. 2002b. 12 March (4, 3). Available at: <http://www.leg.bc.ca/hansard/37th3rd/ h20312a.htm#1808>. Accessed 27 January 2007.

————. 2002c. 15 April (6, 7). Available at: <http://www.leg.bc.ca/hansard/37th3rd/ h20415p.htm#bill34-1R>. Accessed 10 January 2007.

————. 2002d. 29 April (6, 14). Available at: <http://www.leg.bc.ca/hansard/37th3rd/ h20429p.htm#3004>. Accessed 26 January 2007.

————.   2005. 21 Nov. (5, 5). Available at: <http://www.leg.bc.ca/hansard/38th1st/ h51121p.htm#2003>. Accessed 26 January 2007.

Edmonton Public Schools. 2008. '2007 District Satisfaction Survey Results'. Available at: <www.epsb.ca/district/survint/dasr.shtml>.

Education Statutes Amendment Act. 2007. First Reading. Available at: <http:// www.leg.bc.ca/38th3rd/1st_read/gov22-1.htm>.

Goldman, J.P. 1999. 'Edmonton's Entrepreneur Won't Tolerate "Dumb Rules"', The School Administrator. Available at: <http://www.aasa.org/publications/saarticledetail.cfm? ItemNumber=3711&snItemNumber=&tnItemNumber=>. Accessed 13 January 2007.

Human Resources and Skills Development Canada, Council of Ministers of Education, Canada and Statistics Canada. 2004. *Measuring Up: Canadian Results of the OECD PISA Study: The Performance of Canada's Youth in Mathematics, Reading, Science and Problem Solving, 2003*. Vol. 2. Catalogue number 81-590-XIE2004001.

Imagine BC Dialogues on the Future of British Columbia. 2006. 'Learning and Culture: The Future of Education in British Columbia'. Available at: <http://www.sfu.ca/dialogue/ imaginebc/pdf/BowenConsensus2006.pdf>. Accessed 13 January 2007.

Jago, Charles. 2006. 'Working Together to Improve Performance: Preparing BC's Public Education System for the Future. B.C. Progress Board'. Available at: <http://www.bcprogress-board.com/2006Report/EducationReport/Education_Final.pdf. Accessed 13 January 2007.

Kilian, C. 1985. *School Wars: The Assault on BC Education*. Vancouver: New Star Books.

Kuehn, L. 1988. 'The B.C. School Wars', *Our Schools/Our Selves* 1, 1: 75–84.

———. 2007. 'BC International Student revenue and FTE Enrollment 2001–2 to 2005–6'. Research Report RT07 – 0001. Available at: <http://bctf.ca/uploadedFiles/Publications/Research_reports/2007ef01.pdf >. Accessed June 2008.

Public Education Choice and Flexibility Act, 2002. Available at: <http://www.leg.bc.ca/37th2nd/3rd_read/gov28-3.htm>. Accessed 27 January 2006.

Ungerleider, C.S. 1987. 'Inequality and Education: The Ideological Context of Educational Change in British Columbia', *Journal of Educational Administration and Foundations* 1, 2: 17–27.

———. 1994. 'Politics, Power, and Professionalism: The Impact of Change in British Columbia on the Status of Teachers and Their Professional Conduct', in L. Erwin and D. MacLennan, eds, *Sociology of Education in Canada*. Toronto: Copp Clark Longman, 370–9.

———. 2003. *Failing Our Kids: How We Are Ruining Our Public Schools*. Toronto: McClelland & Stewart.

CHAPTER 17

Painting the Mountain Green: Discourses of Accountability and Critical Practice

Ann Vibert

Introduction

Over the past few decades, a number of multiple-case studies in Canada have attempted to identify characteristics of exemplary schools (Gaskell et al., 1995), schools that successfully engage students in learning and school life (Smith et al., 1998), and schools that work effectively with students identified as 'at risk' (Portelli, Shields, and Vibert, 2007). One disturbing insight emerging from these studies is that the teachers who seem most dedicated to promoting equity and social justice are also the ones most likely to burn out, suffer professional marginalization, or leave teaching. Principals and teachers suggest that in schools serving the students most **at-risk** in our society, stress, pressure, and frustration contribute to the high staff turn-over rates. They also say that the challenges of such work are exacerbated by a general lack of systemic support (Vibert and Portelli, 2000).[1] Indeed, **social justice education** itself could be described as 'at risk'; by shifting the emphasis to psychological factors, the **discourse** of 'students at risk' signals that social analyses of educational inequities are not welcome (Fine, 1990).

This chapter draws on information collected in the course of two recent research projects exploring, among other things, the experiences of public school administrators and teachers attempting to practise a critical/democratic pedagogy in an increasingly conservative policy context. After more than a decade working with schools serving communities that schooling has historically failed, I have learned that those schools are the ones most likely to offer a lively critical pedagogy. Without disputing the fact that the pedagogical methods to which poor and working-class students are subjected are often mind-numbing (Shannon, 1989; Apple, 1988), I want to draw attention to the shining moments that the schools serving those communities can offer. It is demonstrably the case that students from economically marginalized backgrounds often receive an impoverished education; yet there are teachers and principals who have devoted their careers to just such communities, and they have much to teach us about the possibilities of a critical practice focused on social justice. In my experience, the 'leafy suburbs' are generally untroubled by challenging and explicitly political pedagogies. It is the high-poverty communities—perhaps because traditional approaches have so clearly failed them—that have taught me what a critical practice might mean in public schooling.

The work entailed in teaching in or administering schools that serve disadvantaged communities has rarely been recognized. However, Thomson (2002) has documented the particular demands faced by teachers and principals in the post-industrial 'rustbelt' schools of South Australia, demonstrating how centralized policy discourses failed to acknowledge the realities of schooling there. In this chapter I take up a related aspect of the struggle for a democratic critical practice in disadvantaged schools: the collision of critical/democratic practice with the current educational fetish called 'accountability'. I will begin by offering working definitions of what I mean by 'critical democratic practice' and 'accountability discourse', and identifying the central theoretical contradictions between the two pedagogical positions. I will then turn to teachers' and principals' accounts of their experiences attempting a critical practice in an age of accountability, examining what they see as the tensions between critical practice and accountability discourses and how they experience these tensions in their work lives.

Critical Practice and Accountability Discourses: Tensions and Contradictions

Critical democratic practice in education is the subject of an entire field of inquiry and is not easily defined. Nonetheless, there are a number of principles that those aspiring to such practice might accept. The first is that critical democratic practice is based not on a set of techniques but on a set of political and moral principles central to democratic life. Among the things it values are dialogical inquiry, open-mindedness, and social justice. These values—and democratic action itself—in turn imply critical examination of the social world and interrogation of the common-sense assumptions that underlie social inequities (Portelli and Solomon, 2001). Central to this endeavour is an understanding of education as an irreducibly political and philosophical pursuit; as Freire (1998) pointed out, there are no neutral pedagogies. A critical perspective commits us to examining the 'taken for granted' (Simon, 1992) in education, in this case the implicit claims to objectivity and neutrality of standardized curricula and assessment methods and market-based management models.

Accountability discourse, by contrast, is a **neo-liberal** phenomenon that originated in management studies but has left few institutions, public or private, untouched (Blackmore, 2002). On the face of it, accountability makes a kind of straightforward sense: an organization defines its central goals, devises procedures for measuring its progress towards them, and holds its members accountable for that progress. Applied to public education, however, accountability discourse tends to obscure or elide the very debates most crucial to the undertaking—debates over matters such as 'the purposes and aims of education'. Proponents of accountability assume that the central purpose of education is to serve the economy—and in so doing they advance a potent neo-liberal vision of education in which difficult questions of principle and practice are reduced to matters of efficiency. Accountability demonstrates the characteristics of a discourse in that the language of accountability constitutes and is constituted by a particular political ideology, in that the ideological claims of the discourse are largely implicit or unspoken, and in that critique of accountability is not linguistically possible from within the discourse (Fairclough, 1989).

The rise of the neo-liberal vision has put educators committed to social justice work in a difficult bind. On the one hand, the system that employs them demands accountability, standardization, improved test scores, and managerial efficiencies (Apple, 2001; Allington, 2002; Blackmore, 2002; Kohn and Shannon, 2002). On the other, their pedagogical principles call for local curricula and assessment sensitive to the contexts of students' lives, recognition of social difference and its implications, de-standardization, flattened institutional hierarchies, and informal, humane school cultures (e.g., Canella and Viruru, 2004; Dei, 2002; Portelli and Solomon, 2001; Shields and Vibert, 2003.)

What the **corporatization** of public education might mean for teachers' work and lives, for democratic and socially just educational policies, and for informed and engaging curriculum development has become a widespread concern in the educational literature. Blackmore (2002), writing about the global **marketization** of education from an Australian perspective, describes how market discourses in praise of things like 'evidence-based research' spawn a kind of monolithic, techno-curriculum incapable of communicating the much more nuanced and powerful 'local knowledges' offered by individual teachers and places. Kohn and Shannon (2002) examine the market opportunities cultivated by a standardized testing industry offering 'quick fix' packages to schools anxious to escape the dire fiscal consequences of falling scores under the United States' No Child Left Behind policy. Barlow and Robertson (1994) detail the encroachment of the corporate sector into public schooling in Canada, explaining how its objectivist, standardizing agenda amounts to an assault on the culture's most vulnerable students and communities.

Social justice principles are not the only considerations that suggest very different directions for educational policy and practice: so does the professional literature, as well as teachers' lived experience. Against an overall policy that demands a standard curriculum focused on developing decontextualized skills, researchers in the field emphasize the importance of local, culturally relevant, critical, and integrated curriculum (Dei, 2002; Knapp, 1995; McMahon and Portelli, 2004; Vibert et al., 2002). Whereas accountability measures call for standardized assessment, educational research shows how standardized testing reproduces disadvantage for students at risk and argues instead for contextualized 'alternative' assessments (Gipps and Murphy, 1994; Oakes, 1985). And against increased calls for accountability in the form of rational hierarchies and managerial efficiencies, research in social justice pedagogy and disadvantage calls for de-institutionalized schools, communal and collaborative school cultures, and a concern for leadership rather than management (Ryan, 2003; Shields, 2003; Thomson, 2002).

While the above studies identify and analyze inequitable effects of corporate ideologies and accountability discourses on disadvantaged communities and schools, fewer studies have documented the lived experience of teachers and principals themselves as they attempt critical and social justice pedagogies within the sphere of accountability discourses. The following sections offer selected insights from sample narratives of teachers' experiences of the effects of accountability discourses on key aspects of their work. By attending to accounts of the lived experiences of public school educators attempting socially just pedagogies in contemporary school systems, we can begin to imagine necessary directions for support of critical social justice work in public education in an age of accountability.

Teachers' Perspectives

On Curriculum

Central to a critical pedagogy is an understanding of curriculum as a *process* rather than a predetermined product. Freire (1998), for instance, critiques the 'banking' notion of curriculum—according to which teachers simply deposit knowledge capital in students' minds—as an over-simplification in which the political ends of education are disguised as neutral. In the critical model, by contrast, curriculum is developed by teachers and students working together through real and consequential material and social contexts. In other words, the contexts of students' (and teachers') own lives are seen not as extraneous factors to be overcome, remedied, or set aside, but as the critical ground of curriculum. This concept—described elsewhere as a 'curriculum of life' (Portelli and Vibert, 2001)—re-imagines the disciplines that constitute the official curriculum as disciplined ways of inquiring into the world.

Accountability discourses, on the other hand, are designed to promote 'improvement on measurable outcomes'—predetermined products generally consisting of scores on standardized tests, particularly in literacy and numeracy. Despite decades of research showing that standardized testing reproduces social inequities (Oakes, 1985; Persell, 1979), produces bad pedagogy, and is an inherently inferior approach (Taylor, 1991), accountability discourses still treat standardized assessment as the 'bottom line' on student achievement. Here the underbelly of the accountability movement begins to show itself as schools under pressure to improve their scores resort to strategies such as excusing marginalized students from participation, or giving students extra drill on test items. So highly do proponents of accountability value the demonstration of improvement that the *appearance* of improvement becomes the primary consideration. As in the market, perception is reality.

The interview excerpts that follow are drawn from 'Pedagogies at Risk: Social Justice and Accountability Discourses', a project funded by the Social Sciences and Humanities Research Council of Canada. The interviewees are all currently employed in the public system as teachers (classroom and/or learning support), principals and vice principals, or district consultants. In the course of the interviews they talk about the supports for and the obstacles to their work as social justice educators.

An important concern for teachers attempting a critical practice in the current landscape is the effect of the accountability movement on curriculum. In particular, experienced teachers whose pedagogies were forged in the heyday of constructivist curriculum worry about the disembodied and disconnected teaching they see sweeping the schools presently.

> It changes everything. It changes every part of the day, and the way that teachers interact with kids. Teachers feel this pressure to produce a student at a certain level, you know, and they feel that they will be judged in their teaching abilities, if their children are below a certain level. And the reason they think that, is because it actually happens. You know, the talk of the staff room this week, is that a school in our board is . . . under the magnifying glass, because their grades primary and ones scored poorly on the observational surveys, and honest to goodness, I knew it was coming. They apparently compare the schools across the board, and your school didn't perform as well as it should, now you have to explain to us why. And so, the natural reaction for teachers is to take some of the joy out of teaching. . . . Much of my job is talking to teachers about individuals, and so when I talk about individuals, teachers are there with me. Yes, of course, it doesn't make sense to ask them to do that kind of homework, or to punish him because he didn't do his homework, or it doesn't make sense to have the spelling tests on Fridays because . . . their gut feeling is [that] doing that drilling on spelling really doesn't teach kids anything about spelling. But—so when I deal with them on an individual basis . . . they're with me and they're supportive, but when they go back, when they put it into the context of their classroom, they can't maintain that focus, which I thought that they were much better at years ago.

Teachers like this one are astonished by the ease with which accountability discourses have transformed understandings of curriculum. 'It's as if everyone's forgotten everything we know about learning', this teacher said later. Working against their 'gut feelings'—that is, against their lived knowledge of learning as always irreducibly embodied and contextualized—teachers are prodded by surveillance regimes to dislocate curriculum from the lives of their students and treat it as a set of disembodied facts and skills, the outcomes so central to this discourse. In the process, knowledge is re-established as a matter of 'banking' and decades of constructivist, critical, and post-structuralist insight into knowledge as located, contingent, and dynamic are effectively rendered irrelevant.

Many teachers express their dismay with this commodification of knowledge by critiquing the managerial sub-discourses of accountability. 'We have a new "Diversity Management Coordinator" in our system', one teacher said. 'I guess that's what we're doing with difference these days—we're "managing" it.' Implicit in the language of management is an 'us against them' relationship in which students, knowledge, and social difference are essentially objects to be managed and/or dispensed by a privileged (most likely white male) 'us'. Lost are critical opportunities to use curriculum to examine the world that students inhabit.

> I always used to say that you wrote your curriculum in hindsight. It isn't that you weren't prepared, but whatever happened would actually happen, and the learning was located in

what was actually occurring. But now developing curriculum around the students is gone . . . teachers don't make any decisions any more. They're told that they can make content decisions, but if you go off on the students' tangents, you can't, they give you the content, they give you the how, and they expect mastery and, you know, everybody's at the same time. . . . And I don't even recognize this as curriculum, I recognize it as a list of things, that somebody, some math person, or science person, or social studies person at a university level, that's not connected to the children at all, is decreeing, is creating. Curriculum involves kids taking a topic and bringing in all sorts of extra content that is relevant to them . . . My kids were always sent out to study their own questions about a thing, to research, to use research methods—writing about it, publicizing it, just getting involved. There's no room for that now, in this corporatized learning, now it's all about managing bits of knowledge and skills and testing and hoop-jumping—it's not about kids, it's not about learning.

This teacher is speaking less about her own pedagogy than about official versions of curriculum represented in system discourses. Of course teachers and principals have strategies for resisting and getting around the negative consequences of those discourses, perhaps especially in the disadvantaged schools where the effects are most damaging. In the context of this chapter, however, it is the interface between critical practice and accountability discourses that we are examining, and most of the teachers and principals in the study describe official pressures toward a reductionist view of curriculum as both far-reaching and disturbing.

A teacher who had become a system consultant for English language arts began by talking about several critical initiatives that she had undertaken as a classroom teacher: a study of marketing strategies for adolescents' clothing with her high-school students, for instance, and a 'humanitarian project' in which students researched social justice and resistance by studying people who had dedicated their lives to changing the world. When asked how she pursued this kind of work as a system consultant, she replied:

> I try, but you know, I find it harder. Because this job really is about literacy and strategies . . . to improve reading and writing skills. I try and do it in terms of the kinds of articles, for example, that I might use as a demonstration or an example piece. . . . but I miss getting into the nitty gritty of issues with kids—that doesn't happen in this job. That was one of the things that I loved the most about teaching, getting into those kinds of conversations with kids. . . . My job is a result of . . . the results on the literacy assessments that the board did for all the grade nines, [which] identified areas of weakness. So the job that I'm doing is intended to be very explicit instruction around strategies, the strategic kinds of interventions, but for the whole class. Which is—you know, it's beneficial to sort of make those kinds of things explicit—what do readers do who are proficient readers . . .

This teacher had, in past teaching contexts, successfully addressed reading and writing strategies in the context of her students' inquiries into their social worlds. But as a consultant she struggles to find ways to insert critical issues into the official curriculum of reading and writing skills and strategies, an emphasis clearly dictated by the general accountability discourse in which she is embedded as a system representative. This reversal of priorities, such that 'curriculum' is reduced to particular measurable facts and skills, and the substance, context, processes, and consequences of curriculum—the central concerns in the critical model—become incidental matters, to be inserted around the details of fact, is characteristic of the way accountability discourses reframe the terms of the curriculum debate. A board consultant for equity and social justice spoke to this issue explicitly when she said, 'No one questions the need for literacy and math in-service, but my work is an add-on—and apparently not seen as a part of the literacy and math curriculum.'

In a number of ways, the tendency of accountability discourses to reframe curriculum as a set of disembodied and decontextualized facts and skills required by all contradicts central tenets of critical practice, constraining and marginalizing the pedagogical commitments of critical practitioners. But the consequences for students at risk are more insidious. Educational generalizations are invariably restatements of dominant values and world views: claims about 'children' in general tend to be generalizations from dominant groups (white middle-class children, in this case), just as claims about generally required knowledge and standards reflect the dreams of the professional classes. The first teacher cited above suggests that the practical dictates of accountability are ill-suited to students at risk. Using as an example her board's prescription of reading recovery as the 'system fix' for 'struggling readers', a principal in a disadvantaged school elaborates on the ways in which such generalizations overlook and further disadvantage her students:

> Well it's just a difficult thing, because reading recovery really relies on home support, and when we look at who the bottom 20 per cent of reading levels in our grade one class are, the parents aren't able to do it . . . it's not possible if you're working nights . . . and the two [students] at the bottom are twins, single mom, you know, she's on her own. How is she going to work with one, let alone two? . . . The other day I had to send some sort of a report about the number of [Individualized Program Plans] in our school, and I pretty much knew them all off by heart. . . . In our school, every single IPP student lives in the trailer park. . . . And what's reading recovery going to do to the fact that every one of the IPP kids in the class lives in the trailer park? How is reading recovery going to address that? Or any other neat little program?

The passion and anger in such educators are directed at the dehumanizing vision of curriculum represented in accountability discourses, and at the deeply political ways in which the latter frame curriculum as apolitical or politically neutral. It is from their moment-by-moment experience of how curriculum affects the school-lives of flesh-and-blood children that these teachers draw their commitment to a critical practice. The tensions between critical practice and the abstract dictates of a fashionable neo-liberal organizational theory seem to centre on the collision between the authority of lived experience and located knowledge and the authority of increasingly bureaucratized, remote, and management-focused school systems. In the next section I look more deliberately at the implications of accountability discourses for the working lives and conditions of critical practitioners in schools.

Accountability Discourses and the Work-Lives of Teachers and Principals

One of the hallmarks of the 'new managerialism' of which accountability discourses are an expression is the decentralization of decision-making to local sites (Moos, 2003). An example is the school improvement movement, which promotes the devolution of planning for improvement from school boards to individual school councils (usually composed of local school faculty, students, and community members). But the approach to decentralization represented here has much more in common with neo-liberal moves toward privatization and contracting-out than with a genuine shift of authority to local sites. School improvement schemes may offer local sites a choice from a limited menu of possible areas for improvement, but the framework is always pre-determined: the parameters of 'improvement' are defined in advance, as are the terms in which improvements can be conceived, implemented, and tracked, and the process through which all sites must work is pre-scripted. Typical of the unclaimed authoritarianism of accountability frameworks is the fact that, once a plan has been adopted, local sites are not permitted to opt out or even to modify the terms of engagement.

It is not surprising, then, that accountability discourses have consequences for critical practitioners that go well beyond classroom and school curriculum to infect school and system cultures and definitions of teachers' and principals' work. A concern for many of the principals interviewed in this study was their growing sense that while their work responsibilities were increasing exponentially, their authority to act was being eroded and curtailed. Critical practitioners offered trenchant analyses of this intensification of work and time, its effects on their ability to do their work, and its significance for the pedagogical priorities of the system ('T' is teacher; 'P' is principal):

T: The negatives are the system itself. There's so much paperwork, documentation, meetings, that there are days when I literally feel like I'm on a treadmill spinning. Just paperwork, just keeping up . . . It's all about accountability. Everything has to be documented, and documented. You have program planning meetings every week. All the notes taken at every one of those meetings, photocopied twice so the people have copies of them. Then any assessments that I do, any—oh my, it just goes on and on.

P1: Someone went to one of those [principals and central administration] meetings and kept a list of all the new initiatives, there were something like forty of them. She listed them all off. I almost fell off the chair . . . health and safety regulations and things like that. Now, I think health and safety are important, but these policies just have no idea what life is like in schools . . . in schools that are challenging places to work there is just more stuff coming at you all day, more support for the kids, more support for the teachers, more support for the communities. . . . The supervisors really don't understand difficult schools. They just want you to get your paperwork in, so that the next level up isn't hounding them.

P2: Of course what is valued now is all-around standardized testing and how you're doing, and what your school plan looks like and how it's posted and how pretty it is, as opposed to the nitty gritty work that's being done in schools. . . . It's seen as being soft, that social justice work, and I don't think the board takes those people seriously. You need to nego- tiate this constantly. There's a lot of negotiating you do in this whole thing, a lot of extra work . . . there's some anger and frustration when you have a school that's doing this kind of work and it's not valued . . . so you turn your focus to the school and community and the work you do there, but *still* fulfilling your obligation around the system, around testing, around improvement, because that's a responsibility you have as a school leader. And you spend a lot of time and energy trying to protect your staff from the down-loading from the board—you say 'This is what the board is asking us to do, and it's no big deal, we're going to do it and get on with our real work', and you're constantly negotiating these conflicting demands.

Accountability discourses, placing a premium on *measurable* outcomes, naturally increase the demand for documentation; principals referred to bookcases filled with proliferating policy binders, as though central administration conceived of policy as a 'book of rules and regulations'. The consequence for teachers and especially for princi- pals is that their time is increasingly taken up with documenting their work, filing forms, and sending information back to the system. In the process, of course, the work of teachers and principals is redefined in technocratic terms: no longer agents in the ongoing debate about purposes and practices that historically was central to education, they become technicians who 'implement' a given curriculum and 'administer' prescribed tests. What is most interesting, though, is that the practitioners interviewed in no way acquiesced to this reconstruction of their work. Instead, rejecting the authority of the system, they described these managerial imperatives as so much misguided busy-work foisted upon them by bureaucrats 'who have no idea what life is like in schools', and they found ways to negotiate these annoyances in order to get on with 'the real work'.

Yet teachers and principals know that the managerial demands of the system must be met, and that opportunities for career recognition and advancement have much more to do with efficient servicing of the system than with the quality of their work in schools. Within accountability frameworks the purpose of public systems appears to have been inverted: one might think that the point of a school system is to serve and support the work of schools, but in the discourses of the new managerialism it seems that school personnel are there to serve the system. The parallel with the logic of the market, in which human beings become 'human resources', is unmistakable.

The consequences of accountability discourses for teachers and principals, then, are similar to the consequences for students. Commodifying and objectifying indi- viduals in a system framework that is interested only in productivity along pre-deter- mined lines, these discourses fundamentally alienate both teachers and students. At the same time they do serious damage to the system and school cultures that they purport to serve. Just below the surface anger and frustration expressed in these narra- tive fragments is a marked nostalgia for a more human and humane time: more than one teacher remarked that 'the heart' has gone out of the system. Closely connected to this sense of heartlessness is a sense that the system has become a sham in which appearances—whether of performance improvement, represented by rising scores on standardized assessments, or of seamless equanimity in the school's operations—are all important. As one principal put it:

> All [board administration] wanted was for that phone not to be ringing from a parent complaining about a decision that you've made. They don't want any parent calling and questioning why it was done that way. They don't want to hear that phone, with the parents, and they really get pretty upset when they've got these calls coming. One time my supervisor said 'It's not good to have all these phone calls.' And I said, 'Well, that's how you know I'm doing something.'

These educators' accounts of the ways in which discourses of accountability have affected their work lives, pedagogical commitments, and school and system cultures are far from idiosyncratic, however deeply rooted they may be in personal experience. Scholars in the area of organizational policy have identified, among the central characteristics of market ideologies, the reordering of system values such that managerial priorities dominate; the impoverishment of system trust through continuous performance surveillance and implied threat; and the displacement of blame from governance structures to individuals (Jones, 2003; Moos, 2003). In his study of trust in an age of performance accountability, Avis (2003) writes:

> I am reminded of the arguments of Beck (1999) and Bourdieu (1998), who suggest that risk has been passed further down the social structure so that the costs are often carried by those who are at the base of organizational hierarchies, such as the classroom teacher or lecturer.

The organizational strategems through which teachers' authority is being restricted and redefined should be of intense interest to all of us committed to critical practice and democratic education, if we recognize this blame-shifting for what it is: a local manifestation of the market ideology that has allowed the state to recast its own failure to address egregious social inequities as a matter of failure on the part of individual citizens.

Painting the Mountain Green

A recent *Guardian Weekly* article outlined an inventive approach to environmental degradation taken by unknown local officials in Fumin County, southwest China, who ordered that the bare slopes of Laoshou mountain, denuded by decades of industrial development, be painted green. According to the author, China has 'a long . . . tradition of confusing appearance with reality' (Hilton, 2007). We may wonder why she would identify the phenomenon as particularly Chinese, for the metaphor will resonate widely among critics of accountability in education.

One of the benefits of discourse theory is that it draws our attention to the linguistic and ideological company that particular words keep. 'Accountability' is a word that comes with legions of associated ideological tags—'measurable outcomes', 'management', 'performance monitoring', 'planning for improvement'—some of which I have taken up here. It is perhaps also instructive to remember that at the root of 'accountability' is 'accounting'. In an age of unbridled globalized capitalism, the meaning of 'accounting' seems to be shifting: Enron was not the only corporate swindle made possible largely through sleight of hand on the part of accountants. One might venture the observation that, in the context of current market ideologies, accounting and accountability alike are becoming marketing strategies, specifically designed to confuse appearance with reality.

Note

1. See Portelli, Shields, and Vibert (2007), *Toward an Equitable Education: Poverty, Diversity, and Students 'at Risk'* and Vibert, Portelli, and Shields (forthcoming), *Pedagogies at Risk: Social Justice and Accountability Discourses*. Gratitude is due to the Social Sciences and Humanities Research Council of Canada for funding these projects and to my co-researchers, John Portelli and Carolyn Shields, for their generosity with this research data and their many and continuing contributions to my thinking.

Glossary

at-risk: The current term used to designate students belonging to groups that schools have historically not served well, generally those marginalized by markers of race, social class, language and culture, gender and sexuality, and/or ability difference.

corporatization/marketization of education: Manifestations of neo-liberal ideology in public education, referring to the remaking of public education and schooling along market-friendly lines. This includes both the growing incursion of private interests into public education (in the form of private consultants, commercially produced curriculum packages, the testing industry, for instance) and the increasing influence of market language and ideology in public school systems (for instance, many school district administrations include offices called 'Corporate Services').

discourse: In this chapter 'discourse' is used in the sense explained by Fairclough (1989) in his work on critical discourse analysis. Briefly, a discourse is both a way of speaking and a way of thinking. We acquire different discourses through our participation in communities, cultures, and institutions, all of which teach us to speak (and therefore think) in particular ways. In recognizing discourses we recognize that social organizations are constituted by particular ways of speaking that represent particular worldviews; in this way, a discourse is by definition ideological, though its ideology works implicitly rather than explicitly.

neo-liberal: A broad and often disputed term generally used to describe a variety of economic (and therefore political and social) developments and arrangements associated with globalized free markets. In the present context, 'neo-liberalism' manifests itself in the increasing influence of certain liberal ideologies (e.g., the free market, individualism) into public education, and the related efforts to reify, commodify, and measure knowledge and learning.

social justice education: A broad body of work in education and a significant educational tradition concerned with questions of justice in society and schooling. Kohli describes it as a pedagogy 'that includes a theoretical account of oppression and privilege, as well as practical strategies for changing social institutions' (2007: 125–6), in this case particularly schools, as sites that reproduce inequities.

Study Questions

1. This chapter has focused on the negative implications of the current emphasis on accountability. Imagine that you are a public school educator charged with improving the accountability of your school or school system:

   a. List as many arguments as you can to support the pedagogical soundness of increased accountability within schools and school systems.

   b. Explicitly connect as many of these counter-arguments as you can to furthering social justice pedagogy within schools.

   c. Outline as fully as you can how you think the author of this chapter might respond to your arguments.

2. Drawing on your own experience in schools, identify two or three school policies (rules, governance structures, guidelines for use of school property, extracurricular practices, etc.) that you think had unintended inequitable consequences for some students and/or some families. What were these policies intended to achieve? How would you explain those unintended consequences? How might you modify such policies (and/or the processes through which they were developed) in order to accomplish their purposes without creating inequities?

Recommended Readings

Corbett, M. 2004. 'Knowing a Duck from a Goose: The Real World Education in an Age of Smoke and Mirrors', *Our Schools/Ourselves* 13, 2: 95–122.

Portelli, J.P.P., and R.P. Solomon, eds. 2001. *The Erosion of Democracy in Education: From Critique to Possibilities*. Calgary: Detselig Enterprises Ltd.

Shields, C.M., R. Bishop, and A.E. Mazawi. 2005. *Pathologizing Practices: The Impact of Deficit Thinking on Education*. New York: Peter Lang.

Recommended Websites

Critical Pedagogy on the Web: http://mingo.info-science.uiowa.edu/~stevens/critped/linksarticle.htm

Critical Literacy for Teachers: http://wwwfp.education.tas.gov.au/English/critlit.htm

References

Allington, R. 2002. *Big Brother and the National Reading Curriculum: How Ideology Trumped Evidence*. Portsmouth, NH: Heinemann.

Apple, M. 1988. *Teachers and Texts: A Political Economy of Class and Gender Relations in Education*. New York: Routledge.

———. 2001. *Educating the 'Right' Way: Markets, Standards, God, and Inequality*. New York: RoutledgeFalmer.

Avis, J. 2003. 'Re-thinking Trust in Performative Culture', *Journal of Educational Policy* 18, 3: 315–32.

Barlow, M., and H.J. Robertson. 1994. *Class Warfare: The Assault on Canada's Schools*. Toronto: Key Porter Books.

Blackmore, J. 2002. 'Is It Only "What Works" That "Counts" in New Knowledge Economies? Evidence-Based Practice, Educational Research, and Teacher Education in Australia', *Social Policy & Society* 1, 3: 257–66.

Canella, G.S., and R. Viruru. 2004. *Childhood and Postcolonization: Power, Education, and Contemporary Practice*. New York: RoutledgeFalmer.

Dei, G.S., et al. 2002. *Removing the Margins: The Challenges and Possibilities of Inclusive Schooling*. Toronto: Canadian Scholars' Press Inc.

Fairclough, N. 1989. *Language and Power*. London: Longman.

Fine, M. 1990. 'Making Controversy: Who's "at Risk"?', *Journal of Urban and Cultural Studies* 1, 1: 6–14.

Freire, P. 1998. *Pedagogy of Freedom*. New York: Rowman & Littlefield Publishers.

Gaskell, J., et al. 1995. *Secondary Schools in Canada: The National Report of the Exemplary Schools Project*. Toronto: Canadian Education Association.

Gipps, C., and P. Murphy. 1994. *A Fair Test?* Buckingham, UK: Open University Press.

Hilton, I. 2007. 'China's Deep Pledges Are as Green as a Coat of Paint', *Guardian Weekly*, 18–25 February.

Jones, K. 2003. 'Culture Reinvented as Management: English in the New Urban School', *Changing English* 10, 2: 143–53.

Knapp, M., ed. 1995. *Teaching for Meaning in High-Poverty Classrooms*. New York: Teachers College Press.

Kohli, W. 2007. 'What Is Social Justice Education?', in W. Hare and J.P. Portelli, eds, *Key Questions for Educators*. San Francisco: Caddo Gap Press, 24–7.

Kohn, A. and P. Shannon, P., eds. 2002. *Education, Inc.: Turning Learning into a Business*. Portsmouth, NH: Heinemann.

McMahon, B., and J.P. Portelli. 2004. 'Engagement for What? Beyond Popular Discourses of Student Engagement', *Leadership and Policy in Schools* 3, 1: 59–76.

Moos, L. 2003. 'Educational Leadership: Leadership for/as Bildung?', *International Journal of Leadership in Education* 6, 1: 19–33.

Oakes, J. 1985. *Keeping Track: How Schools Structure Inequality*. New Haven, CT: Yale University Press.

Persell, C. 1979. *Education and Inequality*. New York: Routledge.

Portelli, J.P., C. Shields, and A. Vibert. 2007. *Toward an Equitable Education: Poverty, Diversity, and 'At Risk' Students*. A National Research Report. Toronto: Centre for Theory and Policy Studies, OISE.

———, and A. Vibert. 2001. 'What Is a "Curriculum of Life?"', *Education in Canada* (Fall): 6–10.

———, and P. Solomon, eds. 2001. *The Erosion of Democracy in Education: From Critique to Possibilities*. Calgary: Detselig Enterprises Ltd.

Ryan, J. 2003. *Leading Diverse Schools*. Boston: Kluwer Academic Press.

Shannon, P. 1989. 'The Struggle for Control of Literacy Lessons', *Language Arts* 66, 6: 625–34.

Shields, C. 2003. *Good Intensions Are Not Enough: Transformative Leadership for Communities of Difference*. Lanham, MD: Scarecrow.

———, and A. Vibert. 2003. 'Approaches to Student Engagement: Does Ideology Matter?', *McGill Journal of Education* (Spring): 4–21.

Simon, R. 1992. *Teaching against the Grain: Teachers as Cultural Workers*. Toronto: OISE Press.

Smith, W.J., et al. 1998. *Student Engagement in Learning and School Life: A National Report*. Montreal: Office of Research of Educational Policy, McGill University.

Taylor, D. 1991. *Learning Denied*. Portsmouth, NH: Heinneman.

Thomson, P. 2002. *Schooling the Rustbelt Kids: Making the Difference in Changing Times*. Crows Nest, Australia: Allen & Unwin.

Vibert, A., and J.P. Portelli. 2000. 'School Leadership and Critical Practice in One Elementary School', *Exceptionality Education Canada* 10, 1/2: 23–37.

———, et al. 2002. 'Critical Practice in Three Elementary Schools: Conceptions of Community, Curriculum, and Voice', *Journal of Educational Change* 21, 54: 1–24.

CHAPTER 18

The Neo-liberal Assault on Ontario's Secondary Schools

Goli M. Rezai-Rashti

Since the 1980s neo-liberal policy discourses have had a powerful impact on educational systems throughout the Western world. Reforms inspired by the neo-liberal emphasis on accountability, choice, and market mechanisms have transformed education at the macro level. They have also profoundly affected the day-to-day work of teachers, as we will see in the second part of this chapter. As Ball (2006), drawing on the work of Rose (1989) and Bernstein (1996), argues, neo-liberal reforms have changed not just what people do, but also their social identity and relations with one another.

The impact of **neo-liberalism** on education has been the subject of many studies (Dale, 1997; Dehli, 2004; Rizvi, 2005).[1] Among the most commonly reported consequences have been changes in management, governance, and assessment procedures; increased standardization; budget cuts; privatization; and more centralized state control over curriculum design and content. The overarching theme in these studies, however, is the impact of restructuring on the work of teachers. Hatcher (1994) argued that this new market relationship in education was becoming the organizing principle of the school system and discussed how new management regimes were creating a new organizational culture. This organizational culture, according to Smith (2000), which is characterized by a language of global competitiveness and a 'marketplace' logic, has created new levels of uncertainty for teachers and an impending crisis for the teaching profession. Smyth (2001) argues that the recent reforms have been extremely damaging to the educative and pedagogical relationships in schools. The imposition of standard curricula and standardized testing has placed progressive methods under attack and is a radical effort to redefine 'teaching' (Ball, 1993, 1994). Even as teachers have been overburdened by incessant pressures to meet standards and measure achievement, they have faced an erosion of trust in their professional judgment and a new reliance on 'experts' and record-keeping. In this reconstructed role, the teacher is visible when issues of accountability, standards, and appraisal are raised, but an 'absent presence in the discourses of educational policy' (Ball, 1993: 108).

Increases in the size, intensity, and complexity of teachers' workloads (Easthope and Easthope, 2000) are accompanied by increases in stress (Kyriacou, 2001). Cutbacks in education spending, changes in assessment and administrative structures, and a more diverse student population mean that teachers must perform new tasks as well as more of the old ones. Easthope and Easthope (2000: 55), drawing on Hargreaves and Lo (2000), argue that teachers struggle to live up to their ethical and ideological commitments while adapting to new market-oriented demands (e.g., the demand that teachers become efficient managers). The hegemonic discourses associated with education reform typically claim that it is necessitated by **globalization**: restructuring is said to be essential if the nation-state is to remain competitive in the face of changes in the world capitalist economy. Globalization is thus used as a legitimizing discourse that makes the need for policy changes in education appear self-evident and leaves educators with no alternative but to comply (Bourdieu, 1999). Educational globalization, then, is an attempt to create global policies around education that will make the movement of labour around the globe easier. Rizvi criticizes the recent theorization of globalization that 'assumes it to be an objective self-evident entity, and does not attend sufficiently to the task of historicizing it, pointing to the hegemonic role it plays in organizing a particular way of interpreting the world' (2005: 1). He concludes that even though the influence of economic globalization on educational governance is undeniable, it is important to show how this influence operates and, more broadly, the nature of the relationship between the 'global context' and educational change.

Macro-level analysis of **educational restructuring** and reform (Apple, 1993, 2000; Burbules and Torres, 2000; Torres, 2002), although politically significant, has little to say about their impact at the level of practice. According to Ball (1994), 'Any decent theory of education policy must attend to the workings of the state. But any decent theory of education policy must not be limited to the state control perspective.' He argues that policies are shaped at the local level of practice:

> Policy is both text and action, words and deeds, it is what is enacted as well as what is intended. Policies are always incomplete insofar as they relate to or map on to the 'wild confusion' of local practice. Policies are crude and simple. Practice is sophisticated, contingent, complex and unstable. Policy as practice is 'created' in a trialectic of dominance, resistance, and chaos/freedom. Thus, policy is no simple asymmetry of power: Control [or dominance] can never be totally secured, in part because of agency. It will be open to erosion and undercutting by action, embodied agency of those people who are its object. (1994: 10–11)

It is in the light of this understanding of state policy formation that educational policy in Ontario from 1995 to 2003 should be seen. The reforms introduced by the Conservatives have been implemented in complex, unexpected, and unstable ways.

Policy Changes in Ontario, 1995–2003

In 1995 the Ontario Progressive Conservatives under Mike Harris defeated Bob Rae's New Democrats and formed a majority government. Having promised to cut the 'waste' (specifically non-classroom activities) from Ontario's schools, Harris introduced a series of major changes to the education system. Not all these changes, however, originated with the Conservatives. A number of them—the introduction of standardized assessment and evaluation procedures and report cards, the creation of Educational Quality and Accountability Office (EQAO), the elimination of grade 13, the establishment of the Ontario College of Teachers—had been strongly recommended by the Royal Commission on Learning (1995), established under NDP premier Rae.

In 1997 the Harris government introduced two bills—Bill 104 (the Fewer School Boards Act) and Bill 160 (the Education Quality Improvement Act)—aimed at reducing costs and centralizing decision-making in its own hands. Until then, local school boards had the power to levy property taxes to supplement the grants they received from the province. The new legislation took that power away and introduced a per-pupil funding system under the control of the Minister of Education. In addition, the government reduced the number of school boards in the province by almost half (from 129 to 72), changed governance at the school board level, amended the collective bargaining process for teachers, and cut secondary school teachers' preparation time by half (Gidney, 1999: 260).

The details of the secondary school reforms were made public in 1998. They included new streaming arrangements for grades 9 and 10; a mandatory literacy test for grade 10; a requirement that students complete 40 hours of non-credit 'community involvement' before graduation; and additional compulsory credits in math and science (Gidney, 1999: 239). In the spring of 1998, a government-contracted team (consisting mostly of teachers) began rewriting the curriculum with an eye to the new standardized assessment and evaluation procedures. Two years later, in 2000, Bill 74 (the Educational Accountability Act) further centralized educational decision-making by introducing mandatory extracurricular duty for teachers and empowering the government to take over a school board if its policy or practice contradicted ministry guidelines (Shaker, 2000). Also in 2000 the government announced a new teacher-testing program requiring, in addition to an initial qualifying test administered by the Ontario College of Teachers, re-testing and re-certification every five years.

All these policy reforms served to centralize educational decision-making and increase the ministry's control over matters of finance and curriculum that had previously been under the jurisdiction of local boards of education. In just five years (1996–2001) the Ministry of Education and Training became the main source of funding and principal regulator of education, drastically reducing the power of school boards. The following section will focus on the consequences of these reforms for teachers.

Consequences for Teachers

The interviews on which this chapter is based were conducted in 2003, following a semi-structured method influenced by the work of Dorothy Smith. As Smith put it,

> institutional ethnography is distinctive among sociologies in its commitment to *discovering* 'how things are actually put together', 'how it works'. The colloquialisms leave what

'things' are or what 'it' is undefined but establish the ideas of encountering the actualities of people's everyday experience, of research that discovers the social as the ongoing co-ordinating of people's activities, and of the researcher as being changed in the dialogic of research. (2006: 1–2)

Institutional ethnography is particularly useful for investigating the connections between the work of frontline workers and the macro-level influences of policies and practices of the institutions. As DeVault and McCoy describe it:

Frontline professionals, such as teachers, nurses, trainers, social workers, community agency personnel, and bureaucrats, often become informants in an institutional ethnography. Individuals in such positions are especially important because they make the linkages between clients and ruling discourses, 'working up' the messiness of an everyday circumstance so that it fits the categories and protocols of a professional regime. (2006: 27)

Twelve teachers were interviewed for the present study: five men and seven women. Specializing in social sciences, history, and English, four came from a school in a predominantly white working-class neighbourhood in London, ON, and eight from two schools in Toronto: one in an upper-middle-class area and the other in a lower-middle-class neighbourhood with a diverse student population. Interviews were tape-recorded and transcribed.

Based on these interviews, the consequences of the reform program for Ontario's teachers can be classified in two categories: intensification and reorganization. Intensification was attributed in part to the new curriculum and in part to budget cutbacks that had led to increased class sizes while reducing preparation time and support mechanisms. The 'reorganization' category included the new assessment and evaluation procedures for students and teachers alike, along with changes in organizational structures and responsibilities.

School Board Amalgamation

Amalgamation reduced the total number of Ontario's school boards from 129 to 72. The impact of this exercise depended to some extent on local circumstances. The Toronto Board has become the largest in Canada with 560 schools, 15,700 teachers, and 284,000 students who are among the most diverse in North America. As one teacher explained:

. . . suddenly the board became huge. . . . There are 600 schools . . . 300,000 students. Attempting to make anything work in that kind of massive structure suddenly becomes an administrative nightmare. . . . Just the size of this new formation itself is a huge impediment to any kind of systematic change, because the system itself is just too large to manage.

Before restructuring, the Toronto District School Board had more than twenty years of experience dealing with various equity issues. It had developed several curriculum materials and its work with teachers and students was a model for school boards across the country.[2] But cutbacks and restructuring led to the abandonment of several programs: When amalgamation happened there were about a dozen people who had different kinds of equity portfolios in the amalgamated board. . . . Well, this year [2003] the equity department consists of one district-wide coordinator, three [consultants] and just two student program workers left over, so basically there are six people. . . .

One teacher who was still working as an equity consultant described his current work as consisting of crisis intervention, troubleshooting, and a workshop here and there. Meanwhile, increasing administrative work and 'stuff that is not particularly interesting and exciting' left no opportunity to conduct ongoing systematic work with teachers and students.

In addition, the teachers mentioned that the high speed of the restructuring process and the profound changes in the nature of teaching and learning left them feeling bitter:

Teachers are at their wit's end, and fed up, and any kind of talk of anything that may seem as more work or something beyond what they're already doing, in a situation where they're incredibly stressed, seems like add-on—they just don't want to do it.

Class Size and Support Systems

Class size was a concern for all the teachers, affecting their teaching workload and their ability to attend to students' individual needs. Class size was especially troublesome in Toronto, because of its English as a Second Language students and inner-city schools. One of the teachers from the Thames Valley District School Board commented that class size had come full circle since he began teaching in 1972:

When I started, I had about 47 students in a [grade 13] class. And regularly for my first several years of teaching, I would always be over the grievance number of 190 students a year. . . . What I saw then, over the middle part of my teaching career, was a steady decline in class sizes, and a steady improvement in teaching workload, until . . . if we go back prior to the current government, it was not uncommon for me to be . . . down to around 160 to 170, and even then History was considered a fairly heavy loaded subject. It was even possible to find teachers with 150. . . So, the number of students we taught declined. We also had a cap on class sizes. Twenty-five students in applied level courses, and 28 in academic level courses.

The head of the history department in an affluent area of Toronto said that the government calculation that results in an average class size of 22.5 is mythical. The average classes, in her experience, are usually over 30. Another teacher with more than 30 years teaching experience also said that 'the class of 22 is a statistical average that doesn't really exist. Most of my classes are in the 30s, and have been for the last few years.'

Support for teachers was another issue raised by most of the interviewees. This is especially important in the context of Ontario because the possibility of earlier retirement meant that there were fewer experienced teachers available to offer advice and assistance. Thus newer teachers in particular tended to say that they were not getting enough support. One of the more experienced teachers contrasted her situation 10 years earlier with the one that faced new teachers after restructuring:

> When I was hired, I actually sat in the room for a week and observed other teachers, and then I look at the new hired person in this department who came three weeks into the job, and because the administration has been streamlined and a lot of the resources have been cut back, the support is certainly a lot less.

It is important to keep in mind here again that the impact of restructuring was felt most strongly in Toronto, where more progressive ideas and support mechanisms had been in place. As one teacher explained, cutbacks and amalgamation into one extremely large board together reduced the support available: 'They are stretched, and I think they do a really good job, but it's no longer the relationship we used to have in the past.' As Ball (2006) and Rose (1989) argue, reforms change not only what people do, but their relationships with one another.

A new teacher who had been teaching for a year and a half described her department as her main source of support:

> I had found the best support I've had has come from within my department. But in terms of Board staff, I don't find the stuff they give out very useful. I myself have not been to meetings where they talk about how to evaluate in a French class or History class, and people will come back and give me the forms they gave out, but basically they are photocopies of the documents, I don't find the exemplars all that useful. I find they are based on the highest achievers, and they don't really work at a school like this one, where there are so many kids whose first language isn't English.

Lack of job security puts additional pressure on new teachers to take on more extracurricular activities and please the administration in order to be asked to stay in the same school for the following year:

> I find it so overwhelming . . . in addition to doing all this paper work, in addition to planning my lessons for a class I've not taught before, dealing with teachers and parents. . . . And then to also have to go and be on the show an extra two or three hours every week or every day, to go and participate in extracurricular activity. . . I don't think there's a job in the whole world, where they expect you to be on the ball all the time, upbeat, positive . . . .

Reductions in preparation time came up in several interviews. Again, new teachers were especially affected, but heads of departments also found it difficult to keep up:

> I used to have a spare every day to deal with departmental issues, and work with other teachers, that kind of thing. Once that was taken away, it really put a big roadblock in the way of doing those kind of things. . . . My own class workload has increased quite a lot—I

have far larger classes than I used to have. Just the general amount of paperwork seems to increase constantly. You always have the feeling you're playing catch-up with your job, and that you never really quite have enough time to do the things you know need doing properly, to the level that you would like to do them. So it's really just a case of trying to do in the limited time with the limited resources that you have, all the while dealing with an ever-increasing workload, and more pressure. It is not easy . . .

The new system for teacher appraisal and re-certification was seen as adding to teachers' workload and 'paperwork'. Most of the teachers explained that they were not against evaluation and constructive feedback, but found that the new system was creating extra work for them without producing much benefit for students. One teacher said the system seemed to be designed not to help teachers but 'to catch something wrong'. Another experienced teacher talked about the extra paperwork involved: 'Now, it's going to become much more serious, because in addition to the evaluation, you have to indicate that you are doing professional development the Ministry requires you to do. You have to prepare an annual teaching plan. It is a lot of paperwork.' Furthermore, he said, teachers in the early to middle years of their career 'look at this with trepidation. They don't like it.'

Standardization

Teachers' responses to the standardization of curriculum and assessment procedures varied. In general, they did not object to the idea of standards, but they were critical of the new curriculum both in terms of quality and in relation to other changes in the education system. In addition, most teachers noted that the new curriculum was designed for the academic stream and that applied-level students were expected to meet similar demands with less remedial or specialized support than they received in the past. Many teachers saw the evaluation process as positive in setting out clear expectations and communicating them to students ahead of time so that there are no surprises: 'if you do this, this is the mark you're going to get. I like that. . . . I think that was a problem before, where you got teachers who would just give 80 per cent on an essay, and [students would] have no idea why.' Nevertheless, many teachers were still ambivalent about the criteria for assessing students' work. In general the new teachers were more concerned; the more experienced teachers explained that they were able to adapt the new curriculum as they thought best:

I have been teaching long enough to see a number of different things come and go through the years, and generally what you do, if you're in a position where you already have a permanent contract, and it is unlikely you would be called up on the carpet, and you have seniority, what you tend to do is to take what you like from these changes that come about, and the things you think are best suited to the particular subject area that you're teaching, and go with those. . . . Now if I were a beginning teacher or even mid-career looking at another ten or fifteen years, then I would definitely address these things in a much more serious way. . . . But my situation is somewhat different, so I have been picking and choosing a little bit.

Most of the teachers interviewed believed that the new curriculum was aimed primarily at academic-level students: 'it's truly designed for the academic kid—[the] high-end academic kid. They can do well in school, the kind of kid that wants to sit in a chair with a book.' This issue was discussed in several interviews. Those with more experience of teaching strongly believed that the new curriculum would be a 'disaster' for applied-level students:

> I think these new academic courses are challenging. They've crammed a lot of stuff in, and they are saying to these students: 'Do this'. And I've got some great work out of my students, because I've finally been able to ask for it. . . . I have been really impressed with the quality of the work I have been getting from my academic kids. But on the other hand, I think the real disaster of this curriculum is the applied courses. If you look through the history of academic and applied, the applied level course in grade 10 is just a watered-down version. If the academic kids need to learn five causes of the war, the applied kids don't care about that, so just say: 'Well, then only three.' We knew a long time ago that you teach general level courses differently. . . .You had to cater to different learning styles. . . .The kids who are getting burned in this curriculum revision are the applied level kids. . . . Even in history, English, geography, failure rate have risen [from about 8 per cent] as high as 25, 26 per cent.

The Reorganization of Teachers' Work

Most of the interviewees discussed how their work has been intensified by larger class sizes, the additional demands that came with the new curriculum and assessment procedures, the lack of support mechanisms, and increasing paperwork. In addition, however, several structural changes were introduced. These changes were more profound than a simple increase in the quantity of work. Most of them involved standardization, increased assessment and evaluation, and amalgamation of schools in order to facilitate government control of teachers' work.

Curriculum

The new Ontario curriculum is more prescriptive than its predecessor and lays out both general and specific expectations for each course. Its primary focus, however, is the assessment, evaluation, and formal reporting of students' progress. Teachers must adhere to both curriculum expectations and an 'achievement chart'[3] at every stage, from lesson planning through student work to assessment and evaluation (Ministry of Education and Training, 2000):

> When planning courses and assessment, teachers should *review the required curriculum expectations* and link them to the categories [of the standard achievement chart] to which they relate. They should ensure that *all* the *expectations are accounted for in instruction*, and the achievement of the expectations is assessed within appropriate categories. The descriptions of the levels of achievement given in the chart should be used to identify the level in which the student has achieved the expectations. Students should be given *numerous and varied opportunities to demonstrate their achievement of the expectations across the four categories* (13; emphasis in original).

A major justification for introducing the achievement chart was to ensure that teachers would plan lessons appropriately so that students will follow the curriculum and their achievement can be measured accurately. Repeated references to 'accuracy' and 'standardization' suggest that the achievement charts are intended to control teachers' evaluation of students' performance (Ministry of Education and Training, 2000). The achievement chart provides a province-wide method for teachers to use in assessing and evaluating their students' achievement. A variety of materials is being made available to assist teachers in improving their assessment methods and strategies and, hence, their assessment of student achievement (142).

Teacher Performance Appraisal

The teacher appraisal was designed in 2002–3 to provide a standard against which school boards could evaluate teachers' classroom performance throughout the province as specified in the Quality in the Classroom Act (2001), which sets clear province-wide standards and procedures. According to this policy, teachers must have an evaluation year in each three-year period. During the evaluation year, the teacher must be evaluated at least twice. Teachers new to the profession or new to the board are to be evaluated twice in each of their first two years. In addition, principals and teachers may request extra appraisals. Parents and students will also evaluate teachers' performance through surveys developed by the board of education. Its main objectives as stated by the Ministry of Education are:

> To ensure that students receive the benefit of an education system staffed by teachers who are performing their duties satisfactorily. Provide for fair, effective, and consistent teacher evaluation in every school. (Ministry of Education, 2002: 3)

At first glance these objectives seem fair, equitable, and conducive to both students' learning and teachers' professional development. But a close look at the document suggests a tendency to reduce teachers' professional autonomy and ensure that they teach the prescribed curriculum.

The Ministry of Education specifies 16 competencies that must be evaluated for every teacher. However, individual school boards can identify additional competencies related to knowledge, skills, and attitudes for the teachers they employ. In addition the appraisal includes a number of specific behaviours known as 'look-fors'. It appears that one of the main intentions of the new appraisal system is to ensure that teachers adhere to the prescriptive curriculum and assessment procedures.

For example, in the sections on professional knowledge and teaching practice the Ministry of Education manual states that teachers must:

> Know their subject matter, the Ontario Curriculum, and educational-related legislation. (6)

> Conduct on-going assessment of their pupil's progress, evaluate their achievement, and report results to pupils and parents regularly. (ibid.)

And the section for 'look-fors' requires that the teacher be evaluated on whether s/he:

Teaches the Ontario curriculum by exhibiting an understanding and ability to explain subject areas. (4)

Assesses and reviews program delivery for relevancy, uses provincial achievement standards and competency statements as a reference for evaluation of teaching. (9)

Thus the teacher performance appraisal system serves to control, regulate, and standardize teaching and learning across the province. The Ministry also indicates that it 'will monitor the application of the Teacher Performance Appraisal System' (2).

Reorganization of Schools

Several of the teachers working in Toronto said there were plans to change their schools' organizational structures in order to reduce costs and improve accountability, and that the changes would likely affect support mechanisms within the school. For example, they said that until 2002–3 most subject areas had their own departments, headed by experienced teachers who were experts in their subject areas and could provide support to other members of the department. Under the new organization, however, two schools were to create a new position called 'curriculum leader'. Individual subjects would lose their department heads and be organized in four new divisions, each headed by a 'curriculum leader' with a specific mandate to deal with instruction, assessment, evaluation, and reporting, but no particular expertise in most of the subjects under his or her direction. The structure of responsibilities of the four 'curriculum leaders' appointed in one Toronto school is presented in Table 18.1.

This change facilitates standardization by limiting opportunities for individual interpretation and professional autonomy. In addition, the elimination of department heads for each subject makes the curriculum leaders more responsible for administrative and managerial control of teachers' work, creating a larger layer of 'middle management' (Hatcher, 1994: 59) or what Ball (2006) describes as 'teacher-managers' whose main responsibility is to administer government-mandated policies in local schools.

Conclusion

The reforms introduced by the Conservative government in Ontario have had a profound impact. Not all teachers have been affected equally, however. The impact and intensity have been greater for new teachers, and for those working with larger bureaucratic organizations—notably the Toronto District School Board. In general, the technical aspects of teachers' work seem to have increased, while their professional autonomy has been reduced. Significant changes in the provincial curriculum tied to standardization of assessment procedures have been creating major changes in teachers' work. In addition, the introduction of 'teacher-managers' to ensure adherence to Ministry policies represents a significant change to workplace relationships. Overall, then, the changes to Ontario's education system are profound. As Ball puts it, 'In its crudest form, what is happening here is that human complexity is reduced to most simple possible form—a category or a number in a table' (2006: 17–18).

Table 18.1 Organizational Chart of a School in Toronto

Curriculum Leader	Curriculum Leader	Curriculum Leader	Curriculum Leader
Student Support (Student Support)	Information Technology (Program and School-Wide Initiatives)	Instruction/ Assessment/ Evaluation/Reporting and two Assistant Curriculum Leaders (Program and School-Wide Initiatives)	Staff Development and School Improvement (Program and School-Wide Initiatives)
Guidance and Career Education, Incl. TAP, AEP, etc. Co-operative Education Special Education Grade 8–9 Transition	Business Studies Computer Studies Technological Studies Learning Resources	Geography, etc. Math/Numeracy Science Health and Physical Education Visual Arts Music Drama	Literacy-English, ESL/ESD History/Social Studies International Languages French Immersion Media Studies Community Partnerships Special Projects

Source: Anonymous, 2002.[4]

It is important to note that not all school boards are following the mandated policies in the same way. Changes in the organization of individual schools, for example, have been most visible in the Toronto District School Board; other boards did not go through the same shifts. Different combinations of context, history, and interests can mean that the same policy plays out quite differently in different places, and may not always produce the results policy-makers intended (Taylor, Rizvi, Lingard, and Henry, 1997). Similarly, different teachers will interpret the same policy in different ways:

> Practitioners do not confront policy texts as naïve readers, they come with histories, with experience, with values and purposes of their own, they have vested interests in the meaning of the policy. Policies will be interpreted differently as the histories, values, purposes and interests which make up any arena differ. . . . Furthermore, interpretation is matter of struggle. (Bowe, Ball, and Gold, 1992: 22)

Levin (2001) similarly argues that although policies are driven by particular logics or ideologies, they are also shaped by local histories, cultures, and political factors. Therefore it is important to go beyond macro-level analysis and look at the local dynamics at micro-level:

The task of the analyst . . . is to consider the ways in which policies are driven by a particular logic or ideology, but also the ways in which they are shaped by other factors—historical, cultural, institutional, and political—that they are less predictable. At the macro level, long term changes in societies and the role of the state are important. At the micro level, chance, in the form of individual personalities or unexpected events, is also an important consideration in understanding reform. Neither the importance of means-ends rationality nor the underlying contingency of life can be ignored—both must be accommodated in an adequate theoretical account.

Although the Conservative government was defeated by the Liberal Party in 2003, there have been no substantial structural changes in the everyday practices of schooling. The reorganization of the education system institutionalized by the former Conservative government is now so entrenched that the potential for any substantial changes to the system are limited.

Notes

I would like to acknowledge the financial support of the Social Sciences and Humanities Research Council of Canada through the Standard Research Grant 410-2001—1622.

1. See also Apple, Kenway, and Singh (2005); Bourdieu (1999); Griffith (2001); Rezai-Rashti (2003, 2004); and Stromquist (2002).
2. For a better understanding of the impact of educational restructuring on equity issues see Rezai-Rashti (2003) and Dei and Karumanchery (2001).
3. 'The Achievement Chart identifies four categories of knowledge and skills in social sciences and humanities: knowledge/understanding, thinking/inquiry, communication, and application. These categories encompass all the curriculum expectations in courses and in the discipline. For each of the category statements in the left-hand column, the levels of students' achievement are described' (Ministry of Education and Training, 2000: 142).
4. From the records of an individual school. Confidentiality prohibits its identification.

Glossary

educational restructuring: Changing the institutional and organizational structure of education systems.

globalization: In the context of this chapter, transnational economic and technological processes as they affect education systems.

neo-liberalism: A body of principles and policies opposed to state intervention in economic and social life and favouring deregulation, decentralization, and privatization. On the other hand, as Stromquist observes, 'many note that these measures, while tending to weaken the state, in some instances end up making the state more centralized and controlling as it institutes measures to ensure compliance with new procedures and similarity of outcome' (2002: 6).

Study Questions

1. What were some of the main characteristics of Ontario's education reform program?

2. What were the reasons for these changes in the education system?
3. What is the relationship between globalization and education?
4. How has education reform affected Ontario teachers' work?
5. What are the main issues discussed by teachers about some of the recent changes in their work produced by educational reforms? How do these compare to the experiences of teachers in other provinces/territories? In other countries?

Recommended Readings

Ball, S. 1994. *Education Reform: A Critical and Post-structural Approach*. Philadelphia: Open University Press.

McNeil, L.M. 2000. *Contradictions of School Reform: Educational Costs of Standardized Testing*. London and New York: Routledge.

Portelli, J., and P. Solomon, eds. 2001. *The Erosion of Democracy in Education: Critique to Possibilities*. Calgary: Detselig Enterprises Ltd.

Recommended Websites

Ontario Secondary School Teachers' Federation: http://www.osstf.ca/
Elementary Teachers' Federation of Ontario: http://www.etfo.ca
Ontario Ministry of Education: http://www.edu.gov.on.ca/eng/
Canadian Education on the Web: http://www.oise.utoronto.ca/canedweb/
List of Canadian public policy organizations: http://www.policy.ca/policy-directory/Policy-Organizations/index.html
People for Education: http://www.peopleforeducation.com

References

Apple, M. 1993. 'Constructing the "Other": Rightist Reconstructions of Common Sense', in C. McCarthy and W. Crichlow, eds, *Race, Ethnicity and Representation in Education*. New York: Routledge, 24–39.

———. 2000. 'Racing toward Educational Reform: The Politics of Markets and Standards', in R. Mahalingam and C. McCarthy, eds, *Multicultural Curriculum: New Directions for Social Theory, Practice, and Policy*. New York: Routledge, 84–107.

———, J. Kenway, and M. Singh, eds. 2005. *Globalizing Education: Policies, Pedagogies, and Politics*. New York: Peter Lang.

Ball, S.J. 1993. 'Education Markets, Choice and Social Class: The Market as a Class Strategy in the UK and the USA', *British Journal of Sociology of Education* 14, 1: 3–19.

———. 1994. *Education Reform: A Critical and Post-structural Approach*. Buckingham, UK: Open University Press.

———. 2006. 'The Micro-economics of Education and the Creative Destruction of Public Sector Modernization'. Unpublished paper, Keynote address to the Taiwan Association for the Sociology of Education.

Bernstein, B. 1996. *Pedagogy, Symbolic Control and Identity: Theory, Research, Critique*. London: Taylor and Francis.

Beznanzon, K., and F. Valentine. 1998. 'Speaking Out' periodic report #2: 'Act in Haste . . . The Style, Scope and Speed of Change in Ontario'. Ottawa: Caledon Social Policy Institute.

Bourdieu, P. 1999. *Acts of Resistance: Against the Tyranny of the Market*, trans. Richard Nice. New York: New Press.

Bowe, R., S.J. Ball, and A. Gold. 1992. *Reforming Education and Changing Schools: Case Studies in Policy Sociology*. London and New York: Routledge.

Burbules, N.C., and C.A. Torres. 2000. 'Globalization and Education: An Introduction', in N.C. Burbules and C.A. Torres, eds, *Globalization and Education: Critical Perspectives*. New York: Routledge, 1–26.

Dale, R. 1997. 'The State and Governance of Education: An Analysis of the Restructuring of the State–Education Relationships', in A. Halsey, H. Lauder, P. Brown, and A. Stuart Wells, eds, *Education: Culture, Economy and Society*. Oxford: Oxford University Press, 273–82.

Dehli, K. 1996. 'Travelling Tales: Education Reform and Parental "Choice" in Post-modern Times', *Journal of Education Policy* 11, 1: 75–88.

———. 2004. 'Parental Involvement and Neo-liberal Government: Critical Analyses of Contemporary Education Reform', *Canadian and International Education* 33, 1: 45–73.

Dei, G.S., and L.L. Karumanchery. 2001. 'School Reform in Ontario: The "Marketization of Education" and the Resulting Silence on Equity', in J.P. Portelli and R.P. Solomon, eds, *The erosion of democracy in education: Critique to possibilities*. Calgary: Detselig Enterprises Ltd., 189–215.

DeVault, M., and L. McCoy. 2006. 'Institutional Ethnography: Using Interviews to Investigate Ruling Relations, in D. Smith, ed., *Institutional Ethnography as Practice*. New York and Toronto: Rowan and Littlefield Publishers, Inc., 15–44.

Easthope, C., and G. Easthope. 2000. 'Intensification, Extension and Complexity of Teachers' Workload', *British Journal of Sociology of Education* 21, 1: 43–58.

Gidney, R.D. 1999. *From Hope to Harris: The Reshaping of Ontario Schools*. Toronto: University of Toronto Press.

Griffith, A. 2001. 'Texts, Tyranny, and Transformation: Educational Restructuring in Ontario', in J.P. Portelli and R.P. Solomon, eds, *The Erosion of Democracy in Education: Critique and Possibilities*. Calgary: Detselig Enterprises Ltd., 83–98.

Hargreaves, A., and L. Lo. 2000. 'The Paradoxical Profession: Teaching at the Turn of the Century'. *Prospects* 30, 2: 167–79.

Hatcher, R. 1994. 'Market Relationships and the Management of Teachers', *British Journal of Sociology of Education* 15, 1: 41–61.

Kyriacou, C. 2001. 'Teacher Stress: Directions for Future Research', *Educational Review* 53, 1: 243–62.

Levin, B. 2001. 'Conceptualizing the Process of Educational Reform from an International Perspective', *Education Policy Analysis Archives* 9, 14. Available at: <http://epaa.asu.edu/epaa/v9n14.html>.

McNeil, L.M. 2000. *Contradictions of School Reform: Educational Costs of Standardized Testing*. London and New York: Routledge.

Ministry of Education and Training. 1995. *For the Love of Learning: Recommendations*. Available at: <http://www.edu.gov.on.ca/eng/general/abcs/rcom/recommen.html>. Accessed 12 November 2002.

———. 2000. *The Ontario Curriculum, Grade 11 and 12: Social Sciences and Humanities*. Toronto: Author.

———. 2002. 'Supporting Teaching Excellence: Teacher Performance Appraisal System'. Toronto: Author.

Portelli, J., and P. Solomon, eds. 2001 *The Erosion of Democracy in Education: Critique to Possibilities*. Calgary: Detselig Enterprises Ltd.

Rezai-Rashti, G. 2003. 'Educational Policy Reform and Its Impact on Equity Work in Ontario: Global Challenges and Local Possibilities', *Education Policy Analysis Archives* 11, 51. Available at: <http://epaa.asu.edu/apaa/v11n51/>.

———. 2004. 'Educational Restructuring and Teachers' Work in Ontario: Regulation, Intensification and the Limits of Professional Autonomy', *International Journal of Learning* 10: 1269–81.

Rizvi, F. 2005. 'Postcolonial Perspectives on Globalization and Education'. AERA 2005 Postcolonial SIG AGM Invited Talk. Montreal, Quebec.

Rose, N. 1989. *Governing the Soul: The Shaping of Private Self.* London: Routledge.

Shaker, E. 2000. *Bill 74: Clawing Back Democracy.* Ottawa: Canadian Centre for Policy Alternatives.

Smith, D.E., ed. 2006. *Institutional Ethnography as Practice.* Toronto: Rowman and Littlefield.

Smith, D.G. 2000. 'The Specific Challenges of Globalization to Teaching and Vice Versa', *Alberta Journal of Educational Research* 46, 1: 7–27.

Smyth, J. 2001. 'What Is Happening to Teachers' Work?' Landsdowne Lecture. University of Victoria, BC. 18 July.

Stromquist, N. 2002. *Education in a Globalized World: The Connectivity of Economic Power, Technology, and Knowledge.* New York and Oxford: Rowman and Littlefield Publishers, Inc.

Taylor, S., and M. Henry. 2000. 'Globalization and Educational Policy Making: A Case Study', *Educational Theory* 50, 4: 487–503.

———, F. Rizvi, R. Lingard, and M. Henry. 1997. *Educational Policy and the Politics of Change.* London: Falmer.

Torres, C. 2002. 'Globalization, Education, and Citizenship: Solidarity versus Markets?', *American Research Journal* 39, 2: 363–78.

CHAPTER 19

'Race', 'Parents', and Education Policy Discourse in Ontario

Kari Dehli

This chapter will discuss the discursive practices of Ontario's neo-conservative Harris government (1995–2003) and some of the groups that challenged it. Who spoke for education in this tumultuous period? How were their **discourses** performed and recognized? In one sense the chapter is about what Michel Foucault (1972, 1991) called **'discursive formations'**: the anonymous and unspoken rules and regularities that determine what can be stated and regarded as true and normal in particular discourses at particular times and places. In another sense it is about the way speaking and writing positions are made (differently) available and taken up in education policy discourses. In turn, the regulation of speaking and writing positions makes it possible for some—but not others—to 'do things with words' (Blain, 1994) and be recognized as entitled to assert or challenge norms and truths in the domain of education politics.

I am particularly interested in the way two terms—'race' and 'parents'—came to be used in policy discourses during 'the Harris years'. I examine how race operated as a category of truth integral to the institutional and discursive 'regularities' of education, and I link that examination to the emergence and circulation of 'the parent' as a key term in education policy discourse in the late twentieth century. Considered together, I ask: how did 'race' and 'parents' come to matter in the articulation of education policy and politics by specific actors in the 'education policy arena' (Scheurich, 1994) in a particular time and place? Thus the chapter is also about how discursive categories are organized and how they circulate in everyday political strategies and discourses. How does 'race' determine who can be recognized as a 'parent', and who can speak in parents' name? How does it operate to qualify and disqualify groups and individuals as political subjects (Hesse, 2004), and as subjects capable of speaking in the name of truth?

The discussion that follows will focus on the racial organization and effects of particular texts that were current in the education policy arena in Ontario in the 1990s. I do not mean to suggest that the people who produced these texts intended them to have racist effects. Nor do I argue that the government at the time was deliberately racist. It is quite clear, however, that the Harris government deliberately dismantled a number of policy initiatives designed by previous governments to address racism and racial inequities in Ontario's schools (Carr, 2006).

Regularities of Educational Discourse

This chapter examines the 'rules of reason' (Popkewitz, 1998) and the techniques of power by which the terms and truths of education politics and policy discourses are organized. Its central ideas are suggested by Foucault's 'archaeological' investigations into the discursive organization of the human sciences, including psychology, linguistics, and medicine (Foucault, 1972). Foucault was interested in how it was that of all the statements that could be made about something only *some* were regarded as scientific truth. He wanted to understand how ideas about what was true changed over time and between places. According to the conventional view, change and innovation in scientific thought could be attributed either to brilliant individual thinkers or to the progressive development of better theories. Foucault saw scientific statements as 'events' that could be examined by tracing the implicit and explicit rules and procedures that organize scientific discourses, as well as the social and material conditions that allowed some statements, rather than others, to come into 'the true' (Foucault, 1972, 1991). One of the questions that runs throughout Foucault's archaeological investigations is why, out of the multitude of human experiences and phenomena, only some come to the attention of scientists as topics that warrant their attention. I have written elsewhere about some of the ways in which the category of 'parents' came to the attention of educators in new ways in the 1970s and 1980s (Dehli, 1996). How, at the end of the twentieth century, did 'the parent' come to be seen as a topic for education researchers and as both a problem and a resource for education policy-makers? I argue that parents were deliberately brought into education policy discourse, as a category of education knowledge, as a resource in curriculum and pedagogy, and as subjects who are invited to relate to schools as partners, stakeholders, or consumers (Dehli, 2003).

Scheurich (1994) uses Foucault's archaeological approach to analyze how some social experiences and populations become 'policy problems'. In particular, he asks how social problems come to be studied and represented, how interventions are formulated and targeted in relation to specific populations, and how policy researchers contribute to these processes. Scheurich develops the term 'social regularities arena' (1994: 306) to show how education policy discourse reproduces, and operates within, limits that define what or who can be conceived of as a problem, while also providing the means or terms through which the problem can be known and addressed. Thus social regularities are ontological, in that they construct 'who the problem group is', and epistemological, in that they regulate 'how the group is seen or known as a problem' (Scheurich, 1994: 107).

Schools and education policies generate both formal and informal norms, standards, and expectations, and they develop practices of qualification, recognition, and correction in relation to students who adapt to or deviate from them (Henriques et al., 1984). Normative thinking and interventions in schools are mostly framed as benevolent responses to individual need or as corrections to, or compensations for, histories of collective exclusion and disadvantage (Popkewitz, 1998). At the same time, norms operate to position some individuals and populations as embodying the problems to be addressed, and others as subjects who are capable of action and intervention. While appearing to address inequality and exclusion, normative thinking leaves the structures of schooling and society, as well as the terms and effects of norms themselves, unexamined. Two related questions follow from this. The first asks how norms, and normative forms of reason and rationality, are expressed in education policy and governance in ways that organize inclusion and exclusion (Popkewitz, 1998). The second asks how such norms and forms of reason are taken up (or not) in the practices of those who act in the field of education politics. In other words, how is it that some individuals and groups come to be recognized and even respected as political agents or subjects, while others are cast as members of populations to be managed? To examine these questions, and to show how they are infused with race, I will now turn to the case of Ontario.

Acting in the Name of 'All': Doing 'Racial' Things with Words

During periods of intense political confrontation, such as Ontario experienced during the 'Harris years', the strategic uses of words, images, and metaphors become very clear. In such moments we can see how political discourse is organized to persuade supporters, justify action, mobilize participation, and convince 'the public' of the truth and morality of protagonists' positions (Blain, 1994). In many ways, education politics in Ontario during the late 1990s resembled a melodrama, with heroes and villains, good and evil, right and wrong, us and them. At the same time, historical narratives and legacies, visions of a present crisis and future danger were invoked, encouraging 'us' within the province or community to protect ourselves against 'them'. At times the threat was identified with groups or individuals among 'us', those whose unruly conduct, traditional culture, or lack of effort posed dangers to social order and economic prosperity; at other times, with entrepreneurial societies competing from without by working harder and smarter (and cheaper) in the global economy. In these melodramatic narratives race was at work both implicitly, in 'discursive regularities' dividing 'us' from 'them', and more overtly, in the ways political actors named themselves and the constituencies on whose behalf they spoke.

If political mobilization operates, at least in part, through discursive strategies of differentiation, persuasion, and performance, it is important to consider how political aims are defined through the language used to talk about them. Perceptions of an issue will vary with the terms in which it is described: as a matter of citizenship and rights; of individual, community, or universal interest; or of a need identified with a particular population (Fraser, 1989). In numerous press releases and newsletters following their election in 1995, the provincial Conservatives repeated versions of the story that the education system was 'broken' and that only they were tough enough to fix it. But what, exactly, was it that was broken? Among the many specific themes raised by the Conservatives, failing standards, poor performance, inefficiency, bureaucracy, and cost were among the most prominent. One storyline compared Ontario's education system with the systems used elsewhere in the OECD and suggested that even though it was among the most expensive, its results did not measure up. The strategy behind this kind of narrative is one of differentiation, in which 'we' are compared unfavourably to some external others who perform better with less. A second differentiation strategy is to make distinctions within and among 'us'. In these narratives 'ordinary' parents or taxpayers are contrasted with 'special interest' groups who are depicted as diverting the system to meet their special demands. This strategy is often used to drive a wedge between urban and rural communities: the former will be said to profit at the expense of the latter. Thus the Ontario government argued that its school funding formula would 'restore' equality by standardizing provincial grants to school boards. Student-focused funding, it said, would reduce 'administrative waste' while increasing 'account-ability for student achievement'. In an explicit strategy of differentiation, this initiative was hailed as enabling parents 'to see how their school board compares with others in the province through the provincial testing program' (Ontario Ministry of Education and Training, 1998a). As many critics pointed out at the time, these claims made sense only if we assumed that all children live similar lives and all schools operate under similar conditions. The municipally funded programs that most irked the government were those developed by urban school boards to address racism and poverty, or to maintain heritage languages.

Designing funding, programs, and curricula around norms that ignore social difference has the effect of consigning large numbers of students to what Popkewitz (1998) calls 'spaces of deficit' or exclusion. When such norms are the basis on which judgments about achievement and performance are formed, they serve to identify excluded students as constituting a 'problem', as if 'deficit' were somehow inherent in their nature, culture, or community. Now, in order to gain access to an adult literacy class or an English as a Second Language program, individuals must qualify as special and deserving. Before long, those who seek out such programs come to be seen as making excessive demands on government resources, asking for programs that 'we can no longer afford'. Rather than waste money on such 'extras', the Conservatives said, they would make the education system simpler, less expensive, and more accountable. Standards and uniformity would be restored through a more centrally controlled curriculum and regular, province-wide testing. The difficult 'jargon' of educators (and researchers) would be replaced by regular and accessible reports and tests designed to reveal the real level of each child's achievement and each school's performance. Parents in particular were targeted with promises that the government would secure their interests by 'regularly tracking children's progress' (Ontario Ministry of Education and Training, 1998b). At the same time, the government promised to focus on the 'basics', instilling respect for authority, and encouraging good conduct. The revised high-school curriculum introduced in 1998, for example, promised that it would 'increase emphasis on math, language and science while promoting responsible citizenship'. As well, schools were asked to 'return to streaming', in order to enable 'all students to achieve their best' (Ontario Ministry of Education and Training, 1998c: 2).

From their initial appropriation of the term 'common sense' to their populist appeals to local empowerment and individual choice, the Tories were astute in portraying themselves as courageous heroes doing what was necessary to wrestle control of the province, and particularly its schools, from the grasp of a 'bloated bureaucracy' and self-interested teachers' unions. School board officials and elected trustees made easy targets when provincial governments across Canada sought to 'reform' the school system. When the Ontario Tories targeted school boards and teachers' unions as the 'villains' in the melodrama of education, they at once demonized their opponents and positioned themselves as heroes who could hold their own against powerful opponents. At the same time they aligned themselves with 'ordinary' people—notably parents and taxpayers, especially in rural and small-town Ontario—while characterizing previous governments as weak and submissive in relation to 'special interest' groups (Gidney, 2000). Without referring directly to racial categories, discursive strategies like these implicitly align the urban and the 'special' with racialized spaces and populations. Drawing on racial codes, they have powerful racial effects.

The 'Ordinary' Parent in Education Politics

Ontario's Conservative government (and its Liberal successor) frequently appealed to 'the parent' to justify its education initiatives. Positioning itself on the moral high ground, in contrast to its weak, free-spending predecessors, the government claimed to speak for 'ordinary parents' against school boards, teachers' unions, and 'special' interests. In itself, the notion of 'the Common Sense Revolution' implied an alignment with 'the people' in opposition to the state. As Knight (1998) has suggested, it is remarkable how the Conservative party continued to position itself rhetorically 'with the people' and against the state long after its election victory in 1995. In the government's rhetoric about education, 'the people' became the 'ordinary parents' on whose behalf the government called for higher standards, greater accountability, more involvement, and wider 'individual' or 'consumer' choice. Thus arguments for choice brought into the education arena a market-based discourse while terms with strong corporate associations, such as 'stakeholders' and 'partners', were increasingly used to refer to parents, families, and communities. In fact, various social movements had been using terms such as accountability and involvement since the early 1970s, when coalitions of community groups, at times joined by teachers, mobilized to hold the schools and the Board of Education accountable to Toronto's diverse communities (Dehli, Restakis, and Sharpe, 1988; McCaskell, 2005). In the harsh political climate of the 1990s, however, the meanings of such terms were transformed as the context shifted from one of community and group rights to one of individual competition and consumption (Carr, 2006).

'Parents' had a mixed career as a political category in this period; I will discuss below how some of the government's opponents mobilized in the name of parents, claiming that they had a more legitimate right to the term than the government did. One of the alternative categories available to the government for use in appeals to righteous victimhood was 'taxpayers'. 'Taxpayers' is less attractive than 'parents' as a category for self-identification; few people take pleasure in paying taxes (Knight, 1998). Yet as Knight suggests, to claim to speak on behalf of taxpayers can be an effective political tactic, affording identification with the many anonymous 'good people' who live respectable lives, work hard, and contribute to society by paying their taxes. Furthermore, like many other identity categories in political discourse, 'taxpayers' evokes its own opposite in the form of those less virtuous and deserving others who spend the taxpayers' hard-earned money, in particular those who use their 'special' status to justify the claims they make on the state.

Among the many enemies of the aggrieved taxpayers, then, are those who work for or depend on government-funded programs—including education and health care as well as social assistance—that would, according to the logic of these arguments, be better governed if they were subjected to the discipline of the free market. Among the 'regularities' that organize this type of discourse are notions of the individual as an independent and self-sufficient actor who makes rational decisions based on economic calculation, who carefully weighs risks and benefits, and who takes responsibility for his or her actions. Such individuals are presumed to be unencumbered by racial, gendered, or classed histories and experiences, or by disabilities and sexualities that set them apart from the norm (Adkins and Lury, 1999). Speaking in the name of 'homo economicus' is a way for politicians to render a majority of people 'special' in a negative sense, as if they (as if we) lacked the capacities required to be full human subjects.

An additional benefit of speaking in the name of 'ordinary' people is that it may serve to differentiate the provincial 'we' from the urban 'them'. In the case of Ontario the division between Toronto and the rest of the province has a very long history, during which it has served many different functions. While the hinterland's negative feelings about Toronto can be traced historically to the city's economic, political, and cultural dominance, in the late twentieth century they were increasingly focused on notions of Toronto and its people as unruly and 'other', not like 'us', not quite Canadian. During the 1990s the city was variously celebrated for its multicultural diversity and decried as a place of violence, excess, and danger, all of which were implicitly linked to race and fear of the racialized other.

Speaking as and for 'the People' in Education

The discourse of the Conservative government's critics also offers evidence of the way systems of differentiation operate. Especially interesting in this respect is the organization called People for Education, which worked hard and quite successfully to position itself as a legitimate representative of the people in educational matters. In part the group's name is a direct challenge to the Conservatives' populist pretensions. But it also evokes a broad notion of 'the people' that lifts it above partisan interests. While the group shared many of the views and positions of teachers' unions and political parties, People for Education has made a point of asserting its freedom from partisanship and avoiding identification as a 'special interest' organization (see the group's website at <www.peopleforeducation.com>).

As I have suggested above, the Harris government sought to align itself with 'ordinary' parents and taxpayers in its assault on school boards and teachers' unions. In one sense, People for Education competed with the government for the job of representing 'everyone'. At the same time the simple generality of the phrase 'for Education' suggests that the group genuinely cares about *all* children and *all* public schools. This notion is underscored by the organization's website, which describes it as 'a group of parents who are working to preserve fully publicly-funded education in Ontario'. In describing themselves as 'parents', the group's members differentiate themselves not only from the government but also from those whose interests in education are political, professional, or particular. At one level, then, the group asserts a general subject position, representative of anyone interested in preserving fully publicly funded education. Indeed, People for Education's regular assertions of independence from political, union, or other 'special' interests have allowed the organization to successfully claim a position of speaking for 'the people' and for 'education' in general.

On the other hand, paradoxically, only certain 'people' can claim such a universal position. Those who speak or write in the name of 'everyone' do so in the context of a normative racial economy (Passavant, 2000; Scheurich, 1994) in which whiteness, or at least the absence of racial markers, is assumed of anyone who would speak as a representative of general truths and norms. To be recognized as someone entitled to speak in the name of 'ordinary parents' it might be tolerable, even preferable, to be a mother, in so far as mothers are presumed to have a natural investment in children and their education (David, 1993). In this discursive context, however, it would not be persuasive for a group of mothers 'of colour' to claim to represent 'parents' in general.

People for Education was founded in Toronto in 1996 by mothers of children attending a public school in a middle-class neighbourhood near the University of Toronto. The issue that provoked them to take action beyond their local schools was a request from the principal to help raise money for math textbooks. In its mission statement People for Education describes its objectives as follows:

> Public education is the foundation of a civil society. People for Education is dedicated to the ideal of a public education system that guarantees every child access to the education that meets his or her needs. At People for Education, we work toward this ideal by doing research, by providing clear, accessible information to the public, and by engaging people to become actively involved in education issues in their community. (People for Education, n.d.)

This statement asserts the centrality of public education for 'civil society'; it assumes that any reasonable person will share this ideal and might therefore 'become actively involved in education issues in their community'. While 'other' groups might represent 'special' interests, or pursue political and self-interested aims based on sentiment or ideology, People for Education serves the public—everyone—with its research and 'clear, accessible information'. This self-representation suggests a voice of reason and knowledge that can be understood and trusted where others—including the government, the unions, and, yes, university-based researchers—either cannot be understood or should not be believed.

While the Harris government presented itself as challenging the expertise of an educational 'establishment' that was out of touch with the 'real' concerns of students and parents, People for Education presented itself as challenging the expertise of school boards and teachers' unions regarding the state of the provinces' schools. It was, and has continued to be, spectacularly successful in positioning itself as a source of trustworthy knowledge about education. It has engaged in an impressive range of research activities, mobilizing hundreds of members across Ontario to generate data for annual reports on the state of the province's schools, touching on everything from school libraries to physical education, special education, and the quality of teaching in English and French as Second Language classes. Although its research is conducted using specialized, 'scientific' concepts, calculations, and technologies, the results are presented in the easily understandable form of surveys and reports. The release of the annual report is a well-attended media event, and the group's findings have been widely cited as reasonable and authoritative by politicians and university-based researchers as well as education activists, who have used its tracking surveys to show the concrete effects of budget cuts and curriculum changes. At the same time, the group has enhanced its reputation for rationality and reason by positioning itself as non-political and free of attachments to teachers' unions, school boards, or political parties. This distancing from 'political' and 'special interest' organizations has encouraged the perception that People for Education does not interpret (or manipulate) the information it gathers, as a 'self-serving' union or 'single-issue' group might.

People for Education's research activities are important, but it is also important to note how those activities allow the group and its network of activists to 'constitute themselves as political power subjects' (Blain, 1994: 812). One remarkable feature of the annual reports is the network of parent activists that produces them. In many ways, recruiting parents to gather information transforms 'ordinary' individuals into researchers who learn to observe schooling in particular ways. Moreover, by collating and analyzing data from schools across the province, and by distributing their reports back to local communities, People for Education contributes to the development of popular and public knowledge about education. The organization provides discursive resources—access to educational facts and figures, comparisons among schools, and trends over time—so that other parents, in particular, can become informed activists in their local school communities. There is a gender dimension to this type of local involvement, whereby the paradigmatic active citizen—the one who is invited or required to become involved in the affairs of the local school—is most often a woman who is addressed in her role as a mother (David, 1993; Dehli, 2004). Across political positions, it seems that the call for more active citizen participation in local communities and school affairs today is deeply gendered in both its assumptions and its effects (Keating, 2004), in so far as many of the functions and responsibilities, and much of the labour, in these areas involves the 'feminine' work of caring for children, young people, and the elderly. Parents may see active involvement in their local schools as a matter of ethical and moral commitment to their children, but it takes a considerable amount of labour, resources, knowledge, and time. Thus it is not surprising that almost all the public faces of People for Education are women. In many ways, the 'parental turn' in education policy resulted in an intensification of mothers' labour and responsibility (Smith and Griffith, 2004).

During the 1990s, as education budgets were cut back, parents were increasingly urged to assume greater responsibility for activities in support of their children's experience and achievements in school (Dehli, 1996). At the same time, it became increasingly clear that parents' ability to volunteer varies, and that the resources that different communities are able to mobilize through parental involvement are not equal; thus an emphasis on parental participation can serve to entrench social and educational inequalities. In this context, it is interesting to see how People for Education has appropriated the discourse of parental responsibility and rights. Indeed, the group makes strong links between rights, responsibility, and reason, in a language infused with outrage that a cherished institution is under attack by a very powerful adversary. Annie Kidder, the founder of People for Education, described the initial outrage that galvanized her and her middle-class neighbours, into action: 'It seemed amazing to us that a government could launch an assault on a public institution without any notice. It rocked a core belief of mine that Canadians could just stand by and let this happen' (Kidder quoted in Makhoul, 2000: 2).

People for Education was not the only group to take action in defence of public education. There were numerous protest activities in the late 1990s, including rallies, protests, deputations, and letters to the media. In 1997, more than 100,000 teachers went on a two-week strike to protest against legislation that undermined their collective bargaining rights and reduced the autonomy of locally elected school boards. During this period of intense public protest, representatives of People for Education were frequent speakers at demonstrations and rallies organized by teachers' unions, where their role was to speak for 'ordinary' parents. Annie Kidder, in particular, became a very public face and voice of parents.

During these events, as well as in their own public rallies and publications, People for Education became fond of telling a very specific and proud story of education and of Canada. Perhaps as a counter to the story told by the Conservative government of a 'broken' and 'bloated' system, People for Education described a system based on democratic principles and universality, operating in a country where 'anything was possible' (Kidder, 1999)—until a disrespectful authoritarian provincial government put it under threat. I will quote Kidder at length as she outlines this history in an article on the People for Education website:

> Our public education system wasn't built by accident. . . . Two decades before Confederation, Egerton Ryerson set out to build a Canadian educational system. In 1843 he said: 'Education is the first charge on the wealth of the province and full public funding is the very foundation of a public system of education. Education is everyone's responsibility and access to a quality education is the birthright of every child in this province.' (Kidder, 1999: 1)

Annie Kidder and People for Education often repeated Ryerson's own arguments in favour of a publicly funded school system—particularly the argument that education matters for everyone and that 'full public funding is the very foundation of a

system of public education'. As a discursive strategy in an ideologically charged political space, the defence of an honoured historical legacy seems an astute choice, particularly as a counter-narrative to a government that also claimed to be defending
traditional values. Yet it is important to question the terms in which Ryerson was resur-
rected—or rather, to ask which aspect of Ryerson's legacy People for Education was
invoking in defence of public education. Indeed, much of the critical and revisionist
historiography of education in Ontario since the 1970s has focused on the ambivalence
of his legacy (Chaiton and McDonald, 1978; Curtis, 1988; Katz and Mattingly, 1975;
Prentice and Houston, 1975). The general thrust of that literature suggests that Ryerson
would have rejected many of the arguments mobilized by People for Education in the
1990s. While he favoured a publicly funded, state-regulated school system, for
instance, he was distrustful of teachers and local communities; while he saw the
'common school' as a crucial feature of democracy, his model of democracy was hierarchical, governed by 'good men of character'; and while he wanted a school system that
would instil the values and habits required of good citizens, the model he had in mind
centred on respect for bourgeois Anglo-European values (Curtis, 1988; Prentice, 1977).

Thus People for Education makes selective use of Ryerson to persuade people that
something important and valuable is under threat. Of course all history is partial, and
if we call on stories of the past it is usually in order to accomplish something in the
present. However, even if we agree that public education should be defended, it is
important to recognize that the stories we select from the past, and the ways in which
we tell them, may have implications that we did not intend. A historical narrative that
makes Ryerson a father figure of democratic schooling and the country a model of
progressive thinking effectively denies the reality that the advantages of public
schooling have never been equally distributed in Canada. Such a narrative does not
easily accommodate the long and ongoing history of struggle over virtually every
aspect of education: who should have access and who should not; what to teach and
how to do it; even what constitutes 'proper' knowledge (to name only a few). Nor does
this narrative recognize the inequalities that schooling has systematically produced
and perpetuated from Ryerson's time to the present (Curtis, Livingstone, and Smaller,
1992).

In terms of its discursive organization, People for Education's version of the
Ryerson story is structured around the individual at the centre of public schooling and
education policy, inviting readers to identify with the difficult work of making,
governing, and ordering the schools. In order to do this work well, 'people' must be
knowledgeable and informed, and they must care for others as well as themselves. A
similar subject position is assumed in much of People for Education's work and publications. Thus a 2005 report on urban schools is prefaced by the following quotation
from Governor General Adrienne Clarkson:

> We have to fight for the right of others to have what we in our generation had—schools
> which helped to bring together children of all backgrounds, income and cultures. . . . If we
> don't preserve it, we are really going to pay a terrible price for it. . . . Public education is
> everyone's responsibility because the future of children is to become citizens of tomorrow.
> (People for Education, 2003: 7)

Adrienne Clarkson, a successful broadcaster who was born in Hong Kong and raised in Ottawa as the daughter of wartime refugees, was quoted here during her tenure as the representative of the British monarchy in Canada. Her statement about fighting for the rights of others assumes the presence of some unspecified adversaries who seek to curtail those rights—specifically Ontario's Conservative government, but also more generally anyone who is not willing or able to fight for public education. At the same time, she is speaking for the values of public education and democracy with the authorizing signature of the Governor General, a position that links these virtuous ideals to Canada's place in the British Empire. Thus Canada's colonial history is glossed as bestowing democracy and progress on the nation.

Conclusion

In this chapter I have worked with some of the concepts and approaches introduced by Michel Foucault to discuss the ways race operates as a constitutive regularity of education policy, albeit one that is often unintentional and masked as something other than race. I have traced how some issues, individuals, and populations, but not others, came to be seen as problems for education, focusing on the category of 'parents'. How are race and racism rendered both visible and invisible, both central and exceptional, in education policy discourses that take 'parents' as one of their main categories? What are some of the effects of racial rules of reason and discursive regularities for the everyday work and relations between students, teachers, and parents? Foucault's concepts have been useful, but as I conclude this chapter I would suggest that it is necessary to go beyond his work to sharpen the analytic focus on race as a discursive category, as a technique of power, and as a pervasive rationality that is an important component of the way our society is governed. While race is a category in discourse that distorts and imposes violent truths, it is also an aspect of the way life is organized and experienced by people who are 'racialized'. In this sense, race and racism are ordinary, unexceptional features of daily life, as much the effects of 'race-less' discourses and stories as they are the intended consequences of wilful ideological untruths (Hesse, 2004).

Through this chapter I have been concerned with the part that race played in shaping the way education problems were defined in Ontario in the 1990s. My argument is that 'race' is at work even when it is not an explicit topic or politic. Race operates as a grammar that helps to determine which individuals will be recognized as reasonable, capable of representing large and general categories, such as 'the people', in debates about education. As well, notions of the past and the future are often framed in terms that take whiteness as the norm or assume speaking positions at the centre of stories of democracy and progress, and therefore have exclusionary effects. At the same time, definitions of problems and actions, and the specification of speaking positions, do not fully determine how concrete individuals will 'take up' those positions, nor do they 'capture' the ways in which people live their lives or experience the world. The discourses and political practices that allow some individuals or collectivities to speak and be recognized as citizen-subjects serve to reduce others, suggesting that they are somehow compromised or incapable of speaking on their own behalf. There is an economy of discourse at work here in which race plays a central role in organizing the terms of qualification, inclusion, and exclusion, indicating how some bodies come to have access to status as universal and knowing subjects, while others are positioned as special, self-interested, unruly, or pathological, not qualified for the responsibilities and rights of citizenship (Lewis, 2000; Dean, 2002). In this way, race is at work in political and policy discourse even when racialized subjects are neither present nor visible.

Glossary

archaeology of knowledge: A term used by Foucault to describe a particular approach to the history of science. Historians of science usually credit change and innovation either to brilliant individuals or to the development of progressively better theories. Foucault challenged this idea, suggesting that changes in scientific thinking are arbitrary and largely attributable to rules and patterns in discourse. He used his archaeological method to analyze the rules and conditions that allow some statements rather than others to be asserted as true, and he traced the way that patterns and repetitions in discourse shape scientific speaking and writing.

discourse: A 'serious' or formal type of speech or writing that conforms to a particular set of rules. In this sense, discourses are authoritative, often generated in and attached to specific institutions, such as governments, universities, and media.

discourse/discursive formations and regularities: Ways of speaking and writing that have become so entrenched as common sense that they are taken for granted by those who regularly use the language. Implicit rules in discourses enable language users to distinguish among objects and sort them into unities. For example, even as the category 'race' has become discredited, it continues to operate in discourse as a regularity that permits the sorting of individuals into particular 'kinds'.

Study Questions

1. One of the arguments in this chapter is that in education policy and politics, the category of 'race' is at work even when racialized individuals are absent. Can you think of other educational contexts where this would also be the case?

2. This chapter has focused on the operation and effects of 'discursive regularities' in education policy. How does looking for such 'regularities' differ from analyzing education policy as an ideology or as an expression of particular ideologies?

3. This chapter suggests that in education policy debates, racialized individuals are positioned on the margins of reasonable and disinterested speech. How does this work? What are some of the consequences? Can you think of other categories that operate similarly?

4. Until the mid-1970s parents were, for the most part, considered outsiders in relation to education except when called on to volunteer, raise funds, or take responsibility when children were in trouble. Today, by contrast, parents are described as central to education and are invited to take part in a wide range of functions. What are some of the reasons for this change? How 'real' is parent participation? What are some of the positive and negative consequences of greater parent participation?

5. People for Education can be seen as an example of a grassroots social movement in education. What are some other organizations that take an active interest in education? What social interests do these groups represent?

Recommended Reading

Curtis, Bruce, David Livingstone, and Harry Smaller. 1992. *Stacking the Deck: The Streaming of Working-class Kids in Ontario Schools*. Toronto: Our Schools–Ourselves Education Foundation.

McCaskell, Tim. 2005. *Race to Equity: Disrupting Educational Inequality*. Toronto: Between the Lines.

Popkewitz, Tom, and Marie Brennan, eds. 1998. *Foucault's Challenge: Discourse, Knowledge, and Power in Education*. New York: Teachers' College Press.

Tamboukou, Maria, and Stephen J. Ball, eds. 2003. *Dangerous Encounters: Genealogy and Ethnography*. New York and London: Peter Lang Publishers.

Vincent, Carol. 2000. *Including Parents? Education, Citizenship, and Parental Agency*. Buckingham, UK: Open University Press.

Recommended Websites

People for Education: http://www.peopleforeducation.com

Foucault Resources: http://www.foucault.qut.edu.au/

Foucault Studies (on-line journal): http://www.foucault-studies.com/

References

Adkins, Lisa, and Celia Lury. 1999. 'The Labour of Identity: Performing Identities, Performing Economies', *Economy and Society* 28, 3: 598–614.

Blain, Michael. 1994. 'Power, War, and Melodrama in the Discourses of Political Movement', *Theory and Society* 23, 5: 805–37.

Carr, Paul. 2006. 'Social Justice and Whiteness in Education: Colorblind Policymaking and Racism', *Journal for Critical Education Policy Studies* 4, 2. Available at: <http://www.jceps.com/?pageID=articlaeID=77>. Accessed 25 October 2007.

Chaiton, Alf, and Neil McDonald, eds. 1978. *Egerton Ryerson and His Times*. Toronto: MacMillan.

Cruikshank, Barbara. 1999. *The Will to Empower: Democratic Citizens and Other Subjects*. Ithaca: Cornell University Press.

Curtis, Bruce. 1988. *Building the Educational State: Canada West, 1836–1871*. London, ON: Althouse Press.

———, David Livingstone, and Harry Smaller. 1992. *Stacking the Deck: The Streaming of Working-class Kids in Ontario Schools*. Toronto: Our Schools-Ourselves Education Foundation.

David, Miriam E. 1993. *Parents, Gender and Education Reform*. Cambridge: Polity Press.

Davies, Bronwyn. 2005. 'The (Im)possibility of Intellectual Work in Neo-Liberal Times', *Discourse: Studies in the Cultural Politics of Education* 26, 1 (March): 1–14.

Dean, Mitchell. 2002. 'Liberal Government and Authoritarianism', *Economy and Society* 31, 1: 37–61.

Dehli, Kari. 1996. 'Travelling Tales: Education Reform and Parental "Choice" in Postmodern Times', *Journal of Education Policy* 11, 1: 75–88.

———. 2003. '"Making" the Parent and the Researcher: Genealogy Meets Ethnography in Research on Contemporary School Reform', in Maria Tamboukou and Stephen J. Ball, eds, *Dangerous Encounters: Genealogy and Ethnography*. New York and London: Peter Lang Publishers, 133–51.

———. 2004. 'Parental Involvement and Neo-liberal Government: Critical Analyses of Contemporary Education', *Canadian and International Education* 33, 1: 45–75.

————, John Restakis, and Erroll Sharpe. 1988. 'The Rise and Fall of the Toronto Parent Movement', in Frank Cunningham et al., eds, *Social Movements/Social Change: The Politics and Practice of Organizing*. Toronto: Between the Lines, 209–28.

Dua, Enakshi. 2003. 'Towards Theorising the Connections between Governmentality, Imperialism, Race, and Citizenship: Indian Migrants and Racialisation of Canadian Citizenship', in Deborah Brock, ed., *Making Normal: Social Regulation in Canada*. Scarborough, ON: Thomson, 40–62.

Foucault, Michel. 1972. *The Archaeology of Knowledge and the Discourse on Language*. New York: Pantheon.

————. 1991. 'Governmentality', in Graham Burchell, Colin Gordon, and Peter Miller, eds, *The Foucault Effect: Studies in Governmentality*. Chicago: University of Chicago Press, 87–104.

Fraser, Nancy. 1989. *Unruly Practices: Power, Discourse and Gender in Contemporary Social Theory*. Minneapolis: University of Minnesota Press.

Gidney, Robert D. 2000. *From Hope to Harris: The Reshaping of Ontario Schools*. Toronto: University of Toronto Press.

Gordon, Colin. 1991. 'Governmental Rationality: An Introduction', in Graham Burchell, Colin Gordon, and Peter Miller, eds, *The Foucault Effect: Studies in Governmentality*. Chicago: University of Chicago Press, 1–52.

Henriques, Julian, Wendy Hollway, Cathy Urwin, Couze Venn, and Valerie Walkerdine. 1984. *Changing the Subject: Psychology, Social Regulation and Subjectivity*. London: Methuen.

Hesse, Barnor. 2004. 'Im/plausible Deniability: Racism's Conceptual Double Bind', *Social Identities* 10, 1: 9–29.

Hoskin, Keith. 1979. 'The Examination, Disciplinary Power and Rational Schooling', *History of Education* 8, 2: 135–46.

Hunter, Ian. 1996. 'Assembling the School', in Andrew Barry, Thomas Osborne, and Nikolas Rose, eds, *Foucault and Political Reason: Liberalism, Neo-liberalism and Rationalities of Government*. Chicago: University of Chicago Press, 143–66.

Katz, Michael B., and Paul H. Mattingly, eds. 1975. *Education and Social Change: Themes from Ontario's Past*. New York: New York University Press.

Keating, Christine. 2004. 'Developmental Democracy and Its Inclusions: Globalization and the Transformation of Participation', *Signs* 29, 2 (Winter): 417–37.

Kidder, Annie. 1999. 'How to Be an Advocate: The Margot McGrath Harding Memorial Lecture 1996', People for Education Newsletter, 8 April. Available at: <http://www.peopleforeducation.com/newsletters>. Accessed 10 June 2002.

Knight, Graham. 1998. 'Hegemony, the Media and New Right Politics: Ontario in the Late 1990s', *Critical Sociology* 24, 1–2.

Larner, Wendy. 2000. 'Neo-liberalism: Policy, Ideology, Governmentality', *Studies in Political Economy* 63 (Autumn): 5–25.

Leithwood, Ken, Michael Fullan, and Nancy Watson. 2003. *The Schools We Need: A New Blueprint for Ontario. Final Report*. Toronto: Ontario Institute for Studies in Education, University of Toronto.

Lewis, Gail. 2000. *'Race', Gender, Social Welfare: Encounters in a Postcolonial Society*. Cambridge: Polity Press.

McCaskell, Tim. 2005. *Race to Equity: Disrupting Educational Inequality*. Toronto: Between the Lines.

Makhoul, Anne. 2000. 'People for Education: Reviving Public Debate'. Caledon Institute of Social Policy. *Communities and Schools* April: 1–8.

Ontario Ministry of Education and Training. 1998a. Backgrounder, 'Increased Accountability'. 25 March: 14–23. Available at: <http://www.edu.gov.on.ca>. Accessed 20 July 2001.

———. 1998b. *Update: Education Reform*. Spring/Summer.

———. 1998c. *Update: High Schools*. Spring/Summer: 2.

Passavant, Paul A. 2000. 'The Governmentality of Discussion', in Jodi Dean, ed., *Cultural Studies and Political Theory*. Ithaca: Cornell University Press, 115–31.

People for Education. n.d. 'About Us'. Available at: <http://www.peopleforeducation.com/aboutus>. Accessed 25 November 2007.

———. Annual Reports, 1998–2006. Available by year of publication at: <http://www.people-foreducation.com/newsletter>.

——— . 2003. 'Public Education in Ontario's Cities'. Toronto. September. Available at: <http://www.peopleforeducation.com/reports/urban>. Accessed 17 October 2004.

Popkewitz, Thomas S. 1998. *Struggling for the Soul: The Politics of Schooling and the Construction of the Teacher*. New York: Teachers College Press.

———. 2000. 'Reform and the Social Administration of the Child: Globalization of Knowledge and Power', in Nikolas C. Burbulus and Carlos Alberto Torres, eds, *Globalization and Education*. New York: Routledge, 157–86.

Prentice, Alison L. 1977. *The School Promoters: Education and Social Class in Mid-Nineteenth Century Upper Canada*. Toronto: McClelland and Stewart.

———, and Susan E. Houston. 1975. *Family, School and Society in Ninetenth-Century Canada*. Don Mills, ON: Oxford University Press.

Razack, Sherene. 1998. *Looking White People in the Eye: Gender, Race, and Culture in Courtrooms and Classrooms*. Toronto: University of Toronto Press.

Rose, Nikolas. 1999. *Powers of Freedom: Reframing Political Thought*. Cambridge: Cambridge University Press.

Scheurich, James. 1994. 'Policy Archaeology: A New Policy Studies Methodology', *Journal of Education Policy* 9, 4: 297–316.

Sears, Alan. 2003. *Retooling the Mind Factory: Education in a Lean State*. Aurora, ON: Garamond Press.

Smith, Dorothy, and Allison Griffith. 2004. *Mothering for Schooling*. New York: Routledge.

Vincent, Carol. 2000. *Including Parents? Education, Citizenship and Parental Agency*. Buckingham, UK: Open University Press.

CHAPTER 20

Public Schooling, Public Knowledge, and the Education of Public School Teachers

Don Dippo, Marcela Duran, Jen Gilbert, and Alice Pitt

Those of us who are charged with preparing prospective teachers to inhabit the contradictory space of schooling have a significant responsibility. On the one hand, we must be committed to thinking through the intellectual dilemmas of teaching and learning; on the other hand, if we are to prepare teacher candidates for professional certification we must help them begin to think about how to negotiate the discourses and practices of professionalism that will envelop them before they even begin to teach. The idealization of 'professional knowledge' in schools casts doubt on the value of 'academic knowledge'. The much maligned theory–practice divide is, in this case, a repudiation of how academic work and a university **experience** might contribute to the development of the teaching profession.

And yet, even as schools deride the university for being irrelevant and out of touch with the reality of classrooms, they too have been subject to skepticism. Their own capacity to greet all who enter their doors is open to question. Schools have not always enjoyed mutually collaborative and sustaining relationships with the communities they serve. Schools often accuse the university of being isolated and solipsistic; yet they themselves have tended to operate on the assumptions that (a) the only valuable knowledge is knowledge that can be measured, and (b) such knowledge is available only within schools. They are more likely to think of the community as an obstacle to learning than as a resource or partner for education (Pease-Alvarez and Schecter, 2005). Schools educate communities; they do not, as a rule, learn from them. But neither, of course, do universities. As the historian Thomas Bender (1998) has observed, universities located within cities have not engaged with the surrounding urban culture; instead, they have seen themselves as bulwarks against the corrupting influences of urban life, spaces for thinking unencumbered by the exigencies of social reality. In this chapter we take up these complicated relationships among the university, the school, and the communities in which both live in order to consider how faculties of education might come to think of teacher education as an engagement with communities and the city, and so begin to see the city as a rich resource for learning and, ultimately, teaching.

We begin with Bender and his vision for a **university _of_ the city**. He explores how the university might be affected by the city and come to embody what he calls '**worldliness**'—a desire to give voice to complex and controversial ideas in the public sphere, to recognize that life may not be so easy outside the privileged space of the academy, and to use theory to critique and redress injustice. Can the city instruct the university in the art of living? Can the university offer the city theoretical tools for social justice? How might a different conceptualization of the relations between the university and the city help us understand the conflicts of teacher education? Can teacher education become worldly?

Later in this chapter we will look at the dilemmas of teacher education and its ambivalent relations with the university, schools, and school communities. This ambivalence can be attributed to several factors: the recent transformation of 'normal schools' into university-based faculties of education; the close relationships that faculties of education enjoy (or tolerate) with teachers' professional bodies; the contested status of academic knowledge in schools and communities; and the university's tendency to build walls—real and metaphoric—around its campuses. This section draws on the efforts undertaken by the Faculty of Education at York University to refashion its pre-service program around an explicit commitment to community engagement and to think differently about the intellectual grounds of teacher education. Here we consider the ways epistemological debates about worldliness and pedagogical concerns for reaching out to and being affected by communities can inhabit a faculty of education.

To structure a teacher education program around reaching out to communities, challenge schools to re-think their reliance on discourses of professionalism, and push teacher candidates and schools to see themselves as students _of_ the city are all laudable goals. Nevertheless, in the final section of this chapter readers will be reminded that a serious engagement with the epistemological and pedagogical challenges of worldliness will require us to re-think some sacred concepts in teacher education, including 'experience' and 'learning'. Teacher candidates' initial reflections on their experiences in communities reveal deep-seated beliefs about the nature of 'experience' in education and learning. Teacher candidates arrive at faculties of education speaking a language of 'proto-professionalism', and they are often suspicious of kinds of experiences that don't confirm their preconceptions about how one learns to teach. We are working towards a new kind of teacher education, one that is less concerned with the problem of teaching than with the problem of learning, so that our students' preconceived ideas and concerns become part of our project to centre questions of learning. To our surprise, we have found that the community organizations that have become our partners in this program tend to hold views about 'experience' and 'learning' that are very similar to those of our students. In this way, we encounter some qualities of the engagement between the city and the university not anticipated by Bender. We shall return to this observation towards the end of the chapter.

The Necessity of Worldliness and Public Culture

The case for re-defining the relationships faculties of education, schools, and their neighbouring communities parallels, in many respects, Bender's arguments about the relationship between the university and the city. In 'Scholarship, Local Life, and the Necessity of Worldliness', Bender (1998) begins by expressing his commitment to the idea of a university that is *of* the city, not simply *in* it: that is, a university that is engaged in, not disconnected from, the compelling social, political, economic, and environmental issues of concern to the community. He notes that in the history of the modern university there has always been 'an impulse to withdrawal and an affinity with the purified, safe, and calm life of the suburbs. Both the university and the suburb are privileged locales with the feel of wealth and security of self-containment; and they are characterised by diversity of the most benign sort' (1998: 18). He sees this withdrawal from the affairs of the city, this affection for semi-cloistered heterogeneity, as leading to scholasticism and self-referentiality. To begin to counter this tendency, Bender acknowledges the important contributions made to knowledge production and public debate by intellectuals outside the academy, and argues that 'city knowledge' and 'academic knowledge' both need the counterweight of the other. He writes:

> The university is best at producing abstract, highly focussed, rigorous and internally consistent forms of knowledge, while the city is more likely to produce descriptive, concrete, but also less tightly focussed and more immediately useful knowledge whether this is generated by businessmen (*sic*), journalists, or professional practitioners. The academy risks scholasticism, but the culture of the city is vulnerable to the charge of superficiality and crude pragmatism. (1998: 19)

As an inherently interdisciplinary field, education draws on a range of academic disciplines and employs a variety of methodological approaches to produce what counts as knowledge of, and knowledge in, education—knowledge that conforms to Bender's description of university-based academic knowledge. Parent organizations, advocacy groups, social service agencies, merchants' associations, artists, journalists, and politicians, on the other hand, drawing on different traditions and employing different means, contribute different kinds of knowledge to public discourse and debates and to processes of 'making public culture' (1998: 25).

Part of the reason for inquiring into the interrelatedness of city knowledge and academic knowledge 'is to better devise ways of obtaining their respective virtues' (1998: 19). What Bender finds interesting about these knowledge-generating and knowledge-legitimating institutions—the university and the city—is that 'there is in each a complex ecology of intellectual cultures and social purposes (or interests) that are organized on multiple scales of time and space, with varying degrees of institutional closure and boundary permeability' (ibid.). Within the context of the city, various interests and interest groups, finding academic knowledge inadequate, 'have created institutions that are at once devoted to research and advocacy' (ibid.). Hundreds of these organizations exist in New York City, where Bender teaches (at NYU), and hundreds of similar organizations exist in metropolitan Toronto. In distinguishing the city from suburbia, Bender observes that city life is marked by plurality and diversity of all sorts, which transform traditions, institutions, and even geography, while suburban life may be best known for its relief at having escaped the city.

For our purposes, the historic/geographic distinction between urban and suburban life no longer holds. We want, therefore, to begin to imagine the city as a state of mind. For instance, the Jane–Finch community, which surrounds York University, once lived at the very northern edge of Toronto in a municipality called North York. Neither a real part of the city nor a suburban refuge from it, this community is now home to hundreds of thousands of refugees, new and not-so-new immigrants to Canada, as well as more established Canadians who might once have believed they were living in the suburbs. And yet the Jane–Finch community is urban. Like New York City, this community is home to dozens of organizations—advocacy groups, social service agencies, cultural centres, not-for-profit organizations, voluntary associations—that create programs, conduct research, lobby governments, write for community papers, organize cultural events, appear on community radio, make documentaries, and otherwise advocate for and participate in the making of a vibrant and diverse public culture. In New York City Bender is confident that these groups 'represent a growing influence in our intellectual and cultural life' (1998: 20). The influence of the equivalent groups may not be as strongly felt in the Jane–Finch community, but Bender's reasoning illuminates our context as well. When he looks to the city and sees the influence of non-academic 'public intellectuals' (Said, 1994) and 'organic intellectuals' (Gramsci, 1971), he refers to their rich and vibrant contributions as 'city knowledge'. We have observed that in our own context the boundaries between the city and the suburbs are not so clear, and that we may not be so confident about the degree of intellectual influence on public culture. Moreover, we are acutely aware that, as we turn our sights to the north, east, and west of our campus, a similar blurring of boundaries is under way in most of the communities we work with, even those that have historically been called suburban. For these reasons, what Bender calls 'city knowledge' we prefer to call 'public knowledge'.

Still, following Bender, we in York's Faculty of Education see compelling reasons for looking to the organizations and the 'public' and 'organic' intellectuals who are creating programs and doing research and advocacy work in the Jane–Finch community. Examples of what constitutes an urban-style, community-based, intellectual milieu—one that already exists and could become a complementary partner of the university—would include those 'public' and 'organic' intellectuals who often serve as 'spokespersons' in the media, writers, artists, activists, journalists, organizers, civil servants, health care workers, jurists, and so on; in the context of York University, it would include people who work in and for organizations such as People for Education, the Caring Village, the Jane–Finch Community and Family Centre, PEACH (Promoting Economic Action and Community Health), the Black Creek Community Health Centre, the Upfront Theatre, and Friends In Trouble, among others. Engagement between the university and the city, between academics and public/organic intellectuals, between the Faculty and community organizations, would create a ferment of contested but useful knowledge that could enhance and enliven public discourse about local, national, and global issues and their relationship to teaching and learning in schools. In such a lively context, Bender writes, 'Truth making becomes more participatory and dialogic' (1998: 21).

Referring to those community settings where knowledge and interest are mobilized in advocacy work, Bender writes:

> In these alternative settings the very process of making knowledge is coterminous with the diffusion of knowledge, thus dissolving the old categorical distinction between production and popularisation. Bringing production and use of knowledge into closer relation may actually increase sensitivity to the broader implications of particular knowledges. The humanities once claimed this domain, the realm of values and ethics. But as they become more self-referential in their accelerating professionalization, they cannot speak to the ethical issues of our quotidian existence. (ibid.)

As universities and traditional academic disciplines, including education, have turned away from the local, the particular, and the everyday, communities have been developing their own sources of 'really useful knowledge' (Cohen, 1990). Although this does not necessarily signal the end of disciplinary and professional knowledge, it does suggest a need for academic revitalization. One way of filling that need might be to reconsider the relation between academic knowledge and public knowledge and the relation of the university to the organizations where public knowledge is produced. 'The challenge facing advanced thought and contemporary theory in the human sciences', as Edward Said observed, 'is to bridge the gap between the academy and the conditions (and politics) of everyday life' (Said, 1983: 147, cited in Bender, 1988: 21). The way forward, according to Bender, 'is to work toward a pattern of partially localised and purposive academic knowledge that is honed in the world of power and complexity that is the metropolitan environment' (ibid.). He urges contemporary academics not to work so hard at keeping the life of the city at bay, for 'it is a source of energy, of wonderfully complex intellectual problems, and of non-academic intellectuals who have much to offer' (1998: 22). Part of our challenge then, in faculties of education, is to think about how we might use this 'public knowledge' to energize our thinking and find ways, through our research, projects, and programs, for it to energize schools' relations with neighbouring communities as well. Responding to this challenge has meant, in part, re-imagining our teacher education programs. In the next section we will review changes made to one program and discuss how our thinking about 'public knowledge' has found its way into our pedagogical structures.

Encounters with Public Knowledge

Serious thinking about the place of community in our teacher education programs began in the mid-1990s with our adoption of the Report of the Academic Framework Committee as a planning document. The purpose of the 'Academic Framework' (Britzman et al., 1995) was to help us think about our own pre-service programs in relation to the field of teacher education, our university context, and the large urban and suburban communities that constitute our fields of practice. Our mandate is conceptually broad and asks us to think about how pedagogical structures might emerge from our theoretical, intellectual, and social commitments:

> An academic framework supports a common conceptualization of the work that we do, a conceptualization of knowledge, social relations, structures, desirable practices, intellectual frames, and questions. It is an occasion for engaging critically with our present and our future. Centrally, an academic framework is also a language for expanding, thinking, interpreting, and articulating the underlying reasons and purposes for our work. As a language, an academic framework is also an attempt to envision a culture of teacher education capable of change, flexibility, and relevancy to diverse populations. (Britzman et al., 1995: 1)

In addition to calling for serious intellectual engagement with the dilemmas and possibilities of both education and the education of teachers, the framework identifies several qualities of 'professional discourse' that have come to inhabit the language, imagination, and practices of the teaching profession, making the latter susceptible to fantasies of scientific legitimation. Bender criticized the university itself for being disconnected from the city, but for our Faculty the problem was somewhat different: we needed to address the disconnection of compulsory schooling from both the university and the city. In our efforts to re-orient ourselves and discover a worldliness *within* teacher education, we shifted our focus from the pragmatic question of how we teach others to teach (others) to the more philosophical question of how people learn. This was a deliberate intervention into the training model, inherited from the normal schools, that prevails in most, if not all, pre-service teacher education programs and continues to dominate the profession's various articulations of what is required to become a teacher. Our conceptual and practical shift requires us to be attentive to everyone's learning, to the ways in which learning might affect institutions and communities, and to the possibility not only that significant learning may occur outside school, but that it may even interrupt school learning. In addition to thinking about the range of theories, debates, and pedagogical commitments our students should encounter, the academic framework expands our notion of the practicum so that it becomes a three-part experience involving classrooms, whole schools, and—significantly for this discussion—neighbouring communities.

The academic framework is organized around four motifs: 'Professional Curiosity', 'Communities and Cultures', 'Knowledge and Learning', and 'Teaching Practices and Interpretive Frames of Knowledge'. An elaboration of the thinking behind community-based practicum is found in the section entitled 'Communities and Cultures', in which the question of 'how communities are made' (24) is central. Among other things, **community-based practicum** experiences ought to help students develop 'an awareness of the range of cultures within a school and its geographical areas'; a deeper knowledge and understanding of 'a child's, adolescent's, or adult's everyday life in a community'; and a sensitivity 'to cultural and community perspectives in terms of history and present preoccupations' (ibid.). Part of this imperative is addressed in the required course 'Inquiries into Learning'. Designed to encourage students to explore the range of things that qualify as 'learning' both inside and outside the classroom, this course covers a variety of learning situations—everyday problem solving (how to work an ATM), technical training (how to drive a car), learning from trauma (dealing with a death in the family)—that can arise anywhere: in private, in public, or at work, as well as in non-formal (driving school), informal (standing in line), and formal (school) learning environments.

Another part of the community practicum imperative is addressed in the required 'Inquiries into Schooling' course. Some aspects of this course are designed to provoke the question, 'What, within the broad range of events and activities that can be understood as "knowing" and "learning" in the world, qualifies as "knowing" and "learning" in schools?' Observing and reflecting on experience in formal school settings (both inside and outside the publicly funded systems) helps students develop an appreciation and analysis of what counts as knowledge and learning in schools, from the narrowly focused sets of assumptions that underpin curriculum and pedagogy in many back-to-basics and denominational schools to the open-ended (sometimes presumptuous) assumptions that underpin practice in many elite and alternative schools.

The practicum itself consists of short-term field work in the community. Students are placed for 50 hours in a community organization. The range of 'community sites' is broad—Early Years Centres, Children's Aid Societies, programs run by local public libraries, immigrant–refugee reception centres, concerned citizens organizations, university–community projects, small bookstores doing neighbourhood outreach, theatre, arts, and environmental programs, homeless youth shelters, mental health clinics, community gardens—offering many possible understandings of learning, participation, and advocacy. The experiences and work the students engage in are negotiated with the organizations, in consultation with the Faculty. Students keep a journal, produce a culminating reflection paper, and also discuss the work they do for the organization with their peers in class conversations and through online conferencing.

The point of this more intensive community experience is to put our students into contact with non-academic public/organic intellectuals working in community organizations to talk broadly about teaching and learning, theory and knowledge, equity and social justice, and to consider what thoughtful people outside of the field of education might imagine are the appropriate aims and purposes of schooling in relation to community life. Thus the community practicum has less to do with specific activities than with the knowledge, commitments, and understandings of those who initiate, organize, coordinate, and work in such programs. (This helps to explain why community placements must be organized around a set of specific topics, questions, and concerns, and supported by a seminar in which students are expected to think deeply about their community experiences.) The point is for our teacher candidates to learn how to listen, to make sense of local community knowledge, to engage with people outside education, and to contribute to public discussion and debate—abilities that they could not develop within the self-referential (and 'professional') confines of the school or the university. Hence the value of community placements: they provide a sustained engagement with public, organic intellectuals outside the field of education regarding public knowledge and public discourse about teaching, learning, and the fundamental aims and purposes of education. Through such encounters and engagements our students will learn how to become advocates both for children and for schools; they will also learn how and why it is important to participate more effectively in public discourse around issues such as hunger, homelessness, poverty, violence, and AIDS—to name only a few—and what Kozol (1991) has described as the 'Savage Inequalities' that characterize life in many North American cities.

On Bringing Experience into Discourse

The community placement reflects a longer-term commitment on the part of the Faculty to change the nature of its relationships with parent groups, social service agencies, and other community organizations by shifting the emphasis from 'studying' to 'participating' in community. The community placement serves as a touchstone for teacher candidates' entry into their professional education. The required companion courses, 'Inquiries into Learning' and 'Inquiries into Schooling', and a 24-hour practicum seminar open up conceptions of what it means 'to know' and what it means 'to learn', in the hope of preparing students to move from 'observations of' to 'encounters with' communities. The extent to which this shift has been achieved becomes apparent in classroom talk and course assignments. We have learned that it requires much deeper and more complicated notions of experience and understandings of how people learn from experience than our students typically hold. In developing the courses and placement seminars we worked with the following description of experience:

> For experience to be seen as meaningful, purposeful and hence as a basis from which knowledge is made and rethought and for experience to become the grounds to provoke ethical and pedagogically justifiable actions, experience must be socially articulated, argued over, and conceptually engaged. Experience must be brought into discourse. What can matter most in teacher education is the language of experience: how an event, condition, concept, interaction, worry, or learning becomes narrated, rethought, and an occasion for learning. (Britzman et al., 1995: 6)

This conception of learning from experience troubles the assumption that experience makes knowledge—an assumption fundamental to teacher education and the popular literature on 'service learning'. If 'experience must be brought into discourse', then community placements are only as educative as the pedagogical structures, discussions, literatures, and conflicts brought to bear on them. The meanings of the placement experience are not transparent to either the students or the course directors. Something must be actively made of those experiences if they are to become pedagogically meaningful.

We are reminded of the importance of bringing experience into discourse when reading interviews with teacher candidates who had completed the first year of our new program. Most students thought highly of their instructors, but many were mystified by their classroom activities and/or their placement projects. Their comments suggest that introducing new occasions for thinking about how people learn is not enough, and that we need to do more to help teacher candidates use their experiences for their own growth and development. For instance, students seemed willing to embrace community placements that had 'direct' connections to classroom teaching: tutoring programs, ESL programs, and literacy programs for children were deemed relevant because they were understood as 'practice teaching' in a community setting. By contrast, placements that were not so clearly related to the classroom required that students make them relevant by finding connections between their experiences and their implicit theories of teaching and learning. Students come into teacher education with a deeply ingrained idea of what teaching is; they are already overfamiliar with schools, and they are reluctant to accept the place of the beginner. One question that is frequently asked—'What does this have to do with teaching?'—betrays both a narrow, mechanistic notion of education and a certain anxiety about interpretation. Yet students are required to approach the placement without any preconceived idea of what it will (or should) mean for their teacher education. One student described a 'good placement' as 'one where you interact with people. Not working with 60-year-olds.' According to another, 'the first half of the year was really successful and good but the second half has been really tedious. I don't see the point anymore. We're not learning about a community that way.' Observations like these suggest a utilitarian view in which the function of the placement is to accumulate an experience, to learn 'about a community'—once the 'lesson' has been extracted from it, the experience itself becomes meaningless.

To respond effectively to complaints about placements, we need a theory of experience that moves beyond the simple equation of experience with knowledge. First, we need to furnish students with the conceptual tools to make relevance from their experience. This is one of the university's contributions to thinking about the city. What questions, ideas, debates, theories, and controversies might students bring to their experience that would render it pedagogical? How many ways can we connect *this* with *that*? What happens to the experience of the community placement when it is 'brought into discourse', when it is subject to scholarly debates on the nature of community? Crucially, in this encounter between the event of the placement and the experience of interpretation, where does learning take place?

Second, we need to recognize that the learning 'outcomes' of the community placements are inevitably delayed, out of sync with the placement experiences. Students do have an implicit sense that learning takes time. As one said, 'It was a rough start to the year and I know a lot of people who really haven't been satisfied with it. It's probably fifty/fifty (happy/unhappy) which is probably not good. At the beginning of the year probably twenty per cent were happy but it's evening out a bit more now.' In this assessment, the student seems to recognize that the value of the experience cannot be ascertained in advance, and that one's own experience of the placement shifts over time. We must assume, as well, that the meaning of each student's experience will shift again when it is brought into conversation with more traditional practice teaching. It may be that the experience of the placement will be remade over and over again throughout the student's teacher education and into her career.

This view of experience as made through interpretation conflicts with some myths of the teacher, identified by Britzman (2003)—myths that students absorb and defend even before they begin their teacher education. The first myth that must be dismantled if the community placements are to become educative is that teachers are self-made. This myth, according to Britzman, 'serves contradictory functions, for it supports the conflicting views that teachers form themselves and are "born" into the profession' (2003: 230). In effect, it dismisses teacher education as irrelevant before it has even begun: in this view, the structures that we create to support the development of beginning teachers can speak only to whatever innate aptitudes the student already has. Experience, therefore, is merely a commodity to be accumulated on the way to being certified as a real teacher. There is no possibility of considering how a teacher education program might change the way the student imagines the work of teaching and learning.

This anticipates the second myth that Britzman identifies: the myth that experience makes the teacher. If teachers make themselves as they accumulate experience, any experience that cannot be rendered immediately intelligible and transparent can only be discarded as inappropriate, irrelevant, and inauthentic. This dynamic explains why the students, in reflecting on their first year, described their placements in terms of 'good' or 'bad' experiences. This language of judgment cannot address the qualities of experience that are perhaps neither good nor bad, but interesting. The idea that interest must be made comes as an insult to students who regard the meanings of experience as obvious. For this reason, even though the placement is supported by pedagogical structures designed to create a space where unintelligible experiences can be brought into significance, we must also give students time to move past the initial phase of good/bad judgments and make something more interesting out of their experiences.

Bender argues that the university, to be worldly, must become an 'essential site for democratic debate and deliberation' (1998: 26). In our view, what he is calling for is the creation of spaces for students to think about their experiences in and of the city. If we are to support teacher candidates in their cultivation of worldliness, we need to do more than facilitate the accumulation of experiences: we need to help bring those experiences into discourse and make 'debate and deliberation' central to the work of teaching and learning—both our own and our students'.

Today, in the third year of this initiative, we have come to realize that our students are not the only ones who struggle on their way to making knowledge from experience. Many of the instructors who embarked on the new program with hope and enthusiasm also found their own understandings of experience, learning, and the relations between the two unsettled by the students' complaints and difficulties. Conversation, debate, and study have helped all of us to become more articulate about our theoretical commitments, to hone these commitments in our work with students, and to revise many of our contradictory habits of thought. Discussions have extended as well into our work with the community organizations that host the community placements. We had not anticipated that representatives of these organizations, armed with the alternative public knowledge that we were seeking to encounter, could also be influenced by the kinds of myths about learning and experience described above. For example, during one debriefing discussion, an animated exchange focused on a small number of students who did not seem to take seriously the requirements of the placement, and several community participants wondered if this problem could be alleviated by changing the Pass/Fail evaluation to a letter grade. Others, however, were quick to point out that such a solution would merely mimic familiar forms of school authority; they thought we would be better off ensuring that the placements were well-designed and that there were many opportunities to discuss with students why they were doing what they were doing.

When the University Meets the Community . . .

Most students expect their community placement experiences to be transparently related to teaching—only to find that instead of learning to teach, they are asked to consider the work of learning. What follows are extracts from the placement journals of two students who were initially concerned that they were not getting the 'teaching practice' they had expected. Our first example comes from a student assigned to the Office of the Education Advocate at the Catholic Children's Aid Society (CCAS), which does research and advocacy related to schooling for children who are wards of CCAS. Teacher candidates helped with the research and discussed their findings both with CCAS staff and among themselves. A student in the second year of the program reflects in her journal:

> I noticed in the research we were doing how much [the CCAS wards] generally seemed to struggle in school. While there were a few individuals who did very well in school a vast majority of the youth in care were just getting by. In order to get a better understanding of why this tends to be a problem I again discussed it with my supervisor and the youth worker. My supervisor theorized that a lot of the problems come from a lack of direction in these children's lives and the youth worker added that it is very difficult for these youth to think about school when they have much deeper issues to deal with. I also decided to discuss the issue with the other teacher candidates. We all looked at our lives to try and understand what set us apart from others and allowed us to get as far as we have today. . . I sat in with the youth worker while he met with a few of the youth. After hearing their stories I was increasingly moved by their spirit and sincerity. All of the youth I met had part time jobs and all of them were struggling in school. . . . When I asked them what they like and do not like about school they all seemed to give me similar responses. All the youth liked teachers who were strict but fair and that were willing to help them and listen to them. They confided that they were not regular kids and they need a teacher that is willing to listen to their problems. This was good to hear because I had always worried that such efforts go unnoticed, but the youth reassured me that these efforts are necessary. As for what they didn't like, they didn't like unfair teachers and they didn't like when a teacher acted as though they are always right. For these kids humanity and some authority is what they wanted from their teachers, not just instruction.

Our second example comes from a student assigned to a long-established NGO that provides support and information services to immigrant and refugee families in the Jane–Finch community. Teacher candidates were asked to help prepare and deliver information packages and a presentation for newcomers about the school system. This assignment required much negotiation and dialogue with their supervisor, a woman with much experience welcoming newcomers. In this journal entry, the student reflects on a discussion about teaching and teachers:

> My supervisor suggested that knowledge of people's backgrounds is the key to understanding them. Teachers need to become familiar with how to convey information across cultures. It is critical for teachers to keep communication open with the parents, they need to involve the parents by asking them questions . . . teachers should not leave it up to the children to explain things to the parents, instead, they need to engage the parents to participate so they do not feel useless. As adults, teachers should put themselves at the same level as other adults and share information as opposed to talking down to the parents. [. . .] It is only when one makes an effort to learn about their community as well as other communities and cultures that assumptions and stereotypes are replaced by awareness and a better understanding.

In both cases, the students' reflections developed out of conversations with supervisors and others at the placements. It has been interesting to see how often the placement experience has helped students see where their notions about teaching were mistaken. Encounters with 'public knowledge' enrich students' understanding and push them to focus on the problem of their own learning. In particular, students need to see how their own experiences, rather than being a source of knowledge, can prevent them from seeing other realities. Moving outside the university into the city opens students to alternative realities. Although the program focuses on helping students learn about the communities they are working in, the state of mind that the city represents gives them the conceptual framework to consider how we go about learning from our encounters with otherness.

Notes from Borders: Concluding Remarks

Early on in this chapter, we wondered if teacher education could become worldly. The characteristics of worldliness that Bender associates with both universities and cities are 'secularity, tolerance, specialization, concentration, diversity' (1998: 18). As we consider the constraints on the worldly potential of teacher education—constraints originating in a normal school tradition more conducive to self-referential professionalism than intellectual and political worldliness—we return to Bender, who 'worries . . . that the university may increasingly have qualities in common with the suburbs. There may even be a trend towards making the university more like the suburbs than like the city, or even a part of the city' (ibid.). This concern may be well-founded, and the presence of professional programs, such as teacher education, in the university might even be hastening such a development. Our initial goal in forming new kinds of relationships with community organizations was to address concerns that teacher education and schools were increasingly isolated from and irrelevant to their communities. Bender invites us to turn our attention also towards our university and to insist on the contributions that city or public knowledge can make to the generation of 'useful' academic knowledge.

At the same time, Bender sees in the university a significant investment in globalization. This investment suggests to him, on the one hand, a departure from the nineteenth-century association of the university with the nation and, on the other hand, a sign that the university still has more in common with the city, as a swirling, multicultural, and pluralist metropolis connected in network fashion to other metropolitan centres, than it has with the suburbs. The fruitful potential for mutual influence lies in what universities have to gain from throwing their lot in with cities:

> To talk about new cultures built from the materials brought by immigrants and from previously suppressed groups is very threatening in the context of national identities. Yet if we think of cities, of metropolises, instead of nations, as the key units of society and culture, the prospect of diversity is less threatening. Cities have always had this quality, and they have always continually redefined their culture through the work of inclusion. They have always been more successful at this work than have nations. Nations are falsely thought to be unitary and homogeneous, but cities have always been understood to be diverse, local, having their own distinctive mixes. (1998: 27)

If urban schools, by virtue of existing in this new global culture, are to become worldly, they too have to find ways to think of themselves more as *of* the city and less as a microcosm of the nation. There are two things to consider here. First, if faculties of education, schools, and communities work at forging the kinds of relationships that Bender advocates, they will generate new knowledge, which in turn will support a more inclusive, humane, and vibrant social life that put us all in a better position to address the social reality of the new urban spaces where the suburbs used to be. Faculties of education, like the university, may need to resist what Bender calls 'suburbanization', but this resistance may most provocatively and productively take its cue from the social reality of the city, even if the city is not actually on the faculty's doorstep. Second, the fact that the city represents the social life of the future for more and more of the planet requires that we reconsider what we mean by and want from what has become known as urban education.

Without diminishing urban education's commitment to the most vulnerable populations within cities, Bender's vision of productive encounters between city and university knowledge may require new metaphors and a more creative understanding of public culture. As a product of the evisceration of cities in the United States, urban education may not be able to grasp the intricacies of life in and of the metropolitan city. In Canada we do not have many cities, and certainly not many that could be considered great metropolises. What we do have are cities, small and large, that have never been truly segregated (though they have certainly had their demarcations) and cities across the country with relatively long histories of immigration, bringing together earlier and more recent arrivals. There is no need to romanticize the city as a place. However, if we do not find the knowledge we need in the culture, conversations, and art forms of the people who live in the city, we will never be able to locate, let alone elaborate on, its unruly resources.

So far this conclusion has focused on what we have learned from Bender as we think about our work in teacher education. We now turn to what we believe we might contribute to discussions about encounters between the city and the university. Our own focus on learning and experience has helped us to recognize something that we already understood conceptually. This has to do with what happens when individuals bearing knowledge encounter each other. It is never enough to imagine that one kind of knowledge will simply refine, revise, or refute another, since we can never be sure what people will make of their experience. This is something that the field of educational studies might contribute to the life of the university as well as the life of the city, as it makes its own way towards both.

Glossary

community-based practicum: Sustained participation in a community organization where students might shift from observing communities to becoming engaged with and participating in the communities that schools serve.

experience: Experience in education is not simply accumulated, transparently meaningful, or easily translated into knowledge. Experience must 'be brought into discourse' (Britzman, et al., 1996: 6). That is, its meanings are belated; it must be narrated, argued over, and made into knowledge.

university of the city: A university that opens itself up to both 'city knowledge' and 'academic knowledge' and is engaged in, not disconnected from, the compelling social, political, economic, and environmental issues of the community.

worldliness: An engagement with 'democratic debate and deliberation' (Bender, 1998: 26); an opening up onto the conflicts and pleasures of living with others.

Study Questions

1. What questions, ideas, debates, theories, and controversies might we bring to our experience in order to render it pedagogical? In how many ways can we connect *this* with *that*?
2. As discussed in this chapter, worldliness is a demand to give voice to complex and controversial ideas in the public sphere, to recognize human injury beyond the privileged space of the academy, and to use theory as a form of criticism to redress injustice. Can the city instruct the university in the art of worldliness, and can the university offer the city theoretical tools for social justice?
3. How might a different conceptualization of the relation between the university and the city help us understand the conflicts of teacher education? Can teacher education become worldly?
4. What happens when experience with and in communities is 'brought into discourse'—that is, when it is subject to a range of scholarly debates on the nature of community?
5. What happens to learning when encounters with and in communities meet interpretation?

Recommended Reading

Anyon, Jean. 2005. *Radical Possibilities: Public Policy, Urban Education, and a New Social Movement*. New York and London: Routledge.

Bender, T. 1998. 'Scholarship, Local Life, and the Necessity of Worldliness', in H. van der Wusten, ed., *The Urban University and Its Identity: Roots, Locations, Roles*. Boston: Kluwer Academic Publishers.

Canadian Centre for Policy Alternatives-MB. 2006. Inner-City Voices Community-Based Solutions: State of the Inner-City report: 2006. Winnipeg, MB.

Cohen, P. 1990. *Really Useful Knowledge*. Stoke-on-Trent: Trentham Books.

Warren, Mark. 'Communities and Schools: A New View of Urban Education Reform', *Harvard Education Review* 75, 2. Available at: <www.edreview.org/harvard05/2005/su05/s05warren.htm>.

Recommended Websites

The Simon Fraser University Community Education Program: www.sfu.ca/cstudies/community

Canadian Centre for Policy Alternatives/Centre canadien de politiques alternatives: http://www.policyalternatives.ca

Winnipeg Inner-City Research Alliance (WIRA): www.usaskstudies.coop/socialeconomy/WIRA_main

Center for Community Partnerships at the University of Pennsylvania: http://www.upenn.edu/ccp/index.php

Grow Your Own Teachers, Illinois: http://www.growyourownteachers.org/

References

Bender, T. 1998. 'Scholarship, Local Life, and the Necessity of Worldliness', in H. Van Der Wusten, ed, *The Urban University and Its Identity: Roots, Locations, Roles*. Boston: Kluwer Academic Publishers.

Britzman, D. 2003. *Practice Makes Practice: A Critical Study of Learning to Teach*. Albany: State University of New York Press.

———, D. Dippo, D. Searle, and A. Pitt. 1996. 'Toward an Academic Framework for Thinking about Teacher Education', *Teaching Education* 9, 1: 15–26.

Cohen, P. 1990. *Really Useful Knowledge*. Stoke-on-Trent: Trentham Books.

Gramsci, A. 1971. *Selections from the Prison Notebooks*, trans. and eds Q. Hoare and G. Nowell-Smith. New York: International Publishers.

Kozol, J. 1991. *Savage Inequalities*. New York: Harper and Row.

Pease-Alvarez, L., and S. Schecter, eds. 2005. *Learning, Teaching and Community: Contributions of Situated and Participatory Approaches to Educational Innovation*. Mahwah, NJ: Lawrence Erlbaum.

Said, E. 1983. 'Opponents, Audiences, Constituencies, and Community', in H. Foster, ed., *The Anti-Aesthetic: Essays on Post-Modern Culture*. Port Townsend, WA: Bay Press.

———. 1994. *Representations of the Intellectual: The 1993 Reith Lectures*. New York: Pantheon Books.

CHAPTER 21

The Privatization of Higher Education in Canada

Claire Polster

With the possible exception of health care, there are few things that Canadians value more than public education. Our education system has traditionally been quite successful at simultaneously helping students to develop their individual personalities and potential, prepare to make a living, and become thoughtful citizens who will help shape their society, and it has performed these functions with an impressive degree of efficiency and equity (Robertson, 2005: 6). While Canadians' commitment to education remains at historically high levels (Livingstone and Hart, 2005), the nature of our public system has been quietly, gradually changing in recent years. Rather than being publicly supported for public purposes, it is becoming privatized, both in the sense that it is increasingly seen as an individual rather than a social responsibility and in the sense that it is increasingly shaped by and oriented to market values and practices rather than public or collective ones.

This **privatization** of Canadian education is visible at all levels of the system. It is reflected in the frequent knocks on our doors by youngsters selling chocolates or collecting bottles to help purchase not just the 'extras' but, increasingly, the basics that their schools cannot afford because of cuts in public funding. It is manifested in the ubiquitous advertising on school walls, bathroom stalls, and vending machines, and in the various arrangements (such as Wal-Mart's adopt-a-school and Campbell's labels programs) between cash-strapped schools and wealthy corporations seeking invaluable publicity and opportunities to 'grow' their customer bases. Privatization is also evident in our schools' adoption of a growing number of private-sector principles and practices such as the contracting out of various services and the growing use of standardized performance measures (Froese-Germain et al., 2006). It is at the level of the university, however, that the privatization process is most clear and advanced. As numerous analysts have observed, a university education in Canada is increasingly regarded and treated as a private rather than a public good, much less a citizenship right (Turk,

2000b). As well, our universities are increasingly seeing themselves, and operating, as businesses in the research, teaching, and other work that they do.

This chapter focuses on the nature and implications of the ongoing privatization of Canada's universities. It does this to highlight some of the main ways in which public education in our country is being transformed and to address what this means for our citizens and our nation. My main argument is that we can and should resist the privatization of our universities in particular and of our public education system more generally. For although this process may provide some benefits to some individuals and corporations, it does not serve the majority interest and may undermine even the interests of its advocates.

The Privatization of Canadian Higher Education

Before proceeding, I want to address the term 'privatization' and how I approach it in this chapter. In its simplest form, 'privatization' refers to the process through which a resource or service is moved out of the public or collective sphere and into the private sphere, generally through sale. In the 1980s and 1990s, for example, the federal and provincial governments of Canada privatized many firms that had been owned and operated by the state (including Teleglobe Canada, Air Canada, Petro-Canada, the Potash Corporation of Saskatchewan, and BC Ferries), selling them to private interests, sometimes at rock-bottom prices (Padova, 2005). In the case of Canadian education in general and higher education more particularly, however, privatization is not so straightforward. Here privatization is not a matter of outright sale to private corporations; rather, a more complex relationship is developing in which our universities are increasingly influenced by and oriented towards the needs of the private sector (and some wealthy individuals), while still being funded largely by the public purse.[1] In other words, the university itself is not being sold, but the uses and benefits of its resources are being ceded to private interests at the public's expense, both literal and figurative.

I also use the term 'privatization' to call attention to a second development in Canadian universities that stems from and contributes to the one discussed above. This is the cultivation and normalization within Canadian universities of an individualistic, self-serving ethic rather than a collective, public one. As our universities become more market-driven, those who work and learn within them are encouraged and/or compelled to place their private interests over and above collective interests, including those of their peers, their academic departments or faculties, and even the broader community that the university is charged to serve.

Together, these two general trends are changing what Canadian universities do and what they fundamentally are. Once public-serving institutions that met a wide variety of social needs in a plurality of ways, our universities are becoming private-serving institutions in which people are increasingly oriented towards their own needs and interests and those of well-resourced organizations and individuals. This transformation jeopardizes the value—real and perceived—of Canada's institutions of higher learning. It also poses significant threats to the well-being of many, if not all, Canadians, both now and in the future.

Two additional points regarding this chapter's approach to privatization are worth noting. First, as it is not possible to provide a complete account of how our universities are being turned from public-serving into private-serving institutions, the following discussion focuses only on selected aspects of this transformation occurring within three areas or functions of the university, namely academic research, governance, and teaching.

Second, the primary analytic tool I use to track the transformation of Canadian higher education is that of social relations. These are the ongoing courses of human activity through which people produce a given feature of the social world—in this case, the university—in its particular shape or form (Campbell and Gregor, 2002; Smith, 1987). In this analysis, I explore how the social relations of Canadian higher education are being reorganized or reconfigured so that the university changes from a publicly oriented institution into an institution that increasingly works for, with, and as a business, and so that those within the institution become more attuned to private than to public interests. One way of conceptualizing this analysis is as tracking the reconstruction of the various pathways through which key players in higher education (including university administrators, academics, students, and the broader community outside the university) are brought into contact with one another. As old pathways are dismantled and key players are brought together (or kept apart) for new purposes and/or in new ways, both their own roles and the role of the university itself begin to shift in a new direction.

University Research

A useful entry point into the ongoing privatization of Canada's universities is through the transformation of their knowledge production or research function. Before the 1980s there was relatively little research collaboration between Canadian academics and members of the private sector. Although some academics did some research and other work (such as consulting) for corporations, such alliances were few in number and kind, and were held in relatively low regard (Naimark, 2004: 54–5). For the most part, university research was conducted by academics with academics in response to emerging problems within their fields and in the service of the broader community. Instances of privatization and **commercialization** of university research (i.e., its conversion into intellectual property and exploitation for profit) were rare. Rather, research results tended to be widely disseminated and/or freely shared both within the academic community and beyond it (Tudiver, 1999: 11).

Since the 1980s, in response to factors including government cuts in university operating budgets and concerns about Canada's global competitiveness, research alliances between academics and the private sector have been strongly promoted, supported, and rewarded. As a result, such alliances (small-scale research contracts, collaborative research centres and networks, technology transfer offices, innovation parks, etc.) are now widespread on all Canadian university campuses. While these alliances are quite varied, they generally involve corporate partners footing a portion of the bill for some academic research. In exchange, partners may shape the topic of the research and some of the conditions under which it proceeds; they may also acquire intellectual property rights to some or all of the research results.

Collectively and cumulatively, these research partnerships help transform our universities from public- into private-serving institutions. First, they alter both the process through which research decisions are made and the kinds of research that are done within the university. As opposed to being shaped by the professional judgements and choices of autonomous academics, research decisions are increasingly made by well-resourced parties external to the university. Furthermore, these research projects are designed to serve corporate partners' particular interests—which may or may not also serve, and may even conflict with, the collective good (such as when technological innovations cause job loss or environmental harm). In addition to allowing corporate sponsors to command disproportionate shares of academics' time, energies, and talents in the short term (and at a fraction of their real costs), such alliances help skew the general scientific research agenda toward industry needs and interests in the long term. Because the research needs of other social groups are neglected in favour of those of paying clients, academics' capacities and willingness to meet the needs of the former may decline and/or fail to get passed on to the next generation of Canadian researchers. This is already happening in fields like biology, where the shift toward molecular biology is eroding other approaches, such as organismic biology, which can offer citizens less costly and more environmentally friendly solutions to various problems such as pest control (Press and Washburn, 2000: 50).

As well as changing the kinds of research that our universities do, alliances with industry are transforming how academic research is done. Whereas university research has traditionally been an open, collaborative, and collective activity, corporate partnerships are helping to convert it into a more closed and competitive, business-like affair. For example, academics working with or for industry partners are routinely obliged to sign secrecy agreements that prohibit them from discussing, much less sharing, their research with colleagues until, and sometimes even after, intellectual property rights have been secured. Academics involved in corporate partnerships may also be compelled to work within very short time lines and with an eye to profitability, and may no longer be free to pursue all promising research avenues that emerge. These market-driven norms and practices may, in turn, spill over into the broader academic enterprise, further eroding the collective nature of academic science (colleagues who are not working for industry may keep research results secret as a defensive measure, for example) and the many social benefits that flow from it (including less costly, more efficient, and higher-quality knowledge production) (Atkinson-Grosjean, 2006: 23–8).

Finally, research alliances with business transform the ways in which and conditions under which academic research is accessed and used. Instead of being a public good that is freely shared, the research produced in these alliances is increasingly becoming the private property of research partners. If and when research results are made available to other academics or members of the public, it is more frequently through some kind of commercial transaction (e.g., direct purchase, or payment of a licensing fee). The privatization of academic research thus renders it far less accessible to most academics and citizens, who must now pay for previously free knowledge, often at the very high prices that stem from monopoly conditions. This form of privatization also helps to promote another, by transforming university administrators' and academics' perceptions of their interests and the ways in which they respond to them.

In recent years, spurred on by federal and provincial governments as well as their growing entrepreneurial expertise, university administrators have realized that they need not limit themselves to serving the research needs of paying clients, but may also exploit the fruits of academic research on their own. As a result, they have pursued a range of entrepreneurial activities based on faculty members' research: establishing commercial development offices, selling ringside seats to leading edge research, setting up spin-off companies, licensing valuable intellectual property, and so on. Such initiatives are not small-scale ventures that are peripheral to universities, but complex undertakings that are consuming more and more of their money, effort, time, and other resources (Read, 2003). Administrators' growing involvement in entrepreneurial activities further entrenches private-sector values and practices within our public universities. It also leads universities to prioritize their own interests over those of the general public. Indeed, one might argue that it is producing a reversal in the relationship between our universities and the broader community, for instead of using public funds for public purposes, our universities are using those funds to finance private ventures aimed at enriching themselves.

The university's greater involvement in entrepreneurial activities also transforms individual academics' interests and either entices or compels them to prioritize those new interests. For example, as universities currently share the spoils of business initiatives with those researchers who produce profitable knowledge, some academics have unprecedented opportunity to become rich from their research. This gives them greater incentive to pursue lucrative research questions and areas which are not always the most scientifically valuable or socially useful ones. A classic example is medical researchers' growing attention to the minor but profitable 'lifestyle' concerns of wealthy people, such as erectile dysfunction, and their marked inattention to widespread and serious diseases of the poor, such as malaria and tuberculosis (Mahood, 2005). The growing importance of corporate partnerships and commercialization to universities is leading administrators to reward academics involved in these activities in various ways, both formal (through the tenure and promotion process, for instance) and informal (by according them greater institutional prestige and influence). This too encourages faculty to become involved in privately oriented research activities instead of more publicly oriented ones. It is worth noting that those academics who refrain from allying themselves with private partners or privatizing their research must not only forgo those benefits but may thereby compromise their position within the university. It is also not uncommon for faculty who criticize the university's entrepreneurialism as a conflict of interest or betrayal of its public service mission to face various forms of sanction within the institution, ranging from mild disapproval to harassment and even job loss (see, for example, CAUT, 2003b). Thus, in supporting the public's interest, academics may end up jeopardizing their private interests. This makes it progressively more difficult to sustain a public-service ethic.

University Governance

In the post–Second World War period, universities were run as collegial and democratic institutions (sometimes more in theory than in practice). At all levels, academic decisions were made collectively, by professors, through established collegial structures and processes, such as those of academic senates and faculty councils. While administrators, who were relatively few in number, had substantial power in the institution, they tended to see themselves and to behave as leaders of the collegium, whose job was to support academics' work and to protect the university's autonomy from undue outside influence. Particularly in response to their activism in the 1960s, students were afforded considerable opportunity to participate meaningfully in academic affairs. As well, the university's relatively autonomous and democratic nature resulted in high degrees of responsiveness to a variety of social constituencies and of accountability to the wider community (Cameron, 1991: ch. 7; Tudiver, 1999: ch. 4).

Beginning with funding cutbacks in the 1970s, and continuing with university corporate partnerships and entrepreneurial activities, the nature of Canadian university governance began to change. These (and other) developments led to a significant increase in the size of academic administrations and substantial changes in their nature and practice. Administrators began to see themselves—and to behave—not as leaders of collegial and democratic universities, but as managers of these increasingly complex organizations. This has resulted in their centralizing institutional power and adopting a range of values and practices that predominate in the business world, both of which render our universities more like private-sector institutions and more amenable to the latter's desires and demands (Newson, 1992).

One of the ways in which university administrators are centralizing power is by bypassing collegial bodies and making decisions either on their own or by way of hand-picked advisory committees. Such actions are often justified by the need to capture fleeting commercial and other opportunities that might be lost if decision-making were to get 'bogged down in democracy'. Another way of centralizing power is by replacing traditional collegial processes with various 'consultative' exercises (frequently conducted on-line), that offer a more limited—and malleable—form of academic participation. Perhaps most troubling is the growing secrecy that pervades university operations. Instead of being open to academic (and public) scrutiny and deliberation, research and other agreements (including monopoly sales agreements) between university administrators and external partners are increasingly being made and kept under a cloak of secrecy. This practice, which is frequently justified by the need to protect partners' proprietary information, sacrifices academic tradition and community interests to the desires and demands of particular individuals and corporations (Newson and Polster, 2001: 59).

University administrators are changing university operations in other ways that render them more like corporations. One significant aspect of this transformation is the adoption of private-sector practices, such as the use of various performance indicators, which reduce professors' autonomy and increase managerial scrutiny and control (Bruneau and Savage, 2002). A more general feature of this transformation is the progressive displacement of academic by economic criteria in decision-making related to a growing number of university issues ranging from who is hired and rewarded, to how resources are allocated to academic units, to what research areas are and are not prioritized. Another subtle but powerful change is the importation into our universities of corporate language in which presidents are 'CEOs', faculty members and staff are 'human resources', and students are 'clients' (Turk, 2000a: 6). Such terms are not merely new forms of address: they imply—and produce—very different roles for, and relationships between, those who work and learn in the university.

The university is not simply being run more as a business, however. To an unprecedented degree, it is being run *by* members of the private sector and other wealthy individuals. Not only are private sponsors gaining greater say over what academic research is done and how it is done; they are also being granted extraordinary say over other academic matters, such as hiring and curricular decisions, and even given voting positions on university committees, in exchange for donations in cash or in kind. (Such was case when the mere loan of some high-end equipment gave Sony Classical Production a seat on the curriculum committee of McGill University's Faculty of Music; Shaker, 1999). This change in academic governance is facilitated by, and in turn reinforces, the changes in university administration addressed above. For instance, the increasing exclusion of academics and members of the general public from university decision-making processes makes it more difficult to challenge either the particular actions or the broader cultural transformation within the university that open the way for corporate influence and control.

These changes in the social relations of academic governance also serve to alter the interests of those within the university and to encourage them to prioritize their personal well-being over the common good. For example, these changes are reducing the payoff that academics get from participating in university governance, given that important decisions are less frequently made within established collegial bodies and that university service is progressively less valued and rewarded (particularly relative to income-generating activities) in the context of academic performance review. As a result, many professors are opting to minimize if not abandon their university service work in favour of their research and teaching work, which may be more personally and professionally rewarding (Newson and Polster, 2001: 69–70). While this retreat from **collegialism** may serve academics' immediate individual interests, it undermines their collective interests and ultimately the public interest.

The changing social relations of academic governance are also leading some faculty and others, such as lower-level administrators, to alter the ways they participate in planning and decision-making processes, so that they act less as members of a collective pursuing common goals than as individual agents pursuing their private goals. For instance, as university planning decisions are increasingly made outside the traditional collegial bodies, academics, department heads, and/or deans have fewer opportunities to collectively negotiate positions that would serve the majority interest. For this reason, many are attempting to informally influence planning processes as individuals (or small groups) advocating only for their particular needs. This strategy leads others to follow suit, if only to ensure that their own interests are not compromised. Thus the well-being of the collective is increasingly subordinated to that of the individual, and academic solidarity and power vis-à-vis increasingly managerial senior administrations is further fragmented and diminished.

University Teaching

Teaching was at the heart of the post-war university. While professors were expected to contribute to knowledge production and academic governance, it was understood that teaching students was their first priority (Pocklington and Tupper, 2002: 11). Thus most university courses were taught by full-time faculty members. Class sizes were also kept relatively small. With the dramatic expansion of Canada's university system in the 1960s, higher education progressively came to be seen as a citizenship right, rather than a privilege of the rich. Accordingly, tuition and other fees were kept low and student grants and loans were made widely available to ensure that higher education was accessible to all qualified Canadians (Axelrod, 1982; Rounce, 1999).

Beginning in the 1970s, however, and continuing relatively consistently since, governments have been reducing the funding they provide to assist universities with their operating costs, which include teaching costs (see, for example, CAUT, 1999 and 2005b).[2] At the same time, universities have been entering into a variety of private initiatives that are frequently very expensive. To cope with rising costs in a context of diminished operating revenues, university administrators have adopted a number of strategies related to teaching that further erode the public-serving character of Canadian higher education.

One such strategy is to substantially reduce teaching costs (CAUT, 1999). Thus, across most if not all Canadian campuses, class sizes have swelled, library holdings have diminished, general classrooms and facilities have deteriorated, and courses and programs have been slashed, particularly in areas like the arts and humanities. Universities have also upped their use of part-time and graduate student instructors who are paid far less than full-time faculty and receive fewer benefits (Tudiver, 1999: 163–4). Steps such as these both stem from and contribute to the growing influence of private-sector values within the university, particularly the 'bottom-line thinking' alluded to in the previous section.

In addition to reducing the resources they invest in teaching, university administrators have opted to increase tuition and other student fees. According to the Canadian Federation of Students (CFS), average undergraduate tuition fees have increased substantially—from $2,000 in 1993–4 to over $4,000 in 2003–4 (CFS, 2005)—and the increases have been even more dramatic in professional programs (CAUT, 2003a: 1). Raising fees privatizes higher education by making it more of an individual and less of a social or collective responsibility, and therefore less accessible to growing numbers of Canadians. It also privatizes education in that many students must work longer hours to finance their schooling and thus have less time to socialize or get involved in other campus activities (CAUT, 2003a), making the university experience more isolated and less communal, both for themselves and for others. More recently, as they have developed their entrepreneurial acumen, administrators are regarding university teaching not simply as a cost to manage, but as an untapped money-making opportunity. Thus they are becoming involved in a variety of lucrative teaching ventures ranging from providing exclusive, 'boutique' programs (such as Executive MBAs that cost tens of thousands of dollars per year), to developing or delivering courses for private companies, to hosting foreign programs on Canadian campuses for a cut of the profits (see, for example, Day, 2006). Administrators are also attempting to capitalize on the huge commercial opportunities opening up in the international education market, by expanding the profitable courses and programs they offer to students overseas and more aggressively recruiting foreign students who pay increasingly exorbitant differential fees—up to $26,000 per year at some Canadian universities (CFS, 2004). Such initiatives further erode the quality of the education that is provided to the general student body, as they divert university resources and efforts towards more valued 'clients', be they the students who pay substantially higher fees or the private partners whose education ventures make money for the university. They also further erode public values, such as equity in, and access to, higher education, and public serving practices, such as providing openness and accountability in university affairs.

As our universities are becoming more business-like in relation to the education they provide, they are also becoming more business-like in relation to the students they serve. This is manifested in the growing amounts of time and resources they are investing in branding, advertising, and other marketing activities aimed at attracting greater numbers (and different kinds) of students. This is reflected in the greater use of technology and standardized procedures and protocols to manage student affairs. And this is apparent in the widespread use of teaching evaluations, student exit surveys, and other instruments to assess and improve 'customer service' and satisfaction (Newson, 2005). These and other such measures erode public education by diverting resources away from the practice of teaching itself and towards the corporate services that promote and manage it. They also reflect, and help entrench, a different relationship between the university and its students, who are increasingly treated as isolated consumers of services rather than participating members of an educational community.

The changing relations of university teaching also transform the interests of those within the academy and encourage them to place their private well-being over that of the collective. In the case of students, reduced opportunities to collaborate to shape university education are leading them to act on, and for, their individual interests. Thus, for example, rather than allying with their peers to improve the quality of education for all, high achieving students (for whom universities are competing) are entering into more frequent and more aggressive negotiations with academic institutions to secure the best possible terms and conditions for their education only (Alphonso 2006a; Reich, 2001: 203–4). More generally, as students are increasingly treated as customers, many of them are relating to their education as customers, expecting teaching practices and decisions—particularly those surrounding grades— to please them. This is evident in the growing number of accounts of students challenging evaluations of their work and even demanding A's for their courses 'because they paid for them' (Alphonso, 2006b: A3; Newson, 2005: 35–6). In a context where administratively imposed performance indicators, such as standardized student evaluation forms, carry increasing weight in academics' performance reviews, some faculty members feel pressured to prioritize their own interests over students' interests by tailoring their teaching expectations and standards to conform with their customers' demands (Churchill, 2006: C1). In so doing, these faculty members also compromise the interests of their colleagues who opt to resist this pressure and the interests of the public that is harmed by the diminished quality of higher education.

This account addresses only some of the ways in which Canadian higher education is currently changing. But it does provide a general picture of how the privatization process is taking place and how it is transforming our universities from public- into private-serving institutions. While previous sections alluded to a number of particular consequences that flow from this transformation, the following sections address its implications for two more general concerns, namely power and inequality in our society.

Power

In general, the ongoing privatization of higher education—and all education—in Canada serves to entrench and intensify inequality within our society. It does this, in part, by shifting resources and power upwards, concentrating them in the hands of those who already have resources and power. For example, as tuition fees escalate, privileged youth and adults are making up a growing proportion of the university student population. They are also more able to take full advantage of their educational opportunities than are their less affluent peers. Similarly, as universities become more involved in various research partnerships and business ventures, the institutions' research resources and results are increasingly being made available to those who can afford to pay for them, to the detriment of those who cannot. In addition to greater access to the university's resources, wealthy citizens and corporations are gaining greater control over the direction of the institution as a whole. As administrators run universities more and more like corporations, they are closing down the spaces for members of the academic community and the broader community to influence university affairs, while expanding the opportunities for members of the private sector and other wealthy individuals to shape academic decisions and decision-making processes. Not only does privatization thus undermine the redistributive function of public higher education but it actually serves to reverse it: instead of the rich subsidizing the education and research needs of those who are less fortunate, the general public is subsidizing the rich, paying most of the costs of teaching and research that they are less able to use or control.[3]

The upward shift of university resources serves to entrench and intensify inequalities in our society in a multiplicity of ways. As fewer disadvantaged students—and, increasingly, middle-class students—can afford the growing costs of higher education, the relative advantages of the wealthy stand to increase.[4] Further, as corporations and some individuals gain greater access to university research resources and results, their ability to sustain and expand their advantages over their competitors and consumers in general increases. For instance, companies that obtain broad patents on important academic discoveries are often able to stifle competition, pre-empt the development of alternative products and processes, and charge monopoly prices for their products (Washburn, 2005; Shulman, 1999). The upward shift of control over the university further reinforces inequalities in our society, providing the well-resourced with 'an inside track' into university policy- and decision-making that they can use to privilege, and perpetuate, both their individual interests and the collective interests of their class. Given that transparency and accountability in university affairs are being reduced at the same time, wealthy individuals and corporations can advance their agendas with an unprecedented lack of scrutiny and a high degree of impunity.

Privatization does not simply further privilege the privileged, however. It simultaneously harms the majority of citizens—particularly disadvantaged citizens—by diminishing various resources that enable them to resist increasingly unequal power relations in our society and to otherwise enhance the quality of their lives. For instance, as our universities become more influenced by and oriented to corporate needs, the knowledge produced and transmitted within them becomes increasingly instrumental and narrow in nature, and thus less critical and diverse in nature. This limits the opportunities for academics and the public alike to question and critique the status quo. It also deprives them of the knowledge they would need to transform the status quo in ways that more closely conform to their interests. As universities have become more involved in partnerships with agri-business and pharmaceutical companies, for example, it has become more difficult—both scientifically and politically—to question and challenge the assumptions and implications of genetic engineering and the curative approach to health (Sanders, 2005; Schafer, 2005; Washburn, 2005). At the same time, there is relatively little alternative knowledge being developed and transmitted in the university, such as knowledge of organic farming or holistic approaches to illness prevention, that citizens could draw upon—even were they so inclined—to better serve their own needs and enhance the collective well-being.

The privatization of higher education also erodes important skills that enable citizens to achieve greater equality and advance the public interest. For instance, when Canada's universities were run more openly and communally, they served as important training grounds for democracy. Many civic leaders cut their political teeth on university politics, and for many more citizens it was during their university years that they developed a sense of their right to become actively involved in public institutions, as well as the skills and savvy to do so effectively (Pitsula, 2006). As universities limit the ability of students and others to participate meaningfully in academic affairs, treating them instead as customers or employees, they rob them of opportunities to develop some of the democratic sensibilities and capacities that are key to achieving progressive change within the institution and the broader society.

Perhaps most troubling, however, is that privatization undermines various values and commitments that inspire and reinforce efforts to promote social equality and justice, such as service to the common good. The university deals a serious blow to the common good through its involvement in the privatization of knowledge, which not only leads it to make withdrawals from our common stock of knowledge without depositing much in return, but also makes it more difficult for others to replenish our rapidly diminishing knowledge commons (Washburn, 2005; Shulman, 1999). To an alarming degree, growing numbers of university administrators and academics are even betraying the common good by knowingly jeopardizing citizens' well-being in the pursuit of profit, as is revealed in the growing number of scandals and lawsuits in which universities have become embroiled. (For a chilling account of many of these, including the wrongful death of Jesse Gelsinger in the United States and the sagas of two Canadian doctors who were penalized for prioritizing patients over university partners' interests, see Washburn, 2005.)

Academic administrators and others are failing to nurture the common good in numerous other ways. They are reducing the resources and rewards that are provided to those involved in communally oriented programs and projects in the university, and suppressing and penalizing various forms of resistance to privatization that students and staff undertake in defence of the collective good. At the same time, they are promoting greater individualism and competitiveness, such as when they bestow honours and privileges on those academics who privately profit from their research, and when they encourage—and even help train—graduate and some undergraduate students to do the same. Perhaps the greatest threat to the common good, however, is the progressive normalization of the corporate perspective within the university. For the more that this perspective is taken for granted and passed on by those who work and learn in the institution, the more the pursuit of private interests is placed above question, and even redefined as the principal means of achieving the common good.

It is worth noting that even as privatization serves the interests of the privileged at the expense of the majority of citizens, it also fundamentally undermines their interests in several ways. Wealthy students may be getting more education, and superior education, than others, but the overall quality of their educational experience is declining because of growing homogeneity, isolation, and competitiveness within the student body, and the university's growing tendency to treat education as a business and students as an income source. Similarly, while particular corporations may derive immediate benefits from the research alliances in which they are involved, privatization harms the longer term interests of the corporate sector as a whole by eroding many features of academic research, such as its open and collaborative nature, which enhance its quality and its actual and potential economic contributions (Atkinson-Grosjean, 2006: 23–8; Polster, 1994: ch. 7). More generally, although privatization may enrich privileged individuals and organizations, it simultaneously impoverishes (and imperils) the larger social and natural contexts that they inhabit. While wealth and power may insulate them from some of their harmful effects, ultimately, the only way to deal with these problems is through collective solutions, whose development privatization impedes.

While its implications are thus very serious and troubling, it should nonetheless be borne in mind that the privatization of higher education in Canada is an ongoing process, not a completed one. The university is indeed becoming more privately oriented in all of its aspects and activities; however, there are still many places and individuals within the academy that remain dedicated to the public interest. There are also growing numbers of opportunities, arising both inside and outside the university, to generate and mobilize resistance to the privatization of higher education.

Resistance

Despite (or perhaps because of) the isolating and disempowering effects of privatization, various groups around the country have taken steps to expose, and oppose, it in recent years. Among the most active in this respect are Canadian students. Through their local, regional, and national organizations, many students have launched actions to resist specific impacts of privatization and the process in general. These have included campaigns to oppose tuition hikes and monopoly deals between universities and corporations (most notably those involving Coke and Pepsi), as well as efforts, such as the Corporate Free Campus project at the University of Toronto, to educate students and others about the general nature and implications of the privatization of Canadian higher education (CCPA, 2005: ch. 1). Many faculty members have also resisted privatization by opposing developments—such as the growing use of performance measures, increases in class sizes, and the greater emphasis on income generating activities—that erode the quality of their own working lives and the service they can render to the public. Students and faculty have also collaborated with one another and with various public interest groups to raise awareness about privatization and opposition to initiatives that entrench and advance it. Beyond their direct and immediate impacts, such efforts help to build alliances and solidarity as well as valuable knowledge and experience that can inspire and strengthen future efforts to oppose privatization. Thus, whether they win or lose particular struggles, those involved in these forms of resistance make an important contribution to preserving public higher education in our country.

While these forms of opposition to the privatization of Canada's universities are extremely important, there are some additional approaches that could be adopted to further enhance resistance. First, rather than simply reacting to various initiatives and practices that promote privatization, opponents of the process might proactively establish alternative initiatives and practices that model the kind of public serving university they hope to preserve and revitalize. One example of such an initiative would be to establish on Canadian campuses institutions like the Dutch science shops, which make academic resources and expertise available to local citizen groups to resolve various problems or serve other needs that they have (Sclove, 1995). Two key principles of science shops are that the groups involved be unable to pay for the research that is done and that any research results be kept in the public domain. The presence on our campuses of such institutions could challenge many of the assumptions and practices associated with privatization, such as the desirability of commercializing academic knowledge and the privileging of the research needs of paying clients. Equally if not more important, science shops could revitalize or instil a public service ethic in both academics and students, and encourage all citizens to take greater interest in and ownership of our universities.

A second approach to strengthening resistance would be to organize a number of broad and coordinated national campaigns, each highlighting one aspect of the privatization process. This approach would allow opponents of university privatization across the country to concentrate their resources on the same issue, instead of diffusing them on a multiplicity of isolated actions. Prime candidates for such campaigns are those aspects of the privatization trend that are most deeply intertwined with the others. Those issues also speak to deeply held and widely shared values and concerns and thus could mobilize a large cross-section of the Canadian population.

One issue around which a national campaign could be built is the privatization and commercialization of academic research. The university's involvement in intellectual property ties into a number of aspects of privatization, including the skewing of the academic research agenda toward industrial interests, greater secrecy and managerialism, rising tuition fees, and the university's growing involvement in various scandals and conflicts of interest. It also touches on widespread, deeply felt concerns within our society and could thus help mobilize a very broad coalition of support. Within the university, a campaign against commercialization could bring together students who are suffering from intolerable debt loads, academics whose access to increasingly expensive research materials is being reduced, and members of departments and faculties that are being penalized for their inability or unwillingness to engage in private knowledge production. It could also bring together a wide range of groups outside the university who have more general concerns about the ongoing privatization of knowledge including farmers, health professionals, Aboriginal people, artists, and even a growing number of corporate leaders and entrepreneurs (Bollier, 2002; Shulman, 1999). Not only would such a campaign stand a good chance of succeeding, but it would also enhance the chances of success of subsequent campaigns against the privatization of higher education[5] and perhaps even of other valued public institutions, such as our medicare system.

One final strategy that opponents of privatization might embrace would be to focus more of their efforts on developments outside the university that are contributing to developments within it. As has been signalled in various places in this article, much of the impetus for the privatization of the university has come from government, particularly the federal government of Canada. Beginning in the mid-1970s and intensifying since then, the federal government's conception of the university has shifted from a resource for social development to an instrument of economic competitiveness (Polster, 1994: ch. 2). This has led politicians to reduce the basic operating funds they provide to universities while encouraging them to form alliances with the corporate sector and undertake entrepreneurial initiatives of their own. These shifts in the government's conception and treatment of the university are largely the product of a shift in the nature of government itself. Instead of producing university policy in-house, the government has increasingly been ceding responsibility for higher education policy-making to unelected and unaccountable advisory bodies, such as the Advisory Council on Science and Technology, which are dominated by corporate and academic executives and people who support their interests. Not surprisingly, these groups have used the opportunity to advance and institutionalize visions and policies for the university that serve their particular needs rather than those of the broader society (Polster, 1994). Thus, as part of the effort to resist the privatization of the university, citizens might also resist the privatization of government. They might work to ensure that those elected by the public (along with other public servants) produce policy for the public, and that they do so in ways that are transparent, accountable, and responsive to a broad range of social interests and needs. This strategy could go a long way towards undercutting many of the conditions that sustain privatization in the university and elsewhere. In so doing, it would reduce and ease the work that opponents of privatization have to do and further enhance the effectiveness of their resistance.

Notes

1. While there has been an increase in private and for-profit higher education in Canada in recent years, the vast majority of our universities are still public.
2. The dynamics of Canadian higher education funding are too complex to address in detail here. However, it should be noted that at the same time that the federal government has reduced support for university operating costs, it has also increased the support it provides to universities for academic research—in particular, for industrially oriented and partnership research. This shift in funding has contributed to many of the aspects and consequences of privatization discussed here.
3. Although the proportion of university operating costs paid by students increased from 16.9 per cent to 34.2 per cent from 1990 to 2003, the share of these costs paid by the public remained consistently higher: 79.7 and 58.6 per cent, respectively (CAUT, 2005a: 3). Many authors on the right have used the 'reverse subsidy' argument to support calls for greater privatization in higher education and elsewhere ('Why should the poor continue to pay for resources that the rich disproportionately take advantage of?'). However, an equally feasible, more just, and ultimately more productive solution would be to reverse privatization and increase public access to public resources by, for instance, dramatically reducing, and eventually eliminating, university tuition fees.
4. Although this discussion focuses primarily on class inequalities, privatization also intensifies other inequalities, such as those of gender, race, and (dis)ability. For example, since women tend to earn substantially less than men, even with equivalent education credentials (CFS, 2003), they are less able, and may become less willing, to assume the heavy burdens associated with higher education.
5. Other issues around which broad national campaigns could be organized include the erosion of democratic control over the university and the mismanagement of public resources that stems from increasingly intense competition within and between universities (an issue that could not be developed in detail in this chapter). There are also many proactive initiatives, in addition to science shops, that could be pursued, such as creating Free Universities (Collins, 2003) and integrating universities into local and regional community economic development projects (Polster, 2000).

Glossary

academic collegialism: The values and practices with which academics collectively govern the university. Key collegial structures include university senates and faculty councils.

commercialization: The process through which a product is introduced into the marketplace. In the case of academic research, commercialization means that knowledge produced in whole or in part with public funds is not made freely available to the public, but becomes private property, accessible only to those who are able and willing to pay for it.

privatization: Most simply, the transfer of assets from the public to the private sector. It may also involve the incorporation of values and practices characteristic of the private sector into public institutions, as well as the formation of partnerships between public and private bodies.

Study Questions

1. What impact has rising tuition had on your own experience at university and on the experience of your peers?
2. How are students currently involved in shaping policy at your university? How does this role differ from students' role in the past? How might the situation be improved in the future?
3. What kinds of business ventures and alliances with industry is your university currently involved in? How do these affect the institution's teaching and research activities?
4. What other forms of privatization are visible at your university (e.g., corporate advertising on campus)? How do they affect the general university environment? What actions have been taken by members of the university community to draw attention to such issues? What further actions could be taken?
5. In what ways is privatization at other levels of the education system similar to and different from privatization at the university level? What are the main benefits and harms of privatization at these other levels?

Recommended Readings

Doherty-Delorme, D., and E. Shaker. 1999–2005. *Missing Pieces 1–5, An Alternative Guide to Canadian Post-Secondary*. Ottawa: Canadian Centre for Policy Alternatives.

Newson, J., and H. Buchbinder. 1988. *The University Means Business*. Toronto: Garamond Press.

Reimer, M., ed. 2004. *Inside Corporate U: Women in the Academy Speak Out*. Toronto: Sumach.

Tudiver, N. 1999. *Universities for Sale: Resisting Corporate Control over Canadian Higher Education*. Toronto: James Lorimer.

Turk, J. 2000. *The Corporate Campus: Commercialization and the Dangers to Canada's Colleges and Universities*. Toronto: James Lorimer.

Washburn, J. 2005. *University Inc.: The Corporate Corruption of Higher Education*. New York: Basic Books.

Recommended Websites

Canadian Association of University Teachers: http://www.caut.ca

Canadian Centre for Policy Alternatives (see the Education Project): http://www.policyalternatives.ca

Canadian Federation of Students: http://www.cfs-fcee.ca

Forum on Privatization and the Public Domain: http://www.forumonpublicdomain.ca

University Watch: http://www.uwatch.ca

References

Alphonso, C. 2006a. 'In Academia, the Early Bird Gets to Learn'. *Globe and Mail*, 27 January: A3.

———. 2006b. 'Among Brazen Undergrads, A is for Aggressive'. *Globe and Mail*, 1 May: A3.

Atkinson-Grosjean, J. 2006. *Public Science, Private Interests: Culture and Commerce in Canada's Networks of Centres of Excellence*. Toronto: University of Toronto Press.

Axelrod, P. 1982. *Scholars and Dollars: Politics, Economics, and the Universities of Ontario 1945–1980*. Toronto: University of Toronto Press.

Bollier, D. 2002. *Silent Theft: The Private Plunder of Our Common Wealth.* New York: Routledge.

Bruneau, W., and D. Savage. 2002. *Counting Out the Scholars: The Case against Performance Indicators in Higher Education.* Toronto: James Lorimer.

Cameron, D. 1991. *More than an Academic Question: Universities, Government and Public Policy in Canada.* Halifax: Institute for Research on Public Policy.

Campbell, M., and F. Gregor. 2002. *Mapping Social Relations: A Primer in Doing Institutional Ethnography.* Aurora, ON: Garamond Press.

Canadian Association of University Teachers (CAUT). 1999. 'Not in the Public Interest: University Finance in Canada 1972–1998', *CAUT Education Review* 1, 3: 1–21.

———. 2003a. 'University Tuition Fees in Canada, 2003', *CAUT Education Review* 5, 1: 1–4.

———. 2003b. *Report of the CAUT AF&T Committee into Complaints Raised by Professor David Noble against Simon Fraser University Regarding Alleged Infringements of Academic Freedom.* Ottawa: CAUT.

———. 2005a. 'Paying the Price: The Case for Lowering Tuition Fees in Canada', *CAUT Education Review* 7, 1: 1–5.

———. 2005b. 'Financing Canada's Universities and Colleges', *CAUT Education Review* 7, 2: 1–8.

Canadian Centre for Policy Alternatives (CCPA). 2005. *Challenging McWorld II.* Ottawa: CCPA.

Canadian Federation of Students (CFS). 2003. 'Equal Minds, Equal Education', *CFS Fact Sheet* 9, 4.

———. 2004. 'Differential Tuition Fees for International Students', *CFS Fact Sheet* 10, 11.

———. 2005. 'Tuition Fees in Canada: A Pan-Canadian Perspective on Educational User Fees', *CFS Fact Sheet* 11, 1.

Churchill, L. 2006. 'Professor Goodgrade', *The Chronicle of Higher Education* 52, 25: C1.

Collins, M. 2003. 'The People's Free University: Counteracting the Innovation Agenda on Campus and Model for Lifelong Learning', *Saskatchewan Notes* 2, 9: 1–4.

Day, T. 2006. 'Private for-Profit College to Open at SFU'. Available at: <www.universityaffairs.ca/issues/2006/mayfor_profit_college_02.html>. Accessed 26 May 2008.

Froese-Germain, B., et al. 2006. *Commercialism in Canadian Schools: Who's Calling the Shots?* Ottawa: CCPA.

Livingstone, D., and D. Hart. 2005. *Public Attitudes Toward Education in Ontario 2004.* Toronto: OISE/UT.

Mahood, S. 2005. 'Privatized Knowledge and the Pharmaceutical Industry'. Paper presented at Free Knowledge: Creating a Knowledge Commons in Saskatchewan Conference, University of Regina, 17–18 November.

Naimark, A. 2004. 'Universities and Industry in Canada: An Evolving Relationship', in P. Axelrod, ed., *Knowledge Matters: Essays in Honour of Bernard J. Shapiro.* Montreal and Kingston: McGill-Queen's University Press, 53–61.

Newson, J. 1992. 'The Decline of Faculty Influence: Confronting the Effects of the Corporate Agenda', in W. Carroll et al., eds, *Fragile Truths: 25 Years of Sociology and Anthropology in Canada.* Ottawa: Carleton University Press.

———. 2005. 'The University on the Ground: Reflections on Canadian Experience'. Paper presented at CEDESP Conference on the Impact of Research on Public Policy on Higher Education, Rincon, Puerto Rico, 2–3 June. *Puerto Rico Higher Education Research and Information Centre Journal.* Available at: <http://cedesp.cespr.org/revista>.

———, and C. Polster. 2001. 'Reclaiming Our Centre: Towards a Robust Defense of Academic Autonomy', *Science Studies* 14, 1: 55–75.

Padova, A. 2005. *Federal Commercialization in Canada.* Ottawa: Library of Parliament, Parliamentary Information and Research Service, Economics Division.

Pitsula, J. 2006. *As One Who Serves.* Montreal and Kingston: McGill-Queen's University Press.

Pocklington, T., and J. Tupper. 2002. *No Place to Learn: Why Universities Aren't Working*. Vancouver: University of British Columbia Press.

Polster, C. 1994. 'Compromising Positions: The Federal Government and the Reorganization of the Social Relations of Canadian Academic Research'. Unpublished doctoral dissertation. York University.

———. 2000. 'Shifting Gears: Rethinking Academics' Response to the Corporatization of the University', *Journal of Curriculum Theorizing* 16, 2: 85–90.

Press, E., and J. Washburn. 2000. 'The Kept University', *Atlantic Monthly* 285, 3: 39–54.

Read, C. 2003. *Survey of Intellectual Property Commercialization in the Higher Education Sector, 2003*. Ottawa: Statistics Canada, Science, Innovation and Electronic Information Division.

Reich, R. 2001. *The Future of Success*. New York: Alfred A. Knopf.

Robertson, H.J. 2005. 'The Many Faces of Privatization'. Paper presented at the BCTF Public Education Not for Sale II Conference, Vancouver, 18 February.

Rounce, A. 1999. 'Student Loan Programs in Saskatchewan, Alberta and at the Federal Level: An Examination Using the Neo-Institutionalist Approach'. Unpublished master's thesis. Regina: University of Regina.

Sanders, J. 2005. 'Monsanto, Lawyers, Lies, and Videotape: Seeds of Censorship Sown at the University of Manitoba', *Canadian Dimension* 39, 5: 34–7.

Schafer, A. 2005. 'Who're Ya Gonna Call? Not the Corporate University', *Canadian Dimension* 39, 5: 26–9.

Sclove, R. 1995. 'Putting Science to Work in Communities', *The Chronicle of Higher Education* 41, 29: B1–B3.

Shaker, E. 1999. 'The Privatization of Post-Secondary Institutions', *Education Limited* 1, 4.

Shulman, S. 1999. *Owning the Future*. Boston: Houghton Mifflin.

Smith, D. 1987. *The Everyday World as Problematic: A Feminist Sociology*. Toronto: University of Toronto Press.

Tudiver, N. 1999. *Universities for Sale: Resisting Corporate Control over Canadian Higher Education*. Toronto: James Lorimer.

Turk, J. 2000a. 'What Commercialization Means for Education', in Turk (2000b: 3–13).

———. 2000b. *The Corporate Campus: Commercialization and the Dangers to Canada's Colleges and Universities*. Toronto: James Lorimer.

Washburn, J. 2005. *University Inc.: The Corporate Corruption of Higher Education*. New York: Basic Books.

Index